INDIAN STATES

INDIAN STATES

A Biographical, Historical, and Administrative Survey

COMPILED BY
SOMERSET PLAYNE, F.R.G.S.

ASSISTED BY R. V. SOLOMON AND J. W. BOND
EDITED BY ARNOLD WRIGHT

GYAN

Published by

GYAN

Gyan Publishing House
5, Ansari Road
Daryaganj, New Delhi-110002
Phone: 011-47034999, 9811692060
E-mail: books@gyanbooks.com

Distribution Network
gyanbooks.com
India, USA, Canada, UK, Australia, France

ISBN : 978-81-212-4609-5 (HB)
First Published, 1921

2nd Impression 2022

Printed at: Gyan Press, Delhi.

INDIAN STATES
Author: SOMERSET PLAYNE

INDIAN STATES

A Biographical, Historical, and Administrative Survey

COMPILED BY

SOMERSET PLAYNE, F.R.G.S.

ASSISTED BY R. V. SOLOMON AND J. W. BOND

EDITED BY ARNOLD WRIGHT

1921–1922

PREFACE

THIS work is the final volume of a series descriptive of India in its varied aspects—administrative, industrial, ethnological, and social. Dealing exclusively with the Indian States, it constitutes a survey, unique in its exhaustive character of that part of the vast Eastern Dominion which is not directly under British rule. The Indian princes, their genealogies and their racial affinities and personal traits are here treated with the authoritative force derived from information specially supplied, and at the same time a complete picture is given of their States, the facts and statistics in every case being brought up to the latest possible date. As a whole the volume is a marvellously graphic representation of the many-sided life of those parts of India which are nearest in outward appearance to a past in which European influences were unknown. It has been said that the Indian aristocracy is the oldest in the world, and the truth of that assertion will be found in the family histories of many of the princes, not a few of whose ancestors had a venerable lineage when the Norman William descended upon the shores of England. Ancient, too, in a large number of instances are their possessions as centres of Eastern civilization, and a glance at the pages of the volume only is needed to see what a wealth of historic monuments they hold within their limits. For pure romance there is nothing in the East to compare with the capitals of several of the Rajpoot States, and there is hardly one of the States of importance described in the work which does not possess some feature of exceptional archæological interest.

The recent visit of the Prince of Wales to India has served to familiarize people at home with many of these historic and picturesque homes of the Indian princes. But strenuous as were the activities of His Royal Highness, it was only possible to bring him into contact with a few typical examples of this princely India which lives its leisured life in conditions, in some cases, of practical independence. Only a volume like the present can adequately bring home to the average citizen the magnitude of the Indian States and the singular rarity they exhibit, in origin, in racial characteristics, and in economical importance. The visits paid to the States by the compiler and his assistants, in furtherance of the objects of the work, entailed journeys by rail and motor car, camels, elephants, and native conveyances, of many thousands of miles, and occupied over two years. Some States were visited several times, and as time is not always regarded as a valuable asset in the territories of the Indian princes, sojourns of weeks had occasionally to be made to complete the photographic record which constitutes so striking a feature of the work. What the enterprise in its completeness meant, measured in terms of personal exertion, may be gathered from the fact that there are upwards of 1,500 photographs in the pages following. The vast majority of these pictures were taken by the compiler's staff, and the extremely intimate character of not a few of the examples involved elaborate preparations to comply with the etiquette of the palace or to suit the convenience of the princely sitters. Onerous and costly as this preliminary work was, it will be generally conceded that the results completely justify it. No such complete survey of the Indian States has ever before been made by private enterprise, and, owing to the enormous expenditure involved, none is likely to be made for many years.

The difficulties involved in the production, inevitably considerable owing to the great distances which had to be travelled and other local causes, have been materially accentuated by the troubles of the post-war period at home. Printing has become considerably more expensive than when the work was first planned, and there have been unavoidable delays arising out of the disturbed conditions of industry generally. Moreover, the death of two of the compiler's principal assistants and the illness of other members of the staff have interrupted the final stages of the work. In such circumstances the compiler feels that he can legitimately appeal for consideration from those who were led to expect an earlier fruition of his labours.

It should be stated that the order in which the States are given in the volume is that of the list of the Order of Precedence of the Indian Princes which is officially published in the India Office List. The names there given are placed in alphabetical order in different sections, each section referring to the number of guns for salute purposes to which the princes referred to are entitled. A further note should be made of the fact that this book does not exhaust the Indian States, and reference must be made to the previous volumes of this series—"Southern India," "Bengal and Assam," "Bombay and the United Provinces"—where full and complete accounts of the remaining States may be found.

CONTENTS

CONTENTS

INDIAN STATES

A Biographical, Historical, and Administrative Survey

THE STATE OF BARODA

THE State of Baroda is in direct Political relationship with the Government of India, although from a geographical point of view it is situated within the boundaries of the Bombay Presidency. It is 8,182 square miles in extent, and the census of 1911 showed that the inhabitants were at that time 2,032,798 in number. It may be true that there are several States in Central India, or Rajputana, or elsewhere in India, which have a larger acreage than Baroda, but in the efficiency of its administration, and the conspicuous progress made during the past 25 or 30 years, it is not excelled by the dominions of any other Ruler in India. His Highness the Maharaja has high ideals of statesmanship, and his extensive travels in foreign countries, as well as in India, have stimulated him to inaugurate many notable measures of reform, in which he has manifested a masterly grasp of the intricacies of good government. These characteristics are undoubtedly the secret of the well-established position held by Baroda to-day in the history of this vast country.

The early history of the State commences at the time of the dissolution of the Moghul Empire, and the entry into power of the great Mahratta race. A notable leader of the latter, Khande Rao Dabhade, was engaged in several battles against the remnants of the Moghul forces, and he emerged from these so triumphantly that he was appointed *Senapati*, or Commander-in-Chief, by the King of Satara. This was in 1716, when he was residing at his headquarters at Satara. Damaji Gaekwar, an officer serving under him, distinguished himself so greatly in ensuing conflicts, that he was honoured with the title of " Shamsher Bahadur," meaning the " illustrious swordsman," and this name has from that date (1720) been borne by the Gaekwars.

Damaji Gaekwar died in 1721, and was succeeded by his nephew, Pilaji Gaekwar, who is regarded as the founder of the present ruling family at Baroda. Pilaji was entrusted by the *Senapati* with the collection of tribute in Gujarat, a right which has been conferred upon him by the King of Satara. Pilaji established his headquarters at Songadh, where they remained up to 1766, when Pattan became the capital. Two other Mahratta leaders, Kantaji Kadam Bande and Udajirao Powar, had also similarly been authorized to collect tribute from the Province. For a time the three leaders worked together, and levied tribute from the Surat Attavishi, or 28 subdivisions. In 1723 Pilaji marched on Surat, and defeated the Governor, and from that date began to levy tribute regularly in Gujarat. Differences between him and the other leaders ensued in regard to the division of the revenues, and in 1725 it was arranged through the mediation of the Moghul Governor, that Pilaji should levy tribute from the districts to the south of the Mahi, and Kantaji Kadam to the north of the same river. Pilaji thus secured the right to the tribute of the districts of Baroda, Nandod, Champaner, Broach, and Surat.

There was constant rivalry between the Peshwa Bajirao and the *Senapati*, on whose behalf Pilajirao was acting. In the year 1727, the former obtained from Sarbulandkhan, the newly-appointed Moghul Viceroy, the right to levy *chouth* and *sardeshmukhi* in Gujarat, on condition that he should support him against Pilaji and other Mahratta leaders. In the same year, however, Pilaji succeeded in capturing both Baroda and Dabhoi. In 1730 Sarbulandkhan was recalled, and Abhai Singh was appointed Viceroy in his place.

Bajirao concerted with him to turn the *Senapati* out of Gujarat, and this led to the battle of Bhilupur, near Dabhoi, in 1731, in which the *Senapati* was defeated and slain. Bajirao, not deeming it politic utterly to crush the other Mahratta leaders, appointed Yeshwantrao Dabhade, the infant son of the late *Senapati*, to his father's office, and appointed Pilaji as his deputy. Pilaji thus had all the resources of the *Senapati* at his disposal, but his career was cut short in 1732, when he was compelled to take his departure from Gujarat. Momin Khan was appointed the next Viceroy, but finding it difficult to maintain his position at Gujarat, he made friends with Damaji, and granted to him half of the revenue of that Province.

When the young *Senapati* came of age he did not manifest ability to rule, and in 1747, after the death of the late *Senapati's* widow, Damajirao himself was appointed the representative of the Satara Raja in Gujarat.

Tarabai, widow of Raja Ram, invited him to the Deccan in order to rescue the Raja of Satara and the Mahratta kingdom from the thraldom of the Brahmin party, he willingly responded to the call, and set out on the expedition with an army of 15,000 men, with whom he attacked and defeated, at Nimb, a much stronger force which opposed his march. Disaster, however, befell him, and his forces being in danger of annihilation by the Peshwa's army, he was compelled to accept terms

LAKSHMI VILAS PALACE, BARODA.

assassinated at Dakor by the agents of Abhai Singh.

Pilaji was succeeded by his son, Damaji, and almost immediately after his installation, Abhai Singh, taking advantage of the confusion caused by Pilaji's death, assaulted and captured the city and fort of Baroda, whereupon Damaji retired to Dabhoi, whence he decided to take revenge upon his enemy by leading an expedition against Ahmedabad. His efforts met with some success, and one of the prizes won by him was the recapture, in 1734, of Baroda, which has since that time been in the undisturbed possession of the Gaekwars. Damaji's power increased rapidly from this date, and Abhai Singh was, in 1737,

Momin Khan died in the year 1742, and his successor, Fida-ud-din, pursued a policy of opposition towards Damaji. He came into conflict with Rangoji, Damaji's general, whom he defeated, but Damaji, who had been engaged in an expedition in Malwa, subsequently defeated the Viceroy, and drove him from the country, while he became practically master of Gujarat, although vestiges of the Moghul Empire remained for some time longer.

In the year 1749, Raja Shahu, King of Satara, died, and the real power of the Mahratta Government passed into the hands of the Peshwa. Damaji was from the beginning opposed to the policy which enabled the Peshwa to usurp the powers of his master, and therefore, in 1751, when which involved the cession of half of Gujarat, and of all future conquests. He was also required to maintain 10,000 horse to assist the Peshwa in time of need, and to pay Rs. 5,25,000 as tribute. Two years afterwards, Damaji, aided by the Peshwa's army, besieged Ahmedabad, and captured it. The Moghul Empire then came to an end, and Gujarat was divided between the Peshwa and the Gaekwar.

Damaji Gaekwar distinguished himself greatly in the fateful battle of Panipat, and after the defeat of the Mahratta army on that field he was able to effect an honourable return to Gujarat, where he continued with undiminished vigour to crush the combined efforts of the Mahom-

HIS HIGHNESS FARZAND-I-KHAS-I-DOWLAT-I-INGLISHA, MAHARAJA SIR SAYAJI RAO GAEKWAD, SENA KHAS KHEL, SHAMSHER BAHADUR, G.C.S.I., G.C.I.E., MAHARAJA OF BARODA.

HER HIGHNESS MAHARANI CHIMNA BAI SAHEBA GAEKWAD, C.I.

1. SHRIMANT MAHARAJ-KUMAR JAISINH RAO GAEKWAD.

2. SHRIMATI MAHARAJ-KUMARI INDIRA RAJA GAEKWAD.
(Now Her Highness the Maharani of Cooch Behar.)

3. SHRIMANT MAHARAJ-KUMAR DHAIRYASHIL RAO GAEKWAD.

4. SHRIMANT MAHAR-KUMAR PRATAPSINH RAO GAEKWAD.
(Grandson of His Highness.)

edans, who had hoped to win something by the great disaster which had befallen the Mahrattas. Shortly after his return he conquered from Kamal-ud-din Khan Babi all the territories which now comprise the Kadi division of the State, and transferred his capital from Songhad to Pattan. Damajirao died in the year 1768, and left behind him six sons, among whom disputes at once arose on the question of the succession to the *gadi*. Sayaji Rao and Govind Rao, the first and second sons, were the earliest claimants for the throne, but as they were unable to agree upon the matter the Peshwa was invited to become arbitrator. His decision in favour of Govind Rao (who was weak and vacillating in character) was only made after payment of a large sum of money had been made to him. The third son, Fateh Sinh Rao, then proceeded to the Mahratta Court at Poona, and succeeded in obtaining a reversal of the Peshwa's selection of Govind Rao. Sayaji Rao was thereupon declared *Sena Khas Khel*, and Fateh Sinh was appointed his deputy, as Sayaji Rao, owing to his weak intellect, was unable to manage the affairs of the State.

Fateh Sinh was not slow to realize that the disturbed condition of Baroda, owing to the continued feuds between his brother and himself, made it comparatively easy for the Poona Government to acquire Gujarat, and with the object of preventing such a calamity he endeavoured to enter into an alliance with the British, who had just previously captured the city of Broach. The overtures made by Fateh Sinh were not acceptable to the Government, and thus the claimants for the *gadi*, who had been wrangling among themselves for eight or ten years, were left to fight their own battles. In 1778, however, Fateh Sinh obtained from Poona the title of *Sena Khas Khel* for himself, while Govind Rao was compensated by the grant of a *jagir*, of the annual value of Rs. 2,00,000, Sayaji Rao being still alive.

In 1779, when war broke out between the British and the Poona Agency, Fateh Sinh allied himself with the former, and in a treaty executed in 1780 it was arranged that the Gaekwar should thereafter be independent of the Peshwa, and should retain his share of Gujarat, while the British should take over that portion of the Province previously held by the Peshwa. This proposal was cancelled by the treaty of Salbai, by which Fateh Sinh was left in the position held by him before the war. Fateh Sinh died in December 1789, and in spite of the remonstrances of Govind Rao, another brother, Manaji Rao, at once assumed the reins of government. Sindhia, however, supported the cause of Govind Rao, and the rivalry between the brothers continued until Manaji's death, which occurred in August 1793. Sayaji Rao, the eldest son of Damajirao, had died in the previous year.

Govind Rao was now allowed to assume the title of *Sena Khas Khel* Shamsher Bahadur, although he had to pay a very heavy *nazar* to the Peshwa in order to secure it. Govind Rao's reign was taken up with the rebellions of his son, Kanhoji, and his cousin, Malharrao, and by the war with Sheluker, the Peshwa's deputy. Govind Rao died in the year 1800, and he was succeeded by Anandrao, his eldest legitimate son, who was of weak mind, and whose position was soon disputed by his illegitimate brother, Kanhoji, and the latter's old ally, Malharrao. Both parties sought the aid of the British Government, who decided to assist and uphold the authority of Anandrao.

A treaty was signed in July 1802, under which a considerable area of territory was ceded by the Maharaja Gaekwar to the East India Company, but this and other engagements were in 1805 consolidated into a definite treaty of offensive and defensive alliance between the two Governments, by which arrangements were made for the establishment of a subsidiary force, and the cession of certain districts for its maintenance. It was also provided that the foreign policy of the State should be conducted by the British Government, and all differences with the Peshwa should be similarly arranged.

Owing to the infirmities of Anandrao, the affairs of the State were, during his reign from 1802 to 1818, carried on by a commission, presided over by the Resident. One of the first acts of the new administration was to disband the Arab mercenaries, who had in recent disturbances taken the side of Kanhoji, and had imprisoned the Maharaja himself. They refused to leave Baroda unless the arrears of their pay were met in full, and the British Government took over from them, and fulfilled, the guarantees which they had given to many Baroda subjects and bankers who had advanced loans to the State. Their conditions were accepted, and they were compelled to leave Gujarat altogether. The Maharaja's younger brother, Fateh Sinh Rao, became Regent in 1807, and in 1812 the celebrated Gangadhar Shastri was appointed Minister. The long-pending claims of the Peshwa against the Gaekwar then came up for settlement. Moreover, the term for which the farming of the Peshwa's territory in Gujarat had been granted to the Gaekwar with the view of removing conflict of jurisdiction was about to expire. Gangadhar Shastri was sent to Poona to carry on the negotiations for the settlement, and to get the lease renewed through the mediation of the Resident at Poona. As a result of the machinations of a party formed at Baroda, in opposition to the Government of the day, the Peshwa refused to listen to the overtures of the Shastri, and the latter was murdered while the matter was still under discussion. The relations between the British Government and the Peshwa then became very strained, and extensive preparations for war were made on both sides. A treaty was, however, entered into between the two parties in 1817, and by its terms the Gaekwar was declared to be independent of the Peshwa, who, in return for an annual payment of Rs. 4,00,000, relinquished all past claims on the Gaekwar on account of arrears. The Peshwa also agreed to "farm" in perpetuity his possessions in Gujarat, excepting his share in the tribute of Kathiawar (which had been assigned to the British Government), to the Baroda State for an annual payment of Rs. 4,50,000. A treaty was entered into in the same year between the British and the Baroda Governments, by which the latter consented to make additions to the subsidiary forces, and to cede the territories obtained by the perpetual "farm" of Ahmedabad to the British Government, for the regular payment thereof. Okhamandal was by this treaty ceded to the Baroda Government, and the latter also agreed to establish a contingent of 3,000 horse to act with the subsidiary force in time of war.

The Peshwa's power was overthrown in 1818, and as a consequence the annual payment of Rs. 4,00,000, which the Gaekwar had to make to the Peshwa on account of past claims, was remitted.

Fateh Sinh Rao died in the year 1818, and his younger brother, Sayajirao, became Regent. Maharaja Anandrao died shortly afterwards, and British interference, which had until then been necessary, owing to his infirmities, was withdrawn. Sayajirao was recognized as independent in the administration of the State in 1820, on condition of his respecting the guarantees taken over by the British Government from the Arabs, as well as

THE STATE OF BARODA.

1 AND 2. PAST RULERS OF BARODA.

THE STATE OF BARODA.

1. H.H. The Maharaja Gaekwad and His Ministers from 1875 to 1920. 2. Principal Officers of the State, 1920. 3. Durbar at Dwarka on the Occasion of Assumption of Control over the Waghers.

THE STATE OF BARODA

the additional guarantees which that Government had themselves given to State officers and bankers who had advanced funds to the State in order to remove its embarrassments. At the same time the new Maharaja was induced to agree to have no direct dealings with his tributaries in Gujarat and Kathiawar, on the British Government undertaking to collect the tribute in question free of charge.

Differences soon arose between the Maharaja and the British Government, which continued more or less for a period of 20 years. In 1828, in order to pay the instalments of the guaranteed creditors, Sir John Malcolm, Governor of Bombay, sequestrated districts yielding about Rs. 10,00,000. Two years subsequently, further districts yielding an equal revenue were similarly dealt with, for the reorganization of the contingent of 3,000 horse. This sequestration was disapproved by the Court of Directors, and the districts were restored. Sir John Malcolm's successor, Lord Clare, pursued a conciliatory policy, allowing the Maharaja to pay off the guaranteed debt at once, instead of by fixed instalments, and he accepted the Chief's undertaking to keep the contingent in an efficient condition. The amicable relations thus restored only lasted for a few years, however. The Maharaja and the British Government did not agree, among other things, as to the extent to which the latter could interfere in order to support the claims of guaranteed persons, and matters reached a crisis in 1838, when the deposition of Sayajirao was contemplated, but in 1839 he agreed to conform to the wishes of the Government. Sir James Rivett Carnac, the newly-appointed Governor of Bombay, visited Baroda in 1841, and effected a settlement of the outstanding questions. At that time, however, the Maharaja, with great reluctance, agreed to pay Rs. 3,00,000 annually for the expenses of a force, known as the Gujarat Irregular Horse, which had been levied in order to perform police duties in the territories which had been temporarily sequestrated.

Maharaja Sayajirao II died in 1847. The next Ruler was Ganpat Rao, eldest son of the former Prince, and the early years of his reign were marked by continual disagreements with the Resident, stationed at the Court of Baroda. He, however, profited by British influence, and to his credit, be it said that he effectually suppressed the practice of the sale of children, he sternly prohibited infanticide, as well as slavery in any form; he constructed roads, bridges, and public buildings, and in a general way endeavoured to pursue a path of progress and reform. In 1854 the political supervision over Baroda was transferred from Bombay to the Government of India. A notable event, which had far-reaching effects upon the commercial interests not only of Baroda, but also of the whole of Northern India, took place in 1856, when the first sod was turned of the Bombay-Baroda and Central India Railway Company's system. His Highness the Gaekwar transferred, free of cost, all land within the boundaries of his State which was required for the purpose, on condition that he should be compensated for loss of revenue from transit duties. Ganpat Rao died in November of the same year without leaving lawful male issue, and therefore the successor to the *gadi* was his eldest surviving brother, Khande Rao Gaekwar.

Only a few months had passed away when the never-to-be-forgotten Sepoy Mutiny broke out, spreading its unspeakable terrors throughout the greater part of Northern India. Even Gujarat did not escape a rebellious outbreak, but the Gaekwar steadfastly supported his British allies, and generously rendered them all assistance which it was in his power to give, in quelling the trouble. In recognition of these valuable services, Khande Rao was granted the right of adoption, he was created a Knight Grand Commander of the Most Exalted Order of the Star of India; and he was presented with a magnificent pair of peacock fans, and the annual payment of Rs. 3,00,000 agreed to in 1841 for the maintenance of the Gujarat Irregular Horse, was remitted. His Highness had commenced his reign in a most commendable manner, he inaugurated a revenue survey of land, improved the administration, and introduced many beneficial changes, but his passionate love for the chase, athletic contests, jewellery, beautiful mansions, and other expensive objects of self-gratification, deprived him of the means to carry out public works of a necessary character.

In 1859 the Waghers of Okhamandal rose in rebellion, but the insurrection was put down with the help of a British subsidiary force. With the object of keeping these turbulent people under proper check the control over them was entrusted to a newly-appointed Assistant to the Resident at Baroda, and a battalion of infantry was raised under his command to preserve order in the peninsula of Okhamandal. In 1909 the British Government inaugurated a policy of gradually withdrawing from control over the Waghers, which has now been entirely handed over to the State, including the control over the Okha battalion.

As the climate of the city of Baroda did not appear to be suitable for His Highness Khande Rao's health, he constructed, at a small village named Makarpura, about three miles distant from the capital, a most beautiful palace, which has from that time been the country residence of the Gaekwars. Khande Rao died in 1870 without leaving male issue, and the succession to the *gadi* fell to the lot of Malhar Rao, brother of the previous Gaekwar, who was at the time in prison at Padra for having been engaged in a plot to dethrone his predecessor. Malhar Rao was accordingly released and proclaimed Maharaja.

Malhar Rao was, at that time, smarting under his so-called grievances, and determined to wreak his vengeance upon the dependants and followers of the preceding Ruler. He tyrannized over the people, oppressing them with unjust taxation, and he spent his days in reckless extravagance, not even desisting from gratifying his sensual passions at the expense of the poor down-trodden subjects.

Annuities due to members of the Gaekwar family were left unpaid, and the Queen-Dowager—herself a sufferer from the spendthrift's folly—proceeded to Poona, in order to protest formally against the conduct of the Gaekwar. Colonel Phayre, who was at this juncture appointed British Resident at Baroda, heard of the barbarous manner in which the people were being treated, and he promptly asked that definite complaints might be lodged with him in order that an inquiry might be made. A commission, under the Presidency of Colonel Meade, was appointed by the British Government, and the report, which was entirely unfavourable to the Gaekwar, made certain recommendations. Eventually the Government sent a letter to the Gaekwar, calling upon him to restore order in the State, and to abstain from further ill-treatment of his subjects.

On account of the strained relationship between Colonel Phayre and the Maharaja, the former was replaced by Colonel Sir Lewis Pelly, who was appointed Special Commissioner and Agent to the Governor-General. On the eve of Colonel Phayre's departure from Baroda,

THE STATE OF BARODA.

1. Durbar Hall, Lakshmi Vilas Palace. 2. Hathi Hall, Lakshmi Vilas Palace. 3. Maharani's Drawing-room, Lakshmi Vilas Palace. 4. Bird's-eye View of Lakshmi Vilas Palace Gardens.

THE STATE OF BARODA.

1. Makarpura Palace, Baroda State. 2. Nazarbaug Palace, Baroda.

an attempt was made to poison him, and the Maharaja was alleged to have instigated the same. A Commission, presided over by Sir Richard Couch, Chief Justice of Bengal, was, therefore, appointed by the Government to inquire into the matter, the Maharaja having, in the meantime, been suspended from the exercise of power, and placed under arrest.

An authentic State record gives the following result of the Inquiry: "The three English Members of the Commission came to the conclusion that an attempt to poison Colonel Phayre had been instigated by Malhar Rao, while the three Indian Members did not consider him guilty. It was finally decided, as stated in a Proclamation issued in 1875, that the Maharaja must be deposed, not because the British Government has assumed that the result of the inquiry has been to prove the truth of the imputation against His Highness, but because, having regard to all the circumstances relating to the affairs of Baroda from the accession of His Highness Malharrao, his notorious misconduct, his gross misgovernment of the State, and his evident incapacity to carry into effect necessary reforms, the step was imperatively called for." In accordance with this resolution, Malhar Rao was at once deported to Madras, where he resided, under the surveillance of a British officer, until his death in 1882.

The British Government then authorized Her Highness Maharani Jamna Bai, the widow of His Highness Khande Rao Gaekwar, to adopt a successor to inherit the power and wealth of her late husband. Search was made for a suitable Prince, and eventually the choice fell upon Gopal Rao, son of Kashi Rao, a descendant of Pratap Rao, the third son of Pilaji Rao Gaekwar, the founder of the State.

This fortunate youth was then in the thirteenth year of his age, and on May 27, 1875, was adopted by Jamna Bai, with all the sacred rites prescribed by the Hindu *Shastras*. The name of the young Ruler was changed to Sayaji Rao, and under this appellation he ascended the *gadi* in 1875. During minority, the State was administered by Raja Sir T. Madhava Rao. His Highness was given a first-class education and a thorough training in the work of the management of State affairs, and on December 18, 1881, Sayaji Rao Gaekwar was invested with ruling powers by His Excellency Sir James Ferguson, Governor of Bombay, who acted as the representative of the Right Honourable the Marquis of Ripon, the Viceroy and Governor-General of India.

Desirous even in the early portion of his career to give expression of his devotion to the Sovereign of the British Empire, His Highness attended the ceremony at Delhi on January 1, 1877, when Her Majesty the late Queen Victoria assumed the title of "Empress of India."

It was on this occasion that he was invested with the title of "Farzandi-i-Khas-i-Daulat-i-Inglishia," signifying "favoured son of the British Empire."

In 1880 His Highness married a gifted Princess, belonging to the House of Tanjore, in the Madras Presidency. Two children were born, a daughter and an heir-apparent, Yuvaraj Fateh Sinh Rao, whose promising life was cut short by death in 1908. He has left behind him two daughters and one son—Shrimant Maharaj-Kumar Pratap Sinh Rao.

After the demise of Her Highness the Maharani, the Maharaja, in 1886, entered into wedlock with Chimnabai Saheba, of the Ghatge family of the Dewas State, and the union was blessed with three sons and one daughter. The eldest son, Maharaj-Kumar Jai Sinh Rao, was sent abroad for his education, and he returned to the ancestral home laden with honours gained in his collegiate course of study. The second son, Maharaj-Kumar Shivaji Rao, distinguished himself at Oxford University, but his life was cut short prematurely by influenza in 1919. The youngest son, Maharaj-Kumar Dhairyashil Rao, attended a prominent public school in England, and he now holds a Commission in the Indian Army. The Princess, Maharaj-Kumar Indira Raja, married His Highness the Maharaja of Cooch Behar.

Their Highnesses the Maharaja and Maharani paid their first visit to Europe in 1887, and after spending several months in Northern Italy, Switzerland, and France, they proceeded to England, where they were for a time the guests of Her Majesty the late Queen Victoria at Windsor Castle. During an interview, Her Majesty was graciously pleased to bestow upon His Highness the Maharaja the insignia of a Knight Grand Commander of the Most Exalted Order of the Star of India.

The physical strength of His Highness was severely taxed shortly after that time by reason of the enormous energy which he threw into the work of administration, and it was necessary for him to court restoration to health by making another trip to Switzerland. A short stay in the bracing climate of that lovely country in the year 1888 was attended by beneficial results, but the toll levied upon his constitution by a close application to State affairs rendered it essential that the Gaekwar should return to Europe in the years 1892 and 1893, 1895, 1900, and 1905. Her Highness the Maharani accompanied her husband in these tours, and in 1892 she was personally invested with the Imperial Order of the Crown of India by Her Majesty the Queen-Empress Victoria.

Once again His Highness was compelled to leave Baroda on the ground of ill-health, and on March 30, 1910, he, together with Her Highness the Maharani Saheba, C.I., and Princess Shrimati Raj-Kumari Indira Raja, sailed from Bombay for the shores of Japan. During the voyage he was received by leading Government officials at Colombo, Penang, Hong-Kong, Macao, Canton, Shanghai, Nagasaki, Kobe, Yokohama, Kyoto, Tokio, and Honolulu. San Francisco was reached on June 17th, and after viewing Seattle, Banff, and other places, the party arrived at Toronto, inspected the Niagara Falls, and proceeded to New York, where they embarked on July 13th for London. Their Highnesses had the honour of being received at Marlborough House by the King-Emperor and Queen-Empress, and had interviews with several leading statesmen, but, as a rule, His Highness the Maharaja led a quiet life, under the orders of his medical advisers. After paying a flying visit to Paris, the party sailed from Marseilles on December 2nd, and arrived at Baroda on the 19th of the same month.

His Highness had again to visit England the next year, when he attended the Coronation ceremonies of Their Imperial Majesties the present King-Emperor and Queen-Empress, which took place in London in the summer of 1911, and he returned to India in order to be present at the Coronation Durbar held at Delhi in December of the same year. Ill-health compelled His Highness to visit Europe again in 1913 and 1914.

In the course of these extended tours in foreign countries, it was the practice of His Highness the Maharaja to make a thorough study of political, industrial, and social conditions, and it is impossible to exaggerate the value, to the State of Baroda, of the experience thus gained by His Highness and utilized by him in the administration of the State.

An important event occurred in the year 1909, when His Excellency the Rt. Hon.

THE STATE OF BARODA.

H.E. Lord Chelmsford Inspecting Guard of Honour on Arrival at Baroda, March 24, 1919.
2. State Banquet at Baroda in Honour of H.E. Lord Chelmsford, March 24, 1919.

THE STATE OF BARODA.

1. Nyaya Mandir, Baroda. 2. Baroda College.

THE STATE OF BARODA.

1. Museum at Baroda (Front View). 2. Picture Gallery, Baroda.

the Earl of Minto, P.C., G.C.M.G. (Viceroy and Governor-General of India), together with the Countess of Minto, and their daughter, Lady Eileen Elliott, visited Baroda. The Viceregal party arrived in the State on November 13th, and were welcomed by His Highness the Maharaja and a large number of notable personages, the customary salute of 31 guns being fired by the State artillery. Elaborate ceremonials were observed in connection with the exchange of visits and interviews, and on the evening of November 15th, a State Banquet was given to Their Excellencies and Staff in the Durbar Hall of the Laxmi Vilas Palace.

The next Viceroy to visit Baroda was His Excellency Lord Chelmsford, who arrived at Baroda on March 24, 1919, and stayed for a brief period of two days. His Excellency was received with the greatest enthusiasm, and was accorded all the honours due to his exalted rank. A State Banquet was held in his honour on the 24th March.

The State of Baroda is, as stated above, 8,182 square miles in extent, and it is divided into four distinct tracts, separated from each other by intervening British territory. The most southerly portion, Navsari, is situated near the mouth of the river Tapti; to the north of the Nerbudda river is the central district of Baroda, containing the capital city; to the north of Ahmedabad is the district of Kadi; and to the west, in Kathiawar, are tracts of land, isolated from each other, which are comprised in the district of Amreli. The inhabitants, who were 2,032,798 in number at the census of 1911, consist of 1,696,146 Hindus, 160,137 Mahomedans, 43,462 Jains, 7,955 Parsis, 7,293 Christians, and 115,411 persons of animistic creeds.

The highest officer of His Highness the Gaekwar's Government is called the Diwan, who corresponds to the Prime Minister of other countries. He is constantly in touch with His Highness, and it is by him that affairs pertaining to the foreign relations of the State with the British Government and the Indian States are conducted through the Resident at Baroda. His Highness shows great care and judgment in the selection of his Diwan, by inviting the best man available in India to work under him, and to assist him in his administration. Caste, colour, or creed do not influence him, and he has no favourites to deviate him from the path of righteousness and impartiality. This will be evident from the list given below of the gentlemen who have had the honour of holding the office of Diwan under Maharaja Sayaji Rao Gaekwar: (1) Raja Sir T. Madhava Rao, K.C.S.I., who served from May 16, 1875, to September 28, 1882; (2) Khan Bahadur Kazi Shahabuddin, C.I.E., from September 29, 1882, to July 31, 1886; (3) Diwan Bahadur Laxuman Jagannath Vaidya, from August 1, 1886, to May 30, 1890; (4) Diwan Bahadur Manibhai Jashbhai, from May 31, 1890, to November 21, 1895; (5) Diwan Bahadur S. Shrinivas Raghava Iyengar, C.I.E., from July 15, 1895, to October 2, 1901; (6) Diwan Bahadur R. V. Dhamnaskar, from October 3, 1901, to June 30, 1904; (7) Mr. Kersaspji Rustamji Dadachanji, M.A., LL.B., from July 1, 1904, to February 28, 1909; (8) Mr. R. C. Dutt, I.C.S., C.I.E., from June 1, 1909, to November 30, 1909; (9) Mr. C. N. Seddon, I.C.S., from December 1, 1909, to January 3, 1912; (10) Mr. B. L. Gupta, I.C.S., C.S.I., from January 4, 1912, to March 16, 1914; (11) Mr. V. P. Madhava Rao, B.A., C.I.E., from March 17, 1914, to May 7, 1916; and (12) Mr. Manubhai Nandshankar Mehta, M.A., LL.B., C.S.I., from May 9, 1916, who continues to hold office.

With the Diwan are associated a Joint Revenue Minister, and a Deputy Minister, to whom certain powers of the Minister are delegated. These officials form the Council of the State. There is also a Legislative Council, by whom, with certain limitations, laws and regulations are made for the government of the State. This body is composed of the Diwan, as President, four *ex officio* members, six official nominated members, five non-official nominated members, and 10 elected members.

The highest Judicial tribunal is the *Varishta*, or High Court, but the power of revising the decisions of that Bench is reserved for His Highness the Maharaja Sahib, who is advised by a Committee of not less than three members—the Legal Remembrancer, a Judge of the *Varishta* Court (not previously concerned with the case), and the *Huzur Kamdar*. The other Courts are: Five District Judges' Courts (including that of the City District Judge); four Assistant Judges' Courts; 24 Subordinate Judges' Courts; four District Magistrates' Courts: 86 *ex officio* Revenue Magistrates' (Executive) Courts; 24 ordinary Magistrates' Courts; 26 Revenue Magistrates' Courts, exercising second-class and third-class powers (Judicial); three village *Munsiffs'* Courts; five other officials invested with Civil powers; and 90 Courts of village *Panchayats*, exercising civil and criminal jurisdiction.

The Regular forces of the State consist of 93 artillery, 1,500 cavalry, and 3,182 infantry, and the Irregular troops comprise 2,000 horse and 1,806 foot, the annual expenditure being about Rs. 14,00,000.

The sanctioned strength of the police force is 1,024 officers and 3,958 men, 199 of whom are mounted.

It was evident from the commencement of the *regime* of His Highness that he intended to reorganize all Departments of State, and to introduce beneficial measures of progress and reform. He initiated a scientific land-revenue survey as one of his first acts. The new settlement introduced fixity of tenure and order where previously there had been uncertainty. It equalized the land tax to a large extent, basing it on the capabilities of the soil, and it imposed rates which were somewhat lower than the previous demands. It swept away the *Bhagbatai* system, or "payment in kind," which then prevailed in some parts of the Raj. The system of collecting revenue was also thoroughly revised, and rules relating thereto were codified.

Transit duties were abolished, and customs taxation was lightened. A number of miscellaneous *Veros* which existed before, and were levied on people residing in villages following several occupations and trades, were abolished, and a simple and uniform system of income-tax was introduced.

His Highness the Maharaja Sahib has gained a high reputation for his wisdom and foresight in his administrative duties, and it would not be incorrect to observe that in furthering the cause of education, and in his warm support of commercial and industrial enterprises, especially agriculture, his activities are not exceeded by those of any other Prince in India.

One of the most important aids to the development of agriculture was the establishment by His Highness of model demonstration and experimental farms in favourable positions in the State. Cultivators are instructed in the best methods of tillage, the relative values and modes of application of different kinds of manures, and in a thousand and one other matters connected with farming on a scientific basis. Most interesting and

THE STATE OF BARODA.

1. Female Training School, Baroda. 2. Record Tower, Baroda.

THE STATE OF BARODA.

1. Equestrian Statue of H.H. Maharaja Sayaji Rao III, Gaekwad, Baroda. 2. View of Sayaji Ganj, Baroda. 3. Sayaji, Sarovar Baroda. 4. General Hospital Baroda.

THE STATE OF BARODA.

1. Hira Gate and Temple of Kalila Mata, Dabhoi. 2. Ancient Temple at Modhera.

THE STATE OF BARODA.

1. Rudra Malai Sidhpur. 2. Kirti Stambh, Vadnagar.

effective work is being carried out on the experimental portions of the farms, and important results have been obtained as to the most suitable varieties of wheat, cotton, tobacco, oilseeds, millets, and other crops. Four Graduate Inspectors pay visits to villages, demonstrating to cultivators the use of improved implements, and delivering lectures on general improvement in agriculture, and the advantage to be derived from co-operation. During the tours of these officials, in the year 1917-18, they secured 53 orders for improved ploughs, sickles, and cane-crushers, and they also distributed more than 20,000 lb. of pure seed of cotton, ground-nuts, indigo, lucerne, and hemp. A Superintendent of Entomology visits the holdings of intelligent occupiers for the purpose of giving lectures upon the life history and the depredations of insects which cause such serious losses in crops of tobacco, mangoes, sesamum, sugar-cane, cotton, and other vegetable produce.

These "talks to the people" are rendered more interesting and profitable by the use of magic lantern slides, upon which fascimiles of many varieties of injurious pests are depicted. Eight veterinary dispensaries have been opened at Baroda and other central places in the State, and the Surgeons in charge gave treatment to 5,810 animals during the year 1918-19.

His Highness the Maharaja Sahib recently appointed a Committee to inquire into the economic conditions of the people, and the measures to be taken for the further development of the industrial resources of the State. One of the questions under consideration was the manufacture of woollen goods. Information was collected regarding the quality and quantity of wool available in Baroda, and samples of some of the principal types were secured for examination. Investigations are also being made as to the suitability of the wood in the State forests for the purpose of distillation, and a prospecting licence has been granted to an Industrial Syndicate, who propose to make further experiments. The same Syndicate is also interested in the question of salt and other chemicals and minerals, and quite recently it has been discovered that magnesium salts can be successfully manufactured from brine obtained at Dwarka. Among the more important industrial enterprises are several cotton mills, dyeing and bleaching works, chemical works, and factories for making tiles of the Mangalore type, *terra-cotta* ornaments, China clay utensils, ropes, and other goods. Demonstrators, appointed by the State for the purpose of giving instruction in weaving and in the use of improved machinery, have done excellent work during the past few years.

Improved fly-shuttle looms and other appliances have been imported, and many of the weavers have already realized the advantages to be obtained by their use.

Under the present generous policy of fostering new enterprises, the State either secures for them the necessary financial help on easy terms through the Bank of Baroda, or, in exceptional cases, vouchsafes such help directly by giving debenture loans, or by agreeing to keep long term deposits with the Company at easy rates of interest. The State also assists new concerns by helping them to acquire the necessary land on easy terms.

The past few years have presented a wonderful spectacle of new industries fast coming into being, owing to the generous policy referred to above. There will soon rise into existence no fewer than 12 new spinning and weaving textile mills; one mill for woollen fabrics, and four miscellaneous textile mills, dealing with waste cotton and yarn. There will be two large cement factories, with sound financial foundations, one at Dwarka, and the other at Kodinar; two alkali manufactories, with large capital, at Dwarka and Kodinar, and four other chemical works for the preparation of acids and medicinal drugs and essences; wood distillation works, for the manufacture of acetic acid, spirits, and tar; three potteries and two tanneries, saddlery works; four oil mills, and four other miscellaneous factories. These are only the new factories that have already been registered, and have commenced their preliminary operations. All the old industrial concerns are in good working order, and the old cotton mills are flourishing, and additions are being made of new machinery, a greater number of spindles and looms. The Hind candle factory has worked wonderfully well, and its products of chocolate, glycerine, and candles had a marvellous sale during the late Great War.

Another generous and useful attraction offered by the State is that of co-operative investigation and scientific exploitation. In order to assist the promoters of new industries in the preliminary investigations, the State has set apart a large sum, and it has also made arrangements with a number of experts and firms of Consulting Engineers to give the necessary technical advice to the projectors of new industries. Under these arrangements the following problems are under scientific investigation, namely: the manufacture of glass, *Reh*, buttons, and conchshell bangles, tannin and extracts, casein, lactose, and pottery ware, while tests are made of minerals, recommended by former economic surveys, and of forest products.

The State has recently engaged the services of a ceramic expert, and has also undertaken to employ a professional tanner, with the object of improving the old indigenous and wasteful methods of curing and tanning hides and skins.

The fishery and weaving demonstration branches of the State are doing steady and useful work. The most important undertaking of the future will, however, be the cement and salt industry in Dwarka and Kodinar, the latter industry especially having a bright future before it now that the Government of India has agreed to allow the State to export its Okhamandal salt into British India. The industry of manufacturing soda, soda ash, chloride of potassium, sulphates of soda, and other alkalis, is also capable of changing the economic aspect of the above-mentioned parts of the State, and it is being carefully fostered.

For a full development of the cement and alkali works at Dwarka and Kodinar, the improvement of the Adatra and Velan harbours is being undertaken, marine surveys have been completed, and the projects will soon be matured. A railway communication for Dwarka, with the main system of the Kathiawar railways, is also being provided, with the co-operation of the Baroda and Jamnagar States.

Financial assistance is also given to Co-operative Credit and other Societies. There are 417 of these registered in Baroda; two are central Banks, two are Banking Unions, 369 are Agricultural Credit Societies, eight are Agricultural non-credit, 34 non-agricultural credit, and two are non-agricultural non-credit Societies. The membership increased from 11,958 in 1918 to 13,956 in the following year.

The total forest area of Baroda consists of 633·8 square miles of reserved, and 4·9 square miles of protected, tracts. These figures include 3,120 *bighas* of mountainous land, at an elevation of more than 3,000 feet, situated near the Salher fort. Nearly the whole of the forest area is dealt with by the Conservator on the "coppice-with-standards" system, and upon a rotation of 40 years for the regenerating crop. In addition to teak and other valuable timber, the forests yield minor produce, including lac, *mahua* flowers and seeds, *rosha* seeds, and *asinta* and *timru* leaves. The distillation of *rosha* oil has just been carried out experimentally for the first time in the forest tracts of Songhad.

The Public Works Department comprises eight executive divisions, namely, City, Palace, Gardens, Electrical, and the Baroda, Kadi, Navsari, and Amreli Districts. The amount annually expended by the Department amounts to about Rs. 25,00,000.

The total open mileage of railways owned by the State is 535, and construction is being carried on over a distance of 93·17 miles. The total budget grant sanctioned for railways during the past year was Rs. 12,10,000, and the actual expenditure amounted to Rs. 11,85,897.

The cause of education is one of the most popular movements in the State, and one, moreover, in which the deepest possible interest is taken by His Highness the Maharaja. In the year 1893 compulsory and free instruction was tentatively introduced by the State in one *taluqa*, and since 1906 the system has been made universal.

The total number of educational institutions in Baroda at the close of the year 1918-19 was 2,862, in which there were 2,02,034 pupils. These figures were slightly lower than those of the preceding 12 months, but this decrease is more than accounted for by an epidemic of influenza, which necessitated the closing of several schools.

The latest available State Administration Report gives the following particulars of institutions giving an English education, namely, the Baroda College, 15 High Schools for boys, one of a similar standard for girls, 37 Anglo-Vernacular Schools, 9 higher standard classes, one Prince's School, and two special institutions. For instruction in the Vernacular there are four Training Colleges for males, and one of a like nature for women, 2,316 schools for boys, 389 of the same kind for girls, one *Kala Bhuvan*, and 85 classed as "other institutions." The Baroda College, founded in 1882, is recognized by the Bombay University for the full course in Arts and Sciences. It is now attended by 571 students—including 13 ladies—and boarding accommodation is provided for more than 200 of these pupils in the three hostels attached to it. The College is ably controlled by the Principal, who is assisted by a staff of 16 Professors, three Lecturers in French, Sanskrit, and logic, and about half a dozen other teachers. The College possesses an excellent library of more than 10,000 volumes, as well as an Observatory, at which meteorological readings are taken twice daily. The Prince's School is an institution specially set apart for the grandchildren of His Highness the Maharaja Sahib, and a few selected pupils who are regarded in the light of companions. There are in the State 2,983 Government, 23 aided, and 30 unaided primary schools, and one orphanage. The annual expenditure on these institutions is nearly Rs. 12,00,000, and almost Rs. 4,00,000 are spent upon English educational facilities, but when it is observed that the total amount devoted yearly to giving instruction in all standards of learning reaches a sum of about Rs. 23,00,000, one cannot do other than admire the deeply-rooted determination of His Highness to throw open as widely as possible the only avenue by which a State, or even a country, can be raised to a position of material and social prosperity.

A Central Institution, called the "Kala Bhuvan," was founded in the year 1890 with the object of "popularizing and promoting polytechnical education among the masses." Provision is made for courses in theory and practice in the following six subjects, namely, art, civil and mechanical engineering, chemical technology, the manufacture of textiles, and training in elementary commercial principles. The art section includes the painting of portraits, modelling in clay, wood-carving, and photo-mechanical work. The students, about 400 in number, belong for the most part to Baroda, but several hail from remote districts of India.

There is a splendid Museum, with a Picture Gallery, in Baroda city, and it is highly appreciated by students of the local colleges and schools, as well as by others belonging to several outlying districts. The average daily attendance is about 600.

In the year 1910 11 His Highness the Maharaja Sahib established a Library branch of the Educational Department, with the object of promoting the dessemination of general knowledge. The Central one, at Baroda, has more than 64,000 printed volumes, nearly 7,000 Sanskrit manuscripts, and 222 newspapers and periodicals. The Ladies' Library possesses 1,500 books, chiefly in the Gujarati language, and it receives 1 vernacular newspapers and periodicals There are now in the State 536 town and rural Libraries, in which are found 243,842 volumes. A "Travelling" Library, recently founded, sends out annually about 180 cases, containing 15,275 volumes, all of which are circulated in villages throughout the State.

The State maintains, at an annual cost of about Rs. 4,52,000, 61 hospitals and dispensaries, the average daily attendance of outdoor and resident patients being respectively 4,839 and 319 persons. Proposals are now being considered by the State authorities for making medical relief available for all villages within five miles from a hospital or dispensary, and for offering assistance to expectant mothers.

Endeavours were made from the commencement of the settlement operations to preserve as much of the old forms of self-government in villages as was possible, and provision was made in every rural district to appoint a *Panchayat*, and to maintain the services which it previously enjoyed. The unity of villages was thus preserved under *patels* and *talatis*.

In 1904 His Highness decided to introduce the elective system in the village *Panchayats*, and to bestow upon them powers of administration. The supervision of village roads, wells, tanks, schools, *dharmashalas, choras*, and *devasthans*, was vested in them. They were to co-operate with village *Munsiffs* in settling civil disputes; they were to help in the work of medical and famine relief in times of emergency, and some of them are now invested with civil and criminal powers.

In 1904 *taluqa* and district boards were also created. The duties vested in them were the construction of roads, tanks, wells, and water-works, the management of *dharmashalas*, dispensaries, and markets; the supervision of vaccination, sanitation, primary education, and arboriculture, and the inauguration of relief works on a small scale in times of famine.

Every town has been constituted a Municipality, and some of the most important of these are self-governing, certain sources of revenue, adequate for their present expenditure, having been assigned to them.

An Ecclesiastical Department has recently been created for controlling temples, public charities, Sanskrit *Pathshalas*, and religious education in general. It also deals with Sanskrit, Oriental, and Archæological research. Itinerant

THE STATE OF BARODA.

1. North Side of Khan Sarovar, Pattan, North Gujarat. 2. Temple of Shri Dwarkadhish, Dwarka.

THE STATE OF BARODA.

1. Gold Gun, Baroda. 2. Silver Gun, Baroda. 3. Golden Carriage. 4. Gold Ambari, Baroda. 5. Elephant Fight, Baroda.

THE STATE OF BARODA.

1. Waterfall, Lakshmi Vilas Palace Garden, Baroda. 2. Sursagar Tank, Baroda. 3. Suspension Bridge in Public Park, Baroda.

THE STATE OF BARODA.

1. MAIN ROAD, BARODA CITY. 2. BIRD'S-EYE VIEW OF BARODA CITY FROM NAZAR BAUG PALACE.

preachers are engaged, who travel from village to village, explaining social and religious questions on liberal and advanced lines.

His Highness the Maharaja Sahib has been a most loyal and generous supporter of the British Government during the late Great War, and a brief summary of the assistance rendered by him and the State may be tabulated as follows: (I) Men: (*a*) 157 men from the State Regular forces were allowed to join the British Army, and Rs. 1,447 due by them to the State on account of loans were remitted; (*b*) three European Officers from the State army were permitted to proceed to England on special leave to join the Expeditionary Force, and a fourth was also granted special leave to join the British Army at Muttra; (*c*) the services of Dr. C. A. L. Mayer, M.D. (London), were placed at the disposal of the British Government, and he was paid a salary of Rs. 1,200 per mensem from the Baroda treasury, in addition to the allowance drawn by him in British service; and (*d*) 200 *sowars* and six officers were sent to Muttra to train remounts.

The number of subjects of the State who joined the British Indian Army up to the end of November 1918 as combatants, non-combatants, and skilled and unskilled labourers, was 1,417.

(II) Gifts of money: (i) By His Highness the Maharaja Gaekwar: (*a*) for the provision and equipment of aeroplanes, Rs. 5,00,000; (*b*) for the War Gift Fund, Rs. 5,00,000; for "Ford" motor vans, Rs. 15,00,000; (*d*) contribution of Rs. 12,000 a month from January 1916 to June 1919, Rs. 5,04,000, making a total of Rs. 30,04,000; (ii) contribution to the Imperial Indian War Relief Fund: (*a*) by His Highness the Maharaja Gaekwar, Rs. 2,10,000; (*b*) other subscriptions, Rs. 84,586, making a total of Rs. 2,94,586; (iii) contributions to the Prince of Wales's Fund by His Highness the Maharaja Gaekwar, Rs. 30,000; (iv) Red Cross contributions: (*a*) by His Highness the Maharaja Gaekwar to "Our Day" Fund, Rs. 35,000; Red Cross Fund, Simla, Rs. 5,000; (*b*) other subscriptions, Rs. 27,464, giving a total of Rs. 67,464.

The grand total of all money gifts is therefore Rs. 33,96,050. Besides the above, miscellaneous donations to several institutions and Relief Funds in Europe and India, organized in connection with war, amount to Rs. 75,937.

(III) Materials: (i) free gifts: (a) 154 horses from the State cavalry, valued at Rs. 55,786; (*b*) 13 tents, of the aggregate value of Rs. 8,722, for hospital use with the expeditionary force in France; (*c*) 12 sets of chessmen, sent by His Highness the Gaekwar through Her Excellency Lady Willingdon. (ii) Loans: (*a*) the "Jaya Mahals Palace" in Bombay, with bungalow attached, lent as a hospital for officers; (*b*) one State steam tug, for transport purposes. (iii) Supplied on payment: (*a*) 157 horses from the State cavalry; (*b*) railway stock, comprising four X-class engines, 35 open bogies, four brake vans, four trolleys, 22 steel open four-wheeled wagons; (*c*) three "Dumpey" levels, and three theodolites.

(IV) Purchases of War Loan: (i) by His Highness the Maharaja Gaekwar, (*a*) War Loan Bonds of 1917, Rs. 32,00,000; (*b*) War Loan Bonds of 1917, purchased by conversion of old G.P. Notes, Rs. 38,00,000; (*c*) War Loan Bonds (1928) of the second Indian War Loan, Rs. 30,00,000; (ii) by Her High-

THE STATE OF BARODA.

GROTTO, MAKAPURA PALACE.

ness the Maharani Gaekwar, War Loan Bonds of 1917, as a contribution to the Bombay Women's War Loan, Rs. 2.00,000 ; (iii) by Khan Saheb Framji Cowasji, Contractor, Baroda, War Loan Bonds of 1917, Rs. 2,00,000, making an aggregate of Rs. 104,00,000 ; (iv) non-official War Loan, purchased by State subjects, Rs. 8,24,180.

From the foregoing it will be seen that His Highness is one of the most progressive and intelligent Rulers among the Native Princes of India. He emerged from the seclusion of his early home life in an obscure village in Western India, and by his great natural capabilities, developed by experience gained in visiting the leading social, political, and commercial centres of Europe, he has risen to a position in which he is beloved by his own subjects, regarded with respect by those with whom he comes into contact in every-day life, and honoured by His Imperial Majesty the King-Emperor, for whom his unswerving loyalty is ever manifested.

The full titles of the Maharaja are His Highness Farzandi-i-Khas-i-Daulat-i-Inglishia Maharaja Sir Sayaji Rao Gaekwar, III Sena Khas Khel Shamsher Bahadur, G.C.S.I., G.C.I.E.

Baroda city, the capital of the State, is situated on the right bank of the Vishwamitri river, which is spanned by four bridges, connecting the city with the Cantonment. Near to the railway station are the magnificent buildings of the Baroda College, and the "Countess of Dufferin" Hospital, while high above all other structures is the Mandwi, or the famous clock-tower. Within a stone's throw from the last-named structure is the Nazar Bagh palace, built by Malhar Rao Gaekwar, in which the priceless gems of His Highness the Maharaja are kept. These include a necklace of diamonds, one of which, known by the name of "the Star of the South," is 125 carats in weight, and is estimated to be worth Rs. 9,00,000. There is also a cloth, embroidered with precious stones and seed pearls, which was designed as a covering for the Prophet's tomb at Mecca. It is 10 feet by six, woven entirely of strings of pearls, and is valued at Rs. 30,00,000.

The Lakshmi Vilas palace, built in the Hindu-Saracenic style of architecture, at a cost of Rs. 60,00,000, is the next to claim attention. In it is a large Durbar Hall, with walls and floor beautifully decorated in mosaics by Italian experts ; the furnishing is of gorgeous character ; and its further adornment comprises a fine collection of bronze statues, and of costly paintings by European artists.

THE TOWN HALL, HYDERABAD.

THE DOMINIONS OF HIS EXALTED HIGHNESS THE NIZAM OF HYDERABAD

HYDERABAD is the premier Indian State in India, and the chief of the Mahomedan, as well as of all the tributary sovereignties of the King-Emperor, although it is of modern origin when compared with many other Principalities. It is situated in the Deccan, a plateau lying roughly between the Bombay Presidency, the United Provinces, the Central Provinces, and the Presidency of Madras. It is believed that in prehistoric times the territory was included in the Great Dravidian zone, but there are clear proofs that in the reign of the famous King Asoka (272–231 B.C.) the kingdom over which he ruled embraced the northern and western portion of Hyderabad. At least three Hindu dynasties held sway over this part of India in succeeding years, but at the close of the thirteenth century, the Mahomedans, under Ala-ud-din Khiliji, appeared on the scene, their advent being the commencement of a long series of struggles against the Hindu kingdoms of the south. The Emperor Aurungzeb having asserted his power over the wide area conquered by him, appointed one of the bravest of his Generals—Asaf Khan, a Turkoman, connected with a distinguished family—as *Subadar*, or Viceroy, of the Deccan, bestowing upon him the title of "Nizam-ul-Mulk," signifying "Regulator of the State," an appellation which has become hereditary in the family. This official was as sagacious in administration and political economy as he was courageous in battle, and he speedily justified the confidence placed in him by his Royal Master.

The Moghul Empire was about this period tottering towards its downfall, and when the death of Aurungzeb was followed by general confusion, especially in the scramble for territory by minor Powers, Asaf Khan declared his independence against the weak authority of the Delhi Court. This attitude assumed by Asaf Khan created a spirit of intense jealousy at Delhi, where orders were actually issued to the Governor of Khandesh to employ force of arms against the Ruler of Hyderabad.

The decisive defeat of the invading army greatly strengthened the position of Asaf Khan, who established his seat of government at the town of Hyderabad, and thus founded the dynastic line of which His Exalted Highness the present Nizam is a direct descendant.

After the death of Asaf Khan in 1748, the right of succession was claimed by Nasir Jung, his second son, as the eldest of his descendants who held an important position at the Imperial Court at Delhi. This plan was opposed by Muzaffar Jung,

D

nephew of the deceased Ruler, and a serious revolt was soon in existence. The English and French were at this time struggling for supremacy in India, and with the object of furthering their projects, the former espoused the cause of Nasir Jung, while the latter gave their support to the nephew.

Owing to disaffection among the troops of Muzaffar Jung, the latter was compelled to submit to his uncle, who caused him to be imprisoned in a dungeon. Nasir Jung was subsequently assassinated by Pathans, serving in the French army, and Muzaffar Jung was released from captivity and placed upon the throne, although Dupleix, the French Governor, exercised considerable control over the new Nizam. The reign of the latter was of short duration, as he shared a fate similar to that which had befallen his predecessor.

The French thereupon declared Salabat Jung, third son of Nizam-ul-Mulk, to be the legal successor, but the eldest son, Ghazi-ud-din, relinquished his post at Delhi, and at the head of a large army, assisted by the Marathas, marched towards Hyderabad with the view of dethroning Salabat, and of assuming sovereignty for himself. His sudden death, however, put an end to further trouble.

From the date of Salabat Jung's accession to the *masnad*, the French wielded extensive powers at the Court of Hyderabad, and it was not until the British General, Lord Clive, was pushing his way towards the Nizam's dominions that they turned their attentions more closely to the possessions which they had previously acquired in India. The British at this juncture obtained from Delhi the right of trading in certain districts and at several ports on the west coast, but Ali Khan, successor in 1761 of Salabat Jung as Nizam, protested against the arrangement, and prepared a large army to oppose the advance of the British. The questions at issue were, however, amicably settled by an agreement under which the British were allowed to retain the districts above referred to, but in return were required to pay annually to the Nizam the sum of Rs. 6,00,000, and to furnish him with military assistance wherever required. The districts are now known by the name of the Northern Circars.

About the year 1780, trouble arose which had a far-reaching effect upon the future of Hyderabad, and the relationship subsisting between the Nizam and the British Government. Briefly, they were as follows: The death of the notorious Haidar Ali, of Mysore, had brought to the throne of that territory his son, Tipu Sultan, who carried his encroachments against districts occupied by the British as well as by the Hyderabad Ruler. These two Powers entered into a league for a combined attack upon the dominions of their common enemy, but Tipu was in command of so large a force, and was so crafty as a strategist, that hostilities dragged on for several years. Indeed, it was not until 1798 that the Sultan's army was completely defeated by the British, and he himself slain. In the division of territory yielded to the conquerors, the share falling to the lot of the Nizam was of the annual value of Rs. 24,00,000. Lord Wellesley, the Commander of the British troops in these engagements, wrote in an official report: "It would have been impossible to conquer the dominions of Tipu had it not been for the active support and co-operation of Nizam Ali." In October 1800 a new treaty was concluded between the Nizam and the British Government, the terms of the document requiring the former to employ a further contingent of 8,000 infantry, 1,000 cavalry and artillery, and further stipulating that he should not make war upon any of the recognized Powers without the consent of the latter. The Government, on the other hand, undertook to settle all differences arising between the Nizam and his enemies. The area of land transferred from Tipu's dominions to Hyderabad were, further, ceded to the British for the purpose of meeting additional military supplies. Three years later the Nizam rendered conspicuous service to the British in an expedition against the Raja of Berar, and in recognition of this support, a large portion of the territory acquired from that Chief was added to the State of Hyderabad. After a lengthy reign, brimful of vicissitudes of fortune, Nizam Ali Khan passed away in 1803, and was succeeded by his son, Sikandar Jah, who took practically no interest in the welfare of his subjects, and left the full responsibility of administration in the hands of Wazir Mir Alam, his Prime Minister, and subsequently of Munir-ul-Mulk, the latter's son-in-law. This functionary was, however, almost as indifferent as the Nizam, and the British Government, feeling it their bounden duty to interfere, appointed Chandu Lal, of the Kayastha community, a man of wide experience, great intelligence, and rare energy, to take supreme control of all State affairs. The government of Chandu Lal proved advantageous to the State as a whole, but it was far too neglectful of the true interests of struggling *ryots*, and referring to the policy of this Minister, a leading Government official reported that "his method of administration was extremely primitive in theory, and in action oppressive. He 'farmed' the revenue of the several districts to middle-men. The State was thus made secure of a certain revenue, without the trouble of collection, while the taxpayers and people were absolutely without protection." The position of Chandu Lal became so powerful that the jealousy of the sons of the Nizam caused them to devise means for thwarting him in every possible manner, but their opposition was of little avail against so astute a Minister, and they became mere State prisoners, at the mercy of the man whom they desired to overthrow.

Nizam Sikandar Jah died in 1829, when the *masnad* was occupied by his eldest son, Nasir-ud-daula. Chandu Lal, who was retained as Minister, placed the collection of revenue in the hands of his own personal acquaintances, and this act subsequently led to the depletion of the State treasury. Chandu Lal died shortly afterwards, and although his policy on some occasions may be open to criticism, he was such a capable administrator that he is held in high esteem by his successors, even to the present day, and the Deccan Hyderabad is still distinguished from other towns of the same name by the epithet, "Chandu Lal's Hyderabad." In 1853, an inquiry into the financial position of Hyderabad revealed the fact that a very large sum of money was due from the Nizam to the British Government, for the maintenance of a subsidiary force of militia, and fresh stipulations were agreed upon, which provided for a very considerable reduction in the strength of this contingent.

The treaty in question contained the following conditions: "Nizam, while retaining the full use of the subsidiary force, is released from the obligation of furnishing a large force in times of war; the contingent ceases to be the Nizam's army, and becomes an auxiliary force, kept up by the British Government for the Nizam's use." The annual charge was also reduced from Rs. 40,00,000 to Rs. 24,00,000. In order to provide security for the payment of arrears, and the regular discharge of the new obliga-

LIEUT.-GENERAL HIS EXALTED HIGHNESS ASAF JAH MUZAFFAR-UL-MULK WAL MAMILIK NIZAM-UL-MULK, NIZAM-UD-DAULA, NAWAB MIR SIR USMAN ALI KHAN BAHADUR FATEH JUNG, FAITHFUL ALLY OF THE BRITISH GOVERNMENT, G.C.S.I., G.B.E., NIZAM OF HYDERABAD.

THE DOMINIONS OF H.E.H. THE NIZAM OF HYDERABAD.

1. His Highness the Late Nizam. 2. Inauguration of His Exalted Highness the Nizam's Executive Council, October 1919.

tions, the fertile provinces of Berar was leased to the British Government.

The arrangements agreed upon at this period did not meet with approval; the State treasury was empty, revenues were still exacted by officials, who openly oppressed the poor cultivators, crime followed upon the heels of extortion, life and property were insecure, and while the wealthy increased their wealth at the expense of the *ryots*, the Nizam took no steps whatever to put an end to such a terrible state of affairs. The Minister, Wazir Siraj-ul-Mulk, whose laxity had made it possible for such irregularities to exist, was removed by death in May 1853, and he was succeeded by his nephew, the famous Sir Salar Jung, whose high character and brilliant attainments were destined to raise Hyderabad to a position of honour and respect which it has never lost. Sir Salar, entirely reversing the policy of his predecessor, took immediate steps for the reorganization of the police force, with the object of restoring order in the Dominions, and of giving them security against the hordes of depredators who had carried on their nefarious practices with impunity during the previous regime. He effected retrenchment in each State Department, and at the same time introduced reforms which struck at the root of the jobbery and trickery of previous years. With a firm hand he prevented the settlement of lawless tribes within the borders of the Nizam's territories, and thus gave encouragement to the inhabitants to prosecute their avocations without fear of molestation. This "cleaning of the Augæan stable" provoked the hostility of a number of wealthy Mahomedans, who endeavoured to secure the dismissal of the Prime Minister by poisoning the mind of the Nizam against him.

His Highness, who was now thoroughly awakened from his lethargy, could not, however, close his eyes to the fact that the reforms introduced by Sir Salar had been productive of excellent results, and instead of heeding the slanderous reports made to him he entrusted the Premier with still greater powers, and gave him supreme control in administrative duties. The fruits of Sir Salar's able government were manifested by a considerable increase of revenue, and by the prosperity and consequent happiness of the people. At this juncture, the Nizam Nasir-ud-daula died, and was succeeded by his son, Afzal-ud-daula. Immediately after the accession of the new Nizam to the *masnad*, the Sepoy rebellion broke out. In view of the position of affairs in the State, the British Government were seriously alarmed lest the fanatical rebellion should spread to the dominions of the Nizam, and possibly eventually involve that part of India between Bombay in the north-west and Madras in the south.

His Highness was, however, true to his plighted word, notwithstanding the suggestions of some of his reckless followers that he should participate in the revolt, and in recognition of his unswerving loyalty, and of the invaluable aid rendered to the British by his troops, a new treaty was concluded, under which Naldrug and the Raichur Doab, yielding a revenue of more than Rs. 20,00,000, were restored to Hyderabad; a debt of Rs. 50,00,000 was cancelled; certain tracts on the left bank of the Godavari river were transferred to His Highness; and the assigned districts of Berar, with a revenue of Rs. 32,00,000, were taken in trust by the British Government for the purposes specified in the treaty of 1853. Lord Canning, Viceroy and Governor-General of India, wrote a letter to His Highness the Nizam, when peace was fully restored, warmly thanking him and his Minister, on behalf of the Crown, for the great help afforded in quelling the rebellion. Further than this, Rs. 1,00,000 were presented to His Highness. Her Gracious Majesty the late Queen Victoria bestowed upon His Highness and Sir Salar Jung the insignia of the Most Exalted Order of the Star of India, and the Indian Government also made a grant to the Minister of a sum of Rs. 30,000.

Sir Salar Jung again found time to devote his whole-hearted energies to the inauguration of progressive measures, and as was the case in previous years, his actions were strongly opposed, especially by wealthy Mahomedans, whose interests centred in their own personal gain.

Attempts were made upon the life of the Minister, but they were fortunately unsuccessful, and the affairs of State reached a higher standard of efficiency than even before.

His Highness the Nawab Afzal-ud-daula died in February 1869, and his successor was the late Ruler, Prince Mahbub Ali Khan Bahadur, who was then about three years of age. His Excellency the Viceroy and Governor-General of India placed the sole administration of the Dominions in the care of Sir Salar Jung, who was assisted by a Council of Regency. The education of the young Prince was entrusted to distinguished British officers, who proved to be eminently qualified for the highly important duties assigned to them. His Highness became proficient in Persian, Arabic, and Hindustani, and acquired a very fair knowledge of the English language. It is impossible to over-estimate the value to the Dominions of the Nizam of the magnificent services rendered by Sir Salar Jung in his capacity as administrator. He was a statesman in every sense of the word, courageous in the face of difficulties, patient, tactful, and withal endowed with wisdom and intelligence of a very high order.

Sir Salar was as unswerving in his loyalty to the Throne as he was faithful in his devotion to the youthful Prince and the members of his family, and at the same time he never for a single moment allowed any slackening of his interest in the welfare of the State. As His Highness progressed in years he was intelligent enough to appreciate the worth of his Minister, not merely as the virtual Ruler of the State, but as a wise counsellor and faithful friend to himself.

In the year 1875 His Highness the Nizam was invited to visit Bombay, in order to meet His Royal Highness the Prince of Wales (subsequently His Majesty King Edward VII), but as he was unable to leave Hyderabad on account of ill-health, Sir Salar Jung was deputed to represent him. The Minister was cordially welcomed by the Royal Guest, who presented him with several valuable tokens, among them being a sword, encased in a silver scabbard, attached to which was a belt studded with precious gems. Sir Salar Jung proceeded to England in 1876 with the object of conferring with the officials of the India Office upon matters connected with Hyderabad, and during this visit the worthy Minister—whose fame had long preceded his arrival in the Old Country—was the hero of the London season. He was honoured by having an invitation to dine with Her Most Gracious Majesty the late Queen Victoria, at Buckingham Palace.

Sir Salar returned to India in time to accompany the young Prince to the gorgeous Durbar held at Delhi on January 1, 1877, when Her late Majesty assumed the title of Empress of India.

From the year 1881, to the time of his death in February 1883, Sir Salar Jung was sole Regent and Administrator of Hyderabad, and his large-hearted sympathies and liberal policy won for him the sincere admiration of the Paramount

Power, His Highness the Nizam, and practically every subject of the State. A Council of Regency was then appointed to control the administration.

His Highness the Nizam was invested with full ruling powers on February 5, 1884, by His Excellency the Marquis of Ripon, K.G., Viceroy and Governor-General of India.

His Highness, in the course of his training, became profoundly impressed with the privilege of being a faithful ally of the British Government, and on several occasions he offered them his assistance when the political horizon of India was darkened by gathering clouds of disaffection. This loyalty was especially manifested in the year 1887, when Russia appeared to be contemplating encroachments upon India, in its northern frontier, which His Highness offered to help in guarding. This, as well as other acts of devotion, were cordially recognized by successive Viceroys of India, including Lord Ripon, Lord Dufferin, Lord Lansdowne, Lord Elgin, and Lord Curzon, some of whom were visitors at the Royal palace at Hyderabad. His Highness also had the honour of entertaining Their Royal Highnesses the Duke and Duchess of Connaught, the late Prince Albert Victor, and Their Imperial Majesties the present King-Emperor and Queen-Empress, when they toured in India as Prince and Princess of Wales.

His Highness was honoured in 1885 by being created a Knight Grand Commander of the Most Exalted Order of the Star of India, and he was also granted the rank of Lieutenant-General in the British Army.

His Highness, although supreme Ruler in Hyderabad, was no mere figure-head, as he made personal investigation into the management of many Departments of State, and, where necessary, he promptly introduced measures of reform. He thoroughly overhauled the Departments dealing with such important matters as Finance, Education, Sanitation, Revenue, and Land Administration, and he took active steps for the improvement of the condition of his subjects.

Profound expressions of grief were manifested in August 1911, when it became known that His Highness had succumbed to a stroke of paralysis, after a most successful reign of about 27 years. Messages of condolence with the late Nizam's family were flashed from the Royal House of Great Britain, from the Viceroy and Government of India, from Ruling Princes, high Government officials, and others, but perhaps the most striking testimony of all was the spontaneous outburst of grief exhibited by his subjects, for whom he had toiled, and whose love he had gained in no ordinary degree.

The late Ruler left as his heir Nawab Usman Ali Khan Bahadur, who was born April 6, 1886.

The early life of the young Prince was spent in the precincts of the palace, under the careful supervision of especially qualified guardians, but when he had attained the age of youth his education and general training were entrusted to Mr. (afterwards Sir) Brian Egerton, an accomplished English gentleman of good family. He also received excellent instruction in oriental languages and customs from Nawab Imad-ul-Mulk, an Indian gentleman of great scholarly attainments.

It is generally admitted that the choice of tutors was a very happy one, for, as their charge grew in years, he manifested those traits of high moral character, lofty ideals, and perseverance, which are indispensable to the successful career of a Ruler over vast possessions. The Prince not only obtained an accurate knowledge of the English language, as well as a correct accent, but he also acquired that polish of manners which is so essential in one of his high position. In oriental learning the Nizam is remarkably proficient, and he has developed a marked literary talent which has already borne fruit in the form of several volumes of poems and other works, composed in Urdu, which are considered to be of high merit, and which will be an acquisition to Urdu literature.

In 1906 His Exalted Highness married Dulhan Pasha, daughter of Nawab Jehangir Jang, a nobleman representing one of the side branches of the Nizam's family.

The issue of this union are the Nawab Mir Himayat Ali Khan Bahadur, Azam Jah, the heir-apparent; the Nawab Mir Shajant Ali Khan Bahadur Muzzain Jah; and one daughter, named Shahzadi Begum.

His Excellency Lord Hardinge, Viceroy and Governor-General of India, visited Hyderabad in October 1911, for the purpose of investing the present Nizam with administrative powers, and special mention may be made of his touching allusions to the life and character of the previous Ruler.

The present Nizam had enjoyed the very great advantage of parental training in the ancestral home, he was a student at the feet of his revered father, who was rightly looked upon as a man of more than ordinary ability, intelligence, and nobility of character, and in the few years which have elapsed since his accession to power he has amply justified his sincerity, when, at his investiture, he declared that his highest ambition was to be a faithful friend of the Paramount Power, and a beneficent Ruler of his subjects.

In the year 1912 His Highness appointed as his Minister, the third Nawab Salar Jung, grandson of Sir Salar Jung, whose immense services to the Ruling family of Hyderabad, as well as to the inhabitants of the Dominions, have already been referred to. About a year later this Minister resigned, and for several years afterwards the Nizam was his own Minister, until the appointment of an Executive Council towards the close of the year 1919.

His Excellency the Viceroy and Governor-General of India, Lord Hardinge, visited Hyderabad in October 1913, and at a banquet given in his honour, he referred, in terms of high approval, to the numerous improvements effected in the State, which testified to the warm personal interest evinced by His Highness in all matters tending to the welfare of his subjects.

Reference will be made hereafter to the immense assistance given by the State to the British Government during the late Great War, but an announcement made by His Highness when Great Britain declared war against Turkey, was of such great importance, not only to the Moslems of Hyderabad, but also to those of other countries, that it may be quoted here: "In view of the present aspect of the war in Europe, let it be generally known that at this critical juncture it is the bounden duty of the Mahomedans of India to adhere firmly to their old and tried loyalty to the British Government, especially when there is no Moslem or non-Moslem power in the world under which they enjoy such personal and religious liberty as they do in India, and when, moreover, they are assured by the British Government that, as it has in the past always stood the best friend of Islam, so will it continue to be Islam's best friend, and will always protect and cherish its Moslem subjects. I repeat and reiterate that in the crisis before us, the Mahomedan inhabitants of India, especially the subjects of this State,

THE DOMINIONS OF H.E.H. THE NIZAM OF HYDERABAD.

1. The Gateway (Front View), Falaknuma Castle. 2. Falaknuma Castle (View from the Approach). 3. The Falaknuma Castle.

THE DOMINIONS OF H.E.H. THE NIZAM OF HYDERABAD.

1. Entrance, Marble Hall, Falaknuma Castle. 2. Drawing-room, Falannuma Castle. 3. Another View of the Drawing-room, Falaknuma Castle. 4. Dining-room, Falaknuma Castle. 5. Ball-room, Falaknuma Castle.

should, if they care for their own welfare and prosperity, remain firm and whole-hearted in their loyalty and obedience, swerve not a hair's breadth from their devotion to the British Government, whose cause, I am convinced, is just and right, keep sacred the tie which binds subject peoples to their Rulers, and, lastly, that they should in no case allow themselves to be beguiled by the wiles of any one into a course of open or secret sedition against the British Government. Finally, I give expression to the hope that as I, following the tradition of my ancestors, hold myself ever ready to devote my own person, and all the resources of my State, and all that I possess, to the service of Great Britain, so will all Mahomedans of India, especially my own beloved subjects, hold themselves whole-heartedly ready in the same way."

His Exalted Highness attended the never-to-be-forgotten Imperial Durbar at Delhi in 1911, and took part in the magnificent pageant in connection with the coronation ceremony of Their Most Gracious Majesties the King-Emperor and Queen-Empress, and while visiting the historic city he was created a Knight Grand Commander of the Most Exalted Order of the Star of India. He is entitled to a personal salute of 21 guns.

The titles of the Nizam are His Exalted Highness Asaf Jah, Muzaffur-ul-Mulk, Wai Mum Alik, Rustan-i-Dauran, Arastu-i-Zaman, Nizam-ul-Mulk, Nizam-ud-daulah, Nawab Sir Usman Ali Khan Bahadur, Fateh Jung, G.C.S.I.

The dominions of His Exalted Highness are 82,698 square miles in extent, and occupying the centre of the Deccan plateau, lie between 15° 10 and 20° 40′ N. and 74° 40′ and 81° 35′ E. They are bounded on the north by Berar, in the Central Provinces; the Khandesh district of the Bombay Presidency on the north-west; on the south by the Kistna and Tungabhadra rivers, which separate them from the districts of Guntur, Kurnool, and Bellary, in the Madras Presidency; on the west by the Ahmednagar, Sholapur, Darwar, and Bijapur districts of Bombay, and on the east by the Wardha and Godavari rivers, and the Kistna district of Madras. The territory may be described as a polygonal tract, at an average elevation of about 1,200 feet, but with peaks ranging in height from 2,500 feet to 3,500 feet. The rivers Godavari and Manjra divide the country into two portions, which are geologically and ethnically distinctly different in characteristics. The districts in the north and west, inhabited by people speaking the Marathi and Canarese tongues, belong to the Trappean system, and consist of rich black soil, producing good crops of wheat and cotton, while the granitic and calcareous area in the south and east, occupied by persons speaking Telugu, is noted for its rice fields, hills bare of vegetation, rough boulders, and scattered brushwood. The principal mountain ranges are the Balaghat, extending from east to west for a distance of about 200 miles, and a breadth of nearly five miles; the Sahyadriparvat, in the northern part of the Dominions, and traversing them for 250 miles; the Jalna hills, running from the Daulatabad fort in Aurangabad to Berar, with a length of 120 miles; and the Kandikal Galta range, extending for 50 miles in a north-westerly direction from the district of Warangal.

The largest rivers in Hyderabad are the Godavari and the Kistna. The former of these traverses several districts for a distance of fully 670 miles, and it finally enters the district of Godavari, in Madras, where it finds an outlet into the Bay of Bengal. Its chief tributaries are the Purna, Wardha, Painganga, Manjri, and Maner. The Kistna has a total course, within and around the State, of about 400 miles, and its tributaries are the Bhima, Tungabhadra, Musir, and Munnir.

There are not any natural lakes in the Dominions, although many of these which have been constructed, by throwing up dams across valleys traversed by rivers or streams, might in all fairness be classed as such. Many thousands of these, the majority of which are invaluable as sources of irrigation, are now in existence, and the largest of these, known as the Pakhal lake, in the district of Warangal, has an area of nearly 13 square miles.

The whole of the territory is subject to the influences of the two periods of monsoons, and the average amount of rainfall for the past 10 years is 27·52 inches.

It is firmly believed that the mineral wealth of the Dominions is much greater than has up to the present time been disclosed, but several mining companies have been floated, especially in connection with gold, coal, and garnets. These include the Hyderabad (Deccan) Company, and the Hutto Gold Mines Company. Coal is chiefly found at Madhavaram, Singareni, Allapully, Kamawaram, Bandela, Chinur, Tandur, Aksapur, Antergaon, Sasti, and Paoni. During the year 1916–17 about 680,629 tons of coal were raised to the surface, upon which a royalty of Rs. 76,646 was received; and the output from the Hutti gold mine was 13,466 oz., bringing in a royalty of Rs. 43,057. A licence to prospect for mica in the district of Raichur, and another for coal in the Godavar-Maner valley, were granted during the same period; and mining leases for mica and red ochre were also executed.

Graphite, certified to be suitable for lead pencils, is found in large quantities in the Paloncha *taluk*, and a prospecting licence has been granted to a Hyderabad capitalist. Deposits of iron ore occur in the districts of Warangal, Gulbarga, Adilabad, Kareemnagar, Elgandal, and Medhal.

Garnets may be obtained in considerable quantities in a few districts, but mining operations, which gave promise of good results, were suspended on the outbreak of the Great War. Mica is plentiful in the Raichur and other districts; China clay is even more widely distributed; and red ochre, yellow ochre, felspar, galena, jadeite, marbles, and limestone, may be obtained in various parts of the Dominions.

A review of the history of the famous predecessors of the present Nizam clearly shows that they were indefatigable in their efforts to inaugurate and support industrial enterprises, notably that of agriculture, and great as were the results achieved by them, it is confidently expected that under the watchful eye of His Exalted Highness still greater successes may be obtained.

The practice of agriculture in all countries necessarily depends to a very large extent upon the nature of the soil, the equability of the climate, the amount of rainfall, the facilities for irrigation in waterless areas, and the manner in which cultivation of the land is performed. In Hyderabad there are, as already shown, the rich black soil tracts of the north-west, as well as the lighter ones, with a substratum of granite, which are less unproductive than the remaining portion of the territory. There are two well-defined seasons, dry and rainy, and the two harvests of the year, in summer and the following spring respectively, are known by the names of *kharil* and *rabi*. The principal *kharil* crops are: yellow *jowar*, or large millet; *bajra*, or small millet; maize, cotton, peas, paspalum, *til*, and others. These are sown in June and July, and are reaped between September and December, but as their success depends upon the supply of rain during the early monsoons, the ultimate issue is somewhat precarious. The chief *rabi* crops consist of white *jowar*, or large millet; Bengal grains, wheat, barley, linseed, tobacco, and peas. These are not so dependent upon rain, and therefore they are usually grown upon heavy black soils, which are retentive of moisture. Rice and sugar-cane are the principal irrigated crops, and garden vegetables of all kinds are raised in the neighbourhood of wells. In an Administration Report published by the Government of His Exalted Highness for the year 1916–17, it was shown that 31,99,587 acres of cotton, 28,05,221 acres of oil-seeds, 13,44,413 acres of wheat, and about 76,00,000 acres of *jowar* were cultivated.

In connection with manufactures and industries, it may be observed that these two essential branches of trade were exceedingly prosperous many centuries ago. The fame of the industrial products of Hyderabad had, in the early years of the Christian era, extended to Egypt, Greece, the Persian Gulf, and the Red Sea, and the highest reputation was gained for brocades, cloth of gold and silver, silk fabrics, fine muslins, carpets, rugs, filigree work, and beautifully inlaid ornaments and household requisites. At the present time there are in the Dominions, 80 cotton ginning and pressing factories, three cotton spinning and weaving mills, 62 flour mills, 33 rice mills, a silk factory, three distilleries, a tile factory, an ice factory, an iron foundry, an aerated-water factory, and a water-pumping station. Gold and silver wire, locally manufactured, is now worked into costly loom-made garments of all descriptions. What is known as *karehob* work consists of embroidery on silk, cotton, muslins, or velveteens, intended for dresses, shawls, and head-dresses. *Pitambars*, or waist-cloths, worn by Hindu men and women, are made either wholly or partly in silk, and are usually in two colours. Those prepared specially for zenana ladies are beautifully brocaded, and are sold at prices ranging from Rs. 75 to Rs. 500, or even more than this sum. Aurangabad is famous for gorgeous gold-embroidered velvets, and these are generally prepared for canopies at State functions, umbrellas of dignity, covers for elephants in processions, and in furnishings for royal palaces. *Mashru* and *Himru* cloths consist of a cotton warp with a woof of soft silk, and these are woven for Mahomedans, who are not permitted to wear pure silk when engaged in religious worship. The town of Bidar is celebrated for its *bidri* ware, which consists of an alloy of zinc, copper, tin, and lead, the surface of the articles being inlaid with silver or gold.

This work is seen chiefly in ewers, jugs, basins, portions of bedsteads, fancy boxes, cups, and other vessels. Excellent specimens of this highly-artistic handicraft were presented in 1875, during the visit to India of His Royal Highness the Prince of Wales (afterwards the King-Emperor Edward VII). Tasar cocoons are collected in the jungles of the southern and eastern districts of the Dominions, and a very durable silk cloth is manufactured at Warangal, Mathwara, Hasanparti, Kosgi, and other places.

With the object of encouraging the development of manufactures and industries, His Exalted Highness sanctioned the holding of an Exhibition at Hyderabad in the year 1917, and about the same time certain officials of the State Government published interesting pamphlets bearing upon the industrial potentialities of the Dominions. Most valuable suggestions were made by the writers, to whom acknowledgment is due for some of the following particulars. A striking feature connected with the industrial resources of Hyderabad is revealed in the fact that the Dominions of His Exalted Highness export fully one-third of the total quantity of the principal oil-seeds sent abroad by the whole of British India.

Cotton, of the annual value of more than Rs. 7,00,00,000, is exported from Hyderabad, and yet the Dominions import cotton goods worth at least Rs. 2,23,38,000 in a single year. This statement is significant of the need for the erection of spinning and weaving mills. Again, thousands of tons of stalks of the cotton plant are consumed as fuel, or are ploughed into the ground as manure, although they could with great profit be manufactured into good paper. Very large quantities of wool and hair from sheep and goats respectively, now sent to Europe, might be profitably utilized if there were a sufficiency of up-to-date clothing factories.

Very large quantities of hides and skins, if manufactured into leather in Hyderabad, would more than meet the requirements of the Government for military accoutrements and boots and shoes, while horns of animals could be turned into knives, spoons, buttons, and other articles.

There is an excellent opening for the manufacture of sugar, vegetable dyes, tobacco, glass-ware, and numerous other substances, which find a ready sale in all parts of India. It is extremely satisfactory to learn that a laboratory has been erected, and as it is fully equipped with all necessary appliances, it is certain to be of immense assistance in the scientific development of the latest industrial wealth of the Dominions.

The extensive forests, situated chiefly in the Telingana country, in the south-eastern portion of the Dominions, are of very great value, and the revenue derived from all sources is an important item in the State financial returns. The total area covered by forests, namely, 9,967 square miles, comprises 7,068 square miles scheduled as "protected," and 2,899 square miles described as open or unclassed forests. Steps are now being taken to constitute reserved forests under the revised Forest Act, and also for the selection and demarcation of village forests. The principal trees include: teak, rosewood, satinwood, gallnut, ironwood, margosa (alleged to be proof against depredations of white ants), Indian laburnum, elsu, banyan, *pipul*, tamarind, bamboo, and many others. The work of the Chief Forest Officer and his Assistants, in natural as well as artificial reproduction of trees, has been attended with good results, excepting in those places where damage has been caused by animals or fires.

The aggregate value of the trade of the Dominions during 1916–17 amounted to Rs. 19,31,00,000, but some figures extracted from the Administration Report will throw considerable light upon this important subject. Values are given in thousands of rupees. Imports included piece-goods, Rs. 18,845; yarn, Rs. 7,585; salt, Rs. 4,223; sugar and jaggery, Rs. 4,691; gold, Rs. 5,586; livestock, Rs. 2,270; fruits, Rs. 1,884; iron, Rs. 754; and miscellaneous goods, Rs. 22,566. The chief exports for the same period were in thousands of rupees, grain, Rs. 11,849; cotton, Rs. 36,876; castor seed, Rs. 9,970; linseed, Rs. 4,565; hides, Rs. 5,128; cattle, Rs. 3,473; sesamum, Rs. 3,514; and oil and ghee, Rs. 2,060.

The establishment of a Department of Commerce and Industries is one of the fruits of the progressive administration of His Exalted Highness, and this agency will undoubtedly very materially assist in the development of the immense natural resources of the Dominions.

Adverse trading conditions, owing to

THE DOMINIONS OF H.E.H. THE NIZAM OF HYDERABAD.

1. His Exalted Highness the Nizam's Chewmahalla Palace. 2. Panorama of Afzal Gunj Bridge. 3. Clock Tower, Afzal Gunj Bridge. 4. The Charminar, Hyderabad.

the closing of European markets, and the shortage of tonnage in ships, and wagons on railways, naturally affected Hyderabad as well as other countries, but an era of greater prosperity has dawned since the cessation of hostilities.

The success of commercial enterprises depends to an enormous extent upon the means of communication existing between important trading centres, and in this respect the Dominions of His Exalted Highness are favourably circumstanced.

The railways in Hyderabad now open for traffic extend for a distance of 910.57 miles, and these are controlled and worked by the Nizam's Guaranteed State Railway Company.

Extensions sanctioned, and even commenced, prior to the Great War, have necessarily been delayed, owing to the impossibility of obtaining rolling stock and other goods from Europe. It may be observed, however, that during the reign of the present Nizam, about 100 miles of a new metre-gauge railway have been completed, and this section will be of immense advantage to the State, seeing that it has been extended to the seaport of Mormugao, where shipping facilities are obtainable for the export of some of the vast agricultural and industrial products of the State. During the year under review, already referred to, the broad-gauge line from Wadi to Bezwada, with a length of about 330 miles, had net earnings amounting to Rs. 40,40,100, giving 7.63 per cent. on capital outlay; and the Hyderabad-Godavari Valley Railway, 391 miles in length, returned 6.09 per cent. In addition to the above there were earnings upon the Secunderabad-Gadag line, and upon several branches running from important centres. The Government of His Exalted Highness recently purchased five per cent. shares on broad-gauge lines to the value of £12,700; and debentures on metre-gauge sections to the amount of £101,000. The details of Government holdings for the year 1917 were: five per cent. railway shares, £88,500; four per cent. broad-gauge unguaranteed debentures, £600,000; and three and a half per cent. metre-gauge line debentures, £463,000.

Administrative control of all State affairs is vested in His Exalted Highness the Nizam, but until a few years ago it centred in His Excellency the Minister, although in actual practice no action involving consequences of an important or permanent character was taken without the permission or knowledge of the Nizam. Matters specially reserved for the decision of the Nizam included: the introduction of new legislation, the granting of State lands or funds, the imposition of fresh taxation, appointments to Government service where salaries exceeded Rs. 500 per mensem, the confirmation of sentences of death promulgated by the High Court of Justice, and a few other subjects of a similar kind. Associated with the Minister, but subject to his control, were five Assistant Ministers, in charge of various Departments. Each Assistant Minister, with the exception of the one controlling the Finance Department, had under him a Departmental Secretary, who was required to submit to his superior officer a detailed memorandum upon every matter on which orders were desired, and this note was subsequently forwarded to the Minister for final instruction. It must, however, be borne in mind that Hyderabad, with its traditions of the Moghuls, is an autocracy, and therefore the position of a Chief Minister exercising prerogatives, as mentioned above, was an anomaly. Some 30 years ago the late Nizam made an attempt to define the powers of the Minister as differentiated from those which he reserved for himself, but no practical results ensued. To the present Nizam, with his keen intelligence and shrewd foresight, belongs the credit of having decided to adopt a form of administration, not only more efficient, but also more in accordance with modern ideas and requirements.

Soon after his accession to power His Exalted Highness began to be out of sympathy with the somewhat dilatory and sometimes inefficient methods of administration of former days, and after mature consideration of the matter, he tried the daring experiment of taking upon himself the duties of Prime Minister. The assumption of so responsible a position naturally involved a tremendous amount of heavy work, but he resolutely bore the strain for about five years. At the termination of that period the Nizam had gained such an intimate acquaintance with the machinery of government that in 1919 he determined to effect a radical change in the constitution, a change which seemed to be demanded by the rapidly growing political ideas of the times. His Exalted Highness, therefore, in the same year formed an Executive Council, based upon the lines of others in British India, consisting of a President and eight members, each one of those being in charge of one of the great Departments of State. No better selection of President could have been made than Sir Ali Imam, K.C.S.I., who has had several years' practical experience as a member of the Executive Council of His Excellency the Viceroy of India, and also of that of the province of Behar and Orissa. The members were selected from among highly-trusted noblemen and senior officials of the State. It will be obvious that it is too early to form a correct estimate of the value of the Council, but it is undeniable that it has commenced its duties under most favourable auspices.

The existence of an Executive Council seemed to be impotent without a representative Legislature, elected by and responsible to the people, therefore His Exalted Highness has, in a recent decree, foreshadowed the early formation of such a body, as well as the granting of the franchise to his subjects. This bold stroke of statesmanship is in accord with the spirit of progressive government, and will clearly illustrate the far-sighted policy of the Nizam.

Land is let to registered occupants, whose rights are hereditary and transferable, subject to payment of the annual assessment. Assessments of revenue are fixed for a period of years, excepting in the case of unirrigated land, or of fields which are dependent upon wells for water for their crops. Concessions are made by way of encouraging capable persons to bring waste land under cultivation, and in these instances leases are granted for 30 years, a mere nominal rent being charged.

The total net collections made under all heads of land revenue, including arrears, amounted in the year 1916–17 to Rs. 2,93,14,918.

It may not be out of place to refer at this juncture to the *Paigah* estates, held on a quasi-feudal tenure by some of the great nobles of Hyderabad, and which comprise vast tracts of land and villages, granted by former Rulers in return for military service or the maintenance of troops. The relations subsisting between the Nizams and these nobles have always been of a very friendly character, and indeed, they have been cemented by frequent intermarriages. His Exalted Highness is, therefore, not only Paramount lord, but also head of their families. The present Nizam found that these important estates were heavily encumbered with debts, lands and villages having been actually given into the possession of grasping creditors, and he therefore conceived the idea of placing the administration of these territories on a different footing, and thus sav-

THE DOMINIONS OF H.E.H. THE NIZAM OF HYDERABAD.

1. New High Court, Hyderabad. 2. Metre-gauge Railway Station (Kachiguda Station). 3. Mecca Masjid, Hyderabad.

2

3

THE DOMINIONS OF H.E.H. THE NIZAM OF HYDERABAD.

1. City High School, Hyderabad. 2. New General Hospital (under Construction). 3. The Victoria Memorial Orphanage.

ing the young nobles from inevitable ruin. He accordingly appointed Sir Brian Egerton as Administrator, and this official has succeeded in paying off all liabilities, and in restoring the estates to their rightful holders.

For the administration of justice there are in the city of Hyderabad the High Court, the Khazis Court, and the City Court and Criminal Courts, but a large number of other Courts, presided over by 151 highly-trained judges, have been established in various parts of the Dominions, while there are also 211 judges specially appointed for disposing of criminal cases. The recent institution of a special body, consisting of the highest judicial officers of the State, presided over by the Nizam, and called the Judicial Committee, whose duties consist of hearing the most important appeals that lie from the decrees of the High Court, is another instance of the progressive reforms which are attributable to His Exalted Highness. In former days, the procedure in vogue for the admission and hearing of such appeals was not clearly defined, nor were the grounds clearly indicated upon which such appeals could be entertained. These two arguable points, as well as the exact functions of the Committee, have now been settled by legislation. The city police force comprises 42 officers and 3,290 men, while 10,583 of all ranks are employed in various districts.

The total expenditure in the Military Department amounts annually to about Rs. 46,00,000, the troops being composed of the irregulars, 11,630 men; the regulars, 3,726 men; the Golconda brigade, 1,338 men; the Nizam's regiment, 1,148 men; and the Imperial Service Lancers, 1,264 men.

The Public Works Department employs a large staff of well-qualified assistants, who supervise the construction, maintenance, and repair of public buildings, roads, irrigation, and sanitary schemes, and waterworks.

Special reference should, however, be made to the excellent services rendered by this Department when called upon by His Exalted Highness in 1911 to undertake certain works with the object of repairing the immense amount of danger caused in the city of Hyderabad by devastating floods which had then recently occurred.

In the first place, a dam was constructed across the river Musi, upon whose banks the principal city is built, with the view of minimizing, if not altogether preventing, the violence of overflows in the future. The dam proved to be an admirable preventive, but at the same time an enormous reservoir of good fresh potable water was created, which is capable of supplying the needs of the large population of the city, and of the British Cantonments of Secunderabad and Bolaram. Another dam was built across the Isi river, a confluent of the Musi, and the two reservoirs are named respectively the "Osman Sagar," after His Exalted Highness, and the "Himayat Sagar," after the heir-apparent. The provision of pure water was a stepping-stone to the equally important questions of drainage and sanitation, and these schemes have been pushed forward rapidly owing to the energetic action of so enlightened a Ruler as the present Nizam. The work of beautifying the city followed as a natural sequence, and several large public buildings of exquisite architectural design have already been completed, or are in course of construction, all of which will serve as lasting monuments to His Exalted Highness.

Among the completed structures may be mentioned the noble Town Hall, the Central Station on the main-gauge railway, and the spacious High Court, which was formally opened by the Nizam on April 15, 1920.

The incompleted edifices include a new General Hospital, which will cost more than Rs. 20,00,000, and a High School, upon which a sum of fully Rs. 7,00,000 will be spent.

The area which suffered so greatly from floods has been converted by the City Improvement Board into a beautiful recreation park; some of the narrow streets in city and suburbs are being widened; and good residential quarters for the poor are taking the place of unhealthy slums. Several portions of the country districts are being opened up by new roads; waterworks have been established at several provincial towns; and hospitals and jails have been built at places remote from the capital city.

Nearly 2,300 miles of road are at the present time maintained by the Department, and 100 miles of new roads are opened up annually.

Medical relief is afforded in 103 hospitals and dispensaries in the Dominions; 88 of these are maintained from State funds, 13 by the ***Sarf-i-khas*** Department, and four from local funds, while the remaining eight were partially aided. The various institutions include the Victoria Zenana Hospital at Hyderabad, the foundation stone of which was laid in 1906 by His Royal Highness the Prince of Wales, now King-Emperor George V. There is also an English Medical School, as well as one for teaching the ***Unani*** method of treatment. The total number of patients treated in the year 1916-17 was 9,82,326, and 7,917 of these were admitted into hospital wards. The total annual amount expended by the State is about Rs. 10,00,000, but His Exalted Highness has sanctioned the cost of the construction of other hospitals and dispensaries, which are greatly needed in the Dominions.

There is no subject in which His Exalted Highness evinces a deeper interest than that of encouraging, both by precept and practical assistance, the spread of education in the Dominions. The results of these labours have, in a general way, been very gratifying, but it would appear that the necessity of educating the girls in the Dominions, although fully recognized by His Exalted Highness and his officials, has not yet been fully realized by the people. That great progress has undoubtedly been made is evident from the fact that the budget of the Education Department, which was less than Rs. 12,00,000 at the commencement of His Exalted Highness' reign, has increased to more than Rs. 37,00,000. The number of schools has also undergone a very considerable increase, as there is at the present time scarcely a village of any importance which is without a school of some kind. The total number of maintained institutions for general and special education is about 2,600, and these are attended by 1,50,000 pupils. In addition to these figures, however, there are about 4,300 unrecognized schools, with about 74,000 scholars. Statistics show that about 10·7 of children of school age are now receiving instruction

The Nizam College is attended by 110 students. The ***Dar-ul-Ulum***, or Oriental College, has now been expanded into the Osmania University. There are 20 English High Schools for boys, and two English High Schools for girls; 76 Middle Schools; and 2,158 are classed as Primary. Nearly 15,000 girls are taught in 304 schools. There are two Arts Colleges, and valuable scholarships are given to students desiring to proceed to England for a further course of study. Classes in handicraft work, such as weaving, carpentering, and the making of paper and other goods, are held in the Nizam Industrial and five other schools.

Probably the most notable educational

achievement which will for ever stand to the credit of His Exalted Highness was the foundation in Hyderabad of the Osmania University, which is a unique institution of its kind in India, as it represents a great experiment in education, namely, the teaching of various advanced subjects through the medium, not of English as in other Universities in India, but of Urdu, the vernacular of the State. This institution is still in its infancy, but great expectations of its usefulness are entertained.

Connected with the University is the Translation Bureau, the object of which is to enrich the Urdu language in a permanent manner, by translating into its phraseology numerous standard European publications on history, mathematics, science, philosophy, political economy, and other kindred subjects. It is also intended that the teaching of Arabic shall receive special attention.

The Nizam, who is a highly educated man, is fully cognizant of the fact that there are many of his subjects who, owing to custom or prejudice, have been denied the privilege of receiving even primary instruction, and, with characteristic thoughtfulness, he has established special seats of learning for those who may be desirous of becoming pupils. Not longer than a quarter of a century ago there were members of noble families, too, in Hyderabad, who were unable to spell their own names, and who regarded it as undignified to be educated, but the late Nizam expressed his strong disapproval of such prejudices, and took steps to remedy the evil, while the present Ruler has taken upon himself the task of directing the course of instruction. These are the *Paigah* families, who have already been referred to. His Exalted Highness has manifested his desire to raise the normal and social status of future generations of these people by selecting a certain number of their children and sending them to colleges or schools either in the Dominions or at suitable places elsewhere.

The education of girls, which was much neglected up to about 30 years ago, has received special attention during the regime of the late and the present Nizams, and the latter has further established separate high schools for daughters of noble and gentle birth, these academies being under the control of highly-qualified English ladies. In connection with this progressive movement, it may be observed that His Exalted Highness, recognizing the necessity for healthy and suitable surroundings for proper physical development, has sanctioned the institution of a special boarding-house for Wards of State—young Rajas, *jagirdars*, and landholders whose estates are administered by the Durbar during their minority. A really magnificent building is now being erected on a picturesque site, situated at such a distance from the capital city as will give the inmates security against those insalutary influences which it is most desirable that they should avoid.

There are several public libraries in the State, the principal one being the Asafia State library, in which there are 23,663 volumes, of which 15,927 are in Arabic, Persian, and Urdu; and 7,736 in English and other European languages.

The decennial census of 1911 showed that the inhabitants of the Dominions were 13,374,676 in number, this being an increase of 20 per cent. above the previous tabulation. The growth of population is attributed to various causes, the principal of which were steady agricultural prosperity and the extension of railway facilities. Including the city of Hyderabad, there were 85 towns and 20,151 villages, and no fewer than 90·3 per cent. of all the people were residents in villages of less than 5,000 inhabitants. Classed under the heading of "religious," the census figures were: Hindus, 86·93; Mahomedans, 10·32; Sikhs, 0·04; Jains, 0·16; Christians, 0·40; Parsis, 0·01; and Animists, 2·14.

It may not be out of place to refer at this juncture to the assistance rendered by the Government of His Exalted Highness the Nizam towards the prosecution of the late Great War.

An official statement was published in August 1918, and the following particulars are extracted therefrom:

The 1st Hyderabad Imperial Service Cavalry regiment was despatched to Egypt in 1914, and served in Egypt and Palestine. The regiment was in action on several occasions, and sustained a number of casualties. Special commendation has since been accorded to the Regiment, and to individual officers, for their conduct in action.

One hundred rough-riders and two officers were deputed to Muttra in 1915 to train horses for the cavalry.

In order to encourage recruiting within the Dominions, Assistant District Recruiting Officers were appointed to work under the orders of the Divisional Recruiting Officer at Secunderabad. Salaries of these officers and their establishments, together with all expenditure in connection with recruiting, were borne by His Exalted Highness' Government; 4,955 men were recruited for the Indian Army within the Dominions up to June 1918. Since the appointment of the special establishment, the average number of recruits has risen from 217 men per month to 700.

Special concessions were also given in the matter of leave and pay to Government servants called up for general training in the Indian Defence Force.

The 20th Deccan Horse, of which His Exalted Highness is an Honorary Colonel, were re-armed with new pattern swords, at a cost of Rs. 10,000, before proceeding to the war. Chargers were also presented to the Officer Commanding and five other officers of the 20th Deccan Horse.

167 mules, 150 cavalry horses, and 35 artillery horses, belonging to His Exalted Highness' Army, were sold to the Government of India to assist the work of mobilization, and the State Army remained temporarily short of strength in consequence.

The financial contributions in aid of the war consisted partly of subscriptions to the war loans, and partly of free gifts.

(a) Subscriptions to the War Loans were as follows: 4 per cent. Loan of 1916–17, Rs. 39,00,000; 5 per cent. War Loan of 1917, Rs. 75,00,000; 5½ per cent. War Bonds of 1918, Rs. 50,00,000.

(b) The free gifts amounted to Rs. 1,82,09,600. The major subscriptions were: Towards the payment of the War charges of the 20th Deccan Horse and the 1st Hyderabad Imperial Service Cavalry, Rs 1,44,00,000;[1] Prince of Wales' Relief Fund, Rs. 1,00,000; Imperial Relief Fund of India, Rs. 1,00,000; to the Admiralty in aid of the anti-submarine campaign, Rs. 15,00,000; "Our Day" collections for the "Red Cross" Society, Rs. 1,00,000; special donation towards the prosecution of the war, Rs. 15,00,000; to Their Imperial Majesties for the relief of the sufferers from the war on the occasion of their silver wedding, Rs. 3,75,000; and other subscriptions amount to Rs. 1,34,600.

His Exalted Highness' Government were further able to assist the financial situation in British India in 1916, by a loan of Rs. 50,00,000 in silver bullion, pending the arrival of the dollar silver ordered by the Government of India in the United States of America.

[1] This is exclusive of the pay of officers and men of the Imperial Service Cavalry, and is made up of regular subscriptions of Rs. 3,00,000 or Rs. 36,00,000 per annum—a contribution which His Exalted Highness undertook to provide till the end of the war, and which had then been paid for 48 months.

THE DOMINIONS OF H.E.H. THE NIZAM OF HYDERABAD.

1. The Residency, Hyderabad. 2. Zenana Hospital—Surgical and Theatre Room. 3. Zenana Hospital—Maternity Ward.

In connection with materials provided, it may be said that the State workshops were fully occupied from an early date on munitions work. A complete list of the articles supplied need not be given, but the most important works were the construction of cordite boxes, shells, and transport carts. The total value of the works completed and then in hand was fully Rs. 9,00,000. This was paid for by the Government of India ; but, as far as possible, the Hyderabad Government aimed at charging only cost price, without making any profit.

In a territory such as Hyderabad, which has been under the sway of Rulers belonging to many dynasties, there are, naturally, a very large number of objects of supreme interest to the archæological and antiquarians. A few years ago, Mr. Henry Cousens, M.R.A.S., Superintendent of the Archæological Survey, Bombay, was deputed by the Government of His Exalted Highness to prepare particulars regarding important archæological remains in the Hyderabad Dominions, and the following information is derived mainly from the report then prepared. The principal relics described by Mr. Cousens include rock-temples, caves, mosques, tombs, forts, gateways, watch-towers, columns, stone circles, and stones carved with zodiacal signs.

Amongst the rock-temples, or caves, those of Ellora and Ajanta, in the Aurangabad district, are well known. The former group is described as the finest group of caves in India. It is situated 14 miles north-east of Aurangabad. It contains caves dedicated to the service of three religions, Buddhist, Brahminical, and Jain ; and they vary in age from the fifth to the ninth or tenth centuries. The caves of the Buddhist series are 12 in number ; of the Brahminical, 17 ; and of the Jain there are five. The principal building, known as Kailas, measures 138 feet in front, the interior is 247 feet in length, 150 feet in breadth, and its height is about 100 feet. This cave-temple is believed to date from the eighth century. It is dedicated to Siva, but it is surrounded by figures of Vishnu and other deities.

The Ajanta caves, in the village of the same name which is 38 miles distant from Jalgaon, a station on the Great Indian Peninsula Railway, and 261 miles from Bombay, comprises 24 monasteries, and five temples have been cut out of the solid rock, many of which are supported by richly ornamented and sculptured designs. These temples furnish a consecutive history of Buddhist art between the years 200 B.C. and A.D. 600.

Besides these important cave groups, which are still in a good state of preservation, there are other minor groups in the Aurangabad district.

The leading characteristic of the mosques in the Hyderabad Dominions is a profusion of plaster decoration over the façades and minars. The contour of the minars, which have deeply ornamented arched galleries around them, is also quite different from that of minars in Mahomedan centres. There are not many mosques of note from an archæological point of view, but the following are deserving of mention, either on account of their age, or the historical or architectural interest attaching to them. The oldest mosque of any pretension, excluding an unfinished mosque in Gulbarga, appears to be the Jami Masjit, in the city of Hyderabad, which is said to have been built in A.D. 1598. The courtyard of this mosque contains the relics of an old Turkish bath. Another important *masjid* in Hyderabad city is the Mecca Masjid, which is reputed to be the largest in the Deccan. It was commenced about A.D. 1637, but was not completed till after the conquest of Golconda by Aurangazeb, i.e. some time between 1688 and 1707. It is capable of accommodating about 10,000 people. Very large blocks of stone have been used in the structure. The stone which forms the niche, facing which prayers are offered, is described as a huge piece of rock, which occupied some five or six hundred masons about five years in hewing out, and which had to be dragged to the site on rollers drawn by 1,400 oxen. The Kali Masjid, in Jalna (Aurangabad district), so called from the black stone of which it is built, dates from 1600. Twenty of its pillars have been taken from some Jain temples. There are two other mosques in Jalna, one of which contains six sculptured pillars, which once formed parts of an old Hindu shrine, and the other has, besides such pillars, a doorway that belonged to a Hindu temple. In the village of Kamatur, four miles east of Medak, there is a fine *masjid*, solidly constructed of beautifully dressed stone, without mortar. There is an unfinished mosque in the Fort of Gulbarga, which is stated to have been designed on the model of the great mosque of Cordova, and which was commenced in the reign of Feroze Shah Bahmani (1397 1422). It is an extensive building, occupying an area of 38,000 square feet, and it is described as the only great mosque in India, the whole area of which is covered in.

The most famous tombs in the Hyderabad State are those of the Kutubshahi kings, at Golconda, some five miles to the west of the city of Hyderabad. All the kings of the Kutubshahi dynasty, except the last, Abul Hasan, who ended his days as a prisoner in the Daulatabad fortress, are interred here. The earliest of these tombs was constructed some years before 1543, by the first Kutubshahi king, Sultan Kuli, for himself. They are massive structures, of grey granite, oblong or square, surmounted with domes. Some of them are richly decorated with enamelled tiles and other architectural embellishments. Most of them were surrounded by their own separate gardens in former times, but both the tombs and the gardens suffered considerably at the time of Aurangzeb's invasion of Golconda. After this, they remained in a neglected state for a long time, till the first Sir Salar Jung took steps to repair and preserve the buildings, and to replant the gardens. Since then, His Exalted Highness' Government looks carefully after these ancient remains, and much of the wanton destruction which visitors used to inflict has been checked of late. In Gulbarga there are similar tombs, though of less elaborate workmanship, in which the Bahmani kings of Gulbarga are buried. Some of these buildings are now used as Government offices. The Bahmani kings who died after the removal of their capital from Gulbarga to Bidar are interred in ten tombs, situated some five or six miles north-east of Bidar. All of them have richly-ornamented interiors. The Bibi-ka-Makbara, in Aurangabad, is a well-known mausoleum, modelled after the Taj Mahal of Agra. It was erected by Aurangzeb in memory of his wife, Rabia Durani, 1660. A large quantity of marble was used in the structure, which was brought in bullock carts all the way from Upper India. The cost of the building is said to have amounted to Rs. 18,00,000, according to one authority, and Rs. 6,68,000 according to another. One of the minarets was destroyed by lightning many years ago, and the others also are more or less in a damaged condition. Roza, or Khuldabad (City of Paradise), situate about 14 miles north-west of Aurangabad, may be described as a city of sepulchres, containing the mortal remains of a number of illustrious Mahomedans, including Aurangzeb and the first Nizam. There are about 20 domed mausoleums, and 1,400 plain tombs. The tomb of Aurangzeb is a simple and unpretentious structure of limestone, the only noticeable feature about it being a marble screen. The tomb of Yusuf Adil Shah, King of Bijapur, is situated at Gugi, a village 14 miles north of Shorapur, in the Raichur district. There is no structure or dome over it, and the only remarkable thing about it is the grave of a king who died 400 years ago.

There are some 29 forts, large and small, throughout His Exalted Highness' Dominions, enumerated in the classified list prepared by Mr. Cousens. Amongst the principal ones may be mentioned the following: Daulatabad, Raichur, Golconda, Kandahar, Yadgir, Naldrug, Warangal, Nalgonda, Nirmal, and Bidar.

The Dominions of His Exalted Highness comprise the four civil divisions of Aurangabad, Gulbarga, Medak, and Warangal, and these areas are sub-divided into 101 *taluks*, in which there are more than 14,000 villages.

Hyderabad, the capital city of the whole territory, is situated on the left bank of the river Musi, a tributary of the Kistna, and although it is built upon an unfertile plain, the absence of forests and luxuriant vegetation was a most effective safeguard against surprise attacks by the Marathas and other enemies. It was founded in the year 1589 by Mahomed Kuli, the fifth king of the Kutb Shahi dynasty, who named it after his son, Haidar.

The headquarters of the Rulers were at Golconda, about five miles distant on the western side of Hyderabad, which was even in those days a prosperous trading centre. In 1687 the fort of Golconda was stormed, and Hyderabad fell into the hands of the Moghuls, who retained possession of it unti. the first Nizam proclaimed his independence and transferred his capital to Hyderabad.

The city is surrounded by a stone wall, which is now considerably dilapidated; it is flanked by a number of bastions, and is approached by 13 gates, and several posterns and bridges. The area of the city proper is about $2\frac{1}{2}$ square miles, but if the numerous fine suburbs, which have now sprung up, be included, it is not less than 12 square miles in extent.

Thanks to the energetic action of the Municipality, new thoroughfares of considerable width have taken the place of the old tortuous streets, in which insignificant houses, packed closely together, did not conduce to healthy surroundings. Residences are now being constructed of stone, and the general appearance of the city has been immensely improved by the plantation of trees, sometimes in avenues, and by the opening of public parks and gardens.

Numerous bungalows, somewhat European in character, and enclosed in well-kept gardens, are springing up rapidly in the outskirts of Hyderabad and in its charming suburbs.

At the close of the year 1917 the Municipal Board controlled and maintained about 100 miles of roads, 18 miles of which were lighted by electricity; and the drainage system supervised by the local authorities extended for a distance of 421,607 feet.

Hyderabad is 986 miles distant via Bezwada, by railway, from Calcutta; 490 miles from Madras; and 491 miles, via Wadi, from Bombay.

The seat of the British Resident, or Political Representative of the Supreme Government, is situated at CHUDDERGHAT, a suburb of Hyderabad, which comprises the area lying to the north of the river Muci.

THE DOMINIONS OF H.E.H. THE NIZAM OF HYDERABAD.

THE GOLCONDA FORT, HYDERABAD.

The Residency, standing in a wide expanse of park-like grounds, in which are exceedingly beautiful gardens, is a really handsome and spacious edifice, which in some respects resembles Government House at Calcutta. At the main entrance there is a noble portico of Corinthian pillars, and on either side is a large wing, capable of accommodating many guests. The principal apartment is the Durbar Hall, measuring 60 feet in length, 33 feet in width, and 50 feet in height. Several busy bazars, containing a population of more than 16,000 inhabitants, surround the Residency.

Wealthy merchants carry on commercial transactions which extend to every part of India; many of the principal Banks have established branches there; and the vendors of various kinds of merchandise have secured a thriving trade for their goods. Many of the officials employed in State Departments have taken up their residence in attractive bungalows, and a large and prosperous community of Anglo-Indians and Indians have made homes for themselves in areas lying to the north and west of the Residency. The Political Agent exercises civil and criminal jurisdiction over the whole of Chudderghat.

SECUNDERABAD, one of the largest military stations in India, is situated about six miles distant from the city of Hyderabad, and it derives its name from its founder, Nizam Sikandar Jah. The Cantonment, which includes BOLARAM and TRIMULGHERRY, formerly consisted of a line of barracks, extending for about three miles, but since the days of the Sepoy Mutiny, the area devoted to the accommodation of troops is 22 square miles in extent. Greatly improved quarters have been erected for European as well as Indian soldiers, and the inhabitants increased in number from 85,000 in 1901 to nearly 114,000 in 1911. The town is an important trading centre and contains numerous commercial establishments.

There are several large stores and fine shops at TRIMULGHERRY, but the chief building is the military jail, which is locally referred to as "Windsor Castle," on account of some similarity in its external architectural features.

BOLARAM is a military sanitorium, at an elevation of 1,890 feet, and it was here that General Colin Mackenzie, C.B., was cut down by rebellious native cavalry, about a year and a half before the Mutiny of 1857.

THE STATE OF BHOPAL

THE outstanding feature of public interest connected with the Mahomedan State of Bhopal, in Central India, lies in the fact that during the past one hundred years its government has been most successfully administered by four female Rulers in succession. In order to understand the events which led to the foundation of the State, it is necessary to refer to the year 1696—7, when an Afghan, named Dost Mahomed Khan, arrived in India. This man was a soldier of a roving and adventurous disposition, and he soon satisfied his craving for active service on the field of battle, by associating himself with petty rulers who were hankering after more extensive possessions.

In the course of time he entered the division of Malwa, and found that the *pergana* of Berasia was held on lease by Taj Mahomed Khan. The latter had entrusted the management of his estate to Agents, who, it appeared, were entirely unable to grapple with the Rajputs, who were continually invading the territory. Dost Mahomed Khan acquired possession of Berasia by offering an annual payment of Rs. 30,000 to the owner, and he induced a considerable number of his relatives and supporters to proceed to Malwa, where they assisted him in subduing the unruly Rajputs of the neighbourhood. These punitive measures resulted in the acquisition of further territory, and Dost Mahomed built a fort at Islamnagar, which was then made his headquarters. He subsequently obtained possession of Bhilsa, Gyaraspur, Doraha, Sehore, Gulgaon, and other places, and he further seized the fortress of Ginnurgarh. In 1722, Dost Mahomed commenced the building of the town of Bhopal, with the object of making it his capital, and in the same year he assumed the title of Nawab. In 1723, the Nizam, on his march to Hyderabad, to put down disturbances caused by his second son, entered Bhopal with the object of crushing or expelling its Nawab, as the latter had some three years previously assisted Dilawar Ali Khan in attacking him.

Dost Mahomed Khan, being unable to meet the Nizam's forces, which were encamped near the fort of Islamnagar, gave his eldest son, Yar Mahomed Khan, as a hostage. Bhopal State records show how in the space of a few years Dost Mahomed Khan "purchased the lease of an imperial (Moghul) district, and rose by the power of his sword alone to be the founder of a line of independent Princes." He died in the year 1726, leaving six surviving sons.

The nobles in the State ignored the claims to succession of Yar Mahomed Khan, the eldest son, who was still in Hyderabad, and placed on the *masnad*, Sultan Mahomed Khan, a boy of eight years of age. Yar Mahomed Khan had, however, found favour in the eyes of the Nizam, who sent him back to Bhopal with insignia of royalty, and an escorting force of considerable strength. No opposition was offered, and Yar Mahomed Khan quickly deposed his brother, and took up the reins of government.

The new Ruler evidently inherited the desire to possess enlarged territories, for which his late father was noted, and during the course of his reign of 15 years he added considerably to the State. He died in 1724, leaving five sons behind him, the eldest of whom was Faiz Mahomed Khan. Opposition to his succession was raised by a party in the State who desired to reinstate the deposed Sultan Mahomed, and although there was severe fighting between the followers of the contending forces, an arrangement was ultimately made through the personal intervention of Mamola Bibi (the widow of Yar Mahomed) and Bijai Ram (the Chief Minister of the State), under which a small territory was granted to Sultan Mahomed, on his renouncing all claims to the Chiefship. Faiz Mahomed Khan was a religious devotee, who left the control of the State in the hands of Mamola Bibi and his *Wazir*. In 1745, however, they were compelled to part with several *perganas*, after an onslaught made by the Mahrattas. The Nawab died in 1777, without leaving issue, and he was succeeded by his brother, Hayat Mahomed Khan. But objection was raised to his accession by the widow of the previous Chief, who desired to be invested with administrative powers.

Although Hayat Mahomed remained on the *masnad*, his management of the State was anything but satisfactory, owing to his extreme devotion to religious exercises, and he, therefore, appointed Faulad Khan, a Gond, as his Chief Minister. It was about this time that an annual allowance of Rs. 5,00,000 was made to the Nawab for his subsistence, the remainder of the revenue, Rs. 15,00,000, being devoted to State purposes.

In 1776, when the treaty of Purandhar was repudiated by the Hon. the East India Company, Warren Hastings determined to support the Bombay Government. He therefore sent an armed force of infantry, artillery, and a body of Moghul horse from Bengal, and on its passage through

HER HIGHNESS NAWAB SULTAN JAHAN BEGAM, G.C.S.I., G.C.I.E., G.B.E., C.I.

RULER OF BHOPAL STATE (CENTRAL INDIA).

(Photo by Bremner.)

THE STATE OF BHOPAL.

1. Nawab Sir Mohammad Nasrulla Khan, Alijah Bahadur, K.C.S.I., Heir-Apparent, Bhopal State.
2. Lieut.-Colonel Iftikharulmulk Nawabzada Mohammad Hamidulla Khan Bahadur, B.A., Chief Secretary, Bhopal Government.
3. The Armoury, Bhopal.

Bhopal, it was aided in every possible way by Nawab Hayat Mahomed Khan.

Faulad Khan was murdered in 1780. He was succeeded as Minister by Chhote Khan, an able administrator, who established and maintained friendly relationships with the Marathas. His strong control of affairs exasperated Bahu Begam, widow of Faiz Mahomed, who resented his interference, and she accordingly instigated a rebellion against him. He, however, succeeded in defeating the troops which had been raised with the object of removing him from his high office. Intrigues and rebellions continued for some years, but Chhote Khan overcame them, and contrived to uphold the traditions of good government, and also to benefit the State, by undertaking many public works, which have been of inestimable value to Bhopal.

Chhote Khan died in 1795, and was buried in the Fatehgarh fort. The post of Minister was held in succession by Amir Mahomed Khan and Himmat Ram. The internal condition of the State was becoming deplorable, owing to the weakness of Nawab Hayat Mahomed, and as a consequence there were numerous intrigues between Ministers and their supporters.

The Marathas overran the State, and the treasury was well-nigh emptied. At this juncture (1795), Murid Mahomed Khan was invited to become Minister, and he arrived at Bhopal with a force of 1,000 followers, but during an interview with the Nawab he declared his unwillingness to accept the position until all possible opponents had been removed from the State.

Murid succeeded in his plan of expulsion, and then commenced a heartless policy of unjust taxation, in order to provide funds for the payment of the State army. He was concerned in the death of Asmat Begam, wife of the Nawab, and then attempted to deal in a similar manner with her son, Ghaus Mahomed Khan, and Wazir Mahomed Khan, great-grandson of Dost Mahomed Khan. The Nawab was now roused to take action against Murid, but a strong force of Marathas threatened the capital town, and they would probably have been successful in their object had they not been recalled by Sindhia of Gwalior. On their retirement, however, they took Murid and imprisoned him, but he afterwards committed suicide.

Wazir Mahomed Khan was then raised to the post of Chief Minister, and his authority was soon manifested to such an extent that even Ghaus Mahomed became alarmed at the probable result of this demonstration of power. The latter succeeded Hayat Mahomed Khan in the year 1808, but he was only nominal Ruler, as Wazir had acquired too strong a hold upon the administration of State affairs.

The Nawab, however, invited the Nagpur Chief to assist him in an advance upon Bhopal, with the object of expelling Wazir from the State, but the attempt to accomplish this was frustrated by the Minister, who drove the Marathas out of the town. Ghaus Mahomed, it appears, was then persuaded by Wazir to retire to Raisen, and the Gazetteer of the State remarks that "from this date the rule of Bhopal practically passed to Wazir's branch of the family."

Proposals for a treaty with the British were made by Wazir in 1811 and 1812, but they were rendered ineffectual by reason of attacks by the Marathas and others. Troubles of this nature continued until 1816, when the death of Wazir took place. The latter left two sons, Amir Mahomed Khan and Nazar Mahomed Khan, but the latter was chosen to succeed his father, owing to the indolence and weakness of body and mind of the elder brother.

Nazar Mahomed Khan thus became virtual Ruler of Bhopal, but he did not assume the title of Nawab, as it was still held by Ghaus Mahomed Khan, who was living in retirement, and did not take any part whatever in administrative duties.

In 1818 Nazar married Gohur Begam or Kudsia Begam, daughter of Ghaus Mahomed, and in March of the same year he concluded a treaty with the British, one of the clauses being an undertaking to assist them, when called upon, with an auxiliary force of 600 horses and 400 foot soldiers. In order to comply with this condition, Nazar voluntarily disposed of a large quantity of jewellery, which realized more than Rs. 50,00,000. This act of chivalry appealed so strongly to the British, that they transferred to him the fort of Islamnagar, then held by Sindhia, in addition to five valuable *perganas*. After securing these rich possessions, it seemed as if there were a magnificent future before this promising young administrator, but while on a hunting trip to Islamnagar, in 1819, he was accidentally killed by his young brother-in-law, who was playing with a loaded pistol.

Nazar Mahomed Khan left an infant daughter, named Sikandar Begam, and the British Government acquiesced in a proposal that his nephew, Munir Mahomed Khan, should succeed his uncle, under the regency of Gohur Begam, the widow of the deceased Nazar. It was understood that Munir should subsequently marry Sikandar Begam, but when the former in 1827 caused great unpleasantness by assuming dictatorial manners to the Regent, the British Government arranged for his resignation, in favour of his younger brother, Jehangir Mahomed Khan. The latter was married to Sikandar Begam in 1835, although Gohur Begam continued to act as Regent. Serious differences of opinion which arose between Nawab Jehangir and Gohur Begam were not amicably arranged until 1837, when the Political Agent induced the Begam to retire from the Regency, she being granted a life annuity of Rs. 5,00,000. Gohur Begam's services were recognized at Delhi in 1877, by the bestowal upon her of the Imperial Order of the Crown of India.

Nawab Jehangir's literary tastes led him to take delight in the company of men of learning, but he at the same time devoted great care and attention to the material welfare of the State, and the prosperity of his subjects. His life unfortunately terminated in December 1844, at the early age of 27 years. Jehangir, in his will, expressed a desire that his illegitimate son, Dastgir, should succeed him, and that his daughter, Shah Jahan, should be united in wedlock with a direct descendant of Wazir Mahomed. The British Government set aside the will, and recognized Shah Jahan as the rightful successor, and it was further decided that "the future husband of Shah Jahan, who was to be selected from the Bhopal family, with a view to the amalgamation of the two branches descended from Ghaus Mahomed Khan and Wazir Mahomed Khan, should be Chief of Bhopal."

Shah Jahan Begam was, therefore, proclaimed Ruler of Bhopal, she being seven years of age at the time. It was proposed that during her minority the control of the State should be vested in a Regency, consisting of Sikandar Begam and Mian Faujdar Mahomed Khan, the youngest son of Nawab Ghaus Mahomed, the latter being also appointed Minister.

In the course of the following twelve months it was apparent that this dual authority was no longer possible, and the Political Agent obtained the resignation of Mian Faujdar Mahomed Khan, and arranged that Sikandar Begam should be the sole Administrator until her daughter,

THE STATE OF BHOPAL.

1. Habib Manzil, Bhopal. 2. General View of Bhopal from the Jame Masjid. 3. Shaukat Mahal, Bhopal. 4. Sardar Manzil Palace, Bhopal. 5. A View of the Benazir Palace Gateway.

THE STATE OF BHOPAL.

1. View of Sanchi Tope, Bhopal State. 2. Simla Kothi, Bhopal State. 3. Rahat Manzil Palace, Bhopal. 4. Qasr-i-Sultani (Her Highness's Residence), Bhopal. 5. Edward Museum, Bhopal.

THE STATE OF BHOPAL

Shah Jahan Begam, born in 1838, attained her majority. The next few years covered a period of remarkable progress in each department of the State, and the wisdom of this clever lady was manifested by her encouragement of general trading activities, the abolition of the vexatious system of farming revenues, of monopolies, and other measures of a progressive character, which enabled her to discharge many financial obligations to the State. In the month of July, 1855, Shah Jahan Begam was married to Bakshi Baki Mahomed Khan, the Commander-in-Chief of the Bhopal army, who was duly recognized as Nawab consort, and was granted the title of Nawab-Nazir-ud-daula Umrao Dula Bahadur, but Sikandar Begam was to remain as Regent until her daughter arrived at the age of 21 years. The Mutiny of 1857, which changed India into a seething cauldron of rebellion and bloodshed, will for ever be remembered in Bhopal, not merely for the distress which it occasioned, but also for the unparalleled loyalty of the Regent, and the extremely valuable assistance rendered by her to the British.

Sikandar Begam maintained peace within her territories, and although she herself was threatened with violence, she gave home and protection to a considerable number of British refugees; her troops were despatched to places where British residents were in need of reliable guards, and she generously supplied British regiments with an abundance of food for men, and grain for their horses. When peace had been restored, an application was made to the British Government by Sikandar Begam, that she might be installed as Ruler of Bhopal, on the ground that she was the legitimate heir, although her later husband, Jehangir, had been incorrectly raised to the position of ruling Nawab. Her services during the Mutiny were also urged as another reason for her application. Further than this, her daughter, Shah Jahan, supporting her mother's contention, waived her claims to the *masnad* until the death of Sikandar Begam. The matter was favourably entertained by the Government, and in March 1860, Her Highness Sikandar Begam was formerly installed as Ruler of Bhopal.

In January 1861, Her Highness attended a Durbar held at Jubbulpore, and His Excellency Lord Canning, the Viceroy, addressing her, used the following words: "Sikandar Begam! Your Highness is very welcome at this Durbar. I have long desired to thank you for the services which you have rendered to the Queen's Government. Your Highness is the Ruler of a State which is conspicuous in history for never having been in arms against the British Power; and lately, when that State was beset and threatened by our enemies, you, a woman, guided its affairs with a courage, an ability, and a success that would have done honour to any statesman or soldier . . . such services must not go unrewarded.

"I now place in your hands the grant in sovereignty of the district of Berasia. This district was formerly a dependency of the State of Dhar, but Dhar has by rebellion forfeited all claim to it; and it is now given in perpetuity of Bhopal for a memorial of loyalty, under your wise and brave guidance in a time of trial. . . ."

In the same year Her Highness was invested with the insignia of a Knight Grand Commander of the Most Exalted Order of the Star of India, and in 1862 she was granted a *sanad* of adoption. She undertook a pilgrimage to Mecca in 1864, and on October 30, 1868, she passed away at the age of 51 years.

Her Highness Nawab Shah Jahan Begam, who it will be remembered had stood aside in 1845 in favour of the accession of her late mother, was now invested as Ruler of Bhopal, and her daughter, Sultan Jahan, was recognized as heir-apparent. The Nawab Baki Mahomed Khan, consort of Her Highness, died in July 1867, and in May 1871, she married Maulvi Sayad Sadiq Husain, who had for the previous 17 years filled many important positions in the State, he being granted the title of Nawab Wala Jah Amir-ul-Mulk, together with a personal salute of 17 guns. The great ability displayed by Her Highness in the control of State affairs, was acknowledged by the Government by the bestowal upon her in 1872 of the insignia of a Knight Grand Commander of the Most Exalted Order of the Star of India. Her Highness, at subsequent dates, agreed to bear the cost of the Hoshangabad-Bhopal railway, and also granted land for the Bhopal-Ujjain line. Maulvi Sayad Sadiq Husain the Nawab's second husband, died in 1890, and from that date until her death in 1901, the Begam exercised sole control over State affairs.

Her Highness Shah Jahan was succeeded by her daughter, the present Ruler, Her Highness Nawab Sultan Jahan Begam Sahiba, G.C.S.I., G.C.I.E., C.I. Before six months had elapsed, Her Highness suffered a great bereavement in the death of her husband, the Nawab consort. In 1904 Her Highness proceeded on a pilgrimage to Mecca, and in the following year she had the honour of being presented at Indore to Their Royal Highnesses the Prince and Princess of Wales, now Their Imperial Majesties the King-Emperor and Queen-Empress, when the Begam was the recipient of the insignia of a Knight Commander of the Most Eminent Order of the India Empire.

Her Highness evinces the deepest interest in the welfare of her subjects, and by personal visits to the various districts of the State she has opportunities for making herself thoroughly acquainted with the conditions of her people.

The question of education has taken a deep root in the heart of the Begam, and one has only to read remarks made by her at public meetings to realize how earnest she is in affording facilities for the teaching of children.

The State of Bhopal was honoured in December 1909 by a visit from Lord Minto (the Viceroy) and Lady Minto, and at the Sultana Girls' School, Her Highness, in the presence of Lady Minto, said: "In no State in India should the condition of its female population be so well-considered as here in Bhopal, having as it has had, a succession of four female rulers. Under such unique circumstances, it is peculiarly fitting that the womanly heart of the ruler of Bhopal should turn in sympathy with female education. The influence of woman is as great, as vast, and as beneficial in India, as in the western hemisphere. All over the world it is the mothers who have influenced past generations, and who will still exert that influence over the generations of the present and of the future; but it must be remembered that in order to maintain a healthy influence, the women of all nations must be in sympathy and in touch with the times."

In 1910 Her Highness was created a Knight Commander of the Most Exalted Order of the Star of India. During the course of the year 1911 Her Highness travelled to England, in order to be present at the Coronation ceremony of His Imperial Majesty the present King-Emperor. The Begam attended a *levee* and a garden party at Buckingham Palace, and she subsequently toured through Europe, visiting France, Germany, Austria, Switzerland, and Turkey. His Majesty the Sultan of Turkey accorded an interview to Her Highness at Constantinople, and presented to her the priceless gift of a hair from the beard of the Prophet. The Nawab's impressions of Great Britain are well expressed in her own words : " I have returned after my travels a greater believer than ever in the justice, peace, and freedom of the British Empire." Her Highness accepted an invitation to attend the Coronation Durbar at Delhi in 1911, when His Imperial Majesty King George conferred upon her the distinction of the Order of the Imperial Crown of India.

Their Excellencies Lord Hardinge (the Viceroy) and Lady Hardinge paid a visit to Bhopal in December 1912.

One more reference may be made to the earnest and practically-expressed sympathy of Her Highness in all questions tending to raise the status of her subjects, but particularly of women and children, who have a true benefactress in their beloved Ruler. The Sultan Sahiba desired to commemorate the auspicious visit to India of Their Imperial Majesties on the occasion of their Coronation ceremony at Delhi, and she made it known by means of an open letter, circulated throughout the country, that in her opinion no memorial could better serve the purpose than a well-endowed and well-conducted institution at Delhi for the education of women. The letter contained the following notable passage : " My idea regarding the institution I have proposed, is that we should begin with a well-equipped school, which, in the course of time, will become a model for the education of girls of rich as well as poor families. Twelve lakhs of rupees are, in my opinion, necessary at the outset—four lakhs for building purposes, and eight lakhs for endowment. The details of the scheme are being worked out, and I shall be very pleased to receive suggestions in this connection. For my own part, I shall be delighted to give a lakh of rupees from the State, and Rs. 20,000 from my private purse. My daughters-in-law have also expressed practical sympathy with my scheme, the eldest and the second contributing Rs. 7,000 each, and the third Rs. 5,000.

" I have every reason to hope and believe that my scheme will commend itself to all friends of India who have the education of women at heart, and to all my sisters, from Ranis and Begams down to ladies in humbler walks of life, and with their assistance, moral and material, I am absolutely confident of unqualified success."

Her Highness has three sons, namely : Nawab Mahomed Nasrulla Khan Bahadur, who renders valuable assistance to his august mother in the administration of the Forest Department of the State, and in connection with matters specially entrusted to him ; Nawabzada General Mahomed Obaidullah Khan Bahadur, Commander-in-Chief of the State troops, to whom the title of Commander of the Order of the Star of India has been granted by the Indian Government ; and Nawabzada Hamidulla Khan Bahadur, who holds the rank of Lieutenant-Colonel in the State forces, who is a graduate of Allahabad University, and is now Her Highness' Chief Secretary. He is one of the very few scions of ruling houses in India who hold a University degree. His appointment at the head of Her Highness' Secretariat has justified expectations, and the value of his work for administrative efficiency and industrial progress has been repeatedly acknowledged by Her Highness.

Bhopal, the largest Mahomedan State in Northern India, is 6,859 square miles in extent, and the inhabitants are more than 720,000 in number. The territory, which forms a compact block, is bounded on the north by the States of Gwalior, Baroda, Korwai, Maksudangarh, Narsinghgar, and Tonk, and the Saugor district of the Central Provinces ; on the south by the Nebudda river ; on the east by the Saugor and Narsinghpur districts of the Central Provinces ; and on the west by the Gwalior and Narsinghgar States.

The country is naturally divided into a table-land—part of the Malwa plateau covering an area of more than 4,000 square miles, and a hilly portion being an arm of the Vindhya range. The first of these is conspicuous for its undulating downs of yellow grass, and fertile fields of black soil, suitable for the cultivation of cotton, while the other division includes the rich valley of the Nerbudda.

The principal rivers in the State are the Betwa, the Parbati, and the Nerbudda, which flows for a distance of more than 120 miles along the southern border.

The inhabitants consist of Hindus, 73 per cent. ; Animists, 14 per cent. ; and Mahomedans, 13 per cent. ; while the principal cultivators are Khatis, Kachhis, and Kurmis.

Turning to economic matters, it is noticed that the practice of agriculture occupies the attention of 43 per cent. of the people, the principal landholders being Brahmans and Rajputs. The soil varies considerably in quality owing to different altitudes, but speaking in a general way, it produces profitable crops such as are usually grown in Central India.

The two seasons for cultivation are the *kharif*, lasting from May to October, and the *rabi*, extending from October to March. Out of a total area of 4,417,483 acres of land, about 1,170,000 acres are placed under crops in a normal year, and the principal products are wheat, *makka*, *jowar*, cotton, poppy, *bejra*, sugar-cane, and oil-seeds of various descriptions.

Cultivators do not seem to have yet realized the importance of cultivation according to modern scientific principles ; in many instances successive crops are taken without any nutrition, in the shape of natural or artificial manure, being given to the soil ; and although the most important practice of rotation of crops is understood by a large number of cultivators, it is only rarely put into operation. A very large area of land, still uncultivated, is available for pastoral farming, and therefore there is every inducement for occupiers to increase their earnings by breeding cattle and other animals. The Malwar type of cattle, found in large numbers in Bhopal, is exceedingly valuable for agricultural work, being very strong and active, and having deep and wide frames, together with hard and shapely feet.

According to the latest available return of livestock issued in the State, it appears that these are approximately : 155,000 bullocks, 210,000 cows, 15,000 male and 62,000 female buffaloes, 3,000 horses, 4,300 mares, and 3,100 asses.

The whole of the land belongs absolutely to the State, and occupiers, who have no proprietary rights, are allowed to continue their tenancies so long as they pay the State demands, which are classed as revenue.

The principal mineral is the valuable sandstone, which is used extensively for building purposes.

The State forests, 1,187,000 acres in extent, are not in such a thriving condition as they might have been if greater care had been taken in former years to prevent the indiscriminate felling of trees, to re-plant devastated tracts, and to adopt deterrent measures against thefts. There are now two forest officers, who supervise an establishment of guards, consisting of Gonds, Kols, Korkus, Dhanok, and other jungle tribes, but further protection is obtained by granting to villagers residing

THE STATE OF BHOPAL.

1. Fatehgarh Fort, Bhopal. 2. Tomb of Her Late Highness Nawab Shah Jahan Begam, in the Hayat Afza Garden, Bhopal. 3. Tajulmasajid, Bhopal. 4. The Bhadbada Waterfall, Bhopal.

THE STATE OF BHOPAL.

1. La Kothi, Bhopal. 2. Guest House, Bhopal. 3. Lady Lansdowne Hospital, Bhopal. 4. The Jame Masjid, Bhopal. 5. The Big Lake and its Surroundings, Bhopal. 6. Sultania Girls' School, Bhopal.

on the borders of forests the privilege of obtaining wood free of charge, on the understanding that they report any breach of forest rules which may come under their notice.

Poppy was formerly grown in the State, but, in accordance with the advice of the Government of India, its cultivation has, since the export of opium to China was prohibited, been restricted to a smaller area. About 42 maunds (3,360 lb.) were produced in the last year, and the total income, inclusive of arrears, amounted to Rs. 1,85,531. Other manufacturing and industrial enterprises produce stone mortars, fine and coarse cloth, muslin, leather boxes, and other goods, while Bhopal, the chief town, is famous for the making of native jewellery, turbans, and cloth worked with gold and silver thread. An all-India Ladies' Industrial Exhibition was held at Bhopal about six years ago, under the patronage of Her Highness the Begam, and several medals were presented as rewards for artistic articles of remarkably fine workmanship. About the same date a horse show was held in the capital town, with the object of encouraging the breeding of horses.

Good facilities for the transfer of agricultural produce and general mercantile commodities are afforded by the Great Indian Peninsula Railway and the Bhopal-Ujjain section of the same system. The former of these traverses the State for a distance of about 73 miles, and has stations at Budni, Midghat, Barkera, Hirania, Dip, Misrod, Bhopal, Sukhi-Siwania, Gulgaon, Satamatpur, and Sanchi, while the latter connects with the Rajputana-Malwa line at Ujjain, and has stations at Bhopal, Beragarh, Phanda, and Sehore. In the year 1885 the Durbar contributed a sum of Rs. 50,00,000 towards the construction of the Bhopal State Railway, which runs from the capital to Itarsi. and a sum of more than Rs. 22,00,000 was about the same date granted for the Bhopal-Ujjain line. A large proportion of the traffic consists of gram, linseed, wheat, horns, hides, and skins, which are exported to Bombay ; wax to Delhi ; honey to Gujarat ; lac and gum to Mirzapur ; horns and skins to Cawnpore and Madras ; and combs, melons, and timber to Calcutta and other places. The chief imports carried along the railways comprise kerosene oil, sugar, salt, tobacco, cutlery, shoes, cloth, and paper.

The State is administered by the Nawab Begam, who is invested with full ruling powers, including the passing of sentences of death. Her Highness is assisted by two Ministers, who are in charge of revenue, judicial, and police matters, while there are also advisory councils dealing with finance, legislative work, and other subjects, in addition to officials in charge of the Public Works, police, forest, and other departments.

For administrative purposes the State is divided into three districts, namely, Nizamat-i-Mashrik, Nizamat-i-Maghrib, and Nizamat-i-Janub, each of which is in charge of a *nazim*, who is the chief revenue officer, district magistrate, and a civil judge.

In former days, the administration of justice was not controlled by any properly constituted legal tribunals, nor were there any judges such as are met with in the majority of the Native States of India in the present day. A certain amount of evidence was given before high officials, and the only volume taken as a guide in the giving of decisions was the Koran itself.

During the *regime* of Sikandar Begam, however, steps were taken to give a more judicial aspect to the procedure, and since the year 1820 a new order of things has prevailed, largely owing to the influence and advice of British Political Officers. The laws and regulations in force in the State are framed chiefly in accordance with the spirit of those recognized throughout British Indian territories.

There are 44 Courts in Bhopal, comprising the Chiefs' Court, two Judges' Courts, two Assistant Judges' Courts, two City Magistrates' Courts, one *Sadar Amin's* Court, one Munsif's Court, six District and Assistant Magistrate's Courts, and 27 *tahsildar's* Courts. The *Sadar-ul-Muham*, at Bhopal, enjoys the powers of a Sessions Judge, and he hears appeals from the Courts of the *nazims* and City Magistrates, while the final Court of Appeal is that of the Chief.

The State of Bhopal is fortunate in having had Rulers who have been deeply interested in the advancement of education among the people, but even to-day it has to be admitted that the Mahomedan portion of the inhabitants has not manifested much interest in this most important subject.

The first regular school in the State was opened in the year 1860, and about ten years later it was decided by the Durbar that the people might be induced to have their children instructed even in primary knowledge if they were to publish an order that appointments to positions in the State departments would not thereafter be given to any individuals who had not obtained a certificate from a recognized college or school. A Regulation to that effect was actually issued, and progress was noted almost immediately afterwards. The principal educational institution at the present time is the Sulimania High School, affiliated to the University at Allahabad, in which instruction is given in the Persian, Urdu, and Hindi languages, and in the text of the Koran. The students are more than 800 in number.

The Alexandra High School has a daily attendance roll of about 185 youths, and the good work performed by the teachers is apparent from the satisfactory percentage of pupils who have been successful in matriculation examinations.

The institution in which English was first taught in Bhopal is the Jahangiria school, in which there are about 320 pupils. There are also the "Madrassa Ahmadia," specially reserved for instruction in religious subjects ; the Victoria Girls' School, erected in 1891, and the Sultania School, for daughters of parents in good positions, which has a large number of pupils on the rolls. There are also about 75 primary schools, a medical school for instruction in the *Yunani* system of medicine and surgery, and an Art school, commenced in 1905, for the purpose of enabling widows and destitute women to earn a decent livelihood.

The arrangements made by the State for the granting of medical relief are warmly appreciated by the subjects of the State. The Department was organized more than 60 years ago by Her Highness Sikandar Begam, the treatment being given on what is known in India as the "*Yunani*" system, while the first hospital conducted upon English methods was opened in 1870. There are now 40 dispensaries (37 of which are *Yunani*) ; a military hospital at Jahangirabad ; the Lady Lansdowne hospital, opened in 1891, which affords advice and treatment to *purdah* women ; and midwifery schools of instruction. There is also the Bhopal Agency Hospital at Sehore, which is supported partly by an Imperial grant, and partly by money from the Bhopal Agency local fund contributions from other States.

This hospital has accommodation for about 50 resident patients. The out-door and in-door cases attended to in the year

THE STATE OF BHOPAL.

1. View of Taj Mahal from the Tank. 2. View of Minto Hall, Bhopal. 3. Hamidia Library, Bhopal. 4. Alexandra High School. 5. Yacht Club, Bhopal.

1918 were 18,498 in number; 951 operations were performed; and beds were found for 672 persons.

The intense loyalty and devotion to the British Throne of past Rulers of Bhopal has never for a single moment been called in question, and that stainless record has been nobly upheld by Her Highness the present Begam and her subjects during the exceedingly trying period of the Great War.

Acting on the principle that example is better than precept, Her Highness, and various members of her household, as well as State officials, opened wide their private purses, and thus encouraged the people to make some sacrifices for the righteous objects for which the Allies were reluctantly compelled to take up arms.

A statement of the help rendered by the State was recently issued by Her Highness' Political Secretary, and the following particulars have been extracted therefrom. Under the heading of special military expenditure owing to the war, the items include: Enhancement of pay of the Bhopal Imperial Service Lancers, Rs. 14,256; free rations to the same contingent, Rs. 27,404; increase of pay to State motor drivers, Rs. 7,000; extra wages given to men of State infantry serving in Army Reserve Corps, Rs. 22,342; cost of stores granted to cavalry and infantry, Rs. 63,542; cost of horses, yachts, and motor cars, Rs. 92,300; and amount granted to heirs of men on active service during 1918, Rs. 9,180.

Contributions for direct war purposes included: Towards maintenance of the hospital ship *Loyalty*, Rs. 2,00,088; St. John's Ambulance Association, Rs. 5,000; grant to troops, Rs. 25,000; for purchase of two motor launches, Rs. 14,000; the cost of two aeroplanes, Rs. 33,750; in aid of war expenses, Rs. 1,00,000; annual subscription for general expenses for duration of war, Rs. 50,000; bonuses and expenses of recruits, Rs. 33,075; to "Our Day" and similar funds, Rs. 25,000.

In the list of donations to war charities may be mentioned: To Prince of Wales's Relief Fund, Rs 90,000; Imperial Relief Fund (India), Rs. 1,00,000; to Belgian Relief Fund, Rs. 5,000; to British Women's Hospital, London, Rs. 3,000; Bombay Relief Funds, Rs. 2,500; Imperial Relief Fund, Rs. 50,000; to St. John's Ambulance Association, the Y.M.C.A., and various other funds, more than Rs. 30,000.

State officials subscribed Rs. 83,500 to War Loans in 1917 and 1918; and the Bhopal Municipality purchased War Bonds to the amount of Rs. 15,000. War Loan subscriptions from the State comprised the Indian Fund, Rs. 6,00,000; and the National Fund (England), Rs. 1,99,500. The State also contributed Rs. 1,00,000 to various Funds through its *jagirdars* and others.

With regard to assistance given in materials, it is noticed that tents, costing Rs. 12,000, were presented; Rs. 3,000 were expended on books for wounded soldiers; and clothing and comforts, valued at Rs. 16,000.

Lieut.-Col. Nawab Nasrulla Khan Bahadur (the heir-apparent) gave two motor cars, Rs. 22,000; eight horses, Rs. 20,000; portable telephones and motor accessories, Rs. 10,000; subscribed to Red Cross and other funds, Rs. 3,000; to general expenses of war, Rs. 35,000; contributed to British war loans, Rs. 50,000; invested in postal certificates, Rs. 1,36,000; and spent on fuel, grass, and other commodities, Rs. 11,000.

Brigadier-General Nawab Obaidulla Khan Bahadur presented three motor cars of the value of Rs. 41,000; horses, Rs. 1,20,000; and purchased War Loan Bonds, Rs. 75,000.

Lieut.-Col. Nawabzada Hamidulla Khan Bahadur, Chief Secretary of Bhopal Government, invested Rs. 50,000 in the National War Loan of 1915; Rs. 1,50,000 in the Indian Fund in 1917 and 1918; and he also contributed Rs. 52,000, the value of bedsheets and other necessaries for men, and also fodder for horses.

The aggregate amount, therefore, raised through the different agencies of the State was not less than Rs. 28,34,575.

MAHESHWAR GHAT.

CONSTRUCTED IN THE LAST DECADE OF THE EIGHTEENTH CENTURY.

THE STATE OF INDORE

INDORE is the premier State in the area comprised at present in the Central India Agency, and is in Political relationship with the Government of India. It is composed of several blocks. It is bounded on the north by the State of Gwalior; on the east by the States of Bhopal and Dewas, and the Central Provinces; on the south by the district of Khandesh; and on the west by the States of Gwalior, Barwani, and Dhar. Its area is 9,500 square miles, with a population of 11½ lakhs, including the Indore Residency and the Mhow Cantonment; and its revenues from all sources are one crore and five lakhs a year.

The ancestors of the rulers of Indore resided originally near Muttra, but they afterwards removed to the Deccan, remaining for a considerable period first at Chitore and afterwards in the district of Aurangabad. They then took up their residence at a village called Hal, or Hol, situated about 40 miles distant from the present city of Poona. Although the family name of the ruling house is Veerkar, the Maharajas have for centuries assumed the patronymic of Holkar, probably on account of their connection with the village of Hol.

The Holkar dynasty was founded by Malhar Rao Holkar, son of Khandoji, who followed pastoral avocations while residing in the village of Hol, situated on the banks of the river Nera, near Phaltan, in the estate of Nimbalkar. His father died in 1696, when he was only three years of age, whereupon his widowed mother took him to reside with her at the house of her brother, Bhojraj Bargal, who was a landowner of Talauda, in the district of Khandesh. When the boy grew older he was sent by his uncle to tend his flock of sheep; and one has to narrate an interesting family tradition relating to an incident which was curiously prophetic of the distinguished position to be eventually filled by the boy. The legend is to the effect that the youth was one day overcome by the intense heat of the sun, and that he slept on the roadside, being fully exposed to its rays. A cobra, it is said, taking pity on him, expanded its hood and interposed it like a parasol between the sleeper's beaming face and the burning sun in order to protect him from the killing heat. Bhojraj, on hearing of the miraculous occurrence, deemed it a good omen for the boy's future greatness, and transferred him from the obscurity of an attendant upon sheep to a post in the cavalry, which his uncle held in readiness for his overlord, Sardar Kadam Bande, a *Maratha* noble.

Malhar Rao was soon after placed *in* charge of a detachment of cavalry, and in the conflict which was then *raging* between the Mahomedans and the Marathas, the latter of whom were then rising to power. Malhar Rao gained the favour of the Peshwa, Baji Rao I, the

MAHARAJA TUKOJI RAO III (1903).

Photo by Ramchandra rao & Pratap rao, Indore.

leader of the Maratha forces, who in 1725 placed him in command of 500 horses. Just at this time, Nizam-ul-Mulk of Hyderabad was rapidly consolidating his position as an independent ruler, and the Moghul Emperor, fearing him, had given the charge of Malwa to Raja Girdhar to put a check upon his disloyal Viceroy. Jai Singh, the Raja of Jeypore, had a great influence in the Moghul Court, and he favoured the Hindus, who were being persecuted by the Mahomedans. Finding that Raja Girdhar was acting against his wishes, Jai Singh invited the Marathas to conquer Malwa. The Marathas accordingly many times invaded Malwa. On one occasion, in 1727, they met Raja Girdhar at Sarangpore, on the bank of the river Parvati, nearly 50 miles north-east of Dewas. The Maratha armies were led by Chimnaji Appa, the Peshwa's brother, and Malhar Rao Holkar. In the battle that was fought Raja Girdhar was killed. The Marathas had then no time to make good their conquest, as their attention was engaged in their fight with the Nizam. The Peshwa recalled his armies from Malwa, and the Moghul Emperor thereupon appointed Daya Bahadur, the cousin of Raja Girdhar, as the latter's successor.

Young Malhar Rao manifested great skill and bravery in this and in a number of other such engagements, and he was rewarded by the Peshwa with a grant, in 1728, of 12 districts in Malwa; but this number was subsequently increased in 1731 to 82, in return for further valuable services rendered to the Maratha cause.

Three years after the battle of Sarangpore, the Peshwa again sent his armies to Malwa, under the joint command of his brother Chimnaji and Malhar Rao Holkar. Malhar Rao met Daya Bahadur at Tirla, near Dhar; and a battle was fought between them in December, 1731, in which Daya Bahadur was slain, and Malhar Rao took possession of the whole of Malwa, proclaiming the suzerainty of the Peshwa and appointing Vithoji Bolia as Manager at Dhar. The Peshwa divided Malwa between Ranoji Sindhia and Malhar Rao, who efficiently managed affairs there.

In 1737 Malhar Rao accompanied the Peshwa on his expedition to Northern India. The Moghul Emperor, hearing of the advance of the Maratha armies upon Delhi, called upon the Nizam of Hyderabad for help. The Nizam at once set out with 34,000 men and a great battery of guns to help the Emperor. He met the Maratha armies near Bhopal, but without making a stand he took refuge in the fort there. The Marathas besieged the town. Safdar Jang, the nephew of Sadat Khan, a great noble at the Moghul Court, and the Raja of Kotah, meanwhile, were on their way to relieve the Nizam. But Malhar Rao Holkar, with the aid of Jeswant Rao Powar, opposed them at once, and killed 1,500 men of the enemy's army. The Nizam lost all hopes of success. The seige of Bhopal continued for 27 days, and it was conducted by the Peshwa Baji Rao, assisted by Malhar Rao Holkar and Ranoji Rao Sindhia. Food became scarce and ammunition was all spent. The Nizam was thus forced to submit, and the Moghul Emperor recognized the supremacy of the Marathas over the part of the country lying between the rivers Chambal and Nerbuda.

In 1739 Malhar Rao was sent to the Konkan to help Chimnaji Appa in the operations against the Portuguese, who had been persecuting the Hindus for years past. The Fort of Bassein was taken by the Marathas after strenuous operations. Malhar Rao acquired great fame on this occasion.

In 1743 Malhar Rao was invited by the mother of Raja Umed Sing of Bundi to assist him against Ishwar Sing, Raja of Jaipur, who had usurped a part of his territories. Assistance was given, and the Jaipur troops were defeated near Lakheri. In return for this help Bundi substantially rewarded Malhar Rao, and the latter secured for the Raja of Bundi the *Sanads* from Jaipur for his territorial rights.

In 1745 Malhar Rao was requested by the mother of Madho Sing, the younger son of Sawai Jai Sing of Jaipur, to help in securing for her son the *gadi* of Jaipur, which had been wrongfully seized by Ishwar Sing, the eldest son of Sawai Jai Sing. Ishwar Sing was not entitled to the *gadi*, having been born of a mother not belonging to the family of Udaipur; whereas Madho Sing, though younger, was so entitled, having been born of a daughter of the Rana of Udaipur, and it having been agreed in the time of Sawai Jai Sing that a son born of a Princess from the Udaipur family was to have precedence in succession over any other son born of a mother belonging to another family. Malhar Rao marched to Jaipur with his troops to instal Madho Sing on the *gadi*. Ishwar Sing, despairing of the future, committed suicide. Madho Sing was thus enabled to secure the *gadi* of Jaipur. In consideration of these services Madho Sing assigned to Malhar Rao the districts of Rampura, senior and junior, and Hinglasgarh: he promised a tribute of Rs. $3\frac{1}{2}$ lakhs per year, and also gave him a lump sum of Rs. 76 lakhs.

During 1746-47 Malhar Rao took part in the operations against Ajaigarh, Kalinjar, and Jetpur, in Bundelkhand; and was applauded by the Peshwa for the bravery he displayed on that occasion. In 1751 Malhar Rao was with the Peshwa in the action at Kukri river, in which the Nizam was defeated. In 1751 Safdar Jang called in the Marathas to preserve Oudh from the Rohillas. Malhar Rao took a prominent part in this war against the Rohillas. He surprised the enemy by a night attack which he made with a very small body of troops; but this success was due to an old stratagem. He tied torches and lights to the horns of many thousand cattle, and drove them in one direction, while he and his small number of men attacked the enemy from the other side in the dark. The enemy, seeing thousands of lights all round, thought themselves besieged by a very large army; they were confused, and they fled in all directions, leaving everything behind to be plundered by the victors.

In 1752 there were again hostilities against the Nizam, in which Jayappa Sindhia and Malhar Rao Holkar took a prominent part on the side of the Peshwa. This action was fought at Bhalki, in which the Nizam was defeated.

In 1754 there was an expedition against the Raja of Bharatpur, who had espoused the cause of Sujaud Dowla, the Vizir, as against the Emperor Alamgir II; and Najaf Khan, the Commander-in-Chief, had, on behalf of the Emperor, invited the Marathas to punish the hostile faction. The Maratha armies were led by Ragholba, the Peshwa's brother, assisted by Holkar and Sindhia. The Marathas laid siege to the Fort of Kumbher, in Bharatpur territory. During the siege, Khande Rao, son of Malhar Rao, was killed by a cannon-ball from the fort. This infuriated Malhar Rao, who vowed to raze the fort to the ground and throw its material into the river Jamna. The Raja of Bharatpur became alarmed and sued for peace, which was agreed to. In order to pacify the anger of Malhar Rao he gave to him three villages, Gagar Soli, Tamrel, and Set, together with the salt works there, all yielding Rs. 15,000 a year, for the maintenance of the Chhatri to be built in honour of Khande Rao. The Emperor on his part, in order to appease Malhar

PRINCE YESHWANT RAO BALA SAHIB (BORN 1908).

Photo by Ramchandra rao & Pratap rao, Indore.

MAHARAJA SHIVAJA RAO (1886-1903).

Rao, gave him specially in the name of his wife, Gautama Bai, the Pargana of Verul, in the Aurangabad District, and in the name of his grandson Male Rao, the Pargana of Ambar, in that district.

During 1756 Malhar Rao took part in the operations against the Nawab of Savnur, in Deccan; and in 1759-60 he was engaged in taking forts in the district of Jeypore. In the great battle of Panipat, in 1761, the Maratha supremacy in Northern India received a great blow. Malhar Rao was amongst those who were able to retreat to the south. Shortly after this time he acquired from the Peshwa Madhao Rao I, territories worth about 30 lakhs in the Deccan as a reward for his exertions in obtaining a victory over the Nizam at the battle of Tandulja, or Rakshash Bhuwan. To these were added further territorial rewards in Khandesh, in the valley of the Narbuda, and elsewhere. Malhar Rao proceeded in 1764 to the north, on the invitation of Vizir Sujaud Dowla of Oudh, who had been defeated by the British, and who consequently asked for military help from the Marathas. Malhar Rao marched to his help and obtained a signal victory over the British, in the course of which he inflicted heavy losses on them. The British retaliated by making a surprise attack at night on the troops of Malhar Rao, and he had to make a retreat as far as Kalpi, in Bundelkhand. Here he found that the Rana of Gohud, the Raja of Datia, and other Bundela Chiefs, were in combination to throw off the Maratha suzerainty, and that the district of Jhansi had actually been taken from the Marathas by Himmat Bahadur. Entering with vigour into the struggle, Malhar Rao beseiged Jhansi, and recovered it after three months fighting. The Raja of Datia was defeated after four days battle, and was compelled to tender his submission to Malhar Rao. The Rajas of Orchha, Shevda, and other places, were next to be dealt with. In the meantime troops arrived from the Deccan, under the command of Raghoba, to help Malhar Rao, but while a concerted action was being planned against the Bundela Chiefs, Malhar Rao died, at an advanced age, in about April, 1766, at Alampur, or Malharnagar, where a cenotaph stands to his memory.

Malhar Rao was one of the most intrepid warriors of his day, having taken an active part in no less than forty battles; and in administration he stood on a level with many of the leading statesmen then wielding powers in India. He left behind a vast State, yielding about a crore a year, and enjoying the benefits of peace and good government.

Malhar Rao had only one son, named Khande Rao, who had been killed as related, but who left a son, named Male Rao, who succeeded to the *gadi* on the death of his grandfather. The rulership of the young Chief continued for only about nine months, when he died. Tukoji Holkar, a relative, was then appointed Subhedar by the Peshwa; but the management of the State devolved solely on Male Rao's mother, Ahilya Bai, who had already been associated with the administration (civil and military) from the time of her father-in-law. This lady was remarkably clever and hard-working. She succeeded in gaining the affection of her own subjects as well as the confidence of the rulers of neighbouring States. She made herself personally acquainted with the social life of the inhabitants of the State, and she was ever ready to hear, and if possible redress, grievances which were laid before her. The people even of those days indulged freely in litigation, and with the object of ensuring justice, in cases of disputes, this wise ruler established Courts of Equity and Arbitration. Being of a religious turn of mind she spent large sums of money on the construction of temples, *dharamshalas*, and other useful institutions, in various important centres over the length and breadth of India. This gifted lady died in 1795, at the age of 70 years.

Sir John Malcolm in his "Memoirs of Malwa," says, "The facts that have been stated of Ahilya Bai rest on grounds that admit of no scepticism. It is, however, an extraordinary picture: a female without vanity; a bigot without intolerance; a mind imbued with the deepest superstition, yet receiving no impressions except that promoted by the happiness of those under its influence; a being exercising in the most active and able manner despotic power, not merely with sincere humility, but under the severest moral restraint that a strict conscience could impose on human action; and all this combined with the greatest indulgence for the weakness and faults of others. Such, at least, is the account which the natives of Malwa give of Ahilya Bai. With them her name is sainted, and she is styled an *Avtar*, or incarnation of the Divinity. In the most sober view that can be taken of her character, she certainly appears, within her limited sphere, to have been one of the purest and most exemplary rulers that ever existed; and she affords a striking example of the practical benefit a mind may receive from performing worldly duties under a deep sense of responsibility to its Creator."

The late Ahilya Bai received invaluable assistance in her administrative duties from Tukoji Rao I, who was the Commander of her army, and fulfilled those duties which, as a female, she could not perform. Nevertheless, when the time came to offer battle she displayed wonderful fortitude and the tactics of a consummate general. Thus, in the year 1767, when Raghoba Dada, the Peshwa's uncle, threatened to invade her territory at the instance of her faithless Dewan, Gangadhar Chandrachud, in order to coerce her to adopt a boy and appoint Chandrachud as Administrator, which she had declined to do in consultation with the Peshwa Madhav Rao I, Ahilya Bai raised some companies of female warriors, besides other troops, to oppose Raghoba under her own command. Raghoba realized the difficulty of the situation, and wisely sent a message that he had come only to pay a visit of condolence on the death of Male Rao.

Tukoji Rao was a worthy successor of Malhar Rao. He distinguished himself as a general of great tact and ability in several engagements, and it was he who introduced the European system of warfare and discipline into the army. In association with Sindhia he took an active part in the expedition which was sent by the Peshwa in 1769, under the command of Ramchandra Ganesh Kanade and Visaji Biniwale, to punish the Rohillas who had sided with Ahmadshah Abdali against the Marathas at the battle of Panipat. At first the Maratha army divided itself into three parts for separate actions-Sindhia marched against Udaipore, and levied a tribute of 60 lakhs on it; Tukoji Holkar marched to Kotah and Bundi, and levied tributes; while the other two generals remained in Saugor in order to collect the tributes from the Bundelkhand Chiefs. Later on the combined army marched against the Raja of Bharatpur. This Raja had now joined Shuja Ud Dowla, who at the battle of Panipat had deserted the Maratha cause and treacherously joined the Abdali. The Raja had also taken the Agra Fort and District from the Marathas. The action between the Marathas and the Raja took place about 16 miles from Bharatpur, and the Raja was completely defeated. The Raja (Nawal Singh) pur-

1. SUBHEDAR MULHAR RAO I (1728-65). 2. DEVI AHILYA BAI (1765-95). 3. SUBHEDAR TUKOJI RAO I (1795-97).

1. MAHARAJA YESHWANT RAO (1805-11). 2. MAHARAJA HARI RAO (1834-43). 3. MAHARAJA TUKOJI RAO II (1844-86).

chased peace from the Marathas by giving them 65 lakhs in cash and surrendering the Agra Fort and District. The victorious army then proceeded to Delhi. The Marathas also secured at this time (1770) from Najib Khan Rohilla, as the price of making friendship with the Rohillas, the Districts in the Doab which had been lost to the Marathas after the battle of Panipat. The Marathas then proceeded on their march against the Pathans of Farukkabad, who had been their enemies at the battle of Panipat. The Pathans and the Rohillas had, however, a secret understanding to help each other against the Marathas, and the latter had therefore to fight with both the Rohillas and the Pathans. There were several battles between them, in the course of which the Marathas took all the forts, Etawa, etc., with the exception of Farukkabad. One of the battles was at Phattargarh, at the close of 1770, where both the Pathans and the Rohillas, numbering 70 000 were totally defeated. Nawab Ahmed Khan Bangash of Farukkabad, the Chief of the Pathans, now sued for peace, being afraid that he would otherwise lose his territories; and his request was granted by the Marathas, in 1771, on his making restoration of all the territories he had taken from them.

The Emperor Shah Alam was at this time at Allahabad under the protection of the British Government, having been dethroned in 1765 in favour of another aspirant. Knowing that the Marathas were in communication with him with a view to reinstating him on the throne, the British came forward to assist him in that object, as soon as it was possible to do so. The Emperor was impatient, and settled with the Marathas the terms on which they should assist him. These required him, *inter alia*, actually to co-operate with the Marathas in their various projects, to restore to them all the *Jagirs* they had before the battle of Panipat, and to pay to them the *Chouth* which had remained unpaid since 1748. The Emperor was accordingly, with the help of the Marathas, installed on the throne of Delhi at the end of 1771.

In the beginning of 1772 the combined armies of the Emperor and the Marathas marched against Zabita Khan, the Chief of the Rohillas, who had not yet come to terms, though defeated at Phattargarh. The Rohillas retreated to Shukratal Fort for protection. The Marathas besieged the fort, and inflicted many casualties, and Zabita Khan had to escape for his life to Bijnor. The Marathas pursued him and completely defeated him beyond Chandi Ghat. He fled with his *Sardars* to the jungle of Tarai. His forts of Najibgarh, Najibabad, Goshgarh, and Phattargarh were taken, together with all his territories; and the Marathas also recovered from Phattargarh almost all the property that they had lost at the battle of Panipat. The Marathas then returned to Delhi, leaving a part of their army in the Doab.

While the Marathas were in Delhi a conspiracy was formed against them, headed by Shuja-ud-Dowla, assisted by the British, and initiated with the assent of the Emperor. Mahadji Sindhia had obtained from the Emperor for Narayan Rao, the Peshwa's brother, the office of Commander-in-Chief, which until then was held by Zabita Khan Rohilla, and this had given the Marathas predominance at the Moghul Court and influence over the Emperor. Shuja-ud-Dowla and others became alarmed, and they formed the conspiracy. Tukoji Holkar and Visaji Biniwale felt inclined to restore to Zabita Khan his office and *Jagir*, but Mahadji Sindhia disagreed and departed in resentment to Rajputana. The Emperor, however, was not reconciled to the Marathas, influenced as he was by Najib Khan, the Commander, and he mustered his troops, including those furnished by the British, to fight with the Marathas. Hostilities ensued, and the Marathas, led by Tukoji and Visaji Biniwale, defeated the Imperial troops. The Emperor had to retire, and was compelled to accept the arrangements which he had made before with the Marathas.

The Rohillas had yet made no peace with the Marathas, who consequently marched against them, giving it as their reason that the sum of 50 lakhs, promised to them by the Rohillas long before, yet remained unpaid. The Rohillas, led by Ahmed Khan, offered battle, but were defeated at Asadpur, and Ahmed Khan was taken prisoner by Tukoji Khan, who overran the whole of the District of Muradabad. Shuja-ud-Dowla and the British now sided with the Rohillas, remembering that Madhoji Sindhia was away and the Peshwa Madhav Rao had just died. Visaji Biniwale and Tukoji Rao Holkar realized that the odds were heavily against them, and with great strategy they retired to Delhi in face of the forces of their enemy. From Delhi the Marathas marched to Bharatpur, where they had to fight with the Bharatpur troops some miles from Bharatpur City. Nawal Sing, Raja of Bharatpur, was defeated, and the Marathas having settled terms with him, in 1773, proceeded to the South, Tukoji Rao going to Indore and Visaji Biniwale to Poona.

The death of Madho Rao Peshwa, and the murder of his younger brother, Narayan Rao, in 1773, at the instigation of Raghoba Dada, his uncle, was engaging the attention of all the Maratha Chiefs, and a combination of them was formed against the murderer, who had usurped the Peshwaship. On the birth of Madho Rao, the posthumus son of Narayan Rao, Raghoba was deprived of the Peshwaship by the Council of Regency, and Raghoba proceeded towards Malwa with the object of securing the help of Shuja-ud-Dowla and the British, as against the Poona Government. He entered the territories of Sindhia and Holkar, and was permitted by them to remain there. The Poona Government sent Hari Pant Phadke, the Commander-in-Chief, to pursue Raghoba. Sindhia and Holkar took no decided steps to espouse the cause of Raghoba. Negotiations were then set on foot to hand over Raghoba to the Poona Government on certain terms, but Raghoba kept on intriguing, now going to Dhar and now to Bhopal. At last he was forced by Sindhia and Holkar to proceed towards Poona. While on his way he managed to escape, though watched by the combined forces of Sindhia and Tukoji Rao Holkar; Raghoba secured the help of Govind Rao Gaekwar and other Maratha Chiefs. The combined forces of Haripant, Sindhia, and Holkar overtook him near Baroda, and a battle was fought near the Mahi river in 1775, where Raghoba was completely defeated, and had to retire. His troops retired in two different directions and were pursued by the victors. Raghoba asked the Nawab of Cambay to help him, but this was refused. He then approached the Agent of the British at Cambay with the same object, and acting on his advice he proceeded to Bhavnagar, where the British ships were available for him, and he was taken to the British Factory at Surat. The refuge thus given by the British to Raghoba, combined with their atack on Salsette (Sashti), and their occupation of it, led eventually to the first Maratha war.

This action of the Bombay authorities was disavowed by the Governor-General (Mr. Warren Hastings), who made it clear that under the Constitution the former had no power to declare hostilities without his consent. He wrote to the Governor

THE STATE OF INDORE.

1. Shiva Vilas Palace, built in 1891 by H.H. Maharaja Shivaji Rao. 2. Lalbagh Palace, Indore, rebuilt in 1917–21 by H.H. Maharaja Tukoji Rao III. 3. Yeshwant Nivas Palace, Indore, built in 1907.

accordingly, and also to the Poona Government, to whom he also sent a *Vakil* (Col. Upton) to restore the amicable relations. Hostilities were thereupon suspended, and the Treaty of Purandhar was made in 1776, whereby the English bound themselves, *inter alia*, to give up the cause of Raghoba.

There had been some misunderstandings between the Poona Government on the one hand, and Sindhia and Holkar on the other. These were amicably settled, and both the latter pledged their fidelity, which was given practical effect to immediately, in connection with putting down the disturbances raised in 1776 by an imposter, who, styling himself Sadashiva Rao Bhao, of Panipat fame, and cousin to Balaji Rao Peshwa, was able to rally to his support some of the Maratha Chiefs and soldiers. The two Chiefs also helped in restoring order in the southern Maratha Country. In the year following Tukoji Rao Holkar marched against one Narso Govind, who had usurped the Thana of Karkamb of the Patwardhan family, and succeeded in recovering the Thana and arresting him.

The Bombay authorities had not yet given up the cause of Raghoba, in terms of the Treaty of Purandhar, though warned constantly by the Governor-General and also by the Poona Government. They even brought Raghoba from Surat to Bombay, and their Agent at Poona (Mostyn) put forward the plea that the Poona Government had made no provision for Raghoba's maintenance. This plea was of course inadmissible under the Treaty, and the Poona Government felt the necessity of taking precautions against possible hostilities. About this time one Moroba, cousin of Nana Farnavis, put forward his own claim to be one of the Ministers, and this led to the formation of two parties. Some of the Chiefs and officials siding with Nana, and some with Moroba. Moroba commenced his intrigues with the British to restore Raghoba to the Peshwaship, but nothing came out of it. Raghoba continued to receive protection from the Bombay authorities, and the Poona Government finding their protests ineffectual received a *Vakil* from the French Government. The Bombay authorities took alarm and wrote to the Governor-General, who now consented to restore Raghoba to the Peshwaship, and to send some troops from Bengal to carry out the project. This was in the autumn of 1778. Before, however, these troops arrived from Bengal, the Bombay authorities had proceeded on their march to Poona in November 1778, accompanied by Raghoba and his adherents. When the British troops ascended Borghat, they had a desultory fighting with the Marathas, in the course of which Captain Stewart and Captain Kaye were killed. As the British approached Talegaon they found a large Maratha army awaiting them, commanded by Sindhia, Tukoji Holkar, and others. The British retired, and by January, 1779, they reached Wargaon, where there was a big battle between them and the Marathas. The tremendous attack made on the British army on this occasion by Bapu Holkar, nephew to Tukoji Holkar, was most effective. The British were defeated with a great loss, and Mr. Holmes, on their behalf, had to sue for peace, which was granted. This is called the Convention of Wargaon, under which the British bound themselves to surrender Raghoba to the Poona Government, to restore to the Peshwa all the territories, Salsette, etc., that they had taken, and to confirm the provisions of the Treaty made by them in the time of Madhav Roa I. The British gave hostages (Mr. Holmes and Mr. Farmer) for the fulfilment of these terms, and were allowed to retire with their troops to Bombay under the protection of the troops of Sindhia and Holkar. As a reward for the conspicuous service done by Holkar in the battle, the Poona Government accorded to him an extremely cordial reception, and gave to him in *Jagir* the districts of Kunch in Bundelkhand and Rawar in Khandesh.

The Poona Government, after having secured Raghoba, decided to keep him at Jhansi, under the control of Sindhia. While he was being escorted to that place by the troops of the Peshwa, Sindhia and Holkar, he made an attack with his troops on the escort near Onkar Mandhata, and managed to get away to Surat, where he placed himself again under British protection. Col. Goddard had by this time arrived with fresh troops from Bengal; and the British set at naught the provisions of the Convention of Wargaon. Fighting ensued, and the British secured some places in Gujerat and Konkan. They then marched towards Poona, and had fighting on their way until they reached Borghat. Here they met a large number of Maratha troops, commanded by Haripant Phadke, who was joined soon after by Patwardhan and Tukoji Holkar. There was a desultory fighting in which there were losses on both sides, and Col. Goddard soon found out that he was hemmed in by the Maratha troops and his provisions cut off. He had, therefore, to retreat in April, 1781, and had to fight his way back to Bombay via Panwel, suffering a great deal of loss. The British again sued for peace, and this resulted, in May, 1782, in the Treaty of Salbai, under which the British finally abandoned the cause of Raghoba, and restored to the Poona Government almost all the territories that they had taken from them.

In 1783 Raghoba retired to Kopargaon on pension, under assurances of safety from Tukoji Rao Holkar and others, but he died soon after. This event relieved the Poona Government from a heavy load of anxiety, as the intrigues of Raghoba had compelled that Government to purchase the good will of the States of Hyderabad and Mysore by grants of territories and making other concessions. The Poona Government now sent letters both to the Nizam and Tippoo Sultan to demand the arrears of *Chouth* and tribute respectively. In 1785 there was a meeting at Yadgiri between the Nizam and the Poona Government, as represented by Nana Farnavis, Tukoji Holkar and Haripant, when the points of differences were talked over, and a secret arrangement was also made to invade the territory of Tippoo, against whom both the States had grievances on account of his aggressive actions. Tippoo having received information of this, sent a *Vakil* to Poona to settle differences; but simultaneously he despatched 10,000 troops to the States of Nargund and Kitore, which were subordinate to the Peshwa, though under an arrangement of 1780 the tributary rights over them had been assigned, along with certain tracts, to Hyder Ali, on condition of his rendering military assistance against the British and paying a tribute of Rs. 6,00,000 a year. Tippoo forcibly seized these two States, which he annexed to his dominions, and he also wrested parts of Belgaum. In December, 1785, Nana Farnavis planned his operations against Tippoo, and Tukoij Holkar, in company with other Chiefs, took an active part in them with his 25,000 troops. The Marathas marched in two separate divisions. The one headed by Ganesh Pant Behare and Bapu Holkar took most of the *thanas* on the Kitur side from the enemy, but Kitur itself could not be taken. The State of Savnur was warned the Marathas against paying any tribute to Tippoo; and when the latter sent an army to compel payment, Tukoji Holkar and Ganesh Behare re-

THE STATE OF INDORE.

1. Indore Old Palace, rebuilt in 1818 by H.H. Maharaja Malhar Rao II. 2. The Manik Bagh Palace, Indore. 3. Interior of Gopal Mandir, Indore.

THE STATE OF INDORE.

1. State Officers' Club, Indore, built in 1903 by the State.   2. The Residency Bungalow Indore, built about 1820.

THE STATE OF INDORE.

1. Durbar Office, Indore, built in 1894 by H.H. Maharaja Shivaji Rao. 2. Tukoji Rao Hospital, Indore, built in 1901-2 by H.H. Maharaja Shivaji Rao.

paired to the place with their army by making the astonishing march of forty coss in 24 hours. A division of the Maratha army then took the New Hubli, but before they could take the Old Hubli Tippoo sent his troops to defend it. Here there was some fighting between the parties. The scene of operations was then shifted to Savnur, where Tippoo was leading his army in person in opposition to Hari Pant. The scattered troops on both sides marched to this place. Hostilities went on for some time, in the course of which the Marathas achieved a great success, and took Badami Fort from Tippoo. At the end of 1786 Tippoo, despairing of success, opened negotiations for peace through Tukoji Holkar. This peace was finally settled in April, 1787, and Tippoo had to restore to the Poona Government all the territories and rights which he and his father had taken from them, as also to pay to them the arrears of tribute (Rs. 65,00,000). On this occasion, too, Tukoji was given a special reception, the Peshwa going out of the town to meet him.

From 1787-90 there was peace in Maharashtra. But in Northern India the Maratha ascendency, which was being exercised through Mahadji Sindhia, received a severe blow by his defeat at Lalsut, in 1787, at the hands of the combined armies of Gulam Quadir, Jodhpur and Jeypore; Agra and Ajmer were seized by the Rajputs, and Bundi was also in revolt against the Marathas. In these circumstances Sindhia wrote to the Poona Government and also to Devi Ahilya Bai for military help. Ahilya Bai offered to help, if Sindhia would give her the share in the territories in Northern India as settled in Malhar Rao's time. The Poona Government directed Ali Bahadur and Tukoji Rao, in 1788, to march with troops to the help of Sindhia. About this time the troops of Mewar inflicted a defeat on Holkar's troops in that quarter, and Ahilya Bai sent fresh troops to avenge the wrong. These troops inflicted a defeat near Rutlam. Kashi Rao Holkar was sent ahead to join Sindhia, while Tukoji Holkar went to Nathdwar, in Mewar, to settle matters. Here Ali Bahadur joined him, and both then proceeded to Muttra, in November, 1789, to join Sindhia. By means of these measures the Maratha power in Northern India was re-established; and Sindhia offered to give to Holkar his share of territory, worth Rs. 9,21,000 a year, whereof a territory (Gadmukteshwar and Hapat), worth Rs. 2,00,000, was offered immediately, subject to the reservation that the *Savar* rights in them and *Inams* should remain with Sindhia. Tukoji objected to the reservation and declined the offer. This circumstance is of importance, for it accounts for the serious differences which continued in later years between Sindhia and Holkar. Another potent cause of misunderstanding between the parties was that Sindhia wanted the surrender of one Gunsai Himat Bahadur, against whom he had a grudge; but Himat Bahadur took the refuge of Jaripatka, the Peshwa's flag, with Ali Bahadur, which impelled both Ali Bahadur and Tukoji to give him protection.

In 1790 Sindhia was on his way to Poona via the Thana of Satwas, which was Holkar's territory, and he seized it by force.

Tukoji Holkar remained behind in Hindusthan. In 1790 the reasserted his rights to the villages which had been assigned by Bharatpur for the upkeep of the *Chhatri* of Khande Rao Holkar. The differences which arose between him and Sindhia led to hostility between respective troops, and the troops of the former suffered reverses at Laheri, Patan, and Banas between 1791 and 1793. Tukoji returned to Indore about 1794.

Mahadji Sindhia was in Poona from 1792 onwards. He endeavoured while there to secure the recall of Tukoji Holkar and Ali Bahadur, as also to obtain for himself undivided control over the affairs in Hindusthan. He died in February, 1794, leaving his vast possessions to his adopted son Dowlat Rao, then 14-15 years old, to whom the Peshwa confirmed the possessions.

Differences with the Nizam and the Peshwa had in the meantime been taking a serious turn. The Peshwa summoned all the Maratha Chiefs, including Tukoji Holka, with their troops. Holkar reached Poona by the end of 1794, just when the Peshwa was about to start on his expedition against the Nizam. The opposing armies of the Peshwa and the Nizam met at Kharda on March 11, 1795, the Nizam leading his forces in person, and the Peshwa Sawai Madhao Rao leading the various Maratha forces, combined together for the last time, and commanded by their various Chiefs Sindhia, Bhonsla, Tukoji Holkar, Patwardhan, Phadke. The Nizam was signally defeated after a severe action, and had to make peace after considerable cessions of territory and payment of money.

In the following August Devi Ahilya Bai died at Maheshwar, and two months later the Peshwa died at Poona by an accidental fall from an upper storey. The question of succession again opened in the House of Peshwa. The *Sardars*, at first, were for setting aside Bajee Rao in favour of a boy to be adopted by the late Peshwa's widow; but in the end, all, except Patwardhan, espoused the cause of Baji Rao, who consequently received the insignia of Peshwa from the Raja of Satara in December, 1796.

All this time Tukoji Holkar remained in Poona watching the developments, but keeping increasingly bad health. His illness took a serious turn on August 15, 1797, and he breathed his last, leaving behind him two legitimate sons, Kashi Rao and Malhar Rao, and two illegitimate sons, Yeshwant Rao and Vithoji. The succession of Kashi Rao had been confirmed by the Peshwa on Tukoji's request on January 29, 1797, and the latter had also on the eve of his death patched up the differences between Kashi Rao and Malhar Rao. But all this was of no avail. Kashi Rao was of a very weak intellect, with no administrative or military qualities, while Malhar Rao had many of the qualities desired in a military leader. Differences with Sindhia had not yet been settled, and many of the adherents of the House of Holkar—such as Yeshwant Rao, Vithoji, and Hariba—wanted Malhar Rao to be at the head. Kashi Rao's cause was espoused by Sindhia in consideration of a big reward (relinquishment of a debt of 60 lakhs due by Sindhia from Ahilya's Bai's time, and 16 lakhs in cash), and Malhar Rao had at first the support of the Peshwa and Nana Farnavis (the Peshwa's Chief Minister). But Sindhia was at this time all powerful. In the early morning of September 14, 1797, Sindhia sent his troops ostensibly to arrest Malhar Rao, who had a hostile design against Kashi Rao and had seized some of the Holkar territories. In the altercation which ensued Malhar Rao was killed, with some of his adherents. Yeshwant Rao, Hariba, and Vithoji managed to escape, while the widows of Malhar Rao and Bhima Bai, the infant daughter of Yeshwant Rao, were taken into custody by Sindhia's men, together with all the property of Malhar Rao. Yeswant Rao and Hariba repaired to Nagpur, where they were made prisoners by the Bhonsla, at the instance of Sindhia, while Vithoji made depredations in the Peshwa's territory, and was on that account arrested

THE STATE OF INDORE.

1. Edward Hall Indore, built in 1905 by the State. 2. The Daly College, Indore, built in 1911.

THE STATE OF INDORE.

1. High Court, Indore, built in 1905 by the State. 2. Shivaji Rao High School, Indore, built in 1918 by H.H. Maharaja Tukoji Rao III. 3. Holkar College, Indore, built in 1904 by H.H. Maharaja Shivaji Rao.

by Sindhia's men, and was eventually punished with death by the Peshwa. Whatever the real inclinations of the Peshwa were, he was at this time a mere tool in Sindhia's hands. Even Nana Farnavis was imprisoned by Sindhia in December, 1797, and the troops of Sindhia also captured and plundered the camp of Amrit Rao, the Peshwa's brother.

Yeshwant Rao remained for months in confinement at Nagpur, and then managed to escape towards Khandesh and Malwa. In the course of these wanderings he arrived in Dhar, where its ruler, Raja Anand Rao, was threatened with ruin by an attack from his usurping Dewan, Rung Rao Odekar, assisted by Pindhari troops. In the action which was fought Yeswant Rao displayed remarkable courage, and actually turned the anticipated defeat into a victory for the Raja. He had, however, soon to leave Dhar, as Sindhia had threatened the Raja with his extreme displeasure if Yeswant Rao were not seized or expelled. Yeswant Rao proceeded to Depalpur, which he managed to take from Kashee Rao's troops. These successes raised Yeshwant Rao's reputation as a military leader. Feeling convinced of the extremely hostile attitude of Sindhia against him, and realizing that Sindhia was virtually absorbing the Holkar's territories by keeping Kashi Rao in his hands as a mere puppet, he started ravaging the Sindhia's territories and recovering those of Holkar in the name of Khande Rao, the infant son of Malhar Rao. His arts of conciliation and winning manners, coupled with his judgment, activity and vigour, soon gained for him a large following, and he received the allegiance of Ameer Khan and many Pindarri leaders. Having no money, he had, in order to maintain these troops, to plunder the territories of Sindhia. At Kasrawad he gained a decisive victory over Kashi Rao's troops, led by Dudernae, and he achieved another success over Kashi Rao's troops at Satwas. Dudernae joined Yeshwant Rao. Ameer Khan proceeded to Saugor, defeated the Raja of that place, and obtained other victories. During 1800—1 Yeshwant Rao had several engagements with Sindhia's troops in the vicinity of Narbuda and Ujjain; and he was often successful. In July 1801 he obtained a signal victory over the combined armies of Sindhia at Ujjain, which were led by European officers, and who had a large train of artillery. Yeshwant Rao seized the guns and what else he could, but he scrupulously saved the city of Ujjain from devastation.

Sindhia retaliated at once. He sent a considerable army against Indore, where a big action was fought, in the course of which Yashwant Rao was defeated, the palace of Indore demolished and the town of Indore looted by Sindhia's men. It took some time for Yeshwant Rao to rally, and he again began devastating Sindhia's territories. Sindhia gave up the cause of Kashi Rao. He let him go to Maheshwar, and offered to release the infant son of Malhar Rao, together with the possessions of Holkar, if Yeshwant Rao refrained from further devastations. The latter insisted, however, upon receiving his share of territories in Hindusthan, as arranged in Malhar Rao's I's time, which share had remained unsettled in Mahadji Sindhia's time. Sindhia was not agreeable to this request, and Yeshwant Rao resumed his course more vigorously than before.

By this time Yeshwant Rao had come to entertain a strong ill-will against the Peshwa, by whose order Vithoji Holkar his brother had met with death, as stated above, and who had also sent his troops to seize the *jagirs* of Holkar in Khandesh. Yeshwant Rao tried, nevertheless, to accommodate his difference with the Peshwa, but his attempts proving unavailing he opposed the Peshwa's troops early in 1802, and inflicted defeats on them. In the succeeding months he marched into Sindhia's and the Peshwa's territories, levying contributions and engaging in actions whenever necessary. All this time he kept on corresponding with the Peshwa, to whom he put forward the following propositions, which, if agreed to, would put an end to hostility.

(1) Release by Sindhia of the son of Malhar Rao; (2) Recognition of this son (Khande Rao) as head of the Holkar family, in place of Kashi Rao; (3) Restoration by Sindhia of the possessions of Holkar; and (4) Allotment by Sindhia to Holkar of the share of territories in Hindusthan as settled in Mahadji Sindhia's time.

But the Peshwa was powerless to cause Sindhia to accept these propositions. Hostilities consequently went on. Yeshwant Rao marched southward, fighting with Sindhia and Peshwa's troops on the way. In October, 1802, there was a severe action between the combined troops of Peshwa and Sindhia, on the one hand, and those of Holkar on the other, and Yeshwant Rao obtained a decisive victory. The Peshwa left the capital and sought the protection of the British, while Yeshwant Rao became the dictator of Poona. Attempts were made by Yeshwant Rao to induce the Peshwa to return, but the Peshwa showed want of confidence. Yeshwant Rao then thought of placing Amrit Rao at the head of the Government, but the latter showed hesitation. The Peshwa was in the meantime negotiating with the British, and he concluded with them the Treaty of Bassein in December, 1802. This Treaty enabled the Peshwa to secure the military help from the British and the Nizam to leave Poona, and Baji Rao re-entered it with the help of the British army.

The Treaty of Bassein estranged Sindhia, the Bhonsla and the Holkar from the Peshwa, as they saw in it the destruction of the Maratha empire. Sindhia and Bhonsla entered into a league to fight with the British; and they invited Yeshwant Rao to join them on the promise that his demands, described above, would be satisfied. The Bhonsla stood as guarantee to this engagement on the part of Sindhia, and the possessions of Holkar were restored, along with Bhimabai (daughter of Yeshwant Rao) and Khanderao, son of Mulhar Rao, though the share in the territories of Hindusthan was not actually given. Hostilities broke out between Sindhia and Bhonsla on the one hand, and the British on the other. Yeshwant Rao stood aloof, as he had no funds, and Sindhia and Bhonsla did not give him assistance, though he was asking for it. The armies of Sindhia and Bhonsla were defeated at Assaye and Argaum in the south and at Aligarh and Laswari in the north. Sindhia and Bhonsla had to sue for peace, and this was granted on their making large cessions of territories and rights to the British.

These events tended to raise the position of Yeshwant Rao Holkar far higher than that of Sindhia and Bhonsla, and the British Government naturally looked upon him as a rival in the contest for supremacy in India. He had also by this time secured from the Delhi Emperor the title of Mahrajadhiraj Raj Rajeshwar Alija Bahadur, which gave him a high status amongst the princes of India. The British Government did not at first wish to molest him, but during the war with Sindhia, and later on, they had entered into alliance with Rajput Princes, some of whom were subordinate to Holkar. Early in 1804 Yeshwant Rao entered the territories of these subordinate princes for the exercise of his rights. The British officers warned him against doing so, on the ground that they had become allies of the British Government, and they also reminded him that it was Kashi Rao who was at the head of Holkar Government. They considered him as a robber and plunderer. Some negotiations nevertheless went on between the parties, in the course of which Yeshwant Rao made it clear that what he wanted was :—

(1) That the right of Holkar to collect the tribute, as of old, should be recognized ; (2) that the ancestral claims of the Holkar family in the Doab, and the right to one *pargana* in Bundelkhand, should be recognized ; (3) that the country of Hurreanea, which formerly belonged to Holkar, should be surrendered ; and (4) that the country now in Holkar's possession should be guaranteed.

But these negotiations proved ineffectual, and Yashwant Rao was desired to return to his country. About this time Yeshwant Rao was carrying on correspondence with the Sikh and Bundela Chiefs to form a league against the British. He also corresponded with Sindhia, Bharatpur and the King of Kabul, with a similar object. By May, 1804, the British decided to commence hostilities against Holkar, who had by then entered the Jaipur territories ; and they decided also, in the event of Yeshwant Rao's submission, to give him a *jagir* under British guarantee, to make a suitable provision for Kashi Rao from Holkar's territories, and assign the rest of these territories to Sindhia. Naturally, therefore, Sindhia joined the British in the war against Holkar.

This war went on until the end of 1805. There were several engagements between the parties. The British forces under Lucan were defeated. Colonel Monson and Baou Sindhia, who had with them numerous forces, including those from Jaipur and Kotah, were defeated near Mukundra, and they had to beat a disastrous retreat with considerable loss. The Fort of Hinglasgarh was retaken by Holkar. Monson was chased by Yeshwant Rao's troops and there were skirmishes on the way, in which Yeshwant Rao inflicted great losses on the British and was able to seize their baggage. There was an indecisive action near the Banas river, and another near Fatepur Sikri. The successes of Yeshwant Rao, and especially the retreat of Monson, raised the military reputations of the former very high in the estimation of the princes of India. Yeshwant Rao marched in the direction of Muttra, and there was an action in which his troops engaged British forces between Faroh and Muttra, but the result was not decisive. Yeshwant Rao then marched to Brindaban, and Lord Lake arrived at Muttra. There was again skirmishing between the troops on both sides, which lasted for several days, and Lord Lake could only retire to Delhi with great difficulty, so harassed was he by Holkar's troops. A division of Holkar's army attacked the Delhi Fort, but this was repulsed by the British. Yeshwant Rao marched to Shamli and Farukkabad, where he had fighting. He then proceeded to Dig. While there he resumed negotiations with the Bharatpur Raja, and succeeded in enlisting his active support. The British army marched on Dig. Here there was severe fighting for seven days, and the fort was at last taken by the British, in which, however, they suffered a severe loss. The British army then marched to Bharatpur, where Holkar had retired. The British attacked the Fort of Bharatpur no less than seven times, but all these attacks proved ineffective. Ameer Khan was sent to devastate British territories and he looted Gokul Murabad and other places.

In March, 1805, Sindhia tried to bring about reconciliation between the British and Holkar, but these attempts were unsuccessful. By May, Sindhia and Holkar were reconciled to each other, and they actually met at Sabalgarh with their armies. Yeshwant Rao sent letters to the Peshwa, Maharaja Ranjitsingh of Lahore, the Bhonsla and others, to combine against the British. Jaipur and Bhonsla offered to join him, and so also Maharaja Ranjitsingh. In June the British Resident at Sindhia's Court had some misunderstanding with him, and wanted to withdraw, but he was detained by Sindhia. About this time Lord Wellesley offered to Sindhia tempting terms to bring him over to the side of the British, the terms being the cession of the Forts of Gwalior and Gohad, ten lakhs of rupees in cash, and a part of the Holkar territories. Sindhia was not at first disposed to accept this offer, but later on he fell out with Yeshwant Rao, in August, 1805, as the latter was pestering him with demands for money. Sindhia sided with the British and eventually got the reward, as mentioned in the Treaty with him dated November, 1805. Bharatpur had already, like Sindhia, been induced in April, 1805, to join the British.

Yeshwant Rao marched through the Jaipur territory in September, 1805, and by October he arrived in Patiala via Narnaul and Jhind. He had had offers of help from some of the Sikh Chiefs, but when he actually arrived in that country they went back on their promises, having been won over by the British officers to their side. Realizing that the British forces were pursuing him from different sides, Yeshwant Rao, much to the mortification of the British, performed the remarkable feat of crossing the Sutlej at Ludhana Ghat with all his troops and guns, in face of these forces, and thus he got into a place where he could make a stand and obtain support from Maharaja Ranjitsingh and the other Sikh Chiefs. Both parties had by this time become exhausted and their financial position had especially become embarrassing. The way was paved for the opening of peace negotiations to put an end to the fruitless war. By the end of December, 1805, a treaty of peace was concluded between the parties, and two months later some modifications were made in it in order to conciliate Yeshwant Rao.

The wars of 1802 and 1805 made Holkar a completely independent power. He secured all the possessions and rights of the Holkar State as in Tukoji's time, including the rights over Jaipur, Udaipur, Kotah, Bundi and other Rajput Princes, and he thereby acquired a position superior to that of Sindhia, not to speak of other Indian States.

Yeshwant Rao returned from the Punjab by slow marches. He continued writing to the British regarding his claims in the Doab, which had remained unsatisfied, and about which he felt very keenly. But he was unsuccessful in these endeavours, though he managed to secure Alampur and some small possessions to himself, and a few more possessions for his dependents. On returning to the Rajputana country he levied his tributes from Jaipur and Udaipur and he helped Jodhpur, to which he was indebted for giving a refuge to his family during the war. He had numerous troubles with his troops, which frequently mutinied for want of pay. On one occasion (September, 1806) he was compelled to hand over to the mutinous forces his small nephew, Khande Rao, as a pledge for the payment of arrears, and the troops at once proclaimed the child as a real head of the House of Holkar. Yeshwant Rao paid off the troops, and secured the child ; but the child unfortunately, shortly afterwards, died in Shahapura of cholera while Yeshwant Rao was yet on his way to his head-

THE STATE OF INDORE.

1. Maharaja Hari's Chhatri, Indore, built in 1863. 2. The Chhatri Bagh, Indore. 3. The Sidhanath Temple at Nemawar, on Narbada River.

quarters at Bhanpura. The child was not killed as some writers allege.

The war had brought home to Yeshwant Rao the necessity of having a disciplined army, with a large train of artillery; and he applied himself at Bhanpura with remarkable vigour to carry out these objects. He gave himself no rest, often working himself at the manufacture of cannon, and freely indulging in strong drinks to brace his spirits. Either this overwork at the furnace, or the influence of drink, or some other predisposing cause, developed symptoms of insanity in him in 1808, and the malady went on increasing and it hastened his death. Early in 1808 he had given orders for the removal of his brother, Kashi Rao, from Maheshwar, where he had been detained in the fort for hostility towards him. Kashi Rao was rescued by Bharmal Dada, but was ultimately taken to the Fort of Sendhwa for detention. While there his partisans made an attack on the guard to rescue him, and they even dispersed the guard. But in the scuffle which ensued Kashi Rao was killed. Some writers have falsely represented that he was killed by order of Yeshwant Rao. The malady of Yeshwant Rao dislocated to some extent the machinery of Government. He remained, however, throughout his life true to his Treaty with the British Government. So great was his personality that, even in those troublous times, no State or Power could venture to commit aggressions on his territory; and this influence kept the Holkar territory secure even for some years after his death. Yeshwant Rao died at Bhanpura in 1811, where a beautiful *Chhatri* stands to preserve his memory.

His wife, Tulsi Bai, who had administered the State during his incapacity, now became Regent on behalf of Malhar Rao II, the only son, four years old, of the late Ruler, by Krishna Bai *alias* Masaheba. His succession was universally recognized, and in reply to a reference made to the British Government by the State, it was explained that having regard to the position of Indore, the succession required no recognition from the Peshwa or from any other Power. During the minority of the young Prince the Regent experienced the greatest difficulty in managing the State, owing to the refractory conduct of her military Chiefs—Nawab Amir Khan, and others—who made raids upon neighbouring States and plundered money and valuables, ostensibly for the payment of troops. Confusion existed in parts of the State, and disaffection became so acute that the Regent was compelled in 1815 to seek shelter in the stronghold of Gangrad. From that time forward the whole of her actions were controlled by Ganpat Rao, her Dewan. Rebellious military leaders continued to prevent good government, and she had, in 1817, to take refuge in the Fort of Alote. It was at this juncture that the Peshwa had turned his arms against the British, and a part of the Holkar army, led by rebellious military leaders, felt disposed to join him in the expectation of booty, but especially of rewards from the Peshwa. Tulsi Bai was murdered by this section of the army as she was for remaining in peace with the British, and was, in fact, secretly negotiating with them to enter into closer relationship. Her Ministers, who had fully shared her views, were kept in confinement by this military party, and the Maharaja, then 10 years old, was seized, in order that power might be exercised in his name. By this time the British troops, which had come to Central India with the avowed object of suppressing the Pindarries, crossed into the Holkar territory, thinking the State to be hostile. The rebellious section of the Holkar army felt convinced that the British had hostile designs, and it prepared at once for battle. When, however, the battle was actually fought on December 21, 1817, it was only the Holkar artillery that took part, and it inflicted very great losses on the British troops, but the Holkar cavalry stood quite aloof, and thus it helped the British to obtain an easy victory. The British dictated very harsh terms of peace to the Holkar Government. Tantia Jog, the Minister, pleaded that the battle was brought about by the rebellious portion of the Holkar army, quite against the wishes of the Holkar Government; but this pleading had no effect, and he had to subscribe to the terms offered. By the Treaty of Mandsore, which was signed on January 6, 1818, the Holkar State was deprived of almost two-thirds of its territories and rights: Nawab Amir Khan of Tonk was made independent in respect of his Jaidad, rights over the principal Rajput Princes were taken away, but not those over the minor Princes of Pertabghur, Narsingarh, and Jhabua, and large slices of territory were taken over by the British themselves, or secured by them for their allies who had helped them in these operations. In return for the cessions thus made, the British Government undertook "to support a field force to maintain the internal tranquillity of the territories left to Malhar Rao Holkar and to defend them from foreign enemies." The Treaty bound the Holkar State to certain terms in respect of the employment of Europeans and Americans, and in respect of the conduct of relations with other States. In other respects, the status of the State remained as before, and its internal autonomy was specifically assured. On the conclusion of peace the Minister threw himself whole-heartedly into the reform of State affairs. He disbanded the superfluous troops, effected a regular settlement of land revenue, and inaugurated a new era of commercial advance. So successful was he in his administration of affairs, that the amount derived from land, which had for some time previously, owing to the predatory excursions and consequent devastation, not exceeded the annual sum of Rs. 5,00,000 a year, soon increased to the high figure of Rs. 27,00,000. The death of this able and accomplished Minister in April, 1826, was a sad blow to the State, as it was entirely through his efforts that Indore had resumed so soon a state of peace and prosperity. Malhar Rao took little or no interest in State affairs. He was always in poor health, and he died on October 27, 1833, in Indore City, which he had made his capital in 1818.

Malhar Rao died without leaving any issue; but shortly before his death his wife, Gautama Bai, and his mother, Krishna Bai, *alias* Masaheba, had adopted as his heir Martand Rao Holkar, a relative. Martand Rao was duly installed on the *gadi*, with all the customary ceremonies, on January 17, 1834: and this was recognized by the British Government "as the spontaneous unopposed act of the Holkar Government in which the people of the State seemingly acquiesced." In the following month Hari Rao, the nephew of Maharaja Yeshwant Rao, and hence a better claimant, was liberated by his partisans from the hill fort of Maheshwar, to which place he had been consigned by Malhar Rao. He was taken by his followers to the Political Officer at Mandleshwar, where he was openly proclaimed to be the rightful heir of Indore.

The inhabitants of the State, including the soldiers, forsook Martand Rao, and flocked to the side of Hari Rao. The Masaheba requested the Resident to uphold the existing order of things, but was prevailed upon by him to agree to the succession of Hari Rao, as the Govern-

THE STATE OF INDORE.

1. The Indreshwar Temple, Indore, built in the Seventh Century. 2. The Pandharinath Temple, Indore, built by H.H. Maharaja Malhar Rao II. 3. Maharaja Yeshwant Rao's Chhatri at Bhanpura, built in 1811.

ment of India had declared that "in the event of Hari Rao Holkar succeeding in establishing his own ascendency, it will be proper to consider him as the sovereign of the Holkar State." Thus supported on all sides, Hari Rao was enabled to occupy the *masnad* of the Holkar Raj on April 17, 1834, in the presence of the Resident. Hari Rao appointed Rewaji Phanse as Dewan of the State. Rewaji was a person of bad character and had no experience of administration. His appointment was a source of much discontent and consequent trouble. The revenue of the State fell to nine lakhs a year, while the expenditure amounted to twenty-four lakhs. Nearly twelve lakhs were spent on the State army. The chaotic condition turned the public opinion in favour of Martand Rao. Martand Rao's followers were joined by a strong body of three hundred Makranees and some of the commanders of the State forces. The combined forces surrounded the palace on the morning of September 8, 1835, and tried to persuade Krishna Bai to support them, but the sagacious old lady did not approve of the action. They were thus foiled, and the followers of Martand Rao were repulsed. Rewaji's ill-fated ministry soon terminated, as the financial crisis was too perplexing to admit of his continuing in the office any longer. In the month of November, 1836, Rewaji vacated the Dewanship, and the State affairs became worse. Hari Rao's favourite, BhawaniDin, who succeeded as Minister, proved as troublesome as the late Dewan, Rewaji Phanse. Bhawanidin was accordingly dismissed, and Hari Rao girded up his loins to direct the administration himself in 1841. Hari Rao's health was not so strong as to admit of his guiding the administration single-handed, and consequently he called Rajabhow Phanse to his aid. Rajabhow Phanse, who was addicted to strong drink, was not likely to be of much help to Hari Rao, who then called Narayan Rao Palsikar to assume the Dewanship. Death, however, overtook this Dewan in October, 1841, and his son, Ram Rao, was too young to manage the administration. The failing health of Maharaja Hari Rao greatly influenced the course of administration. Raja Bhao Phanse was again entrusted with the duty of the Dewanship. While the State was witnessing a severe financial breakdown, attended by other concomitant evils, Maharaja Hari Rao became unconscious on October 16, 1843, and his death occurred on October 24, 1843.

During Maharaja Hari Rao's illness he had been advised by the Resident to select an heir, as he had no issue. He had adopted Khande Rao, son of Bapu Holkar, on July 2, 1841. Khande Rao was seated on the throne on November 13, 1843. Raja Bhao Phanse was placed at the head of the administration. He succeeded in bringing the young Maharaja completely under his guidance and influence, and thus secured absolute power in the State, which, however, he did not improve in any way. Khande Rao was of a weak constitution, and died suddenly on February 17, 1844, at the age of 15, without, of course, leaving any issue.

Khande Rao's death again opened the question of succession. The Masaheba was in favour of Martand Rao, and so also were the people. But the policy of the Government of India had changed from what it was in 1834. They now interfered in the internal matter of succession, ignored the claims of Martand Rao, and only permitted the Masaheba to select a younger son of Bhau Holkar, then nine years old, "as the sole act of the British Government." When, however, the Resident in open Durbar declared the resolution of the British Government to perpetuate the Holkar State, and to nominate the said son of Bhau Holkar as successor to the *gadi*, and when the young Maharaja was actually installed by him on June 27, 1844, according to the ceremonial observed on previous occasions, including a royal salute of 21 guns, the Government of India disapproved of these proceedings, as they had rather the character of succession by right to the *gadi* of the Maharaja's ancestors. The Government of India then, to mark the act as an act of free grace, required the Maharaja to accept a *Kharita* from them as a formal *Sanad* of appointment, and the boy Maharaja had to agree, though the measure was opposed both to the Treaty and usage.

During the minority of the Maharaja the administration was conducted by the Masaheba, with the help of three Councillors, the senior of whom was Raja Bhau Phanse. The Resident (Sir R. Hamilton) always took a keen interest in the affairs of the State, and gave his friendly advice whenever needed. He was deeply attached to the Maharaja, almost treating him as his own child. The Maharaja appreciated throughout his life these kindly feelings, and raised a statue at his capital in honour of Sir R. Hamilton. Raja Bhau was removed from his office in 1848 for misconduct, and Ram Rao Narayan Palsikar then became senior member. In 1849 the Masehaba died. The Maharaja had all the while been receiving training at the hands of private tutors in English, Sanskrit, and Persian; and the manly forms of exercise—riding, shooting, and Indian gymnastics—were not neglected. On the Masaheba's death he associated himself with the administration, paying particular attention to finance and accounts. On December 19, 1850, the Maharaja, with a small retinue, went on an extensive tour to various places in Northern India, performing all his journeys on horse-back, and he returned to Indore on March 3, 1851. For one year following the Maharaja again associated himself with the administration. By this time Sir R. Hamilton was able to report about the Maharaja's remarkable aptitude, his very retentive memory, and his grasp of administration, and especially in the matter of accounts. On March 8, 1852, the Maharaja assumed the full powers of Government at a grand Durbar attended by the Resident (Sir R. Hamilton) and all the guaranteed Thakurs and land-holders, besides the public functionaries. The Resident impressed upon the Thakurs and all present, "that the full powers of sovereignty devolved upon the Maharaja, that every one must obey him, and that it beholds every one to be obedient and loyal as an imperative duty." Next day there was another Durbar, when the Maharaja granted *jagirs* and rewards to various persons. In the following December the Maharaja proceeded on a tour to the Deccan, where he visited various places of importance.

The dawn of 1854 witnessed the Maharaja grappling with the details of administration in right earnest. Hardly had three years elapsed before the Mutiny broke out at Meerut, on May 10, 1857. It spread like wildfire throughout the country. The British contingents at Mehidpur and Bhopal mutinied, and the contagion spread to Indore, Mhow, and other places. On June 9, 1857, the Maharaja urged Colonel Durand, who had succeeded Sir R. Hamilton a few weeks previously as Resident at Indore and as Agent to the Governor-General, to send away the ladies, children, and the treasure to Mhow; but his advice was not accepted. On July 1, 1857, the Residency was attacked and plundered by the mutineers. Even on this day the Maharaja had written to Colonel Durand offering his help to the best of his ability, as his

THE STATE OF INDORE.

1. Bolia Chhatri, Indore, built in 1858 by Sirdar Govind Rao Bolio.
2. Ahilya Bai's Chhatri, Maheshwar, built by Herself.
3. Temple of Raj Rajeswar, Maheshwar.
4. Malhar Rao's Cenotaph at Alampur.

troops, too, had got out of control; but Colonel Durand retreated suddenly in the direction of Sehore. After the above occurrence the Maharaja sent out detachments to bring in and secure wounded Europeans, and he also gave asylum to the Residency people who had come to the Palace. He recovered what was left in the Indore Residency Treasury and forwarded it to Captain Hungerford, the Commander at Mhow, to whom he also gave all the assistance in his power. The Maharaja's officers and troops in other places—Amjhera and Sirdarpur – gave much valuable help to Captain Hutchinson, the Political Agent in Bhopawar, and to other officers. All this help was warmly acknowledged by Lord Canning, the Viceroy, at the Jubbulpore Durbar, which was specially held for the Maharaja in 1860. The restrictions imposed by the *kharita* of 1844 had been removed by this time—first by the Royal Proclamation of 1858, and secondly by the assurances from the Government of India that the House of Holkar should be perpetuated and flourish. It is unfortunate, however, that the Maharaja was not given the territorial reward, like the Maharaja Sindhia and the Nizam, though an intention to grant the reward had been indicated in the Right Hon. the Secretary of State's Despatch of 1858, and the grant was promised by Sir R. Hamilton, on behalf of the Government of India, at an open Durbar in Indore in 1859. The Maharaja continued to feel throughout his life the injustice done to him in refusing this territorial reward; and he always ascribed this result to the adverse influence of Colonel Durand (afterwards Sir Henry Durand), who was Resident at Indore and Agent to the Governor-General in Central India till December 1857, and was Foreign Secretary to the Government of India during 1859 64, as also to the adverse influence of his son (Sir Mortimer Durand), who occupied later on the position of Under-Secretary and Secretary in the Foreign Department. Colonel Durand had been equally prejudiced against Sindhia and against various other States; but Maharaja Sindhia was fortunate in having by his side Major Macpherson, Resident at Gwalior, and Sir Dinkar Rao, the Maharaja's Minister, in both of whom Lord Canning had full confidence, and who was able, therefore, to counteract the adverse opinion of Colonel Durand.

Before and after the Mutiny the Maharaja realized that a number of rights of the State, i.e., over Jhabua, Jaora, and other guarantee-holders, were in danger of being lost, and he took these cases up with characteristic energy. The policy of the British officers of the day was not favourable, but the Maharaja persisted in his endeavours as best as he could. For the prosecution of these cases, as also for the general reform of the administration, the Maharaja wanted an able Minister, and he selected Sir T. Madhav Rao in 1872 for this purpose, on the strong advice of Sir R. Hamilton and other well-wishers. Sir T. Madhav Rao reorganized the Judicial and the Police Departments, and improved the other Departments also. The new Dewan ably handled some of the Political cases referred to. On December 3, 1872, Lord Northbrook, the Viceroy, paid a visit to Burwaha, where, in the presence of a large gathering of ruling princes and eminent British officers, he laid the foundation-stone of the Narbada Bridge, and highly eulogized the public spirit of Maharaja Tukoji Rao in having been the first to bring a railway into Malwa.

In 1873 the Maharaja went on a pilgrimage to sacred places in the south, in the course of which he also visited Bombay and Poona. He took occasion when at Poona to make friends with many of the Deccan *Sardars*, and also with Maharani Jamna Bai Saheba Gaekwar, to whom he promised his utmost help in Baroda affairs. In December, 1874, the Maharaja paid a visit to the Viceroy at Calcutta, where he was His Excellency's guest, and was treated with marked distinction. About this time Maharaja Malhar Rao of Baroda was charged with various acts of misconduct, and a Commission was appointed to investigate into them. Maharaja Holkar was invited by the Viceroy to sit on the Commission, but this he declined to do on the ground of principle. In May, 1875, on the earnest request of the Viceroy, the Maharaja permitted Sir T. Madhav Rao to proceed to Baroda to preside over its administration, and Dewan Bahadur Raghunath Rao was appointed in his place. Raghunath Rao continued the reforms undertaken by his predecessor. In November, 1875, Lord Northbrook visited Indore as the guest of the Maharaja, this being the first occasion on which a Governor-General had visited Indore. In the following March His Royal Highness the Prince of Wales visited Indore, and was received with all honour. In 1877 there was the Delhi Assemblage, on which occasion the Maharaja was present. The Maharaja, who was already a G.C.S.I., was now made a C.I.E., and a Councillor of the Queen-Empress. His salute, which was a Royal salute before, but which happened to be shown as 19 later on, was now raised to 21 guns. While at Delhi the Maharaja was the central figure, to whom the other Rulers looked for advice and guidance, on account of his conspicuous wisdom and statesmanship; and the Maharaja was thus able to cultivate friendship with almost all the Rulers of Indian States.

In 1879 Maharaja Sindhia was invited by Maharaja Tukoji Rao to visit his capital. The former arrived at Indore and remained for a week as the guest of the Maharaja. The event was significant. The two Maharajas had never before visited each other at their capitals.

In 1882 the Maharaja and the Maharanees, with a large retinue, went on a pilgrimage to Badri Narayan, which was then considered extremely difficult. On his way to Hardwar the Maharaja paid visits to Jaipur and Rampur-Bareilly, where he was received with magnificent hospitality by His Highness Maharaja Madho Singhji and His Highness Nawab Kilbeali Khan respectively. On his return from Badri Narayan the Maharaja paid a visit to Nainital and Simla to see Lord Ripon, the Viceroy. Here the Maharaja discussed a number of Political cases with the Viceroy and the Foreign Secretary (the Hon. Mr. Grant), to whom he gave written statements of all these cases. Messrs. Garud, Shintre, and Sakharam Gopal were the officers left at Simla to prosecute these cases. The Maharaja created a very good impression, and circumstances seemed to be favourable both in the time of Lord Ripon and Lord Dufferin, but in the end the Policy of the British officers came in the way, and he could not secure justice to his claims.

Maharaja Tukoji Rao passed away on June 17, 1886. His reign of 42 years was of exceptional distinction. To Malhar Rao I and Tukoji I is due the credit of founding a vast State by means of conquests; to Devi Ahilya Bai must be given the credit for unstinted charity and beneficent rule; to Yeshwant Rao belongs the credit of rescuing the State from extinction, of restoring it to its former greatness and making it fully independent; but it is to Tukoji Rao II alone that credit is due for developing a State, diminished in size in 1818, to a remarkable degree of prosperity and strength. When Tukoji Rao assumed the reins of

THE STATE OF INDORE

Government in 1852, the income of the State was 22 lakhs, with a population of 5½ lakhs, and the State Treasury was empty. But by the time of his death the State revenues had risen to 85 lakhs a year, the population had risen to 11 lakhs (i.e. nearly double), large cash balances had accumulated in the Treasury, besides sound investments, and agriculture, trade, commerce, and various local industries had developed enormously. How all this was achieved may be summed up in a few words. The Maharaja signalized his assumption of powers in 1852 by the grant of *sanads* for the upkeep of the Indore English Madressa and of the Medical Hospital, intended to treat patients according to the European system. These were supplemented later on by other schools and dispensaries; and a Sanskrit Vidyalaya was established at Indore, where education was given in religious matters and various branches of ancient learning. In 1865 a complete survey was made of the State lands. *Takavi* advances were freely made to cultivators for the improvement of agriculture. A liberal scheme of irrigation policy was put into force whereby no less than 40 lakhs of rupees were spent on various irrigation works during 1865–85. Substantial concessions were made to cultivators in order to reclaim wastes, and to increase wet cultivation. Besides the assistance thus afforded to cultivators, the Maharaja kindled enthusiasm amongst his *ryots* by making frequent tours of inspection in the districts, making personal acquaintance with his people, and freely mixing with them. The Excise and Customs Departments were reorganized so as to secure a stable income. The Indore City Municipality was brought into existence in 1863 through the efforts of Bakshi Khuman Singh and Ramchandra Vithal, for which purpose an annual grant of Rs. 12,000 was made by the Maharaja. The needs of the Indore city for water were met by constructing water-works at a great cost, and distributing water therefrom to the various streets by means of pipes. The Judiciary and the Police were thoroughly reorganized, and Laws and Rules were passed for the disposal of judicial and military matters. The military workshop was brought to a high state of efficiency. Suitable quarters were provided for the troops and the Mulki Fouz Police). A strong stimulus was given to trade by increasing the importance of the Body known as Gyara Panchas, whom the Maharaja utilized in devising schemes for the commercial advancement of Indore and in the settlement of intricate disputes relating to trade and commerce. The State money was lent at a low rate of interest on approved security for commercial undertakings. The needs of State employees and of the *ryots* were met by advancing loans to them at a very reasonable rate of interest, and fixing easy instalments for their recovery. The scattered condition of the State territory involved heavy management charges; these were reduced by arranging with the British Government and other States suitable exchanges, whereby the State territory became compact. The Maharaja was able to make a great advance towards the settlement of the long standing question of the demarcation of the boundary between Khandesh and the Indore State. He also brought about the capitalization of payment towards the United Malwa Contingent and the Malwa Bhil Corps, whereby the work of keeping the accounts was simplified, and at the same time the State was absolved by the Government of India from all liability to them for assistance with troops. The Maharaja was the first Ruler in Central India to realize the advantages of the introduction of railways, and he financed the railway line connecting Southern with Northern India by giving a loan of one crore to cover the cost of the Holkar State Railway. The State Postal Service was efficiently organized; and the Maharaja deserves the credit for being the first amongst the Indian Rulers to establish, in 1869, a spinning and weaving mill at Indore, at a total cost of about 15 lakhs. The object aimed at by this mill was not so much the monetary gain to the State (though this, too, brought a couple of lakhs a year as net profit), as the stimulus it should give to cotton cultivation in Malwa, and the provision of cheap clothing to the people. In order to popularize the coarse cloth turned out by the mill the Maharaja himself used to wear it occasionally, and induced his officers to do the same. The Maharaja's idea was to make the State self-dependent for all the necessaries of life; and to ensure this object he, amongst other things, tried without much success to run the iron works in Burwaha, which he had purchased from the British Government, and he also started a paper factory. By means of these salutary measures the Maharaja raised the State to a very flourishing condition, and he may justly be described as the second founder of the political greatness and financial prosperity of the Holkar dominions, whose patriotic life and history must ever continue to be an inspiration to the Princes of India.

Maharaja Shivaji Rao assumed the reins of Government on July 3, 1886, being then 33 years old. His Highness was very particular in promoting cordial relations with the British Government. In pursuance of this policy he abolished, on their invitation, the transit duties which had been interfering with the free movement of goods, although they brought considerable revenues to the State. He gave a large tank (Berchha tank), with its drainage area over three miles, for the use of the Mhow garrison, and he raised and maintained at his cost a regiment of cavalry for the assistance of the British Government, although the capitalization arrangement of 1865 had for ever absolved the State from any such assistance.

Dewan Bahadur R. Raghunath Rao, who had before been a very successful Minister of the State, was invited to assume that office again in 1887. Having made these preliminary arrangements, the Maharaja proceeded to England, accompanied by Sir L. Griffin and others, and attended the Jubilee of Her Majesty Queen Victoria. He produced a great impression while in England, and made many acquaintances. Her Majesty conferred on him the high insignia of G.C.S.I. His Highness travelled extensively in France, Switzerland, and other countries, and saw a great deal of European life, and this was supplemented later on by extensive travels in India, where he visited almost all places of interest and made personal friends with many Princes and a number of other personages.

His Highness will be especially remembered on account of his very liberal policy in the development of trade and commerce, of education, and of medical institutions. He abolished the transit duties in the State, and established a duty-free market at Shiva Ganj, in Indore, whereby the city has become a most important centre of trade. In February, 1887, a new hospital was opened at Indore in commemoration of the Queen-Empress' Jubilee, and in 1901 was opened the Tukoji Rao Hospital. In 1889 a Technical Institute was opened at Indore, to which was added an Arts School in 1891. Both these Institutions were unique in Central India and gave training which was not available in other States. In 1891 he established a college, named

THE STATE OF INDORE.

1. The Ghats at Indore, built by H.H. Maharaja Tukoji Rao II.

2. The Narbada Bridge at Nurwan, constructed in 1873.

THE STATE OF INDORE

"The Tukoji Rao Holkar College," for teaching up to the B.A. degree, in order to meet the growing wants of the people of Central India in general and of the Holkar State in particular, and to secure highly educated men for the State. The College buildings cost over a lakh of rupees, and provision was made for the appointment of a very competent Principal and an able staff. The education at the College was intended to be free at the outset, and a number of scholarships were also provided for deserving or poor students. The College soon developed into a big institution, and additional professorships were added to it, which enabled it to turn out a number of graduates and under-graduates.

Maharaja Shivaji Rao was highly educated. He was perfectly at home with English and various other languages spoken in India. He had a commanding personality, and was noted for his ready wit and presence of mind, while his knowledge of State affairs was remarkable, due no doubt to his keen intellect and extensive studies and travels. His liberality and charity were widely known, and many institutions like the Fergusson College, Poona, were benefited by his generosity. The Maharaja's love of architecture was equally remarkable, and the State owes to his reign a number of fine and durable buildings—the Shiva Vilas Palace, the new Secretariat Buildings (Durbar Offices), the Sukhnivas Palace, and the Daryao Mahal at Barwaha.

During the reign of His Highness, Indore had the honour of visits from Their Excellencies Lord Lansdowne and Lord Elgin, both of whom were much impressed with the personality of the Maharaja. His Highness the Maharaja Madhao Rao Sindhia also visited Indore, and was received with special consideration by Maharaja Shivaji Rao. Their relations were always very cordial, and the Maharaja throughout his life fostered them by making a visit to Gwalior and by other means.

During 1899-1900 the State was visited by a severe famine, which, in spite of an expenditure of several lakhs on relief measures, took away a large portion of its population, and materially affected its revenues. Before the State had time to recover, a terrible epidemic of plague broke out in 1903, which lingered on for some years, whereby a large portion of the population was again destroyed and the resources of the State crippled. Maharaja Shivajee Rao, who for some time had felt that his health was not equal to his arduous duties, retired in January, 1903, placing on the *gadi* his beloved son, under the title of Maharaja Shree Sawai Tukoji Rao Holkar Bahadur. As the age of the latter was then only 13 years, the Council of State was transformed into the Council of Regency, which, under the general supervision of the Resident, was to administer the State till His Highness should come of age. The Council was to work on certain conditions laid down by Maharaja Shivajirao, the most important of which were the preservation of the rights and privileges of the State and the encouragement of local talents.

The minority administration continued till November, 1911, and it deserves the fullest credit for introducing many reforms; and this it was enabled to do by means of the large cash balance which the sound fiscal policy of the previous *regimes* had enabled the State to accumulate. The Council thoroughly reorganized almost all the Departments in the State – Judicial, Police, Revenue, Forest, Education, Medical, Jail, Public Works, Municipalities, Sayer, Excise, and the Secretariat,—and it revised the scale of pay of public servants so as to attract competent men. Steps were taken to train local men in various lines for State service, and post graduate scholarships were also awarded. Dispensaries, Law Courts, and various buildings of public utility were constructed at a cost of Rs. 53,13,503, and 281 miles of metal roads were added at a cost of about Rs. 45,24,853. A sum of Rs. 42,81,042 was expended on repairs to old buildings and roads, and Rs. 4,23,037 were spent on the construction of tanks and wells. A gigantic project for the storage and supply of water to the city was inaugurated, which cost about 20 lakhs of rupees; and these additional waterworks have been of immense benefit to the people. An electric installation was completed and inaugurated in the city and palaces. A model *Sarai*, called Maharani Waransi Bai's *Sarai*, with a coffee-house for the convenience of travellers, was completed in 1908. A Town Hall, named the King Edward Hall, was built, and was opened in 1905 by His Majesty the King-Emperor, then Prince of Wales. In the same year the New High Court building was erected to commemorate the Royal visit to Indore. The Maharani's Hospital for Women was constructed to supply a keenly felt want. The whole city of Indore was covered by a network of telephone lines, these meeting the requirements of an increasing commercial life. A new railway line, named the Nagda-Mathura Railway, was constructed by the Bombay-Baroda and Central India Railway Company, for which lands were given free by the State; and this line has opened the northern districts of His Highness' Government. A fire brigade, consisting of one 500-gallons, four 200-gallons, and two 100-gallons steam fire-engines, together with an adequate supply of hose and appurtenances, was established and placed under the State Police. Reorganization of the Judicial Department, and the separation from the Judicial of the Executive, were carried out; and measures were taken in right earnest for the prevention and suppression of plague. The survey of the State lands and settlement of the land revenue were made by means of experts kindly lent by the British Government, and these measures have increased the value of agricultural holdings. The Forest Department was thoroughly reorganized under trained officers, resulting in the augmentation of timber supply and an increase of revenue. Much encouragement was given for building quarters outside Indore city so as to relieve its congestion, and facilties were afforded for the development of cotton industries. The codification of laws and the translation into English of the existing legal circulars were taken up and completed.

While all these beneficent measures were being taken mostly on the initiative of the Resident, Mr. (afterwards Sir) Oswald Bosanquet, the young Maharaja was assiduously fitting himself up for his responsibilities under able guidance. He was educated first at the Indore Daly College, and latterly at the Mayo College, Ajmer, from which latter institution he took his diploma in the year 1908. He stood first in tent-pegging at the college games. About this time His Highness lost his beloved father, for whom he had the highest regard. In 1910 His Highness went on a tour to Europe. While in London he had the honour of several interviews with His Majesty King George and Her Majesty the Queen-Empress Mary, whose coronation he attended. During this trip His Highness made the acquaintance of the King of Italy, the Prince of Montenegro, and other high dignitaries and personages. After an absence of 21 months His Highness returned to Indore on October 21, 1911, when the people of Indore gave him an ovation of a unique character. He soon after, that is, on November 6, 1911, took up the reins of Government. On December 12th following, His Highness attended at Delhi the Coronation Durbar of Their Majesties the King-Emperor and the Queen-Empress. In November, 1912, His Excellency Lord Hardinge visited Indore and was given a hearty reception by His Highness, at the Lalbag, where he had put up. At a banquet given in his honour the Viceroy spoke highly of the administration of Indore, alluded eulogistically to the various reforms introduced, and described the State as a very progressive one.

A month later His Highness proceeded on a short tour of three months to Europe. He stayed partly in England and partly in Scotland.

In August, 1914, the Great War broke out in Europe, and His Highness at once placed at the disposal of the British Government the resources of his State for the successful prosecution of the war, though under the Treaty of Mandsore almost two-thirds of the Holkar territory had been ceded to the British Government (and their allies) in consideration of their maintaining sufficient field force for defending the Holkar State, and although the capitalization agreement of 1865 had freed the State from any obligation to render military assurance to that Government. The Holkar State Transport and Escort were on active service in the various theatres of war, and the expenses on their account, ordinary as well as extraordinary, which amounted to nearly 15 lakhs of rupees, were defrayed entirely by the State. Recruiting was carried on for purposes of war; and His Highness freely gave contributions towards the Prince of Wales's Fund, the Imperial Relief Fund, the Red Cross Fund, including the hospital ship "Loyalty" scheme, "Our Day" Fund, and other objects—the total contributions under these heads being over 26 lakhs. He gave besides horses, mules, and *Tongas*, with harnesses; and also subscribed to the extent of 30 lakhs towards the 4 per cent. Conversion Loan, and to the extent of 22 lakhs towards the War Loan. Gifts in money and kind for war purposes were given by Their Highnesses the Maharanees and by the State people. The Indore people also subscribed towards the War Loan, one of them—Sir Hukumchand—making the unique contribution of one crore. On the termination of the war in 1918 His Highness received the warm thanks of His Majesty the King-Emperor and of the Government of India for "the staunch support and substantial aid rendered by the Indore State during the whole period of the war," in the manner described.

In August, 1918, Their Excellencies Lord and Lady Chelmsford paid a visit to Indore as His Highness' guests. His Excellency opened the new High School, called the Shivajee Rao High School, and he took occasion to compliment His Highness on the educational policy of the State. This visit led to the establishment of cordial relations between His Highness and his distinguished guests, on whose invitation he paid a visit to Simla in June, 1920, when he was received with special consideration.

His Highness feels boundless interest in the welfare of his subjects. This was most noticeable during the influenza period of 1918, when His Highness, regardless of the advice of his doctors, visited the affected areas to encourage the volunteers and cheer up patients. During the war days there was a great rise in prices of commodities (a condition of affairs which still continues), but His Highness has, by taking measures to prohibit the export of foodstuffs, and to import quantities of them from cheap markets, managed to secure a steady supply of provisions for his people at rates lower than those prevailing in most other parts of India. His Highness has also sanctioned allowances to State servants in respect of the high cost of living. Turning to the sphere of permanent improvements, it may be mentioned that the Maharaja has set up at Indore agricultural and horticultural institutions, the twofold object of which is to find out the possibilities of improving agricultural and fruit-growing industries, and to publish the results of the incidental experiments for the benefit of the people. His Highness has also established Co-operative Credit Societies, with well-managed Co-operative Central Banks at Indore, Sanawad, Kannod, Petlawad, and Maheshwar, primarily for removing the indebtedness of peasants and for their thorough uplift. Recently one more bank, with a capital of one crore, has been established at Indore, mainly with the object of developing commerce and promoting industries. His Highness realizes the importance of mass education, and is working towards the ideal of free and compulsory education. A number of school buildings have already been constructed to promote the furtherance of this liberal policy. Scholarship and stipends are being freely given to deserving students for the prosecution of studies both in India and foreign countries, and thus the benefits of liberal education are secured to State subjects. The Maharaja has thoroughly reorganized the Sanskrit Maha Vidyalya so as to impart education on improved lines. He has contributed Rs. 2,50,000 to the Daly College at Indore for the founding of a chair; has given Rs. 5,00,000 to the Benares Hindu University; and it is mainly due to him that Indore has the unique institutions of the Mahila Vidyalaya (a Girls' School named after the senior Maharani) and Ahilyashram, Widows' Home, named after his illustrious ancestress, Devi Ali'ya Bai. There are other institutions, too, which give practical proof of the deep interest His Highness takes in education. His Highness has given handsome donations to the Indore General Library, whereby its financial position has become thoroughly sound, and it is consequently rapidly increasing its stock of books, and it allows to the people of Indore the benefit of free reading of various papers and periodicals in English and the vernacular. Early in 1916 a local newspaper, called the "Malhari Martand Vijaya," was started under the patronage of His Highness. It is published at the State Electric Press, and under able editorship it is doing useful work in making it possible for the State subjects, scattered in different districts, to discuss through its columns questions of general interest. His Highness has very progressive views on social questions, and he has already passed the Widows' Remarriage Act and the Civil Marriage Act. Realizing that Municipal administrations afford excellent training grounds for self-Government, His Highness has recently conferred municipal powers upon his subjects in the city of Indore.

About three years ago His Highness' Government secured the services of the distinguished town planner, Professor Patrick Geddes, for the improvement of the Indore City. The Professor has submitted a voluminous Report, and the City Municipality is working out its details. His Highness has paid attention to the village arbitration courts, known as Gaon Panchayat, and a special officer is now engaged to put the scheme into operation in the various villages of the State. The development of industries has also been engaging His Highness' attention. The State has financed the Prince Yeshwant Rao Brush Factory at Indore and the

THE STATE OF INDORE.

1. The Fort, Indore, built by Maharaja Tukoji Rao II. 2. Bosanquet Market, Indore, built in 1911. 3. The Duryao Mahal, Burwaha.

THE STATE OF INDORE.

1. Sir Nukamchand Tower, built in 1921. 2. The State Mills, Indore, erected in 1869 by H.H. Maharaja Tikoji Rao II. 3. The Malwa Mills, Indore, built in 1908.

Thymol Factory at Rao (near Indore). A glass factory has been established at Rao under similar conditions, and a mill for the manufacture of paper is nearing completion at Palia, which is some six miles from Indore.

Side by side with these endeavours to develop the resources of the State, His Highness is displaying zeal in maintaining intact its rights and privileges. Especially is he desirous of reviving those rights and privileges which, as stated above, formed the subject of representations from the late Maharaja Tukoji Rao to the Government of India, but which his untimely death left undecided. All these cases, with others which have arisen in recent years, are at present engaging His Highness' attention, and they are being one by one represented to the Government of India, in the fullest confidence that justice will be done to them.

His Highness is blessed with three children. The eldest is Prince Yeshwant Rao (aged 13 years), who is receiving his education in England; and the other two are the Princess Manorama, aged 12 years, and Princess Snehalata, aged 6 years. His Highness is only 31 years of age, and a long career is thus probably before him. He has been faithful to the noble ideal set up by his illustrious grandfather, and has already done a great deal in that direction. May His Highness' rule be long and happy!

A few words must here be added to give an idea of the modern Indore State and the Indore City, which is rapidly increasing in importance. The State administration is conducted by His Highness, who is assisted by his Chief Minister and a Council, to whom His Highness has delegated most of his powers. Below the Chief Minister there are heads of various departments, with a hierarchy of subordinate officers, each having prescribed powers. The Judiciary consists of Courts of Sessions and District Courts, Court of Munsiffs and Magistrates, presided over by trained lawyers, with a High Court of three Judges above all, who exercise almost all the highest powers in judicial matters. For the disposal of revenue appeals there is a Board of Revenue, from which appeals lie to the Chief Minister and the Council. The various services of the State—Police, Revenue, Forest and Medical—are manned by officers specially trained for the purposes; and there are in operation laws, regulations, and circulars for the disposal of matters in which the public are interested.

The army of Indore is nearly 3,000 strong, besides artillery. It was nearly double before the Regency administration. About 1818 it was nearly 40,000, and still prior to that it was far larger. Two sections of the State army—Escort and Transport—are meant for the assistance of the Government of India. The Police force has taken the place of the previous irregular troops.

The area of the Indore State, its population and revenue, have been given above. The State is divided into five districts, with *tahsils* and *Thanas*, and comprises 4,295 inhabited villages. The tenure is mainly *Raiyatwari*, and settlements are made with the *Rayats* for a fixed period. The *Rayats* have occupancy rights, and have also the power of transferring their holdings on certain conditions. Out of the area of the State almost one-third is under cultivation, 2,601·01 square miles under forest, and the rest is culturable or unculturable waste.

The Indore City and Indore district enjoy the advantage of a very healthy climate all the year round. The rainfall is generally 30 inches per year, and the heat during the two months of summer rarely exceeds 105° Fahrenheit, while the nights are invariably cool. The Nemad and the Rampura-Bhanpura districts are comparatively hotter during summer, and the rainfall in the latter district is at times precarious. But the Mahidpur and the Nemawar districts are more or less akin to Indore district in point of rainfall and climate. The Nemad and, to some extent, Nemawar district are noted for their cotton crop, the Indore district is noted for the wheat crop, while the Northern districts are suitable for opium cultivation. The State grows more than enough of wheat, cereals, and pulses for its requirements. The cotton cultivation is steadily increasing, and the yield is already sufficient to feed more than six spinning and weaving mills. Oil-seeds and grass are produced in abundance, and are often exported abroad. The State forests contain large varieties of timber and firewood. These more than suffice for the State's requirements, and are often exported to neighbouring territories. Small game is found in abundance throughout the State forests, and big game is found particularly in parts of Nemad, Bhanpura, and Nemawar. Cultivation is mainly done by means of bullocks, of which there is an excellent breed in Indore and Mahidpur districts. Milch cattle are especially good in these two districts and also in Nemad.

The State maintains one College in Indore City, teaching up to the B.A. and B.Sc. degrees, which has 200 students on its rolls. The City has one High School for boys, containing about 2,000 students, and one High School Chandravati Mahila Vidyalaya) for girls, where there are 269 pupils, whereof 31, who are widows, are maintained at State expense. There is, besides, one Jain High School in the City, having 350 students. In the Indore Residency there is one Canadian Mission College, teaching up to the B.A. standard, which has about 103 students, one Mission High School for boys which contains 345 students, and one Mission High School for girls containing 139 students. There is the Residency High School, besides the Daly College, which is for the sons of Princes and nobles. The State maintains, besides, one training school for teachers, and there are also a number of Anglo-vernacular and primary schools, maintained by the State or by private organizations, whose number is steadily rising. There is at Indore one Sanskrit Mahavidyalaya, with eight branches in the districts, where students are trained in Sanskrit literature, grammar, Vedic scriptures, and other ancient systems of learning.

The medical institutions of Indore consist of the Tukoji Rao Hospital, which is a first-class institution, having a big staff of doctors, with about 102 in-patients and 516 out-patients, and 45 other hospitals and dispensaries in the city and districts. The Indore Residency has also a first-class large hospital, called the King Edward Hospital, maintained by various States, including Indore; and there is attached to it a Medical School, where students from Central India, Rajputana, and other places, are trained as Sub-Assistant Surgeons. There are two more hospitals in the Residency, one maintained by the British Government and one, a female hospital, maintained by the Canadian Mission.

These educational and medical institutions provide facilities rarely obtainable elsewhere, and the result is that there is a large percentage of people from outside who come up specially to Indore to participate in these benefits.

A reference has been made to the Municipality at Indore, to which the State at present contributes one lakh of rupees

THE STATE OF INDORE.

1. Patalpani Waterfalls (Three Miles from Mhow). 2. The Caves at Dhamnar (160 Miles from Indore), and excavated between the Fifth and Seventh Centuries

from its own revenues, as the local rates levied by the Municipality are insufficient for its purposes. There are besides municipalities in almost all *tahsil* towns of the State.

The Indore State has two very big rivers, the Nurbudda and Chambal, running through parts of its territories, and there are besides rivers like the Sipra, Kalisindh, and others. These watercourses contain immense potentialities for the development of electric power and irrigation, but at present irrigation is mostly confined to tanks and wells, which, as stated above, were constructed at a great cost mainly in the time of His Highness the late Maharaja Tukoji Rao. The plateaus of Vindhya and Satpura, covering miles of territory, also contain similar electrical and irrigational potentialities, and they only await scientific treatment for their successful development.

A reference has been made to the agricultural and horticultural institutions at Indore, from which much good is expected, and an allusion has also been made to the Co-operative Credit Societies, banks, and village *Panchayats*, designed for the benefit of the rural population. A veterinary hospital on approved lines exists at Indore, and also in a few places in the districts. Industries, other than agrarian, are looked after by the Department of Commerce and Industries. During the past four or five years this department has been actively engaged in making investigations with regard to industrial possibilities, and also in taking measures for giving support to concerns already in existence or those to be set up hereafter. It may be interesting to note here that 12 new joint stock companies, with a total capital of several lakhs, have recently been registered under the Indore Company's Act. Enquiries have been made with regard to the lac and various industries, the making of cement, pencils, the nature and value of chemicals, the prospects of coal, iron, copper and lead mining, the distillation of wood on a commercial basis, and the equipment of a laboratory for the analysis of chemical and other raw materials. These inquiries have been followed by demonstration work, which has shown that, from the raw materials available in the State, it is commercially profitable to start the industries of chalk-making, manufacture of type-writing ink, carbon-papers, boot-polish, fast-wall colours, and water-proofs. It has also been brought to light that there are in abundance good iron ore and material for making cement on the Burwah side.

Allusion has been made to the Rao Glass Works which are successfully working, and the material for which is locally available, and the thymol actually produced has been considered quite a first-class stuff in the markets.

At time of the compilation of this work there were in the State nearly 60 cotton presses, five cotton spinning and weaving mills (one of which was nearing completion), two roller flour mills, one of which was to be shortly set up, 29 corn grinding factories, three sugar grinding factories. One oil extracting factory alluded to above is a model of its kind, containing the latest automatic machinery driven by electricity. A new industry for the making of sugar from cane and palm-juice by means of machinery has been set up at Indore on the joint stock basis, and it promises to yield excellent results. There are two factories at Indore for the manufacture of

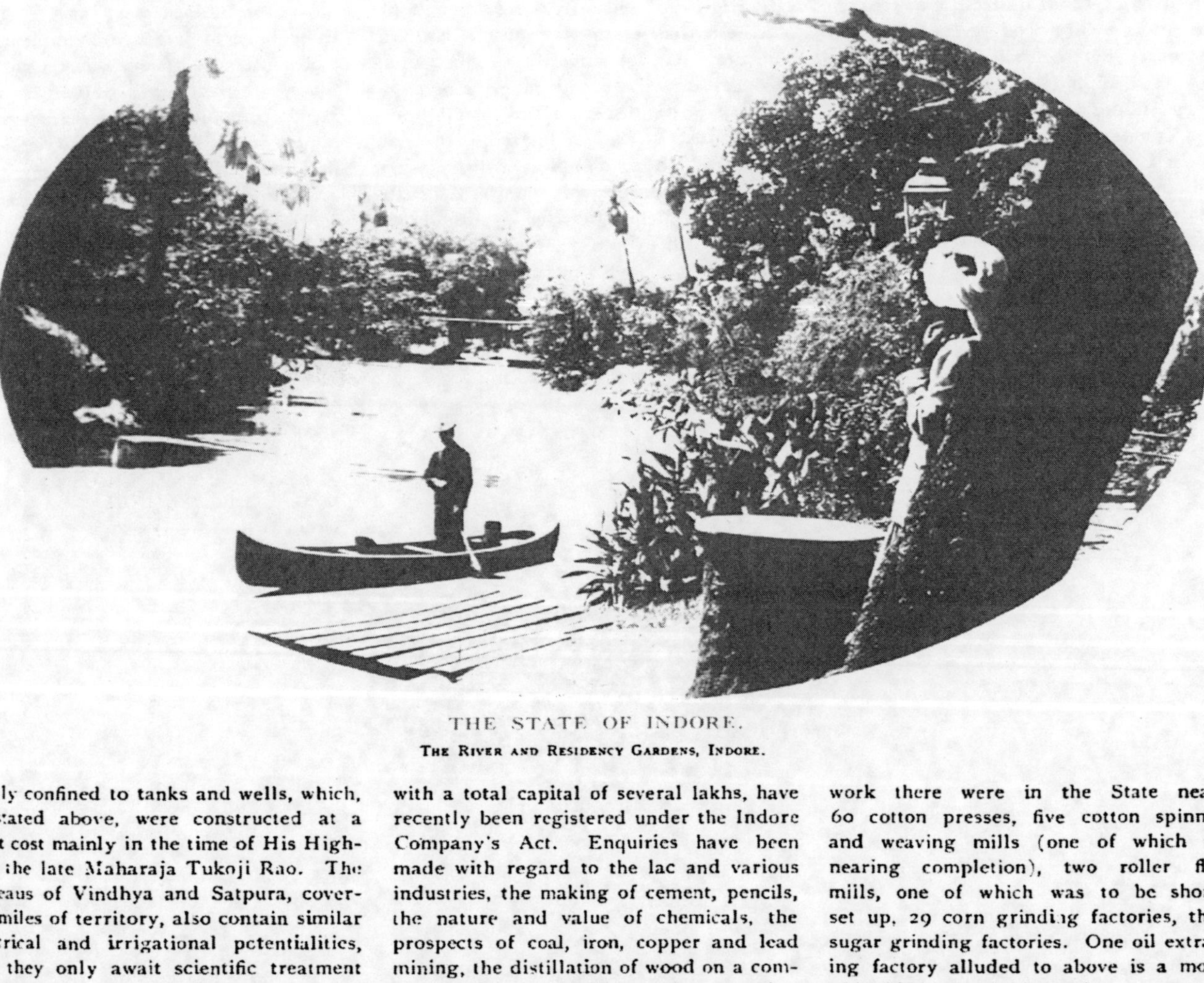

THE STATE OF INDORE.

THE RIVER AND RESIDENCY GARDENS, INDORE.

first-class pressed bricks and tiles, and two foundries for the making of screws and bolts, and for turning out vessels and utensils of various descriptions.

Allusion must also be made here to the industries existing from old times, and to some of which the State is giving financial help. These are the manufacture of superior cotton fabrics at Maheshwar, which have a ready market everywhere in India, and the manufacture of engraved silver work, swords, and knives. On the Rampura side, the making of blankets in the last-named districts, the manufacture of superior *Khadi* in the Nemad district, the dyeing industry at Gautampura in Indore district, the manufacture of tobacco in the Indore City, and the manufacture of molasses in the various parts of the State. The high commercial rank occupied by Indore is well known.

The number of carts bringing in food-stuffs in Siyaganj and Mulhar Gunj, the crowds in Sarafa engaged in the purchase and sale of jewellery, the numbers of purchasers of cloth in Bazazkhana, should all convince one, even on a flying visit, of the immense magnitude of trade and commerce carried on in Indore. The Merchants' Association to settle business disputes deserves mention. Commerce depends upon means of communication. The Indore State is traversed by the Khandwa-Ajmer branch of the Rajputana-Malwa Railway. The Rutlam - Godra branch line of the Bombay-Baroda and Central India Railway passes through the Petlawad Furgana of the Holkar State. The Bhopal-Ujjain Railway serves the district of Mahidpur with a station at Tarana ; and the Nagda-Mathura branch, as said above, was constructed during His Highness' minority, and opened his Northern district of Rampura Bhanpura. The State has for some time looked upon the question of a broad-gauge connection as an important step in the development of its industries and commerce. A survey has already been completed with a view to connect Indore via Dewas by a broad-gauge with Tarana on the Ujjain-Bhopal Railway. This connection is eventually to form part of the projected Jhansi-Manmad Railway, thereby bringing the Indore State nearer both to Northern and Southern parts of India.

Other excellent means of communication are a sufficient number of well-constructed metalled roads. Eighty miles of the Agra-Bombay road are within the borders of the State, and of the Indore-Simrol-Khandwa road and the Mhow-Neemuch road the State has respectively 50 and 12 miles. There are also several other important metalled roads, like the Indore-Nemawar and Indore-Betma roads. The existence of these roads has rendered easy the carrying of passengers to and fro by means of bullock-carts and *Tongas*, and these have of late been supplemented by motor-car services in various parts of the State, which have provided a means of rapid communication to its commercial population. Postal communications exist in almost all places, and there are telegraph communications in important towns. In the Indore City there exists the telephone system already referred to.

THE STATE OF KOLHAPUR

THIS State, in the Presidency of Bombay, under the Political Resident at the city of Kolhapur, is historically interesting from the fact that its Rulers trace their descent from the younger branch of the House of the illustrious Sivaji, the founder of the great Mahratta power. Details of the history of the family and the foundation of the Kolhapur dynasty will be found later in the biography of His Highness the present Maharaja. It suffices to state here that on the death occurring, in 1883, of Maharaja Sivaji V, who left no male issue, his widow, with the approval of the British Government, adopted Yashwant Rao, son of Aba Sahib, Chief of Kagal, who had been acting as Regent. The young Prince, the present Maharaja, was then only 10 years of age, he having been born on June 26, 1874, and the affairs of State were accordingly controlled by the Political Agent and a Council of Regency during his minority. His Highness made great progress in his studies under the capable guidance of Mr. S. M. Fraser, and on attaining his majority in 1894, he was invested with full ruling powers by Lord Harris, Governor of Bombay. His Highness Maharaja Sir Shahu Chhatrapati, G.C.I.E., G.C.S.I., G.C.V.O., LL.D., M.R.A.S., to give him his full title, received an excellent training in administrative duties at the hands of notable British officials, and has shown during his reign how greatly he benefited by it. He is in every way a progressive Ruler, zealous for the good of his subjects, and untiring in his efforts to advance the interests of his State. As regards externals, he has ever been loyal to the British throne, and has manifested the greatest tact in cementing the friendship between himself and neighbouring Chiefs. His Highness, together with the Maharajas of Baroda, Gwalior, and Indore, are the four great Mahratta Chiefs in India, and he holds leading rank among the ruling Princes in the Presidency of Bombay.

His Highness was in London in 1902 in order to witness the ceremonies connected with the Coronation of His Majesty the late King Edward VII, and in 1911 he was a guest at the Delhi Coronation festivities of Their Imperial Majesties the present King-Emperor and Queen-Empress. The honoured distinctions of a G.C.S.I., G.C.V.O., and G.C.I.E. have been conferred upon His Highness, and the University of Cambridge has bestowed upon him the dignity of an LL.D.

It may be interesting to refer now to some of the most important events, chiefly of a personal character, which have occurred during the past few years in connection with the daily life of His Highness the Maharaja of Kolhapur.

On June 22, 1911, His Highness the Chhatrapati Maharaj held a Durbar at Kolhapur to celebrate the Coronation in London of Their Most Gracious Majesties the present King-Emperor and Queen-Empress, and the occasion was made memorable by the presentation of staffs of gold, dresses of honour, special powers of jurisdiction, and other honours to certain Jagirdars and Officials of the State and to close personal relatives of His Highness.

Later in the same year His Highness left Kolhapur *en route* to Delhi in order to be present at the Imperial Coronation Durbar, and he enjoyed the high privilege of attending the magnificent functions connected with that auspicious event. In addition to this His Highness was granted the honour of paying personal homage to His Imperial Majesty, and of receiving from the Royal visitor the insignia of a Knight Grand Commander of the Most Eminent Order of the Indian Empire. Before his departure for the north His Highness the Maharaja had set aside a considerable sum of money for holding festivities in the State, and he had arranged for copies of the Royal Proclamation, in English, Marathi, and Canarese, to be distributed in every village, while photographs of Their Imperial Majesties were circulated widely throughout the Principality.

His Excellency Lord Willingdon, the Governor of Bombay, arrived at Kolhapur on November 23, 1913, and spent the first day of his visit in the inspection of hospitals, schools, the old palace, and other places of interest. On the 25th His Excellency unveiled statue busts of Their Imperial Majesties, the late King Edward VII, the Dowager-Queen Alexandra, the present King-Emperor and Queen-Empress, and Their Royal Highnesses the Duke and Duchess of Connaught, which had been presented by His Highness the Maharaja as (using his own words) " humble tokens of my loyalty and devotion to the Sovereigns and members of the Royal family."

The city of Kolhapur presented a very gay appearance on the morning of April 8, 1914, when Mr. Robertson, Political Secretary to His Excellency the Governor of Bombay, arrived for the purpose of performing the opening ceremony in connection with an Industrial and

HIS HIGHNESS COL. SIR SHAHU CHHATRAPATI MAHARAJA, G.C.I.E., G.C.S.I., G.C.V.O., LL.D., M.R.A.S., ETC.
MAHARAJA OF KOLHAPUR.

THE STATE OF KOLHAPUR.

1. The Yuvaraj Shri Rajaram Maharaja. 2. Principal Officers of the State.

Agricultural Exhibition. Four days later great enthusiasm was manifested when according an exceedingly hearty welcome to Their Highnesses the Maharaja and Maharani Saheba of Indore, who for the first time paid a visit to Kolhapur.

His Excellency the Governor of Bombay and Lady Willingdon journeyed to Kolhapur early in the month of May, 1915. A *shikar* trip had been arranged, the camp being laid out in a beautiful valley near the Western *Ghats*. Shooting covered a period of four days, and a remarkably good "bag" was obtained, His Excellency securing a fine tiger measuring 10 feet in length and weighing 280 lb., in addition to a panther and two bears.

Reference must not be omitted to the Great War of 1914 18, news of the outbreak of hostilities being received at Kolhapur on August 5, 1914. On the following day His Highness the Maharaja telegraphed to His Excellency the Governor of Bombay in these words : "Respectfully offer my cordial sympathy and support to Government in the present war crisis, and would be happy to place at the disposal of Government the whole resources of my State and my own personal services should necessity arise." A reply to this message was couched in the following terms : "His Excellency thanks His Highness most warmly on behalf of Government for loyal and devoted offer, of which advantage will be taken when the need arises." A public meeting under the presidency of His Highness was subsequently held, at which the political significance of the war was lucidly explained, and arrangements were made for the collection of subscriptions to various War Relief Funds. The ladies of the State, at the invitation of Her Highness the Maharani Saheba, also formed a branch for securing donations of money and hand-made articles of clothing and other goods.

His Highness the Maharaja subscribed Rs. 20,000, and the Relief Fund amounted to Rs. 40,729, and the same was remitted to the Bombay Branch of the Imperial War Relief Fund. The subscriptions of the Women's Branch of the same Fund amounted to Rs. 5,743 in cash, and a number of sewn and knitted articles worth Rs. 458. These were forwarded to Bombay.

A public meeting was convened in March, 1917, for the purpose of rendering practical aid to the War Loan Fund which had been opened by the Government of India, and it is reported that the amount of subscriptions to the Indian War Loan by the Kolhapur Durbar, Feudatory *Jagirdars* and subjects in the Kolhapur Principality has come up to Rs. 19,34,617, the particulars of the items being as under : Rs. 5,00,000 subscribed by His Highness ; Rs. 54,200 subscribed by Her Highness ; Rs. 2,25,455 subscribed by Feudatory Jagirdars ; and Rs. 11,54,962 subscribed by subjects of the State ; making a total of Rs. 19,34,617.

The State of Kolhapur is bounded on the north by the river Warna, which separates it from the British district of Satara, on the north-east by the river Krishna, on the east and south by the district of Belgaum, and on the west by the Sahyadri range of mountains.

It has an area of 3,217 square miles, of which 2,124 square miles properly belong to the State, while the remaining portion is held by Feudatory *jagirdars* under His Highness the Maharaja.

According to the census of 1911 the inhabitants of the State were 833,441 in number, of whom approximately 760,000 were Hindus, 33,000 Mahomedans, and 38 000 Jains, the remainder being classed as Christians and Parsis.

In connection with the physical aspects of the State, it may be said that the surface consists roughly of hilly areas in the southern and western portions, and, secondly, the Deccan plateau. The central tract has several ranges of hills.

The district lying between the *ghats* and the Krishna river is favourably situated as regards rainfall owing to the proximity of the *Ghats* and the spurs of mountains thrown out by the Sahyadri range. This portion abounds in rich valleys watered by eight rivers which flow through the territory. These streams overflow their banks during the rainy season and fertilize the soil by alluvial deposits caused by inundations. Cultivators have manifested considerable intelligence in the construction of dams, at favourable places, for the conservancy of water necessary for the irrigation of cotton, sugar-cane, and other valuable crops.

While it is generally understood that rather more than 50 per cent. of the people depend almost exclusively upon agricultural pursuits as a means of livelihood, a Government census report shows that 90 per cent. have something to do with land. Officials of the State, members of the legal profession, artisans, and even personal servants are usually occupiers, although their holdings may be diminutive as regards acreage.

The latest available State returns supply the following figures as regards cultivation : Cereals, 823,900 acres ; pulses, 114,730 acres ; and non-food crops, such as tobacco, sugar-cane, oil-seeds, cotton and other fibres, 218,460 acres ; making a total cropped area of 1,157,090 acres.

Special attention is given to the breeding of livestock, particularly of camels, of which there are usually about 250 in the State paddocks.

An event of exceptional interest illustrative of the desire of His Highness to promote the best interests of his subjects was the holding, in 1914, of an Industrial and Agricultural Exhibition, which the Maharaja Sahib rightly believed would be of great educational value to artisans as well as to agriculturists and the inhabitants generally.

The exhibition was divided into three sections, namely : (*a*) cattle, (*b*) agriculture, and (*c*) arts and industries ; 674 animals were entered for competition, there were about 2,000 exhibits of agricultural products, and 1,700 articles of industrial art were shown. Silver and bronze medals, in addition to a large sum of money, were awarded as prizes to successful competitors.

Reserved and protected forests cover an area of about 490 square miles, and the chief products are : blackwood, sandalwood, teak, grass, honey, lac, and myrabolams. The total annual receipts from the sale of major and minor products amount to about Rs. 2,25,000.

The State of Kolhapur cannot boast of being an important manufacturing or industrial centre, but the following enterprises may be mentioned. The Shri Shahu Chhatrapati Spinning and Weaving Mills at Kolhapur are equipped with 11,388 spindles, and the total annual value of the output amounts to about Rs. 6,00,000.

There are also six cotton-ginning factories, one oil-mill, 11 ground-nut factories, five mills for grinding corn, and one saw-mill.

The Kolhapur State Railway, 29 miles in length, is the property of, and was constructed by, the Kolhapur Durbar, and in terms of an agreement dated July 17, 1891, it is maintained, stocked, and worked by the Madras and Southern Mahratta Railway Company. The total capital outlay at the close of the year 1916–17 was Rs. 28,26,251, and the net earnings amounted to Rs. 1,62,122.

Consistently steady progress has been

THE STATE OF KOLHAPUR.

1. Old Palace. 2. New Palace.

THE STATE OF KOLHAPUR.

1. Rajaram College. 2. Town Hall.

THE STATE OF KOLHAPUR.

1. KOLHAPUR NATIVE GENERAL LIBRARY. 2. ALBERT EDWARD HOSPITAL.

made in the cause of education during the rulership of His Highness the Maharaja, who deems no sacrifice too great to make in order that the rising generation may have the advantage of receiving instruction in general subjects.

The technical institutions in the State comprise the Rajaram College and High School, and about 385 secondary, primary, vernacular, and other schools. Included in this number are night schools, two Sanskrit *Pathshalas*, and a technical institution for instruction in drawing, carpentry, and other subjects. There are also nine hostels or boarding-houses, which have been erected and are maintained by Mahomedan, Jain, and other communities for the benefit of children of their own particular sect or caste. The annual expenditure of the State upon educational establishments is about Rs. 1,75,000, but several of the schools are entirely supported by Christian Missionary Societies.

Medical treatment is given at the Albert Edward Hospital at Kolhapur and at 15 dispensaries scattered at various places throughout the State.

The percentage of lepers in the State is somewhat high, but this is accounted for by the fact that at Narsoba Vadi, a suburb of the town of Shirohi, there is a famous temple dedicated to Dattatraya, a deity who is credited with having the power to drive out evil spirits and of curing insanity, leprosy, and other dreaded diseases. It follows, therefore, that large numbers of afflicted persons are sent there in the hope of securing relief, and they usually remain there, as several charitable institutions have been opened there for the purpose of housing and feeding them. The Victoria Diamond Jubilee Leper Asylum at Kolhapur city now contains about 45 patients, some of whom belong to neighbouring States or districts. Tuberculosis cases are treated at the Tryambuli Sanatorium, near the Tryambuli temple, which was constructed in the year 1916–17.

Land tenures are divided into three classes, namely, (*a*) alienated, (*b*) State lands, and (*c*) *ryotwari* holdings. State lands are the personal property of His Highness the Maharaja, and are controlled by Revenue Officers, who let them on lease to suitable tenants. The third division consists of occupiers who pay cash rents under the revenue settlement, which has been extended to every portion of the Principality with the exception of the Bavda *jagir*, and about 40 villages in various parts of the State.

There are 64 Courts for the trial of criminal charges, their powers ranging from those held by Magistrates of the First Class to those granted to Sessions Judges. The Civil Courts are 40 in number, and the highest appellate bench is that which is presided over by His Highness the Maharaja Sahib.

The gross revenue of the State for the year 1916–17 was Rs. 65,36,947, and excluding debts, deposits, and alienations, the net revenue was Rs. 29,57,849, this being an increase of Rs. 3,93,117 over the amount of the previous 12 months.

The Feudatories of Kolhapur are as follows:

VISHALGAD, in the hands of Meherban Abajirao Pant Pratinidhi, who resides at Malkapur. The estate is 235 square miles in extent, the gross revenue is Rs. 2,54,558, and the inhabitants are 30,807 in number.

BAVDA, in the hands of Meherban Madhavrao Moreshwar Pant Amatya, who resides at Bavda. The estate is 243 square miles in extent, the gross revenue is Rs. 1,64,853, and the inhabitants are 45,465 in number.

KAGAL (Senior), in the hands of Meherban Pirajirao alias Bapusaheb Ghatge, C.S.I., C.I.E., Sarjerao Vajarat Ma-ab, who resides at Kagal and Kolhapur. The estate is 115·1 square miles in extent, the gross revenue is Rs. 3,40,257, and the inhabitants are 44,220 in number.

KAPSHI, in the hands of Meherban Santajirao, alias Balasaheb Ghorpade Senapati, who resides at Kapshi. The estate is 33·1 square miles in extent, the gross revenue is Rs. 1,11,452, and the inhabitants are 11,560 in number.

TORGAL, in the hands of Meherban Narsojirao, alias Balasaheb Shinde, Senakhaskhel. The estate is 137·2 square miles in extent, the gross revenue is Rs. 78,559.

CHALKARANJI, in the hands of Meherban Narayanrao Govind Ghorpade, Pant Sachiva. The estate is 241 square miles in extent, the gross revenue is Rs. 5,20,790, and the inhabitants are 59,641 in number.

KAGAL (Junior), in the hands of Meherban Dattajirao, alias Balasaheb Ghatge, Sarjerao. The estate is 17·3 square miles in extent, the gross revenue is Rs. 76,085, and the inhabitants are 6,333 in number.

HIMMAT BAHADUR'S ESTATE, in the hands of Meherban Udajirao, alias Abasaheb Chawan Himmat Bahadur, who resides at Kolhapur. The estate is 49·1 square miles in extent, the gross revenue is Rs. 70,672, and the inhabitants are 18,391 in number.

SARLASHKAR BAHADUR'S ESTATE, in the hands of Meherban Sultanrao Hanmantrao Nimbalkar, Sarlashkar Bahadur, who resides at Kolhapur. The estate is 21·6 square miles in extent, the gross revenue is Rs. 74,144, and the inhabitants are 5,859 in number.

The city of Kolhapur, the capital of the State, is about 190 miles distant from Poona by the Madras and Southern Mahratta Railway Company's system. It is picturesquely situated opposite a gap in the Sahyadri mountains through which cool sea breezes blow for the greater part of the year. The city is celebrated for its ancient shrines, particularly the one dedicated to Mahalakshmi, the external portions of which are now buried several feet below the level of the ground. Recent excavations have revealed many treasures of undoubted antiquity, such as, for example, a crystal casket bearing an inscription in characters which were in use at the time of the great King Asoka, who reigned in the third century prior to the Christian era. Several small temples of ancient construction have been unearthed during the present century, but complete details regarding these interesting discoveries have not yet been published.

H.H. SIR SHAHU CHHATRAPATI, MAHARAJA OF KOLHAPUR

KOLHAPUR occupies a very high rank among Indian States, as the Ruler is the direct descendant of Shivaji the Great, the founder of the Mahratta Empire, and bears the distinctive title of "Chhatrapati Maharaja." The Rajas of Kolhapur, who are Kshatriyas by caste, are the representatives of the junior branch of the family of Shivaji. After the death in 1700, of Rajaram (Shivaji's younger son, who was the head of the Mahratta power during the captivity of his nephew Shahu in the Moghul camp), his widow Tarabai placed her son Shivaji on the *gadi*. In 1707, Shahu, the rightful

THE STATE OF KOLHAPUR.

1. Ambabai's Temple. 2. Ahilyabai Girls' School. 3. Jotiba Temple.

heir, was released from the captivity of the Moghuls and came to Satara to claim the Mahratta Raj. After a struggle Shahu was successful, and fixed his capital at Satara. Shivaji, with his ambitious mother, repaired to Kolhapur and established a separate principality for himself. He died in 1712, and was succeeded by Sambhaji, son of Rajaram's younger widow. The Kolhapur family, supported by Ramchandra Pant Amatya and other powerful Chiefs, made strenuous endeavours to retain its supremacy among the Mahrattas, but they were compelled to yield precedence to Shahu, who, by the Treaty of 1731, recognized Kolhapur as an independent State.

On the death of Sambhaji in 1760, the direct descendants of Shivaji became extinct. A member of the Bhosle family was adopted as successor under the name of Shivaji II, and the Dowager Rani, Jijabai, conducted the administration during the minority of her adopted son. After her death in 1772 the young Raja was, for a long while, engaged in war with other States, particularly with the Patwardhans, the Sanwant, and the Nipanikar; and, moreover, his government was weakened by internal factions. On several occasions during these struggles, the British Government was requested to interfere, but it declined to do so. In 1811, during a war between the Nipanikar and Kolhapur, when the British Resident at Poona was engaged in the settlement of the Southern Mahratta country, peace was negotiated between the contending parties, and the Raja of Kolhapur concluded a treaty of friendship with the British Government. Shivaji II died in 1812, and was succeeded by Sambhaji II or Abasaheb (1812–21), and the latter was followed by Shahaji or Buwasaheb (1821–38). On his death in 1838, a Council of Regency was formed to govern the State during the minority of his successor Shivaji III, or Babasaheb; but the members of the Council disagreed and the British Government appointed a minister of its own selection in 1844.

It was only after this event that Kolhapur enjoyed some peace and happiness. It remained as a faithful ally of the British Government during the critical times of the Mutiny in 1857. A treaty, whereby the Maharaja of Kolhapur agreed to be guided by the advice of the Paramount Power in all important matters, was concluded with the British Government in 1862, when the administration of the State was handed over to its Ruler, Shivaji III, who died in 1866. He was succeeded by Rajaram, who died at Florence in 1870 during his tour in Europe. His widow adopted Shivaji IV, who also did not live long. He died at Ahmednagar, and was succeeded, by adoption, by the present Maharaja, His Highness Colonel Sir Shahu Chhatrapati Maharaja.

His Highness the Chhatrapati Maharaja was installed on the *gadi* with full powers, except in regard to capital punishment, on April 2, 1894, by His Excellency Lord Harris, the then Governor of Bombay. The restriction in criminal powers requiring the sanction of the Bombay Government to sentences of death was removed in 1895, and in the same year the title of G.C.S.I. was conferred on His Highness by Her Majesty the late Queen-Empress. In 1900 His Excellency the Viceroy and Governor-General of India conferred upon His Highness the title of "Maharaja" as an hereditary distinction. Two years later His Highness was invited to England on the occasion of the Coronation of His Majesty the late King-Emperor Edward VII. During His Highness' sojourn in England the University of Cambridge conferred upon him the honorary degree of LL.D., and the Royal Agricultural Society of England marked their appreciation of His Highness' keen interest in agriculture by making him an honorary member. The high distinction of G.C.V.O. was conferred upon him at Delhi in 1903, and that of G.C.I.E. was bestowed by His Majesty the King-Emperor George V, on the occasion of the Coronation Durbar at Delhi, in 1911. The year 1903 was also marked with the appreciation by Government of His Highness' administration by their withdrawal from the exercise of residuary criminal jurisdiction in the feudatory Jahagirs, which was reserved by the Government of Bombay by section 8 of the Articles of Agreement of 1862.

The military force of the State consists of two separate establishments: (1) the Kolhapur Infantry, commanded by two Europeans, numbering 553; and (2) the Cavalry, known as the red-coated *Risala* or His Highness' bodyguard with 156 horsemen, under the command of a State officer, designated Risaldar-Major. There are 57 guns in all, of which only 10 are mounted and used for purposes of salutes.

In 1918-19 the net receipts, exclusive of alienations, debts, deposits, and other items, amounted to Rs. 38,00,017, while the net expenditure amounted to Rs. 43,22,859.

Inclusive of its Feudatory States, the area of the Kolhapur State is 3,217·1 square miles in extent, and it comprises 1,079 villages, with a population of 8,33,441 persons, according to the census of 1911. The capital town is Kolhapur, originally called Karvir, with 45,000 inhabitants.

The Maharaja is entitled to a salute of 19 guns, and holds a patent, or *sanad*, of adoption. The present Maharaja's salute was increased by two guns on January 1, 1909, as a personal honour, in recognition of His Highness' loyalty to the British Throne.

The Kolhapur State, under the *regime* of the present Maharaja, far from adding to the cares and anxieties of the British Raj, is being administered with great success; its people are contented, and the Maharaja has shown by his acts that he is worthy of the trust reposed in him. He has proved an intelligent and upright Ruler, fully alive to the duties of his position. There is probably no State in India where the Ruler and the ruled are on more satisfactory terms, or in which the great principle (upon which His Highness has always acted) that government should be for the happiness of the governed, received a greater measure of practical recognition. He feels genuine interest in the real welfare of the masses, whose cause he always fearlessly advocates.

There is, perhaps, no better test of the soundness of an administration than its ability to pass, without discredit, through a period of exceptional difficulty. The Kolhapur State has, on many occasions during the present Maharaja's reign, encountered such trials, and has each time surmounted them successfully. Whenever such calamities occurred, so effectual were the measures taken by His Highness' direction, that his Minister, whose energy and administrative capacity are of the highest order, has been able to report to him that during such periods the death-rate did not rise above normal, and that there were no deaths clearly traceable to starvation. But this is not all. Advantage is taken of the opportunity thus offered, to set on foot a system of relief works, under which the water supply available for the use of His Highness' subjects has been permanently improved, with the result that the danger to be apprehended from future periods of scarcity has been largely diminished.

THE STATE OF KOLHAPUR.

1. Rankal's Tank. 2. General View of Panhala Fort from the Residency. 3. Ruins of Old Fort and Gateway, Panhala. 4. Hill Sanitorium.

His Highness the Maharaja has shown himself mindful of the best interests of the people committed to his charge; good progress has been made with the important work of revenue settlement, which was only half completed when His Highness succeeded; new roads have been constructed, hospitals and dispensaries have been opened; attention has been paid to the improvement of the breeds of cattle, and, lastly, the State has liberally supported educational institutions.

The relations of the Kolhapur Durbar with the Government of India have always been specially cordial. The Kolhapur State upon more than one occasion in its history has given evidence of its deep loyalty and attachment to the Government and its loyalty to the Crown, and it has been of great help to Government in rooting out sedition.

Since His Highness' installation on the *gadi* 24 years ago, he has borne a high character as a Ruler and has displayed many qualities which call for sincere admiration. Among these may be mentioned more especially the generosity which he has shown to all useful public institutions, whether within the limits of his State or not. His Highness, apart from being a Ruler of high character, is a kind and thoughtful host, whose hospitality the officials have many times enjoyed.

In other respects the administration of Kolhapur under the present Maharaja has been most creditable to those concerned in it. The finances of the State, the condition of which must at one time have occasioned His Highness some uneasiness, have been placed on a sound basis; crime and outlawry have been put down, and His Highness has personally bestowed much attention upon the wise project for reclaiming the criminal tribes. Courts of justice have been established not only at the capital, but also throughout the State, and are working under well-considered rules.

The Maharaja is fond of ancient forms of *shikar*, such as hawking, hunting the cheetah, pig-sticking, elephant fights (for which a special arena has been put up), and tiger shooting, which are his favourite kinds of sport. He is an excellent horseman, and made a record ride to Mahableshwar, a distance of 114 miles, in eight hours.

In private life His Highness the Maharaja is very unostentatious, amiable, and courteous, and he is dearly loved by all those who come in contact with him.

The Maharaja has one son, Rajaram Maharaja, his heir-apparent, and Shivaji Maharaja, his second son, died as the result of an accident while pig-sticking on June 12, 1918. His Highness has one daughter, who is married to His Highness the Maharaja of Dewas (Senior), and is the mother of a son, the heir-apparent of the Dewas Raj.

WAR SERVICE RENDERED BY THE STATE

Recruiting work was carried on by Regimental Parties, single-handed, under the supervision of British Officers. But it was afterwards found advisable to secure the co-operation of the local Civil authorities, a measure which was promptly adopted. But this did not much improve matters. Meharban Pirajirao Bapusaheb *Jagirdar* of Kagal Senior was, therefore, entrusted with the work. He took it up wholeheartedly, and with his usual energy and zeal laboured night and day and achieved splendid success. Several arbitration courts to summarily decide matters of a judicial nature were opened. This gave no small stimulus to the recruiting work. In February, 1918, the work of arbitration was handed over to Shri Yuvaraj Maharaja and his brother, the late lamented Shri Shivaji Maharaj. They followed suit, with the result that the total number of recruits enlisted came to 1,926. The expenses incurred by the Durbar in this connection amounted to Rs. 80,000 all told.

Besides this, Rs. 39,527 were collected by voluntary subscription for the purchase of five ambulance cars to be presented to Government. The Durbar contributed a sum of Rs. 82,739 to Imperial War Relief Fund; Rs. 16,147 to Women's Branch; Rs. 14,731 to "Our Day" Fund; Rs. 8,174 to the Silver Wedding Fund; and Rs. 6,024 to Lady Willingdon's War Relief Fund. His Highness also contributed some articles of the value of Rs. 5,318 to the War Fête, Bombay, and Rs. 1,000 to the Lucky Bag at Hyderabad opened by Mrs. Fraser. In addition to this, the Kolhapur Durbar purchased War Bonds to the value of Rs. 5,54,200, and the Kolhapur public subscribed Rs. 13,80,417 to the War Loan.

JAGNIVAS WATER PALACE, FROM THE NORTH-EAST.

THE STATE OF UDAIPUR (MEWAR)

UDAIPUR is the premier Indian State in the Province of Rajputana. It is bounded on the north by the British district of Ajmer; on the north-west by a portion of the British district of Ajmer and by Marwar; on the west by the States of Marwar and Sirohi; on the south-west by the States of Danta and Idar; on the south by the States of Dungarpur and part of Banswara; on the south-east by the States of Partabgarh and Gwalior; on the east by the States of Tonk, Gwalior, Indore, and parts of Jhalawar, Kotah, and Bundi; and on the north-east by the State of Bundi and a portion of Jaipur.

The districts of Indore, Gwalior, and Tonk, bordering on the east, originally belonged to Mewar. In the same way Gorwad, a part of Marwar, on the west, belonged to Mewar, and a part of Mewar is also included in Merwara.

The Maharana, for that is the title of the ruler of Mewar, holds the highest rank among the Rajputs, and Hindus universally recognize him as the legitimate heir to the throne of the deified Rama, styling him *Hindua Suraj*, or "Sun of the Hindus." Genealogists, in tracing the history of the Rulers of Udaipur, usually commence with Ikshvaku, king of Ajodhya (now the Province of Oudh), the son of the great Manu, "the progenitor of the Sun-born race," from whom a large number of illustrious princes claim descent. Most prominent of these successors was Shri Rama, whose heroic feats of skill and chivalrous valour led his subjects to deem him an incarnation of the Deity, and to worship him as "the embodiment of the Divine Spark."

Lava, the eldest son of Rama, transferred the seat of government to Lahore, the present capital of the Punjab, and the branch from which the Princes of Udaipur are descended, resided there until Kanksen migrated to the Province of Gujrat. The last-named Chief, in the year 144 A.D., deposed a Mori Parmar Ruler, and usurping the throne, made himself master of an extensive tract of country. He built the city of Vadnagar, which he made his capital, and four generations later his successor, Vijaysen, founded the famous city of Vallabhipur. Several rulers in succession, of whom little is known, occupied the palace at Vallabhipur, but about the year 523, when Shiladitya VI was monarch, the territory was invaded and plundered by foreign hosts, and the beautiful capital was razed to the ground. Pushpavati, the favourite consort of the Ruler, and a daughter of the Parmar Prince of Chandravati, happened to be at that time visiting the shrine of Amba-Bhawani, in the present State of Danta, and was already pregnant. She alone of the royal household escaped destruction. Shortly after this date the Queen gave birth to a son, who was entrusted to the care of Kamlawati, a Brahmin lady residing at Vadnagar.

The infant received the name of Goha, or "cave-born," and as he grew in years

H.H. MAHARAJADHIRAJA MAHARANA SIR FATEH SINGH BAHADUR, G.C.S.I., G.C.I.E., OF UDAIPUR (MEWAR).

1 THE LATE MAHARANA H.H. MAHARANA PRATAP SINGHJI 1.
2. MAHARAJ KUNWAR SHRI PHUPAL SINGHJI BAHADUR.
(Heir-Apparent.)

he began a wandering life in the jungles in company with the Bhils of Idar, who were of a turbulent and predatory nature. Goha became a great favourite with the Bhils, who formed such extravagant ideas of his martial spirit that they proposed to make him king of Idar, over which territory one of their own tribe then ruled. Eventually the old forest chief drew blood from his own finger, and smearing it upon the forehead of Goha, installed him on the *gadi* of Idar. Goha's name became the patronymic of his descendants, who have from that time been termed Gehlote Rajputs.

During the rulership of Aparajit, a successor of Goha, the Bhils killed their own Ruler while out hunting, and once again Idar and its citadel fell into the hands of the predatory Bhils. In referring to this event, Col. Tod, in his "Annals and Antiquities of Rajasthan," says: "The descendants of Kamlavati (the Vadnagar Brahmini) who retained the priestly office in the family, were again the preservers of the line of Vallabhi." On the death of Aparajit, his infant son, Bappa, was conveyed for safety to Nagda, where the infant and his mother lived under the protection of the family priest, Vasishta Rawal. Nagda is situated at a distance of 13 miles from the spot upon which the present famous citadel of Udaipur is erected. In 734 Bappa took Chittor from the then reigning Mori Chief, Raja Man Singh, and himself ascended the throne of Mewar. Bappa succeeded in adding to his territory by making various conquests, his victorious army penetrating on one occasion as far as the kingdom of Persia. Bappa assumed the titles of "Sun of the Hindus," "Preceptor of Princes," and "Universal Lord." He also added the designation of Rawal to the name of his race in memory of his family priest, Vashishta Rawal. Bappa died in 753.

During the following three centuries after the death of Bappa, much of the history of Mewar is unfortunately buried in oblivion. In the twenty-fifth generation after Bappa, authentic information is obtained of Samarsingh, who ruled from 1274 to 1284, and who was followed by his son, Ratan Singh. The latter's reign is memorable owing to the fact that the city of Chittor was twice attacked by the Khiliji Emperor, Ala-ud-Din, and although it was not actually sacked on the first occasion, its safety was only secured at the cost of the lives of the majority of its brave defenders. This assault took place in 1303. Historians agree in saying that the Moslem Emperor, Ala-ud-Din, of Delhi, assailed Chittor, not for the gain of the city, but in order that he might carry away as a prize the extremely beautiful Queen Padamni, wife of Ratan Singh. The Emperor devised many tricks and plans to gain his object, but he was foiled in all his attempts, and he then threatened that he would destroy Chittor unless he accomplished his purpose. The treacherous Emperor seized Ratan Singh, and thrust him into prison. This crafty action provoked the adoption of a ruse by the valiant men of Chittor, who succeeded in defeating the threatening Moslem Emperor, and in liberating Ratan Singh. Ala-ud-Din, however, was not a man to bear opposition calmly, and once again he laid siege to the fortress, attacking the walls with a large number of selected troops. The chivalrous Rajputs were determined to fight to the last drop of blood; they attacked with desperate valour against fearful odds, and the Rana and his faithful warriors, rushing upon the powerful enemy, were mercilessly cut down by them. The faithful Rajput wives within the fort realized the awful position in which they were now situated, and rather than fall into the hands of the Mahomedans, to be carried away to Delhi to work as slaves, they preferred death, and therefore they prepared a funeral pyre in the subterranean passages of the fort, and one by one they committed themselves to the flames.

There was then no obstacle to the victor's entrance into the fort, but what an entry! battered walls and buildings, desolate halls, and widespread ruin, while the ashes of noble women testified to their marvellous courage and their unswerving loyalty to their lords.

Ratan Singh was succeeded on the throne by Karan Singh, who had two sons, Mahap and Rahap. Bhuvan Singh, seventh in order of generation from Rahap, recovered Chittor, and in the time of Maharana Laxman Singh, third in order of generation from Bhuvan Singh, Chittor was again attacked by the Emperor Mahomad Tuglaq of Delhi, in 1326. In this battle Laxman Singh was killed, together with his sons, excepting the youngest, Ajai Singh, who had been previously sent away to the hills, far away from Chittor. Ajai Singh was succeeded by his nephew, Hamir Singh, who remained at Kelwada, at which place Ajai Singh had set up a *gadi* for himself. After the capture of Chittor by the Mahomedans, the Emperor Mahomad Tuglaq appointed one Maldeo, Raja of Jalore, to be his Viceroy at the late capital of Chittor.

Hamir Singh married Maldeo's daughter, and it was through her that her husband was successful in retaking the fort of Chittorgarh. The Mahomedan Emperor of Delhi was soon apprised of the capture of Chittor, and, raging with anger, he turned the head of his army in the direction of the city, in order that he might wrest it from the Rajputs.

Hamir Singh marched boldly with his army to meet the Mahomedan forces, and in the terrific battle which followed he pressed back the Imperial troops, and ultimately defeated them with great slaughter. The Emperor Mahomad Tuglaq was captured, and kept in confinement in the fortress of Chittor, and was only liberated some three months later on his surrendering several important towns, in payment of a sum of Rs. 50,00,000 in cash, and on presentation to Hamir Singh of 100 elephants.

After Hamir Singh came a succession of rulers, who, amid troubled conditions, maintained the Rajput traditions of bravery.

The State reached the zenith of its prosperity in the reign of Sangram Singh I, who succeeded to the *gadi* in 1508. In 1527 an exceedingly fierce battle took place between the Mahomedans, led by Babar, the founder of the Moghul Empire, and the Rajputs of the district, who had attached themselves to the standard of the Maharana. The Imperial troops were unable to withstand the furious onslaughts of the Rajputs and their ranks were considerably thinned by heavy losses, the Emperor sustaining a decisive defeat. In the same year Babar renewed his attack on Mewar with fresh forces, and the tide of fortune was on this occasion turned by the treachery of a Rajput *Sardar*, who assisted the Mahomedan with his followers. The Rajputs were compelled to retire, although the Maharana fought with an almost diabolical fury, forcing his way into the thickest part of the conflict, but he seemed to bear a charmed life, which remained wondrously vigorous notwithstanding the severe wounds which covered nearly the whole of his body. Sangram found refuge in the Aravali mountains, where he solemnly vowed that he would not again enter Chittor until he had gained a complete victory over the followers of Islam. Poison, administered

THE STATE OF UDAIPUR (MEWAR).

1. A View of the City from the Palace. 2. Another View of the City.

THE STATE OF UDAIPUR (MEWAR).

1. The Palace, from the North-east. 2. Palace, with Tripolia Gate.

THE STATE OF UDAIPUR (MEWAR).

1. Shiv Nivas Palace: No. 5 Room, Interior View. 2. Palace: The New Minto Hall and Shambhu Nivas, from the Lake. 3. Palace from the Lake, North-west.

to the Chief by a menial, robbed the Maharana of his ability to redeem his sacred promise.

In 1567, during the reign of Udai Singh, the territory of the Maharana was invaded by Akbar, Emperor of Delhi, and Udai Singh, hearing of the approaching invasion, left Chittor, and retreated to the hills. The army of Mewar that remained behind in Chittor met the Imperial forces, and in the battle that ensued the chivalrous Rajputs fell while fighting heroically. Rao Patta, Jaimel Rathor, and others died for the cause of their master, after gallantly thinning the ranks of the Imperial forces. The fortress fell into the possession of the Emperor. Udai Singh constructed the Udaisagar (lake) in 1559, and the famous capital of the State, named Udaipur, was built not far away from this sheet of water.

Udai Singh was succeeded in 1572 by his son, Pratap Singh, who found himself without a kingdom to govern, or a capital city where he might set up his standard of authority. He, however, in furtherance of a determination to attempt the recovery of Chittor, gathered round him a considerable number of the nobles of the State, and on several occasions made attacks upon Akbar's forces. He expired in 1597, and his death brought Amar Singh on the throne of Mewar in the same year. He, too, like his predecessors, at first refused to accept the sovereignty of the Delhi Emperor, and many times he repulsed his invading forces, but when the major part of his forces was annihilated, and his country was laid desolate, as the Maharana's forces always made raids upon the enemy with great fury and gallantry, the Maharana acceded to the repeated entreaties of his son, Karan Singh, in 1615, and made peace with Jehangir, Emperor of Delhi.

On Amar Singh's death, in 1620, Karan Singh ascended the throne. During his *regime* the condition of the State improved, and the country was re-inhabited. Prince Khurram (afterwards the Emperor Shahjahan) sought the protection of this Maharana, when he incurred the displeasure of his father, Jehangir.

Jagat Singh followed Karan Singh on the throne, and he in turn was succeeded by Raj Singh.

During the great civil war which ensued in connection with the succession, on the death of the Emperor Shahjahan, the Maharana of Udaipur, Raj Singh, with many other Rajput potentates, took the part of Prince Dara, the rightful heir, and thus they incurred the hatred of the other brothers. In this reign the Maharana threw off all allegiance to Delhi, and directed the affairs of the State without any reference to Moghul authority.

When Aurungzeb succeeded as Emperor of Delhi he became intensely bitter against those of Hindu faith, and in a proclamation he imposed the hateful *Jezeya*, or capitation tax, on the whole Hindu race, this act drawing from Maharana Raj Singh the protest which is historic.

The effect of the high-spirited appeal of the Maharana acted as fresh fuel placed upon a fire, and the Emperor called forth the bravest of his soldiers with the object of teaching a lesson to the Udaipur Maharana. The latter was not in any way perturbed, and he rallied the flower of his army, but, fearing that his followers might not be numerically sufficient to overcome the Imperial army he resolved upon stratagem to defeat the foe. He sallied forth to meet Aurungzeb, and, simulating retreat, he drew the relentless foe into a narrow defile, when he killed the majority of the enemy, and pursued the remainder to the very gates of Delhi. Maharana Raj Singh died in 1681.

Sangram Singh ruled from 1716 to 1734, and in his reign the powerful Moghul Empire was dismembered. During this *regime* Udaipur was more highly respected, and the greater portion of her lost territories was regained. The power of the Mahrattas had at this period become exceedingly strong in Rajputana, and when their army invaded Udaipur in 1735 the troops plundered and laid waste lands in every direction. These raids produced disunion among the feudatory Rajputs, and the helpless Maharana Jagat Singh was compelled to make peace with his new adversaries. Predatory bands of this warlike race continued to harass Udaipur, however, during the succeeding three decades, and in 1770 Sindhia of Gwalior advanced into Udaipur and laid siege to the capital city. Maharana Arsi resisted the attack as long as possible, but at length he was obliged to mortgage a considerable portion of the State in order to raise a large sum of money to secure Sindhia's withdrawal to his own country. This respite from raids was only short-lived, and the Maharana, Bhim Singh, growing tired of the unbearable misery and desolation that attended every inroad of the Mahrattas, resolved in 1818 to seek an alliance with the British Government.

The advancement and prosperity of Udaipur had been seriously checked by the numerous wars of spoliation and desolation which preceded the signing of the treaty, and the Paramount Power deemed it advisable to appoint an Agent (temporarily) to administer the affairs of Udaipur, and endeavour as far as possible to evolve order out of chaos.

The Government selected Lieut.-Col. James Tod, the famous author of "Annals and Antiquities of Rajasthan," for the newly-created office. His able control of affairs introduced an era of great prosperity, and the fiscal reforms introduced by him were so thoroughly sound and effective that the revenues of Udaipur were doubled in amount in less than three years.

Maharana Bhim Singh died in 1828, and was followed on the *gadi* by Jawan Singh, Sardar Singh, and then by Sarup Singh, in whose reign the British Government remitted a portion of the tribute which had been fixed in 1818. The same Maharana rendered most valuable assistance to the British Government in the suppression of the Sepoy Mutiny of 1857. Sarup Singh died without leaving issue in 1861, and as the successor to the *gadi*, Shambhu Singh, nephew of the previous Ruler, was then only 17 years of age, the administration of the State was entrusted to a Council of Regency. When full ruling powers were granted in 1865, it was found that owing to the prudent management of affairs, the State treasury had a surplus of Rs. 30,00,000, which included the surplus of Rs. 13,00,000 left by Maharana Sarup Singh, who gave away Rs. 4,00,000 in charity on his death-bed. The Maharana was created a Knight Grand Commander of the Most Exalted Order of the Star of India, and he was also granted a *sanad* of adoption. Universal regret was felt in the year 1874, when this promising career was terminated by the hand of death. There was no male issue of the late Maharana, and therefore Prince Sajjan Singh was appointed to the *gadi*.

This reign was made notable by the commencement of a system of land settlement, by inaugurating schemes for the construction of irrigation works, and by the introduction of many useful measures of reform. His Excellency Lord Northbrook, Viceroy and Governor-General of India, paid a visit to Udaipur in the year 1876, and in January 1877 His Highness attended the Imperial Assemblage held at Delhi by His Excellency Lord Lytton,

THE STATE OF UDAIPUR (MEWAR).

1. Palace: View from the South. 2. Gangaur Ghat, from the West. 3. Shambhu Nivas Palace from the North.

THE STATE OF UDAIPUR (MEWAR).

1. Padmini Palace, Chittor. 2. Lake View, from the South-east. 3. Jagmandir Water Palace, from the East. 4. Lake View, from the East.

THE STATE OF UDAIPUR (MEWAR).

1. Jagdish Temple. 2. Fountains—Sahelion-Ki-Bari (Inside). 3. Fountains—Sahelion-Ki-Bari (Outside). 4. Victoria Hall and Museum, Udaipur.

in honour of the assumption of the title of "Empress of India" by Her Majesty the late Queen Victoria. On this occasion the salute of the Maharana was raised from 19 guns to 21 as a mark of distinction. In 1881 the Maharana was created a Knight Grand Commander of the Most Exalted Order of the Star of India, he being decorated with the insignia at Chittor by Lord Ripon, who went there for the purpose. The Maharana unfortunately died three years later at the early age of 26, and in the absence of male issue Prince Fateh Singh of Shivarati, a descendant of Maharana Sangramsingh, was adopted as successor, his full title being His Highness Maharaja-Dhiraj Maharana Sir Fateh Singh, Bahadur, G.C.S.I., G.C.I.E., G.C.V.O.

His Highness was for a few months assisted in the administration of the State by the Resident, and he was shortly afterwards invested with full ruling powers. In 1887 the Maharana was decorated with the insignia of a Knight Grand Commander of the Most Exalted Order of the Star of India. Ten years later he was accorded a personal salute of 21 guns, and at the Imperial Durbar, held at Delhi in 1911, he was created a Knight Grand Commander of the Most Eminent Order of the Indian Empire. He was appointed a Knight Grand Commander of the Victorian Order in 1918, and the local salute of the State was increased from 19 guns to 21 in the year 1921.

On the occasion of the visit of His Majesty the King-Emperor to India, when Prince of Wales, he was most enthusiastically received at Udaipur, and at a State banquet given in honour of the Royal Guest, His Highness the Maharana delivered a memorable speech.

Among the Chiefs of Rajputana His Highness the Maharana is held in the greatest esteem, and he is accredited as the leading representative of Hinduism in the Province.

It is a justifiably proud assertion of the Maharana of Udaipur that not one of his predecessors ever gave his daughter in marriage to a Mahomedan Emperor, nor contracted such alliance with a daughter of any Rajput family who had entered into a similar foreign alliance, nor gave his daughter to such Rajput families.

His Royal Highness the Duke of Connaught paid a visit to Udaipur in 1889, and in the following year His Royal Highness Prince Albert Victor visited the capital.

The following Viceroys paid visits to Udaipur, namely: Lord Lansdowne in 1890, Lord Elgin in 1896, Lord Curzon in 1902, Lord Minto in 1909, Lord Hardinge in 1912, and Lord Chelmsford in 1916.

It may be of interest to refer very briefly to some important works of construction carried out during the reign of the present Maharana. A railway line has been constructed from Chittor to Udaipur, and in the capital city the Shivniwas palace has been built as an addition to the main block of the original palace; and Minto Hall has been built since the year 1909 for the holding of large Durbars. At Chittor, a palace on the fort, as well as a protecting wall, are in course of erection, and on the summit of the Aravali hills there is the famous fort of Kumalgarh, where the Maharana also constructed a palace. Many tanks have been made for irrigation purposes, the largest of which is the Fatehsagar lake, the foundation of the *bund* being laid by His Royal Highness the Duke of Connaught in 1889. A sum of Rs. 1,00,000 is sanctioned annually in the State budget for expenditure in the Irrigation Department, but this sum is always considerably exceeded. There has been a great improvement in the financial condition of the State, and there is a larger surplus in the Treasury at the present time than there has been in any former reign.

The State of Udaipur has an area of about 12,690 square miles, and fully 80 per cent. of the population of 12,72,568 persons are classed as Hindus.

The physical aspects of the country vary very considerably; for example, in the northern and eastern portions one sees an elevated plateau marked by rocky hills covered with jungle; and the mountainous tract in the south-west embraces the wildest part of the Aravalis. This range enters the State from Merwara, at a height of 2,400 feet, and a breadth of only a few miles, but its course is then extended in a south-westerly direction along the borders of the State of Jodhpur, where it attains a width of nearly 60 miles. The far eastern side of Udaipur may be described as a cluster of hills, upon one of which stands the celebrated fort of Mandalgarh.

The principal rivers are the Banas, Chambal, Berach, Kothari, Jakham, Khari, Sabarmati, Wakal, and the Som. The Berach is an interesting stream from the fact that it rises at a point a few miles to the north of the capital city, it flows through the Udaisagar (lake), passes the fort of Chittor, and after a course of about 130 miles it joins the Banas near Mandalgarh. Its banks are rendered especially attractive on account of its fine natural scenery, consisting of rich vegetation, among which may be seen at intervals handsome residences and the domes of many sacred shrines.

There are also a number of pretty lakes, among which may be mentioned the Jaisamand, the Rajsamand, the Pichhola, the Udaisagar, and the Fateh Sagar.

The bund of the Jaisamand is 1,300 feet in length, and 350 feet in width, and 120 feet in height. The lake is 102 feet in depth, and the area of the land under water is 21 square miles in extent.

The bund of the Raj Samand is 1,000 feet in length, 374 feet in width, and 73 feet in height. The lake is 55 feet in depth, and the land under water covers an area of three square miles.

Archæologists will find much to interest them in Udaipur, although the work of exploration has not yet received the attention it deserves.

The State is divided for administrative purposes into 11 *zillas* and six *parganas*. It also includes the Bhumat of Kherwara and Kotra, held by petty Girasia Chieftains. There are 24 *Jagirdars* of the first class, including Bhai Betas (Kinsmen), and 32 nobles of the second class, and many other fief-holders.

Administration is carried on by the Maharana, assisted by two Ministers and their staff, who conjointly form an executive department, and a *Hakim* is in charge of each of the 17 divisions already mentioned.

Proceedings in civil and criminal courts are guided generally by ancient Hindu law and local customs, but the codes and regulations in force in British India are frequently taken as the basis of decisions.

The practice of agricultural pursuits claims the attention of nearly 60 per cent. of the inhabitants, but the methods of cultivation are still of a somewhat primitive character, and few occupiers have realized the advantages to be derived from the use of modern farming implements.

In the absence of authenticated State statistics, it is estimated that there are about 2,500 square miles of land under settlement, and that of this quantity 743 square miles are placed under cultivation in a normal season. About one-fourth of the cultivated area is irrigated, chiefly

THE STATE OF UDAIPUR (MEWAR).

1. Hotel Udaipur. 2. Walter Zenana Hospital. 3. H.H. The Maharana's High School. 4. Lansdowne Hospital.

THE STATE OF UDAIPUR (MEWAR).

1. Jain Tower, Chitor (Chota Kirtisthamba). 2 and 3. Carvings in Jagdish Temple. 4. Tower of Victory, Chitor, built by Rana Kumbha

THE STATE OF UDAIPUR (MEWAR).

1 and 2. Bund of Fateh Sagar Lake. 3. Bund of Fateh Sagar Lake (Overflow). 4. Jaisamudra Lake and Bund. 5. Rajsamudra Lake and Bund.

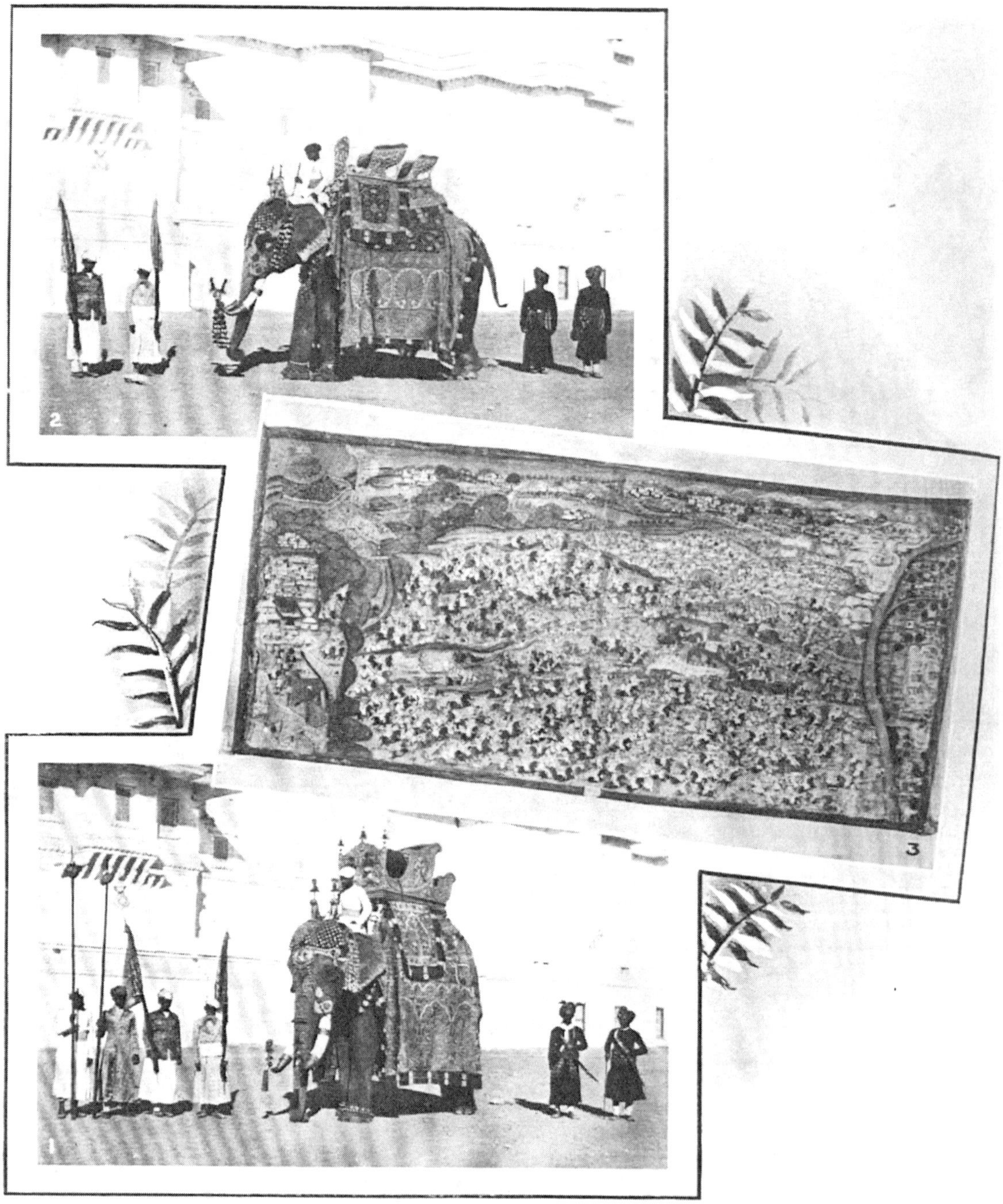

THE STATE OF UDAIPUR (MEWAR).

1 and 2. State Elephant. 3. Battle of Huldi Ghat (the most Historic Battle fought with the Moghul Forces).

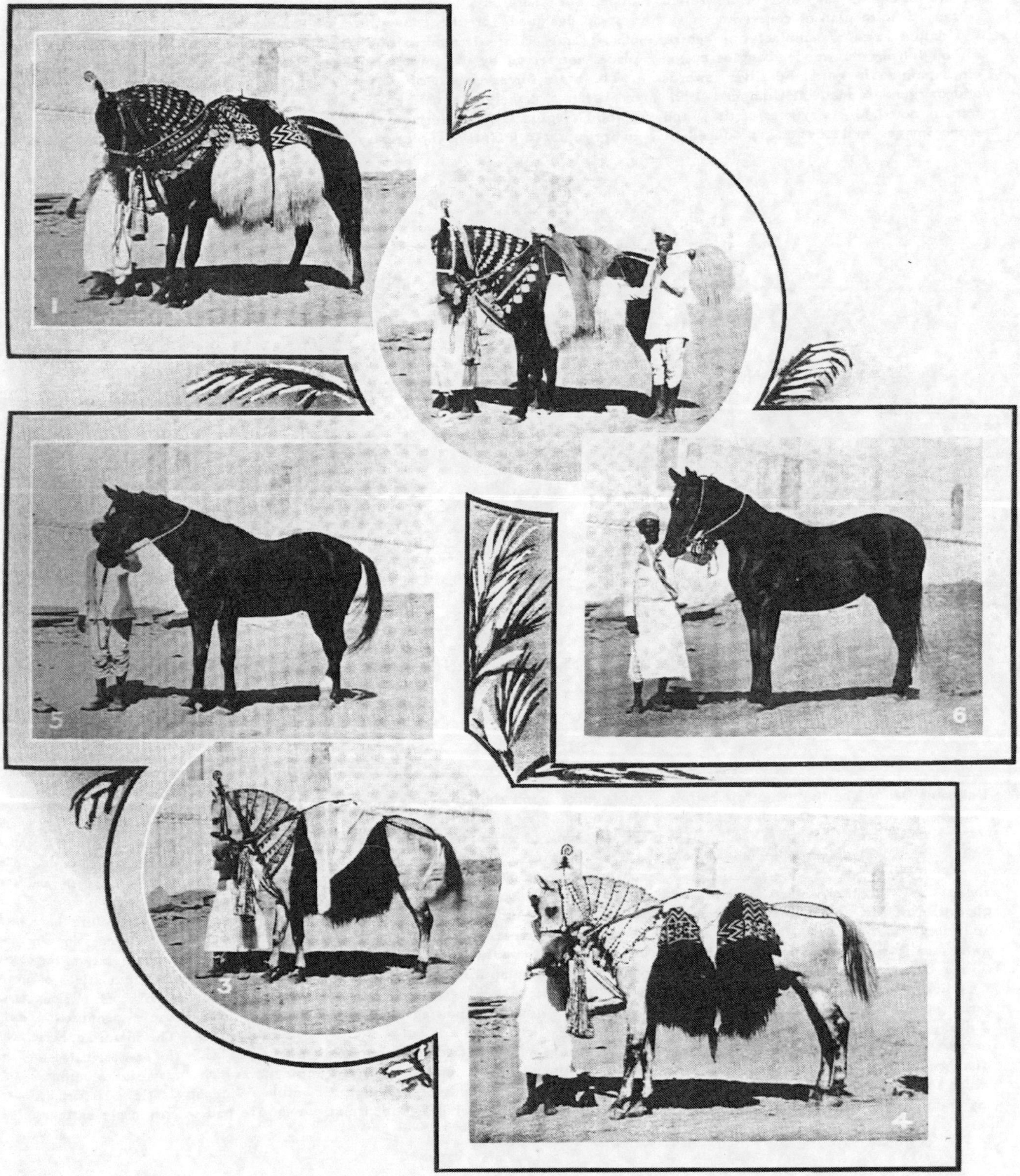

THE STATE OF UDAIPUR (MEWAR).

1 2 3, 4. State Horse with Ornaments. 5. "Red Lad," Presented by H.M. King George V. 6. "Expert," Presented by H.M. King George V.

from approximately 100,000 wells, 25,000 of which are in settled districts.

It is calculated that the forests in Udaipur cover an area of about 4,600 square miles, but they are not controlled by any definite plan of conservancy.

Udaipur is not a manufacturing centre, although ivory and wooden bangles, cotton cloth painted in gold and silver, swords and daggers are made at Udaipur; Bhilwara is noted for its articles of tin; and stone images and toys are produced at Rakhabh Deo. The State controls cotton ginning and pressing factories at Bhilwara, Kapasin, and Gulabpura.

The principal exports include wool, cotton, opium, *ghee*, cooking utensils, and sheep and goats, while considerable quantities of salt, sugar, tobacco, metals, and piece-goods are imported. The State owns and is responsible for the working of the Udaipur-Chittor Railway, which is 67 miles in length, and it has other transport facilities by the Rajputana-Malwa Railway, which traverses the eastern half of the State from north to south for a distance of 82 miles, in the course of which there are 10 stations. The Durbar maintains more than 140 miles of metalled roads, and nearly 300 miles of country highways.

There are 40 British post offices—four of which are also telegraph offices—in the State, but there is also a local postal system designed for the conveyance of official and private letters to and from places not served by the Imperial offices.

The State forces consist of 6,015 men of all ranks, namely, 2,549 Regulars, and 3,466 Irregulars. The former of these comprise 1,750 infantry, 566 cavalry, and 239 gunners, and the latter are made up of 3,000 infantry and 466 cavalry. There are 128 guns, of which 50 are serviceable.

The progress made in educational matters has not been rapid. The State maintains 53 schools for boys and girls, while 10 others are supported entirely by Missionary Societies. The amount expended annually by the Education Department of the State approaches Rs. 40,000, one-half of which is recovered by means of a special tax assessed upon agriculturists in settled districts.

The capital of the State, Udaipur, or "city of sunrise," is beautifully situated on the slopes of a low ridge, overlooking the charming lake of Pichola. Maharana Udai Singh hastened to this part of the country after the fort of Chittor was taken by the Emperor Akbar in 1568, and the refuge which he built for himself amid the surrounding wooded hills was the commencement of the city. One of the most charming views in India is presented from the embankment of the lake, the palaces of the Maharana and the heir-apparent, the great temple of Jagannath, imposing residences of the nobility, and a number of elegant shrines, all of which, with their turrets, domes, and spires standing out clearly from the forest glades, are visible from a considerable distance. The palace of His Highness is an imposing pile, measuring 1,800 feet in length, and from 600 to 800 feet in width.

THE STATE OF UDAIPUR.
VIEW FROM KHAS ODI.

Additions to the structure have been made by each Chief in succession since the year 1571, the probable date of the oldest portion, but the different styles of architecture, representative of various eras, have rather curiously produced a most pleasing effect. The historian, Fergusson, says: "This is the largest palace in Rajputana, which in size and outline is not unlike Windsor Castle. Its details, however, are bad when closely examined, and

THE STATE OF UDAIPUR

it will not bear comparison with many other residences of Rajput Princes."

The Pichola lake, $2\frac{1}{2}$ miles in length, and $1\frac{1}{2}$ miles in width, is notable for two island palaces, known by the names of Jagmandir and Jagnivas, created respectively by Jagat Singh I in the seventeenth century, and by Jagat Singh II about 100 years later.

The former of these was the place of refuge for Prince Khurram (afterwards the Emperor Shahjahan) during the revolt of himself and his brothers against their father, Jehangir. The other edifice comprises a collection of small apartments, courts, and gardens, the last-named containing a large quantity of mango and other fruit trees, which form a perfect roof of overhead foliage. Another object of interest on the islands is a beautiful palace built entirely of 12 enormous slabs of pure marble; visitors rarely miss seeing the well-kept Sajjan-Niwas gardens; the handsome Victoria Hall, used as a library, reading room and museum; a statue of Her Majesty the late Queen Victoria, near the museum; the Maharana's High School, in which English, Sanskrit, and Persian are taught; the Lansdowne Hospital, built in 1894; the Shepherd Mission Hospital, 1886; the fine Walter Hospital for women, 1888; and the cenotaphs of several Chiefs of the State, which are at the old village of Ahar, near to the city.

Udaipur is a station on the Udaipur-Chittor branch of the Bombay-Baroda and Central India Railway, and is 185 miles distant from Ajmer.

About 12 miles distant in a northerly direction from Udaipur, in a narrow defile, is a shrine called "Eklinghji" (signifying, "one lingam"), erected in the eighth century by Bapa Rawal, and dedicated by him to Mahadeo. Inside the temple is a black marble figure of the divinity, represented by a bust and four faces. Since the time of Bapa Rawal the Maharanas of Udaipur have been *Diwans* or vice-Regents of Eklinghji, and in that capacity they supersede the high priest, and perform all ceremonies during each visit to the shrine made by them. About 300 yards distant from the temple is a very beautiful lake, on the picturesque banks of which are numerous smaller shrines.

Chittor, with its celebrated fortress, the object of numerous sieges, is about two miles distant from its railway station, which is the junction of the Rajputana-Malwa and the Udaipur-Chittor railway systems. The fort is an isolated mass of rock, some 500 feet above the surrounding plain, and extending from north to south for a distance of more than three miles. Travellers hold different opinions as to the builder of the fort, but tradition assigns it to Bhim, the second of the Pandavas. It was taken from the Moris by Bapa Rawal in the year 734, and remained the capital of the State until 1568, when Udaipur became the seat of Government. The fort was the scene of many bloody struggles, in which the gallant Rajputs fought for the maintenance of their independence, and on four separate occasions it was taken and sacked by Mussulmans.

About seven miles distant to the north of Chittor is the ancient village of Nagari, where a large number of coins, dating from a period anterior to the Christian era, have been found. Near to Nagari is a pyramidal column, called "Akbar's Lamp," which was built by the famous Emperor during his attack upon Chittor.

Nathdwara, or "portal of the God," a walled town situated on the right bank of the river Banas, and less than 30 miles distant from Udaipur city, possesses one of the most famous Vishnuvite shrines in India, in which is an image of Krishna, traditionally said to date from the twelfth century B.C.

The town is noted for its manufacture of ornaments of gold and silver, artistically decorated with coloured enamel, which are disposed of to worshippers.

IMPERIAL SERVICE MOUNTED ESCORT.

THE STATE OF BAHAWALPUR

THE Nawabs of the Mahomedan State of Bahawalpur (which lies between the Province of the Punjab and Rajputana) are Abbasi Daudputras, who claim descent from the Abbasi Khalifs of Egypt, and tradition is responsible for the story that the children of Abbas migrated via Khorassan and Makran to Rohri Bhakar in Sindh. Legendary accounts are strengthened very materially by existing records, which show that the tribe established themselves as progressive pioneers in their newly-acquired territory, making a special feature of agricultural development, which was only accomplished in an arid region by the construction of canals from the Indus river for the irrigation of their broad acres. Amir Chauni Khan, the thirty-sixth Ruler in descent from Abbas, had two sons, and from the elder, Daud Khan, sprang the line of Abbasi Daudputras, who founded the present State of Bahawalpur.

The modern history of the State dates from July 1866, when, on the death of the reigning Nawab, the administration was placed in British hands during the minority of his successor, Sadiq Mahomed Khan, then a boy of about four years of age.

It was at first arranged that the management of the State should be entrusted to the Commissioner of Multan, but it was shortly afterwards taken over by a Political Agent, acting under the supervision of the Punjab Government, who was faced with the task of re-organizing the whole of the internal affairs of the Principality. When Colonel Minchin became Political Agent in 1867, the State was in a most unsatisfactory condition. It is said that there were not more than two persons of influence in the whole Principality; there were no officials capable of being entrusted with important duties; the Treasury was empty, and salaries were greatly in arrear; the army was inclined to be mutinous; and a large proportion of the owners of land had migrated to other districts, where they had become annual tenants.

A marvellous improvement in the organization of each department under British supervision was soon manifested, and when only a few years had elapsed the State was brought into a flourishing condition. The Nawab attained his majority in November, 1879, when he was duly installed with full ruling powers by His Honour the Lieutenant-Governor of the Punjab.

Nawab Sadiq Mahomed Khan personally conducted the administration after his installation, and in 1879–80 he rendered efficient service to the British during the Afghan campaign.

His Highness received the personal thanks of the Government of India, and on the occasion of the visit to Bahawalpur in 1880 of His Excellency Lord Ripon, Viceroy and Governor-General of India, he was honoured by being created a Knight Grand Commander of the Most Exalted Order of the Star of India.

His Highness died in 1899, after a reign of about 20 years, but during the later portion of his life he unfortunately marred to some extent the successes of his early career by contracting a number of debts, which could scarcely be re-

RUKN-UD-DOULAH, HAFIZ-UL-MULK, NASRAT JANG, MUKHLIS-UD-DAULA, HIS HIGHNESS NAWAB HAJI SADIQ MAHOMED KHAN V, ABBASI.

1. RUKN-UD-DAULA, HAFIZ-UL-MULK, NASRAT JANG, MUKHLIS-UD-DAULA, HIS HIGHNESS NAWAB SIR SADIQ MAHOMED KHAN IV, ABBASI, G.C.S.I.

2. RUKN-UD-DAULA, HAFIZ-UL-MULK, NASRAT JANG, MUKHLIS-UD-DAULA, HIS HIGHNESS NAWAB HAJI MAHOMED BAHAWAL KHAN V, ABBASI.

THE STATE OF BAHAWALPUR.

1. Nur Mahal Palace. 2. Durbar Hall (Nur Mahal). 3. Nur Mahal Gardens.

garded as a desirable legacy for his successor, Nawab Mahomed Bahawal Khan V, who was only 16 years of age at the time of his father's death.

Colonel L. J. H. Grey, C.S.I., was appointed Superintendent of the State during the minority of the young Nawab, and in addition to his successful management, he succeeded in liquidating the liabilities of the former Chief.

The young Nawab studied for about four years at the Aitchison College, Lahore, after which he made himself acquainted with the duties of administering State affairs in order that he might be more fully prepared for the important duties which were soon to devolve upon him. His Highness was invested with full ruling powers on November 12, 1903, by His Excellency Lord Curzon, Viceroy and Governor-General.

During the period of minority the revenue of the State increased to Rs. 24,00,000, and on his accession His Highness proved himself to be a capable and energetic Ruler. There was universal grief in the State when it became known in February, 1907, that His Highness had died at Aden while returning from a pilgrimage to Mecca.

He was succeeded by his minor son, His Highness Haji Sadiq Mahomed Khan Bahadur V, Abbasi, Rukn-ud-Daula, Nasarat-i-Jang, Mukhlis-ud-Dau'a, Hafiz-ul-Mulk, who was born on September 30, 1904. It was decided to place the management of the State in the hands of a Council of Regency, consisting of Indian officials, the members being the President, Maulvi Haji Sir Rahim Baksh, K.C.I.E., Nawab Izat Nishan Khuda Buksh Khan, O.B.E., C.I.E. (Revenue Member), Diwan Asa Naud, Diwan Bahadur (Financial Member), and Khan Bahadur General Mahomed Abdul Rahman Khan (Military Member).

His Highness entered as a student at the Aitchison College, Lahore, and was placed under the guardianship of his tutor, Mr. E. M. Atkinson. He visited Mecca with his late father in 1906-07, and in 1913 he sailed for England with Mr. Atkins, formerly Political Agent in the Punjab, proceeding by way of Egypt, Italy, and France. During his stay in London he was received by the King-Emperor at Buckingham Palace. With the exception of a few weeks spent in paying a flying visit to India, His Highness remained in the Old Country for about two years, and his experiences of Western civilization, manners, customs, and political ideas cannot fail to be of service to him in his relations with his own subjects. His Highness attended the Royal Coronation Durbar held in Delhi in 1911, where he was accorded an interview with His present Majesty the King-Emperor, and during his vacations he has travelled much in Northern India.

His Highness the Nawab ranks second among the Ruling Chiefs of the Punjab, and he is entitled to a salute of 17 guns, as well as to visit and receive His Excellency the Viceroy and Governor-General of India.

The State of Bahawalpur, under the political control of the Bahawalpur Agency, is bounded on the north-east by the district of Ferozepore; on the east and south by the Rajputana States of Bikaner and Jaisalmer; on the south-west by Sind; and on the north-west by the Indus and Sutlej rivers. It has an area of about 17,285 square miles, and nearly two-thirds of the total acreage are either within the limits of the Great Indian Desert or consist of exceedingly light and sandy soil, which is practically useless for agricultural purposes, while the remainder of the land is a fertile alluvial tract in the valley of the Indus and Sutlej.

As the average annual rainfall rarely exceeds five inches, the production of all kinds of crops must necessarily depend to a very large extent upon irrigation, and at the time of writing the area watered by the elaborate canal system is about 800,000 acres in extent, equivalent to about 9·4 per cent. of the total area under cultivation.

The principal crops are wheat, rice, millet of various kinds, and gram, but a considerable amount of revenue is obtained from forests, which cover an area of 394,655 bighas, and from State gardens and plantations. The larger gardens are chiefly of a decorative character, but in others, as well as in nurseries, young timber trees and horticultural plants and shrubs are grown for subsequent transplantation in forests, by the sides of roads, and elsewhere in the State.

A project for utilizing the surplus water of the Lower Sutlej canal is now being considered by the Regency Council, and the materialization of this scheme would undoubtedly lead to a substantial increase in acreage of the cultivated area, and would thus be an additional source of revenue.

The Public Works Department, in charge of the chief engineer, Mr. J. C. Davis, is rendering excellent service in carrying out the construction of new buildings for civil purposes, of maintaining in good order the palace of His Highness and departmental structures, of extending or improving the means of irrigation, and of controlling the State workshops, ice and aerated water factories, and the carpenters' and smiths' shops. The total expenditure during the past year was Rs. 5,28,746.

The State is owner of a railway, 23 miles in length, from Khanpur to Chachran, which was opened in the year 1910, and although the earnings have been gradually increasing each year, they have not yet reached an amount large enough to enable the Council to regard it as a profitable concern.

The Imperial Service Camel Corps is sub-divided as follows: (1) baggage or transport corps, consisting of 372 officers and men, together with 966 camels; and (2) mounted escort with 276 officers, non-commissioned officers, men, and camp followers. The total strength of irregular forces maintained for ward and watch duties is the Bahawal guard of 454 men, the body-guard cavalry with 77 men, and the band with a total of 43 musicians.

In aid of the Allies in the Great War the camel escort served practically throughout the campaigns in Egypt and Palestine, having been amalgamated as infantry with the Alwar contingent.

The camel transport corps did splendid service in the Mahmud Frontier expedition in 1917, and in operations against the Marri tribes in the early portion of the following years, while other detachments were also sent at various times to East Africa and Mesopotamia. The State is now raising a second camel corps at its own expense; it has supplied more than 3,000 recruits to the British army for active field service, and it has—as in former years—proved to be an excellent field in which officers might purchase suitable camels.

Ornamental turbans, silk cloth, and metal cups are manufactured at Bahawalpur and Khanpur; porcelain vessels, shoes, and painted cloth are made at Ahmadpur East and Khairpur; and in various parts of the State there are mills for husking rice and ginning cotton. The chief exports are wheat, gram, indigo, dates, mangoes, and other fruits, wool, and saltpetre, while the principal imports are cloth and unrefined sugar.

The educational institutions in the State consist of the Sadiq Egerton College, and the High Schools at Bahawalpur, together

THE STATE OF BAHAWALPUR.

1. Sadiq Boarding House. 2. Sadiq Dane High School. 3. Military Hospital. 4. Bahawal Victoria Hospital.

THE STATE OF BAHAWALPUR.

1. Maulvi Haji Sir Rahim Bakhsh, K.C.I.E., President, Council of Regency, Bahawalpur State. 2. Daulat Khana, 3. Durbar Office (Bahawlgarh).

THE STATE OF BAHAWALPUR.

1. Daulat Khana Mosque. 2. Daulat Khana Gate. 3. Bahawal Club. 4. Polo Ground and Pavilion. 5. The European Guest House.

with five Anglo-vernacular middle schools, six vernacular middle schools, one Anglo-vernacular primary school, 100 vernacular primary schools, eight Arabic schools, one girls' school, and one training school. In addition, there is a mission school at Bahawalpur, teaching up to the Anglo-vernacular middle school standard, which receives a grant-in-aid for its maintenance, together with a number of scholarships from the Treasury for the encouragement of its students.

the town of Bahawalpur—in the State, and the total amount of income for the past year was Rs. 1,85,968, while the expenditure was Rs. 1,84,061. The sanitary conditions of the several towns have been placed on a satisfactory footing, and some years have elapsed since there was an epidemic of cholera, plague, or other serious disease. The members of the committee have full control over income and expenditure, but the Financial Member, in reviewing their work, states that

(which was established in 1870), and there are, in addition, three District Judges, and five first-class and three second-class *munsifs*.

The inhabitants are about 721,000 in number, of whom 80 per cent. are Mahomedans, and the principal languages spoken are Western Punjabi, Sindhi, and Marwari Rathi.

The total annual revenue of the State has now risen to about Rs. 34,00,000.

Maulvi Haji Rahim Bakhsh, the Presi-

THE STATE OF BAHAWALPUR.

1. Sadiq Egerton College. 2. Band and Guards.

The college above-mentioned prepares students for the first Arts examination of the Punjab University in English, mathematics, history, philosophy, Arabic, Persian, and Sanskrit.

The administration of the State is ordinarily carried on by the Nawab, who is assisted by a council of 11 members, of which the Mushir-i-ala, or Wazir, is President, and the various Ministerial Departments are those known as Foreign Revenue, Judicial, Finance, Commander-in-Chief's, State Forces, Public Works, the Nawab's Household, Private Secretary's, General Secretary's, and Irrigation.

There are 15 Municipalities—including there is a lack of enthusiasm and interest in the well-being of the communities whom they represent. In accordance with an agreement made between the British Government and the State, which took effect on October 1, 1878, customs duties—either on imports or exports—are not to be levied in the State.

The Regency Council maintains two hospitals and some half-dozen dispensaries in outlying districts, while the erection of an outdoor dispensary and staff quarters has recently been completed.

The Chief Judge presides over the *Sadr Adalat*, or principal Court of Justice

dent of the Council of Regency in Bahawalpur, is the son of Chaudhri Shah Nawaz Khan, a landed proprietor at Thaska Miranji, in the district of Karnal in the Province of the Punjab. In early life he held responsible positions in the Chiefs' College at Ajmer, and in the year 1886 he became head teacher of Oriental languages at the same institution. He entered the service of the State in 1892, on his appointment as A.D.C. to His Highness the Nawab, and in 1907 he was chosen for the high office which he now fills with such distinction.

In recognition of his valuable labours on behalf of the British Government as well as the State, he was in 1909 created a Companion of the Indian Empire, and in 1918 he became a member of the Central Publicity Board, while a few months later he was elected on the "Committee of Subjects" in connection with the "Reform" scheme recently propounded by the Hon. the Secretary of State for India and His Excellency Lord Chelmsford, Viceroy and Governor-General.

During the terrible war which has recently struck at the very roots of national life in the continents of Europe, Asia, Africa, and even North and South America, the House of Bahawalpur has again manifested its unquestioned loyalty to the British Throne. Forces raised within the State have been engaged in active field service; fresh recruits have been enlisted; and there has been a splendid response to the request of the Imperial Government for camels, horses, and camp equipment, in addition to officers and men. Further than this, the State has subscribed more than Rs. 82,00,000 to the War Loan Fund; and has contributed Rs. 4,000 to Mrs. Renout's fund for relief of wounded soldiers; Rs. 6 000 to Lady O'Dwyer's fund; Rs. 2,000 in aid of the monument to Indian soldiers at Brighton, in England, and Rs. 5,000 to the Y.M.C.A. for articles of utility and comfort of Indian divisions in France. The large Bahawalpur house at Lahore was offered and accepted for use as a war hospital; and a Durbar tent, equipped with necessary furniture and fittings, was lent to the Y.M.C.A. for convalescent soldiers; and a centre of St. John's Ambulance Society was established in Bahawalpur in January, 1917.

The chief town, Bahawalpur, founded in 1748, and surrounded by a mud wall four miles in circumference, is pleasantly situated on the southern bank of the river Indus.

It contains many handsome buildings, such as the Egerton Sadiq College, the High School, and the Nur Mehal, built in 1875 in the Italian style of architecture at a cost of about Rs. 12,00,000. This extremely fine structure is used as a guest-house as well as a Durbar Hall for State occasions. The palace of His Highness the Nawab, constructed in 1882, is a huge square block with tower at each corner, from which extensive views are obtained of the waterless desert in the Bikaner State. Its reception hall in the centre of the building is 60 feet in length, and 56 feet in height, while the roof of the vestibule is 128 feet in height. There are several flourishing industries in the town, and a very considerable amount of trade is carried on with surrounding districts. About five miles distant from Bahawalpur the river Sutlej is crossed by a splendid iron girder bridge, called the "Empress Bridge," which is more than 4,250 feet in length, and has 16 spans each of 250 feet in length.

Weh, a town of great historical and archæological interest, lies about 38 miles in a south-easterly direction from Bahawalpur. Noted travellers have identified it with a huge city built at the confluence of several Punjab rivers by Alexander the Great, King of Macedon, who flourished between the years 353 and 323 B.C. The ruins are now covered with earth, and the site is marked by three small villages, but nevertheless the place is regarded by Mahomedans as very sacred owing to the large number of shrines in the vicinity.

Khanpur is the chief centre of trade in agricultural produce, and it has mills for husking rice and ginning cotton.

Pattan Munara is an old ruin in the Naushahra *tahsil*, but at the close of the eighteenth century there were the remains of four towers which surrounded a Buddhist monastery. Tradition says that the original city was 100 square miles in extent, and that it was the capital of Mousicanus, who, after submission to Alexander, revolted and was crucified in 225 B.C.

BAYANA FORT (TWENTY-EIGHT MILES FROM BHARATPUR).

THE STATE OF BHARATPUR

THE Ruler of this State is Lieut.-Col. His Highness Maharaja Brijendra Sawai Shri Kishen Singh Bahadur Bahadur Jung, Maharaja of Bharatpur. His Highness has a permanent salute of 17 guns, and a permanent local salute of 19 guns. The area of the State is about 1,993 square miles, and it has a population of 4,96,437 (Census, 1921).

The gross revenue amounts to thirty-six lakhs.

The Heir-apparent is Maharaj Kumar Shri Brijendra Singh Bahadur, who was born in November, 1918.

The present ruling House of Bharatpur are Jats of the Sinsinwar clan, and claim descent from Madan Pal, a Yadaw Rajput. They take the name of Sinsinwar after their paternal village of Sinsini, near Deeg. The first of this House to attain to celebrity was Braj, a contemporary of Aurangzeeb. He was killed in action against an Imperial Army. Churaman succeeded his father, Braj, and made himself very powerful. He invaded the Moghul territory, but when hard pressed, made an honourable peace. Badan Singh succeeded Churaman, and made allegiance with Delhi in 1722 A.D., the year which marks the recognition of Bharatpur as a separate State.

Badan Singh ruled only in name, while his capable son, Suraj Mal, was really at the helm of affairs. It was Suraj Mal who laid the foundation of Jat power and eminence. He was, however, killed in a skirmish with a Mughal squadron while hunting in the Imperial domains. Suraj Mal was succeeded by his son Jawahar Singh, who, during a short rule, extended the Jat possessions to their utmost limit. It was Jawahar Singh who sacked Delhi, to avenge the death of his father. He lived chiefly in Agra Palace, where it was his great hobby to sit on the black marble throne of Jehangir, and it was here that he was murdered in June, 1768. In 1803 Maharaja Ranjit Singh made an alliance with the British, who were assisted by Bharatpur troops in the capture of Agra, and in the battle of Laswari. In 1804, however, a war broke out between the British and Holkar, and Maharaja Ranjit Singh joined the latter. The Mahrattas and the Jats had to fall back upon Bharatpur, and in January, 1805, the memorable siege of Bharatpur began. Three months later Ranjit Singh sued for peace, and a treaty was concluded.

The next most important ruler was Maharaja Jaswant Singh, who came to the *gadi* in 1853. He was then a minor, and a Regency Council was established. During the Mutiny Bharatpur rendered very valuable assistance to the British, which was gratefully acknowledged. Maharaja Jaswant Singh assumed full powers in 1871, and in 1877 was made a G.C.S.I. In 1890 his personal salute was raised from 17 to 19 guns. He died in 1893, and was succeeded by his eldest son,

LIEUT.-COL. H.H. MAHARAJA SRI BRIJENDRA SAWAI KISHEN SINGH BAHADUR, BAHADUR JUNG, OF BHARATPUR.

THE STATE OF **BHARATPUR**.

1. H.H. Maharaja Ram Singh (Father of the Present Ruler). 2. Maharaja Kunwar Brijendra Singh (the Heir Apparent).
3. Gopal Bhawan with Fountains, at Deeg (Twenty-one Miles from Bharatpur). 4. Gopal Bhawan at Deeg (Rear View).

THE STATE OF BHARATPUR.

1. New Palaces inside Bharatpur Fort. 2. Khoti Khas Durbar Hall, Bharatpur. 3. Moti Mahul, Bharatpur. 4. Deeg Fort. 5. Chhatri Goverdhan of the Late Maharaja Balwant Singh (Twenty-nine Miles from Bharatpur).

THE STATE OF BHARATPUR.

1. Victoria Hospital, Bharatpur. 2. Ganga Mandir, Bharatpur. 3. General View of Bharatpur City. 4. Palaces at Sewar (Three Miles from Bharatpur).

THE STATE OF BHARATPUR.

1. Suraj Bhawan (Marble Palaces) at Deeg. 2. Kishen Bhawan at Deeg. 3. Siv. Bhawan, with Old Palaces, at Deeg.
4. Gopal Bhawan, with Gardens, at Deeg.

THE STATE OF BHARATPUR.

1. Band Bareta (Twenty-four Miles from Bharatpur). 2. Chowrasi Khamma: Old Ruins (Twenty-nine Miles from Bharatpur). 3. Fort Weir (Twenty-six Miles from Bharatpur). 4. Old Palaces at Bharatpur.

Ram Singh. The latter was deprived of his powers in 1895, in consequence of his intemperate habits, and was finally deposed in 1900. Maharaja Ram Singh was succeeded by his son, Maharaja Kishen Singh, born in October, 1899.

The present Ruler of Bharatpur, Col. His Highness Maharaja Brijendra Sawai Shree Kishen Singh Bahadur, Bahadur Jung, assumed full powers in November, 1918. He received his education at the Mayo College, Ajmer, and Wellington, England. His Highness is one of the greatest sportsmen in India, a very enlightened Ruler, extremely entertaining host, and a most charming gentleman. He is a great lover of horses, and of all things Indian and old.

During the late Great War the Bharatpur Durbar gave most valuable help to the Imperial Government, both in men and in money, and the famous Bharatpur Imperial Service Infantry fought for the King and country throughout the War in East Africa, and the still more famous Mule Transport Corps saw service in all the theatres of war, except in Africa. In recognition of these services, His Highness received a permanent local salute of 19 guns, and the honorary rank of Major in the British Army. He has now been promoted to the rank of Lieut.-Colonel.

The following are among the most important contributions made by the State during the Great War: (1) Reinforcement sent to East Africa for the Imperial Service Infantry, 714 rank and file, and 64 followers; (2) Reinforcements for the Imperial Service Transport Corps, 430 rank and file and 64 followers; (3) State subscriptions to war loans, 20 lakhs; (4) State subscriptions to Imperial Indian Relief Fund, Soldiers' Comforts Fund, Aeroplane Fleet Fund, Lord Kitchener Memorial Fund, St. John's Ambulance, Serbian Relief Fund, and Red Cross, 2 lakhs; (5) public subscriptions to various war funds, Rs. 26,000; and (6) public subscriptions to war bonds, Rs. 69,000.

Immediately upon their return from Europe the Bharatpur Transport Corps was sent to the North-West Frontier, and remained on active service there during the Afghan War. The Corps returned to Bharatpur at the conclusion of peace in February, 1920.

THE STATE OF BHARATPUR.

1. FORT BHARATPUR. 2. JAL MEHAL, AT KUMHER (NINE MILES FROM BHARATPUR). 3. INTERIOR (DIWAN-I-AM) OF NAND BHAWAN, AT DEEG.

NAOLAKHA TANK, WITH SUNDER GHAT.

THE STATE OF BUNDI

THE State of Bundi, situated in the south-east of Rajputana, between 25° and 26° N. and 75° 1.5" and 76° 19" E., is in subordinate alliance with the British Government under the Treaty of 1818. The British Political Agent resides at Deoli, and is under the Hon. the Agent to the Governor-General in Rajputana.

The Ruling Prince of Bundi is the head of the Hara clan of Rajputs, and is a direct descendant of the ancient Chauhan kings of Ajmer and Delhi. They first settled at Sambhar, and for this reason the word "Sambharik" is attached to the Princes of Bundi up to the present day.

From the time of Rao Surjan, who succeeded to the *gadi* in 1533, the rulers of the State were intimately associated with the Moghul Emperors as feudatories and allies.

In 1707, in the battle for Emperor Aurangzeb's vacant throne, Budh Singhji, the Bundi Prince, held a prominent post, and his unparalleled gallantry and matchless courage contributed mainly to the victory which left Shah Alam Bahadur Shah without a rival. For these signal and distinguished services he was honoured with (1) the title of Maharao Raja; (2) the dignity of *haft hazari*, i.e. the command of 7,000 horse; (3) a grant of 52 districts; and (4) admittance to the intimate friendship of the Emperor, which he enjoyed until the Emperor's death. Budh Singhji shortly afterwards lost his State in consequence of disturbances with Jaipur, but his son, Umed Singhji, making several unsuccessful efforts, at last succeeded, with the assistance of Holkar, in recovering much of his lost possessions, but in this transitory period some portions of the State were usurped by the Mahrattas. It was during the reign of this Prince, Umed Singhji, that negotiations for making treaties and engagements with the Hon. East India Company were opened.

During the latter portion of the eighteenth century the State was practically overrun by the Mahrattas, and in 1804 a British Army was sent, in command of Colonel Monson, for the purpose of suppressing the power of Holkar. In the disastrous retreat which followed, Colonel Monson was very greatly assisted by Bishan Singhji, the Prince of Bundi at that time, but the latter drew upon his own head the special vengeance of the Mahrattas. A safe passage for the retiring army was not only cheerfully granted, but the troops were aided to the utmost of the Raja's means and with an almost culpable disregard for his own welfare and interests.

Thirteen years later the Mahratta flag was flying alongside that of Bundi in the capital city, and the whole of the revenue collected at the time was barely sufficient to provide the means for the personal protection of the Chief, this state of affairs

HIS HIGHNESS MAHARAO RAJA SIR RAGHUBIR SINGHJI SAHEB BAHADUR, G.C.I.E., G.C.V.O., G.C.S.I., OF BUNDI.

1. HIS LATE HIGHNESS MAHARAO RAJA SIR RAM SINGHJI SAHEB BAHADUR, G.C.S.I., C.E., C.I.E.
2. SHRI, LATE MAHARAJ KUMAR RAGHUVENDRASINGHJI SAHEB. 3. KANWAR SAHEB BHAWANISINGHJI.

being mainly attributable, says Colonel Tod, "to our abandonment of the Raja in 1804." When, however, the Imperial

HIS HIGHNESS AND HIS BROTHERS (THE LATE MAHARAJ RANGRAUSINGHJI AND THE LATE MAHARAJ RAGHURAJSINGHJI) ON ELEPHANTS.

Government called upon Rajputs to render help in vanquishing the Mahrattas, the State of Bundi was one of the first to offer the whole of her resources; Princes and dependents forthwith took up arms against the common enemy, and when peace was restored the gallant Chief, Bishan Singhji, was not forgotten. Districts which had been held by Holkar for more than half a century were restored to Bundi without any qualification or reservation, and history is responsible for the statement that the intense gratitude felt by the Raja was expressed in the following words: "I am not a man of protestation, but my head is yours whenever you require it."

This was no meaningless phraseology, it was the sincere tribute of a loyal Prince, and there is every reason to believe that should certain circumstances have arisen he would have kept his word.

On February 10, 1818, Maharao Raja Bishan Singhji concluded a treaty with the British which entirely put an end to Maharatta [illegible]rages. Maharao Raja Bishan Singhji died in the year 18[illegible]24 and was succeeded by his son, Ram Singhji, who was then only 10 years of age. It has been stated in various publications that this Chief was exceedingly apathetic towards, if not to some extent sympathetic with the rebels during the Sepoy mutiny of 1857, but there is documentary evidence in the State archives, including letters and certificates from Government officials, which prove conclusively that His Highness was loyal to the core, that he furnished troops to assist in quelling the disturbances, and that a sum of Rs. 5,000 offered by him to the captor of the rebel, Jaidayal, formerly Commander-in-Chief of the Kotah forces, who was responsible for the death of Major Charles Burton, Political Agent, Harauti, was forwarded from Bundi to the Political Agent at Jaipur to be handed over to the person who had caught the culprit.

Maharao Raja Ram Singhji was an old-fashioned, dignified but popular Ruler, a man of strict integrity, and one who endeared himself to his people by his ceaseless efforts to promote their welfare. It has been said of him that "he was a grand specimen of a true Rajput gentleman." He had inherited his father's love for sports as well as his staunch principles of loyalty to the Crown. In 1862 he received the usual *sanad* conferring upon him the right of adoption. Besides being a G.C.S.I., he enjoyed the proud and unique distinction of being made a Counsellor of the Empire. He died in 1889 after a long and glorious reign extending over a period of nearly 70 years, and was succeeded by his son, the present Ruler, His Highness Maharao Raja Sir Raghubir Singhji Saheb Bahadur, G.C.I.E., G.C.V.O., K.C.S.I., who was born 21 years previously.

The State of Bundi is bounded on the north by the States of Jaipur and Tonk, on the east and south by Kotah, and on the west by Udaipur.

It is 2,220 square miles in extent, and in the census of 1911 the inhabitants were 218,730 in number, of whom 113,212 were males and 105,518 were females.

ARMOURY IN HATIAN SAL.

Its most remarkable physical feature is seen in a double line of hills, called the Ara-Bala range, which traverse the full length of the State from the south-western to the north-eastern boundaries, and the barrier thus formed is practically impassable, excepting in four places, the principal of these being at the town of Bundi where the road between Deoli and Kotah cuts through the obstacles. The highest peak of the range is at Satur, about 10 miles to the west of Bundi.

The soil in the northern half of the State is of a stony character and is dependent entirely upon rain for moisture for vegetation, but the southern portion contains rich alluvial and black cotton soil, while in other parts the soil is a light sandy loam, rendered fertile by means of numerous wells.

The principal crops are wheat, barley, gram, *jowar*, maize, *mung*, *urad*, opium, oilseeds, and cotton.

There are large tracts of woodlands, and the forest area extends to about 480 square miles, but the latter is not now inhabited by hordes of large game as it was a hundred years ago when Maharao Raja Bishan Singhji is reported to have "slain upwards of 100 lions with his own hand; besides many tigers and boars innumerable were victims to his lance."

The present Ruler has also the reputation of being a good shot, and has to his credit a record of having already killed about 100 tigers, besides an immense number of other large game.

Industrial enterprises have not yet advanced beyond those which are met with in almost every village in India, with the exception of a cotton press at Baori, 19 miles distant from the capital town, which is owned by the State, and a ginning factory at Bundi belonging to local traders.

In connection with the manufacture of lime and cement, however, a lease, for 30 years, of land at Lakhari, in the Gaindoli *nizamat*, was granted on December 1, 1913, to Messrs. Killick, Nixon & Co., of Bombay, who have established works thereon under the style of "The Bundi Hydraulic Lime & Cement Co., Ltd.," the registered office being in Bombay. During the year ended December 31, 1917, a sum of Rs. 21,388 was paid by the Company to the State by way of royalty, this being an increase of Rs. 10,578 upon the working of the previous 12 months.

His Highness was invested with full powers of administration in 1890, and for the purpose of management the State is divided into the Hondoli, Gaindoli, Keshoraipatan, Deyi, and Baroondhan *nizamats*, each presided over by a *Nazim*: the *tahsil* of Karwar under a *Tahsildar*; and forts at Nainwa, Taragarh, and Ajitgarh under a *Kiladar*. Assessment rates fixed in 1878 remain in force to-day with some slight modifications, and the readiness with which cultivators pay them is ample evidence of the extremely reasonable nature of the amounts.

There is an Imperial Post and Telegraph Office at Bundi, from which letters and parcels are transferred to the State Head Post Office for dispatch to their several destinations.

Educational matters have not in the past received the support which they deserve, as with a population of about 218,000 inhabitants the State supports only three schools, namely, the Darbar High School at Bundi, and two village schools at Nainwa. There are, however, four private schools at the capital town. Greater encouragement is now being given to this most important subject, several vernacular schools having been erected recently or being in course of construction. Sanskrit is taught up to a high standard, and all education is imparted free of charge.

The State has its own codifications, which are based upon the *Dharma Shastras*, the customs of the country, and on the general spirit of the Laws in force in British India. Civil and criminal justice is administered by Courts in the capital city and at other centres, the Council of His Highness being the highest authority. Sentences of death can only be inflicted when the last-named Court is presided over by the Maharao Raja.

The military maintained by the State comprises 600 infantry, 50 artillery, and 100 cavalry, all of whom are employed in furnishing escorts, guards of honour for State processions and ceremonials, and on other occasions when required. The infantry are armed with smooth-bore, muzzle-loading muskets and bayonets; the cavalry with smooth-bore, muzzle-loading carbines, swords, and lances; and the artillery are provided with swords. The total annual cost of maintenance of these troops is about Rs. 128,000.

There are about 600 men of all ranks in the city and district police forces, the distribution giving one officer to an area of 3·98 square miles, and to 390 persons.

The State maintains a General Hospital at Bundi, and dispensaries at the city jail and Kotwali, but owing to a healthy climate the percentage of individuals requiring medical treatment is unusually small. During the year 1916-17 about 10,550 outdoor and 40 indoor patients received professional aid in the city, and some 120 at Kotwali, the total expenditure being Rs. 6,269. A *Vaid* is in receipt of a *jagir* for providing medical relief to the people free of cost, and there are also several *Vaids* and *Hakims* who are paid by the State for attending patients without charge. Besides this, there are two *Vedic* dispensaries maintained by private enterprise.

The State has an annual gross revenue of nearly Rs. 10,00,000 in local coinage, the average amount for the last five years being Rs. 9,54,287, which is equivalent to Rs. 8,29,810 in British currency, and it pays to the Imperial Government a yearly tribute of Rs. 1,20,000.

Bundi was one of the States honoured with a visit by Her Majesty Queen Mary during the Coronation festivities in 1911, and the recollection of that auspicious event will never be obliterated from the memories of His Highness the Maharao Raja and his subjects. It was announced that December 23rd and 24th had been fixed for the Royal visit, and for several months previously to that date grand preparations were in progress, His Highness personally directing, advising, and encouraging his subjects to dress the beautiful city of Bundi in a garb which would be worthy of the occasion.

Ere daybreak had dawned on the 23rd the streets of the city were animated by a crowd of expectant people, who were putting the finishing touches to the attractive display of decorations, and a visitor would have been struck by the fact that this manifestation of welcome was being completed by State officials and prominent citizens, while the humblest individuals in the State joyously contributed their share to the imposing spectacle.

The rising of the sun added much to the charm of the scene, and thousands of sightseers clad in holiday attire thronged the roads and eagerly discussed the one topic of the day, "the coming of India's Queen-Empress." About two o'clock in the afternoon His Highness the Maharao Raja emerged from the palace. He is possessed of a fine manly figure and was clad in State robes of the costliest description; his head-dress consisted of a magnificent coronet of precious stones around which was wound a handsome saffron puggaree; his neck was adorned with bands of beautiful pearls, and upon

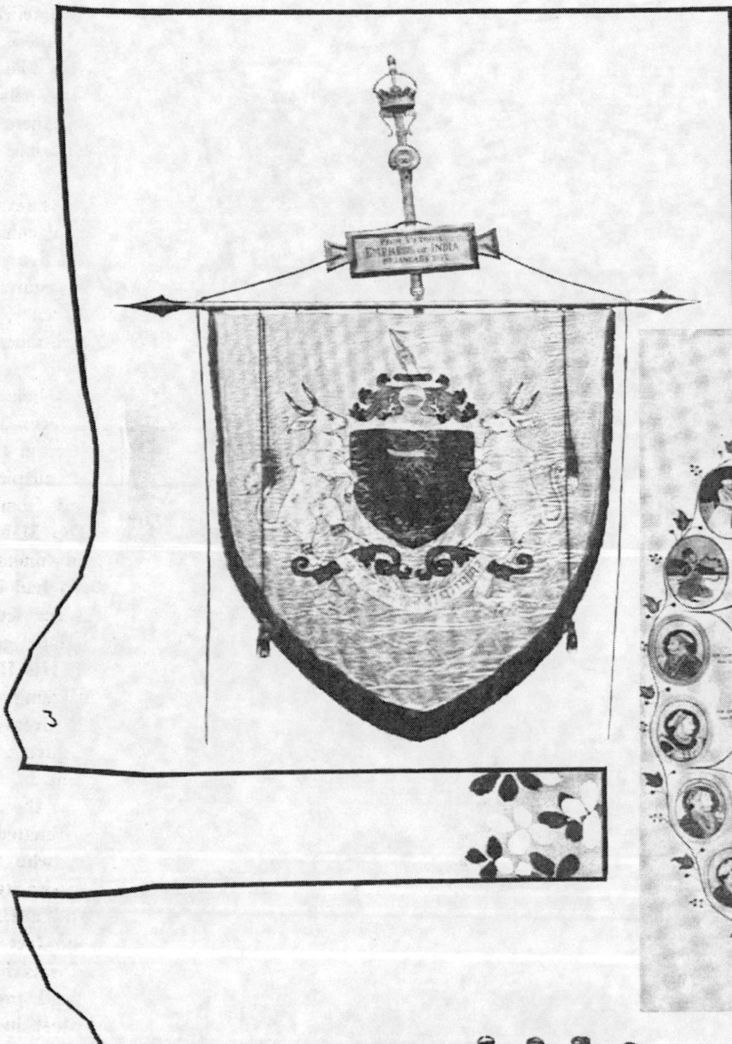

THE STATE OF BUNDI.

Genealogical Group of Bundi Princes. 2. His Highness with Sardars and Officials. 3. The State Flag.

THE STATE OF BUNDI.

1. Chhatar Mahal Palace (Exterior). 2. Chhatar Mahal Palace (Interior). 3. The Ratan Doulat Darikhana. 4. Ranisahee Nathawatji-ki-Baori.

THE STATE OF BUNDI.

2. Group showing H.M. Queen Mary and H.H. the Maharaja Rao. 3. H.M. Queen Mary in Hatian Sal.
4. H.M. Queen Mary's Camp—The Royal Tent. 5. H.M. Queen Mary's Camp, from the South.

his breast he wore a number of distinguished Orders the lustre of which was greatly augmented by the jewelled sword, ***katar***, and belt. Accompanied by Major Peacock, Political Agent, Harauti, and Tonk, and surrounded by ***Sardars*** in glittering apparel, he proceeded by motor-car to Satoor village, about six miles distant from the city of Bundi, where he was to meet Her Majesty.

The ***Sowari*** of the State lancers, a detachment of infantry, guns, and emblems of Royalty such as ***chanwar***, ***chhatra***, ***morchhal***, and ***nau-neza***, i.e. nine spear bearers, and ***Mahi Maratab*** (constituting the full ancestral ***lawazma*** or emblems) had already arrived at Satoor, and His Highness soon satisfied himself that everything was in order for the reception of the distinguished visitor.

After a few minutes had elapsed, motor-cars containing Her Majesty and her suite were brought to a standstill, and His Highness with the greatest respect tendered his homage to the Queen-Empress of India, who warmly shook hands with him and with Major Peacock. The guard of honour presented arms, and the National Anthem was played by bands of music.

The Royal car, immediately followed by that of His Highness, then proceeded in the direction of the city. The route taken was along the main Bazar, beautifully decorated with flags and bunting, which harmonized in a charming manner with various other attractive displays on the premises of bankers, merchants, traders, and private residents. The road was lined by old-fashioned State soldiery, some being armed with muskets and flint-locks, some with lances, and others with ***talwars***, and they were stationed at intervals of five yards, while police were on guard on each side of the streets within the precincts of the city. The arrival of the party at the grounds of the Royal Camp was announced by a salute of 101 guns, fired from the famous fort of Taragarh; the guard of honour presented arms, and the State band played the National Anthem. This fort, on the spur of a hill 2,850 feet in height, towering above the city, commands a magnificent view of the extensive ***maidan*** at its foot, and it is surrounded by defence work of high fortifications and walled terraces each of which is protected by heavy guns. The camp ground was situated in the spacious compound of the State Guest-House, and it had been made most attractive by velvety green lawns interspersed with beds of choicest flowers, while the quarters specially designed for Her Majesty and her suite were most luxuriously furnished with appointments of the latest designs.

RAMGARH—A HUNTING PLACE.

One of Her Majesty's most distinguished characteristics is energy, and this trait was manifested when, after a brief interval for tea, she drove to Sukh-Mahal, or the "Palace of Happiness," a small but very beautiful structure erected on the borders of the Jaitsagar lake by His Highness the Maharao Raja Vishnu Singhji, who ruled between the years 1773 and 1821. It should be observed that one of the principal streets of the city had to be traversed during this journey, and before the Royal Party had actually entered their cars a rumour was current that Her Majesty had expressed a desire that the people should be allowed to assemble on the roofs of houses or shops in the Bazar or any other point of vantage which they might choose, provided they did not interfere with the special arrangements which had been issued by the police for keeping order. The rumour travelled quickly from group to group, but doubt was soon set at rest when it was officially declared that Her Majesty had actually given the instructions referred to. One cannot in cold print convey the slightest conception of the intense enthusiasm and the ecstatic joy which filled the hearts of the people, who quickly availed themselves of the privileges afforded by the Royal command. Faces beaming with delight peered from trees, house-tops, and other heights, but the sightseers were quiet and respectful in their demeanour, regarding their lives as being purified by viewing the sacred ***darshan*** of the Queen-Empress, and there were few persons of mature age in the vast crowd who did not offer prayers for long life for their Most Gracious Majesties.

His Highness personally conducted Her Majesty over the Sukh-Mahal, and after half an hour had been spent in admiration of the building the visitors returned to the Royal Camp. During the evening the whole of the city, and particularly the Fort and Palace, were brilliantly illuminated, and Her Majesty was so delighted with the spectacle that she thereupon caused a telegram to be sent to His Majesty, the King-Emperor, in which she specially expressed her gratification at her reception at Bundi, and her pleasure at the hospitality and courtesies shown to her by His Highness.

A State dinner was given at a later hour, and His Highness in a short but eloquent and impressive speech referred to the honour conferred upon the State by the visit of Her Imperial Majesty, and again declared his unswerving devotion to the British Throne.

A grand display of fireworks proved a fitting conclusion to the first day's proceedings.

THE STATE OF BUNDI.

1. ... and City.—View from the South. 2. Bundi, from the East. 3. View of the City from the Fort. 4. ... Gate.
5. The City, from the North.

On the morning of December 24th the Royal Party visited the palace on the hill, to which the Queen-Empress drove in a State carriage canopied with ***chanwar*** and ***morchhal,*** an escort being furnished by State lancers under the Officer Commanding the Bundi forces. The procession wended its way at a walking pace in order to give the crowds another opportunity of seeing Her Majesty along the city road until it arrived at the commencement of the magnificent steep stone-paved ascent to the palace. His Highness the Maharao Raja, attended by a large number of his *Sardars* and high officials, was waiting at this stage to receive Her Majesty, who, with her suite, was carried in handsome *tonjons*, specially built for the occasion, to the entrance gate of the spacious courtyard of the palace. This gateway, of great architectural beauty, is the only one of its kind in India, and it is formed by massive representations of two elephants facing each other and forming an archway by extending their trunks until their tips are united. This unique work of art was greatly admired by the Royal Party. Passing along the Chowk, when the guard formed by the State infantry presented arms, a fine view was obtained of the palace, to which Colonel Tod refers as follows :

" Throughout Rajputana, which boasts of many beautiful palaces, that of Bundi is placed in the first rank. It is an aggregate of palaces each bearing the name of its founder, and yet the whole so well harmonizes, and the character of the architecture is so uniform, that its fantasies appear only to rise from the peculiarity of its position and serve to diversify its beauties."

In the Nothana courtyard the guard of honour furnished by the State troops presented arms, and the State band played the National Anthem as Her Majesty alighted from the ***tonjon***, and was conducted to the famous audience hall, called the " Ratan Daulat Darikhana," in which is placed the white marble throne.

This hall was built in the seventeenth century by Rao Raja Ratanji, but it is only used on very special occasions, such as the holding of a grand Durbar. The throne was watched—as it is to-day—by the old style of guards of the Rajput infantry (known as the " ***Pakhti*** "), who wore orange-coloured pugarees on their heads and were girt with swords and powder pouches, while they carried old-fashioned but very powerful matchlocks on their shoulders. A visit was then paid to the Chhater Mahal palace, founded and built in 1664 by His Highness Rao Raja Shatrushalji, who was the Commander-in-Chief of Prince Dara's forces in the war against the Emperor Aurangzeb, the Raja falling mortally wounded while fighting for the Imperial cause in a great battle near Dholpur. Here were assembled the principal nobles, ***jagirdars,*** and officials of the State clad in robes worn on the occasion of the Coronation Durbar at Delhi some two weeks previously, all of whom had the honour of being presented by His Highness the Maharao Raj to Her Imperial Majesty. The palace is beautiful beyond description, and after every portion of it had been closely inspected and greatly admired by the guests, Her Majesty was pleased to command that photographs of the incomparable edifice should be prepared for her. Two group photos were accordingly taken.

An inspection was also made of the State Armoury, which contained (***inter alia***) weapons of offence and defence that

THE STATE OF BUNDI.

1. JAITSAGAR LAKE. 2. PUSHPASAGAR PALACE. 3. HINDOLI LAKE.

THE STATE OF BUNDI.

1. [illegible] and Chhatar Mahal. 2. Main Street, with Horse Tirthia. 3. Moti Mahal Palace. 4. Chatserbhuj Temple. 5. City Bazaar.

were used on historic occasion of bloody battles in times gone by.

A visit was also paid to the upper compartments of the palace, and in one of them the ornamental slab ceiling of Badal Mahal, which is a marvel of fine architecture, was greatly admired by Her Majesty. After this, *tonjons* were called into requisition for the descent of the slopes from the hill, and the party reentered their motor-cars and drove to Sar Bagh, the place of cremation of Bundi Chiefs. This is a building of great antiquity, but its chief attractions lie in the remarkably fine carvings on about seventy cenotaphs, which date from the year 1579.

Shikar Burj, one of the prettiest spots in Bundi, was next visited, and its unique charms drew from the Royal Party praises of no mean order.

A small palace overlooking a beautiful tank was erected here by Maharao Raja Shriji Umed Singhji, who abdicated in favour of his son Ajit Singhji for the express purpose of spending the closing years of his life as a religious recluse in this building.

A halt was next called at Phul Sagar, or " flower tank," its name being doubtless derived from the fact that on the banks of a very fine lake a charming garden has been laid out, while on a lower level is a palace which is the summer residence of the Rulers of Bundi. A walk of less than five minutes sufficed for Her Majesty to reach the place where lions, Royal Bengal tigers, panthers, leopards, and other forest-bred animals are confined in huge enclosures built of solid masonry. Several fountains and a waterfall add to the beauty of the scenery, and the visitors spent fully half an hour in admiring the magnificence of the surroundings. Her Imperial Majesty returned at mid-day to the camp, being highly pleased with all that had been seen under the guidance of His Highness the Maharao Raja.

ON BOARD THE S.S. "MEDINA."

The long looked-for and keenly anticipated visit of Her Majesty was now nearly at an end, but there was not the slightest diminution in the respectful demeanour of the Bundi people nor on the part of His Highness, who had carefully supervised the arrangements for the departure of the Royal guests. The Maharao Raja arrived at the Royal Camp at half-past two in the afternoon of that memorable Saturday and was graciously accorded an interview with Her Majesty, who, to the intense joy of His Highness, presented him with a photograph of herself. The Maharao Raja acknowledged in the most respectful terms the unique honour conferred upon him, and he further ventured to express the hope that he might at some future date have the distinguished privilege of welcoming his Royal Guest as well as His Imperial Majesty the King-Emperor.

A guard of honour was furnished by State troops and a salute of 101 guns was fired from the fort as Her Majesty emerged from the camp at three o'clock. After shaking hands with His Highness, who was deeply touched by this gracious act, Her Majesty entered her motor-car and left for Kotah, her departure being witnessed by a group of *Sardars* and others, who demonstrated their feelings in a suitable manner.

On the following morning—Christmas Day—His Highness the Maharao Raja addressed a communication to Her Imperial Majesty at Kotah in which he tendered his loyal devotion and homage, and in reply thereto the following message was sent by the Queen-Empress, namely: " Grateful thanks for your kind wishes. I much enjoyed my stay in Bundi. (Signed) Mary R. Queen-Empress. Camp Kotah."

In order to commemorate Her Imperial Majesty's visit to the State, His Highness the Maharao Raja remitted arrears of revenue amounting to several *lakhs* of rupees, and also gave up in perpetuity grazing fees for cows throughout the State.

In the first week in January, 1912, His Highness the Maharao Raja travelled to Bombay to bid farewell to Their Imperial Majesties, and while on board the S.S. *Medina* His Highness, as a token of loyalty, offered his *katar*—the special weapon of Bundi—which His Majesty graciously accepted, remarking that it would be preserved as a memento of a pleasant meeting.

His Highness the Maharao Raja in August, 1914, manifested his sincere attachment to the Throne, and his practical desire to support the Allies in the Great War, by placing his personal services and the entire resources of his State at the disposal of the Supreme Government, and subsequent to that date he, to the best of his ability, contributed both men and money for the successful

THE STATE OF BUNDI.

...ka Kund. 2. Chorasi Thumbki Chatree (Cenotaph of 84 Pillars). 3. Kashar Bagh, with Cenotaphs. 4. Kedar Nath Temple. 5. Shikar Burj.

prosecution of hostilities. With a view to render assistance in this matter His Highness established a War Board, consisting of five members, to organize, supervise, and carry out various schemes of utility. Under it were appointed a Recruiting Board and a War Loan Committee, with their headquarters at the capital and branches in the various districts.

In his desire to popularize the work of recruiting, His Highness selected four pensioned Government Military Officers, resident in the State, and conversant with local conditions, whom he specially deputed, with a sufficient staff and means of transport, to undertake these duties. By way of encouragement these officers were granted a handsome allowance together with a reward of Rs. 3 for each recruit secured. It speaks well for the lead given by His Highness, the enthusiasm of the recruiters, and, indeed, for the loyalty of the people that over 1,000 men have served with the Indian Army, a large proportion of whom have had the proud privilege of being actually engaged in the fighting line.

By the end of the year 1918 a sum of Rs. 1,82,700 had been contributed from the State to the following funds, for special objects, namely: "The Prince of Wales' Fund (London), The Indian Imperial War Relief Fund, the cost of two aeroplanes, The Belgian Fund, The Roumanian Relief Fund, gift to a Fancy Fair at Simla (through Her Excellency Lady Chelmsford), Lady Munro's Lucky Bag, Lord Kitchener's Memorial Fund, The Soldiers' Memorial in Brighton, The Belgian Children's Christmas Day Fund, The Red Cross Kit-Bags Fund, Their Majesties' Silver Wedding Fund, general war expenses, and bed for wounded in Sydney Hospital and the Curiosity Bureau.

In order to explain the object of the War Loan Fund to the public in general, and to ensure the raising of a handsome amount from the State, a mass meeting, attended by *Sardars, Jagirdars*, representatives of all castes and creeds, and the public at large, was held on May 10, 1917, at Sundar Ghat, Bundi, under the Presidency of His Highness the Maharao Raja Saheb Bahadur, who expressed himself in a few well-chosen words in Hindi.

Great enthusiasm prevailed, every one present being touched to the core, and a sum of Rs. 50,000 was subscribed on the spot.

Local meetings were also held in the *Nizamats* and *Jagir* villages, where subscriptions were collected for the loan, and by the end of November, 1917, a sum of Rs. 3,58,562 had been contributed from the State.

In May, 1918, the flotation of the second War Loan having been proposed by the Government of India, efforts were made by the State to make this one as great a success as the first.

A meeting, attended by all the State *Sardars, Jagirdars*, nobles, officials, bankers, and others, was held at Sundar Ghat, and a touching speech in Hindi was read, on behalf of His Highness, by Major Madan Mohanlal, Member of State Council, which proved very impressive and effective for obtaining loans and recruits. Though the State and its people had only recently suffered heavy afflictions from visitations of plague and influenza, a sum of Rs. 1,00,000 was contributed by His Highness and Rs. 50,000 by the public.

His Highness received the distinction of K.C.S.I. in 1897; he was made a G.C.I.E. in 1904; in January, 1912, His Majesty the King-Emperor bestowed upon him the honour of G.C.V.O. at a Royal Court held in Calcutta shortly after the Coronation Durbar at Delhi, the insignia of which His Highness had the proud privilege of receiving from the Royal hands on the S.S. *Medina*, and a further mark of Royal favour was manifested in June, 1919, when His Majesty the King-Emperor conferred upon His Highness the distinction of G.C.S.I.

Lack of space forbids an enumeration of the many measures of reform carried out by His Highness the Maharao Raja, but it may be observed that the State is more prosperous now than it ever was, and the people are happy and contented with their lot, believing that in their Chief they have a Ruler who makes it the aim of his life to promote their welfare as far as lies in his power.

Rajputs have always been recognized as brave men in battle, but in their fighting, as well as in private life, they manifest a keen sense of justice, and it is this particular characteristic which causes their subjects to place such perfect confidence in them.

It might be added that in the able management of the affairs of State, His Highness receives most valuable assistance from the Members of his Council.

The capital of the State—Bundi—is one of the most beautiful cities in Rajputana, and it is situated in a most picturesquely wooded gorge on the steep side of the Bundi Pass, its many charms being intensified by pinnacled terraces rising one above another to the summit upon which stands the glorious palace and the grim old walls of the Taragarh Fort. The city is entered through four stately gateways, and at once the visitor is treated to a striking panorama of varied scenery of exquisite beauty, the like of which it would be difficult to find in any other part of India. It has a population of nearly 20,000 inhabitants.

THE STATE OF JAIPUR

JAIPUR State is situated in the north-east and east of the Province of Rajputana, and lies between 25° 41′ and 28° 34′ north latitude and between [illegible] 41′ and 77° 13′ east longitude.

On the north of the State are Bikaner, [illegible]haru, and Patiala ; on the west, Bikaner, [illegible]hpur, *Kishengarh*, and the British dis[illegible] *of Ajmer* ; on the south, Udaipur, [illegible]di, *Tonk*, Kotah, and Gwalior ; and [illegible] the *east*, Karauli, Bharatpur, and [illegible]r. The district of Kotkasim, received [illegible] the British Government in recog[illegible] of services rendered by the State [illegible]g the Mutiny, lies near to the [illegible]ri *Tehsil* of the Gurgaon district, in [illegible] north-east of the State.

[illegible]ipur State is named Dhundhar by [illegible] chroniclers, an appellation which it [illegible] retains. The land is replete with [illegible]cal Kshatriya associations. In the [illegible] Age it was known as Matsya Desha, [illegible]a being a race of warriors. In [illegible] *Rig Veda* it is mentioned that they [illegible] against King Sudas. The Shatpatha [illegible]an mentions one King Dhvasana [illegible]ana, monarch of Matsyas, who per[illegible] the *Ashwamedha* or "horse sacri[illegible] According to Manu, it lies in the [illegible]marshi Desha, the land of Brahman [illegible], which comprises the neighbouring [illegible] of Kurukshetra, Braj (Soura[illegible], and Panchala. The name also fre[illegible]tly occurs in the *Mahabharat*. There [illegible] place in the Jaipur territory called [illegible], at a distance of 48 miles from [illegible], where the Pandavas passed their [illegible] of exile.

[illegible]irat is really a place of very great antiquity, inscriptions of the time of Asoka (250 B.C.), and coins of even an earlier date having been found there. Archæological researches show that it was the capital of the old province of Matsya. Hiuen Tsiang, the Chinese pilgrim, visited the place in A.D. 634, and found eight Buddhist monasteries in existence there.

It was here that Asoka issued his famous edict to monks, which was inscribed on a detached boulder of reddish-grey granite, and is now preserved in the rooms of the Asiatic Society of Bengal in Calcutta.

Bairat was invaded by Mahmud of Ghazni in the eleventh century, and is mentioned in the *Aina-i-Akbari*.

The general character of the country is level and open, but the scenery is diversified by the presence of several ranges of hills, ridges, and isolated peaks. Most of them are crowned with forts, around which towns and villages have in the course of time sprung up.

The centre of the State is an elevated table-land, in the form of a triangle, from 1,400 to 1,600 feet above sea-level. A line, running west from Jaipur city, is the base of this triangular table-land. Ranges of hills traversing north and south along the Alwar border, form the eastern side. A portion of the Aravali range, running from near the Sambhar Lake in a north-easterly direction as far as Khetri in a series of broken chain of hills, gives the apex of this triangle. These hills afford a natural boundary between the sandy desert tract of Shekhawati to the north, and the fertile plains of Jaipur proper, to the south and south-east, Raghunathgarh, 3,450 feet in height, being the highest peak. The general level of the country rises gradually towards Kishengarh, on the west of the capital. There are broad and open treeless tracts, where hills, here and there, make their appearance, and there are other ranges in the extreme south and south-eastern portions. The scenery near Rajmahal, where the Banas river forces its way through the hills, is simply charming. The country presents a very wild appearance on the Karauli border, and between the Chambal and Banas rivers, and to the east of the capital it slopes through the valley of the Banganga river to the Bharatpur border.

The principal rivers of the State are the Banas and the Banganga. The former of these flows for about 110 miles, and the latter for about 90 miles, through the State. There are several smaller streams, most of which are dry excepting during the rains, and in the centre of the State is the Amanishah river, which supplies Jaipur with drinking water.

The well-known salt lake at Sambhar, on the Jodhpur border, is owned jointly by Jaipur and Jodhpur, and the excellent product obtained from it is abundantly distributed throughout Northern India and adjoining tracts. The lake is situated nearly 1,200 feet above sea-level, and it covers a wide expanse of about 20 miles in length and from two to seven miles in breadth. In the year 1870, the lake was leased to Government in consideration of the payment of royalty both to Jodhpur and to Jaipur.

The area of the State is 15,579 square miles. To give a comparative idea of its extent it may be interesting to observe that Denmark, in Europe, is 14,840 square miles, and the North-West Frontier Province, in India, is 16,466 square miles in area.

THE STATE OF JAIPUR.

1. Amber Sheesh Mahal (Interior). 2. Amber Ganesh Pol. 3. Jaipur, Sire Deohri, Entrance to Courts and Palaces.

THE STATE OF JAIPUR.

1. Dewan-i-Khas, Sarbata. 2. Dewan-i-Am.

Jaipur is the most populous State in Rajputana. The inhabitants at the census of 1911 were 26,36,647 in number, of whom about 90 per cent. are Hindus; 7 per cent. are Mahomedans; 1 per cent. are Jains; Animists about 0·06 per cent.; Sikhs, 0·005 per cent.; Christians, 0·05 per cent.; and Aryas 0·01 per cent. The majority of the population include nearly all classes of persons, who are now generally known as "Hindus"; of these the Brahmans return the largest number. Then follow the Jats, Minas, Chamars, Gujars, Mahajans, Malis, Rajputs, Kumhars, Balais, and Ahirs, in the order of their numerical strength. It will be seen that though Jaipur is a Rajput State, it does not possess the largest proportion of Rajput persons.

Jaipur, on the score of its area or extent, stands fourth in Rajputana. A very large portion of the State belongs to what has been denominated by geologists "The Aravali Region."

The soil of the country is generally sandy throughout the north and west, but towards the east and south of the capital it is rich or black. The former type yields only one crop, while the other yields two. The food-grains produced are chiefly *bajra*, *mung*, *moth*, *jowar*, maize, wheat, barley, and gram. Rice, of a very inferior quality, is also raised in one of the eastern districts. In some places the soil is suitable for growing cotton, poppy, sugarcane, and *til*.

The climate, though dry, is very healthy, and epidemic diseases are of very rare occurrence. During the hot months the days are very hot, but the latter part of the nights and early mornings are decidedly cool. The average mean temperature is 77°, varying from 59° in January to 91° in June.

The rainfall varies from 15 to 18 inches in the north, and 21 in the west, and about 25 at the capital, to more than 31 inches in the south-east.

The hot season commences in March and April. The monsoon months are July, August, and September. Winter begins during the latter part of October, January being the coldest month of the year.

The hilly tracts in the State are covered with forests, and the area under Forest administration is about 283 square miles. In the districts of Sawai Jaipur and Sawai Madhopur there are reserved forests. Very little valuable timber is produced, *babul* (Acacia Arabica), *ber* (Zizyphus Jujuba), *nim* (Melia Azadirachta), *pipal* (Ficus religiosa), and *shisham* (Dalbergia Sissoo) being the most common trees. In Shekhawati, Rohira, a variety of *Tecoma* is also found, which is admirably suited for cabinet work. Honey and lac are other articles included in forest produce.

The usual kinds of small game are found in the country, and there are also tiger, leopard, hyæna, black bear, sambhar, antelope, wild hog, and wild dog near the capital and Sawai Madhopur.

The land cultivated directly by State agency is the *khalsa* portion of the State. In Shekhawati large plots of land do not come under the plough, this being due to the want of cultivators and the very low fertility of the sandy soil. The well-favoured regions are those near water-courses, rivers, and artificial tanks, which yield magnificent harvests. In Shekhawati camels are yoked to the plough, and it is a very interesting sight to watch the good and docile animal drawing this implement.

At the capital and important towns of the State, there are a number of Seths, who carry on extensive banking and exchange business. The chief articles of export are salt, cotton, *ghee*, oil-seeds, *sanganer* and *bagru* chintz, woollen fabrics, marble statuary, plain and ornamental brassware, and lacquered bracelets, while other articles such as piece-goods, sugar, rice, tobacco, and hardware are imported. Shekhawati exports a very large quantity of wool.

The Rajputana-Malwa branch of the Bombay-Baroda and Central India Railway, with a total length of about 243 miles, runs through the State from east to west, with connected lines from Phulera to Kuchaman Road and Rewari, and from Bankikui to Agra. Besides this, the Jaipur Durbar has constructed a line, called the Jaipur State Railway, from Sanganer to Sawai Madhopur, while another railway from Jaipur to Shekhawati has not yet been completed. The Nagda-Muttra section of the Bombay-Baroda and Central India Railway passes through Jaipur territory for about 85 miles, the capital cost of construction having been contributed by the Jaipur Durbar.

There are also metalled and unmetalled roads, with total lengths of about 283 and 236 miles respectively.

The State is administered by His Highness the Maharaja Sahib Bahadur, assisted by a Council. His Highness the Maharaja exercises supreme civil and criminal authority.

The State Council is divided into several Departments, including the Foreign and Political, and the Financial and Judicial.

For revenue administration the State Council has two *Diwans*, or Revenue Commissioners, presiding over the two main divisions of the State, called the Eastern and Western. The whole State is again subdivided into 12 administrative units, or *nizamats*, each under a *Nazim*. There are altogether 31 *tahsils* under them.

Jaipur has a mint of its own, which coins gold *mohurs*, rupees, smaller silver coins, and copper pieces. These coins are highly valued, as the metal used is always absolutely pure. Jaipur coins are known as *Jhar-Shahi*. They are so called because they have the special mint-mark, the *Jhar*, or spray, of six sprigs. This currency is the legal tender of Jaipur.

The rulers of Jaipur are descended from Kush, son of Rama, the deified king of Ajodyha. Rama, or Ramachandra, is said to have sprung from the Sun. His descendants are, therefore, known as Suryavansi, or "of the family of Surya" (solar line). The Kachhwaha or Kachhawa clan of Rajputs is one of the 36 Royal races, and Kachhwaha, or Kachhawa, is the patronymic name of this family of Rajputs.

The Sun is specially worshipped to this day in Jaipur, where an annual festival in honour of it is held during the month of *Magh* (January or February).

It is said that the Kachhawas, having left Ajodyha, at first settled at Rohtas, on the Sone river. Some time afterwards, Nala, the hero of the famous Sanskrit epic, *Nala and Damyanti*, founded the city of Narwar in A.D. 294, where he built a fort. His descendants were styled "Pal," and from this place they migrated to Gwalior, where they ruled for about 800 years.

An inscription at Gwalior, dated A.D. 977, mentions Vajradama, who was an independent ruler of Gwalior, which he had wrested from Raja Bijaypal Parihar of Kanauj (Udaipur).

In the twenty-first generation after Nala came Sodha-deva, who had his capital at Gwalior, which subsequently fell into the hands of Tawars.

Chroniclers relate that Ishwari Singh, father of Sodhadeva, once consulted the Brahmans with the object of devising means to perpetuate the sovereignty in his house, and they advised him to give away lands in charity in order to secure the desired object. The religious impulse becoming predominant, Sodhadeva abdicated his position at Gwalior in favour of his

1

2

3

THE STATE OF JAIPUR.

1. Chandra Mahal. 2. Sanskrit College. 3. Maharaja's College.

THE STATE OF JAIPUR.

1. Hawa Mahal (Palace of the Winds). 2. Astronomical Observatory. 3. School of Arts.

THE STATE OF JAIPUR

daughter's son, Jaisajee Tanwar, and, accompanied by all his people, he retired to a place at some distance called Nidrari. In A.D. 967, after the death of his father, Sodhadeva became tired of his secluded and retired life, and from various other considerations thought it wise to go to Bareilly.

From this place he sent messengers in every direction, with the object of finding some land upon which they might settle.

Dulha Rai, or Dula Rai, son of Sodhadeva, was married to the daughter of the Chauhan Raja of Moran, who counselled him to take Dausa, half of which, he said, belonged to him, and the other half to Badgujars. Dulha Rai accordingly managed, with the co-operation of his Chauhan relations, to take possession of Dausa, and thus laid the foundation of the present principality of Jaipur. The valiant Prince Dulha Rai invited his father to rule this country.

Sodhadeva (966 1066). At this time the Dhundhar country, now known as the Jaipur State, was for the most part in the hands of powerful Mina Chiefs, as well as Rajput princes. The Rajputs had found the Minas very troublesome neighbours, and Sodhadeva and his son, Dulha Rai, finding Dausa too small for them, they therefore contemplated taking all the Mina strongholds in the vicinity. Dulha Rai accordingly invaded Mach, which he successfully occupied after a severe conflict with the Minas, and he changed the name of this place to Ramgarh, in honour of Rama, the deified progenitor of the family. He also erected a temple near the scene of the battle, and dedicated it to Jamva Mata, the household goddess of the ruling house of Jaipur.

Dulha Rai afterwards acquired three more Mina strongholds, namely, Khoh, Getor, and Jhotwara.

Dulha Rai (1006 1037), in the early part of his reign, had some trouble with the Badgujars, whom he totally routed. Subsequently a prince of Southern India besieged his relative at Gwalior, and at the request of the latter, Dulha Rai marched with an army to render help. He succeeded in beating off the invader, but was wounded in the battle, and on his return, died at Khoh in 1037.

Kakil Jee, also named Maidal Rao, the successor of Dulha Rai, obtained possession of Amber from the Susawat Minas in 1037, and having made it his capital, he built a temple, and dedicated it to Ambikeshwar Mahadev.

During the reigns of his successors the Minas continued to give trouble, as they were anxious to regain possession of their lost strongholds. One of these Rulers, Pujwan, or Pajun, whose death took place about 1192, is well known to the readers of ***Prithviraj Rassa***, the famous ballads of Chand Bardai. At the head of the army of Prithviraj, Emperor of Delhi, he defeated Shahabuddin Mahomed Gori in the Khyber Pass, and pursued him as far as Ghazni, and he obtained Mahoba, in Bundelkhand, from the Chandela Rajputs for Prithviraj, but he was at last killed while fighting with Prithviraj on the field of Kanauj. Prithviraj had given his sister in marriage to him, and the fact that the king of Delhi had formed such an alliance with him shows that he was a man of considerable importance. Prithviraj, the Chauhan, may be said to be the last Hindu Emperor reigning at Delhi.

Seventh in descent from Pujwan was Udai Karan (1367 88). He had five sons, one of whom succeeded to the *gadi*. The fourth, Balojee, through his grandson, Shaikhajee, originated the Shekhajwat sub-clan of the Kachhawas, inhabiting Shekhawati, a portion of Jaipur held by them as feudatories of the State. From the fifth, Barsingh, sprang the Naruka section of the Kachhawas. Fifth in descent from Udai Karan was Prithviraj (1503–28). He had a numerous progeny, 12 of whom survived him. They are the ancestors of 12 families, or estates, called the twelve Kothris of the Kachhawas, who form the present nobility of Jaipur.

Bharmal (1548 74), successor to Prithviraj, flourished during the time of the Emperors Baber and Humayun, to both of whom he was of great service, as Amber was centrally situated. He received from Humayun the ***Mansab***, or commandership, of 5,000 horse.

His son, Bhagwandas (1574 90), strengthened his alliance with the Delhi throne, and was an intimate friend of the great Akbar. He conquered Kabul and Gujrat, which were made a part of the Moghul Empire, and he was also appointed Governor of the Punjab.

Man Singh (1590 1615) was nephew of, and successor to, Bhagwandas. In the Indian military history of his time, he is regarded as one of the most conspicuous and brilliant characters, whose fame as a victorious general, intrepid commander, and tactful administrator, had spread throughout the country. He maintained the Imperial authority, even in Kabul, during most troublous times. From Kabul he brought interesting relics, which are preserved to this day as precious trophies. On behalf of Akbar he conquered Bengal, and Behar, and Orissa, and made a tributary of Assam. He also acted as Viceroy of Bengal, Behar, and the Deccan, and Kabul.

The greatness and extent of the Moghul Empire was due to this valiant prince, who acquired grants of land in several cities of the Empire, in which he built bazars, palaces and temples, the famous Man Mandir in Benares still remaining as a memorial to him. In the latter years of his reign Akbar became jealous of his power, but he died peacefully in Bengal in 1615. The goddess, Sila Devi, whose shrine is at Amber Fort, was brought from Bengal by him.

Another most noteworthy military ruler who followed Man Singh was Jai Singh I (1622 68), his grandson, popularly known in the annals of Rajputana as Mirza Raja, the title which he received from the Emperor Aurangzeb, along with the ***mansab*** of 6,000. He died at Burhanpur in 1668, while on his way to Delhi.

Fifth in descent from Mirza Jai Singh was Sawai Jai Singh (1700 44), who ruled for 44 years. The title of Sawai (meaning one-and-a quarter), signifying his superiority over others, was conferred upon him by the Emperor of Delhi, and this title retained by his descendants, is associated with the name of the State, which is styled Sawai Jaipur. He laid out the new capital, and named it Jaipur, after himself, its plan being in strict conformity with old Hindu rules of survey and measurement. He is entitled to be deemed the first great "planner" of towns in Hindustan, who carried out his work on a regular and geometrical plan.

Sawai Jai Singh was really a remarkable man of his age, and the State reached the zenith of its power and fame during his reign. He lived at a time of exceptional unrest, when the Moghul Empire was about to fall, when the Sayyids, the manly Sikhs, and the sturdy Mahrattas were rising, and when Nadir Shah had begun his devastations. Sawai Jai Singh was not only a courageous soldier, but also a distinguished statesman and diplomatist, and his experience of men and matters enabled him to steer his course safely through positions of great intricacy. He obtained from the Emperor Mahomed Shah the final repeal of ***Jaziya***, a poll tax imposed on Hindus by Aurungzeb.

The three leading States of Rajputana at that time, namely, Udaipur, Jaipur, and Jodhpur, formed a triple alliance, for mutual defence and preservation, against the Mahomedan power.

Sawai Jai Singh governed Agra and Malwa for Mahomed Shah, and it was he who repelled the incursions of the Jats. The Emperor Farrukhsiyar conferred on him the insignia of the *Mahi Muratib*, the emblems of royalty, and the title of Raj Rajendra. The patrimonial State of Amber was considerably extended by him.

He was a great patron of science and art, and being a famous mathematician, astronomer, and engineer, he constructed astronomical observatories at Jaipur, Delhi, Benares, Mathura, and Ujjain, where he erected scientific instruments of his own design.

Isri Singh (1744 51), eldest son of Sawai Jai Singh, succeeded him. Madho Singh, his brother, born from an Udaipur princess, disputed the succession, and his claim was supported by his uncle, the Maharana of Udaipur. This incident occasioned great trouble, and it doubtless tended to shorten his life, which terminated in 1751.

Madho Singh I (1751 68) was a valiant Prince, who inherited his father's learning and talents.

During the reigns of succeeding rulers from 1768 to 1835 Jaipur, and Rajputana as a whole, was the scene of plunder and devastation by the lawless hordes of the Mahrattas and Pindaris, who periodically desolated the country and caused great loss of property as well as lives. There were also internal dissensions among the Rajput Princes themselves, which subjected them to serious miseries and humiliation.

In the year 1818, when Jagat Singh II was ruler, an alliance was formed between the Jaipur Durbar and the British Government.

Ram Singh II (1835 80) was only an infant when he came to the throne, and the period of minority lasted until 1851, when he was invested with powers of government. He was regarded as one of the most enlightened princes in India at that time. He earned a great reputation for his encouragement of art and learning, as well as for his conspicuous loyalty and devotion to the British throne. He placed at the disposal of the Government, during the Mutiny, all his troops, which punished the Mewatis, and rescued several Europeans, and conveyed them safely to the Agra Fort. For this service the Government of India granted him the *pargana* of Kote Kasim. He was a commander of the Indian Empire, and a Member of the Legislative Council of India from 1869 to 1873. He was subsequently created a Knight Grand Commander of the Most Exalted Order of the Star of India.

Maharaja Ram Singh was a very wise and intelligent ruler, who rendered immense service to the State and its people by improving the administration and by promoting the material condition of the Principality. Jai Singh built the city, but it was actually adorned by Maharaja Sawai Ram Singh. For the English and Sanskrit Colleges, the Girls' School, the School of Arts, the Mayo Hospital, and the Ram Newas Gardens, the metalled roads, and the gas and water works installation the people are indebted to Maharaja Sawai Ram Singh. The gift of pure drinking water to a dry and thirsty country is an invaluable blessing. He died on September 18, 1880, after having selected a young relative to succeed him.

Maharaja Sawai Madho Singh II (1880), the present Ruler, adopted this name when he came to the throne, his original name being Kaim Singh. He was born in 1861. Ever since he assumed the reins of government it has been his policy to maintain and steadily improve all the useful measures initiated by the late Maharaja. Those reforms have not only been maintained but have been considerably expanded, and, in addition to these, several new developments, calculated to advance the general welfare of the State and the well-being of the people, have been initiated. His administration is characterized by great liberality, catholicity, and a broad outlook on affairs. He evinces an unrivalled generosity and genuine and active sympathy, which have been chiefly instrumental in bringing about all that tended to the good of the land and its people. His deep religious devotion and piety make him an ideal Hindu ruler, and his toleration for all sections of his subjects, whatever their religion, is proverbial, while his geniality and love command the admiration of all who know him. His Highness stands high in the estimation of the Paramount Power, on account of his staunch loyalty and maintenance of the traditions of his house. He actually rules in the hearts of his people, and thus enjoys unexampled popularity.

The following paragraphs give a short resume of what His Highness has done during his benign rule to ameliorate the material condition of his people who are so dear to him.

Immediately after his accession in August 1881, a happy start was made at the capital to instruct and amuse the common people in a most pleasing and interesting manner, by opening an Economic and Industrial Museum. It presented to craftsmen the best specimens of local manufactures, as well as the finest art work of India. A collection of the raw products of the State and surrounding districts was also formed, with the object of bringing together the economic natural resources of the country. This museum became very popular at once, and an intelligent interest in the exhibition was created both among artisans and the general public of the place.

From the inception of this museum there was an easy transition to the idea of holding an exhibition, which crystallized in 1883, when in the first two months of the year it remained open for general inspection, and was largely attended by all classes of people. A very costly and monumental work, entitled "Memorials of the Jeypore Exhibition of 1883," illustrated in colours with Indian subjects, was published by His Highness the Maharaja, and is now a recognized work of reference on Indian art.

All the interesting exhibits were purchased by His Highness, and these formed the nucleus of a valuable permanent exhibition, started in 1887 in the Albert Hall, a beautiful building, in the Ram Niwas Gardens, near to the city. The foundation stone of the Albert Hall had been laid by His Royal Highness the Prince of Wales (His Imperial Majesty King Edward VII) on February 6, 1876. This institution is not merely a museum, it is also of great educational value.

The establishment of the museum has marked a new epoch in the history of Indian art, and has materially benefited the people both in Jaipur and other places. Jaipur art and Jaipur curios are extremely popular, and the show-rooms of many vendors in the chief cities of India are filled with them.

In order to perpetuate and immortalize all that is best and beautiful in Indian architecture, especially the most charming examples found in the early buildings of Rajputana and Moghul India, His Highness had under his direct supervision, and at considerable expense, published a series of "Portfolios of Indian Architectural details," wherein a number of full-size plates, in colours, and black and

THE STATE OF JAIPUR.

1. Ram Bagh Palace. 2. Ram Bagh Palace (Interior).

THE STATE OF JAIPUR.

1. King Edward Memorial. 2. All Saints' Church. 3. The Residency.

THE STATE OF JAIPUR

[illegible]aite, are collected, with the object of affording help and inspiration in artistic work.

It needs no further testimony to show [illegible]w genuinely solicitous His Highness is [illegible] popularize Indian art in all its phases. His Highness' patronage of letters is [illegible]ually keen. He raised the Maharaja's [illegible]llege to the status of a first-grade [illegible]llege, which is affiliated to the Allaha[illegible] University. This College has also [illegible] Oriental department attached to it, [illegible] Sanskrit is taught, and ample provision has been made to enable candidates to obtain degrees for fluency in the language. These institutions are richly endowed, and there is, besides, a network of primary and secondary schools all over His Highness' domains, and education is entirely free. Deserving students are given stipends and prizes.

Female education also receives sympathetic attention from His Highness. There is a fine Girls' School centrally situated in the city of Jaipur, where daily [illegible]es are given to needy pupils to enable [illegible] to prosecute their studies. The total strength of literate females in the State was 0·9 per million in 1901. At the [illegible]sus of 1911 it was 2·4 per million.

[illegible]he School of Art at Jaipur has lately [illegible] much to enhance the industry in [illegible] manufactures, and gives employment [illegible] number of intelligent skilled artisans. [illegible] relieve and alleviate the distress of [illegible] sufferers and the sick, there is the [illegible] Hospital at the capital, with a [illegible]er of dispensaries at the head[illegible]ers of all important centres. These [illegible]al institutions are maintained by the [illegible] There is ample accommodation for [illegible]g in-patients at the Mayo Hospital, [illegible] is also provided with electric in[illegible]ion, an X-ray apparatus, and a [illegible]ological laboratory. His Highness [illegible]ared nothing to make it a complete up-to-date institution. He has also [illegible]ted and endowed a Zenana Hos[illegible] ard, attached to the Mayo Hospital, [illegible]ory of Lady Hardinge. Its upper [illegible] has separate accommodation for [illegible] patients. Lord Curzon describes it [illegible] one of the best equipped in India." [illegible]ation is also looked after by the [illegible]ical Department.

[illegible]he State Public Works Department [illegible] reorganized by His Highness, and [illegible]s done very useful work. Many [illegible] works, miscellaneous public im[illegible]ments, and irrigation *bunds* have [illegible] completed, and His Highness has [illegible] about Rs. 4,00,00,000 upon them.

There are no perennial streams in Jaipur, and all rain water found at suitable places is collected in these *bunds*.

The invariable policy of His Highness is to add to these irrigation works every year, and they are of incalculable value when there is a deficient rainfall. There are 224 State irrigation *bunds* at present. The total cost of all these works up to August 31, 1917, was about Rs. 80,00,000.

The great famine which devastated so large a portion of India in 1899–1900 evoked His Highness' warmest sympathies. There was acute distress in his State, and most energetic and effective measures were taken to meet the dire calamity. He also realized at this moment how needful it was to have funds at hand to relieve suffering promptly, and thus the idea occurred to him of founding a permanent all-India Famine Fund, which would be available in the event of any such calamity overtaking the country again. He laid his scheme before His Excellency Lord Curzon, who cordially approved of it, and to start it His Highness subscribed a sum of Rs. 16,00,000, and he subsequently augmented this generous contribution to a total of Rs. 25,00,000. The interest of this sum is available for helping famine-stricken people in any part of India. This fund is known as the "Indian People's Famine Trust."

His Highness takes a very keen interest in Imperial matters. For military defence of the British Empire he maintains, at his own cost, an Imperial Service Transport Corps, which he has placed entirely at the disposal of the British Government for use at any time when emergency arises. It is said that during his visit to Jaipur, His Excellency the late Lord Roberts impressed upon His Highness the necessity of raising such a corps, as his own experience had taught him that when nations are at war the highest military talent and the most capable fighting strength are of no avail without the transport service, which supplies the sinews of war.

The Jaipur Imperial Service Transport Corps was raised by His Highness the Maharaja in 1889, and its present strength is 1,200 ponies, 16 *tongas*, 560 carts, and 792 men.

The Corps has also ambulance arrangements for the immediate removal of 500 sick or wounded men at a time. It has its own workshops, where carts, saddlery, and other gear are made and repaired. It is a complete self-contained unit, ready to start at a moment's notice for any place on the face of the globe.

How far His Highness' forethought in making this admirable provision for Imperial defence has proved useful and valuable, is amply proved by subsequent events in the history of India, and in the recent Great War.

The record of the Corps has been most brilliant and glorious since the time of its first organization, in 1889, up to the present time. Its services to the Empire have been mentioned in Despatches, and have been duly appreciated and rewarded.

The Corps was on active service throughout the expeditions of Chitral in 1895–6, and in Tirah in the campaign of 1897–8.

During the Great War it saw continuous service in the front line in positions of danger and responsibility in Mesopotamia and Persia. These magnificent exploits have actually surpassed all previous ones, and have elicited the admiration of the military authorities. The Corps has been selected for service on all important occasions, and it is at present employed on the North-West Frontier, the scene of its former exploits.

For the good and excellent work done by the Corps, and its remarkable record, the Government of India have placed on record their expressions of gratitude to His Highness the Maharaja.

His Highness the Maharaja has devoted special attention to the provision and extension of railways and other communications, to connect the various commercial and agricultural centres of the State. The Rajputana-Malwa Railway traverses the Jaipur territory for a total length of 243 miles. In the year 1907, His Highness the Maharaja constructed a metre-gauge line, 73 miles in length, from Sanganer on the above-named system, to Sawai Madhopur on its south-eastern boundary, where it joins the Nagda-Muttra section of the Bombay-Baroda and Central India Railway. With the object of affording further facilities for trade and commerce, His Highness sanctioned the construction of the Jaipur-Shekhawati Railway from Jaipur city, through the northern portion of the State, to Loharu in the Punjab, a distance of about 142 miles. This new line will extend to the very extreme north-east corner of the State, and will throw open the country for the benefit of traders and for Indian markets abroad. This line has not yet been completed, but a portion was formally opened for traffic by His Excellency Lord Chelmsford on November 9, 1916. There are other projects for railway extension under consideration, and it is hoped that in the near future the whole State will be covered by a network of railways, which will help in the material advancement of the people, as well as in the development of the resources of the State.

Cattle and horse fairs are held every year at the capital, and stallions are kept at Jaipur to encourage breeding of high-class animals.

His Highness the Maharaja has not neglected the preservation of ancient monuments, old buildings having been preserved intact. Maharaja Sawai Jai Singh's astronomical observatories at Jaipur, Benares, and Delhi, have been restored, and are now in thorough working order. Observations made in the Jaipur Observatory are accurate to a degree, and are employed in preparing almanacs. The Observatory at Jaipur is the largest of five which were built by him. Great masonry instruments, restored now to their exact original state, form one of the wonders of the world, and credit for all this restoration is due to the present Ruler.

A syndicate of Astronomer-Pandits is employed in making observations, and an attempt is being made to correct and reform the Indian calendar with the aid of observations.

His Highness also maintains a Meteorological Observatory at the capital, which was erected and equipped at considerable cost in 1881, and it is deemed a first-class institution. The observations recorded here are telegraphed every morning throughout the year to the Simla and Bombay Meteorological Departments. His Highness the Maharaja is greatly interested in the subject, and he consults the daily register which is submitted to him.

At the Coronation of King Edward VII His Highness was present as the chosen representative of the Princes of Rajputana. He crossed the seas, and for the first time showed to the world that even when far away from home, amid strange surroundings, a Hindu could remain a Hindu, provided he had the will power to maintain the social and religious traditions of this country, without in any way running counter to the ideas of the West.

On this memorable occasion His Highness was honoured by an invitation to an audience with His Majesty the King-Emperor.

Before proceeding on his voyage across the *Kalapana* (black waters of the great oceans), His Highness the Maharaja, in accordance with the sacred and time-honoured custom of the Solar house, worshipped the waters, as Rama, the deified progenitor of the family had done long, long ago.

For the comfort of himself and his party, His Highness chartered a new ship of the "Anchor" line, named the *Olympia*, to the upper deck of which some additions and alterations were made, in order to suit his requirements. The ship carried His Highness' five-coloured flag, the "Panch Rang" of the Jaipur State, and it was of great interest to all who saw it on the voyage. His Highness took with him the image of his household deity, Gopaljee, and elaborate arrangements were made for the shipment at Bombay of all supplies, even including Indian earth, which might be required during their stay out of India. While in London, Moray Lodge, Campden Hill, was His Highness' residence, and another large building in the vicinity was taken for his Sardars and retainers, who numbered about 130.

England had seen many thousands of Hindus before, but no royal orthodox member of that community had ever visited that land before. They had not seen a Hindu King most tenacious in his adherence to his own customs, who lived and moved about in strictly orthodox Hindu style. He had his usual holy Ganges water for drinking purposes, of which he took numerous casks with him. At Dover he was welcomed to English soil by the Mayor and Corporation of that ancient borough, and he was cheered enthusiastically by English men and women.

In London he was accorded a right royal reception, and his progress in that wonderful city, headed by his deity, Gopaljee, is still memorable in many Western minds.

Moray Lodge was transformed into an Indian palace, where His Highness' sojourn extended over a period of about three months.

His Highness witnessed and took part in the brilliant pageant of Coronation Day in London, and was present as His Majesty's guest at the ceremony in Westminster Abbey, the venerable historical building that has been the scene of the crowning of so many English Sovereigns.

His Highness had thus an opportunity of seeing how English Sovereigns are crowned, and it impressed him greatly to observe that the function, in its essential aspects, was very similar to the crowning, or the installation, of Hindu Rajas. The anointing of the King, and the holding of a pall, or canopy, over His Majesty by four Knights of the Garter, were ceremonies of quite a Hindu character. Nothing could excel the grandeur and dignity of the whole scene in the Abbey.

His Majesty the King held a Court at Buckingham Palace, at which he received His Highness the Maharaja, accompanied by his *Sardars* and officials. His Highness had also the honour of personal interviews of the most friendly character with our Sovereign, and of frank intercourse and exchange of thoughts with many of the most celebrated Englishmen of the day.

During His Highness' stay in England he experienced nothing but kindness and courteous consideration from every quarter, high and low alike.

Immediately after His Highness' return to India, he (together with 10 other ruling Princes) was invited to take part in the great celebrations to be held at Delhi in December and January 1902-3, in honour of the Coronation of His Imperial Majesty the King-Emperor of India.

In the State entry into Delhi on December 29, 1902, Their Royal Highnesses the Duke and Duchess of Connaught rode on the lordly elephant "Maula Baksh," belonging to His Highness, which was specially selected for their use, and ruling Chiefs followed on elephants, marshalled in prescribed order. His Highness the Maharaja of Jaipur was on the right front of the Rajputana Chiefs, while beside him, His Highness the Maharaja of Gwalior headed the Central India Chiefs. The magnificent cavalcade included a troop of 160 elephants, which served to make the scene memorable. This customary and time-honoured feature in an Indian State *cortège* gave it a truly oriental character.

January 1, 1903, was fixed for the Imperial Durbar, in which His Highness took part, and, with other ruling Princes, occupied a proud place among the guests of the Government, His Royal Highness the Duke of Connaught, and His Excellency the Viceroy, having seats in their midst. His Highness was also present and took part in the Grand Chapter of the two Indian Orders, held in the Diwan-

THE STATE OF JAIPUR.

1. Getore. Sawai Jai Singh's Cenotaph. 2. Sanganer. Jain Temple. 3. Jain Temple (Shrine with Images).

THE STATE OF JAIPUR.

1. View of Amber Fort and Hills. 2. A Street Scene, Jaipur.

THE STATE OF JAIPUR

-Am, in the Palace of the great Moghuls, which was the scene of the most magnificent ceremonial.

Soon after his return from the Delhi Durbar His Highness was honoured by the visit of Their Royal Highnesses the Duke and Duchess of Connaught to his capital, and at a largely-attended Durbar in the Jaipur Palace His Royal Highness decorated His Highness with the Grand Cross of the Victorian Order, in the name of His Imperial Majesty the King-Emperor Edward VII.

In the year 1911, when Their Imperial Majesties the present King-Emperor and Queen-Empress visited India to proclaim in person Their Coronation at Delhi, His Highness the Maharaja again had the honour of heading the Rajputana Princes in the official entry, and the Hon. the Agent to the Governor-General sat on his left hand in a barouche drawn by four horses, there being no procession of elephants on this occasion. His Highness was escorted by a body of feudal Rajput horsemen, clad in mail and steel armour, as well as by a detachment of Jaipur cavalry and guards, wearing dark green dress, and armed with matchlock guns and swords.

The Jaipur camp was entered by two gates, which were exact replicas of those in the city of Jaipur, and they were decorated after the style of the gates at the Amber Palace, with the addition of shields and flags, which are typical Rajput symbols. His Highness was received by His Majesty at his camp, and their personal relationship, formed at previous interviews, was renewed. His Highness, during his stay at Delhi, was treated with great dignity and distinction. His Excellency the Viceroy paid a visit to His Highness in his camp, and at every social gathering throughout the Durbar Their Majesties invariably showed a warm friendly feeling towards His Highness. On the day of the Durbar His Highness was the first among the Rajputana Chiefs to pay homage to Their Majesties, and this was done in true Hindu style. This affecting and picturesque act greatly affected Their Majesties and the great assembly.

After leaving Delhi Her Majesty the Queen-Empress visited Agra and Rajputana, His Majesty the King-Emperor having gone to Nepal, and from Agra the Royal guest journeyed to Jaipur, and was received by His Highness the Maharaja on the railway platform, he offering the customary allegiance.

Four little Hindu girls of the Jaipur Girls' School showered flowers on Her Imperial Majesty, who graciously accepted from them embroidered articles, which were of their own make. On emerging, Byas Jee, a high priest, performed before Her Imperial Majesty the most holy act of adoration by waving lighted lamps (*arti*), while Sanskrit hymns, in honour of Her Majesty, were chanted by a chorus of students of the Maharaja's School.

At a little further distance from the station Her Imperial Majesty was welcomed by a bevy of Hindu maidens, with pots (***kalash***) full of water, and flowers on their heads, a customary form of paying the highest honour to the august Visitor, and chanted rustic songs. This is deemed one of the most auspicious kinds of greeting.

His Highness accompanied Her Imperial Majesty in the procession to the Residency, where the State apartments were shown by His Highness himself. Her Imperial Majesty, while at Jaipur, visited places of interest, and also opened a road, named after Her Majesty, leading to the Jhotwara palace and gardens, where she greatly enjoyed the novel experience of driving in a bullock cart.

In honour of this visit His Highness granted a remission of Rs. 50,00,000 arrears of rent due from cultivators. This generous act brought joy to thousands of Jaipur subjects, with the result that the name of Queen Mary has become a household word in the State.

Since 1913, when, at the invitation of His Excellency Lord Hardinge, the ruling Princes and Chiefs of India assembled in Conference in Delhi, His Highness has made a practice of joining this great assembly every year, and he takes a keen interest in the proceedings, which are fraught with great possibilities. Fully realizing the advantages of such a Conference to the Rulers and their subjects, His Highness has always furthered its aims by lending the weight of his great influence among his brother Princes, as the head of the great Kachhawa Clan of Rajputs, who were always the leaders of men from very ancient times, both in war and in peace. His Highness, though conservative in ideas, is a firm believer in the steady and gradual political development of the country, and in all deliberations at the Conference his views were listened to with the highest respect. Both the Government of India and the Princes and Chiefs fully appreciated His Highness' sober judgment, ripe experience, and his deep knowledge of matters affecting the Indian States and the customs in vogue, especially in Rajputana.

In the fourth year of the Great War, namely, on April 29, 1918, a War Conference was held by His Excellency Lord Chelmsford in response to a gracious message from His Imperial Majesty the King-Emperor to India in the supreme hour of the Empire's history.

In the spacious Legislative Council Hall in Delhi there assembled, under the presidency of His Excellency the Viceroy, the great ruling Princes of India, high officials of the Government of India, leading members of the commercial community, land-holders, and politicians of various shades of opinions. Of all the Princes present His Highness, a picturesque figure in his princely costume, was the cynosure of all eyes. As in the past, so at this juncture, His Highness promptly and generously responded to the appeal in the cause of the Empire, and showed in a practical manner his unswerving loyalty to the Person and Throne of the Emperor of India, and his solicitude for the safety of the Indian Empire.

His Highness the Maharaja's large-hearted generosity knows no limitation in caste, creed, or colour distinction, he having liberally contributed on all great occasions to almost every conceivable charity. A pillar, to commemorate the Royal visit to India in 1911, will be erected at Delhi at his cost, and for this purpose a princely donation has been subscribed.

During the late war, His Highness, besides sending his Transport corps to the front, made large and substantial contributions to various funds, with the object of assisting the Allies. A battery of 10 machine guns was also presented as a thank-offering for the recovery of His Imperial Majesty the King-Emperor from his accident in France.

To the Victoria Memorial at Calcutta he has presented a very valuable historical oil-painting by the Russian artist, V. Rosterhagin, which has for its subject a unique and gorgeous scene, depicting the elephant procession which took place during the time of the late Maharaja, when His Imperial Majesty King Edward VII visited Jaipur as Prince of Wales in the year 1876.

His Highness' donations and subscriptions to works of public utility and charity may be summed up under three heads as follows : (1) Education, Rs.9,32,302-7-3 ;

(2) Charity, Rs. 26,23,500; and (3) Imperial Defence, Rs. 16,60,252-13-0.

His Highness' toleration and catholicity for all creeds is well known, but it may be mentioned that, in addition to a number of Mahomedan mosques throughout the State, there are, at the capital, churches for members of the Church of England, the United Free Church of Scotland, and Roman Catholics.

The full title of His Highness the Maharaja is: Major-General His Highness Saramad-i-Rajai-Hindustan Raj Rajendra Shree Maharajadhiraj Sir Sawai Madho Singh Bahadur, G.C.S.I., G.C.I.E., G.C.V.O., G.B.E., LL.D. (Edin.). His Highness enjoys a salute of 21 guns, of which four are personal.

The State motto is "Yato Dharmastato Jayah," meaning "Where virtue is, there is also victory."

In the history of town-planning, which now occupies the attention of modern administrators, Jaipur ranks first as being the place where, nearly three hundred years ago, in the reign of Sawai Jai Singh, the founder of Jaipur, the idea of a city with broad streets and regular arrangements of lanes, and buildings in blocks, was for the first time in India conceived, and found expression in the creation of a beautiful city.

Jaipur, designed and built by Sawai Jai Singh in 1728, bears the impress of his unrivalled and extraordinary intellect and genius. The merit of the design, the chief characteristic of which is its unusual regularity, rests with this famous Rajput personality and his famous engineer and counsellor, Vidyadhar Bhattachariya, who erected it in the most picturesque surroundings. It is encircled by a natural wall of rugged hills, crowned with forts on all sides excepting the south.

The view of a city of this kind, with hills overhanging it in the rear, can be better imagined than described. It is an entrancing picture seen while driving from the railway station, with its crenellated wall, loop-holes, and parapet, kiosks, towers and bastions, with trees in the foreground, and behind it the rugged hills, studded with forts at important points. The city stretches from east to west, or between the gates of the Sun and Moon, and is laid out in rectangular blocks. Three wide roads cross the central avenue, thus dividing the city into eight equal portions. These are again intersected at equal intervals, and this subdivision is carried on until thoroughfares become merely small lanes. The principal roads are beautified by large temples and mansions of important personages, or by public offices, while the central block is set apart for the Palace, which occupies about one-eighth of the whole town. All the houses in the principal streets are coloured pink, and there are seven gateways.

The principal architectural feature of the city is the palace of His Highness the Maharaja, which occupies a commanding position in one enclosure - called the Sarhhad - which embraces nearly one-seventh of the total area of the capital. In this enclosure may be seen the personal establishments of His Highness and several of the Departmental Offices of the State, in addition to the Diwan-i-Khas, or hall of audience, the Diwan-i-Am, or public hall of audience, the Astronomical Observatory, and the temples of Brajanandji and Anandkrishnaji.

The Chandra Mahal, or principal palace, is a massive building of two storeys, from which a magnificent view is obtained of the surrounding hills, forts, and extensive gardens, which will be referred to hereafter. The ground and other floors of the palace comprise apartments richly decorated with floral designs, embellished with quaint and beautiful paintings, adorned with mirrors, and sumptuously furnished and filled in the most elegant style.

Any history of Jaipur would be incomplete without reference to the Albert Hall (or the Jaipur Museum), which stands in the Ram Newas (Public Gardens), on the south side of the city, between its two principal gates, the Sanganer and Ajmer. The building is in the Indo-Saracenic style, with necessary modifications to adapt it for use as a modern public edifice. The general appearance, and the open courts, with fountains on either side of the Hall, remind one of the Alhambra, the palace of the Moorish kings of Granada. The scheme of decoration adopted makes the building a museum in itself, as all parts of this noble structure are enriched with beautiful examples of art from Rajputana and Moghul India.

The Hawa Mahal, or "palace of the winds," is a remarkable structure of the Saracenic order of architecture, and no better description of it can be given than by quoting the words of Sir Edwin Arnold, as follows: "It is a vision of daring and dainty loveliness, of storeys of rosy masonry and delicate overhanging balconies and latticed windows. Soaring with tier after tier of fanciful architecture in a pyramidal form, a very mountain of airy and audacious beauty, through the thousand pierced screens and gilded arches, of which the Indian air blows cool over the flat roofs of the very highest house. Aladdin's magician could have called into existence no more marvellous abode."

The Ram Newas, or public gardens, covering an area of more than 70 acres, were commenced by the late Maharaja in 1868, and were laid out at a cost of nearly Rs. 4,00,000. A portion of this extremely popular resort is devoted to zoological and ornithological collections, while space has been provided for an open-air gymnasium, cricket, football, and other athletic games. The annual cost of maintenance of the garden is about Rs. 26,000.

The official headquarters of the Political Representative of the British Government is styled "The Residency," and it is situated about one mile distant from the Jaipur railway station. The oldest portion of the building was constructed about the year 1740 by Maji Shree Ranawatji Sahiba, wife of the celebrated Sawai Jai Singh II, the founder of the State, but considerable improvements have been effected in recent years.

The Meteorological Observatory was erected and equipped at the expense of the State during the reign of the late Maharaja Ram Singh, but as its position within the grounds of the palace was considered to be unfavourable, it was removed in 1881 to a more suitable site near the Residency. Observations taken at eight o'clock each morning are sent by telegraph to the Government of India, and the Meteorological Department at Simla and Bombay. Other readings taken include the surface temperature of the soil; records of the force, velocity, and direction of the wind and the fall of rain. Of still greater interest to scientists, however, is the Jaipur Observatory, near to the Royal palace, which is the largest of five erected by Maharaja Sawai Jai Singh early in the eighteenth century. This most accomplished Ruler had a thorough knowledge of the principles of mathematical science, and in pursuance of his astronomical work, constructed several brass instruments, but he replaced them by others made of massive masonry, with the object of preventing vibration, which frequently led to inaccuracies. The observatory was neglected for many years after the death of its founder, but necessary repairs were commenced by the late Maharaja, and

THE STATE OF JAIPUR.

1. Mayo Hospital. 2. Roman Catholic Church (Interior). 3 State Procession. 4. Rajputs, Minas and Nagas.

were completed in 1911 by the present Chief.

Amber, so called after Ambarikha, or Ambarisha, son of Mandhata of Ajodhya, lies to the north of Jaipur, about 7½ miles distant from the railway station. This ancient seat of the Kachhawa Rulers of Jaipur dates farther back than the time of Kakiljee, grandson of Dulha Rai. It was taken from the Minas in A.D. 1037. The founder built a temple, dedicated to Mahadeva (Shiva), and gave it the name of Ambikeshwar. This is well worth seeing. The Minas are still living at Amber, being employed in garrison duty at the fort.

The fort, with its palaces and a series of citadels and fortifications, was an ideal stronghold, erected gradually by a succession of Hindu warriors. The general view of the fort and the city is most romantic and picturesque, yet at the same time it inspires solemnity and peacefulness. Sawai Jai Singh in the eighteenth century gave it a most dignified and lovely gateway, which is an entrance to the earlier palaces inside. From different parts of the fort one witnesses magnificent views, and to those interested in classical ages it recalls the deeds and personages of bygone days.

Galta is the name of a beautiful and remarkable gorge in the hills, about four miles in an eastwardly direction from Jaipur. Its chief feature is that it is crowded from top to bottom with tanks, temples, and other places for the accommodation of the immense number of pilgrims who gather there. The crest of the ridge is about 350 feet above the level of the plain, and quite near the top, on a projecting rock, is the famous temple dedicated to the Sun, curiously enough, by one Rao Kirparam, a Jain.

The Ghat is an intensely beautiful Pass, about a mile in length, leading through the hills along the main road from Jaipur to Agra. It is flanked on either side by high cliffs, on the northernmost point of which is the Ambagarh Fort, which forms part of the outer line of circumvallation, connecting Jaipur with Amber. The road is lined in most picturesque fashion by a continuous row of temples, country residences, and lovely gardens, and it leads to some ancient shrines, whose walls are decorated with very handsome fresco paintings.

ARTS AND CRAFTS OF JAIPUR

IT has already been remarked that Jaipur from very early days was widely known as a seat for the manufacture of artistic products, and it was due to the patronage and genuine interest in fine arts of the rulers of Jaipur that this most desirable result was brought about. Their special interest in arts and industry led many a Ruler of the State to invite, and make arrangement for their perm nent stay at the capital of all the best-known artists from far and near, who could be induced to make their home at Jaipur. Highly-skilled artists and artisans were thus available for carrying out different branches of artistic work ; and in this way there have been raised generations of workmen whose intellect and skill have given Jaipur this prominent and honourable place in the field of Indian art.

Painters, sculptors, goldsmiths, enamellers, ironsmiths, potters, carpenters, dyers, and others now following their various callings in Jaipur, have doubtless acquired their special gifts by heredity. Stones, suitable for building purposes and statuary, are largely quarried in Jaipur, and this abundance of material has from very early times given employment to numerous sculptors, whose artistic products are seen in nearly every part of India. Thus the plastic art became native to the land, and it is generally acknowledged to be a speciality of Jaipur. Several varieties of marble are to be had here, and these, when sculptured, are used as ornaments for decorating temples and palaces.

Images of Hindu gods made here—which are sent to all parts of India—are made in the orthodox style, and the forms given to them are exactly in accordance with the canons of the Hindu scriptures.

The carving of stone gives employment to a caste of workers known as Silavats, who occupy a whole division of the city of Jaipur. Modern requirements have given these men opportunities of producing marvellous tombstones and altars, which now embellish numerous churches all over the country.

These artisans, under trained modern influence, have reproduced in stone, portraits, busts, and statues, which are deemed faithful representations of the originals.

From work in stone there is a natural transition to studies in plaster, and Jaipur plaster (*araish*) is known far beyond the borders of the State ; examples of this form of decoration adorning most of the edifices in the capital cities of India. Jaipur plaster is made of powdered *chunam*, and it is extensively employed in decorating the dados and floors of houses. It takes a high polish and gives a pleasant cooling effect. In hot climes, floors covered with this material can be washed several times during the day without being tarnished or damaged in any way as far as the brilliancy of the surface and its texture are concerned, and on walls this form of decoration gives beautifully designed dados, enriched with floral or other patterns, in black or any other colour, green having been found to be particularly effective. It has also been used with great advantage in reproductions of the famous Taj marble Mosaic panels in the palace at Jaipur.

The Jaipur plaster is again usefully employed in making panels for windows, which are formed of pieces of glass in a variety of colours and patterns. The work is termed *Gach-Li-jali*.

In former days, ceilings and walls of palaces and bathrooms were ornamented with coloured mirrors, and the residences thus decorated are known as *Shish Mahals*.

Carving in ivory is practised to some extent in Jaipur, and some of the work produced is in no way inferior to the best pieces obtained in other parts of India.

Jaipur pottery in blue and white is so popular as ornamental ware, that it meets with a ready sale, although it is not produced in large quantities. It is practically similar to Delhi and Multan ware. All the principal ingredients for its manufacture are obtained in the State, and it is made in a variety of forms, with surface designs, which are chiefly oriental in character.

There are numerous evidences still extant to show that the early rulers of Jaipur were particularly fond of porcelain tiles, and several portions of the palaces at Amber and Jaipur, adorned with these beautiful pieces of work in various colours, are now in a good state of preservation. They are admirably suited for the ornamentation of walls, or of limited surfaces.

The Jaipur School of Art has given a

THE STATE OF JAIPUR.

1. Albert Hall Museum. 2. Interior, Albert Hall. 3. Museum (Interior).

great impetus to the popularity of this industry, and the tiles have latterly been introduced into cabinet work, in which they are most effective. Clay pottery is also made, every article being painted by hand.

Numerous families of braziers, brass founders, and copper beaters live in a busy quarter of the city, and being regular and patient workers, they ply their trade day and night with very short intervals of rest.

The dealers in brass occupy a long range of shops in the great bazar, and on the night of the Devali festival the display of their glittering wares amidst the blaze of innumerable lamps, presents a delightful scene of fairyland.

The wealth of a Hindu householder of an average standing is estimated by the number and weight of the brass utensils in his possession.

Brass vessels for daily household requirements are always made with a plain surface, in order that they may be thoroughly cleansed from all impurities. Cleaning with sand and water gives a very brilliant polish, and the display of these vessels of various sizes and forms in a Hindu house is an attractive sight.

Brass is ornamented in Jaipur in various styles, and the great popularity of beautifully-made articles for daily use, or as decorations, has extended throughout India, as well as in Europe and the United States of America.

The chief styles of surface decoration are *repousse*, chasing and engraving, enamelling or lacquering, and encrusting with other metals. All these modes are very dexterously and artistically practised in the capital of the State, and Jaipur occupies a most prominent place in the manufacture of these art curios. Jaipur is fortunate in having a number of skilled workmen who have been able to produce such exquisite articles which embellish many oriental and Western homes; and have obtained first-class prizes at various industrial exhibitions.

It is very interesting to observe the process of making these valuable articles, how by hammering on the back of metal, and "chasing" it, most beautiful patterns are worked and cleverly delineated. Attempts have been made to portray busts and groups in metal in this manner, and large shields depicting various important scenes in the great Hindu epics, the *Mahabharata* and *Ramayan*, have been executed in a marvellously artistic manner.

Jaipur workmen have obtained a special reputation for this work, and the Government of India recognized this fact several years ago by ordering a silver *howdah* for an elephant to be made for presentation to a ruling monarch. Several sets of door panels of carved wood, and mounted with *repousse* brass-work, similar to those in Jaipur, have been supplied for residences in England and elsewhere, and they are greatly admired.

The next method of decorating brass or silver is plain and simple engraving. Plates of the required shape are first covered with white paint, an artist then draws in pencil the designs which are to be produced, and these are afterwards engraved.

The enamelling or lacquering of brass is a very fine work, demanding the highest skill. The designs are first engraved, then the parts thus worked are treated with the fused colours, and finally the whole is subjected to careful polishing. Almost all of the recognized colours are used in this manner, and the designs for decoration include a large variety of subjects.

This art was formerly practised at Moradabad, in the United Provinces, but the Jaipur workers have proved to be their superiors. The Moradabad workers are mostly Mahomedans, among whom the drawing of animal figures is prohibited by religious ordinances. In Jaipur the craftsmen are entirely Hindus, and as they are not restricted to floral decoration alone, they introduce all kinds of figures, which make the articles most attractive and artistic.

Religious subjects are also enamelled, and sometimes large salvers and shields, depicting subjects borrowed from Hindu sacred writings, are made.

In addition to the processes described above for ornamenting brass, floral designs are very often pierced, this being a variety of decoration which is greatly admired.

Moulding and casting of large and small pieces of metals is a thriving industry, and beautiful figures of animals and deities are thus made. Much of the heavy jewellery in base metal or silver, worn by peasants, is produced by the old method of casting in wax. Bronze chain anklets, cast in one mould, are so cleverly made that it is doubtful if the best foundries in Europe could excel them.

Jaipur has been universally acknowledged to be the only place in India where the best work of enamelling on gold is performed. Silver and copper are also employed, but they are not so suitable for Jaipur enamel.

It is said that this ancient art of enamelling was known to the Phœnicians, who taught it to the Persians, and from Persia it reached India.

Maharaja Man Singh, who was one of the pillars of the Moghul Empire at the court of Akbar, who had governed the kingdom of Kabul, brought Hindu enamel-workers from Lahore, and their descendants carry on to this day work similar to that practised by their forefathers.

The Jaipur enameller enjoys a special reputation for the purity of his colours and the precision with which they are employed. Enamelling is done in two styles, the "Cloisonne," and the "Champleve," the latter named method being followed at Jaipur. The enameller is able to apply all colours to gold, but it is the brilliant pure ruby red and green for which Jaipur is specially noted. The rich transparent lustre which is given to these colours is unique and peculiar to Jaipur enamel.

Silver and copper are also enamelled, but the former can only be used with white, black, or pink colours. Enamelled copper eyes are made for images.

The great increase in the demand for damascened articles has led to the production of cheap and inferior work, and as a consequence, much injury has been done to this indigenous art, in fact it has now become quite impossible to secure first-class work.

Rajputs still possess a great love for decorating their weapons in this form of ornamentation, the art being practised in the palace workshops. Sometimes silver is also employed with gold in damascening, and the combination thus produced is termed ***Ganga-Jumni***, from its supposed resemblance to the confluence of the white waters of the Ganga with the deep blue waters of the Jumna at Allahabad.

The armoury of His Highness the Maharaja of Jaipur has a very large and valuable collection of articles representative of this instructive and most beautiful art.

A large quantity of arms of good steel are manufactured in Jaipur. There are also a considerable number of blacksmiths, who carry on their hereditary occupation in a masterly style.

The lapidary, too, is greatly in evidence at Jaipur.

Having given above a brief survey of indigenous industries in the mineral kingdom, reference may now be made to those connected with vegetable substances.

THE STATE OF JAIPUR.

1. Jaipur Brass 2. Damascening and Arms. 3. Lacquered Wood. 4. Carvings in Ivory, Sandalwood and Ebony. 5. Pottery.

THE STATE OF JAIPUR.

1. Enamelling Gold and Silver Plate. 2. Statuary Marble. 3. Paintings. 4. Sanganer Chintzes and Tie and Dye Work.
5. Corner of the Museum Court, showing an old Jain Pillar and Hindu Deities.

THE STATE OF JAIPUR

Papier mâché is obtained by pounding paper pulp and other ingredients, which forms a mass suitable for the plastic modelling of large and small figures, depicting characters from life, which are afterwards painted and dressed. At the Jaipur Museum there may be seen a large number of heads made of this material, portraying the principal castes in India, which are acknowledged to be exceedingly clever and correct studies, and similar collections have been contributed to several galleries of curios, both in India and in Europe. These figures are highly valued, as they are lighter and less brittle than plaster or clay images, and therefore one can easily carry them without risk of breakage. When they are beautifully dressed in cloth, and adorned with sham jewellery, they become remarkably attractive ornaments.

A very fine collection of these figures, as well as masks, is exhibited every year in one of the Hindu temples at Jaipur, at the time of the *Narsingh Lila*.

An enormous trade is carried on in lacquered wooden goods in almost every town in Rajputana, and Khandela, in Jaipur, is especially noted for the manufacture of such articles.

In the School of Art, at Jaipur, a finer variety of work is done, which is known as incised lacquer. The articles thus ornamented receive several coats of lac of different colours, applied while they are being turned on the lathe, and with the help of sharp tools figures of various kinds and shades are produced. This work is carried on by the artists with great rapidity and skill, and it is wonderful to watch how exact they are in the use of their instruments. In the armoury of His Highness the Maharaja there is a very interesting collection of maces and sticks, carried by royal messengers, which are perfect examples of lacquering.

Wooden covers for manuscripts have also been made, the chief subjects of the writings being inscribed on the surface, which is subsequently painted and lacquered.

Large wooden trays, stools, and thrones for gods, as well as *howdahs* for elephants, are also decorated in this manner, while circular playing-cards are painted and lacquered on leather or fish scales at Sawai Madhopur.

The weaving of coarse or fine variety of cotton is practised in nearly every part of India, and Jaipur is no exception to the rule, as excellent cloths, suitable for wearing apparel, rugs, flooring, and other purposes, are produced in large quantities, but since the making of it is done by hand the material produced is not sufficient to meet local requirements. At the same time, however, it may be said this material is more durable, and will undergo all kinds of wear and tear, better than the machine-made article.

Jaipur enjoys a high reputation in the industry of printing and dyeing cloths, the best class of work being executed at Sanganer and Bugroo.

Sanganer, a very old town near Jaipur city, is the chief seat of this manufacture. The printers, who are hereditary craftsmen, worship Namdeo, the patron saint of the workers who flourished long long ago at Panderpur, in Gujarat. The printers are Hindus, and their manufacturing processes are of the most simple character.

Bugroo is another place in the State where there is a large industry for the production of chintzes on thick coarse materials which are extensively employed for personal wear and other uses.

A very brisk trade is carried on at Jaipur in dyed cloths which are prepared for everyday use both in permanent and fugitive dyes.

Carpets of plain and elaborate designs are manufactured by local weavers. More than three hundred years ago Maharaja Man Singh brought a number of old Persian carpets to Jaipur. They are most splendid pieces of artistic work, and are in wonderful preservation, although mellowed with age. They have, in fact, considerably improved in appearance, and are characterized by that richness of tone and harmony for which they are famous. The existence of these carpets in Jaipur enabled the workmen of the city to take a prominent part in this industry, which has produced numerous copies of bold and graceful designs. There is a large demand for them to-day, but unfortunately the output is very limited.

Malpura, a town in the south-west of Jaipur, is famous for the manufacture of felt, or *numda*, which is made of wool, well washed with soap and water, and then dried. *Chukmas* (floor-cloths), covers for saddles and guns, for waterproof cloaks and *asans*, or prayer-mats, are the most familiar examples, all of which are largely manufactured.

Jaipur has for ages been known as a home of artists, who have flourished under the patronage of its rulers. It is clear, however, that the early progenitors of these painters did not belong to Jaipur, but the mere fact that they were brought to the State bears unmistakable testimony to the inherent love for fine arts which characterized the ruling princes of the past.

The artists belong chiefly to the following castes, namely: *Khatis* (carpenters), *Silawets* (stone-workers), and *Kumhars* (potters). They paint on various kinds of materials, but plaster, wood, cloth, leather, metal, glass, ivory, and paper are most commonly used. They are of different grades, too, the highest being those who paint on ivory and paper.

In His Highness' private library in the Palace, and in the possession of the Rajput aristocracy, are still to be seen a number of old paintings, which are of profound interest. They are good portraits of celebrities of the past, depicting events in the days of the early kings and their courtiers. They form a gallery of historical portraits, and are perfect examples of clever work. Being rare objects they are very valuable.

A large quantity of good paper is manufactured at Jaipur, Sanganer, and Sawai Madhopur, which is consumed in the various State Departments. This paper is very strong and durable, and is admirably suited for writing purposes with Indian reed and ink.

HIS HIGHNESS MAHARAJA DHIRAJ RAJ RAJAISHAWAR, SAR-AMAD-I-RAJ HAI HINDUSTHAN MAHARAJA SHREE, UMED SINGHJI, SAHIB BAHADUR, OF MARWAR.

A VIEW OF THE FORT FROM DECKUND.

THE STATE OF JODHPUR (MARWAR)

MARWAR is the most extensive principality under the political charge of the Resident in the Western Rajputana States Agency of the Government of India, its area amounting to 34,963 square miles. The word is a corruption of "Maru-war" (meaning the region of death), and was doubtless originally applied because of the desert character of a good proportion of the State. The State is bounded on the north by Bikaner, on the north-west by Jaisalmer, on the west by Sindh, on the south-west by the Rann of Cutch, on the south by Palanpur and Sirohi, on the south-east by Udaipur, on the east by Ajmer-Merwara and Kishengarh, and on the north-east by Jaipur. In the last census of 1921 its population was 1,841,642, the number including 1,576,329 Hindus, 154,409 Mahomedans, 103,109 Jains, 6,577 Animists, 622 Christians and 596 others. Its average annual income is a crore of rupees.

The Maharaja of Jodhpur is the head of the Rathor clan of Rajputs, and claims descent from Rama, the deified king of Ayodhya. He holds a unique position in India, having seven salute princes amongst the cadets of his house, viz., the Maharajas of Bikaner, Kishengarh and Idar, and the Rajas of Rutlam, Sitamau, Sailana and Jhabua. The Rashtras (originally termed Rashtriks) are mentioned in some of the edicts of Asoka in the Deccan, to which they migrated from Surashtra, their classic home. The earliest king was Abhimanyu, who reigned in the fifth century A.D. Driven from the Deccan, the Rashtras sought refuge in Kanauj, where they founded a new dynasty under the name Gahadwals: there were seven kings of this line, beginning with Yasovigrah and ending with Jaichand. The latter suffered a defeat in a desperately fought battle at Etawa, and was slain A.D. 1194. Unwilling to submit to the yoke of the conquerer, his near kinsmen sought in the scrub and desert of Rajputana a second line of defence against the advancing wave of Mahomedan conquest.

Jai Chand was succeeded by Rao Siahji (1212), whose descendants secured an immense territory, including a large portion of western Rajputana, and a home was made in the district, which included the area now known as the State of Marwar.

Subsequent Rulers increased their possessions, and one of them captured the town of Mandore from the Parihars, it remaining the capital until the year 1459, when Rao Jodha laid the foundation of the State by transferring the seat of government to the present city of Jodhpur.

Rao Jodha (1454–89) was succeeded by Rao Satal (1489–92), in whose reign (1492–1516) a band of Pathans entered Marwar during the holding of a festival, and carried off 140 maidens from

1. HIS LATE HIGHNESS MAJOR SIR SHREE SUMMAIR SINGHJI, SAHIB BAHADUR.

2. GENERAL HIS HIGHNESS MAHARAJA DHIRAJ SIR PRATAP SINGHJI, SAHIB BAHADUR, G.C.B., G.C.S.I., G.C.V.O., D.C.L., LL.D., ETC., MAHARAJA-REGENT OF MARWAR STATE.

3. MAHARAJ SHREE ZALIM SINGHJI SAHIB BAHADUR, VICE-PRESIDENT, COUNCIL OF REGENCY, MARWAR STATE.

4. MAHARAJ SHREE AJIT SINGHJI, SAHIB BAHADUR, YOUNGER BROTHER OF H.H. THE MAHARAJA SAHIB BAHADUR OF JODHPUR.

THE STATE OF JODHPUR (MARWAR).

1. The Palace. 2. The Palace Drawing-room. 3. The Jodhpur Imperial Service Lancers.

the town of Peepar. The tidings of the raid soon reached the ears of Satal, who, accompanied by a number of vassals, pursued and overtook the captors, but the rescue of the women was effected at the cost of the Rao's life. The itinerant minstrelsy of Marwar are in the habit at the present day of visiting fairs and singing "the rape of 140 virgins of Peepar, and of their rescue by their cavalier Chief at the price of his own blood."

Rao Satal was succeeded by Rao Siya, who reigned till 1516, and was succeeded by Rao Ganga, who died in 1532, and was succeeded by Rao Maldeo.

Rao Maldeo (1532-63) is regarded as one of the most distinguished Rathor Rulers of early days; he acquired new territory, and knew how to retain it; he caused the State to become powerful and influential; and it is no mean tribute to his memory that the Mahomedan historian, Ferishta, speaks of him as "the most potent Prince in Hindusthan."

His increasing prosperity enabled him to enclose the city of Jodhpur with strong walls, he erected palaces and other public buildings, and made considerable additions to the fortress. It is said that the financial means for carrying out these and other important works were derived from the great wealth of the products of the Sambur salt lake, over which the State had control. Ancient histories contain proof that Marwar, at this period, consisted of 38 districts, several of which comprised 360 townships, and that there was not one which did not number 80. The vassals of Marwar were consequently increasing in number and power, a circumstance arising from the fact that the numerous progeny of the several families were granted certain portions of land at birth, and thus it followed that the State was split up into innumerable portions. Maldeo realized that it was due to his position as Chief that steps should be taken to check the subdivision which was going on, and he therefore instituted a system of grading his followers, according to rank, and thus reducing to a very great extent the influence of units.

Some ten years later Sher Shah, who had driven Humayon from the Imperial throne of Delhi, led an army of 80,000 men into Marwar, and Maldeo immediately collected a force of about 50,000 Rajput troops to meet the invader. Both leaders were men of great judgment and skill in battle, and each manifested such caution in making an attack, that the two armies faced each other for 28 days without any further advance being made. Sher Shah, perceiving the difficulties of the situation, managed by stratagem to cause differences of opinion between Maldeo and his subcommanders, with the result that some of the latter, disregarding the orders of their Chief, marched against the opposing force with a mere handful of about 12,000 men. The inevitable followed, and Maldeo's army was almost wholly destroyed.

Near the close of his life Maldeo's castle was again besieged, and although resistance was stoutly offered, the Chief was compelled to yield homage through the person of his elder son, Udai Singh, who was enrolled by the Emperor as "Commander of one thousand," and was shortly afterwards invested with the title of "Moota Raja," or "Fat Raja," the epithet by which he is designated in annals of that period.

After Maldeo's death Chandersen occupied the *gadi*, and he was succeeded by Raja Udai Singh in 1584. This Chief entered into matrimonial alliances with the Moghul Emperor by giving his daughter and sister respectively in marriage to Prince Salim (Jehangir) and Akbar. The latter, in acknowledgment of these unions and of other services rendered by the Chief, restored all the possessions—with the exception of Ajmer—which had been wrested from Marwar during recent wars. On the death of Udai Singh in 1595, his eldest son, Raja Sur Singh, ascended the *gadi*, and by his fearless exploits, added such lustre to the Rathor name, that he was greatly esteemed by the occupant of the Imperial Throne. Notwithstanding his almost constant absence from the State owing to the number of the expeditions in which he took part, he found time to beautify his palace and to construct many fine public works, including the Sur Sagur tank, or "Warrior's Sea." The next Ruler, Raja Guj, had a short but peaceful reign, and in the ordinary course of events he would have been followed by Umra, his eldest son, but as this Prince possessed a most turbulent spirit, despising all restraints, and was always seeking for opportunities for the display of martial skill, the Raja summoned a convocation of the feudality of Marwar, at which sentence of exclusion from succession was passed upon him, and this was accompanied by the solemn and seldom practised rite of exile. This occurred in 1633, and five years later, on the death of the Raja, the reins of government was taken up by Jaswant Singh, who was the first Chief of Marwar to be invested with the title of Maharaja. This Ruler was at an early stage in his career selected to lead an army against Aurungzeb, who, with his brother Murad, had rebelled against their father the Emperor, Shah Jehan, during the illness of the latter, but he failed to overpower the Delhi Prince, who entered Jodhpur city in triumph. This battle cost Marwar the lives of no fewer than 15,000 gallant Rajputs.

After Aurungzeb became Emperor, he recognized the fact that Jaswant Singh was anxious to throw off the Mahomedan yoke, and with the object of counteracting that restlessness, he came to the conclusion that it would be a wise policy for him to keep the Chief engaged in petty conflicts in places where he would be the least dangerous.

Colonel Tod, in his "Annals and Antiquities of Rajasthan," referring to this subject, says: "If Jaswant's character had been drawn by biographers of Court, viewed mainly in the light of a great vassal of Empire, it would have reached us with the stigma of treachery in every trust reposed in him, but, on the other hand, when we reflect on the character of the King, the avowed enemy of the Hindu Faith, we only see in Jaswant a Prince putting all to hazard in its support. He had to deal with one who placed him in these offices, not from personal regard, but because he deemed a hollow submission better than avowed hostility, and the Maharaja, therefore, only opposed hypocrisy with fraud and superior strength with treachery." Jaswant died in 1679, when on one of his ordained excursions beyond the Attock river. He was succeeded by his posthumous son, Ajit Singh, who in his infancy was carefully guarded in a secluded monastery on an isolated rock at Abu in order to prevent his seizure by Aurungzeb. The latter, enraged at his inability to secure the custody of the young heir, invaded Marwar, pillaged the capital city and other towns, and pulled down temples and erected mosques in their places, all these acts of devastation being done with the object of converting Hindus to the tenets of Islam. Ajit Singh was a Prince of great valour, but he inherited the same invincible hatred to the very name of Moslem as his predecessor had done, and he used his intelligent mind in considering measures for ridding the State of the oppression. Maharaja Ajit Singhji was cruelly murdered, and was succeeded by Abhey Singhji in 1750, who was dethroned by his uncle, Maharaja Bakhat Singhji, in 1752. The latter had a very

THE STATE OF JODHPUR (MARWAR).

1. The Guest House. 2. The Sardar Club. 3. The Residency.

THE STATE OF JODHPUR (MARWAR).

1. The Marble Bara-Dari at the Palace. 2. The Racecourse Pavilion. 3. The Palace Swimming Bath.

THE STATE OF JODHPUR (MARWAR).

1. H.H. The Maharaja Regent Sahib Bahadur's Residence. 2. The Jubilee Courts. 3. Maharaj Shree Zalim Singhji Sahib Bahadur's Residence.

short and uneventful reign, and in 1753 Bijoy Singhji became Ruler of the State. Marwar had been in enjoyment of peace for several years, but the Mahrattas, having again assumed a threatening attitude, the Rajputs in that territory deemed it necessary to combine their forces in order to defend their political existence. The Ruler of Jaipur, in 1787, sent an embassy to Marwar with proposals for joint action against the enemy, and in the battle of Tonga, which followed, the Rathors, exhibiting the greatest valour, completely routed the Mahrattas and Scindia, their leader, abandoned the field.

Maharaja Bijoy Singhji was succeeded by Maharaja Bhimsinghji in 1793: he died in 1804, and was succeeded by Maharaja Man Singh.

Early in the reign of the Maharaja Man Singh troubles of a personal character arose between the Rulers of Marwar and Jaipur, and the Pindari leader, Amir Khan, after supporting, in turn, the views of each Chief, deposed Man Singh and assumed control of the affairs of Marwar. This high-handed procedure continued for only about two years, but even in that short space of time the usurper ransacked the Treasury of every rupee, and left the State in a most deplorable condition.

Marwar was placed under British protection by a treaty made in 1818 with Chhatar Singh, the son of Man Singh, and Regent at the time. Man Singh subsequently resumed his occupancy of the *gadi*, but his conduct towards the nobles in the State was of such an unreasonable character that the British Government intervened, and induced the Chief to devote his attention to legitimate State affairs instead of causing needless troubles within his own borders. On his death in 1843, without issue then living, the choice of a successor fell upon Takhtat Singh, who thereupon became Maharaja. Takhtat Singh is remembered chiefly on account of his loyalty to the British during the Mutiny of 1857, the lives of a large number of Europeans being saved by his protection of them in Marwar. He died in 1873, and was followed by Jaswant Singh, during whose reign the State attained a degree of prosperity which had hitherto been unknown. He established Courts of Justice, constructed railways, telegraphs and roads, introduced the system of revenue settlement, and thoroughly re-organized every Official Department in the State. He, further, formed an Imperial Service Cavalry Corps which, as will be shown later, has rendered efficient active service in France in the great European War. Jaswant Singh was honoured by being created a Knight Grand Commander of the Most Eminent Order of the Star of India, and died in 1895, leaving his only son, Sardar Singh, who was then a minor, to succeed him. The administration of the State was entrusted to his uncle, His Highness the Maharaja Sir Pratap Singhji Saheb Bahadur, and the young Maharaja was invested with full powers of government in 1898.

Barely 12 months later the new Ruler was called upon to face the great famine of 1899–1900, and although the prospect would have been discouraging enough for one of maturer age, His Highness did everything that was humanly possible, within the resources of the State, to afford relief to his suffering subjects. The Maharaja was a guest at the Delhi Durbar in 1903 as a member of the Imperial Cadet Corps, to which he was admitted during a visit to England in 1901–2, and he, like his predecessor, was presented with the insignia of a Knight Grand Commander of the Most Eminent Order of the Star of India.

His reign was marked by an exceedingly able administration of affairs, and at the time of his death, in 1911, the various Departments of State were in a thoroughly satisfactory working order, and the people were prosperous and contented. The successor of the late Chief was his elder son, His Highness Raj Rajeshwar Maharaja Dhiraj Sri Sumer Singhji Sahib Bahadur, a minor, and the management of the State was placed in the hands of a Council of Regency, comprising Major-General His Highness the Maharaja Dhiraj Sir Pratap Singh Bahadur and Maharaj Sri Zalim Singh Bahadur.

During the lifetime of his father His Highness was placed under the guardianship of Captain Williams, who also acted as his tutor. After his accession on April 5, 1911, he proceeded to England in the charge of Captain A. D. Strong, and was entered as a pupil in Wellington College. After 2½ years' residence in England His Highness returned to Marwar on January 11, 1914, and he had the pleasure in the following month of receiving at his capital Their Excellencies, Lord and Lady Hardinge, the Viceroy and Governor-General of India and his consort, who had paid a special visit to the State for the purpose of welcoming the Maharaja Saheb Bahadur to his ancestral home. A banquet was held at the Residency on the evening of the 7th of February, which was attended by Their Excellencies, His Highness the Maharaja Saheb, His Highness the Maharaja the Regent Saheb, and a number of European guests. During the evening His Highness the Maharaja Sir Pratap Singhji proposed the health of Lord and Lady Hardinge, and in the course of his remarks, he said: "I will not trouble Your Excellency here by referring at any length to the affairs of this State, with the guidance of which Your Excellency did me the high honour to entrust me during the present minority; I only hope that Your Excellency will, from personal inspection, be satisfied that the confidence reposed in me has been justified.

"His Highness the Maharaja has now returned from England to his own State and people, with his mind and outlook on life enlarged by education at a public school, by travel, and by a general introduction to the affairs of the world under the inspiring influence of a sympathetic and conscientious guardian, Major Strong: and lastly, by the inestimable advantage of having come under the favourable notice and almost parental regard and care of his Sovereign, who honoured him with his close personal friendship. It will now be my proudest duty to be associated with such further measures as Your Excellency may direct for His Highness' administrative training and preparation for the position of Ruler of the splendid heritage to which he has succeeded.

"I wish to bring to Your Excellency's notice, and to express my thanks for, the continual help ungrudgingly given me at all times by my esteemed friends, the Hon. the Agent to the Governor-General, and the Resident, and by all Members of the Regency Council, individually and collectively, and particularly I should like to express the deep obligation I feel to Your Excellency for the kind support and sympathy that I have always received at your hands, without which I should at times have felt my task, as Regent of the State, wellnigh impossible."

In replying to the toast, which was most enthusiastically received, His Excellency remarked: "I desire to thank you, Sir Pratap, very cordially for the kind terms in which you have proposed my health, and for the opportunity afforded me of welcoming His Highness Maharaja Sumer Singh back to his State after two years of public school life in England. I am sure all of us here to-night are delighted to see His Highness return full of health

THE STATE OF JODHPUR (MARWAR).

1. The Central Jail, Jodhpur. 2. Shree Jaswant Serai. 3. Teja Mahi's Temple. 4. Kunj Behari's Temple.

and strength. It was only after the most anxious consideration that I decided, with the full concurrence of the Maharaja Regent, to take the important step of sending His Highness to England, but from what I have heard of the progress which His Highness has made during his stay there, and his popularity both with the masters and his school-fellows, I am confident that the experiment has been crowned with success, and that the public school training, which His Highness has received, will have implanted in him true ideals of morality, honour, and justice, while it has left his love for his country and her noble traditions unimpaired. His Highness' subjects will, I am sure, be gratified to learn that it is proposed that His Highness shall complete his general education in Jodhpur in order gradually to familiarize himself with those local administrative problems with which he will shortly be called upon to deal.

" I would remind His Highness that the task of governing a State of the size and importance of Marwar is one calculated to tax the energy and test the ability of even the most experienced, and that the more assiduously he applies himself to the study of its administration in the time which remains before he is invested with powers, the easier will that task become and the more efficiently will it be performed.

" In the early eighties Marwar was not the peaceful country it is now, but dacoity and turbulence were rampant in the land ; Maharaja Jaswant Singh was on the *gadi*, and called to his aid Sir Pratap, who had already won his spurs as an administrator. Sir Pratap himself took the lead against various gangs of freebooters, and his activity and energy rapidly evolved law and order where chaos and disorder had hitherto prevailed ; and then, under his guidance, boundary disputes were settled, real courts of justice established, criminal tribes reclaimed, the customs reformed, a treasury started, debts paid off, and funds provided for public works. At the time, too, the inauguration took place of the Imperial Service Troops, some of whom served with distinction in the Tirah campaign, where Sir Pratap was also present, and later, under his leadership, maintained their fine reputation in the China Expedition ; and I have no doubt that in the future, as in the past, they will always be ready, and more than ready, for similar service should occasion arise. When, therefore, two years ago arrangements had to be made for the administration of the Marwar State, I had cause to deem myself fortunate in being able to avail myself of the services of a man of ments had to be made for the administrative ability, and integrity of purpose, and I can confidently claim that time has amply justified the wisdom of my choice.

" It will not be long before His Highness the Maharaja will take over the reins that have been held so skilfully during the Regency, and, with the great traditions of the Rathor clan behind him and all the world before him, he may look forward to a career of honourable distinction worthy of his ancestry, and he may rest assured that throughout its course he will carry with him the warm and hearty good wishes of all who know him."

On the 8th of February His Excellency the Viceroy formally opened the new Rajput Schools at Chopasni, about six miles distant from the capital.

Loyalty to the British throne of the staunchest type has ever characterized the relations of the Jodhpur house with the Paramount Power, and when the Great War commenced in 1914, none were readier than the princely representatives of this ancient State to render aid to the British arms in the mighty conflict then opening. Fortunately, at the moment, in a position of authority as Regent was the noble figure of Lieut.-General Sir Pratap Singhji, a Rajput of the Rajputs, the living embodiment of all the chivalrous virtues of that splendid race. In spite of his advanced age (he was then over seventy), Sir Pratap decided to accompany the young Maharaja to the front. Quitting Jodhpur on August 29, 1914, the Maharaja, as Colonel-in-Chief of the Sardar Rissala, and Sir Pratap in supreme command of the Regiment, the two princely warriors proceeded to join the British field army in France. Meanwhile, active preparations were made in the State for the organization of the State forces in order to render the greatest possible assistance to the British Government. In all, during these memorable days of the war, the State despatched to the field 1,369 combatants of all ranks. In addition, in 1918, arrangements were made to raise an infantry battalion 1,360 strong, and recruiting was proceeding when the conclusion of the Armistice rendered further action unnecessary. The Jodhpur Lancers in the West acquitted themselves splendidly, as was to have been expected. In France the method of fighting of necessity restricted their openings for distinction, but, nevertheless, they took a leading and useful part in a counter-attack on the enemy at Festubert on December 21, 1914, losing four men in the operation, and again on November 30, 1917, at Villers Causlan they showed equal bravery in an action in which they lost four men killed and 18 wounded. Proceeding on July 14, 1918, with the Imperial Service Brigade to Palestine, the Jodhpur Lancers participated in an attack on the enemy on the Jordan, and drove them back with heavy casualties, suffering themselves a loss of 15 killed and 7 wounded. Later, on September 23, 1918, the regiment stormed and took the fortified town of Haifa at a gallop, fearlessly charging the enemy across the river in the face of heavy gunfire, killing many Turks at the point of the lance, and capturing 700 prisoners ; twenty were wounded in the action, and of these six subsequently died. On October 25, 1918, the regiment was again engaged to the north-west of Aleppo, and suffered a number of casualties.

His Highness was made an honorary lieutenant of the 3rd Skinner's Horse on October 15, 1914, and on August 1, 1917, was promoted to the honorary rank of Major. Later still, on January 1, 1918, His Highness was made a K.B.E.

His Highness returned to Marwar in June, 1915, and in the following year was invested with full ruling powers by His Excellency Lord Hardinge, Viceroy and Governor-General. A Durbar was held on February 26th, which was attended by the Agent to the Governor-General in Rajputana, the Resident, Western Rajputana States, and a large number of British Officers and high officials of the State.

His Excellency in his address declared that the policy of the Government of India towards Ruling Princes was one of sympathy and trust, of sympathy with their aims and sentiments and their noble traditions, of trust in their fervent loyalty to the person of the King-Emperor, and to the Power whose protection they enjoyed. His Excellency continued : " We have recognized that if a State is to be ruled justly and well, and to be a source of real help to the British Empire, it is only through the Ruler himself, supported by his *Sardars* and people, that these results can be obtained. Irksome restrictions on the exercise of sovereign powers are apt to chafe and irritate a proud and sensitive spirit, with results disastrous not only to the Ruler and his people, but also to the Empire at large. We have, therefore, made it our aim to cultivate close and friendly relations with the Ruling Princes,

THE STATE OF JODHPUR (MARWAR).

1. View of the City from the Fort. 2. View of the City from Deckund.

THE STATE OF JODHPUR (MARWAR).

1. THE DURBAR HIGH SCHOOL. 2. THE POWLETT NOBLES' AND ELGIN RAJPUT SCHOOLS. 3. THE HEWSON HOSPITAL. 4. THE JASWANT FEMALE HOSPITAL.

THE STATE OF JODHPUR (MARWAR).

1. The Jai Pol Gate (The Fort). 2. The Singar Chowki (The Fort). 3. The Gallery of Heroes.
4. Cenotaph of Maharaja Shree Ajit Singhji, Saheb Bahadur, at Mandore. 5. Cenotaph of Maharaja Shree Jaswant Singhji, Saheb Bahadur, at Mandore.

to show by every means that we trust them and look on them as helpers and colleagues in the great task of Imperial rule, and so to foster in them a spirit of responsibility and pride in their work which no external supervision can produce. . . . In the critical times through which we have passed since this terrible war began, the moral and material support given by the Princes and Chiefs of India have been of incalculable value. They took the lead in asserting their enthusiastic loyalty to the King-Emperor, both by word and deed. Many of them, including the gallant veteran warrior, Sir Pratap Singhji Bahadur, who, to-day, will resign his post as Regent of Jodhpur, and the young Prince who will relieve him of his charge, have served with His Majesty's armies in the field, and all with one accord have offered their personal services and lavished their resources in support of the noble cause which Great Britain has espoused.

" The reforms effected by the Council under the able presidency of His Highness Sir Pratap Singhji have extended to every branch of the administration, and Your Highness may well be gratified at the account which the Council are able to give of their stewardship. In spite of a series of lean years, the revenue has risen during your minority from Rs. 75 to 89½ lakhs, while the Reserve Fund of Rs. 65 lakhs has been trebled. The State is free from debt, and its assets, so far as they are calculable, have risen from Rs. 2¾ to 4½ crores. This period has seen, among other less important works, the completion of the Sumer Samand Irrigation scheme, the extension of the old Surpura scheme, the construction of the Rajput Schools at Chopasni, the installation of an electric light and power house, and the provision of a pure water supply for the capital city. For the current year no less than Rs. 33 lakhs have been provided in the Public Works Budget, much of which expenditure is necessitated by the failure of the rains. In railway matters, the Council has wisely pursued the progressive policy of earlier years, and by the construction of the Jodhpur-Phalodi and Jaswantgarh-Ladnu sections, has increased the length of open lines from 525 to 605 miles. In the Judicial Department the period under review has been marked by the institution of the present Chief Court, the introduction of the Marwar Penal Code and the Code of Criminal Procedure, a Court Fees Act and a Police Act, the enrolment of properly qualified *vakils*, the inauguration of an amicable settlement with the *jagirdars* regarding the powers to be exercised by their Courts, and a general improvement in the *personnel* and standard of work in the Department.

" Time will not permit me to do more than mention the marked and steady progress made in education, especially in the Rajput Schools, the reforms and good work carried out in the Land Revenue, Police, Medical, Customs, and other important Departments, but I cannot, in the present circumstances, and in a State with the traditions of Marwar, pass quite so briefly over the working of the Military Department. We all know that, for the last year and a half, His Highness' Imperial Service Lancers have been at the front in Europe, and we all know how well the *Sardar Risala* have answered the calls made upon them. Up to date the State has sent 787 officers and men to the front, of whom over 700 are still on field service.

" On these notable reforms and achievements the Marwar Durbar may well congratulate itself, and mingled with that feeling will be a deep sense of gratitude to His Highness Maharaja Sir Pratap Singhji, whose long experience and whole-hearted devotion to the State have enabled him to achieve results which no other man could have effected.

" Your Highness, I do not propose to trouble you with advice on this momentous day, when your heart must be full of pride in your country's glorious past and of high hopes for its future. I will merely say this, and I say it with all the earnestness of a father to his son, you are undertaking to-day a great burden and a grave responsibility. On you mainly will depend the happiness and prosperity of your people, and in maintenance of the noble traditions of your House. I look to Your Highness to realize this responsibility and, by governing your State wisely, and with due regard to the rights and interests of your *Sardars* and people, to add strength and lustre to your name and to the great British Empire, of which the Marwar State is a part. You have succeeded to a goodly heritage, and you have round you helpers and advisers who wish you well and have the interests of your State at heart. May you prove worthy of the great trust laid upon you, and may God bring happiness and prosperity to you and to your people."

The Viceroy then conducted His Highness the Maharaja Saheb Bahadur to a chair of State representing the *masnad*, and fastened on His Highness the *sirpech*, sword and necklace, and declared him to be invested with full ruling powers. The Political Secretary to His Excellency then recited His Highness' full titles (Lieutenant His Highness Raj Rajeswar Maharaja Dhiraj Summair Singh Bahadur of Jodhpur), and a salute of 17 guns was fired from the ramparts of the Fort in honour of His Highness. His Highness the Maharaja Saheb Bahadur then replied to His Excellency's address, and the following extracts are taken from the speech:

" I am extremely indebted to your Excellency for being so kind as to confer on me ruling powers in my State, and for the honour Your Excellency has done me, my family, and my people in coming all the way from Delhi, at a time when Your Excellency has so many other engagements, to perform the ceremony personally here to-day.

" My sincerest gratitude is also due to Your Excellency for the parental interest you have taken in my education, and the very satisfactory arrangements made for the conduct of the administration during my minority.

" Nor can I help expressing my heartfelt thanks to Sir Elliot Colvin and Colonel Windham for the great interest they have taken in the affairs of my State, and last but not least, to my great-uncle, His Highness Major-General Maharaja Sir Pratap Singhji, who, at a considerable self-sacrifice, abdicated the *gadi* of Idar in order to be able to steer this State during the trying period of my minority.

" I feel my responsibilities are great, but I find comfort in the fact that I shall always have the benefit of obtaining friendly advice from the Resident in all difficult matters. I need not assure Your Excellency that it shall always be my best endeavour to act up to the advice conveyed in the *kharita*, and in the address just delivered by Your Excellency, and to uphold the noble traditions of my House in the matter of unflinching loyalty and whole-hearted devotion to the person and Throne of His Imperial Majesty, who was so gracious as to take parental care of me during my stay in England, and to allow me the privilege of serving under the British flag with my Imperial Service Lancers in France. I shall feel proud when, by the good government of my people, I shall prove myself deserving of the confidence now reposed in me."

The other notable event during the year was the marriage of His Highness the Maharaja Saheb Bahadur with a sister of His Highness the Jam Saheb Ranjit

THE STATE OF JODHPUR (MARWAR).

1. The Motor Garage. 2. The Electric Power-house at Jodhpur. 3. Interior of the Power-house.

THE STATE OF JODHPUR (MARWAR).

1. The Jodhpur Central Jail Industry. 2. Specimen of Lacquered and Embroidery Work on Glass and Camel-hide Ware. 3. Marble and Ivory Industry.

THE STATE OF JODHPUR

Singhji of Jamnagar, which took place at Jamnagar on December 9, 1915. Owing to the continuance of the war there were no festivities, and the loyal subjects of His Highness could not take part on this auspicious occasion.

His Highness Major-General Maharaja Sir Pratap Singhji Saheb Bahadur, the Regent of the State, returned from the war on a short visit in October, 1915, and after His Highness the Maharaja Saheb Bahadur had been invested with ruling powers and had married, Sir Pratap remained in Marwar until March 31, 1916, when he left for the front, sailing from Bombay on April 4th following. The other members of the Marwar Royal Family remained with the Imperial Service troops in France.

A remarkably fine illustration of the whole-hearted loyalty of His Highness the Maharaja to the Throne, and of his fixed determination to uphold the cause of the Allies in their strenuous campaign in Europe, was given in May, 1918, on the occasion of the raising of the infantry regiment to which reference has been made. His Excellency the Viceroy had caused it to be known that he had received from His Majesty the King-Emperor a message addressed to the people of India, urging them to respond to the urgent call of the Imperial War Cabinet for a large number of recruits for active service, and although His Highness was at that time in Southern India, he at once returned to Jodhpur and summoned a meeting of Sirdars, Jagirdars and others with the object of devising measures to enable the State to respond to the summons.

The attendance of every noble and feudatory of the State was a grand answer to the appeal of His Highness, and it is said that a larger or more enthusiastic meeting had not been witnessed in Jodhpur within the memory of the oldest inhabitants.

After introductory remarks relating to the excellent service which had already been rendered by Sir Pratap Singh and his men on the battlefields of France, His Highness referred, in glowing terms, to the patriotism of Rajputs, and continued: "Is your patriotism dead, is your regard for your King and country dead? If so, we are not fit to take our places in the mighty Empire to which we are proud to belong. Marwar will not fail in doing its duty, whatever the circumstances may be. The heavier the blows from the enemy, the greater his success, and the more resolute will we be in our iron determination to secure ultimate victory. Warriors of Marwar, two things are needed to defeat the enemy, and these are men and money. In addition to keeping up our regiment of Cavalry at the seat of war, we have up to now supplied about 5,000 recruits for the British Army, but the number is far below the quota assigned to us. We rejoice that our efforts in this direction are proving successful, as the number of those enlisted during the past month has risen to 432. I have offered to raise a battalion of about 1,400 infantry, and I have called you here for your help and co-operation in the matter. Not only this battalion, but many battalions, one after another, must be raised by us, and if Marwar does its duty—as it has always done in the past—we shall enjoy the fruits of victory." The Maharaja then proceeded to urge his hearers to contribute to the War Loan, and remarked: "It behoves every man and woman in Marwar to subscribe, even the smallest amount each can spare, even at inconvenience to one's comforts, since real sacrifice does not mean that we should secure our comforts first and pay for the war afterwards. I have paid two lakhs of rupees from my private purse; will ask my Dewan to give a substantial sum from the State Treasury; and I now call upon you *jagirdars*, first of all to subscribe liberally from the *thikana* exchequers, and afterwards to press the matter upon the attention of your people." In concluding a speech which was enthusiastically received, His Highness gave utterance to the following striking words: "I have heard it said that England's need is India's opportunity. I do not believe in this philosophy. England's need is India's duty, and as England is doing her duty to the world, India is bound to do its duty to England, whose component part it has become by Divine Will. There should be no bargain, no barter;. Marwar has to stand up by the side of England through thick and thin, and will live or die with her."

A sum of more than Rs. 3,00,000 was subscribed in the room, and additional amounts were collected in various districts, while the rousing call of His Highness for more men met with a most encouraging response.

Apart from the direct military services rendered in the manner narrated, the Jodhpur State made many valuable contributions to Imperial needs during the war. Ponies and horses were supplied for remount purposes, a number gratuitously, munitions were made in the Jodhpur State Railway workshops, and a Turkish prisoners' camp was maintained. Provision was made later for the education of the children of men who had died while on active service. Further, the Durbar offered a lump sum of eight lakhs of rupees to the Government of India as war contribution, to be set off against the extra expenditure incurred in connection with the Imperial Service troops. Actual cash contributions made from the Jodhpur State Treasury in association with the Great War aggregated Rs. 35,96,095.

Unhappily His Highness did not live to see the full fruition of the great work which his State had so nobly accomplished. He died on October 3, 1918, at the early age of 20 years, and was succeeded by his brother, His Highness Maharaja Dhiraj Sri Umed Singhji Sahib Bahadur. This Prince was born on July 3, 1903, and received his education at the Mayo College, under the guardianship of Lieut.-Col. C. W. Waddington, M.V.O., C.I.E. His Highness was gazetted honorary captain in the Indian Army on October 24, 1921.

His Highness is entitled to a salute of 17 guns.

A very large portion of the State land consists of unproductive soil, almost deserving the name of desert, with the result that agricultural pursuits, upon which the great majority of the inhabitants depend for support, cannot be carried on with the success which attends cultivation in many other States in Rajputana. Again, the rainfall is, as a rule, remarkably deficient in quantity and uneven in its distribution, and as there are no perennial streams in the State, the soil is unable to obtain sufficient moisture.

The principal crops are *bajri, jowar*, barley, wheat, cotton, maize, and several varieties of oil and other seeds. The most important industry in the State is the quarrying of the famous white marble found at Makrana, the greater portion of which is being used in the construction of the Victoria Memorial at Calcutta. Sandstone quarries at Jodhpur, Sojat, and Khatu yield large quantities of material, which is in great demand in India for ordinary and decorative building purposes. Other minerals which are being profitably exploited include gypsum, Fuller's earth, wolfram, manganese, molybdenum and tin. About the year 1914 a State industry, known as the Marwar Timber Factory, was established in the city of Jodhpur. Its object is to utilize local timber in the

THE STATE OF JODHPUR (MARWAR).

1. The Sardar Market. 2. A View of Mohamandir. 3. Old Palace at Mandore.

THE STATE OF JODHPUR (MARWAR).

1 The Kailana Lake. 2. View of the Chhota Abu at Jodhpur, from the Kailana Lake. 3. The Old Fort and its Ruins at Mandore.

preparation of articles of furniture, but in order to impart strength, beauty of appearance, and variety to the goods imported, wood such as teak and *sisam* is combined with local forest produce. Other industrial enterprises carried on by the State are: Locomotive and Carriage Workshops of the Jodhpur-Bikaner Railway at Jodhpur; the Durbar Ice Factory, in which steam power is used in the manufacture of ice and aerated waters of various kinds; the Public Works Department workshops; the Marwar State Press; and the Central Jail Factory, in which cloth is woven by prisoners. Factories owned by private individuals or Corporations comprise: the Edulji Cotton Wool Pressing Factory at Pali, which is worked by means of a 20 h.p. steam boiler; the Sankalchand Ginning Factory at Binjwa, equipped with machinery driven by a 10 h.p. boiler; and the Pratap Printing Press at Jodhpur. Industries of minor importance consist of the making of brass articles, leather goods, felt, lacquered woodwork, embroidered goods, and in dyeing cotton materials.

In the year 1913–14 an estimate of Rs. 3,68,654 was sanctioned by the State Council for the installation of an up-to-date electric light and power station at Jodhpur, and within a few months a considerable portion of the work had been completed.

The total volume of trade in the State reached a very considerable amount, in imports as well as exports, prior to the declaration of war, and as good progress had been made for several years previously, the annual returns have not, since that date, been so disappointing as might have been expected.

Outbreaks of famine, too, involving the migration of a large number of families from the State, the loss of cattle owing to the failure of crops, and general stagnation in industrial enterprises have had a prejudicial effect upon commerce, but the vigorous steps taken by the Durbar in securing artificial irrigation of the soil, and in establishing relief works, have had a most beneficial effect. It is noticed in State Administration Reports that in the year 1912–13 goods were imported to the value of Rs. 3,07,32,166, and that in 1915–16, notwithstanding war and drought, they reached the sum of Rs. 2,60,39,671. Exports for the same periods amounted respectively to Rs. 1,01,22,139 and Rs. 64,17,894. The principal imports are *ghee*, piece goods, metals, sugar, yarn, tobacco, rice, and other commodities, while exports include hides, bones, wool, wheat and other grain, quarried stone and cotton.

Statistics relating to the livestock in Marwar show that there are approximately 397,885 bullocks, 682,814 cows, 105,000 buffaloes, 4,302 horses, 6,247 mules, 66,755 camels, 43,459 asses, 2,030,441 sheep and 1,507,489 goats.

The forest area under the supervision of a Superintendent and a number of Assistants consists of the protected portion, 405 square miles in extent, and unclassed forests covering about 447 square miles. This territory is designated for purposes of management as follows: (*a*) Eastern division; (*b*) Western division; and (*c*) Direction division. The total revenue, including the income from fuel and fodder reserves, is about Rs. 1,00,000.

The State has constructed, at its own expense, and is responsible for the maintenance of the Marwar section of the Jodhpur-Bikaner railway (more than 600 miles in length), which traverses the country from east to west, and has several branch lines running in northwardly and southwardly directions. The percentage of returns on railway capital expenditure in the year 1911–12 was 13·53, and in 1915–16 it amounted to 13·49, while the average for the five years was slightly more than 11 per cent. Good internal communications have been established by means of metalled and other roads, many of which have been made when relief works have been started during periods of famine.

Marwar ranks second on the list of Rajputana States in the facilities provided for giving education, in the efficiency of its teachers, and in the successes achieved by the pupils in its scholastic institutions. There has, in the past, been no more persistent advocate of instructing the young than His Highness the Regent, Sir Pratap Singh, and it is a happy augury for the future prosperity of the State that His Highness, the present Chief, since his ascension to the *gadi*, has manifested the warmest sympathy towards every movement calculated to uplift the status of the inhabitants of future years by providing means of education for the boys and girls of to-day. The policy of the Durbar is to increase the number and efficiency of State schools, in which free education is imparted to all classes, and further to give every encouragement to private institutions to attain the best possible results. The teaching institutions comprise: the Jaswant Arts College and the Durbar High School at Jodhpur city, 19 Anglo-Vernacular schools, 48 Vernacular schools, the Hewson Girls' school, and two others for the acquisition of Sanskrit and the principles of commercial knowledge respectively. The total number of pupils on the rolls of the above State schools is 4,166, with an average daily attendance of 3,195, while there are 2,745 children attached to State-aided schools, and an average daily attendance of 2,238. Shorthand and typewriting have been added to the curriculum of the Sanskrit school, and His Highness takes special pleasure in encouraging the boys to cultivate a love for athletics and healthy sport and games of all descriptions.

The State maintains 20 public dispensaries, including the Jaswant Female Hospital, two railway dispensaries, the public hospital at the city of Jodhpur, and four non-public dispensaries at the Fort; Ratanada, the Central jail, and Chopasni, together with the Leper Asylum at Nimba Nimbri.

The military forces of the State comprise (*a*) the Imperial Service Lancers (Sardar Risala); (*b*) Regular Forces, comprising (1) artillery, Perganna Garrison, and (2) Sardar infantry; (*c*) Irregular Forces, composed of (1) Summair Camel Corps, (2) Summair Horse, and (3) Summair Infantry.

The annual cost of maintenance of the above forces amounts to about Rs. 10,00,000, and the contribution of the State towards the strength of the Erinpura Irregular Force is Rs. 1,15,000 per annum.

Further protection is afforded by a police force, consisting of about 2,000 men of all ranks, who are attached to 76 stations and 58 outposts, and the yearly cost of these is about Rs. 4,08,000.

With the exception of one or two minor enactments, the laws relating to civil and criminal jurisdiction are based upon the model of those in force in British India. There are 34 Durbar Courts, and the *Jagir* Courts are 49 in number.

The modern city of Jodhpur is built upon sloping ground in the form of a horseshoe. In the early part of the 18th century a strong and massive encircling wall was constructed; it is 24,600 feet in length, its breadth varies from 37 feet to 9 feet, the height ranges from 15 feet to 20 feet, and it has six gates, studded with sharp iron spikes for protection against the ramming of elephants in times of siege. The principal structures include the Maharaja's palace, or rather succession

THE STATE OF JODHPUR (MARWAR).

1. The Marble Cenotaph at Deckund of H.H. Maharaja Sir Jaswant Singhji Saheb Bahadur. 2. The Ship House. 3. The Raika-Baigh Palace. 4. Balsamand.

of palaces, as each Prince, from the time of the founder, has added memorials of architectural beauty; the Moti Mahal, built by Raja Sur Singh in the early portion of the 17th century, and the Fateh Mahal, both of which are noted for their beautifully carved panels and pierced screens of red sandstone. There are also several very fine residential and public buildings, together with 10 old palaces and 11 temples.

The main streets are paved, and a light tramway, laid between the city and railway station, and worked by bullock power, has proved to be a most acceptable boon to the inhabitants, and has also greatly reduced the expenses of living by cheapening the cost of the conveyance of grain and other produce. In the suburbs one may see a palace of former Maharajas at Rai-ka-Bagh, the splendid new palace at Ratanada, the Imperial Service Cavalry Lines, the Residency, and a number of public offices. The Fort, which is the finest in Rajputana, is erected on an isolated rock about 400 feet above the surrounding plains, and its wall, from 20 feet to 120 feet in height, and from 12 feet to 20 feet in thickness, encloses an oblong space measuring 500 yards in length and 250 yards in breadth. Seven barriers are thrown across the circuitous ascent from the base, each having immense portals and separate guards. The grim old walls and the face of the perpendicular rock bear evidences of assaults made during various attacks upon the capital.

Nagaur, a thriving commercial town in the eastern portion of the State, is surrounded by a wall more than four miles in length, and its battlements have many Arabic and Persian inscriptions on stones obtained from mosques demolished by Maharaja Bakht Singh in order to repair breaches caused in warfare. The Fort, commanding the town, is protected by double walls, the outer one being 25 feet and the inner one 50 feet above the ground.

The principal objects of interest consist of some palaces, a fountain, believed to have been erected by the Emperor Akbar, a mosque, constructed by Shah Jehan, and a cave, which is claimed by both Hindus and Mahomedans as a place of retreat for their respective ancestral saints. Nagaur was a former capital of Marwar, and was the scene of conflicts with Rao Chanda in the year 1400, it was captured by Akbar in 1561, and was restored by him on his marriage with the sister of the then reigning Chief.

Phalodi, a commercial centre of importance of the State, in the north-western part, is said to have been founded in the fifteenth century, and its fort contains capacious reservoirs for the storage of water, and a number of very fine palaces.

Pali, situated about 45 miles to the south-east of Jodhpur, is regarded as the commercial capital, its principal industry being the dyeing of woollen goods.

Jalor is the headquarters of the district of the same name, and is situated on the southern border of the sandy plain of Marwar. Its inhabitants are engaged in the manufacture of cotton cloth, saddles for camels, and drinking vessels made of bell metal. The fort, 800 yards in length and 400 yards in breadth, is only accessible by an ascent of about three miles along a stone road, upon which are three distinct lines of defence.

Didwana, about 130 miles distant from Jodhpur, contains many buildings of considerable interest to archæologists, such as a mosque, said to have been erected by the Emperor Akbar, several old temples, and some cenotaphs bearing inscriptions dating from the ninth century.

THE STATE OF JODHPUR (MARWAR).

A View of the Fort from Gulab Sagar Tank.

GROUP OF TEMPLES.

THE STATE OF KOTAH

THE Ruling Prince of Kotah, an Indian State in Rajputana, under the Kotah Jhalawar division of the political agency of the Government of India, belongs to the Hara Sept of the clan of Chauhan Rajputs. The Chauhans are one of the most illustrious of the 36 Royal races of India, and among their 24 branches, the Haras are the most important. It will be interesting to note that the Chauhans were the last Hindu monarchs to occupy the Imperial Throne of Delhi. Kotah and Bundi (an adjoining State) have been for many years known as Haraoti, or Harawati, signifying " the land of the Haras." About the year 1342, Rao Dewa, a descendant of the Ajmer kings, founded the town of Bundi. In the early portion of the seventeenth century Madho Singhji, the second Chief of Bundi, established a separate kingdom at Kotah. His independence under the title of Raja was recognized by the Emperor Jehangir and later by Shahjehan. The seventh Chief of Kotah, Bhim Singhji (1708–20), who considerably extended his dominions, was the first Ruler to assume the title of Maharao, granted by the Delhi Emperor, and he also obtained from the same source the dignity of the name " Punj Hazari," or " leadership of five thousand," together with the orange-coloured banner used as the State standard. The Maharao Umed Singhji ascended the *gadi* in 1771, but during the course of his long reign of nearly 50 years he was little more than nominal head of the State, the actual Ruler being Zalim Singhji, his famous minister and adviser. The latter, in the year 1817, on behalf of Kotah, made the first Treaty to be concluded in Rajputana with the British Government, and he succeeded in having a supplementary clause added to that document by which the administration of the State was vested in himself and his successors in perpetuity. Scarcely 10 years had elapsed, however, when disputes arose between Maharao Ram Singhji and his Minister, Madan Singhji, grandson of Zalim Singhji, and matters became so strained that the Government of India, realizing that the problem of an hereditary Minister was unworkable, decided, with the consent of the Maharao, to separate 17 of the districts of Kotah from the State and to form them into a new Principality to be bestowed upon Madan Singhji and his heirs and successors. During the occupancy of the *gadi* by Maharao Shatrusalji, the administration of the State was placed by the Government of India under the supervision of its own nominee, but this arrangement terminated on the death of the Chief in 1889, who was in the same year succeeded by his adopted son, the present Maharao, who was then a minor and a student at the Mayo College, Ajmer. It should be mentioned here that on the formation of the new State of Jhalawar in 1899, 15 of the 17 districts transferred,

H.H. THE MAHARAJADHIRAJ MAHAHENDRA MAHIMARAO LIEUT.-COLONEL SIR UMED SINGHJI, SAHIB BAHADUR, G.C.S.I., G.C.I.E., C.B.E.

MAHARAJ KUNWAR BHIM SINGH.

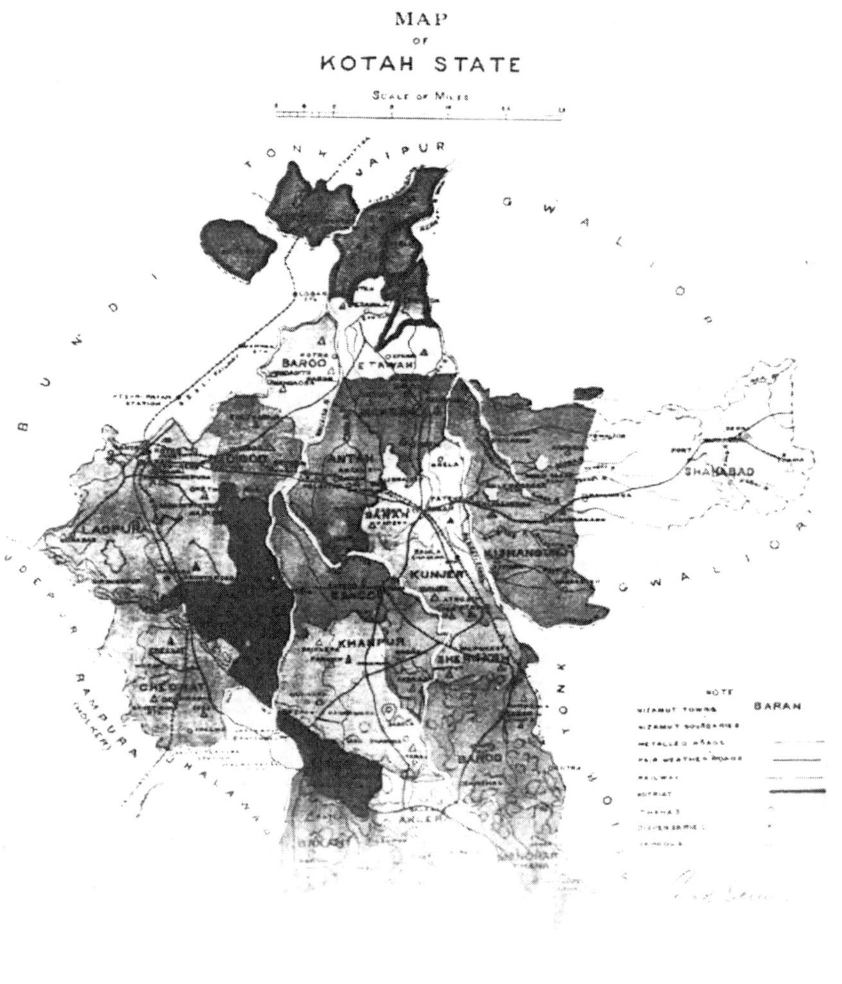

THE STATE OF KOTAH.
Map of Kotah State.

as already stated, in 1838 were restored to Kotah.

The State—including the eight fiefs known as Kotris—has an area of 5,684 square miles, and has a population of 639,089 persons according to the census of 1911.

It is bounded on the north by a portion of the Gwalior State, Jaipur, and the river Chambal ; on the east by Gwalior ; on the south by Rajgarh and Rampura Kilchipur ; and on the west by Bundi, Udaipur, and Jhalawar.

The country is fertile and well watered by the Chambal, Kali Sindh, the Parbati and other rivers, and the Mukandwara range, varying from 1,200 feet to 1,671 feet in height, traverses the State in a north-westerly direction. About 47 per cent. of the inhabitants earn a livelihood entirely upon the land and its products, and 20 per cent. combine agricultural pursuits with their respective trades. The principal crops are wheat, barley, *jowar*, maize, gram, rice, *til*, linseed, cotton, and opium, while the minor products of the forests include gum, resin, dyes, tanning substances, catechu, grasses, suitable for paper pulp and essential oils, honey, beeswax, and fibres of various kinds.

The chief industry carried on is the weaving of cotton, but special mention must be made of white and coloured muslins, which are occasionally ornamented by the introduction of gold or silver threads while the fabric is still in the loom, of silver table ornaments, and rough country paper, all of which are manufactured in the city of Kotah. Embroidered trappings for elephants and horses, inlaid ivory and other similar work, and a large variety of lacquered goods and toys are also made in other towns.

Kotah is a State in which the progressive mind of its Chief is ever on the alert to inaugurate and support industrial occupations for the benefit of his subjects, and at the present time there are several schemes of this nature which it is hoped will be securely established in the near future. These comprise the manufacture of alum from bauxite, of dyes, tanning substances, essential oils, soap, glycerine, morphine, narcotine, and paper pulp, while it is proposed to commence pottery works, oil factories, cement, and hydraulic lime works.

The mineral survey of the State was started during the month of January 1914, and up to the present time the following have been discovered, namely, bauxite, china clay, fire clay, red oxide of iron, red and yellow ochres, calcite, jasper, quartz sand, crystalline limestone, clay and limestone suitable for cement, and slate which is adapted for roofing, flooring, and lithographic purposes. A factory has been started for the manufacture of block glass for bangles, and it is intended to extend the scope of these works by making lamp globes, chimneys, bottles, jars, and other articles.

The principal imports into the State are piece-goods, rice, sugar, *gur*, iron, yarn, and metals, while exports include food grains, oil-seeds, clean cotton, cattle hides and skins.

The Maharao takes a deep personal interest in the question of education, and some interesting facts relating to this important subject are given in the Administration Report of the State for the year 1916–17. Children receive free instruction in all schools, and in the middle and primary vernacular institutions, as well as in the girls' schools in the city, books, slates, and drawing materials are provided gratis for pupils without distinction of caste or creed. There are 92 schools in the State, namely, for girls, four ; Anglo-vernacular, four ; Sanskrit, two ; and Vernacular, 82. The total number of pupils on the roll was about 6,000, with an average daily attendance of 4,000, and a particularly satisfactory feature of the Report is the reference to the middle and three primary schools for girls, in which there are no fewer than 389 pupils, thus emphasizing the fact that parents are awakening to the necessity for raising the mental status of women in

THE STATE OF KOTAH.

1. The New Palace. 2. The Drawing-room.

THE STATE OF KOTAH.

1. Old Palace. 2. The Durbar Hall.

THE STATE OF KOTAH.

1. Raj Mahal. 2. H.M. Queen Mary and Sardars.

THE STATE OF KOTAH.
SARBAGH, WITH CHUTTRIES.

India. The expenditure incurred by the State in this department was Rs. 63,211.

The State supports 20 dispensaries, the past year's expenditure reaching the sum of Rs. 66,589. The troops which the Maharao may maintain are limited to 15,000 men of all grades, but the actual number now on the rolls comprises rather more than 4,000 cavalry, artillery, and infantry.

Kotah is well supplied with means of communication, and during recent years considerable extensions and improvements have been effected upon roads, the extent of those constructed and maintained by the State being 170 miles, metalled, and 492 miles unmetalled.

The Great Indian Peninsula Railway branch line from Goona via Baran meets the Nagda-Muttra section of the Bombay-Baroda and Central India line at Kotah, and thus about ten districts are provided with an excellent service of trains for passengers as well as goods.

General administration is carried on by His Highness the Maharao Sahib, who receives invaluable assistance from the Diwan Bahadur Chaube Raghunath Das, C.S.I., an old and highly-respected servant of the State, and the decisions in Civil and Criminal Courts are guided by the spirit, though not the actual letter, of the laws in force in British territory.

The gross revenue of the State, calculated on the average of the past five years, is Rs. 42,81,261. A tribute of Rs. 2,34,720 is paid to the British Government, and, in addition, a sum of Rs. 2,00,000 is contributed for the maintenance of the Deoli regiment. A further amount of Rs. 14,397 (local Jaipur coin) is paid to Jaipur on account of tribute due from *Kotris*, whose allegiance was transferred to Kotah early in the nineteenth century.

The only municipalities in the State are in the city of Kotah and at Baran. Among the numerous fine buildings in the capital are Uhmed Bhawan, the new palace, the guest house, the Crosthwaite Institute in the public gardens, the "Herbert" High School, the "Wyllie" Memorial Market, and Her Highness Sri Maharaniji Sahiba's school for girls in the Rampura Bazar.

His Highness the Maharajadhiraj Maharaj Mahimahendra Maharao Raja Lieut.-Colonel Sir Umed Singhji Bahadur, G.C.S.I., G.C.I.E., G.B.E., was born on September 15, 1873, and was educated at the Mayo College, Ajmer. He succeeded to the *gadi* by adoption on the death of Maharao Shatrusalji in the year 1889, and was granted full powers of administration in 1896. On the death of his first wife, the eldest daughter of His

"श्री"

राजा हुजूर बहादुर दाम इकबाल हू का
सलामी

बृज नाथ यश प्रवान करे नृप उमेद को ।
बल तेज रवि समान करे नृप उमेद को ॥

"दोहा"

महि महेन्द्र उम्मेद सिंह, हाड़ा कुल सरताज ।
तव प्रताप जग में रहो, सर्वाग्र वंश की लाज ॥१॥
बृजनाथ..........
बल तेज..........

"दोहा"

कोटा नृप उम्मेद सिंह, शूर बीर बलवान ।
रहे सदा आनन्द में, राज्य प्रजा के प्रान ॥२॥
बृजनाथ..........
बल तेज..........

रचियता
हीरालाल सूद

THE STATE OF KOTAH.
KOTAH NATIONAL ANTHEM.

THE STATE OF KOTAH.

1. The Residency. 2. The Guest House. 3. Tank.

Highness the Maharana of Udaipur, His Highness married the daughter of His Highness the Rao of Kutch, of the Jarija clan of Rajputs, and at a subsequent date he also married the sister of the Thakar of Isarda in Jaipur, a Kachwaha Rajput of the Rajawat sub-clan. A son and heir by the last mentioned Rani was born on September 14, 1909, and he has received the name of Bhim Singh.

Since his accession His Highness has evinced a deep interest in the general welfare of the State and the prosperity of his subjects. He has introduced a revised Land Revenue Settlement, and has recognized and greatly strengthened all administrative departments, especially those of Revenue, Customs, Forests, Judicial, Police, and Public Works; he has established unity with the post offices in British India, and has legalized British currency.

His Highness has been the means of inducing his people to avail themselves to a considerable extent of the advantages of education, and to develop manufacturing and industrial arts, while his zeal for real progress in agricultural matters led him to import modern types of machinery, such as threshing machines, chaff-cutters, corn-grinding mills, English ploughs, a reaping machine, and traction engine with wagons attached, which are used for the transport of stone for building purposes.

His Highness is no mere figure-head of Kotah, he is a worker, and he attends daily at his offices, where his practical acquaintance with the details of administration enable him to pronounce well-balanced judgments upon the most intricate questions submitted to him. He is, in the literal sense of the word, a father of his people, and his charming manner causes him to be a sympathetic listener to genuine grievances.

State officials are happy and contented in their services, and for recreation during leisure hours His Highness has kindly provided them with the handsomely furnished Crosthwaite Institute, in which there is a fine library of books, a billiard-room, a general reading-room, tennis and racquet courts, a swimming bath, and public gardens, in which the State band plays twice or thrice a week.

Notwithstanding the Maharao's constant supervision of business matters connected with the State, he is an excellent all-round sportsman, delighting in games which call for the manifestation of athletic capabilities, while as a keen hunter of large game he has few equals in India. His extensive preserves contain tigers, panthers, bears, wild boar, and nilghai, together with other species of the deer tribe, and since his assumption of Rulership a considerable number of all these animals have been bagged by him. *Shikar* parties are frequently attended by European as well as Indian friends from practically every part of India and occasionally from England.

THE STATE OF KOTAH.

1. The Herbert High School. 2. Girls' High School.

His Highness is the owner of several motor-cars by well-known makers, and also possesses a motor launch, which is used on the river Chambal for hunting or pleasure parties.

The most notable events in the year 1911 were the Coronation Durbar at Delhi and the visit to Kotah of Her Imperial Majesty the Queen-Empress.

His Highness, accompanied by a number of State officials, obeyed the Royal command and was present at all the grand and stirring functions which will ever live in the memory of those who were privileged to participate in them, and on the morning of December 12th His Highness was advised that His Majesty the King-Emperor had been graciously pleased to appoint him to be Knight Grand Commander of the Most Exalted Order of the Star of India.

It was a red-letter day for the State when Her Imperial Majesty the Queen-Empress visited Kotah in connection with the Coronation Durbar. Shortly after Her Majesty's arrival at the Agency on December 24th, the ceremony of "*Mizaj Pursi*," on behalf of His Highness, took place, and a deputation consisting of the Diwan, Raj Bijaya Singhi of Kunari, Maharaja Madho Singhji of Gainta, and Kanwar Onkar Singhji of Palaita proceeded to the Agency to inquire after the health of the distinguished visitor. "*Dalis*" were presented at 6 p.m., and this closed the official functions of the day.

Her Imperial Majesty and party on the 25th motored to the Amar Niwas Palace on the Chambal river, through the Public Gardens, and were thence conveyed in motor and steam launches up the river to the waterfalls. There was a Christmas-tree at the Agency in the evening, at which the Maharaj Kumar Sahib and other children of Sirdars, Jagirdars, and high officials were present. Her Majesty was graciously pleased to give toys and other Christmas gifts to Maharaj Kumar Sahib and all other children present.

Her Majesty and party drove in State carriages on the 26th through the city to the Palace, escorted by State cavalry, and His Highness in his Major's uniform rode alongside the Royal carriage. As the Queen-Empress entered the Salar Ghazi gate a salute of 31 guns was fired. In the Raj Mehal were assembled all the Sardars and Heads of Departments, and as Her Majesty passed the gateway to this building all rose to their feet. The party then went round the palace and moved on to the enclosure, where some old arms were shown to them by His Highness.

There was a dinner in the evening, and the grounds of the Agency, the banks and islands of the Chambal, portions of the city walls, the pontoon bridge, and the Kunari House on the other side of the river were illuminated. Her Majesty, after dinner, went out to witness the brilliant spectacle.

After breakfast on the 27th there was an excursion in motors to the Umedganj Rari, where *shikar* arrangements had been made. A tiger and a bear came out and were seen by the Queen-Empress and her party. The animals were fired at, and the tiger escaped, but the bear was shot.

THE STATE OF KOTAH.

1. THE CHAMBAL AT ANARNIWAS. 2. RIVER VIEW.

Before leaving the Agency House on the following day, Her Majesty was pleased to present a jewelled miniature of herself to His Highness, and to give her photographs signed by herself to the Diwan and Kanwar Onkar Singhji.

A photograph of the royal party, in which His Highness and some of his Sardars were privileged to join, was then taken, and at 11.30 Her Majesty left Kotah junction. The road throughout was lined by the police and Raj troops, and all the ensigns of royalty of a State procession were once more in attendance along the route. On arrival at the station Her Imperial Majesty was received by His

THE STATE OF KOTAH.

1. The City Fort. 2. The Clock Tower. 3. View of the City. 4. East Gate of the Fort.

THE STATE OF KOTAH.

1. Crosthwaite Institute. 2. Curzon-Wyllie Memorial.

THE STATE OF KOTAH.

1. City Hospital. 2. State Engineer's Office. 3. Private Secretary's Office.

THE STATE OF KOTAH

Highness and the Agent and General Traffic Manager of the Bombay-Baroda and Central India Railway.

After shaking hands with His Highness Her Majesty entered the Royal saloon, and as the special began to move away, loud and continuous cheers broke forth from all standing on the platform, which Her Imperial Majesty most kindly received and constantly acknowledged.

On the arrival and departure of Her Imperial Majesty salutes of 31 guns were fired.

His Majesty the King—Emperor, on the recommendation of the Government of India, was graciously pleased to appoint Diwan Bahadur Chaube Raghunath Das to be a Companion of the Most Exalted Order of the Star of India on the occasion of His Majesty's birthday, and he was invested with the Insignia of the Order on the night of June 22, 1912, at the Viceregal Lodge, Simla.

This sketch cannot be closed without reference being made to the very able services rendered to the State by the Diwan Bahadur Chaube Raghunath Das, C.S.I., during his 40 years of service. Under his efficient management the revenue of the State has increased greatly, and in controlling the various departments his one aim has been to strive for the best interests of the State and its inhabitants. He has inaugurated many useful reforms, and the people regard him as a close friend who devotes his undoubted abilities for the advancement of their welfare. Another old and trusted official of the State is Khan Bahadur Mir Madar Ali, who, according to a letter of the Honourable Mr. E. C. Colvin, Agent-General in Rajputana to the Governor-General of India, written on November 12, 1917, "has been in the service of the Kotah Durbar for a great many years, his reminiscences dating back to the days of the Mutiny. It was his duty to meet high officials visiting Kotah and accompany them on their tours, and he was always courteous, obliging, and helpful."

VIEW FROM THE RIVER.

THE STATE OF PATIALA

PATIALA is the largest and most important Sikh State belonging to the group known as Phulkian States of the Punjab. It is divided into three portions, of which the most extensive is situated in the plains south of the Sutlej river, the second is hill country stretching to Simla, and beyond as far as Kufri, while the third is the isolated *pergana* of Narnaul, lying 180 miles distant from the capital and contiguous to the Shekhawatti and Torawatti districts of Jaipur and the States of Alwar and Loharu. It has an area of 5,492 square miles with a population of 14,07,659 according to the census of 1911, and the Revenue from all sources according to the figures for the year 1918–19 amounted to about Rs. 1,17,00,000. Urdu and Punjabi are the two languages spoken.

The State of Patiala derives its name from its capital city, which was founded by Raja Ala Singh, the first independent Ruler about the middle of the eighteenth century.

The earliest progenitors of the House of Patiala were scions of the princely Rajput family of Jaisalmer, who left their desert homes about the time of Rai Pithora, the last Hindu King of Delhi, and established themselves in the country round Hissar, Sirsa, and Bhatner. A few centuries later, one of their descendants, Khewa, married the daughter of a Jat *zamindar* of the Naili. Sidhu, the offspring of this union, was known by the caste of his mother, and the Sidhu Jat tribe, of which he was the founder, increased and grew in prosperity until it came to occupy the first position among the people inhabiting the country between the Sutlej and the Jumna rivers.

Ala Singh was descended from Phul, who is also the common ancestor of the Jhind and Nabha Princes. Ala Singh was an altogether remarkable man, and to his genius must be ascribed the rapid rise of the State in the first stages of its history. In a fight against the powerful Mahomedan Chief of Kot and Jagraon, aided by the Afghans of Malerkotla and the Imperial *Faujdar* of the Jullundur Doab, Ala Singh gained a brilliant victory, which spread his fame far and wide.

In 1749 Ala Singh built the fortress of Dhodan (Bhawanigarh), and a few years later was founded the present capital. An expedition against the Chief of Bhatinda resulted in the acquisition of important villages, while the Bhatti menace was finally removed after a successful, though arduous, campaign in 1757. About this time Ahmad Shah Abdali overran the Punjab, and he went as far as Delhi, defeating the Mahrattas in the celebrated battle of Panipat. Ala Singh entered into friendly relations with Abdali, who presented him with a robe of honour and conferred upon him the title of Raja, installing him as the principal Chief in that part of the country. This alliance was greatly resented by the Sikhs, who looked upon the Shah as their national enemy and were just then smarting under the disgrace of a defeat inflicted on them near Barnala, where some 20,000 brave Sikhs had been killed. But Ala Singh was anxious to save his people from the horrors of a foreign invasion, and his foresight was amply proved when in 1764 Ahmad Shah made a virtue of necessity by handing over to him the troublesome but important Province of Sirhind.

Raja Ala Singh died in the following year, but he had already laid the foundation of a rule based not on plunder and force, as was frequently the case in those days, but on the love and respect of his subjects, whose descendants still cherish his memory and always refer to him by the half-reverent, half-loving title of "Baba."

Ala Singh was succeeded by his grandson, Amar Singh, who proved to be a capable ruler and a brilliant soldier. When in 1767 Ahmad Shah paid his last visit to the Punjab, he conferred on Amar Singh the title of Raja-i-Rajgan. In 1766 Amar Singh conquered and acquired Pail and Isru from Malerkotla, and he next sent one of his generals to reduce Pinjaur, the place which lies at the foot of the Simla Hills and is noted for its picturesque Moghul gardens. Bhatinda was reduced in 1771, and in 1774 Amar Singh led a great expedition into the country of his kinsmen, the Bhattis, defeating their Chiefs in the battle of Beghran, and taking Sirsa and Fatehabad. Diwan Nannu Mall also conquered the Governor of Hansi and overran that district as well as Hissar. By several other territorial acquisitions Amar Singh succeeded in making Patiala the most powerful State between the Jumna and the Sutlej. He died in 1781, and was succeeded by his son Sahib Singh, who was only six years of age.

On his accession, Sahib Singh received the title of "Maharaja" from the Emperor Shah Alam. Diwan Nannu Mall ably managed the affairs of State, but when he invited the aid of the Mahrattas in quelling internal disorders, he lost his influence, and Bibi Sahib Kaur, the sister of the young Maharaja, became the Chief Minister of the State. The Princess inherited the valour and determination of the Rajputs, and placing herself at the head of her army she completely defeated the Mahrattas when they again invaded the territory in 1794. At Sahib Kaur's death, the Cis-Sutlej Chiefs, who had been harassed by the predatory warfare carried on by the well-known Irish adventurer, George Thomas,

MAJOR-GENERAL H.H. MAHARAJA SIR BHUPINDER SINGH, MAHINDER BAHADUR, G.C.I.E., G.B.E., MAHARAJA OF PATIALA.

1. MAHARAJA BABA ALLA SINGH, SAHIB BAHADUR. 2. H.H. MAHARAJA AMAR SINGH, SAHIB BAHADUR.
3. H.H. MAHARAJA SAHIB SINGH, SAHIB BAHADUR. 4. H.H. MAHARAJA KARAM SINGH, SAHIB BAHADUR.
5. H.H. MAHARAJA SIR NARINDER SINGH, MOHINDER BAHADUR, G.C.S.I.

1. H.H. MAHARAJA SIR MOHINDER SINGH, MOHINDER BAHADUR, G.C.S.I.
2. H.H. MAHARAJA SIR RAJINDER SINGH, MOHINDER BAHADUR, G.C.S.I.
3. H.H. RAJA SIR RANBIR SINGH, K.C.S.I., UNCLE TO H.H. THE MAHARAJA-DHIRAJ BAHADUR.

appealed to General Perron, who was in command of the Imperial forces of the Scindia of Gwalior, and with his aid he crushed their common enemy.

Friendly political relations with the British Government commenced in the year 1804, when Lord Lake was assured by Maharaja Sahib Singh of his friendship as he passed through Patiala in pursuit of Jaswant Rao Holkar, who had retreated into the Punjab. Lord Lake signed a document in which he assured Sahib Singh that "whereas you have declared yourself to be a staunch friend of the Kingdom, therefore, the country at present in your possession shall continue to remain as it is and no tribute shall ever be demanded."

In 1805, as a result of the Duladdi village dispute which had ended in bloodshed, the Rajas of Nabha and Jhind invoked the intervention of Ranjit Singh, who eagerly seized the opportunity. He crossed the Sutlej, but in an encounter against the Patiala forces, the "Lion of the Punjab" had to sue for peace. After a short stay he returned to Lahore, having considerably enriched himself at the expense of the Chiefs through whose territory he passed on his way.

Alarmed at the menace of the growing power of Ranjit Singh, Maharaja Sahib Singh and the other Cis-Sutlej Chiefs made certain representations to the British Resident at Delhi, which resulted in a definite promise of protection, and the enforced retirement of the Ruler of Lahore from his acquisitions south of the Sutlej. A proclamation of protection against Lahore was issued in May 1809, which, after stating that "the country of the Chiefs of Malwa and Sirhind had entered the protection of the British Government," went on to secure to these Chiefs "the exercise of the same rights and authority within their own possessions which they enjoyed before."

A strong and able Ruler was still the great need of Patiala, and owing to the continuance of internal dissensions, the British Agent at Ludhiana intervened and helped to instal as Regent the ambitious Rani Kaur, whose relations with her husband had been strained for some time. Apart from her ambitious nature and greed for power, Kaur was a very capable woman, and she managed the affairs of the State in a very satisfactory manner.

Maharaja Sahib Singh died in 1813, and was succeeded by Maharaja Karam Singh, who greatly distinguished himself by his wholehearted and unwavering support of the British Arms in several expeditions. In recognition of his services, the British Government awarded to Maharaja Karam Singh, at the close of the war, 10 *perganas* in the Simla Hills.

In 1839 the Maharaja advanced to the British Government Rs. 25,00,000 for the first Afghan War; Rs. 5,00,000 in connection with the second Afghan War in 1842; in the following year he sent two guns and 1,000 cavalry to help British troops in suppressing disturbances in Kaithal State; and in 1845, on the outbreak of the first Sikh War, he provided a contingent of 2,000 cavalry, 2,000 infantry, and followers for service with the British Army, at the same time undertaking to furnish a large quantity of stores and supplies. Before the conclusion of this war Maharaja Karam Singh died, and was succeeded by his son, Maharaja Narindra Singh. For Maharaja Karam Singh's services, the Ruler of the Patiala State was exempted from the presentation of *Nazar*.

The new Maharaja was even more friendly towards the British Government than his father had been, and when the second Sikh War broke out, Maharaja Narindra Singh supplied the British with a loan of Rs. 30,00,000, and he also offered the services of his troops, but no necessity arose for their employment.

During the great Mutiny of 1857–8, no Prince in India showed greater loyalty or rendered more conspicuous service to the British Government than the Maharaja of Patiala. He was the acknowledged head of the Sikhs, and any wavering on his part would have been attended with most disastrous results, while his ability, character and high position would have made him a most formidable leader against the Government. But Maharaja Narindra Singh unhesitatingly placed his whole power, resources, and influence at the absolute disposal of the Paramount Power during the darkest and most doubtful days of the rebellion. From the commencement of the Mutiny to the end of the year 1857 Patiala supported the British with eight guns, 2,156 cavalry, 2,846 infantry, and 156 officers; while in 1858 the drafts included two guns, 2,930 infantry and 907 *sowars*.

The splendid services of the Maharaja were gratefully acknowledged by the British Government, who made a grant to him of the rich *pergana* of Narnaul, forming part of the forfeited State of the Nawab of Jhajjar, on condition of political and military support in times of general danger and disturbances, and he was also permitted to acquire the *pergana* of Kanaud and the *taluqa* of Khamanon in perpetual sovereignty in liquidation of certain loan transactions with the British Government during 1848 and also during the Mutiny. He was also given all the rights of the paramount power over the Bahadur *Sirdars*. His titles were, at the same time, increased by the addition of "Farzandi-i-Khas, Daulat-i-Inglishia, Mansur-i-Zaman Amir-ul-Umra Sri."

In 1860 the Rulers of the Phulkian States received from the Government the right of adoption, and they were further empowered to select successors from the Phulkian family in the event of there being no male heir or if the privilege of adoption had not been exercised.

Maharaja Narindra Singh was one of the first Indian Princes to receive the Knight Grand Commandership of the Most Exalted Order of the Star of India. He had also the unique honour of being appointed a Member of the Governor-General's Council for making Laws and Regulations during Lord Canning's Viceroyalty. His Highness was noted for his measures of reform and progress and for his unbounded charity. He died in 1862, when his eldest son Mohindra Singh was not more than ten years of age. Maharaja Mohindra Singh did not live long, and died when he was only twenty-six, but his administration was marked by several events of considerable importance to the State. The Sirhind canal—the idea of which had originated with Maharaja Narindra Singh—was sanctioned during his Rulership, although it was not opened until 1882. The Durbar contributed a magnificent sum of Rs. 1,23,00,000 towards the construction of this great scheme.

In 1871 His Highness rendered valuable aid to the British Government in suppressing the Kuka rising. The Maharaja gave Rs. 70,000 to the University College at Lahore, and established the Mohindra College at his own capital. His salute was raised from 15 to 17 guns in 1864, and the insignia of a Knight Grand Commander of the Most Exalted Order of the Star of India was conferred upon him in 1871. His Highness donated Rs. 10,00,000 for relief of sufferers during the famine of 1873 which caused such great havoc in Bengal.

The Patiala State contributed a contingent of 1,100 men of all arms of service beyond the frontier in the Kabul War of 1879.

His Royal Highness the Prince of Wales (the late King Edward VII) paid a visit to the Maharaja at Rajpura in 1875, and to commemorate the event the Albert Mohindra Gunj was established at Rajpura.

Maharaja Mohindra Singh died in 1876, leaving as his heir Rajindra Singh, who was only four years of age.

THE STATE OF PATIALA.

1. Interior View of Durbar Hall (Quilla Mubarik), Patiala. 2. Ijlas-i-Khas (Secretariat Offices). 3. Metibagh Palace, Patiala. 4. Baradari Palace, Patiala.

THE STATE OF PATIALA.

1. Statue of King Edward VII, Rajinder Hospital, and the Lake, Patiala. 2. Suspension Bridge, Banaser Tank, Patiala. 3. Rajgarh Villa Palace, Chail. 4. Gardens, Rajgarh Villa Palace, Chail. 5. Shalamar Gardens, Pinjaur, Patiala. 6. Old Nizamat-Gah, Rajpura.

THE STATE OF PATIALA.

1. Cricket Ground and Club Building. 2. Samadh of Maharaja Baba Alla Singh Sahib. 3. Gurdwara Sahib, Natibagh. 4. Polo Ground and Pavilion. 5. Interior View of Mohindergarh Fort. 6. Gurdwara Sahib Futehgarh (Sirhind).

Towards the end of 1887, the Council of Regency offered to place the whole resources of the State at the disposal of the British Government in the event of the outbreak of war on the north-west frontier. This generous offer was given a practical form in an engagement to maintain for service side by side with British troops, especially trained Corps numbering 600 cavalry and 1,200 infantry, fully equipped and ready to take the field at a moment's notice. Two years later these units proved their worth in the Tirah and Mohmand expeditions. The Maharaja served in person with General Elles in the Mohmand country, and was present at the forcing of the Bedmani Pass. Patiala troops also participated in the China War which subsequently followed.

When war broke out with South Africa His Highness presented a large number of trained remounts for the use of British cavalrymen.

During Maharaja Rajindra Singh's time a line of railway 108 miles in length was constructed by the State between Rajpura and Bhatinda. His Highness was created a Knight Grand Commander of the Most Exalted Order of the Star of India in 1893. His munificent donations included Rs. 1,62,000 to the Khalsa College, Amritsar, Rs. 55,000 to the Punjab University, and Rs. 30,000 to the Imperial Institute in London. Maharaja Rajindra Singh died in 1900, and was succeeded by his son, the present Ruler.

His Highness Maharaja Bhupindra Singh was born on October 12, 1891. During his minority, which terminated in 1909, a Council of Regency managed the affairs of the State. He received his education at the Aitchison Chiefs' College, Lahore, and in early life he displayed those qualities which have served to render his rule so memorable in the annals of Patiala. At the Coronation Durbar held in Delhi in 1903 he won the admiration of all present by the gallant way in which, as a youth of 12, he personally led his troops at the Grand Review. His Highness was visited by Lord Curzon in the same year, and in 1905 he was invited to meet His Royal Highness the Prince of Wales (now His Imperial Majesty King George V) at Lahore. On this occasion he gave Rs. 1,00,000 to the Khalsa College, Amritsar, for founding a foreign scholarship. Their Royal Highnesses' safe return to England was commemorated by another donation of Rs. 50,000, which was equally divided between the Victoria Mary Girls' School and Lady Minto's Fund for Nurses. In 1908 the Maharaja was married to the daughter of the Commander-in-Chief of the Jind State army. His Highness assumed the reins of government at the age of 18, on September 30, 1909. In November, 1910, Lord Minto visited the State and performed the opening ceremony of the Patiala City Water-works. During the past 10 years the Patiala State has progressed by leaps and bounds. Almost every department is being overhauled, particular attention being given to education and sanitation. Primary and collegiate education is imparted free in the State.

His Highness granted 69 acres of land at Dharampur for the King Edward Consumptives' Sanitorium. He also gave Rs. 1,00,000 to the Institution, and furnished it with a fully-equipped hospital. A list of some of the more important charitable donations is given below: the Minto Memorial, Rs. 5,000; Victoria Memorial Hall, Rs. 1,00,000; Kangra Relief Fund, Rs. 10,000; King Edward Memorial, Rs. 2,00,000; Khalsa College, Amritsar

THE STATE OF PATIALA.

HIS HIGHNESS'S FAVOURITE HORSES—1. "THE GENERAL" (BEST CHARGER IN INDIA); 2. "MADINA"; 3. "GREY BEAUTY."

Endowment Fund, Rs. 6,00,000; Lady Hardinge Memorial, Rs. 1,25,000; Lady Hardinge Medical College, Rs. 2,00,000; Sikh Kanya Mahavidyala, Ferozepore, Rs. 10,000; Sikh *dharamsala*, London, Rs. 1,20,000 (£8,000); Tibbia College, Delhi, Rs. 25,000; Hindu University, Benares, Rs. 5,00,000 and an annual grant of Rs. 20,000.

His Highness, who has ever been a lover of cricket, captained the Indian team which went to England in May 1911. At the invitation of the Imperial Government he took part in the Coronation ceremony of Their Majesties in England, and he was also a prominent figure at the Delhi Coronation Durbar of 1911. The visitors on that occasion still remember the truly warlike manner in which he led his Imperial Service troops past Their Majesties at the Grand Review of the forces. The dignity of Knight Grand Commander of the Indian Empire was conferred on His Highness at the same Durbar, and he was decorated with the insignia of the Order by His Imperial Majesty himself at the Investiture Ceremony held at that time. Her Highness the Maharani was present at the *purdah* reception of Her Majesty, and had the honour of being selected to present to the Queen-Empress, on behalf of the women of India, an address accompanied by a magnificent jewel. In 1912 Lord Hardinge paid a visit to the State. The heir-apparent was born on January 17, 1913.

With the outbreak of the Great War begins a new chapter in the history of Patiala. It is a magnificent chapter; but it could never have been the brilliant record that it is but for the personal example the Maharaja set to his people by his ceaseless exertions throughout the period of hostilities.

At the very outset His Highness placed unreservedly all the resources of the State at the disposal of the Indian Government, and through his efforts Patiala continued to pour forth a stream of men, money and material until its record of war services stood unsurpassed by any other State in India. After the Russian *débâcle* in 1917, His Highness was invited by the Viceroy to sit on the Central Recruiting Board. In response to the Premier's appeal in April, 1918, His Highness at once offered to raise three new battalions, and he took a leading part in the memorable Indian War Conference, which met at Delhi in the same month. His zealous services in the cause of the Empire were signally recognized by his selection in 1918 as one of India's representatives on the Imperial War Conference and the Imperial War Cabinet, His Highness visited the Allied fronts in Belgium, France, Italy and Palestine, and received the highest honours and titles that the Governments of these countries could confer. His Majesty the King-Emperor invested him with the insignia of a Knight Grand Cross of the Order of the British Empire, and he was raised to the rank of Major-General. Later on, His Highness was appointed as Honorary Colonel of the 15th Ludhiana Sikhs, and also Honorary Colonel of the newly-raised 1-140th Patiala Infantry. In 1917 His Highness and his successors were for all time exempted from the presentation of *Nazar*, a concession which had been originally granted to the Ruler of Patiala State for services rendered by Maharaja Karam Singh; but the perpetual nature of which had, after the time of Maharaja Narindra Singh, been brought into question. The personal salute of His Highness has been raised from 17 to 19 guns.

During the war the Patiala State con-

THE STATE OF PATIALA.

1. His Highness's State Silver Carriage, with Postillions. 2. His Highness's State Elephant.

THE STATE OF PATIALA.

1. A Panorama View of Patiala City. 2. Patiala Bazaar Scene. 3. Bahadurgarh Fort. 4. Bhatinda Fort. 5. Sheranwala Gate, Patiala.

THE STATE OF PATIALA.

1. Gate of Palace, Androon. 2. Main Gate, City Palace (Quilla Mubarik), Patiala. 3. Temple of Rajrajeshwari. 4. Imperial Service Infantry Lines. 5. Mohinder College, Patiala. 6. Nisham Sahib Gurdwara Sahib Metibagh and Motibagh Gardens, Patiala.

tributed about 25,000 men. The Patiala Imperial Service troops served in all the main theatres of war, and won no less than 125 battle distinctions. Besides maintaining its fighting forces at a cost of over Rs. 60,00,000, the State furnished 1,000 camels, 259 mules, and 400 horses for the transport and remount branches. A sum of Rs. 35,00,000 was subscribed to the War Loans, and the Patiala State helped the Government of India to tide over the currency crisis by a timely loan of Rs. 10,00,000 of silver coin without interest. Altogether the State contributions in money amounted to nearly Rs. 1,50,00,000, and in materials to about Rs. 9,00,000.

During the recent disturbances in the Punjab His Highness heartily co-operated with the Government, and detachments of Patiala troops were despatched under responsible officers to take charge of the important railway junctions in the State territory. All lines of communication, roads, telegraphs, and telephones were also properly protected. Owing to these strenuous measures, peace and order were fully maintained in the State and the adjoining British territory.

In the recent Afghan War His Highness at once volunteered his personal services along with those of his troops, which were accepted by the Government of India. His Highness worked as Special Service Officer on the staff of the General Commanding the North-West Frontier Force, and remained at the front until an armistice was asked for by the Amir.

His Highness has been one of the leading lights of the Princes' Conference, in whose deliberations he takes a very keen interest.

With the ultimate aim of associating his subjects in the higher Councils of the State, His Highness is introducing the element of representation in municipalities and district boards.

Agriculture, in which more than 60 per cent. of the people are engaged, is carried on under greatly diversified conditions owing to the isolated position of many portions of the State. The land consists chiefly of an extensive plain with varying characteristics, for example, a large area of the soil is fertile, but it is not productive owing to the deficiency of rain, while in the *nizamats* of Pinjaur, Karmgarh, and Amargarh excellent crops are grown in rich loam.

The principal crops are wheat, barley, cotton, *gram*, maize, *jowar*, mustard, ginger, rice, turmeric, sugar-cane and potatoes.

The chief exports of the State are grain (principally wheat), rapeseed, *gram*, millet, pulses, *ghee*, cotton, yarn, pepper and lime; and the imports include raw and refined sugar, rice, piece-goods, and cloth.

The State has first and second-class forests of about 110 square miles in extent in the hilly *thanas* of Pinjaur, Dharmpur, Srinagar, Dun, and the Siwaliks, which contain considerable quantities of pine, *deodar*, oak and bamboos; and it also possesses 171 square miles of grass land together with some 12,000 acres of reserves on the plains. Avenues of shisham (*Dalbergia Sissoo*) have been planted along the banks of canals, and several roads are bordered with fine trees of the *Acacia Arabica* type.

Patiala has a good breed of strong upstanding cattle for agricultural and general draught purposes, but it has a very limited supply of cows suitable for the dairy. Farmers do not appear to have yet realized the necessity for selecting good sires and dams, and therefore the little breeding carried on is not a profitable undertaking. A good strain of indigenous ponies is found in nearly every portion of the State, and in 1890 the Durbar established a stud farm near the principal city in order to encourage the production of animals of even a better type. The paddock usually contains about five stallions, one pony sire, three donkey stallions, and some 25 brood mares.

The most recent additions to the attractions of the city are the Victoria Memorial Poor House, costing Rs. 80,000; the Victoria Girls' School, the *Sadr* and Lady Dufferin Hospital, and a training school for midwives and nurses at Patiala.

There are four administrative departments in the State, namely, Finance, Foreign, Judicial, and Military, all of which are under the control of His Highness the Maharaja through his Confidential Secretary.

For general administrative purposes the State is divided into five *nizamats* of Karmgarh, Pinjaur, Amargarh, Anahadgarh, and Mohindargarh; and each of these is under the supervision of a *nazim* who possesses executive powers.

Revenue from land was formerly collected by the State taking a share of the produce—usually about one-third—but in 1862 a settlement upon a cash basis was adopted, and in 1901 a regular settlement was undertaken.

The principal sources of revenue, other than land, are the Public Works Department (including irrigation works and railways), excise, octroi duties, stamps, and Provincial rates.

The only industrial enterprises are unimportant in character, and they are confined to a few towns and some of the larger villages.

Courts of justice are guided in their decisions by a code based upon laws usually in force in British Indian territories, and the highest Appellate Court in civil as well as criminal cases is the Chief Court, the confirmation of His Highness the Maharaja being necessary in sentences of capital punishment. Special jurisdiction in criminal matters is exercised by the *Mir Munshi*, or Foreign Minister, who enjoys powers of a Sessions Judge, and certain canal and forest officers have magisterial powers with regard to offences concerning their respective departments.

There are a number of feudatories of Patiala who are *Sardars* of Bhadaur, and they conjointly enjoy a *jagir* of more than Rs. 70,000 per annum. A claim made by the State in 1855 to regard these Bhadaur Chiefs as its own feudatories was disallowed by the British Government, but in 1858 the supremacy over Bhadaur was ceded to the ruling Maharaja as a portion of his reward for his splendid loyalty during the Sepoy Mutiny. The *jagirdars* of the Khamamon villages receive fully Rs. 90,000 yearly from the State in addition to various dues paid by the villagers themselves.

SWINGING GATE, JHULA DARWAZA, REWA FORT PALACE.

THE STATE OF REWA

WITH the exception of the principality of Gwalior, Rewa is the largest first-class treaty State in the Baghelkhand division of the Central India Political Agency. The word "Baghelkhand" is derived from the name of the clan of the ruling family—the Baghels—who are a branch of the Chalukyas or Solankis who, with the Parmars, Parihars and Chauhans, were *Agnikul* Rajputs created from the sacred firepit at Mount Abu. The Solankis originally founded an extensive kingdom in Southern India, but between the tenth and twelfth centuries they held supreme power in the Province of Gujerat. About the middle of the thirteenth century Vyaghra Deva, brother of the Chief of Gujerat, left the Province, and established himself in Northern India, about 20 miles in a north-easterly direction from Kalinjar. The town of Bandhogarh (this name being applied during the Mahomedan period to the country now called Bundelkhand), together with its fort, was granted as dowry to Karan Deva, son of Vyaghra Deva, but at the close of the thirteenth century Karan Deva was driven from his possessions in Gujerat, and he, with a very large number of Baghels, migrated to Bandhogarh, which remained their capital until it was reduced by the Emperor Akbar in 1597. The Baghels, in a quiet but effective manner, extended the area of their possessions, and when Rao Chandra was Chief of Bandhogarh, between the years 1555 and 1592, it had assumed very considerable proportions. This Ruler, who was an able administrator, was renowned for his great consideration for the welfare of his people, seeking their advancement in every possible way, but he unfortunately died in 1592. The next Ruler, Birchandra, did not long enjoy his elevation to the *gadi*, being accidentally killed, and the consequent succession of Vikramaditya, then a minor, produced a sensational panic in the State. When the news of it reached the ears of Akbar, he laid siege to the fort and demolished it, as already stated, in 1597. About the middle of the seventeenth century Anup Singh was the Chief of Rewa, and after he had been driven from his State, he laid his case before the Emperor at Delhi, who ordered the restoration of the country, and raised Anup Singh to the rank of *Seh-hazari*, as well as the command of 3,000 cavalry. The Pindaris, in the year 1812, proceeded from Rewa and raided the district of Mirzapur, but the British Government, believing that the Raja Jai Singh was cognizant of the invasion, compelled the Raja to enter into a treaty with them, by which he acknowledged their supremacy, and agreed to submit for their decision any disputes which might arise between Rewa and neighbouring States. Jai Singh was a man of considerable literary ability, and he was not only the author of several important works, but he took pleasure in the company of men of learning, to whom he was a great benefactor. He was succeeded by the eldest of his three sons, Viswanath Singh, whose administrative capabilities had been proved during the lifetime of his father, and who, on attaining full ruling powers, proved himself to

HIS HIGHNESS MAHARAJA GULAB SINGHJI BAHADUR.

1. HIS LATE HIGHNESS MAHARAJA RAGHURAJ SINGHJI BAHADUR, G.C.S.I. (GRANDFATHER OF THE PRESENT RULER).
2. LIEUT.-COL. HIS LATE HIGHNESS MAHARAJA VENKAT RAMAN SINGHJI BAHADUR, G.C.S.I. (FATHER OF THE PRESENT RULER).

be a very capable Chief. He, too, was highly educated, and spared no pains in encouraging others to make the acquisition of learning one of the chief features of their lives. The next Chief, Maharaja Raghuraj Singh, had only occupied the *gadi* for a period of about three years when the Sepoy Rebellion of 1857 occurred. His Highness at once communicated to the Government of India his determination to do all in his power to protect British interests, and to assist the forces of law and order to quell the rebellion, which soon spread with great rapidity. His first act was to send a detachment of 2,000 men to preserve peace in adjoining territories, and the able manner in which he conducted these operations may be gleaned from the fact that he was subsequently rewarded with a grant of the *parganas* of Sohagpur and Amarkantak, which had been taken from Rewa by the Mahrattas in the early part of the century. About 10 years later His Highness removed all transit duties, and abolished the system of leasing out the collection of revenue, while his earnest desire to reorganize the administrative machinery of the State resulted in the appointment of Raja Sir Dinkar Rao, K.C.S.I., as his Chief Minister. In 1860 the distinction of a Knight Grand Commandership of the Most Exalted Order of the Star of India was bestowed upon him, and in 1870 he attended a special Durbar, held at Agra, in honour of the visit of His Royal Highness the late Duke of Edinburgh. Shortly after this date it became apparent that the financial condition of Rewa was not by any means satisfactory, and therefore, at the request of His Highness, the Government of India undertook the duties of administration. The Maharaja was present at the Durbar, held at Delhi in 1876, in honour of His Royal Highness the Prince of Wales (the late King-Emperor Edward VII), and in the following year he was presented with a banner and medal at the Delhi Imperial Assemblage. His Highness died in the year 1880, and was succeeded by Lieut.-Col. His Highness Maharaja Sir Venkat Raman Singhji Bahadur, G.C.S.I., who was born on July 14, 1876. During the long period of minority of the new Ruler, the administration was conducted by Political Agents of Baghelkhand and Superintendents of the Rewa State. Major (afterwards Lieut.-Col. Sir David) Barr was Superintendent from 1881 to 1888, and Lieut.-Col. (after Sir Donald) Robertson occupied the same position from 1888 to 1894, and the names of these two distinguished administrators will long be remembered in Rewa. A Council consisting of nine *Sardars* was constituted in 1881 in order to give advice and assistance in matters connected with the general management of the State, and while this body was of a purely consultative character until the year 1893, its powers were then enlarged to enable it to pass final orders especially, however, upon questions relating to cases of settlement. The education of His Highness was, in 1883, entrusted to Surgeon-Major Goldsmith, with Pandit Furn Mul as assistant tutor, and at the same time 10 other boys, sons of *Sardars*, were selected to study with the young Maharaja and to be his daily companions. On the retirement of Major Goldsmith in 1888, on the ground of ill health, Col. Gimletts was selected to succeed him. His Highness was invested with full administrative powers in November, 1895, and he found, on assuming the reins of government, that during his minority the various State departments had been thoroughly reorganized and placed on a sound footing, and that the survey of land and settlement of revenue had been completed throughout the whole portion of Northern Rewa.

Although young in years when the prosperity of a large portion of India was threatened by the outbreak of famine in 1896, His Highness the Maharaja showed the metal of which he was made by promptly establishing relief works, by opening homes for poor and needy persons, and by distributing food, clothing and other gifts, to his necessitous subjects. Large sums of revenue were suspended or entirely remitted, while *taccavi* advances were made on a liberal scale. An immense sum of money was expended by the State in its endeavours to minimize the destitution of the people, but His Highness was rewarded by the consciousness that he had saved the lives of thousands of his subjects, and had been able to restore them to their former homes. The Government of India expressed its warm appreciation of the very great services rendered by His Highness, and made the announcement that the distinction of a Knight Grand Commandership of the Most Exalted Order of the Star of India had been conferred upon him.

The State was honoured in March, 1903, by a visit from His Excellency Lord Curzon, Viceroy of India, and at a banquet given in his honour, His Highness the Maharaja referred to the year as an auspicious one, as it witnessed the great Durbar at Delhi, the marriage of His Highness' sister, and lastly, the presence of Lord Curzon himself. The Viceroy, in his reply, humorously, but very appropriately, remarked that His Highness had omitted to mention a very important event connected with the State, which had taken place much nearer his home than Delhi, namely, the birth of a son and heir, the present Maharaja, which had occurred only a few days previously.

His Highness was present at the Delhi Durbar in 1903, where his camp was (according to an official account), "one of the most elaborate in the whole of Delhi. It was lavishly equipped, and so profusely decorated with bunting and so modern in style, that a visitor might have imagined himself in a corner of the Paris Exhibition. The camp contained the whole of the large retinue which the Maharaja took with him, consisting of about 800 men, 18 elephants, and a large number of horses." In the following year he attended a conference at Ajmer, held to consider the reorganization of the Chief's College; in 1905 he went to Indore, where he had the honour of being presented to Their Royal Highnesses the Prince and Princess of Wales (the present King-Emperor and Queen-Empress); and in 1911 he participated in the brilliant functions connected with the Coronation ceremony at Delhi of their present Imperial Majesties.

An event which will in future histories of India be described as one of vital importance to the good government of Indian States, and their relationship to the Paramount Power, was the establishment, a few years ago, of a conference of ruling Princes and Chiefs, who were to assemble periodically for a free and open discussion of matters affecting the welfare of their respective States.

His Highness the Maharaja of Rewa was present at Sessions held at Delhi in the year 1916 and 1917, and he took a deep personal interest in the proceedings which, it is reported, were characterized by a brotherly sympathy which augured well for the future prosperity and happiness of a large number of His Majesty's subjects in the vast Indian Empire.

The news flashed by cable in August, 1914, to every corner of the world intimating that the British Government had been compelled to take up arms against Germany, caused a profound sensation in Rewa, and His Highness the Maharaja Sahib, on the 6th of that month, tele-

THE STATE OF REWA.

1. Maharaj Humar Ramanuj Prasad Singhji Bahadur (Brother of His Highness the Maharaja).
2. The Madhogarh Fort. 3. Main Gate, His Highness's Residence, Rewa. 4. The New Kothi, Rewa. 5. Rewa Fort Palace.

graphed to the Political Agent in Baghelkhand as follows: " Have first learned Great Britain has been forced into war in Europe. Kindly inquire if there are any orders for me and my army from His Majesty the King-Emperor or Government of India." In reply to this offer, a reply was received from the Political Agent, which stated: " Have pleasure to convey to your Highness Viceroy's warm thanks for your message, and to inform you that should course of operation require employment of armed strength of India, advantage will be taken of Your Highness' patriotic offer."

On the 11th His Highness sent a message to His Excellency the Viceroy, couched in these words: " Learn from papers two divisions are to go from India for the war. Does not Your Excellency think it possible that I, with some of my troops, could be attached to one of them? " His Excellency the Viceroy replied as follows: " Thank you very much for your offer, which I greatly appreciate. At present nothing but regular troops are going, and it has not yet been decided whether Imperial Service or other troops are to go." The foregoing message was followed by another one from His Highness, who desired the British Government to understand that he not only offered his personal services in the cause of the Allies, but also that the State treasury, and even his private purse, as well as his jewellery, were at the full disposal of the Government. In the month of August the Maharaja Sindhia of Gwalior initiated a movement—in which he was supported by a number of ruling Princes, including His Highness the Maharaja of Rewa—for the supply of a hospital ship, called the *Loyalty*, containing 300 beds, for the use of the Imperial Government wherever required. This act of devotion to the Imperial cause elicited from the Political Agent in Baghelkhand a reply to the effect that the Secretary of State for India in Council had cabled to His Excellency the Viceroy asking that an expression of his appreciation might be conveyed for the very generous offer. In September the Political Agent was requested to forward to the Government of India the following message: " His Highness has heard that elephants have been used in France, and asks whether gun-elephants would be useful for the siege guns there. If so, the Maharaja of Rewa is prepared to lend about 30 elephants, some of which have already been trained." The Government thanked His Highness for his generous offer, but regretted that it did not appear to be possible to make use of the animals. In addition to his offer of troops, horses and elephants, His Highness the Maharaja also unreservedly placed at the disposal of the Government his State colliery and leather factory at Umaria, the latter being designed for the supply of harness and other similar necessities for the troops. In the same month the Chief Government Mobilization Officer visited Rewa, and selected 81 horses for remount purposes, and in July, 1916, a further draft of 18 was purchased. His Highness presented an aeroplane called " Rewa " for the Indian Army, which cost Rs. 18,000, and after being used successfully in Egypt, it met with an accident, resulting in its partial destruction, but His Highness bore the expense of repairs, which amounted to about Rs. 3,000.

In September, 1915, another aeroplane was purchased for His Highness (which was named " Bandhava," after Bandhogarh, the ancient capital), for presentation to the same army, and the cost of this machine was Rs. 22,500. During the same year His Highness the Maharaja appealed to all the Solanki Chiefs and *Thakurs* in India, requesting them to join him in making a present to the Government of three or four aeroplanes, to be named the " Solanki Squadron," and as a result of His Highness' action, two planes were added to the " Rewa " and " Bandhava," and the fleet was at once transferred to the Government for service wherever required. Included in the long list of contributions for various war purposes, the following are noticed: Rs. 1,000, given by Her Highness the Dowager Pariharin Maji Maharani Sahiba towards the Baghelkhand branch of the Red Cross Fund; Rs. 150, for kit-bags manufactured in the State and sent to France; Rs. 2,00,000, presented by His Highness the Maharaja in May, 1918, and 1,000 *maunds* (80 lb.) of *gram* was supplied by the Durbar.

In order to illustrate the successful rulership of His Highness the Maharaja, it may be said that the total receipts of the State in the year 1894 5 were Rs. 17,08,087, and that in the year 1916–17 the revenue had increased to Rs. 47,65,411. The State of Rewa was singularly fortunate in receiving visits from Viceroys of India, the list including their Excellencies Lord Dufferin in 1888, Lord Lansdowne in 1893, Lord Elgin in 1894, Lord Curzon in 1903 and Lord Hardinge in 1914. His Highness the Maharaja Sahib died in October, 1918, and was succeeded by the present Ruler, His Highness Maharaja Gulab Singhji Bahadur, who was born in the year 1903.

The education of the young Prince was commenced when he was in the sixth year of his age, a capable Indian tutor having been selected as his instructor, until he was succeeded by a European official. The Maharaja entered the Daly College, Indore, in January, 1916, and remained there until August, 1918, studying in Hindi, Sanskrit and English, and he also received special training for the heavy and responsible duties which would devolve upon him as Ruler of a first-class Indian State.

His Highness was married in June, 1919, to the sister of His Highness the Maharaja of Jodhpur. He is fond of all manly games, especially polo, while he has already given proof of his skill in handling a rifle, having shot several tigers.

His Highness appears to be following in the footsteps of his late father as a hunter of large game, the late Maharaja having bagged no fewer than 139 tigers up to the end of September, 1917.

The State of Rewa, with a population of 15,13,299, is about 13,000 square miles in extent, and it is interesting to note that it is about equal to the size of Belgium before the late Great War, and of Bulgaria before the Balkan Expedition. Rewa is bounded on the north by the districts of Banda, Allahabad and Mirzapur, on the east by the feudatory States of the Chhattisgarh division of the Central Provinces and the district of Mirzapur, on the south by the districts of Bilaspur and Mandla, and on the west by the districts of Banda, Jubbulpore and Mandla, and the States of Kothi, Sohawal and Maihar. The State falls into two natural divisions, which are separated by the scarp of the Kaimur range. Lying to the north of the mountains, and surrounding the chief town, is an elevated plateau nearly 4,000 square miles in extent, while to the south the country is traversed by a succession of paralleled ridges of hills enclosing a deep valley, the whole region being covered with dense forests. The plateau ends on the north and south in an abrupt scarp, and the scenery near the hilly tract is remarkably fine. Over the northern scarp the River Tons falls in a series of beautiful cascades, and near Govindhgarh, on the southern boundary, are the waterfalls of Chehai and Keonti, which are respectively 360 feet and 331 feet in height. The

THE STATE OF REWA.

1. His Highness's Residence (Kothi) at Sutna. 2. The Venkat Bhawan, Rewa. 3. The Kothi Palace Gardens, Rewa. 4. Front View, Ragho Mahal, Rewa. 5. Interior of Ragho Mahal, or Audience Hall.

two watersheds of the State are provided by the Kaimur range or branch of the Vindhyan mountains, and the Maikala range, on which is situated the sacred village of Amarkantak. The great rivers, Tons and Son, with their tributaries, constitute the drainage of the State.

The geology of the State is of an interesting character. Rewa, Kaimur, Bandir and Serbu derive their names from the localities in which they are found. The plateau in which the town of Rewa is built consists of rocks of the lower Bandair series, overlaid with alluvium, while some of the hilltops have a covering of laterite. The tract of land lying on the south side of the Kaimur range consists largely of hills of Vindhyan sandstone, superimposed on gneiss, and in other portions of the State there are different kinds of slates, sandstones, iron ores and basic lavas, as well as Gondwana rocks, well known for their coal-bearing properties. Gneiss contains corundum, while mica and galena also occur. It may be remarked that valuable limestone is fairly prevalent, and there is good quantity of red-banded jaspers, similar to those which are found near Gwalior, and which are used by stone workers at Agra. The coal mines in the Gondwana area (which will be referred to more fully hereafter) are a source of considerable income to the State.

The soil in that part of the State lying to the north of the Kaimur range is fertile and bears excellent crops, while to the south of the mountains cultivation is confined to the valleys. Land is usually classified according to the natural formation of the surface and its proximity to villages. The principal crops are rice, *saman*, maize, *kakun*, *bajara* and *kodon*, grown in the autumn ; and wheat, *gram* and barley in the spring, with subsidiary crops of *til* and linseed. Poppy is cultivated to some extent in the low-level tract of the Teonthar *tahsil.*

The reserved forests of the State are 2,016 square miles in extent, and the revenue for the year 1916–17 amounted to Rs. 1,80,946, the items including timber, Rs. 18,000 ; charcoal, nearly Rs. 16,000 ; lac, Rs. 11,000 ; and minor produce, Rs. 91,000. The State lac factory at Umaria was carried on successfully during the year under review, the total receipts being Rs. 6,91,121 and the expenditure Rs. 95,894, showing a net profit of Rs. 5,95,227. The State colliery at Umaria is situated on the Katni-Bilaspur branch of Bengal-Nagpur Railway, at an elevation of 1,500 feet above the level of the sea. The town came into existence on the opening of the mines in 1881. The seams of coal in some places reach a thickness of 31 feet, and borings, which have been made by experts, reveal the fact that an estimated yield of 24,000,000 tons is not an extravagant one. Eight seams have already been opened, two of which are now being worked, and it is stated that the mine could, if necessary, produce 1,000 tons of coal daily, although the maximum output on any one day has not been more than 890 tons. The output for the year 1916 17 was 1,99,758 tons, and about 75 per cent. of this quantity was taken by the Great Indian Peninsula Railway Company. The earnings for the same period amounted to Rs. 6,89,583, and the working expenses were Rs. 4,67,740, leaving a net profit of Rs. 2,21,843. Between the years 1883 and 1903 the extraction of coal was 1·9 million tons. The mine was worked by the State from 1881 to 1885, when it was taken over by the Government of India, but in 1900 it was restored to the management of the Durbar. The workers, about 1,300 in number, above and below ground, consist of Mahomedans, Kols, Gonds, and other tribes. The European staff includes Mr. J. E. Tyers, M.I.M.E., the Manager, and U. N. Roy, M.I.M.E., as Assistant Manager.

Accidents of serious nature are fortunately remarkably few, but a hospital is maintained by the State for use in cases of emergency. The Durbar also maintains works for the manufacture of tiles, leather, shellac, sugar, linseed oil, oil cakes and flour.

The volume of trade carried on in the chief commercial centres and bazars of the State, according to the receipts of weighing fees amounted, during the year above mentioned, to Rs. 95,81,725. The principal articles of export are : wheat, rice, barley, *masur*, *arhar*, *ghee*, *mahua*, betel leaves, *til*, linseed, rapeseed, myrabolums, khair, bamboos, hides and horns, while the chief imports include sugar, salt, coco-nuts, cloth yarns, kerosene oil, and other manufactured articles.

His Highness the Maharaja exercises supreme powers in civil and criminal jurisdiction, even to the passing of sentences of death. Civil cases are heard in the Judicial Commissioner's Court, the Civil Judge's Court in Northern and Southern Rewa, and in the Courts of Deputy and Honorary Magistrates, while criminal jurisdiction is dispensed in the Judicial Commissioner's Court, a Court of Magistrates in Northern and Southern Rewa, and the Courts of Deputy and Honorary Magistrates.

The Public Works department, under the control of the State Engineer, has in recent years been actively employed in the construction and repair of roads, and at the present there are 193½ miles of metalled and 294 miles of unmetalled highways, making a total of 487½ miles, which are maintained by the State. The principal roads are the great Deccan road, 87 miles in length, the Sutna-Bela road, 22½ miles, the Bela-Govindgarh road, 11 miles, the Rewa-Govindgarh road, 10 miles, and the Rewa town roads, 18 miles. A considerable amount of work is done every year in the building and enlarging of tanks and walls, and special care has to be taken to prevent the numerous embankments of both tanks and water channels from giving way under the pressure of abnormal rains.

The number of hospitals and dispensaries is as follows : four hospitals at Rewa (the Victoria, the Military, the Jail and Zenana), two at Sutna (Raghuraj Singh's and the Venkat Eye Hospital), ten dispensaries in the mofussil, and one hospital at Umaria, in charge of an Assistant Surgeon. The average daily attendance varies between 175·20 at Rewa Victoria Hospital to 13·06 at Tala.

The educational institutions of the State comprise the Durbar High School, the Venkat High School at Sutna, two Sanskrit grant-in-aid schools at Rewa, 11 secondary boys' schools, 34 primary boys' schools and three girls' schools. There are about 2,500 scholars on the rolls, and the annual cost of the department is nearly Rs. 29,000. The two high schools above mentioned are affiliated to the Allahabad University.

The State does not pay any tribute to the British Government or any Indian State.

The total receipts in the year 1916–17 were Rs. 47,49,792, and the expenditure amounted to Rs. 41,08,011.

The strength of the military forces of the State is as follows : 816 cavalry and 3,727 infantry.

Rewa, the capital of the State, lying at an elevation of 1,045 feet above the level of the sea, is situated about 31 miles distant by a metalled road from Sutna, on the East Indian Railway. The town became the capital on the capture of Bandhogarh by the Emperor Akbar in 1597, and it is traditionally reported that Raja Vikramaditya constructed a number of

THE STATE OF REWA.

1. Akharghat Temple and Cenotaph. 2. Hindu Parade Temple—Purandas Akharghat. 3. Lakshmanbagh, from the River (The Seat of the High Priest of Rewa). 4. Cenotaph of H.H. Maharaja Raghuraj Singhji Bahadur. 5. Exterior View of Govindagh Palace. 6. Rani Tank, Rewa, showing Temples.

THE STATE OF REWA.

1. DURBAR HIGH SCHOOL, REWA. 2. VICTORIA HOSPITAL, REWA. 3. THE LAKE AT GOVINDGARH. 4. THE UMARIA COLLIERY. 5. THE PURWA WATERFALL, RIVER TONS.

palaces and other fine buildings. The older part of the city is still enclosed by a wall 20 feet in height. On the eastern side entrance to the town is gained through the Jhala *Darwaza*, or swing gate, a finely-carved piece of work, which was taken from the ancient town of Gurgi Masaun, the remains of which may be seen about 12 miles distant from Rewa. A deep ravine, crossed by a causeway, lies between the old town and modern extension, and it is believed that the gateway at the entrance of the causeway was erected by the Bandels after the capture of the city. The chief buildings are the palace of Vishvanath Singh, the Kothi or new palace erected in 1883, and the State offices. A garden known as Lakshman Bagh contains several modern Vaishnavite temples, erected by previous Chiefs, which are supervised by the *Swami* or high priest of the State, the spiritual director of the Rewa Maharajas. Three generations ago the Chief of Rewa became an ardent supporter of Vaishnavism. An annual income of Rs. 40,000 is attached to the post, and the *Swami* has great influence in temporal as well as spiritual matters.

Sutna, or Raghurajnagar, situated on the Jubbulpore-Allahabad section of the East Indian Railway, has been the headquarters of the Political Agent in Baghelkhand since the year 1872. It is a place of considerable commercial importance, and a large centre of trade of a general description, the annual value of the exports and imports passing through it being about Rs. 4,00,000. The principal exports are wheat, rice, linseed and *ghee*, while imports are represented by kerosene oil, cotton cloth and sugar. Among the buildings to be noticed are the residence and offices of the Political Agent, a High School, *dak* bungalow, hospital, dispensary and post and telegraph offices.

GOVINDGARH.—The fame of this town in the *Huzur* tahsil of the State rests upon its picturesque situation on the edge of the Kaimur scarp, at an altitude of more than 1,200 feet. A magnificent view is obtainable over the extensive area of dense forests and across fertile valleys productive of excellent crops of nearly all kinds of grain. The health-giving properties of the climate attract many visitors, but the splendid sport which is offered by the abundance of large game is a considerable inducement to others.

His Highness the Maharaja has a palace in the town, which also contains a dispensary, school and post office.

THE BIHAR-BICHIA SAMGAN AT REWA.

THE STATE OF TONK

THIS Mahomedan State is situated partly in Rajputana and partly in Central India, and is included with two others in the Haraoti—Tonk Political Agency. It has a total area of 16,33,809 acres, equivalent to about 2,553 square miles, and its *perganas*, which comprise Tonk, Aligarh, and Nimbahera in Rajputana, and Chhabra, Sironj, and Pirawa in Central India, are separated from each other by distances varying from 20 to 250 miles.

The present Chief, His Highness Amin-ud-daula Wazir-ul Mulk Nawab Sir Hafiz Mahomed Ibrahim Ali Khan Sahib Bahadur Sowlat-i-Jung, G.C.S.I., G.C.I.E., belongs to a Mahomedan Pathan family of the Boner clan, who resided on the boundary line of Afghanistan, and is descended from Amir-ud-daula Nawab Mahomed Amir Khan, the founder of the State.

The chief physical features of the State are ranges of low hills clothed with forest trees, but there is also a considerable area of flat table-lands of fertile soil, in which excellent crops of various kinds are cultivated, the principal ones being wheat, *gram*, jowar, maize, and cotton. About eight per cent. of the cultivated land is irrigated by water, obtained from a large number of wells which have been sunk by the present Nawab.

A large proportion of the inhabitants are engaged in agricultural pursuits, but His Highness is doing his utmost to encourage the inauguration or development of local manufacturing and industrial enterprises. Cotton ginning and pressing factories, and flour mills, have been started in three *perganas*, and in the capital town, Tonk, and elsewhere, a large number of people are employed in making boots, shoes, cotton cloth, rugs, soap, and *numdahs*, of a superior quality, which are exported to foreign markets, where they command a ready sale at remunerative prices.

The principal imports are salt, sugar, rice, English piece-goods, tobacco, and iron, while exports include cereals, cotton, opium, hides, and cotton cloth.

The State maintains in a thoroughly up-to-date manner the "General" and the "Walter" hospitals at Tonk (the latter being for women only), together with a dispensary at the headquarters of the five other *perganas*. About 78,000 outdoor and 300 resident patients were treated in 1915–16, and the expenditure incurred by this Department was Rs. 17,526.

The Nawab personally interests himself in the cause of education, and considerable progress has been made during the past few years.

The Ajmer-Khandwa branch of the Rajputana-Malwa Railway—which was opened for traffic in 1881—passes for a distance of 16 miles through a portion of the district of Nimbahera, and in 1899 the construction of the Bina-Baran section in the district of Chhabra was completed.

One of the most important measures of reform designed for the purpose of securing greater security for persons and property in Tonk, was the reorganization of the police, a duty which was entrusted by His Highness to Mr. S. T. Hollins, Superintendent of Police, Ajmer-Merwara, now Inspector-General of the Tonk State police.

The present force comprises more than 900 men of all ranks, involving a yearly expenditure of about Rs. 91,352. The State also maintains a military force of about 395 cavalry, 254 artillery, and 1,123 infantry.

The system of administration, as reformed by the Nawab in the year 1905, provided for a Council of four members, controlling the Revenue, Finance, Judicial, and Home Departments—all of which were under the supreme authority of His Highness—but in 1909 the first two-named offices were combined, and placed in charge of Dewan Bahadur Moti Lal, under whose competent guidance old debts inherited from previous Rulers of the State have been liquidated, and the annual income has been increased to about Rs. 19,00,000, while the fact that there is a cash balance in the State Treasury of more than Rs. 12,00,000 is a proof that the financial condition of Tonk is exceedingly satisfactory.

Revenue from land was formerly collected in cash, or "kind," but this system was open to grave abuses, as a number of speculators sprang up between the Durbar and cultivators who "farmed" the revenue, but who relieved their own financial troubles by squeezing money from the unfortunate *ryots*.

His Highness the Nawab put an end to this iniquitous practice in 1887, when the Durbar commenced to make a regular survey and settlement of the land. The present practice is to fix a certain rate per acre, which is assessed in amount according to the classification of soil, and its productiveness, to the distance of the land from town or village, and the facilities for transporting produce to a suitable market.

The laws in force in the State are based chiefly upon those recognized in British India, and civil and criminal Courts of Justice have been established, while ap-

HIS HIGHNESS AMIN-UD-DAULA WAZIR-UL MULK NAWAB SIR HAFIZ MAHOMED IBRAHIM ALI KHAN SAHIB BAHADUR SOWLAT-I-JUNG, G.C.S.I., G.C.I.E., NAWAB OF TONK.

1. SAHIBZADA MAHOMED ABDUL HAFIZ KHAN, ELDEST SON OF HIS HIGHNESS.
2. H.E. THE VICEROY'S GROUP.
3. DEWAN BAHADUR LALA MOTI LAL, RAI BAHADUR (OF DERA ISMAIL KHAN), REVENUE AND FINANCIAL MEMBER, STATE COUNCIL, TONK.

THE STATE OF TONK.

1. An Interior View of Baradari Kothi Nazar Bagh. 2. Idgah Bagh Kothi (Exterior). 3. Idgah Bagh Kothi (Drawing room).

THE STATE OF TONK.

1. View of Tonk (Old City). 2. View of Tonk (New City). 3. Amirganj Bazaar.

THE STATE OF TONK.

1. A View of His Highness's Palace. 2. The Jama Musjid Palace, Tonk. 3. The Guest House, Tonk. 4. A Portion of the Armoury.

THE STATE OF TONK.

1. The Durbar High School, Tonk. 2. Chaterbhuj Temple and Lake. 3. Pucca Bund House and Lake. 4. State Council Building, Tonk. 5. The Office of Mizamat Mal, Tonk.

peals are decided by the Nawab and his Council, confirmation by His Highness of sentences of death being necessary.

His Highness manifests a warm personal interest in the welfare of the State and its inhabitants, and is ever eager to inaugurate measures of reform tending in that direction. He spends a considerable portion of his time in the enjoyment of domestic happiness, and in the performance of religious observances, such as listening to the reading and interpretation of the Koran, or joining in social and instructive discussions with learned and pious men, who have found a haven of retreat at his court. The Nawab is at the same time a rigid disciplinarian in attending to the various duties of administration, in remedying legitimate grievances, and in giving intelligent consideration to all matters connected with the physical and moral development of his subjects. He has constructed palaces, public buildings, and places of worship, in the city of Tonk and elsewhere, and he is mainly responsible for the provision of a number of wells, in addition to several pleasure gardens, for the enjoyment of State officials and the people generally. His charitable gifts to religious, philanthropic, and other deserving causes, have been of the most benevolent description, while his liberality to the needy poor forms the theme of conversation in many a humble home.

His Highness has nine sons and 10 daughters, his heir being Sahibzada Mahomed Abdul Hafiz Khan.

The Nawab has specially manifested his loyalty to the Throne at a recent date by his noble contributions to, and work for, various War Funds, and in this matter he has been ably supported by his Dewan, Lala Moti Lal, who has not only been generous in his gifts, but is now acting as a member of the recruiting Board, and in other ways is showing his desire to follow in the footsteps of his noble Chief.

The State had a gross revenue for the year 1915–16 of Rs. 19,60,607, but it does not pay tribute to the British Government or any other Native State, nor does it maintain Imperial Service troops.

His Highness has had the honour of being created a Knight Grand Commander of the Most Exalted Order of the Star of India, and Knight Grand Commander of the Most Eminent Order of the Indian Empire, and he is entitled to a salute of 17 guns.

The capital and headquarters of the State is the city of Tonk, which lies about two miles in a northwardly direction from the river Banas ; it is 60 miles from the city of Jaipur, with which it is connected by a good metalled road ; and it is 36 miles from the Cantonment at Deoli.

THE STATE OF BANSWARA

BANSWARA is situated in the extreme south of Rajputana, and it is, in regard to size, eleventh among the twenty States of that Province. It lies between 23° 3′ and 23° 55′ north latitude and 73° 58′ and 74° 47′ east longitude, and has an area of 1,946 square miles.

It is bounded on the north by the State of Partabgarh, Udaipur and Dungarpur; on the west by the States of Dungarpur and Sunth; on the south by the Panch Mahals district of Jhalod, the State of Jhabua, and a portion of the Petlawad *pargana* of Indore State; and on the east by an outlying tract of the State of Sailana, and by the States of Ratlam and Partabgarh. Its greatest length from north to south is about 58 miles, and its greatest breadth is nearly 50 miles.

Banswara had a population of 187,468 persons according to the census of 1911.

The word Banswara is said to be a corrupted form of "Vasnawara," and the territory takes its name from a Bhil chieftain, Vasna, whose *pal* or village was on the site of the present capital, and who was defeated and slain about 1530 by Jagmalji, son of Maharawal Udai Singhji of Bagar.

Banswara originally formed part of the territory known as Bagar, and was, from the beginning of the thirteenth century, until about the year 1529, held by certain Rajput Chiefs of the Gahlot or Sesodia clan, who held the title of Rawal, and who claimed descent from an elder branch of the family now ruling at Udaipur.

Towards the end of the eighteenth century, the whole country became more or less subject to the Mahrattas, whose predatory bands plundered at large, while roving companies of unattached mercenaries subsequently appeared and carried off what was left by the Mahrattas. The rise of British power seemed to Rawal Bijai Singhji, the then ruler of the State to present a good opportunity for ridding himself of these plunderers, and, in 1812, he offered to become tributary to the British Government on the sole condition that the Mahrattas should be expelled, but no definite relations were formed with him, and he died in 1816.

A treaty was concluded in September 1818 with his successor, Umed Singhji, by which, in consideration of the protection of the British, the Maharawal agreed to act in subordinate co-operation with Government, to settle his affairs in accordance with its advice, to abstain from disputes and political correspondence with other Chiefs, and to pay a tribute in return for a guarantee of protection from the war-like Mahrattas.

The amount payable annually was definitely fixed in 1904 at Rs. 17,500.

Umed Singhji died in the following year, and was succeeded by his son, Bhawani Singhji (1819 39). The latter died in 1839, but as there was no male heir he was succeeded by Bahadur Singhji, who ruled for five years only. After his death, Maharawal Lachman Singhji succeeded at the early age of five, and in 1862 he received the usual *sanad*, guaranteeing to him the right of adoption. He died on April 29, 1905, and was succeeded by his eldest son, Shambhu Singhji, who passed away in December 1913, and was followed by His Highness the Maharawal Pirthi Singhji, the present ruler.

His Highness the Maharawal was born on July 15, 1888, and was invested with full ruling powers in 1914, on the death of his father, the late Maharawal Shambhu Singhji. His Highness has seven brothers, namely, Maharajo Gulab Singhji, Lal Singhji, Madan Singhji, Chater Singhji, Kishore Singhji, Sawairaj Singhji, and Shankar Singhji; two sisters, one son, Maharaj Raj Kunwar Chandravir Singhji, and three daughters.

His Highness has proved himself to be a wise and efficient ruler, and his practical knowledge of the work of each Department in the State has been an important factor in the progress which has been abundantly manifested in the general well-being of the people. The income of the State has also been more than doubled since he ascended the *gadi*.

His Highness is entitled to an hereditary salute of 15 guns.

It is believed that the State abounds in objects of archaeological interest, but they have not yet been professionally examined. Those known at present are the remains of about a dozen Hindu and Jain temples, belonging to the eleventh and twelfth centuries, situated at Arthuna, in the western portion of the State, and a fine Jain temple at Kalinjra, in the south. The latter has been described by Heber as being built on a very complicated and extensive plan. The temple possesses three inscribed slabs, which, however, have not yet been deciphered. In the Kushalgarh district the ruins of Jain temples exist at Andeshwar and Wagol, and others of a shrine dedicated to *Mangleshwar* (Vishnu), at Magarda, but they also have not been professionally examined.

The administration of the State is in the hands of His Highness, who is assisted by a *Diwan* and his Council. The former exercises general control over various De-

HIS HIGHNESS RAI RAYAN MAHARAWAL SHRI PIRTHI SINGHJI BAHADUR.

1. HIS LATE HIGHNESS MAHARAWAL SHAMBHU SINGHJI BAHADUR.
2. MAHARAJ RAJ JUNWAR CHANDRAVIR SINGHJI. 3. UNCLE AND FOUR BROTHERS OF HIS HIGHNESS.

THE STATE OF BANSWARA.

1 Shrigarh (New Palace). 2. Phul Mahal (Old Palace). 3. Sherbilas Palace. 4. Kushalbag Palace. 5. Bungalow—Private Residence of His Highness.

partments, such as Accounts, Customs, Excise, Judicial, Police, Revenue, and Forests, and each Department has its own responsible head. The whole State is divided into three *tahsils*, namely, Banswara, Khamera, and Kalinjra.

For judicial purposes the Chief Revenue Officer and the *tahsildars* are respectively second and third class magistrates, and they dispose of civil suits not exceeding Rs. 100 in value. Appeals against their decisions lie with the *Faujdar*, who has first-class magisterial powers, and can hear civil suits not exceeding Rs. 10,000 in value. The highest court in the State is the Council. It hears appeals from the orders of the *Faujdar*, and disposes of all cases, civil or criminal, that are beyond his powers, as well as of all important cases such as those in which the first-class nobles are concerned.

Some of the *Jagirdars* have been given second- or third-class magisterial powers, personal within their respective *jagirs*, and appeals against their decisions are heard by the *Faujdar*.

The total State income from all sources during 1917-18 was Rs. 9,55,885, and the total expenditure was Rs. 7,62,674. The Revenue consisted of land revenue, Rs. 2,43,326; Forests, Rs. 27,135; Customs and Excise, Rs. 3,20,415; Judicial, Rs. 11,885; and Miscellaneous, Rs. 2,48,592. Besides the above, additional income amounted to Rs. 1,04,532.

The central and western portions of the State are comparatively open and well cultivated; there is little or no forest, but the landscape is relieved from dullness by numerous *mahua*, babul, and palm trees. The south-west is better wooded, and is much broken up by hillocks and ravines, while the rest of the territory, particularly in the south and east, is a mass of rugged hills, rocks, scrub-jungles, and woodland. The open country in the centre is about 700 feet above the sea, and the ground slopes gradually towards the Mahi river on the west; the eastern half of the State, on the other hand, is traversed by ranges of hills, running generally north and south, and having an average height of 1,300 or 1,400 feet, though there are two or three peaks of 1,700, and one (about six miles north of Kushalgarh) of 1,988 feet. Banswara has been described as the most beautiful portion of Rajputana; and it is seen at its best just after rains, when the varied hues of the foliage, the luxuriant growth of the tall grasses, and the streams dashing down the hill-sides or purling through shady glens between banks fringed with ferns and flowers, present a most pleasing picture.

The State is, on the whole, well supplied with rivers and streams, and an absolute water famine is an impossibility. The principal rivers, the Mahi and Anas, have never been known to fail, even in a season of drought, but their beds are rocky, their banks high and steep, and they are of no use for supplying water to the crops. The minor streams, such as the Eram of Airav, the Chap, and the Haran, are, however, used for irrigation.

The greater portion of the soil of the State is of a fertile character. The average annual rainfall ranges from 25 to 40 inches, but its unequal distribution is frequently a source of great anxiety to the Durbar. Fully two-thirds of the population are Bhils, who have been converted from a marauding tribe to a peaceable and industrious race, and are rapidly becoming more and more proficient in the cultivation of their lands. The position of the *rayats* has been very materially improved since the first regular Land Revenue Settlement of 1906, as prior to that year a lump sum of money was imposed on a whole village as revenue assessment, and that amount was subsequently apportioned (frequently unfairly) to the various holdings.

During the last Settlement, which was completed in 1915–16, the whole of the State, including rivers and hills, has been surveyed. It was found that the total area was 17,73,517 *bighas*, 9,59,251 of which were still uncultivated. One of the most important results of the recent Settlement is that payers of revenue hold land direct from the State, there being no intermediate or *zamindari* class to receive a portion of the rental. It has further been decided that every tenant has a heritable right in his holding, and that he can mortgage or sell his prescriptive right of cultivation, but he is not permitted to dispose of the actual land.

Local trade consists mainly of the export of surplus agricultural produce, which includes grain, *ghee*, *til*, and in the import of cloth, cotton, tobacco, sugar, salt, gur, and other goods.

Forest produce has now commenced to contribute appreciably to the trade of the State, it consisting largely of the export of gum and lac. During 1917-18, 3,96,568 *maunds* of grain and 58,057 *maunds* of *ghee* were exported. The State is doing all in its power to stimulate all branches of trade. It started a Bank six years ago to afford financial assistance to traders, and it is under contemplation to increase its scope considerably in the near future.

There are no indigenous industries of any importance, although a few wooden toys and lacquered goods are made in several villages. A factory for the ginning of cotton has been opened at the capital town on a co-operative basis, and the State has started a printing press at a cost of Rs. 5,000, it being named the "Prithvi Vijay Printing Press." It does all printing work for the various State Departments.

Reserved forests are about 255 square miles in extent, and the areas are known as: (1) Pipalda-Pipalkhunt; (2) Banswara-Kalinjra; and (3) Bhungra-Jagpura.

Education is also being greatly encouraged in the State. There are 14 schools in the whole district, but this number will be increased when the people show a greater desire for instruction for their children. There is an Anglo-Vernacular Middle School at the capital, teaching up to the Rajputana Middle Examination, which is situated in a building known as "King George V School." It was constructed in commemoration of the visit of Their Majesties the King-Emperor and Queen-Empress to India, in connection with the Coronation Durbar at Delhi. There is a separate vernacular section, teaching up to the Vernacular Middle Examination of the Allahabad University. There is also a Girls' School.

During last year there were 286 students attached to the two schools at the capital, and the daily attendance was 199.

The pupils in the village schools during last year (1917–18) were 806 in number, with daily average attendance of 360.

In 1915–16 the Municipality of Banswara provided further education facilities by the establishment of a Sanskrit *Pathshala* for the children of Hindus, and of a Persian-Urdu School for those of Mahomedan birth. It is under contemplation to increase considerably the grant to these institutions, as the number of pupils is growing rapidly. The daily average attendance at these two schools is about 200 pupils.

The only Municipality in the State is at Banswara, the capital, and its record of progress in sanitation, street lighting, the control of building operations, and other matters of vital importance to the

THE STATE OF BANSWARA.

1. Mahakma Khas and Account Office. 2. Colvin Municipal Hall. 3. King George V School. 4. Agency Rest House.

THE STATE OF BANSWARA.

1. View of Banswara Town. 2. Temples of Dhanabad in the Bazaar. 3. Bazaar View, Banswara. 4. Pirthibilas Cenotaphs.

THE STATE OF BANSWARA.

1. Keshavi Rai's Temple. 2. Baneshwar Temple, built A.D. 1588. 3. Tripurasundri Temple, built in the Tenth Century. 4. Nilkanth Mahadeo, built in the Tenth Century. 5. Vithaldeo Temple, built in the Tenth Century.

THE STATE OF BANSWARA.

1. Bhil Dance. 2. Bhil Woman. 3. Bhil with Bow and Arrow. 4. Gangor and Ghumar Dance. 5. Gangor Procession.

chief town, is such as to reflect credit on all concerned.

As soon as the news of the outbreak of the Great War reached Banswara, His Highness wrote to the Government of India, assuring them of the unswerving loyalty of himself and his subjects to the Throne, and placing his personal services and the resources of the State at the disposal of the Government of India. The State then announced the following concessions for the encouragement of recruiting: (1) A grant of 15 *bighas* of land for enlistment in the British Army; (2) a pension to the employees of the Durbar who wished to enlist; and (3) a grant of Rs. 5 per recruit, and a certificate of good service and loyalty to those who supplied recruits.

The State contributed Rs. 44,115 to the various relief funds connected with the war, and it also gave Rs. 5,147 towards the Rajputana Aeroplane and Machine Gun Fund. It further promised to contribute Rs. 1,000 per mensem towards the general expenses of the war, and on the latter account a sum of Rs. 6,000 was actually paid, as hostilities ceased six months afterwards. The State contributed Rs. 58,830 towards the two war loan funds. Further than this, it supplied (on payment) 4,688 *maunds* of babul bark to the Government harness and saddlery factory, Cawnpore, a transaction which involved the State in a loss of Rs. 1,747.

THE STATE OF DATIA

THIS State, situated in the low-lying tract of the Bundelkhund Agency in Central India, is 911 square miles in extent, and it has a population of about 155,000 inhabitants. The regularity of the boundaries of the State is greatly affected by intervening portions of the State of Gwalior, but that area which may be regarded as the main portion is bounded on the north by sections of Gwalior and the district of Jalaun, on the south by Gwalior and the district of Jhansi, on the east by Samthar and the district of Jhansi, and on the west by Gwalior.

In tracing the early history of the State it is necessary to revert to the time of Bir Singh Deo, Maharaja of Orchha, who towards the close of his life bestowed certain *jagirs* upon his sons. Bhagwan Rao, the second in age, received a grant of territory which included the town of Datia and its palace, as well as the revenue of the *tahsil* of Baroni. Bhagwan Rao thereupon (1626) left Orchha, and took up his residence at Datia. While still a young man in his father's house at Orchha, Bhagwan Rao had on several occasions been sent to Delhi to render service to the Moghul Emperor, and after his acquisition of Datia, he assisted the Moghuls in at least two or three campaigns. In return for the aid thus given he was rewarded by the grant of tracts of land in the neighbourhood of Datia. Old records state that Datia then comprised the greater portion of the country lying between the Chambal river on the north, the Belwa on the east, and the Sind river on the west.

Bhagwan Rao died in 1656, and was succeeded by his son, Subha Karan. The latter was, like his father, a zealous supporter of the Moghul army, and in the fratricidal war, which followed the death of the Emperor Shah Jehan, Bhagwan Rao ranged himself on the side of Aurangzeb, and thus gained great favour with the future Emperor. He was continually engaged in warfare, and he distinguished himself in various conflicts with the Mahrattas. He died in the year 1683, the *gadi* being filled by his son, Dalpat Rao. The new Ruler was a brave soldier, occupying a prominent position in the principal campaigns of his day. Two of his successors were of a similar warlike disposition, but there is nothing of particular interest to record here. In 1736, on the death of Ram Chandra, a dispute arose on the question of succession, and the matter was referred for decision to His Highness the Maharaja of Orchha, who decided in favour of a minor, named Indrajit, and he also sent troops to support the young prince in securing the *gadi*. In 1760 the Emperor Shah Alam visited Bundelkhund, and invited the Ruler of Datia to meet him at Bhanda, where he conferred the title of Raja upon Indrajit, and at the same time presented him with a portable throne and two royal standards. The power of the Mahrattas had increased to such an extent about this date that they were constantly invading Datia, Orchha, and other neighbouring States. Raja Indrajit died in 1762, and the *gadi* fell to the lot of his son, Shatrujit, who was almost immediately after his succession called upon by Kunwar Dulaju to assist him, the duly appointed heir of the Orchha State, in resisting the claims of an illegitimate son of his late father, who aspired to become the recognized Ruler. Shatrujit expelled the pretender, and was rewarded with the grant of 17 villages. The chief event of the following reign was the signing, in 1804, of a treaty of alliance and friendship between the British Government and Rao Raja Parichhat of Datia, and this document is still the basis of relationship between the State and the Paramount Power. The Marquis of Hastings visited Datia in 1818, and personally thanked Raja Parichhat for his good services in securing peace in his territory, and at the same time the *tahsil* of Indargarh was added to the area of Datia. In 1836 the Raja, who was without heir, adopted Bijai Bahadur, whom he educated at his own expense. This act, although recognized by the Supreme Government, gave great offence to the Thakores of Baroni, who were direct descendants of Bhagwan Rao, the founder of the State. Serious objections were raised to the succession of Bijai Bahadur in 1839, on the death of Raja Parichhat, but the Government upheld the adoption, and formally installed him on the *gadi*. This Ruler devoted the greater portion of his time to religious ceremonies and literary pursuits, spending large sums of money at Benares, Bindraban, and other holy places in furthering the views which he held. The Raja died immediately after the outbreak of the Sepoy Mutiny in 1857, and was succeeded by the late Ruler, Bhawani Singh, adopted from the Bhasnai family, who were descended from Har Singh Deo, a brother of Raja Bir Singh Deo of Orchha. The administration of the State was placed in the hands of the senior Rani, owing to the minority of the heir, and she greatly distinguished herself by her vigorous support of the British during the rebellion already referred to. On her death, in 1858, the junior Rani who became Regent, espoused the claim

HIS HIGHNESS MAHARAJA LOKENDRA SIR GOVIND SINGHJU DEO BAHADUR, K.C.S.I.

1. HIS LATE AND LAMENTED HIGHNESS MAHARAJA LOKENDRA SIR BHAWANI SINGHJU DEO BAHADUR, K.C.S.I.

2. THE HEIR-APPARENT, RAJA BAHADUR KUAR BALBHADRA SINGHJU DEO.

THE STATE OF DATIA

to the *gadi* of Arjun Singh, an illegitimate son of Raja Bijai Bahadur.

The Rani, at the head of her followers, defied all authority, seized the fortress of Seondha, and caused the outbreak of civil war. A British force, sent to Datia, recovered the fort and restored order, Arjun Singh was banished, and the Rani and her leading supporters were placed in confinement. The Thakores of Baroni again urged their claims to the Datia *gadi*, but the British Government refused to recognize them. A question of considerable importance to the State, namely, the devolution of the shares in the Baroni *jagir*, which had for several years been agitating the administration of the State, appeared to be ripe for settlement in 1882, and the British Government in that year finally ruled that the Thakores of Baroni were the holders of an independent grant from the Moghul Emperor, but that " they were politically subordinate to the Maharaja of Datia."

The long reign of the late Chief, which extended for a period of 50 years, from 1857 to 1907, was made memorable by many important events, some reference to which may now be made. Reforms were introduced, such as the establishment of regular Courts of Justice, the abolition of transit dues, the resignation of His Highness of his rights over the manufacture of salt in return for an annual payment by the Government of the sum of Rs. 10,000 ; the opening of a high school in the principal town, the cession of land for the Betwa canal, and for the extension of railway facilities, and also for amendment of the currency system which made the British rupee the sole legal form of tender.

In 1862 His Highness was granted a *sanad* of adoption, and three years later the title of Maharaja was declared to be hereditary. His Highness had the honour of being presented to His Royal Highness the Prince of Wales (subsequently King Edward VII) in 1875, and in 1877 he attended the Imperial assemblage at Delhi, when the title of " Lokendra " was conferred upon him as an hereditary distinction, and a banner and gold medal were also presented to him. The famine of 1897 was a most disastrous one, but the Datia *durbar*, stimulated by the energy and wisdom of His Highness, responded promptly and most liberally to the cries of the starving population by which it was surrounded. Employment was found for those who were competent to work, and large sums of money were expended in distributing food to those unable to help themselves. In recognition of the meritorious services rendered by His Highness, he was created a Knight Commander of the Most Exalted Order of the Star of India.

In 1903 His Highness, accompanied by his son, the Raja Bahadur Govind Singh—the present Ruler—attended the Coronation Durbar at Delhi, and in 1905 they were presented to Their Royal Highnesses the Prince and Princess of Wales at Indore.

His Highness the Maharaja Lokendra Sir Bhawani Singh Bahadur, K.C.S.I., died on August 4, 1907, and was succeeded by his only son, who now rules under the title of His Highness the Maharaja Lokendra Govind Singh Bahadur.

The State of Datia may be described in a few words as a flat plain lying between the Belwa and Sind rivers, as the only hills are those of the Seondha *tahsil*, and they do not attain an elevation of more than 1,000 feet above sea level. The southern portion is of a rocky character, marked by ridges of gneiss, reefs of quartz, and masses of boulder, the only signs of vegetable life being the low scrub jungle with which it is covered. On the other hand, the northern part has a substratum of rock, but it is hidden by fertile alluvium formed by the waters of large rivers flowing beyond the boundaries of Datia. The only rivers of importance within the State are the Sind and Pahuj, each of which traverses the area for a distance of about 50 miles. The climate is subject to extremes of heat and cold, and the average rainfall is about 38 inches.

Nearly 40 per cent. of the inhabitants support themselves by engaging in agricultural or pastoral pursuits, but this is a somewhat precarious existence, as the productivity of the soil depends upon sufficiency of rain, little being done in the way of irrigation. The cultivated acreage in a normal year amounts to about 49 per cent. of the total area, and among the principal crops may be mentioned : *jowar*, approximately 66.000 acres ; *bajra*, 10,000 acres ; wheat, 85,000 acres ; rice, 3.000 acres ; gram, 75,000 acres ; cotton, 53,000 acres, and a smaller area of sugar-cane. Not more than about two per cent. of the cultivated land is watered from tanks and wells, the supply being conveyed in channels to the fields of the growing crops. Land revenue was in former years based upon a valuation of standing crops, and the assessment was collected " in kind," the proportion taken by the State usually ranging from one-third to one-half. Rents are now fixed by a State official, who takes into consideration the inherent capabilities of the soil and the facilities for irrigation. The amounts due are invariably paid promptly in two equal instalments. Although so large a portion of the State is useless for arable purposes, it is fortunate for the pastoral farmers that in normal years excellent grazing may be obtained in or near to every village, and even in the jungles there is considerable quantities of vegetation which may be safely consumed by cattle and other animals. A return of agricultural livestock, published recently by the Datia *durbar*, shows that there were in the State 41,000 bullocks, 44.000 cows, 4,000 male buffaloes, 17.500 female buffaloes, 700 horses and mares, 3,000 asses, and nearly 80.000 sheep and goats.

Industrial enterprises are limited to the manufacture of country cloth and blankets. Datia, the principal town, is practically the only trading centre of any importance, and its activities have been developing gradually since railway facilities were obtained. The principal exports are grain, oil-seeds, cotton and sugar, and the imports include piece-goods, grain, leather, hides, kerosene oil, salt and various kinds of metal goods. The midland section of the Great Indian Peninsula Railway system, with stations at Datia and Sonagir, traverses the State for a distance of 21 miles, and the opening of this section in 1881 has had a most beneficial effect upon the commercial prosperity of the State.

The State employs regular and irregular forces of about 5,160 infantry and 925 cavalry, exclusive of officers. This number includes the *Rajkumar Risala*, a regiment composed of 170 sons of local Sardars and Thakores, and an irregular force, consisting of hereditary servants, acts as bodyguard to His Highness the Maharaja. For the preservation of order in the State, the *durbar* maintains some 270 police of all grades, whose headquarters are at the town of Datia, and at Unao, Padri, Ronija, Baroni, Indargarh, Seondha, Tharait and Nadigaon. Nearly 900 *chaukidaris*, employed in guarding villages, report breaches of law to the nearest police station.

The education of the young was not, until a few years ago, regarded in the light of an essential in the building up of character in human beings, or in promoting the social as well as the material welfare of a State, but considerable progress has been noticeable during the

THE STATE OF DATIA.

1. Front View of Lokendra Bhawan Palace. 2. Rear View of Lokendra Bhawan Palace and Gardens. 3. The Old Palace. 4. Govind Niwas, the Maharaja's Private Residence, Datia. 5. The Maharaja's Private Residence, Seondha.

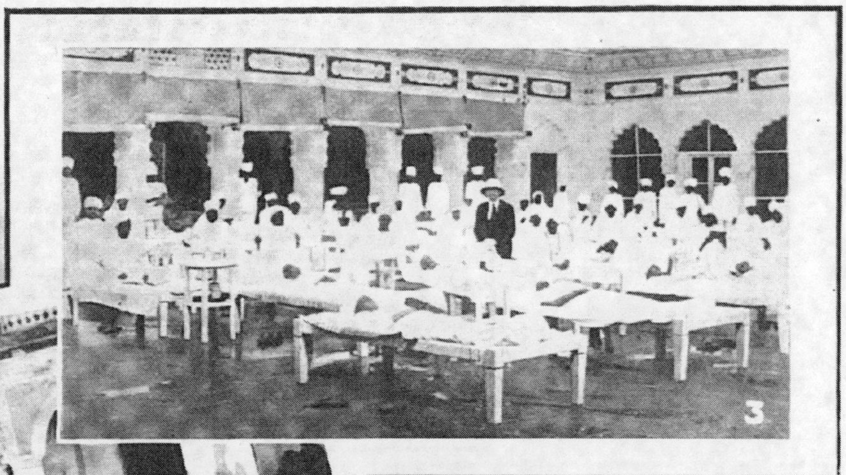

THE STATE OF DATIA.

1. Pandit Panna Lal Tiwari, the Present Minister, Datia State. 2. Exterior View of the Maharaja Govind Singh War Hospital, Datia.
3. Interior View of one of the Wards of the Maharaja Govind Singh War Hospital.
4. Group of Distinguished Visitors and Principal Officers of the State taken on the occasion of the Opening Ceremony of the Maharaja Govind Singh War Hospital, Datia.
5. Datia State Armoured Car, which rendered Valuable Service on the Western Front and in Mesopotamia.

THE STATE OF DATIA.

1. Gate of the Lokendra Bhawan Palace, Datia. 2. The Rajgarh Durbar Offices. 3. The Guest House. 4. The Hardinge Hospital. 5. The Grain Market, Ganj. 6. The Indergarh Fort.

THE STATE OF DATIA.

1. The Maqbara Chhatries, Datia. 2. Panorama of the City from Rajgarh. 3. The Avad Bihari Temple, Datia. 4. The Vijaya Govind Temple, Datia. 5. The Balaji Temple, Unao, Datia. 6. General View of the Fort and the River Sindh Seondha.

regime of His Highness the present Maharaja. The High School, established at Datia in 1892, imparts instruction up to the entrance examination of the Allahabad University, and about 30 primary schools have been opened in various other places in which Persian, Hindi, Sanskrit and Urdu are taught.

His Highness is the supreme authority in the State, final appeals in judicial matters and references on other subjects being disposed of by him. The *Diwan*, acting under instructions from the Chief, controls the working of all departments of administration, namely, the *Durbar*, Revenue, Treasury and Accounts, Forest, Police and Jails, Education and Medical. For governmental purposes the State is divided into four *tahsils*, presided over by officials, whose headquarters are at Datia, Indargarh, Nadigaon and Seondha, but limited powers of management are vested in a few officials in each village. There is no legislative officer in the strict sense of the term, as the Chief, after consultation with the *Diwan*, issues such regulations as may appear to him to be suitable for the several divisions. The Indian Penal Code is followed in criminal matters, and in deciding civil suits, judgments are based very largely upon local customs. His Highness the Maharaja is virtually the High Court, and he alone has power to pass sentence of death or transportation for life. The gross annual revenue of the State amounts to about Rs. 10,00,000, of which some Rs. 6,00,000 represent the value of land assigned to *jagirdars*.

Datia, the capital, with a population of about 17,000 inhabitants, is pleasantly situated on a rocky eminence about 980 feet in height. It is an important station for the despatch of grain and general merchandise, and being on the high road between Jhansi and Gwalior, it commands a thriving trade with country districts. The town possesses an unusually large number of substantial stone dwelling-houses, the majority of which are owned by leading Sardars of the State. Other buildings include a post and telegraph office, hospital, high school, and jail, but the most conspicuous of all is the magnificent palace of Bir Singh Deo. This massive pile, towering high above the town, is a remarkably fine example of Indian architecture. It is built in the form of a square, the monotony being relieved by four octagonal towers, one at each corner, and by string courses of stone lattice work defining the five storeys. The summit is ornamented by numerous graceful *chhatris*, crowned with ribbed domes, while many of the ceilings in its chambers are finely carved. The southern façade overlooks a large lake, the waters of which are held up by retaining walls of stone. The palace of Subha Haran is also a handsome structure, but it cannot be compared with the other in point of elegance. Datia is 718 miles distant from Bombay, and 16 miles from Jhansi.

Not more than five miles from Datia is the sacred hill of Sonagir, or "hill of rest," on the summit and slopes of which there are more than 100 Jain temples. Viewed from a distance the hill presents a picturesque appearance, with the pine-cone spires of its numerous shrines jutting out of rough crags of granite rock, but on approaching nearer some disappointment is experienced, as the structures are not elegant, and their ornamentation is not such as one usually beholds in Indian temples. They are, too, comparatively modern, as the majority have been constructed since the beginning of the eighteenth century. Unao, or Baramjee, a village about 10 miles distant from Datia, and six miles from Jansi, is noted for its temple dedicated to the sun as Brahmanya Deo. The shrine, which faces the east, stands on the bank of the river Phuj. Inside the building is a circular piece of stone, six inches in diameter, and on its edges are engraved 21 triangles, representing phases of the sun. The stone rests upon a brick platform covered with brass plates. As many as 25,000 devotees assemble for worship during certain festivals. Seondha, the headquarters of the *tahsil* of the same name, is situated on the bank of the River Sind, and is 22 miles distant from the railway station at Kunch. A glance at many of the buildings will convince any one of the antiquity of the town, but there are many interesting archæological remains which clearly indicate the former existence of an earlier settlement. Some historians have averred that the relics are those of the Sarna fort, which was taken by Mahmud of Ghazni in 1018.

THE STATE OF DEWAS (SENIOR)

THE Ruler of this State traces his ancestry for many hundreds of years through a line of Kings and Princes who in vicissitudes of conquests or defeats, as well as in rare times of peace, were famous on the one hand for their valour and on the other for their encouragement of the arts and sciences for which India has from immemorial days been so justly renowned.

Descent is claimed from the ancient Pawar family, who about the commencement of the Christian era ruled over vast possessions through the powerful Vikramaditya, King of Ujjain in Malwa, Central India. Successive Rulers of Malwa extended the area of their territory, but the majority of them attained considerable distinction in the field of literature and in striving for the social advancement of their subjects. The sway of the Pawars commenced to decline about the tenth century, and during the following 300 years they lost the whole of their kingdom with the exception of districts in Malwa. This last remaining stronghold was wrested from them by the Mahomedans about the year 1350, and they were compelled to migrate in separate families with the object of seeking their fortunes in various other portions of India. The branch with representatives in a direct line from Vikramaditya eventually settled in Mewar in Rajputana, but the eldest descendant, Shambhu Sinha, incurred the displeasure of his father, who had become Raja of Bijolya, and attended by a handful of followers left his home with the object of establishing a State for himself in another part of the country. About the year 1620 he achieved his purpose after annexing a considerable portion of the territory now known as the districts of Poona and Ahmednagar, but his reign was short as he was treacherously killed by a neighbouring Chief.

A minor son of his—Krishnaji—subsequently found favour at the Court of Shivaji, founder of the Mahratta Empire, and about the year 1680 this Emperor restored to him the possessions of his late father and recognized him as successor, and thus began the connection of this house with the Mahratta Empire. The founder of the Dewas State was a great-grandson of Krishnaji, the famous Mahratta General Tukoji Rao, who inflicted a defeat on the Mahomedan Governor of Malwa and by that means established himself in Dewas territory.

After Tukoji's death in 1750 the *gadi* was occupied by Krishnaji Rao I, who was followed in 1789 by Tukoji Rao II.

During the reign of the latter Maharaja a treaty was entered into with the British Government (1818). His Highness Tukoji Rao II died about ten years later, and was succeeded by his son Rukmangad Rao, whose faithful adherence to the Paramount Power during the Sepoy Mutiny in 1857 was suitably recognized by the Imperial Government. His Highness Krishnaji Rao II next occupied the *gadi*, and enjoyed a peaceful and prosperous reign until his death in 1899 when the succession devolved upon his nephew the present Ruler, His Highness Maharaja Sapta Shahasra Senapati Pratinidhi Sir Shri Tukoji Rao III, K.C.S.I., who was born on January 1, 1888. His Highness was most diligent in studies during his educational career at the Daly College, Indore, and the Mayo College at Ajmer, but those who were responsible for his preparation for the all-important duties which would eventually devolve upon him as Ruler of a State decided that before he attained his majority it would be of the greatest possible advantage to him if he were instructed in the general working of State Departments and in those principles of administration which are so essential to good government. This excellent proposal received the warm approval of the Government of India, who deputed a capable official to supervise the training, and also to accompany His Highness on a tour throughout India, Burma and Ceylon, with the object of enabling the young Prince to broaden and enrich his mind by coming in contact with men holding leading positions in political, commercial, and social circles.

His Highness was invested with full administrative powers in 1908, and he at once set himself the task of reorganizing State Departments, of inaugurating useful public works, of placing finances on a more satisfactory footing, and of promoting the welfare of his subjects in every possible manner.

The territory of the State is intermixed with the area of Dewas (Junior) State, and it is scattered and divided into four *parganas*, namely Dewas, Alot, Sarangpur and Bagod. It is a direct Treaty State, lying in north latitude 22° 24', east longitude 70° 77', and it pays no tribute to the British Government or any Indian State.

It has an area of about 446 square miles and contains over 75,700 inhabitants, the major portion of the adults being engaged in agricultural occupations.

On May 31, 1915 the Maharaja founded an Industrial and Commercial Bank for the benefit, chiefly, of timber-merchants and weavers in the *parganas* of Dewas, Alot, and Sarangpur, and he has more recently interested himself in the erection of new village schools, dispensaries, and other institutions destined to be of considerable benefit to his subjects.

The State maintains one hospital at

HIS HIGHNESS MAHARAJA SIR TUKOJI RAO PUAR, K.C.S.I., OF DEWAS STATE (SENIOR).

1. GROUP OF SARDARS AND STATE OFFICIALS.
2. SHRIMANT JAGADEV RAO PUAR, BHAU SAHEB MAHARAJ (BROTHER OF HIS HIGHNESS).
3. SHRIMANT VIKRAM SINGH RAO PUAR, NANA SAHEB, MAHARAJ (YUVRAJ).
4. SHRI ANAND BHAVAN PALACE.

THE STATE OF DEWAS (SENIOR).

1. The Old Palace in the City. 2. King Edward VII Memorial Arch. 3. The State Guest House. 4. Goddess Hill Temple.

Dewas and dispensaries at Alot, Sarangpur and Bagod.

One of the first measures of reform to which His Highness turned his attention after taking up the reins of office was the survey of the whole State, this being a necessary preliminary to a revised settlement for revenue purposes. A considerable portion of each of the four *parganas* has already been surveyed, and the new assessments have been productive of considerable benefit to occupiers, while they have at the same time resulted in increased revenue.

His Highness is a descendant of the old Mahratta warriors, and a Kshatriya by caste. In 1908 he married Her Highness Shri Radha Bai Sahiba Maharaj, the only daughter of His Highness the Maharaja of Kolhapur, and the heir-apparent, Shrimant Vikram Sinha Rao Pawar Nana Sahib Maharaj, was born on April 4, 1910.

The gross revenue, excluding alienations, amounts to about Rs. 7,00,000, and His Highness is entitled to a hereditary salute of 15 guns.

Immediately upon receipt of news of the outbreak of the late Great War, His Highness elegraphed to the Political Agent in Malwa placing his personal services, as well as the resources of the State, at the unconditional disposal of the Government of His Majesty the King-Emperor. In response to an appeal by His Excellency the Viceroy and Governor-General, His Highness, together with State officials and subjects, contributed liberally to the Imperial Indian Relief Fund, and His Highness has further subscribed most generously to the general expenses of the war and to various other funds such as the Prince of Wales's War Fund, the St. John Ambulance Red Cross Fund, the French Red Cross Fund, and the *Loyalty* Hospital Ship Fund.

His Highness has for several years been a member of the Managing Committee of the Daly College, Indore, and has been President on two occasions of the General Mahratta Conference. The Maharaja was invited to attend the ceremonies connected with the Coronation Durbar at Delhi in 1911, and on that occasion His Imperial Majesty the King-Emperor George V bestowed upon him the dignity of a Knight Grand Commandership of the Most Exalted Order of the Star of India.

Acknowledgment should be made here of the extremely valuable assistance rendered in general administrative affairs to His Highness the Maharaja by his brother, Shrimant Jagdeo Rao Pawar Bhau Sahib Maharaj Vishwasrao Bahadur, Maharaj Samstan Supa Jamgod. His thorough grasp of the details of each Department and his enthusiasm in supporting measures of reform render him a colleague of whom any Ruler might be proud, while his high mental and literary abilities are eminent qualifications for the high position of trust and responsibility held by him.

Similarly this account will not be complete without recording here that in all the affairs of the State and its improvement His Highness has in his Minister, Rao Bahadur Sardar Pandit Narayan Prasad, Morchaldar, Sar-Khawas, *Jagirdar* of Binjana, a most capable, enthusiastic and loyal supporter and administrator. Sardar Pandit Narayan Prasad has been with His Highness from his early days, firstly as his tutor and guardian and subsequently as Private Secretary and Chief Household Officer. In 1908 he was made Diwan of the State, which high position he still most deservedly holds.

THE STATE OF DEWAS (JUNIOR)

THERE are two States of the name of Dewas having capitals at the town of the same name, and the Rulers of each Principality are descendants of an illustrious dynasty which wielded great power more than 1,500 years ago. In those far-off days the Rulers reigned over Malwa, one of the present Native States in the Malwa Political Agency of Central India, and although their territories continued to increase in extent during a period of several hundred years, disasters fell upon the Kingdom between the eighth and twelfth centuries, with the result that only Malwa was eventually left to them. In the fourteenth century the Mahomedans obtained possession of that State also, and the members of the Pawar family, as they were called, migrated to other parts of India with the object of regaining the prestige which they had temporarily lost. They settled in the Deccan, in Rajputana and elsewhere, and for many years were engaged in rendering assistance to powerful monarchs until the early portion of the eighteenth century, when a considerable area in Malwa was granted to Tukoji Rao I as a reward for his faithful allegiance to the conquerors. Tukoji died in 1789 and was succeeded by his elder brother, who assumed the title of Tukoji Rao II. By virtue of a treaty of peace made by this Chief with the East India Company in 1818, the State now pays to the Government an annual sum of Rs. 14,237 in commutation of the expenses of troops.

The present Ruler of the State, who is a high-caste Mahratta and claims a Rajput descent, is His Highness Raja Malhar Babasaheb Pawar, who was born on August 10, 1877, and succeeded by adoption to the *gadi* in the year 1892 upon the demise of his uncle and adoptive father, Raja Narin Rao Dada Saheb.

His Highness is assisted in administration by a Council of which he is President, the members being Shrimant Sadashiva Rao Khasesaheb Maharaj Pawar, the brother of the Chief, heir-apparent, and Minister of State and *ex officio* Vice-President; Mr. B. V. Samarth, B.A., LL.B.; Mr. Haripant Karambelkar; and Mr. V. R. Deshmukh, M.R.A.S., who was appointed Chief Revenue Officer. The State has an area of about 117 square miles, the inhabitants according to the census of 1911 being 63,015 in number, and it is divided into four *perganas*, Dewas, Sarangpur, Ringnod-Gadgucha, and Padlia, but it is probable that an alteration may be made in the future as His Highness considers it advisable that Ringnod should, for administrative purposes, be separated from Gadgucha.

His Highness has always manifested the utmost solicitation for the welfare of his people, and in connection with agricultural matters he has introduced many measures of reform.

A recent Administration Report of the State showed that the total area in holdings was 144,486 acres, while culturable fallows, forest ranges, and outside holdings were 52,850 acres in extent. The total area actually under cultivation was 105,617 acres, the principal crops being *juar*, cotton, wheat, *gram*, maize, *til*, bajra, and *tuar*.

The forest, 9,634 acres in extent, in the Padlia *pergana* has been surveyed by a conservator, who submitted a scheme for making it a valuable asset in the State revenue, and although the working plan was not put into operation until April 1915, the results of less than three years confirm the belief that an annual income of Rs. 12,000 is assured.

Compulsory education for boys between the ages of seven and twelve was adopted in the year 1911–12, and all instruction given in the State is free with the exception of the English language for which exceptionally low charges are made. The Superintendent of the Department, Mr. D. B. Tilak, M.A., has thoroughly revised the curriculum of the schools, making provision for graduated courses in religious and moral instruction, general scientific knowledge, sanitation, first-aid, and hygiene for the home. Encouragement is also given to other subjects such as drill and athletics.

His Highness exercises full criminal and civil jurisdiction in the State, and remarkable progress has been made during the past three or four years in enforcing stricter procedure, not only on the part of Judges, but also by Court officials and legal practitioners engaged in the conduct of cases. A very important event took place when His Highness sanctioned the establishment of *panchayats* or Honorary Magistrates in villages, *tahsils*, and towns. Their Courts have jurisdiction in suits not exceeding Rs. 50 in value, and their criminal powers are those of a Magistrate of the third class under the Code of Criminal Procedure.

His Highness the Raja received an invitation to attend the Coronation Durbar at Delhi in December 1911, and he attended all the functions connected with that memorable event. He paid a visit to His Majesty, which was returned by His Excellency the Governor-General of India on His Majesty's behalf. The occasion was celebrated throughout the State by means of illuminations, acts of charity were performed, and prayers were offered for Their Imperial Majesties.

The loyalty of the Pawar House to the Throne was illustrated in a very practical manner during the Indian Mutiny of 1857.

THE STATE OF DEWAS (JUNIOR).

1. The Shri Laxmi Narayan Bhuwan Club. 2. His Highness with Mr. M. Govindrao, Foreign Minister, and Mr. B. V. Samarth, Home Minister. 3. The Rajwada (Palace).

THE STATE OF DEWAS (JUNIOR).

1. The Gate at Shri Malhar, the Residence of His Holiness Shri Shilnath Maharaj. 2. The Durga Bag Palace. 3. The Law Courts.

and in 1914 when the present Ruler received intimation from the Political Agent in Malwa that war had been declared with Germany His Highness, through his Minister, wrote in reply that he was much concerned with the news, and he ardently and sincerely hoped that the trouble was a mere passing cloud, but if it should be otherwise His Highness gave an assurance that he and all his subjects would totally identify themselves with the interests of England, and that if occasion arose the State, in keeping with its past history, was with its slender resources ready to stand by the Mother Country and thus contribute its *quota* to the preservation of the British Empire. As soon as the Imperial War Relief Fund was started His Highness contributed Rs. 2,000 towards it, and he subsequently made several gifts to soldiers on active service. Shortly after this date a public meeting was convened at the request of the Saheb Raja, who presided and delivered an eloquent speech soliciting assistance to the Fund "from all who called themselves Indians," and in response to this appeal the sum of Rs. 1,532 was subscribed in the room. Prayers were also offered in Hindu temples and Mahomedan mosques for the success of Great Britain and her Allies.

His Highness has gained the entire goodwill of his people by sympathetic and wise administration, and he is ceaseless in his efforts to promote the welfare of every inhabitant in the State by inaugurating measures of reform, redressing grievances, by acts calculated to improve the social, moral, and material welfare of his subjects, and by his tolerance towards all classes and creeds, notwithstanding his own reverence for traditional rites and customs.

THE STATE OF DHAR

DHAR is one of the nine Ruling States of the Central India Agency in direct treaty relations with the British Government.

It is 1,783 square miles in extent, and is composed of one main block, lying around the town of Dhar, and consisting of six *perganas*, namely, Dhar, Badnawar, Nalchha, Mandu, Dharampuri, and Thikri; and of three isolated *perganas* known as Kukshi, Sundarsi, and Nimanpur. The main block is bounded on the north by the State of Rutlam, on the east by parts of Gwalior and Indore, on the west by the State of Jhabua and parts of Gwalior and Indore, and on the south by the State of Barwani and portions of Indore.

The Vindhya range of mountains traverses the State almost through the centre, dividing it into two distinct portions of widely different physical features. On the northern side of the range the land belongs to the area of the Malwa plateau, while rugged hills covered with dense vegetation are the principal characteristics of the southern or Nimar half.

The census of 1911 showed that there were 154,048 persons living in the State, of whom 68 per cent. were Hindus, 24 per cent. Animists, and 8 per cent. Mahomedans. Nearly 30 per cent. of the population are employed in agricultural pursuits, and it may be said here that His Highness the Maharaja is devoting special attention to the encouragement of modern scientific methods of cultivation, seeing that the growth of farm produce forms the chief feature in the commerce of the State.

The quality of the soil varies considerably, but excepting upon hilly ground it is generally fertile, and the somewhat deficient rainfall of the past few years has been to some extent counterbalanced by irrigation from rivers, wells, and tanks. The principal crops are wheat, cotton, *juar*, *gram*, *til*, barley, linseed, poppy, and sugar-cane.

The value of a rotation of crops is understood by occupiers, but up to the present time their efforts in this direction have not been systematically carried out. The average annual quantity of land placed under monsoon and dry-season crops during the past few years is 361,200 acres.

A separate department for the control of forests was established in 1896, and five years later the management was placed in the hands of a European conservator.

Valuable work is being performed by the Department, under the able control of Mr. B. A. Rokeby, in natural and artificial reproduction of trees; young, straight, and vigorous saplings have taken the place of worn-out, diseased, or crooked trees; roads have been opened through the ranges for facilitating the removal of timber; broad fire belts have been cleared; and energetic action has been taken with regard to the multiplication of minor products. The direct revenue during a recent year amounted to nearly Rs. 80,000, which included items for sales of teak and other timber, Rs. 44,000; fuel and charcoal, Rs. 1,650; and minor products, Rs. 6,500.

Coarse cotton cloth is woven into various garments in the principal towns and large villages, while the spinning of cotton into yarn is the chief occupation among women of inferior social positions.

There are eight ginning factories in the State, and it is noteworthy that the opening of each of these has synchronized with a marked increase in the acreage devoted to the cultivation of the cotton plant. The State controls a large factory for the distillation of alcohol from *mahua* flowers, which is well equipped with modern machinery and is worked upon thoroughly scientific principles. The greatest advance made in industrial concerns since the year 1914 has been the enormous growth in the number of thymol factories, owing primarily, it is alleged, to certain natural or indigenous physical conditions which are of the greatest assistance in crystallizing the solid principles of *Ajwan* oil from which thymol is obtained. Another factor tending in the same direction has been the prohibition of production of poppy seed as a crop and the substitution of *Ajwan*, which thrives remarkably well upon black loamy soils of average quality.

Before the outbreak of the Great War the State had for many years been manufacturing thymol on a small scale, even in the face of German competition in the shape of synthetic products, and during the past four years Dhar has been able to meet nearly the whole of the world's requirements of this particular drug. It is claimed that the suitable geographical situation of the State has been an important factor in enabling it to keep well ahead of foreign substitutes, but other reasons may be urged, such as the quality of the crystals produced from the oil, and the cheap rate at which they can be produced. The Shri Gopal Krisna State Chemical Works has quite recently been started by the Department of Commerce and Industry, manufacturing Phar-

H.H. SIR UDAIJI RAO PUAR BAHADUR K.C.S.I. (RAJA SAHIB OF DHAR).

THE STATE OF DHAR.

1. Sardars and Officers. 2. His Highness and the Members of the State Council.

macœpia Thymol at the town of Dhar, and it is completely equipped with modern machinery of the most approved type. Arrangements are now being made for the production of tannin, gum, dyes, and vegetable oils of various kinds, as well as matches and turpentine, all of which can be manufactured in large quantities from the natural resources of the State. Further than this, there is an almost illimitable supply of wood pulp in the forests from which it is proposed to manufacture paper, and there are other valuable natural products in the jungles which can, without great expense, be converted into marketable commodities of a profitable character.

Iron ore is plentiful in many districts of Dhar, but principally in the Nimanpur *pergana*, where it is about to be mined, while traces of ancient workings have led the Durbar to believe that a revival of the industry would in all probability be distinctly advantageous to the State.

Among other minerals may be mentioned jasper, of purple, green, or reddish colours; a large variety of silicious materials; quartz; and agates, all of which are met with occasionally; red and yellow ochres, potter's clay, lime, and road metals are found in nearly every *pergana*, and outcrops of sandstone furnish an abundant supply of stone for building purposes.

Dhar is 34 miles distant from the nearest station, Mhow, on the Rajputana-Malwa branch of the Bombay-Baroda and Central India Railway, and therefore its isolated position is unfavourable for commercial prosperity of a high order. Its principal imports include: Rice, salt, metals, coco-nuts, dates, groceries, kerosene oil, glass, hardware, crockery, paper, yarn, twist and piece goods; while in the list of exports it is noticed that wheat, *gram*, and maize are sent to Mhow, Indore, and Bombay; spices of different kinds to neighbouring States; oil-seeds to Bombay; and cotton, tobacco, and other goods to Marwar and other important business centres.

The economic problem of utilizing the resources of the State to greater advantage, and of obtaining markets to which the expenses of transport are not prohibitive, is one to which the Durbar is giving special attention, and it is confidently expected that before many years have passed, the State will become one of the proportionately large producing and exporting centres among the Native States of India.

The Dhar State Public Works Department came into existence originally in 1867, but it was reorganized in 1899, and especially during the past eight or ten years it has been rendering excellent assistance in works connected with: (1) The Palace; (2) new buildings and repairs; (3) new roads and maintenance; (4) irrigation; and (5) archæology and ancient buildings.

Turning to the subject of education, it may be observed that Dhar, the chief town of the State, was famous as a seat of learning during the rulership of the Paramaras between the ninth and thirteenth centuries, and Raja Bhoja, the ninth Chief, was a renowned scholar and author who is said to have written many valuable treatises on astronomy and divination, rhetoric, Yoga-philosophy, the *Dharmashastra*, engineering, and Sanskrit poetry; while it is also alleged that he compiled a

H.H. MAHARAJA SIR ANAND RAO PUAR BAHADUR, K.C.S.I., C.I.E. (LATE MAHARAJA OF DHAR).

U*

THE STATE OF DHAR.

1. The Old Palace. 2. Her Highness's Residence 3 King Edward Memorial Hospital.

THE STATE OF DHAR.

1. Bara Bungalow (Guest House). 2. Zire Palace (Guest House). 3. Anand High School. 4. The Club.

manual on veterinary science, and *Prakrit* grammar, and a lexicon on the Sanskrit language.

The first English school was opened at Dhar in 1849, and it has grown in importance until it is now known as a High School. A Persian school was established in 1850, and it was followed by others teaching in Marathi, Hindi, and Sanskrit, as well as in English, until the year 1872, when a Department of Education was organized and a regular system of control was put into force.

His Highness the late Maharaja Sir Anand Rao Puar, K.C.S.I., C.I.E., took the deepest interest in educational questions, and it was due to him that several primary schools were opened in some of the larger villages, that scholarships on a liberal scale were granted, and that suitable school premises were provided, of which the Anand High School is an example.

The present Ruler, His Highness the Maharaja Sir Udaiji Rao Puar Sahib Bahadur, K.C.S.I., has been equally as enthusiastic in his support of teaching as was his predecessor, and it is largely due to him that the people have recently manifested a readiness to seek for educational advantages for their children.

Of the 70 schools in the State the curriculum extends to the Hindi middle examination in one school; three give teaching up to Standard VI; 12 give instruction up to Standard III; and the remainder as far as Standard II only.

The Anand High School is the only institution maintained in the capital of the State to supply the need of advanced education, and the average daily attendance of students has been gradually increasing, reports now showing 235 present out of a total of about 300 on the roll. This school is managed so successfully that applications for admission are continually being received from candidates from adjoining States, and about two years ago it was found necessary to revise the regulations relating to entrance, and to make certain additions to the scale of fees.

The establishment of a well-equipped science laboratory, and the arrangements made for regular lectures in connection therewith, have been of the greatest benefit to students, many of whom, by the way, are eventually drafted into the service of the Durbar for clerical and other positions. One of the most encouraging features in connection with education in the State is the fact that parents are now desirous of having instruction given to their daughters, and the Durbar has not been slow in making suitable provision to meet their wishes. The teaching given to the girls in two schools at Dhar, and at others in different districts, is of an elementary character, including reading, writing, arithmetic, sewing, knitting, and general knowledge, aided by maps and pictures. When State supervision of schools was first undertaken, the annual cost to the Durbar was not more than Rs. 1,000 per *annum*, while at the conclusion of the year 1916 the amount expended on education had risen to Rs. 24,420, and it appears that 3,209 boys and 238 girls are now receiving instruction in State-aided institutions. About two-thirds of the total cost is borne by the Durbar, the remainder being derived from collections from local funds and from school fees.

The Medical Department has greatly extended its field of operations under the fostering care of His Highness the Maharaja, who is deeply interested in maintaining the general health of his subjects and in improving the sanitary conditions under which they live.

In 1854 the only institution for the medical treatment of patients was a small charitable dispensary which formed a branch of the charitable hospital at Indore, but about 10 years later the first State hospital was opened at Dhar. The Durbar also maintains four other hospitals, as well as four first-class dispensaries, and nine second and third-class ones.

According to the terms of the treaty entered into with the British Government in 1819 the Maharaja has full control over all general administrative and judicial matters in the State, the principal Departments being Judicial, Revenue, Public Works, Military, Police, Forests, Medical, and Survey and Settlement, and the Diwan is the chief executive officer. The formation of an Advisory Council, consisting of the heads of the several departments just mentioned, was one of the first measures of reform taken in hand by the Maharaja after his succession to the *gadi*, but the policy of His Highness strongly favours decentralization of powers of government whenever favourable opportunities occur. In furtherance of this idea His Highness has encouraged the establishment of Municipal and Local Boards presided over by capable officials, and the people have readily accepted the responsibilities of self-government, and have manifested a praiseworthy desire to make the best use of their privileges.

British laws have been adopted as the basis of the codes by which civil and criminal justice is administered, although reference is frequently made to local customs and regulations with the object of meeting special conditions peculiar to the State. The State Courts are 34 in number, those at headquarters comprising the Durbar Court, the District Magistrate's Court, and the Court of the City Magistrate, while the one presided over by His Highness is the final Court of Appeal. The District Magistrate is empowered to pass sentences of imprisonment up to seven years' penal servitude, and he has jurisdiction in civil matters to the value of Rs. 2,000, while the City Magistrate hears cases in which the amount involved does not exceed Rs. 500.

The whole of the land in the State is deemed by custom to be the property of the Ruler, and thus the contributions paid by land-holders are regarded as revenue, and not as rent.

The system of tenure is known as *ryotwari*, that is a direct holding by the occupier from the State, and revenue is based upon the principle of settlement for a fixed period. His Highness has manifested his desire to deal fairly and yet considerately towards his subjects by making the basis of revenue as flexible as possible, and by causing assessments to be made on broad and generous lines, due regard being paid to any special conditions in individual instances.

For the maintenance of law and order the State maintains about 380 Regulars, comprising cavalry and artillery with five guns; and Irregulars consisting of about 200 cavalry and 200 infantry. The infantry are engaged mainly in guarding the Palaces, Treasury, and other important buildings, but they are sent into various districts for the purpose of preserving the peace in times of scarcity of food.

The military performed all police duties until the year 1872, when a small force was organized for the protection of the town of Dhar, but the men now employed comprise a superintendent, inspectors, constables, and about 320 mounted men for service in rural areas. The central jail in the Fort at Dhar, under the supervision of the State Surgeon, is conducted on reformatory lines as far as is consistent with the character of offences, and as various industries such as weaving and the making of various articles of clothing

THE STATE OF DHAR.

1. Lat Masjid. 2. Pillar of Victory—Lat Masjid, "The Lat." 3. Jama Masjid (Interior). 4. Jama Masjid (Front View). 5. Jahaz Mahal.

THE STATE OF DHAR.

1. Entrance to Fort. 2. Side View of Fort. 3. Rupmati's Pavilion.

THE STATE OF DHAR.

1. Khasbardars in Antique Dress. 2. State Musicians. 3. Artists and Painters.

THE STATE OF DHAR.

1, 2, 3. Training of Vicious Horses for Government. 4. Country and Australian-bred Mares and Foals (Remounts). 5. Thoroughbred Mares (Remount). 6. Mares and Foals at Water.

THE STATE OF DHAR.

1, 2, 3. Jail Industry. 4. Thymol Distillery (Old Process).

are carried on, the period of detention has a salutary effect upon the majority of the prisoners, who in after life become respectable citizens.

He was not destined to enjoy the honours of his position for any length of time, as the disaffected Minister persuaded Scindia and Holkar to make raids upon Dhar, and thus the State was continually being invaded by the forces of these two inveterate foes. In 1803, however, Anand Rao served in the army of Scindia, and after the defeat of the latter he returned to Dhar, where he died in 1807.

The territories lost during this reign comprised a considerable quantity of land in Rajputana, in addition to the districts of Agar, Sunel, Badnawar, Berasia, and Tal Mandawal. On the death of Anand Rao, the responsibilities of control of the State devolved upon his widow, Maina Bai, and no sooner had she taken up her onerous duties than she found that intrigues were being formed against her with the object of securing the succession of a distant relative of her late husband. Shortly after this, however, she gave birth to a son, to whom the name of Ramchandra Rao was given, but owing to his early demise she adopted, with the concurrence of Holkar and Scindia, Lakshman Rao, the son of her sister, Thaku Bai Scindia, who later assumed the title of Ramchandra Rao II. The area of the State had been so reduced during previous years by continual raids of the Pindaris, as well as of Scindia and Holkar, that the Regent had no possessions beyond the town of Dhar and the Fort in which she resided, and her means of subsistence depended entirely upon supplies obtained by force of arms in the surrounding neighbourhood.

In regard to the history of the State it may be stated that the Ruler of Dhar is a descendant of the famous Parmar clan who ruled over Malwa from the ninth to the thirteenth century. The State first came under British influence on January 10, 1819, when a treaty was entered into between the British Government and Raja Ramchandra Rao, the then Ruler, under which the former agreed (*inter alia*) to protect the State of Dhar and its dependencies, namely, Badnawar, Bairsea, Kuksee, Derhampur, Sultanabad, Bulkiar, Nalchha, Loaree, and Khurwarrah in the Province of Jowut, and to secure them and the tribute of Allee to Ramchandra Rao Puar, Raja of Dhar, his heirs and successors.

In 1821 an agreement was made by which the Berasia *pergana* and the tribute from Alirajpur were ceded to the British Government in return for a sum of Rs. 1,10,000 paid annually to the Durbar. Some 10 years later the State was thrown into turmoil by Achyut Rao, who endeavoured to depose the Raja and take possession of the *gadi* for himself, but the British Government again came to the rescue and induced the Pretender to withdraw his claims in return for the promise of a monthly pension of Rs. 200.

STATE CARRIAGE.

The Raja died without issue in 1833, and his widow adopted a son of Yashwant Rao of Malthan in the Deccan, who succeeded as Yashwant Rao II. This selection was made by Anand Rao Puar, Raja of the Dewas State (Junior Branch), as Yashwant Rao of Malthan was his nephew. Full administrative powers were granted to His Highness in 1837, and his reign of 20 years was marked by the adoption of many measures of economic and industrial reform, one of the most important of these being a systematic survey and settlement of land for revenue purposes. He died in 1857, and Anirudh Rao Puar, his half-brother, whom he had adopted as his successor, ascended the *gadi* as Anand Rao III. The new Ruler was only thirteen years of age at the time, and his Ministers being utterly unable to check the mutinous spirit which then prevailed, the State was confiscated in January, 1858. It was, however, restored —with the exception of the Berasia *pergana*—on May 1, 1860, but as the Ruler was a minor, it remained under British supervision until October 1, 1864.

His Highness was a most capable administrator, and his staunch loyalty to the throne was recognized by the British Government, who presented him with a *sanad*, which conferred upon him the right of adoption.

At Delhi, in 1877, he was granted the title of Maharaja, and was, further, created a Knight Commander of the Most Exalted Order of the Star of India. His Highness was an invalid during the last seven years of his life, and he died on July 15, 1895, having previously adopted the present Ruler, his nephew, Bhagoji Rao Puar of Malthan, who took the name of Udaji Rao II.

His Highness the Maharaja Sir Udaji Rao Puar Sahib Bahadur, K.C.S.I., son of Sambhaji Rao Puar, half-brother of the late Chief, was born on September 30, 1886. The first part of his education was received at Daly College, Indore, where he remained until the year 1903, after which he studied in his own home under a European tutor (Mr. F. D. H. Joy), who was assisted by Rai Saheb P. N. Banerjee, B.A., the present Minister of the State. About three years later His Highness passed through a course of practical training in the details of administration, given by Lieutenant-Colonel F. G. Beville, C.I.E., then Political Agent in Central India, and his natural aptitude for acquiring knowledge has since been mani-

THE STATE OF DHAR.

1. Epitome of Sanskrit Inflectional Terminations in Boja Shala. 2. Hindola Mahal. 3. Interior, Hindola Mahal. 4. Hoshang Shah's Tomb.

THE STATE OF DHAR.

1. Kalika Temple. 2. Dhareshwar Temple. 3. The Delhi Gate (Mandu). 4. Paz Bahadur's Palace.

THE STATE OF DHAR

fested in his thorough grasp of the intricacies of State management.

A Superintendent, acting under the guidance of Lieutenant-Colonel Beville, was placed in charge of the State during the minority of the Maharaja, who was invested with full ruling powers on December 6, 1907, by the Hon. Lieutenant-Colonel Sir Hugh Daly, K.C.S.I., C.I.E., Agent to the Governor-General in Central India. A grand Durbar was held for the ceremony, which was attended by *Sardars*, *Jagirdars*, Feudatories, State Officials, and a large number of illustrious European as well as Indian guests.

There were great rejoicings at Dhar on the 25th of the same month, when His Highness was married to the eldest daughter of the Raja of Savantvadi, a Native State in the Bombay Presidency, and again on the 27th when a younger sister of the bride became the wife of Shrimant Saturam Puar Sahib, younger half-brother of His Highness the Maharaja.

From the date of his accession to the *gadi* His Highness has devoted himself with unceasing energy to promote the material prosperity of the State and to secure contentment and happiness among his subjects.

Honour is due to him for the very efficient manner in which he reorganized the various departments of administration in the State, for the very remarkable advance made in the development of new industrial enterprises, and for the encouragement given by him in strengthening others which were already established. His Highness is fully aware that satisfactory trading relationships both within the State and with neighbouring principalities depend largely upon favourable means of transport, and he is making every effort to push forward the construction of new roads, as well as other means of communication, which will open up outlying districts for the free interchange of commercial products.

The Maharaja, who belongs to the high-class Mahratta Rajput clan of Rajputs, possesses brilliant scholarly attainments; he is author of several publications, and he is an earnest supporter of all projects calculated to raise the literary status of his people.

He is, moreover, a keen sportsman and expert horseman, and takes a special delight in encouraging all kinds of games.

His amiable disposition endears him to rich and poor alike, and his genial hospitality to his guests, coupled with a most generous nature, make him a worthy representative of the ancient Puar clan.

Upon the invitation of the Government of India His Highness attended the Delhi Durbar in 1903, when a King Edward Coronation Medal was presented to him. Two years later he was present at a Durbar at Indore, held by His Royal Highness the Prince of Wales (the present King-Emperor), and at the Delhi Coronation ceremonies in 1911 His Imperial Majesty conferred upon him the distinction of a Knight Commandership of the Most Exalted Order of the Star of India.

In recognition of his munificent gifts and other valuable help rendered during the late European conflict, His Highness was, in November, 1917, created a Knight Companion of the British Empire, and on January 1, 1918, he was raised to the dignity of an hereditary Maharaja.

He was nominated by His Excellency Lord Minto as a member of the Managing Committee of the Mayo College at Ajmer, and he is also a member of the Board of Management of the Daly College and the King Edward Hospital, both at Indore.

It is a particularly pleasing duty to be able to refer to the Maharani Sahiba, whose contributions towards various war funds have been recognized by the Imperial Government, who have presented to her the Kaiser-i-Hind Gold Medal, a decoration instituted by her late Majesty Queen Victoria as a reward for valuable public services rendered in India.

It will not be out of place to refer now to a few of the most important events which have taken place at Dhar since the accession of His Highness the present Maharaja.

In November, 1912, His Excellency Lord Hardinge, Viceroy and Governor-General of India, accompanied by Lady Hardinge, paid a visit to the State, and on the morning of the 11th the former laid the foundation stone of the King Edward Memorial Hospital at Dhar.

The State Administration Report for the year 1914–15 contains a lengthy statement of an exceedingly sympathetic character regarding the onerous task which had fallen upon the British owing to the declaration of war by Germany and Austria. The writer of the notes in question stated that His Highness immediately contributed Rs. 7,500 to the Relief Fund inaugurated by His Royal Highness the Prince of Wales; Her Highness the Maharani Sahiba gave Rs. 5,000; and the leading *Sirdars* and officials added another Rs. 1,000. Their Highnesses also warmly supported the Indian Imperial Relief Fund by presenting Rs. 10,000 and Rs. 2,000 respectively, and the Nobles of the State subscribed Rs. 4,077.

The Royal Horse Artillery then stationed at Mhow was ordered to the front, and His Highness presented the Government with two motors for their use while on active service; and he contributed to the equipment of the battery all his best

REWA KUND.

THE STATE OF DHAR.

1. Dassera Procession. 2. Review of Military Forces. 3. Dassera Sports. 4. His Highness in State Carriage on Dassera Day.

horses—including his English team and valuable studs—worth about Rs. 30,000; and he also gave Rs. 7,000 for the purchase of motor-cycles.

Her Highness the Maharani Sahiba voluntarily came forward at this juncture to render assistance to the Government by the establishment of a branch of the St. John's Ambulance Association, under the name of " The Dhar Ladies' Voluntary Aid Association," for the purpose of providing funds and various articles suitable for " Red Cross " work.

Arrangements were so made that at the end of nearly every month consignments were despatched of ladies' handiwork, such as mufflers, bandages, handkerchiefs, pillow-cases, bed-sheets, covers, and other necessities.

This splendid work was continued throughout 1915–16, and it is noticed in the Dewan's Report upon the State that during the 12 months then under review Their Highnesses contributed personally, and on behalf of the " Ladies' Association," Rs. 25,000 towards the Hospital Ship *Loyalty*; Rs. 3,000 for salaries of compounders and dressers; Rs. 1,200 for food and comforts for sick and wounded at Mhow and Bombay; Rs. 850 for chocolates and cigarettes; donations of Rs. 500 to the Aerial Club, London; Rs. 700 for the entertainment of soldiers at Mhow; and other sums for miscellaneous objects, making a grand total of Rs. 48,000. These gifts were exclusive of bundles of *bandis*, *kurtas*, pyjamas, tobacco, helmets, and other requisites, and also of three contributions specially made by Her Highness the Maharani Sahiba consisting of Rs. 7,500 for sick and wounded soldiers, Rs. 3,000 for destitute persons in Belgium, and Rs. 10,000 for a motor-launch for Mesopotamia.

THE STATE OF DUNGARPUR

DUNGARPUR is one of the three States which form the Southern Rajputana Political Agency, and it covers an area of 1,447 square miles, while the population, according to the census of 1911, is 1,59,192 persons, of whom the Bhils are in a majority. It is bounded on the north by the State of Udaipur, on the west by Idar, on the south by Lunawara, and on the east by Banswara. The average annual gross revenue of the State amounts to about Rs. 5,00,000, and the expenditure is nearly Rs. 4,50,000.

With the exception of the southern and eastern portions, the State is traversed by low rocky hills, covered with a dense mass of jungle. The Mahi and Som are the chief rivers, but there are numerous smaller streams, which include the Moran, Majam, Vatrack, and Bhadar. The climate is generally dry and healthy—the average annual rainfall not exceeding 27 inches—but a considerable sum of money is expended annually by the State in the construction and maintenance of tanks and wells, with the result that a sufficient supply of water is usually available.

By far the greater proportion of the inhabitants are engaged in agricultural pursuits, but there are many primitive methods of cultivation still in existence, which if discarded in favour of modern scientific practice, would inevitably lead to heavier yields of produce of considerably better quality. About one-third of the cultivated area is irrigated from wells, tanks, and streams, and the principal crops are maize and rice, although wheat, barley, poppy, sugar-cane, pulses, oil-seeds, and *gram* are also grown.

In the State Administration Report for the year 1910-11, it is stated that the cultivation of poppy, from which opium is derived, had been a thriving industry, and an important source of revenue in Dungarpur for many generations, but as the exportation of the drug was being curtailed, it was decided by the Durbar to make experiments in the growing of cotton. Two experts, possessing practical knowledge of the cultivation of this plant, were employed for the purpose of giving instruction to farmers, and generally assisting them by practical demonstrations. The result of the first year's trial was not entirely satisfactory owing to continued drought in certain portions of the State, but in those areas in which irrigation from tanks or wells was possible, the trial had shown that, with a sufficiency of rain or artificial watering for the plants, a profitable industrial enterprise might be carried on. In conformity with regulations framed upon instructions issued by the Government of India, the cultivation of poppy has now been reduced to the bare necessities for local consumption, and the monopoly for the manufacture of opium has been given to the State Bank.

The principal imports are salt, rice, cloth, sugar, tobacco, *gurh*, coco-nuts, *mahua* flowers, and piece-goods, and the exports include oil-seeds, oil, grain, *ghee*, gum, and other sundries.

All forests belong to the State, and are classified as follows: (1) State forests under the control and supervision of the Forest Department, and (2) Village forests administered by the Revenue Department. The former of these comprise about sixty blocks, covering an area of about 450 square miles; 33 of these are open for the cutting of timber, but the remainder are closed for the preservation of game and for wood for various purposes in the State.

Education on modern lines was introduced into the State in the reign of Maharawal Udai Singhji, and the present Ruler has always specially interested himself in the encouragement of parents to avail themselves of the opportunities provided for giving instruction to their children. Teaching is entirely free in every part of the State, and books are given gratuitously to pupils in village schools who are unable to pay for them.

Their Highnesses the Maharawal and his consort evince the deepest possible interest in the Shri Davendra Girls' school, and although the question of female instruction is still in its infancy it is already noticed that there is a growing awakening among the people to the immense importance of this subject. The annual grant of the Durbar amounts to about Rs. 8,000.

The State maintains dispensaries at Dungarpur and Sagwara, and the sum expended annually on medical relief is about Rs. 7,000.

The highest Court of civil and criminal jurisdiction with jurors was established in the year 1913. It is the highest Court of Appeal in all judicial and revenue cases, and the Dewan is *ex officio* chief judge, while the Sessions Court deals with criminal prosecutions, and also hears appeals from subordinate courts. His Highness the Maharawal is required to confirm sentences of death and imprisonment for seven years and upwards, and as

H.H. RAI RAYAN MAHARAJADHIRAJ MAHARAWALJI SHRI BIJAYA SINGHJI, SAHIB BAHADUR, K.C.I.E., OF DUNGARPUR STATE.

H.H. THE MINOR MAHARAWAL SAHIB SIR LAKSHAMAN SINGHJI, BAHADUR OF DUNGARPUR.

THE STATE OF DUNGARPUR.

1. Udaibilas Palace. 2. The Old Palace.

President of the final Court of Appeal applications for clemency are made to him.

The Durbar maintains 243 police, 99 of whom are armed with smooth-bore Snider rifles, and there is a specially selected company of 108 men, called the Bijai Paltan, who are employed as guards at the palaces and as an escort for Their Highnesses whenever required.

The administration of the State is carried on through the Dewan, who exercises supervision and control over all Departments, including Revenue, Customs, Excise, Judicial, Public Works, Education, Medical, and Court of Wards, while correspondence with the Political Department of the Government of India is conducted by the same official.

THE STATE OF DUNGARPUR.
BANESMARJI'S TEMPLE.

Municipalities have been established at Dungarpur, Sagwara, and Galiakot, the Board in each instance controlling sanitation, lighting, and other matters. The members of the Boards are official and non-official, the latter being composed of bankers, leading traders, and private persons of influence in the several areas.

The State of Dungarpur, with Banswara, which adjoins it on the eastern side, formed a territory which in olden days was known by the name of Bagar. It was occupied chiefly by the Bhils, but Rajputs of the Chauhan and Parmar clans were also inhabitants at that time, although they were subsequently overcome by the Sisodiyas, belonging to the same martial race as themselves.

It may be mentioned here that the Rulers of Bagar, as now represented by the Maharawals of Dungarpur and Banswara belong to the Sisodiya clan of Rajputs who claim descent from Lava, the eldest son of Rama the divine king of Ayodhya (the present Oudh) and the hero of the renowned epic known as the "Ramayan."

The early history of Dungarpur is somewhat obscure. But it is a well-ascertained fact that the Dungarpur rulers were among the few Rajput princes who declined to assist the Moghul Emperors by waging war against their own race.

In 1577, Rawal Askaran, the then Ruler of Dungarpur, entered into political relationship with the Emperor Akbar, and for a period of about 200 years the State enjoyed continued peace and prosperity. The security of Dungarpur was soon afterwards seriously threatened by the rebellious raids of the Mahrattas, Pindaris, and others, and the whole of Rajputana became a hot-bed of anarchy. Extraneous aid was needed in order to evict the marauders, and the Governor-General, acting on behalf of the Government of the East India Company, invited the Ruling Princes to a friendly alliance, and as a result of the appeal Dungarpur joined the remaining Rajputana States in signing an offensive and defensive treaty in the year 1818. The Maharawal acknowledged the suzerainty of the British Government and agreed to pay an annual tribute (which in 1904 was reduced to Rs. 17,500) in return for a promise of protection from foreign invaders and a guarantee that succession to the *gadi* should be given to the Ruler and his heirs in perpetuity.

Dungarpur was then at peace as far as outside foes were concerned, but the Bhils, who were exceedingly numerous in the State, had been instigated to rebellious acts by disaffected nobles, and a military force was necessary to subjugate them.

Troubles arose shortly afterwards which ended in the deposition of Maharawal

THE STATE OF DUNGARPUR.

1. Peer Fakruddin's Shrine in Galiakote. 2. Deo Som Nath's Temple.

Jaswant Singh, and a temporary arrangement was made for the administration of the State by a Prince of Partabgarh until Udai Singh, who had been selected as successor, should attain his majority. The Regency was, however, transferred to an Indian Agent in the year 1852, and five years later Udai Singh assumed control on his own account. The Maharawal, though still young in years, proved himself to be a doughty supporter of the British Government during the dark days of the Sepoy mutiny in 1857, and in 1862 a *sanad* was granted to him, which secured the right of adoption to him and his successors. The terrible famine of 1869-70 presented an opportunity to Udai Singh to manifest his high administrative capabilities, and the sympathetic manner in which he strove for the welfare of his subjects is to-day a cherished memory in the State. He established relief works by constructing tanks in 25 villages, purchased grain at Cawnpore and other producing centres and sold it at nominal rates, gave special help to the aged and the infirm, and remitted customs duties on imports and exports, while his many chharitable acts involved the State in an expenditure of more than Rs. 1,00,000.

THE STATE OF DUNGARPUR.
SHRI NATHJI'S TEMPLE.

Maharawal Udai Singh died in the year 1898 after a peaceful and glorious reign extending over 54 years, and he was succeeded by his grandson—then 11 years of age—the present Ruler, His Highness Rai Rayan, Maharaj Adhiraj Maharawalji Shri Sir Bijoy Singhji Sahib Bahadur K.C.I.E.

The administration of the State during His Highness's minority was vested in a Political Officer, who was assisted by the Dewan and a Council of two members.

His Highness was educated at the Mayo College, Ajmer, where he was placed under the efficient personal tuition and guardianship of the Vice-Principal, Mr. H. Sherring, and during his scholastic course he won the highest praise from the Professors, while at the same time he was exceedingly popular with his fellow Princes. Before leaving the College he passed the diploma examination with distinction, and in 1907 he was successful in another one which is equivalent to taking the Bachelor of Arts degree in an Indian University.

In February of the same year His Highness was married to the eldest Princess of Sailana, a State in the Political Agency of Central India, and in March 1908 the birth of the heir-apparent, the Maharaj Kumar Sri Lakshman Singhi, was proclaimed amid the great rejoicings of the Maharawal's subjects. Two other sons and one daughter have been born since that date.

At the conclusion of his college career His Highness was initiated into the duties of practical administration, and on February 28, 1909, he was invested with full ruling powers by Colonel F. H. Pinhey, the Agent in Rajputana to the Governor-General of India.

Shortly after His Highness had been installed on the *gadi* he was overwhelmed with grief at the unexpected death of His late Majesty King Edward VII, and when he subsequently attended a meeting at Ajmer, called for the purpose of considering a proposal for the erection of a suitable Provincial memorial, the Maharawal in addressing the assembly, observed: "Now that the proposal for an All-India

THE STATE OF DUNGARPUR.

1. Bijaya Garh. 2. Kailash Bhawan.

Memorial has been disposed of. I wish to suggest for consideration a project for a provincial memorial for the whole of Rajputana.

"Most of the other provinces of India are erecting memorials in commemoration of the short but brilliant and beneficent reign of our late Emperor King Edward VII, of happy memory, and in my opinion Rajputana, which yields to no other province in loyalty, should take a leading part in furthering so excellent a project.

"Ajmer is in British territory in the centre of the Rajputana States, and it is the headquarters of the Honourable the Agent to the Governor-General for some months in the year.

"Ajmer also contains the Mayo College, whither the different States send their young nobles to be educated, and the Government College, which has provided the States with some of their most successful and important officials. Hence, I venture to think that no better place can be found for a Rajputana memorial than Ajmer.

"Several of the States, in order to show their love and loyalty to the late King, will probably erect local memorials, but I trust this will not prevent them from uniting to raise a common memorial for the whole province."

His Highness generously contributed Rs. 15,000 towards this project.

The most notable event of the year 1912 was the Grand Coronation Durbar held at Delhi, to which His Highness the Maharawal was invited by the Imperial Government. His Highness left Dungarpur on November 30th, accompanied by his suite, consisting of Thakur Kishan Sinha of Bankora, Thakur Dhirat Sinha of Bichhiwara, Thakur Lal Sinha of Bomasa, Gandhi Kirpa Chand, Shah Kastur Chand, Seth Sobha Chand, Sardar Partab Sinha, Mr. Mohan Lal Tara Chand, Shah Rawat Ram Swaroop, Lala Shiva Prasada, and Mr. Murli Dhar Bhargava, and he arrived at Delhi on December 2nd. A salute was fired as the special train drew alongside the station platform, and His Highness was received by the Deputy Commissioner of Delhi, and other officials, an escort of Indian cavalry being in attendance for the purpose of accompanying the Maharawal to his camp, which was pleasantly situated on the King's Way.

The Royal train reached the city on the morning of the 7th, and Their Imperial Majesties subsequently drove to the pavilion in the fort, where they received the Indian Chiefs who were duly presented to them. The Royal procession was afterwards formed, in which the Ruling Princes took part, Major F. B. Prideaux (Indian Army), Political Agent in Southern Rajputana, occupying a seat in the state carriage of His Highness the Maharawal.

At an early hour on the long-looked-for day upon which the Grand Durbar was to take place, His Highness and his suite offered their dutiful homage to Their Imperial Majesties, and the transcendent splendour of the ceremonies on that occasion will never be effaced from the memory of the Maharawal. His Imperial Majesty presented to His Highness the Durbar gold medal and autograph portraits of His Gracious Consort and Himself, while the title of Rai Sahib was conferred on Seth Sobha Chand, Member of the Dungarpur State Council.

The auspicious event was celebrated with great pomp and enthusiasm at Dungarpur, and His Highness was pleased to commemorate it by distributing food and clothing to the poor, giving sweets to children, releasing prisoners, and providing entertainments and games of various kinds.

The State artillery fired a Royal salute at noon, and the Imperial Proclamation was read in the vernacular by Rai Bahadur Munshi Ganesh Ram Rawat, Diwan of Dungarpur. Prayers were offered in Hindu and Jain temples and Mahomedan mosques, and in the evening the principal buildings were brilliantly illuminated.

In November 1912 His Highness was invited to Ajmer in order to receive from His Excellency Lord Hardinge of Penshurst, Viceroy and Governor-General, the insignia of a Knight Commander of the most Eminent Order of the Indian Empire, this being one ot the Birthday Honours conferred by His Majesty the King-Emperor George V. When His Highness arrived at Modasa, a town in British territory and trading with Dungarpur, the leading citizens of the town desired to present an address, and extended such a cordial invitation for the acceptance of their hospitality that it was impossible for him to refuse compliance. In the evening of the same day, therefore, a crowded public meeting, attended by the Assistant Collector and a large number of other Government Officials and private residents, was held, when a beautiful casket containing the address was tendered to His Highness. On the arrival of the special train at Ajmer on the following morning a salute of 15 guns was fired, and His Highness was welcomed by Mr. A. T. Holme, I.C.S., Commissioner of Ajmer-Merwara, and Major R. E. A. Hamilton, I.A., Political Agent of the Southern Rajputana States. Formal visits were exchanged between His Excellency the Viceroy and His Highness, at one of which the latter received the insignia of the High Order to which he had been admitted.

Before leaving Ajmer His Highness attended the ceremony of laying the foundation stone of the Rajputana Provincial Memorial, as a tribute to the high personal character of His late Majesty King Edward VII.

His Highness is a Ruling Prince of the first class, exercising unrestricted powers in civil and criminal matters, and is entitled to a salute of 15 guns. He is a man of strong religious tendencies, and a staunch adherent of the faith of his forefathers, but the caste or even creed of a person does not weigh for one moment with him when an appeal is made for a charitable gift. Public and private institutions and societies of various descriptions are continual recipients of substantial financial help, and since his accession he has, out of his benevolence, distributed more than Rs. 1,00,000. The high literary attainments of His Highness render him a sincere patron of education, and although he is indefatigable in his endeavours to rule wisely and well, there is perhaps no subject in which he takes deeper interest than that of providing facilities for instruction to the rising generation.

The strenuous life of the Rajputs as a race has caused them to imbibe the love of sport side by side with their ordinary youthful training, and among many Chiefs who have distinguished themselves as hunters of large game, the name of His Highness of Dungarpur is one of the most prominent. He is a sportsman in the best sense of the word, conducting his *shikars* in a manner which stamps him as one who takes the keenest delight in tracking his quarry until he can get to close quarters with it, when it is certain to have fair play in a contest in which the laurels do not always fall to the lot of the man behind the rifle. His Highness has, since his accession, bagged more than 200 panthers and tigers, in addition to other large game. Early in 1918 a pair of fine tigers made their home in the State, and it is the intention of His Highness to protect these animals and their offspring for fully ten years. Some African lions have also been bred, and it is proposed to turn the troupe into the jungles in the near future.

When the news of the outbreak of hostilities in Europe reached Dungarpur, His Highness the Maharawal, in accordance with the traditional loyalty of his House, caused a telegram to be despatched to the Viceroy and Governor-General assuring him of unflinching fealty to His Majesty the King-Emperor, and at the same time placing all the resources of the State at the disposal of the Government, in addition to offering his own personal services. On August 26, 1914, a public meeting was convened at Dungarpur, under the chairmanship of His Highness, who eloquently appealed to his hearers to rally to the cause of the Empire and to subscribe to the Imperial War Fund. A liberal response was made, the sum of Rs. 8,000 being subscribed.

At a subsequent date, when Turkey espoused the cause of Germany, and again in 1915, His Highness renewed his offer to proceed to the front, but to his bitter disappointment His Excellency the Viceroy was unable to accede to the proposal. Further than this, the Maharawal desired to raise signalling infantry and cavalry sections as an Imperial Service Unit, and he also proposed to raise a body of 100 men for garrison duty in India, but the Government expressed its warmest thanks to His Highness, and regretted that the offer could not at that time be accepted. It may be added that the Viceroy and Governor-General subsequently accepted the offer of the last-named unit.

A sum of nearly Rs. 1,45,000 was contributed by the Dungarpur State for war purposes to the end of September 1918, this amount representing about 29 per cent. of the annual revenue of the State. The following list contains particulars respecting some of the contributions from His Highness and the State: A sum of Rs. 1,000 was generously given monthly by His Highness from April 1, 1915, towards providing comforts for wounded Indian soldiers; Rs. 6,500 were subscribed to the Imperial Indian Relief Fund; a motor-car, costing Rs. 11,465, was presented to the Motor Ambulance section; five horses, costing nearly Rs. 5,000, were presented to the Military Department; Rs. 500 were given to the "Comforts Fund of the Merwara Light Infantry," despatched to the front; a sum of Rs. 30,000 was offered towards the Rajputana Aeroplane Fund for two aeroplanes, which were presented to the Government; while various amounts ranging from Rs. 50 to 2,000 were expended upon blankets, cigarettes, "Our Day Gifts," religious services for the victory of the British arms; buildings for disabled soldiers, and various other objects. In May 1918, His Highness further contributed Rs. 20,000 for war purposes in response to the Prime Minister's appeal, addressed to the Princes and people of India. In addition to the above, the State Officials and His Highness's subjects contributed Rs. 6,480 in cash and kind, while those in the service of the State drawing salaries of not less than Rs. 50 a month, regularly contributed one day's pay per mensem from March 1, 1916.

The inhabitants of the State have been no less enthusiastic in contributing to the War Loan Fund, as the following figures will show: The amount paid for cash certificates is Rs. 29,775; for war bonds, Rs. 10,800; and for war loan, Rs. 7,125; making a total of Rs. 47,700, but the nominal value of these securities is now given as Rs. 56,720.

The Durbar, on the instructions of His Highness, offered every possible inducement to subjects of, or persons residing in, the State to enlist for foreign service either as soldiers in the Indian Army or as clerks in the Supply and Transport Corps of the Indian Expeditionary Force. In view of the modest annual revenues of the State, the handsome contribution to the War and the provision made by the Durbar for those who joined the colours was of the most generous description, and reflected great credit on its Ruler.

THE STATE OF IDAR

BIRD'S-EYE VIEW OF THE CITY OF IDAR.

HIS HIGHNESS MAHARAJA DHIRAJ MAHARAJAJI SHREE LIEUT.-COLONEL SIR DOWLAT SINGHJI SAHIB BAHADUR, K.C.S.I., MAHARAJA OF IDAR.

MAHARAJA KUMAR HIMMAT SINGHJI.

His Highness's Eldest Son and Heir-Apparent of the State.

THE STATE OF IDAR.

1. Group (from Left to Right)—Maharaja Kumar Madan Singhji, His Highness's Third Son; Bhanwarji Daljit Singhji, His Highness's Grandson; Maharaja Kumar Man Singhji, His Highness's Second Son.
2. The Pratap Palace at Himatnagar.

THE STATE OF IDAR.

1. The Zenana Palace at Himatnagar. 2. The Juwan Niwas and the Zenana Palace at Idar.

1

THE STATE OF IDAR.

1. "Anand Pole," the Entrance Gate to the Pratap Palace. 2. View of the Hathmati River and Canal Weir.

VIEW OF RANI TALAO, NEAR IDAR CITY.

THE PALACE ON THE FORT.

THE STATE OF JAISALMER

JAISALMER, the most westerly State in the Province of Rajputana, consists chiefly of a vast sandy tract of land, some 16,000 square miles in extent, situated on the borders of the Great Indian desert. Its Rulers belong to the Bhati branch of the Yadava clan of Rajputs, whose power was paramount in India about 3,000 years ago. The present Maharawal is the lineal descendant of Shri Krishna, the most illustrious representative, as statesman, soldier, and philosopher, of the ancient Lunar dynasty. After the death of Shri Krishna, the members of his clan were scattered widely, and some of them left India altogether. One of his successors, Salivahan, conquered the greater portion of the Punjab, and in the southern portion of that province he built a large city, as his capital, which he named Salivahanpur, but which is now known as Sialkot. He avenged the death of his father Guj, the founder of Gajni, and regained possession of its fort. Bhati, grandson of Salivahan, is a notable figure in the history as a great warrior who subdued 14 Princes and annexed their territories, and the tribe thenceforth bore the patronymic of Bhati Yadava. After several changes of capitals, and after many vicissitudes of fortune, they eventually established themselves in a favourable part of the desert.

The modern history of the State may be said to begin in the year 1808, when the then Ruler of the State, Maharawal Moolraj concluded with the British Government a treaty of perpetual friendship, amity, alliance, and unity of interests. By this agreement the Maharawal undertook to act in subordinate co-operation with the British Government, and with submission to its supremacy. From that time to the present the loyalty of the House of Jaisalmer and its devotion to the British Throne has not been excelled by that of any other dynasty in India.

Maharawal Moolraj Sing died in 1820, and the accession to the *gadi* devolved upon his grandson, Gaj Singh.

Gaj Singh ruled his State with considerable ability. In 1829 Maharaja Ratansingh of Bikaner, in violation of his treaty engagements, invaded Jaisalmer to revenge some injuries committed by subjects of the latter. After the invading army was driven back into Marwar territory, the British Government interfered, and through the arbitration of the Maharana of Udaipur the dispute was settled. In 1838–39 the first Afghan War necessitated the dispatch of British troops to join the main army by way of the Indus, and Gaj Singh's exertions to supply camels for transport purposes were such as to elicit the special thanks of Government; while in 1844, after the

HIS HIGHNESS MAHARAJADHIRAJ SHRI MAHARAWALJI SIR JAWAHIRSINGHJI, SAHIB BAHADUR, K.C.S.I.. OF JAISALMER.

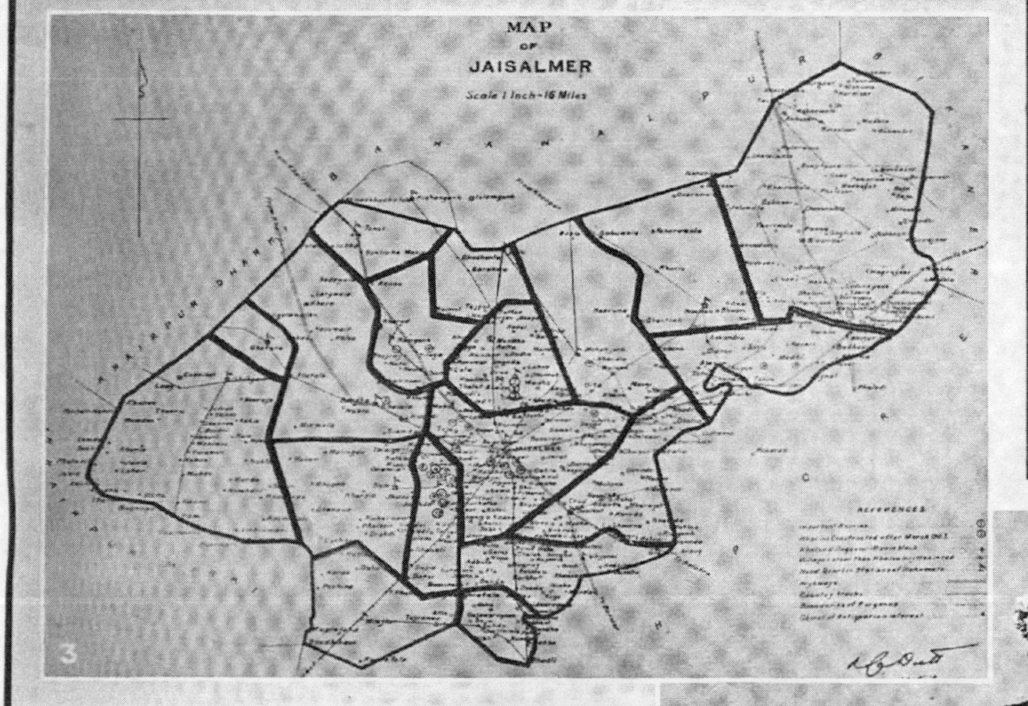

1. HIS LATE HIGHNESS MAHARAJADHIRAJ MAHARAWALJI SHRI BAIRISALJI BAHADUR.
2. MAHARAJ KUMAR SHRI GIRDHARSINGHJI SAHIB OF JAISALMER. 3. MAP OF JAISALMER.

THE STATE OF JAISALMER.

1. Patwon-ki-Haveli. 2. Nathmal-ki-Haveli. 3. Salamsingh-ki-Haveli.

conquest of Sind, the forts of Shahgarh, Gharsia, and Ghotara, which had formerly belonged to Jaisalmer, were restored to the State.

Maharawal Gaj Singh died in 1846 without issue, and his widow, a daughter of the Ruling House of Udaipur, adopted Ranjit Singh, the son of Thakore Keshri Singh, who occupied the *gadi* until he was followed by his younger brother Bairisal in 1865. In 1870 an extradition treaty with the State by the Government of India was concluded. On his death in 1891, his widow adopted Shyam Singh, who assumed the family name of Salivahan and succeeded to the *gadi*. He was a child at the time of his adoption. He received his education in the Mayo College, Ajmer. After attaining his majority, he associated himself personally with the administration, and it was at his initiative that several fiscal reforms were introduced. He died in 1914, and was succeeded by the present Ruler His Highness Maharajadhiraja Maharawal Sir Jawahir Singh Bahadur, K.C.S.I., who was born on November 18, 1882. He is the son of Thakur Sardar Singh, and he was, prior to his succession, adopted, in 1889, by Thakur Man Singh of Etah. A sound education was imparted to His Highness at the Mayo College, Ajmer, and he was one of the first youths to be selected from that institution as a member of the Imperial Cadet Corps.

His Highness was entrusted with the reins of government on June 26, 1914, and the formal installation ceremony took place on the 9th of the following month.

The Bhatis of Jaisalmer are connected by marriage with the Ruling Houses of the following States, namely, Udaipur, Dungarpur, Bundi, Jodhpur, Bikaner, Kishengarh, Sirohi, and Dhrangadra.

The news of the outbreak of the Great War was received in Jaisalmer with mingled feelings; it produced deep sorrow on the part of the Maharawal and his faithful subjects, but it also inspired a manifestation of joy that the devotion and loyalty of the Ruling House, which was proverbial, could once again be displayed by hearty co-operation with the Allies in their desperate struggle for freedom against the oppression and tyranny of the foe.

His Highness was foremost in offering his personal services as well as the resources of his State in support of the British Government. The contributions and investments in connection with the war made by the State and its subjects, in and outside Jaisalmer, roughly amounted to one million rupees. Thousands of sheep and goats were provided free of duty for consumption of prisoners of war. Military rewards were given and grants of land, besides several other easements, were offered to men who came forward to be enlisted as recruits. The number of men, however, enlisted in the Imperial Army was much smaller than the number that preferred serving in the Imperial troops maintained by adjoining States.

The State of Jaisalmer has always maintained its independence—even in the dark days of the Moghul period—and it

THE STATE OF JAISALMER.

1. The Meghadambar Chhatra.

An umbrella, the inner work of which is nearly 5,000 years old and which, according to tradition, Shri Krishna used on occasions of State. It has been similarly used since that date by his lineal descendants and successors, i.e., the scions of the House of Jaisalmer, who are styled "Chhatrala Yadava Pati," the canopied lords of the Yadavas.

2. The Jaisalmer State Standard.

has preserved its pride of race and purity of blood notwithstanding the fact that it has passed through various vicissitudes of fortune. Its historic fort has resounded with the boom of the cannon of invading armies, and it, on one occasion, withstood a siege of eight years, but the State has never allowed its name to be sullied by payment of tribute. The valour displayed by the Bhati Princes in repelling successive waves of Mahomedan invasions earned for them and their descendants the title of "Uttar Bharkinwar," that is, "the mighty portals of the north" (of India).

The Rulers of Jaisalmer are also styled "Pachcham-ka-Padshah," signifying "Emperor of Western India," as up to the days of Amir Singh (1661–1702) and his successor, the territory of Jaisalmer extended northwards to the Sutlej river, and comprised the whole of Bahawalpur; westwards to the Indus, including Sukkur, Bukkur, Rohri, and other tracts in Sind; and to the east and south as far as the districts of Poogal, Pokaran, Barmer, Phalodi, and others. In commemoration of the victories in Sind a part of the palace is built with bricks brought from Amarkot, now in Sind, after its sack,

THE STATE OF JAISALMER.
STATE PALKHI.

and the jewels which the patron goddess of the Ruling House now wears on special occasions are those which the Begums of the great Moghuls were required to give by way of ransom. The Rulers of Jaisalmer, in recognition of their great valour, were presented by the Moghul Emperors with the "Fish" insignia and the "Sash Hazari." Several poets have made allusions to the prowess of the Bhatis, but the two following translations must suffice: "Wealth they gained, but hoarded it not; the earth they carved out with the stroke of their sword; such are the Bhatis, the Lords of the Yadavas, who have learned only the lesson of renown." Again, "Mighty portals of the north are they, the Bhatis, who are capable of bearing the brunt; the pledge of Bijraj they maintain, and in the battle they rush forth armed with their lances."

RAO SAHIB M.R. SAPAT, OF KHERO, DEWAN OF JAISALMER STATE.

One of the oldest and most highly-prized heirlooms of the State is the "Meghadambar," an umbrella which, according to tradition, was used by Shri Krishna on State occasion, and which has ever since been similarly employed by the House of Jaisalmer as his descendants. The reigning Maharawal is accordingly styled "Chhatrala Yadava Pati," meaning "the canopied lord of the Yadavas."

The umbrella, made of eight metals, which surmounts the Jaisalmer palace, towering high above the venerable walls of its historic fort, is emblematic of the proud position which the House of Jaisalmer occupies as the Head of the lunar race and of its offshoots. The only other

THE STATE OF JAISALMER.

1. State Horse.

The gold wagtail on the head of the horse is emblematic of ***Palan***—a bird—in whose shape the patron goddess of the House appeared and helped Maharawal Bijairaj in vanquishing his foes.

2. State Elephant. 3. State Camel. 4. State Rath.

THE STATE OF JAISALMER.

1. A Street in the Bazaar. 2. Barlhwan-para Street. 3. Kachba-para Street.

THE STATE OF JAISALMER.

1. View of the Fort and City from an adjoining Hill. 2. The Fort from the East. 3. Bird's-eye View of the City from the Fort.

THE STATE OF JAISALMER.

1. Moti Mahel. 2. Gaj Vilas Mahel. 3. Badal Vila (a portion of the Mandir Palace). 4. Garden House.

THE STATE OF JAISALMER.

1. The Durbar Hospital. 2. Garsisar Lake and Palace. 3. Amarsagar Lake and Palace. 4. Amarsagar Jain Temple. 5. Moolraj-Sagar and Garden.

House which enjoys the same privilege is (according to Colonel Tod's "Rajasthan") that of Udaipur.

The standard of the State is chiefly orange-coloured; the black portion represents the desert; the embattled line which divides the shield alludes to the famous fort of Jaisalmer and to others in the State; and the supporters are the steeds of the moon, "bezante," or, marked with gold coins because the capital was formerly a place of refuge for the families of wealthy traders from all parts of India. The "bearing" and "crest" have reference to the tutelary goddess of the House, "Swangiaji," a "taker of the *swangi*," or spear.

The head of the administration is the Dewan, Rao Sahib Murarji Rao Sapat, whose valuable services to the State have been recognized by the *Durbar* by the presentation of gold and a *jagir, Tejsi-ro-Kherho*, and it may be added that the distinction of gold has only been accorded to two other premier nobles of Jaisalmer, namely, the Raos of Bikampore and Barsalpore. The Dewan has also been given the *Izzat* of "*Ekori Tazim*."

Jaisalmer is a full-power sovereign State. It enjoys internal autonomy, and pays no tribute either to the British Government or to any Indian State. In regard to size it is the third among the 20 States and Chiefships of Rajputana, and its greatest breadth from east to west is about 170 miles, while its extreme length from north to south is 136 miles. It has a total area of more than 16,000 square miles, and its inhabitants are about 88,000 in number, the majority of whom are Hindus. It is bounded on the north by the State of Bahawalpur, on the west by the Shikarpur district of Sind, on the south and east by the State of Jodhpur, and on the north-east by the State of Bikaner.

The general appearance of the surface of the State is that of a flat sandy waste broken by numerous ridges covered with stunted vegetation. A series of low sandstone hills practically bisects the State; on the northern side of this line the soil is unfruitful, but in the southern portion it is fairly fertile although light in character.

Agricultural pursuits form the occupation of the majority of the subjects of the State, and primitive methods of cultivation have to a very large extent been superseded by modern systems of tillage, including irrigation, especially since a land settlement was completed in the year 1906.

The greater portion of the land which has been or can be brought into cultivation is of a sandy character, but in the region of desert in which Jaisalmer lies, the rainfall, although slight, is usually sufficient for the growing of good crops.

Owing to the peculiar characteristics of the soil camels are more serviceable than bullocks for ploughing and other agricultural work. The chief crops are *Bajra, jowar, moth, mung*, and *til*.

Practically the whole wealth of the people consists of their herds of camels and cattle, the former of these being famous for hardiness, speed, and easy paces.

Many of the inhabitants are employed in quarrying sandstone and limestone, the latter of which is noted for its fine grain and its adaptability for carvings.

Salt of fair average quality is also a valuable production of the State. Brine, found at a depth of about 10 feet, is raised to the surface by the use of buckets, and after it has been subjected to evaporation, it is prepared for general purposes. Manufactured goods comprise bags and druggets made of the hair of camels and goats, blankets of sheep's wool, stone cups and platters.

The principal exports are: Wool, *ghee*, fuller's earth, cattle, camels, and sheep; and imported goods are unimportant, with the exception of piece-goods and tobacco. The import of cereals varies with the sufficiency or otherwise of the seasonal rains.

The State forces comprise 220 men under arms, including cavalry, artillery, and infantry, and there are 17 serviceable guns. About 160 police are enrolled, and 72 of these are mounted on camels.

The State is not traversed by any railway, and the nearest station is at Barmer, on the Jodhpur-Bikaner line, some 90 miles distant from the chief town.

Education is imparted free of charge in all schools, and medical treatment is provided, at the cost of the State, at the town of Jaisalmer.

His Highness the Maharawal is entitled to a salute of 15 guns.

The chief town, Jaisalmer, is situated about 600 miles distant in a northerly direction from Bombay, and 1,200 miles from Calcutta. It was built by Maharawal Jaisal in 1156 at the southern end of a low range of hills, and it is surrounded by a massive stone wall from 10 feet to 15 feet in height, 5 feet in thickness, and having a circuit of about three miles. On the southern side of the town, but overlooking it, is the famous fort which has been erected on a hill 500 yards in length and 250 yards in breadth, while it is 250 feet above the surrounding country.

Within the fort is the imposing palace of His Highness the Maharawal crowned by a huge metal umbrella (already referred to), "a solid emblem of dignity of which the Bhati Chiefs are justly proud." Near to the palace are many substantial buildings constructed of limestone and beautifully carved.

There are also a number of very fine Jain temples, some of which are said to date from the sixth century. In the libraries attached to these temples there is a collection of old and rare manuscripts written on palm-leaves.

THE STATE OF KHAIRPUR

THE State of Khairpur is in the province of Sindh, under the Government of Bombay, and its Ruler is called the Mir of Khairpur. His Highness is a First-Class Chief, and possesses full powers of life and death, with reservation in favour of British-born subjects, who cannot be tried for capital offences without the concurrence of the Political Agent. His Civil jurisdiction is unlimited. He belongs to a Baloch family called Talpur. Previous to the accession of this family, on the fall of the Kalhora dynasty of Sindh in 1783 A.D., the history of Khairpur is included in the general history of Sindh. In that year Mir Fatteh Ali Khan Talpur established himself as Rais or Ruler of Sindh ; and subsequently his nephew, Mir Sohrab Khan Talpur, founded the Khairpur branch of the Talpur family.

About the year 1813 A.D., during the troubles in Kabul, incidental to the establishment of the Barakzai dynasty, the Mirs were able to withhold the tribute which, up to that date, had been paid to the rulers of Afghanistan. Two years earlier, in 1811 A.D., Mir Sorab Khan had abdicated in favour of his son, Mir Rustam, whose unfriendly relations with his brother, Ali Murad, led to the intervention of the British. In 1832 A.D., the individuality of the Khairpur State, as separate from the other Talpur Mirs in Sindh, was recognized by the British Government in a treaty, under which the use of the River Indus and the roads of Sindh were secured to the British. Ali Murad, who gradually succeeded in establishing his hold on the chiefship, cordially supported the British policy, and the result was, that after the battles of Miani and Daba had put the whole of Sindh at the disposal of the British Government, Khairpur was the only State that was allowed to retain its political existence under the protection of the Paramount power.

His Highness Mir Sir Ali Murad Khan Talpur, G.C.I.E., attached himself to the British interests. During the Sind War he rendered valuable assistance to the British Government, and in 1845 he aided them materially both with arms and diplomacy to put an end to the Turki Campaign. In 1857, when in England, hearing of the outbreak of the Indian Mutiny, he sent orders to his eldest son, Mir Shah Navaz Khan, to render every assistance to the Paramount Power. On learning that the Shikarpur jail and treasury were threatened by the rebels, Mir Shah Navaz marched there with troops and assisted in saving them from falling into the hands of the enemy. In 1866 A.D., a Sanad was granted to the Mir, under which the British Government promised to recognize any succession to the chiefship, according to Mahomedan Law.

His Highness Mir Sir Ali Murad Khan died in 1894 A.D., and was succeeded by his son, Mir Faiz Mahomed Khan, who ruled the State up to 1909 A.D., and was bestowed the title of G.C.I.E. by the British Government. After his death, his son, His Highness Mir Sir Imam Baksh Khan Talpur, came to the *gadi*, and was formally installed on July 1, 1909 A.D. The title of G.C.I.E. was conferred on him on the occasion of Delhi Durbar in December, 1911, and the honorary rank of Lieutenant-Colonel on January 1, 1918, in recognition of services rendered in connection with war. He was also a Donat of the Order of St. John of Jerusalem. Mir Sir Imam Baksh Khan died on February 8, 1921, and was succeeded by his son, His Highness Mir Ali Navaz Khan, who was born in 1884. He visited Europe in 1911, accompanied by a Political Officer. His Highness takes a keen interest in the administration of the State, and has introduced several reforms in it, since his accession to the *gadi*, such as abolition of the *Chher* (forced labour) system, excavation of new canals and organization of co-operative societies for the benefit of agriculturists, etc., with the help of his Wazir, Mahomed Kader Shaikh, Esq., M.B.E., whose services have been lent to the State by the British Government.

The total area of the State is 6,050 square miles, and the population is 1,93,152 souls, according to the Census of 1921. The average revenue of the State amounts to Rs. 24,00,602.

His Highness Mir Ali Navaz Khan Talpur is entitled to a salute of 15 permanent and 17 local guns, and is a member of the Chamber of Princes.

Apart from the distinguished part played by the Khairpur Imperial Mounted Service Rifles and Camel Transport in the operations in British East Africa, in Egypt, and in the North-West Frontier of India, the Khairpur Durbar rendered the following services during the Great War :

1. Sahibzada Mir Ghulam Ali Khan Talpur, the youngest brother of His High-

HIS HIGHNESS MIR ALI NAWAZ KHAN TALPUR, RULER OF KHAIRPUR STATE.

THE STATE OF KHAIRPUR.

1 H.H. the Mir of Khairpur, His Son Vazir, and Naib-Vazir. 2. The Faiz Palace, Khairpur State.

THE STATE OF KHAIRPUR.

1. H.H. the Mir of Khairpur with Members of the Ruling Family.
2. H.H. the Mir, the Political Agent, Guests and State Officials, taken at the time of the Visit of the Political Agent, Sukker.

THE STATE OF KHAIRPUR.

1. His Highness the Mir and his Vazir shaking hands immediately after H.H.'s Installation. 2. M. K. Shaikh, Esq., M.B.E., LL.B., Vazir, Khairpur State.

THE STATE OF KHAIRPUR.

1. H.H the Mir of Khairpur on the occasion of his Installation by the Political Agent, Sukkur, inside the Faiz Palace.
2. Group taken on the occasion of the First Visit of the Commissioner in Sind to H.H. the Mir of Khairpur, soon after H.H.'s Installation.

ness the Ruler, served in the various theatres of War as honorary Second Lieutenant in the Indian Army from March 21, 1915, to November 25, 1917. He was mentioned in General Sir A. Murray's despatches.

2. 142 recruits were enlisted for the Indian Army through the State agency.

3. A sum of Rs. 34082 was paid by the Durbar for one Aeroplane, to be called "Khairpur." Besides, a sum of Rs. 200 was subscribed towards the Aeroplane Fund.

4. Donations for the direct War charities were given by the Durbar as under:

(*a*) War Relief Fund, Rs. 5,000; (*b*) St. John's Ambulance, Rs. 5,000; (*c*) Queen Mary's Technical School for wounded, Rs. 5,000; (*d*) Silver Wedding Fund, Rs. 5,000; (*e*) Poona Pageant Fund Rs. 2,000; (*f*) Tobacco for Indian soldiers on front, Rs. 1,000.

5. A sum of Rs. 4,00,000 (four Lacs) was subscribed by the State towards the War Loan, exclusive of public subscriptions, which amounted to Rs. 6,91,053.

THE STATE OF KISHANGARH

THE Kishangarh State is situated almost in the centre of Rajputana, between 25° 49' and 26° 59' north and 74° 40' and 75° 19' east, with an area of 858 square miles and a population of 77,806 souls according to the census of 1921 It is bounded on the north by the Sambhar salt lake, on the west by the State of Marwar, and the British district of Ajmer-Merwara, on the east by the State of Jaipur, and on the south by the Chiefship of Shahpura (Mewar).

Excepting for small isolated patches, the territory consists of two elongated strips which, together, are 80 miles in length from the Sambhar Lake in the north to the Khari river in the south. The breadth varies from 20 miles in the centre to about two miles in the southern extremity. The northern portion is generally sandy, owing to drifts from the adjoining Marwar district in the west. The central portion has poor soil overlying stratified rocks in the northern, and gneiss in the southern half. The southern portion of the State, comprising the district of Sarwar, is generally flat, but the soil is good and fertile, overlying gneiss.

Towards the close of the sixteenth century the reigning Chief of Jodhpur (Marwar) was His Highness Maharaja Udai Singhji, better known as "Mota Raja," and he had 17 sons, of whom His Highness Kishan Singhji the Eighth was born at Jodhpur in the year 1575. At the age of 19 he was presented with the *jagir* of Asop, where he remained for about 12 months, and he then went to Dodur, a more important holding of a similar tenure, which was conferred upon him by his elder brother, Maharaja Surya Singhji, who was then ruling at Jodhpur. He subsequently moved on to Ajmer, where the Emperor Jehangir allowed him to remain by further conferring on him some villages in the vicinity. He kept in close touch with the Moslem Emperors, and was sent with Mahabut Khan to fight against His Highness Maharana Amar Singhji of Udaipur (Mewar), where he was wounded. After his return in 1611 he founded the city of Kishangarh. The revenue of the State at the time of his death in 1615 amounted to Rs. 2,50,000.

His eldest son, Maharaja Sahesmal, succeeded him, but he died in 1618 without male issue, and was accordingly followed by his brother, Maharaja Jagmalji, who ruled for ten years. The absence of a direct heir brought Maharaja Har Singhji to the *gadi* in 1628, and he ruled for 15 years. He was selected by the Emperor at Delhi to undertake a mission to Kabul, but he unfortunately died there in 1643, leaving no male issue. He was succeeded by his nephew, Maharaja Rup Singhji, who also was chosen by the Moghul Emperor for another expedition to Kabul, in which he fought valiantly and gained many victories, and was rewarded with high honours. On his return from Kabul he founded the city of Rupnagar, in the northern portion of the State, which was named after him, and he also built a fort there. Rup Singhji was a second time deputed to proceed to Kabul on military service, and on this occasion he compelled Kabul to accept the Moghul system of weights and measures. On his return he was asked by the Emperor to choose a reward and his reply was a prayer to the Emperor to reinstate Raja Sawal Singh of Jaisalmer, who had been dethroned. The Emperor, pleased with the brave deeds of Maharaja Rup Singhji, granted his request. In 1653 he was further rewarded by the grant of the fort at Mandalgarh. He died in 1658, and was succeeded on the *gadi* by his son, Maharaja Man Singhji, who ruled for about 48 years in peace and tranquillity, and was in like manner rewarded by the Imperial House with the grant of additional *jagirs*, thus enlarging his territory. He died in 1706 and was succeeded by his son Raj Singhji

His Highness Maharaja Raj Singhji, shortly after his accession, was engaged in a battle with the Rana of Dholpur in Rajputana, and after victory had crowned his efforts the Emperor conferred upon him the title of Umdai Rajahe Baland Makan Maharaja Bahadur, and also granted him as a reward the *parganas* of Sarwar and Malpura. He died in 1748, and was succeeded by his third son, Maharaja Sawat Singhji, who led a retired life at Brindaban (Muttra), and died in 1764, leaving as his successor Maharaja Sardar Singhji, who died three years later in 1767. He, however, had adopted his cousin, Birad Singhji, the son of Bahadur Singhji, to succeed him on the *gadi*, but the latter was at the time *de facto* ruler, and was recognized as such by all. It was this Prince who rebuilt the fort at Kishangarh as it now stands, and who also erected a wall encircling the whole of the city.

The *gadi* of Kishangarh was, after his death in 1781, occupied by Birad Singhji and his son Pratab Singhji, but the former was recognized as *de facto* ruler. This joint administration continued for 16 years, that is, until Birad Singhji's death in 1788, when he was succeeded by his son, Kalyan Singhji, who ruled for 41 years. In the early part of the nineteenth century this Maharaja entered into a treaty with the British Government in connection with a general scheme for the suppression of Pindari marauders, by whom the province of Rajputana was at that time overrun.

LIEUT.-COL. H.H. UMDAE RAJHAE BALAND MAKAN SINGH BAHADUR, K.C.S.I., K.C.I.E., THE PRESENT MAHARAJA.

Maharaja Kalyan Singhji, who was a weak ruler, became involved in trouble with his nobles, and this misfortune eventually resulted in his flight to Delhi. Affairs fell into great disorder at Kishangarh, and eventually Kalyan Singhji abdicated in favour of his son, Mokham Singhji. The latter ruled for only two years, and was succeeded in 1840 by his adopted son, Maharaja Dhiraj Prithvi Singhji, who died in 1879, and who conducted the administration with marked ability and success. The present State Council, as well as many other administrative reforms owe their existence to this Ruler. On his death he was succeeded in January, 1879, by the late Maharaja Sardul Singhji, who ruled until his death in 1900, having continued the enlightened policy of his predecessor.

The present Ruler, His Highness Maharaja Madan Singhji, is the only son of the late Maharaja Sardul Singhji. He was born on November 1, 1884, and was 16 years of age when he succeeded to the *gadi* in 1900. He received a good English education under private tutors. His Highness was a member of the Imperial Cadet Corps from January 1902 to January 1904, and was invested with full ruling powers on December 11, 1905. The Maharaja received an Honorary Captaincy in the British Army in March, 1908, and was created K.C.I.E. in January, 1909. He became a Major in the Army in 1911, and in December of the same year he received the title of K.C.S.I. When the Great War broke out His Highness placed the whole of the resources of his State at the disposal of the British Government, and proceeded on military duty to Flanders on August 29, 1914, and returned to Kishangarh on February 22, 1915. In August, 1917, he became a Lieut.-Colonel in the British Army.

His Highness—whose full title is His Highness the Maharaja Sir Madan Singh Bahadur, K.C.I.E., K.C.S.I. — married, firstly, the daughter of the Maharana of Udaipur, by whom he has not had any children, and secondly the sister-in-law of His Highness the late Maharaja of Bhavnagar, by whom he has three daughters.

His Highness is a keen sportsman, and has the reputation of being one of the most renowned polo players in India.

The salute of Maharajas of Kishangarh consists of 15 guns, and they are entitled to pay and receive visits from His Excellency the Viceroy of India. In January 1921 the present Maharaja received an additional personal salute of two guns. The State does not pay tribute to the British Government. The history of the State from the time His Highness came to the *gadi* comprises the initiation and consolidation of the various reforms and improvements inaugurated by his late father, among which may be mentioned the systematic reorganization of the various Courts of Law and of the Police, which has resulted in the diminution of crime and the maintenance of law and order, the improvement and simplification of the system of accounts and audit, the institution and popularization of the Court of Wards, which at present administers the estates of five *Thikan*, 131 *Jagirdars*, and nine private individuals, the organization of the Forest Department, the establishment of more satisfactory central distillery system in the *abkari* arrangements, the improvement of the Customs and Revenue departments, and the inauguration of a better method of preparing revenue returns, together with the introduction of liberal rules for the extension of cultivation. The opening of schools and hospitals and the support of a central jail on a reformed basis, and the increase of masonry irrigation *bunds* throughout the State, and more modern currency arrangements are other matters which have not been overlooked.

The revenue, excluding *jagir* lands, is about Rs. 6,00,000. The Durbar local currency has been abolished in favour of the Imperial coinage, which was introduced in the State in November 1913.

There are no natural lakes in the State, but there are numerous artificial ones, called *bunds*, some of which were constructed many years ago. Two of the latter are situated near the capital, on one of which, the Goondlaw (a picturesque sheet of water) the town of Kishangarh, the Maharaja Fort, and the palace and gardens are situated. A good road suitable for vehicles has been constructed round it, and from this point of vantage a fine view of the *bund*, the city and surrounding hills can be obtained. This *bund* is more than a square mile in extent, and although its catchment area was formerly very limited, it has from time to time been extended, and it now extends to over 20 square miles. There are altogether 207 artificial tanks scattered throughout the State, including *jagir* lands, formed by masonry dams or mud *bunds* thrown across rivers and gullies or by long embankments over low lands. The water held by these reservoirs during the monsoon season enables the agriculturist to irrigate his fields and benefit his crops; but during scanty rains the tanks become dry.

The State is divided for administrative purposes into four districts, namely, Rupnagarh, Kishangarh, Arain and Sarwar.

The Bombay-Baroda and Central India Railway passes through the State, running past the capital near the new town of Madanganj, where the railway station is situated about 1½ miles distant from Kishangarh town.

A substantial fair-weather road, maintained by the British Government, has been constructed from Nasirabad through the Sarwar district or southern portion of the State towards Deoli. The Grand Trunk metalled road leads from Ajmer and passes the capital and the railway station at Madanganj, and is continued to Jaipur and Agra.

In addition, there is an unmetalled road which traverses the entire length of the State from Rupnagarh in the north to Sarwar in the south. There is also a road, which was constructed as a famine relief work, leading from the capital to Srinagar in the Ajmer-Merwara district.

The climate of Kishangarh is similar to that of Ajmer, and is dry and healthy, although in October and November malarial fever is prevalent.

The rainfall is very precarious and uncertain.

There are no extensive forests in Kishangarh, the present area being about 31,200 acres, with an average yearly revenue of Rs. 27,500, derived mainly from the sale of wood, hay and the pods of various kinds of acacia, which are used as fodder.

The Silora stone quarries near Kishangarh supply good roofing slabs, which are pronounced by expert authorities to be as good if not better than the Agra red sandstone slabs.

There are four Imperial post offices in the State, namely, Kishangarh City, Madanganj, Rupnagarh and Sarwar, and these, with the exception of Rupnagarh, are connected with telegraph systems.

There is also a Raj postal system in force in the State, with 21 offices in existence.

Trade in Kishangarh declined since the introduction of the railway, which had the effect of concentrating trade at large commercial centres. In order to remedy this the Durbar reformed the *octroi* system restricting the imposition of duty to a few articles only and making all others free.

The lace industry has for a long time been of some importance in Kishangarh, and a factory which has been working for some years is doing well. There is also a soap manufactory at the capital, which has acquired a good reputation, the products finding a market in all parts of India.

THE STATE OF KISHANGARH.

1. Bird's-eye View of the City from Chauburja. 2. H.H. Maharaja Pirthwi Singh Bahadur (Grandfather of the Present Maharaja). 3. H.H. Maharaja Sardul Singh Bahadur, G.C.I.E. (Father of the Present Maharaja). 4. The Fort, Kishangarh 5. Goondolas Lake.

THE STATE OF KISHANGARH.

1. The Majhela Palace. 2. The Mitra Niwas (Guest House). 3. The Yagbhawan Kothi. 4. The Phul Mahal Palace.

THE STATE OF KISHANGARH.

1. The Mokham Bilas. 2. Buland Durwana. 3. The Chauburja. 4. The Rupnagar Fort and Palace.

Apart from the indigenous industries, the establishment of mills and factories as joint-stock concerns, with limited liabilities, under a local Company's Act (adapted from the Indian Companies Act) has been encouraged, and in connection with this project the following may be mentioned: a steam hydraulic cotton press and ginning factory at Kishangarh and Sarwar, and the Maharaja Kishangarh Some-Yag Spinning and Weaving Mills Company at Kishangarh, from each of which the State receives a considerable royalty.

About two-thirds of the entire area of the State has been permanently alienated, and is held by *Sirdars* and *Jagirdars* on service tenure, or by *Maufidars* and religious charitable institutions.

There are 567 service *Jagirdars*, who are required to supply for State use when required 770 horses.

There is a Maharaja School at Kishangarh, with a boarding establishment attached, which teaches up to the middle standard of the Allahabad University in both the vernacular and Anglo-vernacular departments.

As this school is located in the city, the *Durbar* has arranged to build a new one called the King Edward Memorial School in a very favourable position in the near suburbs. The foundation stone was recently laid by the Honourable the Agent to the Governor-General in Rajputana. There are 23 mofussil schools, those at the headquarters of the districts being vernacular middle schools, and those at the *tahsils halkabandi* schools.

The State mint has been closed for silver coinage since the British Imperial rupee was introduced into the State, but gold mohurs are still coined.

For administrative purposes there are four constituted branches in the State, namely, the Huzuri, Revenue, Public Works and Judicial Departments.

Small as the State of Kishangarh is in area and resources, in point of "Izzat" and reputation it ranks very high in Rajputana, and as far as administration is concerned it is one of the most advanced in that Province; but it is not by any means an easy matter to administer such a State, in which the area is so small, the soil in so many parts sandy and unproductive, the population so scanty, the rainfall so precarious and limited, and where drought and famine have constantly to be faced. In spite of all difficulties—including an expenditure which almost equals the revenue—to be contended against, the State is well administered and is in a prosperous condition.

THE STATE OF PARTABGARH

PARTABGARH, formerly known as the Kanthal, that is, the border or boundary between Malwa and Gujarat, is one of the three Sisodia States in the charge of the Political Agent in the Southern Rajputana States.

The Rulers of Partabgarh trace their descent from one Bika, a descendant of Rana Mokal of Mewar, who relinquished the estates which he possessed in that territory about the year 1553, and, proceeding in a southerly direction, subdued a number of aboriginals and established himself in the conquered tract. In 1561 he founded the town of Deolia, or Deogarh, which was named after Devi Mimi, a local Chieftainess, and he subsequently overpowered Rajput Chiefs residing further to the east and south. About two generations later Jaswant Singh, in the direct line from Bika, was so powerful and was regarded as so dangerous a foe that he was invited to Udaipur, where he and his eldest son were treacherously murdered; the Kanthal was thereafter occupied by Mewar troops. Hari Singh, second son of Jaswant, journeyed to Delhi in 1634, where his personal character and abilities, supported by the influence of Mahabat Khan, gained for him a position of honour at the Court of the Emperor Jehangir. He was subsequently recognized by Shah Jahan as an independent Chief, he agreeing to pay an annual tribute of Rs. 15,000. He at the same time was granted the title of *Haft hazari*, or Commander of 7,000, and the further title of Maharawat.

Aided by Imperial forces, Hari Singh returned to Mewar, and expelled the garrison occupying the town of Deolia, and succeeded in subjugating the surrounding country. He died in 1674, and was followed by his son Pratap Singh, who about 20 years later founded the town of Partabgarh, which gave its name to the State, although many people still make use of Kanthal, the early designation, or they frequently refer both in speaking and writing to Deolia-Partabgarh, thus combining the former and present capitals of the State. At the close of the eighteenth century the country was overrun by the Mahrattas, and the State was only saved by the Maharawat agreeing to pay to Holkar a tribute of *salim shahi* of Rs. 72,720 in lieu of the sum of Rs. 15,000 formerly paid to the Emperor of Delhi.

The first occasion on which the State came into touch with the British Government was in 1804, but the preliminary treaty then made was cancelled by Lord Cornwallis, the Governor-General of India, in 1818, in favour of a new agreement which extended to Partabgarh the protection of the Imperial Power.

The next Ruler, Sawant Singh, was followed in succession by Dalpat Singh (1844–64) and Udai Singh (1864–90).

The present Chief is His Highness Maharaja Dhiraj Maharawat Sri Sir Raghunath Singhji Bahadur, K.C.I.E., who belongs to the Sisodia clan of Rajputs, and is related by blood to the ruling families of Udaipur, Dungarpur and Banswara, and by marriage to the Chiefs of Bikaner, Khetri (Jaipur), Pisangan (Ajmer), Semlia and Sailana (Central India), Terhi in Garhwal, and Dhrangadhra in Kathiawar.

The Chief has the sovereign power of passing sentences of death. He enjoys the right of adoption, although his subordinate *jagirdars*, in default of male issue, cannot adopt successors without the consent of the Durbar. The annual tribute payable to the British Government (in two instalments) is Rs. 36,350 in British currency. The *jagirdars* of the State pay tribute to the Durbar of nearly Rs. 20,000.

One of the most disastrous famines ever known in Rajputana occurred in 1899–90, and in consequence the inhabitants of the State were reduced to a most deplorable condition. His Highness promptly organized an efficient system of giving relief to his distressed subjects, and advances to agriculturists and remissions and suspensions of land revenue caused a loss to the State treasury of more than Rs. 1,50,000.

In 1911 the late Maharaj Kumar Mansinghji Bahadur was a guest as a representative of His Highness at the great Durbar at Delhi, and took part in the Coronation festivities of Their Imperial Majesties the King-Emperor and Queen-Empress. In October of the same year Maharaj Kumar Shri Man Singhji Bahadur was united in marriage to the daughter of the Maharaja of Tehri-Garhwal and grand-daughter of His Excellency the Maharaja Deb Shum Shere Jung Bahadur Rana, ex-Minister and Commander-in-Chief of Nepal. The Chief's younger son, Maharaj Kumar Gordhan Singh, is the Maharaj of Arnaud, and he was married in February 1917 to the daughter of the Thakore of Mahanser in Jaipur.

During the lifetime of Maharaj Kumar Mansingh the administration of the State was conducted under his direction and supervision. He evinced a keen interest in every branch of State work, and by the introduction of a large number of useful reforms promoted the happiness and well-being of the people. His death took place in October 1918.

His Highness the Maharawat is entitled to a salute of 15 guns.

The area of the State of Partabgarh is 886 square miles. The population is 67,110

HIS HIGHNESS THE MAHARAWAT SIR RAGHUNATH SINGHJI BAHADUR, K.C.I.E., OF PARTABGARH

1. MAHARAJ KUNWAR MANSINGHJI.
DIED OCTOBER 29, 1918.
2. BHANWARLAL RAM SINGHJI, THE HEIR-APPARENT.
3. YOUNGER MAHARAJ KUNWAR GORDHAN SINGHJI.

THE STATE OF PARTABGARH.

1. His Highness's Palace at Deolia. 2. His Highness's Palace at Partabgarh. 3. Udey Niwas Palace at Partabgarh Fort. 4. City Palace at Partabgarh.

THE STATE OF PARTABGARH.

1. Raghunath Hospital, Partabgarh. 2. Pinhey Nobles' School, Partabgarh. 3. Mahadeo's Dipnath, Partabgarh. 4. Bird's-eye View of Partabgarh City. 5. Gotamnath Temple, Gotmeshwar.

souls; and it is bounded on the north and north-east by the States of Udaipur, Indore and Gwalior; on the south and south-east by Gwalior territory and the Piploda estates; on the east by the States of Gwalior and Jaora; and on the west by the States of Udaipur and Banswara.

The greater portion of the State consists of a fine stretch of fertile plain, but the north-western tract is hilly. Towards the western border stand a range of hills. This tract is well-wooded, the principal trees being teak, blackwood, *pipal*, and *babul*, but sandalwood—which is a State monopoly—is found extensively in southern districts.

The revenue for land in the State is paid in cash, the amounts being based upon survey and a settlement made in the year 1906.

The principal crops are wheat, sugar-cane, maize, *jowar*, *gram*, barley, cotton, linseed and opium.

Water for irrigation of the land is obtained chiefly from 2,000 wells in the *khalsa* portion of the State.

Partabgarh is noted for its enamelled work of gold upon glass and for other lacquered articles, all of which are keenly sought after by visitors. Its manufactured goods comprise coarse cotton fabrics and black woollen blankets. There is a factory for the ginning of cotton at the capital town.

The State does not yet possess the advantage of having any railway system within its borders, the nearest station being Mandasor, 20 miles distant on the Rajputana–Malwa line, which is connected with the capital by a good metalled road.

The highest Court of Judicature is the State Council, or Raj Sabha, consisting of the Diwan as a Chairman, and seven other members. This Court has full original and appellate jurisdiction in civil and criminal cases, and it is also empowered to make laws and regulations subject to the approval of His Highness the Maharawat Sahib. Appeals are made to the Chief from the decisions of the Raj Sabha and for revision of its orders in cases in which that Court has exercised powers in original suits.

Subordinate to the Raj Sabha are the courts of first-class and second-class magistrates.

The principal *jagirdars*, namely, Dhamotar, Raipur, Arnaud, Salamgarh, Achlaoda, Jhantla, and Bardia, are invested with second-class magisterial and limited civil powers in their own estates, and all appeals against their decisions lie with the civil and criminal judges of the State.

The educational establishments maintained by the State are: the "Pinhey" Nobles' school, and the Raj Verna school at Partabgarh, the Deogarh Verna school, and nine village schools; but in addition there are seven private vernacular *path-shalas* at Partabgarh, Deolia and elsewhere.

The "Pinhey" school prepares boys for the Rajputana Middle examination, and for the English branch of the Matriculation examination of the Allahabad University. Attached to this institution is a boarding-house for the sons of *jagirdars* and other Rajput boys. Athletic exercises and games such as cricket, football and tennis are played on the school grounds.

The whole of the cost of boarding, lodging and clothing for the residents in the hostel is borne by the State.

The late Maharaj Kumar Sahib took great interest in educational matters.

The Court of Wards, which is supervised by the Revenue Officer, has several estates under management.

The gross annual revenues of the State average Rs. 6,00,000, including deposits.

THE STATE OF RAMPUR

RAMPUR is an independent State in Rohilkhand, under the political superintendence of the Government of the United Provinces of Agra and Oudh, and pays no tribute to the British Government. It has an area of 892 square miles and a population of approximately 531,200 inhabitants, of whom the majority are Mahomedans. The cadastral survey of Rampur was undertaken at State expense by the Government of India, and was completed in 1892. The total area is practically a level and fertile tract of country, with an abundant supply of water in the north, the direction of the rivers which traverse the State being from north to south and south-east. The principal of these rivers are three—the Ramganga, the Kosi, and the Gangan, but in addition to these there are several smaller streams which serve to irrigate the northern portions of the State. Here, as in many other parts of India, the greatest difficulty is to contend with the varying courses of the rivers, which in the low-lying tracts is always a serious problem to solve, for it should be borne in mind that the State capital is less than 5,000 feet above sea-level. The Ramganga receives the waters of both the Kosi and Gangan in State territory, and is itself a tributary of the mighty Ganges.

The history of the State is full of interest. It is the sole survival of what may be termed the Rohilla State, which was a tract of country subjugated by the Rohilla Afghans. In the early days of the Moghul Emperors the portion of Rohilkhand which now forms the Rampur State was in the province of Delhi. Bareilly was then practically unknown, and Rampur was merely a Hindu village under another name. The country was then called Katehr, a term still sometimes applied to the upland portion of Rohilkhand. It was held by the Katehriya Rajputs, of whom large numbers are still found in Rampur. They were a very turbulent people, and were constantly coming into violent conflict with the early Emperors of Delhi, and one of the first records of this is in A.D. 1253–4, when Nasir-ud-Din Mahmud sent an army across the Ramganga to pillage Katehr in a manner " that the inhabitants might not forget for the rest of their lives," and which was repeated in 1266. The Katehriyas slowly recovered from these attacks, and in 1379 murdered the Moghul Governor at Budaun, and this act infuriated the then Emperor, Firoz Shah, to such an extent that he laid waste the whole country, which was converted into a jungle. The Rajputs, however, re-established themselves some few years later, and strife with Delhi was a usual thing until the days of Humayun, who captured the new fort of Bareilly and subdued the Katehriyas. During the troublous times after Aurungzeb's death, the Hindu Chiefs once more asserted themselves, and it was then that the real history of Rampur commenced. The country had become populated by a considerable number of Afghan settlers, who had been given grants of land in return for military services, and in addition to these there were numbers of vagrants, chiefly in search of employment, but each owning his horse and accoutrements, who were prepared to enter the employ of any one provided prospects were sufficiently alluring. These Afghans were named Rohillas, signifying mountaineers or highlanders, and their origin as Chiefs commenced during the reign of Mohammad Muazzam Shah, when an adventurer named Daud Khan arrived in India from Tirah, in Afghanistan, and settled in the Katehr country. He was a son of Shah Alam, the son of Mahmud Khan of Kandahar, a family belonging to the Barech clan, with a reputation for sanctity. Daud Khan was a brave and ambitious man, and taking advantage of the troublous times and with the opportunities which such characteristics offered, he got together a small body of fighting men and made several daring expeditions to various parts of the country, soon establishing a reputation for himself. On one occasion a serious fight took place at Bankauli, in Kabar, and in the raid on this village Daud Khan met a boy of six years of age—named Saiyed Mohammad Ali—whom he adopted. His name was subsequently changed to Nawab Ali Mohammad Khan, according to the custom of the Moghul Court, when his position as Nawab of Rampur was acknowledged by the Emperor. This boy was of Saiyid origin and belonged to a family connected with the Saiyids of Bareha, who had migrated and settled at Bakauli. He was destined to add very considerably to the Rohilla history, beginning eight years thereafter, when he was only 14 years of age, and immediately after Sardar Daud Khan had been murdered by the Raja of Kumaun. He then collected a large force of Afghan adherents and became the most powerful man in Katehr. He neglected no means in his power of strengthening his interests and enlarging his connections, and the circumstances of the time afforded him ample scope for the fulfilment of these views by the most easy and obvious methods. The Court of Delhi, being at

THE RULER OF RAMPUR STATE.
COL. H.H. ALIJAH, FARZAND-I-DILPIZIR-I-DAULAT-I-INGLISHIA, MUKHLIS-UD-DAULAH, NASIR-UL-MULK, AMIR-UL-UMARA NAWAB SIR SYED MOHAMMAD HAMID ALI KHAN BAHADUR, MUSTAID JANG, G.C.I.E., G.C.V.O., A.D.C. TO HIS IMPERIAL MAJESTY THE KING-EMPEROR.

THE STATE OF RAMPUR.

Hamid Manzil Palace, Rampur.

the time distracted by the struggles of contending nobles, had lost much of its power and influence, so that Ali Mohammad Khan, conscious of his strength, showed little attention to imperial mandates, and delayed or avoided on various pretexts any payment of revenue into the royal treasury, employing the income of his lands in raising troops, purchasing artillery and military stores, and, above all, in securing the friendship of many of the principal personages of the province, by a judicious and well-timed liberality. Nor was he remiss in cultivating the attachment of the lower orders by the same practices as enabled him to succeed with their superiors, and he only awaited an opportunity to throw off the mask and openly assert his independence, as most of the Governors in the more distant provinces had already done. He took possession of Daud Khan's estates at Budaun and placed himself in command of Daud Khan's forces; and made friends with Amzat-Ullah, Governor of Moradabad, and with Muin-ud-din, Governor of Bareilly, thereby securing possession of the large village of Mananuna, near Aonla, and after some fighting made himself master of the town and pargana of Aonla, in possession of which he was confirmed by the Prime Minister. This was probably about the year 1719, for in the following year he acquired ownership of Shahjahanpur, and in 1737 he received the title of Nawab from the Emperor Mohammad Shah, with the rank of Commander of 5,000 and the grant of a large portion of Katehr in return for his services against the powerful family of Bareha Sayeds in the Muzaffarnagar district. Taking advantage of the invasion of Nadir Shah in 1739 the Nawab proceeded to further enlarge his possessions, and he annexed Richha, in Bareilly, and some neighbouring *parganas*; but his ever-increasing power had at last attracted attention from Delhi, and in 1741 Raja Harnand, Governor of Moradabad, received orders to eject the Rohillas from Katehr. He was joined by Abd-un-Nabi, Governor of Bareilly, and their united forces numbered 50,000. The Nawab advanced to meet them with only 12,000 men, and in the ensuing battle both the imperial Governors were slain and the Nawab obtained possession of a large portion of the territory now known as Rohilkhand. He was officially recognized as Ruler of Katehr, or Rohilkhand, and in that capacity entered the city of Bareilly. He followed this up by acquiring Pilibhit by ejecting the Banjara Chief, Despat, and in 1743 he invaded and subdued Kumaun, which he rented to the Raja of Garhwal. The power now wielded by the Nawab excited the jealousy of Safdar Jung, the Nawab Wazir of Oudh, who persuaded the Emperor Mohammad Shah to take the field against the Rohillas. Ali Mohammad Khan ultimately surrendered to the Emperor, and he was taken to Delhi, but after six months he was sent to Sirhind as Governor, the Emperor retaining two of his sons as hostages. In 1748, when Ahmad Shah Abdali invaded India, Ali Mohammad Khan seized the opportunity of returning to Rohilkhand, when he was immediately joined by his old retainers and soon regained his former possessions, adding to them the *parganas* of Dhampur and Sherkot, the property of Safdar Jung. He was once more recognized by Delhi as Ruler of Rohilkhand, and appears to have come to some sort of understanding with the Nawab of Oudh, whom he supported in his candidature for the office of Wazir.

Nawab Ali Mohammad Khan died in 1749, but before his death assembled ten of his Chief Sardars and made his will in their presence by which his third son, Sadallah Khan, was to be his successor until, if ever, the two elder sons returned, and the four younger sons were to be placed under the care of a steward, who was nominated at the time. The Sirdars were required to consult together when any common danger required concerted action, and all were sworn to be faithful to the Nawab's children. The Nawab's last measure was to pay off the arrears due to his troops, and he advanced them 25 lakhs of rupees, in return for which each soldier gave his written promise of loyalty to the Nawab's sons. The tomb of His Highness is at Aonla, and is still in a fair state of preservation.

The death of Nawab Ali Mohammad Khan was almost immediately followed by quarrels and intrigues amongst the Rohilla Chiefs, and attacks from neighbouring foes, prominent amongst the latter being the Nawab Wazir of Oudh, but his attempted invasion of 1750 was easily defeated by the late Ruler's veteran leader, Hafiz Rahmat Khan. This was followed by an attack by the Bangash Chief of Farrukhabad, which had been instigated by the Nawab Wazir, but it was doomed to failure, for Rahmat Khan was again victorious, and he followed up these successes by reducing the Tarai country east of Pilibhit before returning to Aonla.

Safdar Jung, however, was determined to avenge himself, and invited aid from the Mahrattas, who, nothing loth, joined the Wazir, and marched with a large army against the Rohillas. In 1751 Saidar Jung occupied Aonla, from which the Rohillas had fled northwards towards the foot of the hills, the country being overrun and ransacked by the Mahrattas. Subsequently the Wazir collected his forces and came up with the Rohillas at Laldhang, where he found them too strongly entrenched to be defeated, so he employed blockading methods pending the arrival of his heavy artillery, which were subsequently found to be as ineffective as his blockade. Some weeks passed without any decisive engagement, and then came the news of Ahmad Shah Abdali's second invasion of India. This enabled a peace to be made in 1752 whereby the Rohillas gave securities for an indemnity of 50 lakhs, together with a yearly tribute of five lakhs, which bonds were handed over to the Mahrattas and served as a pretext for later invasions of Rohilkhand.

Ahmad Shah Abdali left India without approaching Delhi, but having previously taken a friendly interest in Nawab Ali Mohammad Khan, he now sent back the latter's two eldest sons, Abdullah Khan and Faiz-Ullah Khan, with a request that the provisions of their father's will might be observed. This did not meet with the approval of Rohilla Sardars, who immediately realized that by the return of the two sons they would be relieved of a great deal of power, and to retain their authority devised a scheme of carrying out the will in such a manner as to produce friction between the sons, thus eventually restoring their power once more. With this object they divided the State into three parts, each of which was assigned jointly to two brothers. Thus Abdullah Khan and Murtaza Khan, the eldest and youngest sons, received Aonla, Faiz-Ullah Khan and Mohammad Yar Khan, Bareilly, and Sadulla Khan and Allah Yar Khan, Moradabad. This soon led to quarrels, as was anticipated, and gave the Sardars an excuse for a fresh partition of the country. Nawab Sadulla Khan was made the nominal head of the State, Nawab Abdullah Khan received a large portion of Budaun, and Nawab Faiz-Ullah Khan most of Rampur and Chhajlet in Bareilly. Murtaza Khan left the country in disgust, and Mohammad Yar Khan, who is not

THE STATE OF RAMPUR.

Khushru Bagh Palace.

mentioned, was probably absent at the time of distribution. Allah Yar Khan died almost immediately afterwards in 1754.

With the reign of Nawab Faiz-Ullah Khan, the actual history of Rampur begins. He appears to have remained in possession of his dominions, but was for years constantly engaged in war in company with the rest of the Rohillas. In 1758, after the third departure from India of Ahmad Shah Abdali, the Mahrattas overran the Punjab, and in the following year they entered the Duab and laid waste the Saharanpur possessions of Najib-ud-Daula. The Mahrattas then crossed the Ganges and devastated the whole of Bijnor and Moradabad. The Rohilla Chiefs could offer no effective resistance and were compelled to retreat to the Tarai, whence they sought assistance from Shuja-ud-Daula, the Nawab Wazir of Oudh, who came to their aid, and the combined forces, in November, 1759, drove the Mahrattas across the Ganges, after inflicting severe losses upon them. Shortly after this Ahmad Shah Abdali invaded India once more, and the Mahrattas advanced to meet him, whilst the Rohillas collected all the troops they could muster and set out to join Ahmad Shah, forming the right wing of his army. At the Battle of Panipat in 1761 the Mahrattas were routed, and the Rohillas were rewarded for their bravery, particularly in the first onset, by the grants of Shikohabad to Nawab Faiz-Ullah Khan and Jalesar and Ferozabad to Nawab Sadullah Khan. The latter died in 1764, and was buried in Aonla, and in the following year the famous warrior, Rahmat Khan, who had reluctantly joined Shuja-ud-Daula against the English, was defeated at Kora by Colonel Carnac, and peace was concluded with the English in August, 1765. The next five years were peaceable, but in 1770 a succession of misfortunes began which almost extinguished the Rohilla power. Rahmat Khan lost Etah and other territory in the Duab to the Mahrattas, and in the same year Najib-ud-Daula and Dunde Khan died, the latter being an old retainer of the State, who was made Commander-in-Chief of its forces by the late Nawab Ali Mohammad Khan. This was followed in 1771 by a Mahratta invasion of the Bijnor territory, with which the Rohilla Chiefs were unable to cope, and they therefore sought a renewal of the alliance with the Nawab Wazir of Oudh as the only possible way out of the difficulty, and in the meantime retreated to the forests of the Tarai. The Wazir declined to interfere unless Rahmat Khan came in person to make terms with him, his object being undoubtedly to seize Rohilkhand for himself, but Sir Robert Barker, who was in command of the English contingent, persuaded him to come to the help of the Rohillas, and Captain Harper was sent to fetch Hafiz Rahmat Khan when a treaty was made, on June 15, 1772, which was countersigned by Sir Robert Barker. By it Shuja-ud-Daula undertook to drive the Mahrattas out of Rohilkhand for a consideration of 40 lakhs of rupees, to which Rahmat Khan agreed.

This agreement, sealed in the presence of General Sir Robert Barker, is a most important document in Rohilla history, for the non-fulfilment of its conditions by both parties led ultimately to the ruin of the Rohillas, which was partly caused by dissensions amongst the Chiefs themselves. Rahmat Khan declined to pay the sum promised as the Wazir had entered into no negotiations with the Mahrattas, neither did he venture to attack them, but, on the contrary, returned towards Fyzabad, thus leaving the Rohillas an easy prey to the Mahrattas, whose demands they were forced to satisfy. As a result of this, Hafiz Rahmat Khan sent a letter of explanation to Warren Hastings, which he concluded by saying that "as a friendship has long been established between us, I doubt not but you will at all times and on all occasions wish to preserve it. Other particulars the Major will inform you of," but obviously little attention was paid to this. Shuja-ud-Daula, after pressing in vain for payment of money not earned by him, attacked Rohilkhand after having obtained a promise of assistance from Warren Hastings. The result was that the Rohillas were completely defeated near Shahjahanpur, where the gallant Hafiz Rahmat Khan was slain. Nawab Faiz-Ullah Khan was forced to retreat to Aonla, and from thence with his family and treasure through the Tarai to Laldhang, on the northern borders of the Bijnor district, where he entrenched himself, and was for some time besieged by the English forces and Shuja-ud-Daula. Eventually, in 1774, a treaty was concluded, at the instigation of the English Commander, Colonel Champion, whereby Nawab Faiz-Ullah Khan was secured in possession of the State of Rampur.

This treaty was renewed under British guarantee in 1778, and was soon followed by a very striking incident when Nawab Faiz-Ullah-Khan came forward to the Governor-General with the offer of all his cavalry, 2,000 strong, when England had declared war against France. He was under no obligation to do this, and it is probably one of the very first occasions when a ruling Chief in this part of India spontaneously came to the assistance of England, a tradition which has been nobly upheld by his House ever since. This offer was acknowledged by the Governor-General in his letter of January 8, 1779, wherein he said that "in his own name, as well as that of the Board, he returned him the warmest thanks for this instance of his faithful attachment to the company and the English nation."

In 1780 the Nawab was asked by the Wazir to supply a contingent of 5,000 men in terms of the treaty, but in 1783 this condition was withdrawn in time of war in exchange for monetary consideration of 15 lakhs, in accordance with an agreement concluded on February 17, 1783, by Major William Palmer.

Nawab Faiz-Ullah Khan died in 1793 after a reign of nearly 20 years, and was buried in a tomb to the north of the city outside the Idgah gate. He was a soldier, statesman, and administrator, qualities which were specially needed during his reign, for without them he could not have held his possessions. He was succeeded by his son, Nawab Mohammad Ali Khan, who was 43 years of age at the time. The new Ruler was a man of hasty disposition and ungovernable temper, and in the course of a few days made himself so unpopular that the Rohilla Sardars determined to replace him by his brother, Nawab Ghulam Mohammad Khan, a man of polished manners and in every respect eminently suited to succeed his father. On August 14, 1793, the Sardars marched to the Nawab's palace with 500 men, and entering the Council Chamber bade Mohammad Ali Khan descend from the throne. The Nawab drew his sword and resisted, but was overpowered and removed to his private apartments, when Nawab Ghulam Mohammad Khan was requested to take his place on the *masnad*. Mohammad Ali Khan was transferred to the fortress of Dungarpur, about two miles from the city, where he was shortly afterwards shot dead in his sleep. His tomb is in the Madrasa Muhalla and has recently been repaired.

The State was now held under British guarantee, and when the news of Mohammad Ali Khan's downfall was received, the Furrukhabad brigade, under Sir Robert Abercrombie, was lent to the Wazir, Asaf-

THE STATE OF RAMPUR.

Offices and Court.

ud-Daula, in order that the new Ruler might be deposed and Ahmad Ali Khan, the infant son of Mohammad Ali Khan, installed on the throne. Asaf-ud-Daula had already communicated with Nawab Ghulam Mohammad Khan, demanding that he should make an allowance of Rs. 25,000 per *mensem* to Ahmad Ali Khan, who would reside in Lucknow, and, in addition, pay a fine of 24 lakhs. These terms were refused by the Rohillas, though it is believed Nawab Ghulam Mohammad Khan was not adverse to such an agreement, for he fully realized the danger of his position, but, nevertheless, was induced by his followers to take the field. He collected some 25,000 men and marched towards Bareilly, taking up a position at Bhitaura, about two miles distant from the British. In the fight which followed the Rohillas fought valiantly, but were ultimately routed by the better trained and disciplined British troops, though not before inflicting severe casualties, for the British losses were 14 officers and a considerable number of men killed. A monument was erected over their graves at Bhitaura, which was renamed Fatehganj, in honour of the victory, and is still to be seen. Asaf-ud-Daula joined General Abercrombie after the battle and advanced into Rampur as far as Ajitpur, two miles south of the capital. Ahmad Ali Khan was then proclaimed Nawab, and Ghulam Mohammad Khan went on a pilgrimage to Mecca. He eventually died in 1828 at Nadaun, near Kangra, in the Punjab. Nawab Ahmad Ali Khan was confirmed in possession of the city of Rampur and lands yielding a revenue of ten lakhs a year, the rest of the State being appropriated by the Nawab Wazir, and the treaty to this effect was signed on November 29, 1794. By its terms Nasrullah Khan, son of Nawab Abdulla Khan, was appointed Regent and guardian of Nawab Ahmad Ali Khan until the latter came of age.

Nasrullah Khan held the office of Regent for 16 years, and his administration was popular and fairly successful, it never being interfered with by the Nawab Ahmad Ali Khan. Nasrullah Khan died in 1225 Hijra, and was buried in a tomb outside the Nawab gate of the city.

In 1801 Rohilkhand was ceded to the British Government, but this did not affect the status and rights of the Nawab, who was simple in his habits and extremely popular with the people gere ally, owing to his generosity and daring, and his love of shooting, hunting, and other manly sports. After a rule of about 40 years he died in 1840, on the anniversary of his succession, and was buried in the village of Nankar, two miles from the city. He had no male heirs and only one daughter, who could claim no right to the throne. This problem was solved by Mr. Robinson, the then Commissioner of Rohilkhand, who proposed that Mohammad Said Khan, eldest son of Ghulam Mohammad Khan, should succeed. This candidate was then serving as a Deputy-Collector at Budaun, and the nomination being confirmed by Lord William Bentinck, the Governor-General, he was installed on the *masnad* on August 20, 1840, after giving an undertaking to govern the State, establishing Courts of Justice, and organising a regular army and important fiscal measures, which resulted in great improvement of the land revenue and in untold relief to the cultivators. He was both a soldier and a scholar, and as a result of his training in the British service, paid very much more attention than his predecessors to the internal administration of the State. He died on April 1, 1855, at the age of 75, after a reign of 15 years, and his tomb is near the new palace in the fort. He left five sons, the eldest of whom, Mohammad Yusuf Ali Khan, was nominated as his successor.

Nawab Mohammad Yusuf Ali Khan was 40 years old when he succeeded to the *masnad* of Rampur. He inherited the administrative capacity of his father, and even excelled him as a statesman. An engagement similar to that given by his father was also given by him, and he justified the trust reposed in him by proving himself a faithful friend to the British Government during the troublous times of the Mutiny, when he not only managed his own territory successfully, but also took charge of the Moradabad district, where he rendered excellent service. In the dark days of 1857 when the whole country was in a state of hopeless chaos, Rohilkhand had its full share of the troubles. Every means of obtaining assistance and maintaining communications had been swept away, and the European officers derived incalculable aid from the support freely afforded them by the Nawab of Rampur. He supplied them with an abundant quantity of provisions and also with gold and silver to the amount they required. He kept a vigilant watch over the movements of the secret agents of the mutineers who visited Rampur State, and it required no little tact to thwart their mission and defeat their intrigues without taking any overt action. Secret communications were continually passing between the local Pathan leaders and their relatives in Bareilly, Bijnor, and Moradabad districts. The Nawab was confronted with the difficult task of making his people understand that the cause of their religion was not bound up with the rebellion, yet he succeeded in preventing any open revolt in Rampur, while he himself did all in his power to help the British Government to suppress the rebellion and restore order and tranquillity. The herculean efforts thus made told very severely upon his health, as is shown by the following letter from Mr. Alexander, then Commissioner of Rohilkhand, in describing a visit paid to the Nawab. He says, "the Nawab's whole mind was devoted to this policy as much as was the attention of any statesman or warrior throughout the same eventful time, and one result to himself personally was in grievous failure of health. Previous to meeting him on April 18th I was told to be prepared for a considerable change in his appearance, and I can only state that notwithstanding this preparation I was much shocked by the very evident signs of the effect which labour and anxiety had had on him." It is interesting to note that the feeling which actuated the Nawab to adopt such a noble and sagacious course was wholly spontaneous, and was not due to the suggestion of any one of his subordinates. It was he, and he alone, who was responsible for the wise and careful administration of the affairs of the State at this critical period.

On the outbreak of the Mutiny, realizing the nature of the approaching troubles, and wishing to keep in prompt and constant touch with events, the Nawab resolved to maintain a thorough supervision of all the divisions of work involved.

One of the most remarkable features in the whole course of events was the manner in which secure means of communication for the British officers was invariably maintained. The Nawab sent his own servants to act as postmen, and also kept the British authorities constantly informed of the movement of the mutineers by means of confidential agents despatched to such centres of revolt as Delhi, Lucknow, and Bareilly.

It so happened that a number of European officers, ladies, and children had entrusted their lives and safety to the

THE STATE OF RAMPUR.

Machi Bhawan Palace.

Nawab at a time when to assist them in any way was looked upon as positive sacrilege. Naini Tal was the refuge of a large number of Europeans, and the Nawab appointed his own trusted agents to look after their comforts and see that none of their requirements were neglected. For this purpose His Highness deputed Ali Bakhsh Khan to visit Naini Tal and minister to the wants of the Europeans there, and this gentleman carried out his master's instructions with much ability and zeal.

It is interesting to note that the representatives of the European community resident in Kumaun held a meeting, with General Sir William Richards, K.C.B., in the chair, and recorded their gratitude to His Highness the Nawab in the following resolution:

"The members of this meeting representing the European community resident in Kumaun, are anxious to record the expression of hearty thanks to His Highness the Nawab of Rampur, who, during their forced exclusion from the plains for the past six months, has, by the supply of the comforts and necessaries of life and other acts of goodwill, shown towards them a staunch and active friendship. This meeting, desirous to present to His Highness the Nawab some token in memorial of its grateful appreciation of his conduct, resolved that a subscription paper be circulated for benefit of all uniting with it in this object, wherewith to purchase a vase or other piece of plate with suitable inscription."

The upshot of this was a handsome silver ornament suitably inscribed, which has an honoured place amongst the many treasures the new palace contains.

Another most important task undertaken by the Nawab was the administration of the Moradabad and other neighbouring districts on behalf of the British Government. Mr. Alexander writes:

"This administration was conducted by the Nawab with as near adherence to the system and principles of our own Government as circumstances could admit of, so that judicial, revenue, and police functionaries were continued at their posts, and the two last departments were in working operation throughout the tenure of the district by the Nawab."

The supreme Government showed itself well aware of the valuable and meritorious services rendered by Nawab Yusuf Ali Khan throughout the Mutiny, and acknowledged these services publicly in a Durbar held at Fatehgarh. Her Majesty's Government was also pleased to grant to the Rampur State an *ilaqa* yielding an annual income of Rs. 1,28,527, taken from the Bareilly and Moradabad districts. Besides this, a *khilat* of Rs. 20,000 was conferred upon the Nawab, and the prefix of Farzand-i-Dilpizir was added to his title.

In 1861 Nawab Yusuf Ali Khan Bahadur was created a Knight Commander of the Most Exalted Order of the Star of India by Her Majesty the late Queen Victoria, and in the following year he was appointed an additional member of Lord Elgin's Council. He died on April 21, 1865, after a reign of a little over 10 years, and was buried in the *Imambara* in the fort. He left three sons, of whom the eldest, Kalb Ali Khan Bahadur, succeeded to the throne when he was 31 years of age. He entered into an engagement similar to that of his predecessors, and his loyalty to the British throne was as marked as that of his father. He was a Persian and Arabic scholar of great repute, so much so that some of his poems were sent to Teheran, and were much praised by the poets there. He was a liberal patron of learning, and by his generosity did much to promote the cause of education, and in addition he was an exceedingly able administrator and greatly increased the financial resources of the State. He was appointed a member of Lord Lawrence's Council, but was compelled to leave Calcutta owing to indifferent health. He was a man of remarkably sound judgment, and his ability to form a correct estimate of the capabilities of his fellow men enabled him to make a most judicious selection of his officials, notably of Ali Asghar Khan, the Commander-in-Chief, and Usman Khan, the Prime Minister. In 1872, when Nawab, Kalb Ali Khan went on a pilgrimage to Mecca, and Medina Usman Khan held the reins of government, but he was eventually assassinated at a religious gathering in the Jama Masjid. The original mosque was erected by Nawab Kalb Ali Khan, but the present Nawab has entirely enlarged and made it far more beautiful than the former structure, the cost of the work being over three lakhs of rupees. The Nawab, unlike his father, was a strict *Sunni*.

In 1875 His Highness went to Agra to meet His late Majesty King Edward VII, then visiting India as Prince of Wales. He received at the hands of His Royal Highness the insignia of the Knight Grand Commander of the Most Exalted Order of the Star of India. In the Imperial assemblage at Delhi in 1877 the Nawab received a standard, and his personal salute was raised from 13 to 15 guns. In 1878 he was created a Companion of the Indian Empire. Towards the end of his reign Nawab Sir Kalb Ali Khan was to a great extent an invalid, in fact, from 1875 onwards, he was a victim to continued ill-health, although he still kept the government in his own hands and personally administered the affairs of the State. In 1878 he lost through death the services of General Ali Asghar Khan, and appointed as his successor Azimud-din Khan, who was related through his mother to the Ruling House. The Nawab died on March 23, 1887, at the age of 53, after a reign of 22½ years, and was buried in the mausoleum of Hafiz Jamal-Ullah, where 100 persons daily attend his tomb to recite passages from the Koran. He had five sons, the two eldest of whom, Bande Ali Khan, and Akbar Ali Khan, died in infancy. The third son, Zulfiqar Ali Khan, died in 1871, at the age of 16 years, while in 1880 his fourth son, Sahibzada Mushtaq Ali Khan, was recognized by Government as heir-apparent, and he succeeded his father when, like him, he had reached the age of 31 years. Just before ascending the *masnad* he had a severe stroke of paralysis from which he never really recovered, despite the best medical skill obtainable, and, as a consequence of poor health, appointed General Azim-ud-Din Khan as his Prime Minister. This appointment was not popular with several members of the Nawab's family, who, in consequence, left Rampur for Moradabad, whence they lodged complaints with the Government of the North-Western Provinces. The Lieutenant-Governor, Sir Auckland Colvin, took steps to redress the grievances, and induced the Nawab to organize a Council of Administration. This Council consisted of His Highness as President, General Azim-ud-Din Khan as Vice-President, Saiyid Ali Hussain, a deputy collector of the North-Western Provinces, as Financial and Revenue Member, and Kunwar Lutf Ali Khan as Judicial Member. The last-named shortly afterwards resigned, and was succeeded by Nawab Yar Jang, who had served in a similar position at Hyderabad. His Highness was unable, through continued ill-health, to take the energetic interest he might otherwise have done in the doings of the Council, but he was fortunate in having got together such progressive ministers. One of their first

THE STATE OF RAMPUR.

Rung Mehal Palace.

efforts was a thorough reform in the land revenue system and in finance, and in the latter instance it should be mentioned that a large sum of money which was lying idle in the reserve treasury was invested in Government paper, which yielded an annual revenue of six lakhs. The army was reorganized by General Azim-ud-Din Khan, who was an enthusiastic reformer, and it was during this reign that the State secured the services of Mr. W. C. Wright as Chief Engineer. Towards the end of January, 1889, the Nawab suffered from another attack of paralysis, from which he never recovered, and he died on February 25th of the same year, leaving two sons, His Highness Nawab Sir Syed Mohammad Hamid Ali Khan Bahadur, the present Ruler, and Sahibzada Nasir Ali Khan.

His Highness the present Nawab was born on August 31st, 1875, and was only 13 years of age when he ascended the *masnad* on February 27, 1889, receiving full powers in 1896. In the meantime, during the minority, a Council of Regency was appointed, with Sahibzada Safdar Ali Khan, son of Nawab Mohammad Said Khan Bahadur, as President, General Azim-ud-Din Khan, Vice-President, Nawab Yar Jang, the Judicial Member, and Saiyid Ali Hussain, Revenue Member. In 1891 the Council was remodelled owing to General Azim-ud-Din Khan having been assassinated in the city when returning from a party given by the sons of Abdullah Khan. The case was immediately investigated, and ultimately four persons were found guilty of murder and executed in 1892. The new Council was formed, with Major H. A. Vincent, of the Central India House, as President, and Sahibzada Hamid-uz-Zafar Khan, the younger brother of the late Vice-President, as Secretary, the old Judicial and Revenue Members retaining their offices until 1892, when Nawab Yar Jang resigned and Sahibzada Wahid-ud-Din was appointed to the vacant post.

In March, 1893, His Highness the Nawab commenced a tour round the world to complete his education and to gain an insight into the underlying principles of good government, as well as to expand his views upon political, social, and economic questions. Whilst in England he had the honour of being presented to Her Majesty the late Queen Victoria, and made the acquaintance of several crowned heads during his travels through Europe.

On April 4, 1894, His Highness was installed by Sir Charles Crosthwaite, the Lieutenant-Governor, when the Council of Regency was dissolved and a Council of Administration formed, and this method of government continued until June, 1896, when His Highness was invested with full powers. In 1894 His Highness was married to the eldest daughter of His Highness Nawab Ismail Khan Bahadur, of Jaora.

From this time forward His Highness' life was an eventful one, for in 1903 he was invited to the great Coronation Durbar at Delhi, and was presented with the Gold Coronation Medal, and in 1905 His Excellency Lord Curzon, the then Viceroy, visited Rampur. In December of the same year His Highness was invited to Lucknow to meet their present Majesties, then Prince and Princess of Wales, when His Highness had the honour of receiving a return visit from His Royal Highness and of meeting him at other functions. In January, 1907, His Highness was invited to meet His Majesty the Amir of Afghanistan at Agra, and on January 1, 1908, His Majesty the King-Emperor appointed him a Knight Commander of the Most Eminent Order of the Indian Empire. In April of the same year the late Lord Kitchener visited Rampur and inspected the Imperial Service Lancers and other troops of the State, and in June, 1909, His Highness was appointed an Honorary Lieut.-Colonel in the Indian Army, being raised to Brev.-Colonel the following year, when it was announced that His Majesty the King-Emperor had been pleased to appoint His Highness his Aide-de-Camp with the rank of Colonel.

In October, 1911, His Highness lost his eldest son, Sahibzada Hasan Ali Khan Bahadur, who was only 11 years of age, and this was a great calamity and severe blow to him. The deceased Sahibzada had been selected to act as page to His Imperial Majesty at the forthcoming Delhi Durbar, but he died before this historic event took place.

In January, 1911, His Highness was invited to England to attend His Imperial Majesty as one of his A.D.C.'s during the Coronation ceremonies, but, to his great disappointment, he was unable to travel on account of ill-health. His Highness attended the Delhi Durbar in December, 1911, and being one of His Majesty's A.D.C.'s, attended him personally, when he was decorated with the insignia of Knight Grand Cross of the Royal Victorian Order from His Majesty's own hands. In 1912 His Highness attended Lord Hardinge's Durbar at Delhi, and in September and October of that year he entertained Sir John Hewett and Sir James Meston, the retiring and incoming Lieutenant-Governors at Rampur. The following June he journeyed to Jansath, his ancestral birthplace, which had not been visited by the Rulers of Rampur for nearly a century. This trip was memorable in that His Highness went not as a Ruling Prince, but a brother to the Saiyids of Bahera.

On the outbreak of the Great War in August, 1914, His Highness, true to the traditions of his House, at once came forward with the offer of his personal services and all the resources of his State, and his contributions in men and money were notable. He commenced by subscribing Rs. 10,000 to the Imperial Indian Relief Fund, and Rs. 7,500 to His Royal Highness the Prince of Wales's Fund, and undertaking to bear a share with other Princes in the expenses of the Hospital Ship *Loyalty*, following this up by donating Rs. 25,000 to the U.P. Special War Fund for the supply of motor ambulances, and by the offer of his large Brook Hill property for the accommodation of sick and wounded, which was utilized as a Convalescent Home for European Officers. Two lakhs of rupees were invested in the first War Loan and five lakhs in the second, while a further sum of Rs. 25,000 was given to the Imperial Indian Relief Fund, of which His Highness became a Patron. On the conclusion of hostilities the Government of India offered to refund the expenditure incurred by the Durbar during the war on the Imperial Service Troops in excess of the ordinary peace expenditure. This sum amounted to Rs. 2,28,813, but His Highness did not wish to claim it, preferring that it should be counted as a contribution towards the war. He also subscribed Rs. 5,000 towards the Our Day Fund and sanctioned substantial increases in the pay of his Imperial Service troops. These are only some of His Highness' donations, but the sum of his financial assistance reaches the highly creditable total of about Rs. 12,50,000—a truly magnificent effort.

As regards His Highness' contributions in men, a detachment of 373 of the Imperial Service Infantry was accepted for East Africa, and drafts of the Lancers were sent to Aurangabad and Bellary to train remounts. These units acquitted themselves, and the Infantry returned from East Africa in March, 1918. For

THE STATE OF RAMPUR.

Khas Bagh House.

services in the field and on garrison duty the following decorations were won by various officers and men in the regiment : (*a*) Order of British India, second class, with title of Bahadur, 4 ; (*b*) Croix de Guerre, 1 ; (*c*) Indian Distinguished Service Medal, 4 ; (*d*) Meritorious Service Medal, 2 ;[1] (*e*) mentioned in the despatches of the Commander-in-Chief, East African Forces, 8.

His Highness also offered 100 Sowars of the Imperial Service Lancers to convoy Government horses to Europe, and he presented seven double-poled tents for camp hospitals in the field. He also offered all the horses of his Imperial Service Lancers, over 100 of which were accepted by the military authorities. The services of the Rampur Durbar during the war were acknowledged in a *kharita* dated June 30, 1919, addressed to His Highness by His Excellency the Viceroy as follows : "On behalf of His Majesty the King-Emperor and myself I thank your Highness most warmly for the staunch support and liberal assistance rendered by the Rampur State during the whole period of the war. Your Highness joined the scheme for the Hospital Ship *Loyalty*, lent houses at Naini Tal for the accommodation of sick and wounded, presented horses and other useful gifts, and generously contributed to the Imperial Indian Relief, Fund. The Rampur Imperial Service Infantry rendered valuable services in the East African campaign, other cavalry training remounts in India, and recruiting was stimulated throughout the State. Your Highness has thus manifested the depth of your steadfast loyalty and devotion to His Imperial Majesty the King and the British Empire, and has thus shared in the great struggle for justice and freedom in which India has so nobly borne her part."

The administration of the State is conducted by His Highness, who is assisted by several secretaries, each of whom is in charge of an important department of Government, and a great deal in the way of progress has been accomplished since His Highness came to the throne. The revenue has steadily increased, and it now reaches the substantial total of 52 lakhs, and particular attention is paid to all measures of reform. Especially is this noticeable in the educational policy of the State, which controls no less than 81 schools in the *mofussil*, in which education is free, and over 30 of others in the capital town, while there is also an Arabic College, which attracts students from all parts of India, and even from beyond the borders of India. The benefits of education are fully realized by His Highness, and to encourage it scholarships are awarded to deserving students for their school as well as college careers.

The Public Works Department is well organized, and supervises the construction of buildings, roads, and canals. There are many handsome structures in and around the city, the majority of which have been erected or remodelled during His Highness' reign, including the various palaces, the fort, and the Jama Musjid, which is generally regarded as one of the most beautiful in India. The city is supplied with electric light generated at the well-equipped power-house which was opened subsequently by Sir James Meston on July 31, 1913. Considerable additions had to be made to the machinery to meet the growing demand for current. The city possesses some thriving industries, and it is situated on the Oudh and Rohilkhand main line of railway, at a distance of about 800 miles from Calcutta.

The State troops are under the direct control of His Highness the Nawab, who is ably assisted by an officer styled "the Commandant of State Forces." They consist of 506 Cavalry, including camel *sowars*, and 2,175 Infantry, including Artillery and Band, making up the following regiments : I.S. Lancers, I.S. Infantry, 3rd Squadron, 2nd Battalion, 3rd Battalion, Artillery, Gurkha Company, and Camel *sowars*. The first two-named units being I.S. troops, are inspected periodically by British officers deputed to this duty from the Punjab.

The full title of the Nawab is Colonel His Highness Alijah Farzandi-i-Dilpizir-i-Daulat-i-Inglishia, Mukhlis-ud-Daula, Nasir-ul-Mulk, Amir-ul-Umara, Nawab Sir Syed Mohammed Hamid Ali Khan Bahadur, Mustaid Jung, G.C.I.E., G.C.V.O., A.D.C. to His Imperial Majesty the King-Emperor. The words Alijah, Mukhlis-ud-Daula, Nasir-ul-Mulk, Amir-ul-Umara, Nawab, and Mustaid Jung are ancient hereditary titles conferred by the Moghul Court on Nawab Ali Mohammad Khan, and they are recognized as such to-day by the Government of India.

His Highness has three surviving sons, the eldest of whom, Colonel Nawab Syed Raza Ali Khan Bahadur, is the heir-apparent, being born on November 17, 1906.

Special mention should be made of the State library, which is one of the finest in India, and possesses 23,000 books and 9,000 manuscripts, to which additions are made yearly. Many of the works are original and duplicates are not available in India. It has been visited by numbers of persons of note, whose remarks in the visitors' book make interesting reading.

His Highness enjoys a permanent salute of 15 guns, and he is a member of the Marlborough Club, London.

THE STATE OF BHAVNAGAR

BHAVNAGAR is a first-class tributary State in the Province of Gujerat within the Kathiawar Political Agency of the Bombay Presidency, and it lies at the head and on the west side of the Gulf of Cambay.

His Highness the Maharaja belongs to the illustrious tribe or clan of the Gohel Rajputs of Kathiawar, of whom he is the Chief, and after whom the eastern part of the Province of Kathiawar is called Gohelwad. According to the writings of ancient bards (which are usually accurate) the Gohels are said to have descended from the celebrated Pandavas, who belonged to the Lunar or *Chandrabansi* race, and trace their line from the renowned Shalivahan, the originator of the Shak Era.

The founder of the present Ruling House of Bhavnagar, according to the bards, was Sejakji (grandson of Mohodas, twentieth in descent from Shalivahan), who migrated into Saurashtra (Kathiawar) and established his sway in the heart of the Peninsula, gradually extending it by conquest, and finally not only establishing his own sovereignty but also bestowing villages upon his younger sons. Historical records show that as far back as the year 812 the Gohels ruled in Saurashtra, and that their authority extended along the coast line from Gogha to Mangrol.

Mahipal III, *alias* Rah Meheloo, whose seat of government was at Junagadh, ruled over an extensive tract of territory in the Province, and he appointed Sejakji to an important position in his State, subsequently making a grant to him of Shahpur and 12 adjacent villages. He also, with the permission of the Raj, built a new village, and called it after him, Sejakpur. Remaining there, he conquered neighbouring districts and established an independent principality.

Sejakji had three sons, named Ranoji, Shahji and Sarangji, whose descendants are said to have founded the principalities of Bhavnagar, Lathi and Palitana respectively. He died in the year 1290, and was succeeded by his eldest son, Ranoji, who founded Ranpur and made it the seat of his Government. In course of fighting with the Mahomedans in 1309 the town of Ranpur fell into the hands of the latter, and Ranoji himself was slain. His son and successor, Mokhdaji, conquered Bhimdad from the Vala Rajputs and Umrala from the Kolis, and took up his residence at the last-mentioned place. He subsequently annexed other territories while driving the Mahomedans from Khokhra and Gogha, and he transferred his capital to Piram, which he wrested from Baria Kolis. Mokhdaji was subsequently brought into serious conflict with Juma Khan, *alias* Mahmud Toghlak, Emperor of Delhi, and in one of the engagements (1347) he was killed by a javelin hurled at him by the Emperor's nephew.

After his death came a succession of rulers of comparative unimportance until the reign of the famous Bhavsinghji I, twentieth in descent from Sejakji, who succeeded his father, Visoji, in 1703, and who, during a long reign of more than 60 years, succeeded in consolidating his position and influence in Kathiawar and in greatly extending the volume of trade carried on in the State. It was at the commencement of his reign that the Moghul power was waning, and the raids of the Mahrattas were spreading confusion over a large territory in Northern India; and Bhavsinghji, in common with other rulers, decided to establish himself more firmly in his possessions. In 1722–3 the Mahrattas, under their leaders, Kantaji Kadam Bhande and Pilaji Gaekwar, laid siege to the fort of Sihor, but they were repulsed by the Chief, although Bhavsinhji lost a large number of his bravest warriors. Fearing a further attack by the enemy, the Rawal left Sihor and took up his residence at a small village named Vadva, situated near the mouth of the creek, a few miles to the north of Gogha. In 1723 Bhavsinhji built a new city on that spot, and naming it Bhavnagar, after himself, he made it his seat of government. The site chosen for the new capital was an admirable one, seeing that its seaport afforded a convenient outlet for the products not only of the Province, but also distant places such as Rajputana and Malwa. Soon after this date Bhavsinhji became very friendly with Sohrab Khan, the Governor of Surat, under the Moghul power, and it was he who assisted Bhavsinhji to build the harbour at the port of Bhavnagar. In 1739 Bhavsinhji entered into an agreement with the Officer Commanding the Surat Citadel for the protection of trading interests at Bhavnagar, and when Surat was taken by the British in 1759 he induced the victors to renew the commercial arrangements made some 20 years previously.

Rawal Bhavsinhji died in 1764, leaving behind him five sons, and the eldest of these, Akherajji I, succeeded as Ruler of the State. At this juncture the fort of Talaja was in the hands of Baria-Kolis, a lawless band of pirates who infested the western littoral from Cambay to the Indus. Their unjust exactions pressed so heavily

H.H. RAVAL SHRI SIR BHAVSINGHJI, K.C.S.I., THE LATE MAHARAJA SAHIB OF BHAVNAGAR.

HER LATE HIGHNESS THE MAHARANI SHRI NANDKUNVERBA, C.I., OF BHAVNAGAR.

Photo by Bourne & Shepherd, India.

1. H.H. RAVAL SHRI KRISHNAKUMARSINGHJI, THE MINOR MAHARAJA SAHIB OF BHAVNAGAR.
2. MAHARAJKUMARS SHRI NIRMALKUMARSINGHJI (seated), AND SHRI DHARMAKUMARSINGHI (standing), BROTHERS TO H.H. THE MINOR MAHARAJA.

THE STATE OF BHAVNAGAR.

1. Ambulance Cars (Part of Bhavnagar's Contribution to the War).
Photo by Bourne & Shepherd, India.
2. The Marble Statue of His Late Highness Sir Takhtasinghji, G.C.S.I., in the Gardens, Bhavnagar. 3. In the Peile Gardens.
4. View in the Peile Gardens, showing Bandstand.

upon merchants in that locality that the large trade previously carried on was almost entirely ruined, even British ships falling into their clutches. The Imperial Government then sent troops, which were assisted by Rawal Akherajji and his army, and it was their combined forces which captured the stronghold of Talaja and caused the extirpation of the whole race of marauders.

Akherajji died in 1772, and was followed by Wakhatsinhji, a vigorous ruler who greatly extended the power and territory of the State. After reigning for about 44 years, during which period he was constantly engaged in warfare, he died in 1816, and the succeeding Rulers were Vajesinhji, Akherajji II, and Jasvatsinhji.

During the Mutiny of 1857 the last-named Ruler acted promptly in offering all possible assistance to the British Government in its suppression, and for his valuable services he was created a Knight Commander of the Most Exalted Order of the Star of India, a distinction which he was the first ruling Prince in Kathiawar to receive. Various improvements were effected during his time; fine hospitals and other public buildings were erected; dispensaries and schools were established; good roads were made; and local self-government was granted to certain towns by the establishment of municipalities.

His Highness Jasvatsinhji died in the year 1870, and was succeeded by his son Takhtsinhji, who was then a minor. By order of the Government the management of the State was placed in the hands of a British official as Administrator jointly with the Chief Minister. The young Prince was educated at the Rajkumar College, Rajkot, as well as by private tutors, and he was invested with full ruling powers in the year 1878. The dignity of a Knight Commandership of the Most Exalted Order of the Star of India was conferred upon His Highness in 1881, and that of a Knight Grand Commandership of the same Order in 1886. The personal distinction of the title of Maharaja was bestowed upon him in 1891.

His Highness the Maharaja had the privilege of attending the Imperial Assemblage held at Delhi on January 1, 1877, on the proclamation of the assumption by Her Majesty the late Queen Victoria of the title of Empress of India. During this visit His Highness was presented with a Royal flag, and as a mark of personal distinction his salute was increased from 11 guns to 15. He subsequently made a tour in Europe, and while in England the University of Cambridge bestowed upon him the honorary degree of LL.D. His useful career was cut short by death in the year 1896, and his elder son, Bhavsinhji II, born in April 1875, succeeded to the *gadi*.

The young Prince received a first-class education at the Rajkumar College, Rajkot, and during his residence there, which extended over a period of more than four years, he won golden opinions from all, delighting his masters by his steady application to his studies, and finding favour with his fellow students by reason of his genial nature and his prowess as an athlete. After leaving College His Highness was, at the express wish of his late father and by arrangement with the Government of Bombay, placed under the tutorship of Mr. S. M. Fraser, C.I.E., I.C.S., with whom he, together with his friend the Maharaja of Kolhapur, remained for nearly four years.

In the year 1890 the young Prince, together with his tutor and some of his companions, visited the chief places of interest in Northern India, and the experiences gained during the trip were so helpful to His Highness that in 1891 it was decided that he should visit Southern India and Ceylon. After leaving Kolhapur on November 5th, he travelled to Bijapur, Hyderabad, Madras, Pondicherry, Tanjore, Tuticorin, Colombo, Kandy, Newara-Eliya, Bangalore and Mysore. The advantages of such a trip were of inestimable value, as His Highness became acquainted not only with the physical aspects of India, but also with various races of people, their languages, customs, religions, and social and economic conditions.

His Highness was married in the year 1893 to Princess Devkunvarba, daughter of Maharaval Shri Mansinhji, a Chauhan Rajput, the ruling Chief of Devgadh Baria, a second-class State in the Rewa Kantha Agency. In June of the same year His Highness proceeded to Poona for the purpose of acquiring military training to fit him for the command of the Bhavnagar State Imperial Service Lancers, a corps which was established mainly for the enrolment of Rajputs of the Gohel Clan. In commemoration of the birthday in 1894 of Her Majesty the late Queen Victoria, His Highness was appointed by his father to be Commandant of the State Imperial Lancers. A most important event in the history of the young Prince occurred in 1894, when his father issued a memorandum stating that, as his son and heir desired to gain some knowledge of the work of several departments of the State, he had nominated him to be an extra member of the Executive and Military Councils of Bhavnagar. Arrangements were then made for His Highness to attend regularly at the head office of several State departments. He commenced his work at the Political Department, which controlled matters relating to the rights and liabilities of the *Bhayats* and *Mulgrassias* subordinate to the State, and he also was charged with the supervision of all alienated lands. He then applied himself to the duties of the Public Works Department, which also had the oversight of railways, municipalities and horse-breeding, and subsequently he undertook the study of Revenue subjects, and civil and criminal justice.

All the inhabitants of the State—from palace to cottage—were plunged into the deepest gloom when it became known that His Highness Maharaja Sir Takhtsinhji, G.C.S.I., LL.D., had on January 29, 1896, succumbed to an attack of illness. It was a great consolation to the heir-apparent to learn from the Political Agent that Her Majesty the late Queen-Empress had desired the Secretary of State for India to express her deep regret at the death of His Highness the Maharaja. The Political Agent also conveyed the condolences of Her Majesty's Secretary of State for India, His Excellency the Viceroy, and His Excellency the Governor of Bombay.

The ceremony of formally investing the new Ruler, Raol Shri Bhavsinhji II, on the *gadi* took place in the Durbar Hall of the town palace on February 10, 1896, in the presence of a large number of European and Indian gentlemen, officials of the State, and other visitors.

His Highness had scarcely witnessed the laying to rest of the remains of his late father before he heard with keen sorrow of the death of Mr. Chester Macnaghten, the highly respected Principal of the Rajkumar College, Rajkot, a man who was personally beloved not only by His Highness and his late father, but also by hundreds of other Princes who had enjoyed the privilege of being trained under his supervision.

In the year 1897 the rainfall in the State, although not seriously deficient in quantity, fell at unseasonable times, with the result that there was a considerable shortage of food grains and other crops. The high prices of the necessities of life prevailing in other parts of India owing to famine naturally tended to increase the hardships of poor people throughout the whole of Bhavnagar, and therefore it became compulsory for the Durbar to establish relief works and in other ways to render suitable help to distressed persons. His Highness promptly

THE STATE OF BHAVNAGAR.

1. The Bhavnagar State Infantry. 2. The Bhavnagar Imperial Service Lancers. 3. Officers of the Bhavnagar Imperial Service Lancers in Full Dress Uniform.

issued a famine code similar to that in force in British India, and he personally visited nearly every part of his territory in order that he might decide upon the best steps to be taken to mitigate the sufferings of his subjects. It may be mentioned that at one time no fewer than 16,000 persons were employed on relief works, the daily average being 14,000.

The sympathies of His Highness were not selfishly confined to his own subjects, as when a severe famine was raging in the southern portion of the Bombay Presidency about this time, His Highness manifested a kindly feeling towards those affected by it, and he not only presided at a public meeting held at the capital city for the purpose of raising funds for their aid, but he also headed a subscription list with a donation of Rs. 10,000. In addition to this, the sum of Rs. 7,000 was collected at the meeting, and a further amount of Rs. 5,000 was forwarded to Bombay at a subsequent date.

The late Maharaja Takhtsinhji was so highly respected by Europeans as well as Indians in the State that on his visit to England he at their request gave a sitting to an eminent sculptor in order that a statue to be erected in some prominent position of the city might serve as a fitting memorial of his beneficent and statesmanlike administration. The work was duly completed and Colonel Hunter, the Political Agent, was requested to unveil the statue, which stands in the Peile Gardens of the city. This gentleman eulogized the high qualities and noble virtues of head and heart of His late Highness, and concluded his remarks by observing that the present Ruler had the incentive of a noble example to follow, and that he was glad to think that His Highness had already shown promise of being a worthy son of a worthy sire.

The loyalty of the House of Bhavnagar to the throne was exemplified by its celebration of the Diamond Jubilee of Her Most Gracious Majesty the late Queen Victoria.

A grand Durbar was held on June 21, 1897, in the Motibag Palace in Bhavnagar, which was attended by Major Ashby, the Assistant Political Agent, Gohelwad, His Highness, European and Indian military officers, State officials, merchants, *Bhayats* and *Mulgrassias*. During the festivities about 10,000 children attended a fête in the Peile Gardens, at which they were regaled with sweetmeats. A garden party was given by His Highness at the Nilambag Palace, and in the evening, prior to a grand display of fireworks, all public buildings in the city were beautifully illuminated, the effect of thousands of small coloured lights lining the steps of the Gangajalia tank down to the water's edge being remarkably fine.

Following the precedent of 1887, the Princes and Chiefs of Kathiawar presented an address to Her Most Gracious Majesty, which was enclosed in a golden casket and handed in to the Political Agent for transmission to England. It may be interesting to mention here that the address was prepared and elegantly printed on velvet at Bhavnagar, and the golden casket with beautiful engravings on it of the 10 images of incarnations of the god of Hindu mythology, and the sandal-wood box were all locally made.

His Excellency Lord Sandhurst, Governor of Bombay, in fulfilment of a promise, paid a visit to Bhavnagar in November 1898, when he was received with all honours and heartily welcomed by His Highness.

The famine of 1899-1900 was more severe than on any previous occasion, and His Highness quickly responded to the first cry of distress in the State. Relief works consisted of the deepening of several large tanks and wells, the distribution of food grains, fodder and money, the opening of State pasture lands for the grazing of cattle, and the construction of roads and other works of utility. Poor-houses were established at the headquarters of every district, and cheap grain shops were opened for the supply of food at exceedingly low rates. The expenditure incurred by the State up to September 15, 1900, amounted to nearly Rs. 23,00,000, which sum was equivalent to more than 50 per cent. of the total revenue in a normal year. The terrible distress caused by the famine impoverished the people to such an extent that it was impossible for them to meet their liabilities for rents of their holdings. His Highness the Thakor Saheb, with characteristic generosity, remitted a large proportion of the revenue which he knew would be a hardship upon the people to enforce. Land revenue for that year amounted to Rs. 25,25,000, and a sum of almost Rs. 14,00,000 was left outstanding.

On the morning of January 20, 1901, His Highness the Thakor Saheb was stricken with grief on receiving the sad news of the death of Her Most Gracious Majesty the late Queen-Empress.

A special *Gazette* was issued by the Durbar conveying the sorrowful intelligence to the people, and ordering the closing of departmental offices, places of business and schools for a period of five days. Religious services were held by the Christians, Hindus, Mahomedans and Parsis in their various places of worship.

In December 1902 His Highness attended the Imperial Durbar at Delhi held to celebrate the Coronation of His Majesty the late King Edward VII.

One of the effects of the famines which have already been referred to was a diffidence among the people with regard to the credit system of trading and the investment of their savings. His Highness the Thakor Saheb gave anxious attention to the matter, and he ultimately established a Durbar Savings Bank, principally with the object of encouraging habits of thrift among the Durbari servants, and also of providing a safe place of investment for them as well as for merchants and others who might choose to deal with it. The transactions include the receipt of money on fixed deposits or current accounts and the granting of loans to substantial persons. The bank has been extremely useful to all classes of the community, and the deposits at the end of the financial year 1920-21 amounted to nearly Rs. 83,00,000.

In November 1903 His Highness suffered a remarkably heavy loss owing to the death of his only consort, Her Highness Rani Shri Devkunvarba, and the sad event caused the greatest grief among a wide circle of friends.

On June 24, 1904, His Highness the Thakor Saheb was proud to receive a telegram from His Excellency the Viceroy stating that His Imperial Majesty the late King Edward VII had been pleased to confer upon him the honourable distinction of a Knight Commandership of the Most Exalted Order of the Star of India. The news was received with immense rejoicing throughout the whole State, and congratulatory messages were received from a very large number of friends and admirers, English and Indian alike. The ceremony of presenting the insignia of this distinguished Order took place at a grand Durbar held at Rajkot in March 1905 by His Excellency Lord Lamington, Governor of Bombay.

His Highness the Thakor Saheb was married on August 23, 1905, to Princess Nandkunvarba, daughter of the Chief of Khirasra.

A subject of vital importance to the trading interests of the State was placed before His Excellency Lord Lamington at an informal conference of the Chiefs of several maritime States of Kathiawar on November 25, 1905. The view of the Government of India on the question of the custom arrangements at their ports was placed before the meeting, but exception was

THE STATE OF BHAVNAGAR.

1. Motibag Palace, Bhavnagar. 2. Durbar Hall, Motibag Palace. 3. Drawing-room, Motibag Palace.
4. Trophies of His Late Highness Maharaja Sir Bhavsinghji, K.C.S.I. 5. Nilambag Palace, Bhavnagar.

THE STATE OF BHAVNAGAR.

1. The Jasunath Temple. 2 The Lila Bungalow in Nilambag. 3. The Lal Bungalow in Nilambag. 4. The Majirabja Marble Chhatri. 5. The Takhteshwar Marble Temple, Bhavnagar.

THE STATE OF BHAVNAGAR.

1. High Court, Bhavnagar. 2. High School, Bhavnagar. 3. Takhtsinghji Hospital, Bhavnagar. 4. Panvadi (Guest House), Bhavnagar.

taken by the Thakor Saheb of Bhavnagar to a frontier line which had then recently been established at Viramgam. It was contended that this line violated the much-valued treaty rights of Bhavnagar, rights which were won by His Highness's ancestors at the cost of great sacrifices. The points in dispute were placed before the Government of India, and eventually before the Home Government, and after correspondence extending over a period of seven years His Majesty's Secretary of State reported, early in the year 1911, that the Paramount Power had been pleased to preserve unimpaired and inviolate the ancestral treaty rights of the Durbar and to rule that it was not open to Government to hinder or tax the land trade of Bhavnagar by the establishment of a customs line.

A day which will long be remembered in Bhavnagar was November 15, 1908, the occasion being a visit of His Excellency General Viscount Kitchener of Khartoum, G.C.B., G.M., G.C.M.G., G.C.I.E., R.E., Commander-in-Chief of India.

Early in the year 1909 great joy was manifested in the State at the news that His Majesty the King-Emperor had graciously bestowed the title of "Maharaja" upon His Highness. His Excellency Sir George Sydenham Clarke (now Lord Sydenham), in a letter congratulating His Highness upon the honour, wrote as follows: "I congratulate you most warmly on the honour conferred on you by His Majesty the King-Emperor, an honour which has been richly deserved by your Highness's excellent work in the State and by your unswerving loyalty to the Crown." His Excellency subsequently visited Bhavnagar and held a Durbar in the Albert Victor Square for the formal presentation of *kharita* together with the *sanad* relating to the honour thus conferred.

The painful news of the death of His Majesty the late King-Emperor Edward VII reached Bhavnagar on May 7, 1910, and His Highness immediately despatched telegrams to His Excellency the Viceroy, His Excellency the Governor of Bombay, and the Agent to the Governor, to convey his heart-felt condolence and sympathy to Her Majesty Queen Alexandra, His Royal Highness the Prince of Wales, and other members of the Royal Family in their sad bereavement. He also ordered the publication of a special *Gazette*, in which he commended the many good qualities of one who has been styled "Peacemaker of the World," and he enumerated in fitting terms His late Majesty's deeply sympathetic treatment of his subjects in India. A salute of 101 guns was fired from the battery, the Royal Standard and the flag on the Palace were hung at half-mast, and all offices and educational institutions were closed for five days. A mass meeting of people of all communities was also held to give expression to the deep sorrow felt at the sad death of the King-Emperor.

The most important event of the year 1911 was the Coronation of Their Imperial Majesties King George V and Queen Mary. His Highness the Maharaja proceeded to Delhi on November 30 for the purpose of attending various functions arranged in connection with the Royal visit, and he had the honour of paying his homage in person to His Majesty.

It may be mentioned that in the month of December the King-Emperor was graciously pleased to bestow upon Her Highness Maharani Shri Nandkunvarba the badge of the Imperial Order of the Crown of India.

A most auspicious event happened on May 19, 1912, when Her Highness the Maharani Saheba gave birth to the Yuvaraj Maharaj Kumar, and a very large number of congratulatory messages were received from many personal friends and acquaintances.

In December 1912 Princess Manharkunvarba, the only daughter of Their Highnesses, was married to His Highness the Mahendra Maharaja Yadavendra Singh Saheb Bahadur, the Ruler of Panna State. For several months prior to the appointed date grand preparations were in progress for the comfort and convenience of the large number of distinguished guests who were expected to visit Bhavnagar. Ten extensive camps were arranged, and each one was placed under the direct control of an officer of the rank of a head of a department. The distinguished bridegroom arrived by special train, and was received by His Highness and the principal officers of the State. He and his party of followers, nearly 600 in number, were accommodated in the Motibag Palace and in its fine garden. A banquet was held after the marriage ceremonies, and it was attended by Mr. Sladen, Agent to the Governor in Kathiawar, European ladies and gentlemen, Raja Sahebs, and other visitors of rank.

It might be mentioned here that in addition to the very large number of leading Europeans, Indian Princes and other notabilities who assembled at Bhavnagar for the wedding festivities, which continued for six days, all the Kumars of the Rajkumar College, by the kind permission of the Agent to the Governor, were entertained in one of the camps, and it will be readily understood that a week's outing of this character, unique in the history of the College, was thoroughly enjoyed by the students.

Shortly afterwards His Excellency Sir George Clarke, then Governor of Bombay, requested His Highness Maharaja Bhavsinhji to lend the services of Mr. Prabashanker D. Pattani, C.I.E., the Diwan, to Government, as it was desired to appoint him a Member of the Executive Council. The Maharaja very cordially accepted the proposal as an honour to his State.

The most important event during the year 1918 was the sad death of Her Highness Maharani Shri Nandkunverba, C.I., which occurred on November 9th. The two elder Princes, together with their mother, were attacked by influenza, and while the former gradually recovered, Her Highness fell a victim to pneumonia, in spite of the best efforts of capable medical men. His Highness was naturally overwhelmed with grief at the sudden loss of one whose presence illumined the home and whose short life was spent in helping to raise the moral and social status of the people, and particularly in fostering the spread of female education.

The Great War which raged from 1914 to 1918 stirred up in the heart of His Highness the Maharaja those feelings of sympathetic loyalty to the Throne for which the House of Bhavnagar has always been distinguished. Prince and people contributed money, various kinds of goods and useful articles to the full extent of their means.

On July 17, 1919, Maharaja Bhavsinghji breathed his last, and all the subjects of the State were plunged into profound mourning. During the minority of Maharaja Krishna Kumarsinhji the State is managed by a Council of Administration.

The State of Bhavnagar is about 2,860 square miles in extent, and it is divided into 10 districts, namely, Daskroi, Sihor, Mahuva, Kundla, Lilia, Umrala, Botad, Gadhada, Talaja, and Port Albert Victor.

The inhabitants, according to the census of 1921, were 426,404 in number, of whom about 86 per cent. are Hindus and 8 per cent. Mahomedans; but there are also about 20,000 Jains, nearly 300 Parsis, 163 Christians, and 14 Jews. The territory presents varied aspects, as, for example, the district of Lilia consists of a rich plain of black cotton soil; in Bhal the chief feature is an extensive salt-flat area; Sihor and Kundla are undulating and in some places hilly, although the country does not in any part rise to a great elevation. The hilly portion appears to be of volcanic origin, and consists of trap and basalt, piercing a

THE STATE OF BHAVNAGAR.

1. Lighthouse, Bhavnagar Fort. 2. View on the Bunder. 3. Godown, Bhavnagar Bunder. 4. View of Gaurishanker Lake, showing Dam. 5. View of Gaurishanker Lake, showing Suspension Bridge.

THE STATE OF BHAVNAGAR.

1. Starting for Procession. 2. Old Palace Gate. 3. Bird's-eye View of Bhavnagar City. 4. A Street Scene in Bhavnagar City, 5. The Terminus Station, Bhavnagar. 5. The Barton Library, Bhavnagar.

THE STATE OF BHAVNAGAR.

1. Collection of White Black-buck and Does. 2. The Paddock, Bhavnagar. 3. Types of Kathi Horses, bred in Bhavnagar Paddock. 4. Greyhound and Cheetah feeding off Black-buck.

course of sandy limestone. In various places laterite of good quality for building purposes and a conglomeration abounding in fossils are found.

The principal rivers are the Sukh Bhadar, Kalubhar, Ghelo, Shetrunji, Bagad and the Malan, none of which is of great length; but the water in the last three continues flowing throughout the year and is used for irrigation. There is a fine artificial lake, about five miles in circumference, near the capital town, formed by a dam across the bed of the Gadhechi river, which supplies water to tanks in the town. The port is supplied with water from this lake. In addition to Bhavnagar, the State possesses the following ports: (*a*) Mahuva and small ports subordinate thereto; (*b*) Kathivadar, now called Port Albert Victor; (*c*) Pipavav; (*d*) Talaja (Sultanpur); (*e*) Jhanjmer; and (*f*) Sonrai. All these enjoy, in virtue of agreements with the Government, the full benefits of British Indian ports.

The total area of arable land under the Revenue Department is about 12,00,000 acres. The revenue collected during the year 1920–1 was Rs. 38,15,360 out of the total demand of Rs. 44,47,260, the balance of Rs. 6,31,900 being the amount ordered to be suspended. The total area cropped by Durbari cultivators is about 7,50,000 acres.

With the object of improving the economic condition of the holders of land His Highness the late Maharaja established Agricultural Co-operative Societies, which were intended to form a sure, ready and immediate means of self-help in either prosperous or adverse seasons. The basis of these societies is co-operation and joint liability. There are now 339 societies in the various districts, with a membership of 11,633 persons and a total capital of Rs. 58,062.

Manufactures and industries have not as yet received the attention which they deserve. There are, however, in the State one spinning and weaving mill, working with 337 looms and 19,600 spindles; three power-loom factories in Bhavnagar; seven cotton presses; and 16 ginning factories at Botad, Dhola, Panchtalavda, Kundla, Dungar, Facharia, Rajula, Mahuva, Jesar, Talaja and Sihor. In the year 1911 the Bhavnagar Chemical Works at Vartej were established for the manufacture of all kinds of tinctures, spirits, liniments and other pharmaceutical and chemical preparations. This concern, which is being satisfactorily worked, is supplying medicines to Bhavnagar and other states in Kathiawar. The practice of weaving by hand has declined considerably during the past few years, but weavers in Kundla produce gold-laced *pachhedis*, silk-bordered *Dhotars* and thick covering sheets of cotton cloth known as *chofals*. Other products are strong woollen blankets, carpets and bed-covers dyed in various colours, pretty wooden and ivory toys, and brass and copper household utensils.

An official statement regarding the trade of the State shows that the value of exports during the year 1920–1 was Rs. 2,32,55,214. Imports increased by more than 5 per cent., reaching a total value of Rs. 2,52,38,811 as against Rs. 2,38,24,475 in the previous year.

With regard to the means of internal communication, it may be observed that the Bhavnagar State Railway, which was one of the main undertakings initiated by His Highness the late Maharaja's illustrious father, and which was the first enterprise of the kind in the province of Kathiawad, dates back to the famine year 1877–8; and it has been found to be of the highest utility to the State and to other parts of the Peninsula. With the extensions constructed by the late Maharaja the line now runs from Bhavnagar to Wadhwan (105 miles), from Dhola to Dhasa (15 miles), from Sihor to Palitana (17 miles), from Dhasa to Kundla (35 miles), and from Botad to Jasdan (33 miles), making a total of 205 miles. Besides these there are 31 miles of sidings.

The Bhavnagar Dock Estate has been connected with the line starting at the Bhavnagar terminus, thereby facilitating the through-booking of goods between the railways and steamer. At the close of the year above mentioned the total capital outlay, including suspense, was Rs. 1,28,38,093, while the total net earnings amounted to Rs. 2,27,38,315, thus showing that the receipts have exceeded the outlay by the sum of Rs. 99,00,222.

There are nine Magistrates' Courts, and two Courts of Sessions, together with two Courts of Appeal for the trial of criminal offences. Civil justice is administered in 11 courts of original and three of appellate jurisdiction.

For the protection of the State the Durbar maintains the Imperial Service Lancers. The armed police known as the Bhavnagar State Infantry comprise about 250 men, including a draft who are specially trained in artillery. The Police force has on its rolls 68 officers, 52 mounted police and 1,552 unmounted.

The foundation of the educational system in the State was laid as far back as the year 1852, when there was not merely indifference but frequently opposition to the giving of instruction in public schools. This apathy, which extended throughout the greater part of Kathiawar, could not have been so strongly manifested in the State of Bhavnagar, as boys' schools were established there some 70 years ago, and even an institution for the education of girls was opened in the capital town in 1856. There are at present in the State one Arts College, one high school, 12 middle schools (including five English classes at Rajula, Umrala, Trapaj, Lilia, and Gadhada), 168 primary schools (including 24 girls' schools, four Sanskrit *Pathshalas* and two Urdu schools), and 11 aided schools. There are mission schools for boys and girls in Bhavnagar, in addition to 13 private schools and 63 indigenous schools. In addition to the liberality of His Highness the Maharaja with regard to education within the State borders, the Durbar maintains a number of pupils at several institutions in other places. In connection with scholastic work it may be added that the Barton Library at Bhavnagar has a fine collection of nearly 9,000 books on general literature, history, philosophy, science, biography and other subjects, including a number of Sanskrit manuscripts.

The institutions giving medical relief in the State comprise three hospitals and four dispensaries in the town of Bhavnagar, 14 dispensaries in the several districts of the State, and a small dispensary in connection with Sir Takhtsinhji Poor-house in the village of Adhewada.

The gross annual revenue of the State was Rs. 69,41,955, while the expenditure was Rs. 52,98,229.

The annual expenditure of the Public Works Department was Rs. 3,68,550, which is spent in connection with means of communication, buildings, lighthouses, harbour works, public recreation, water-works (including irrigation), and other matters.

Municipalities in the State, 10 in number, are maintained as Durbari institutions. The most important of these is the one at the capital town, upon which an annual sum of more than Rs. 70,000 is expended.

The Ganga-Jalia tank and a number of wells, in addition to the flow from the Gouri-Shankar Lake, supply the town of Bhavnagar with water which is brought through main pipes into the town, and delivered to the people by means of tanks erected at convenient places. Filtered water has been available for the whole town since the completion of the Sandhurst Reservoir in 1912.

The State pays an annual tribute of Rs. 1,28,060 to the British Government, Rs. 3,581 8. as *peshkashi* to the Gaekwar of Baroda, and Rs. 22,858 as *zortalbi* to the Nawab of Junagadh.

SIR AJITSINHJI HIGH SCHOOL, DHRANGADHRA.

THE STATE OF DHRANGADHRA

THIS first-class State in the Kathiawar Political Agency of the Bombay Presidency lies to the south of the lesser Runn of Cutch and to the north of the Kathiawar peninsula. The Chiefs of Dhrangadhra belong to the famous clan of Jhala Rajputs, from whom have sprung Rulers of many Principalities, chiefly in Western and Central India. The Dhrangadhra family claim descent from a famous leader, named Harpal Deo, who became Chief of a very large tract of country, which he named Jhalawad, after the tribe to which he belonged.

A portion of Kathiawar was subsequently brought under the sway of this Chief, and considerable prosperity was enjoyed during this *regime* and that of the successor, Sodhoji, during the latter portion of the sixteenth century. Owing to vicissitudes of fortune in subsequent years the family became separated, and several established themselves as Rulers of small Principalities, including Wankaner, Wadhwan, Jhalrapatan, and others.

Early in the eighteenth century the fort of Dhrangadhra was built by Raj Raisinhji, and one of his successors, Raj Jaswantsinhji, made his headquarters there when it became the capital of the State. This event occurred about the year 1800. Shortly after this time the peninsula of Kathiawar and its Rulers came under British protection, and when a firm but just control had taken the place of confusion and sometimes chaos, there began to be signs of prosperity in the condition of the people owing to their ability to prosecute agricultural and industrial enterprises. A most accomplished scholar and illustrious Ruler in the person of Maharana Shri Ranmalsinhji occupied the *gadi* from 1843 to 1869, and in recognition of his great abilities, the Supreme Government conferred upon him the insignia of a Knight Commander of the Most Exalted Order of the Star of India.

Maharana Shri Mansinhji, the next Ruler, emulated his father's example by making great personal efforts to accomplish reforms in the administration of State affairs, and to develop the resources of Dhrangadhra by introducing new features in the industrial work of the inhabitants. He also founded schools and dispensaries, and the well-conducted Prince of Wales Hospital at the capital town was constructed through his instrumentality. Mansinhji died in the year 1900, and was succeeded by his grandson, Maharana Shri Ajitsinhji, who was no less able than his predecessors in administrative ability and in the inauguration of measures of progress and reform.

The most poignant grief was exhibited throughout the State when it was known that His Highness had, on February 9, 1911, succumbed to an attack of smallpox, and numerous expressions of sincere

H.H. MAHARANA SHRI SIR GHANSHYAMSINHJI, K.C.S.I., MAHARAJA RAJ-SAHIB OF DHRANGADHRA.

THE STATE OF DHRANGADHRA.

1. The Ajit Niwas Palace, Dhrangadhra. 2. Durbar Hall, Dhrangadhra.

THE STATE OF DHRANGADHRA.

1. Rana Shri Manisinhji Surajsinhji, Jhala, C.I.E., Dewan. 2. Dewan Sahib's Town Residence. 3. Secretariat, Dhrangadhra.

THE STATE OF DHRANGADHRA.

1. Bird's-eye View of the City of Dhrangadhra. 2. City Gate, Dhrangadhra. 3. Sir Ghanshyamsinhji Tennis Club, Dhrangadhra. 4. Bazaar View, Dhrangadhra.

THE STATE OF DHRANGADHRA.

1. The Shakti Mata Temple, Dhrangadhra. 2. The Clock Tower, Dhrangadhra. 3. Ancient Tower, Halvad Palace.

THE STATE OF DHRANGADHRA.

1. The State Hathikhana, Dhrangadhra. 2. State Elephant Caparisoned with Howdah. 3. The State Silver Carriage.

THE STATE OF DHRANGADHRA.

1. and 3. Wood-carving at Halvad Palace. 2. Temple at Halvad. 4. Old Spiral Staircase, Halvad Palace.

THE STATE OF DHRANGADHRA.

1, 2, 3. Paliyas of Sati Monuments, Halvad. 4. View of the Lake and Temple, Raj Seetapur.

regret were received at Dhrangadhra from all parts of India.

He was succeeded by his son, the present Chief, His Highness Maharana Shri Sir Ghanshyamsinhji Bahadur, K.C.S.I., Maharaja Raj Sahib of Dhrangadhra. His Highness was born at Dhrangadhra on May 31, 1889, and owing to a somewhat delicate constitution he was placed under a private tutor in his own home before he joined the Rajkumar College at Rajkot. He remained at that institution, with Rana Shri Mansinhji, the present *Diwan* of the State, for about four years, and he earned special praise from the Principal on account of his intelligence and capacity for hard work. At the age of 16 His Highness went to England with the dual object of completing his studies and of obtaining a close acquaintance with English social life. The climate of the Old Country benefited his health very considerably, and the five years spent under the care of Sir Charles and Lady Ollivant were carefully employed in furthering his studies, and in training him in the development of principles of conduct which would fit him for the high position which he expected to occupy at a future date. On his return to India in 1909 His Highness was appointed Commander of the State forces, as well as Commissioner of Police, plenary powers being conferred upon him.

His Highness was invested with full ruling powers on March 3, 1911, by Mr. E. Maconochie, Agent in Kathiawar to the Governor of Bombay. One of the first measures of reform of the new *regime* was to give permanency of tenure to holders of land, and this security of occupation naturally induced them to cultivate more thoroughly and also to bring under the plough extensive areas of land which had for a long time been fallow. Scrupulous care began to be taken in the selection of types of cotton which appeared to be most suitable for the climate and varieties of soil in Dhrangadhra, and then great vigilance was exercised to preserve all seed from impurities of every description. The result has been that the Dhrangadhra staple has now earned a high reputation in foreign as well as Indian markets. The quantity of cotton harvested per acre has been doubled during the short period of a decade without in any way interfering with the production of cereals generally.

The construction of works of public utility has been another important feature of the past 10 years, in which a sum of Rs. 11,20,640 has been expended in the erection of hospitals, dispensaries, schools, markets, factories, and workshops, and in the carrying out of schemes of irrigation and the making of new roads. The enhanced prosperity of the State brought about an accumulation of funds out of which the Dhrangadhra Railway has been extended to Halvad, and arrangements are being made for the continuation of this section at an early date to Maliya on the Runn of Cutch, for which work the sanction of the Government has been obtained.

It is fully in accord with the thorough training of His Highness the Maharana Sahib in the best traditions of English social and political life that his rule should have been characterized by a spirit of enlightened and progressive policy, and in inaugurating and carrying out numerous measures of reform he has been ably supported by his *Diwan*.

Immediately on receipt of news of the outbreak of war between Great Britain and Germany in the first week of August, 1914, His Highness the Maharana Saheb telegraphed to Government placing the whole resources of the State at the disposal of the Crown for the support of the Allies. During the period of more than four years that the war continued, the total contributions from the State and its subjects to the various funds and War Loans amounted to Rs. 19,18,000, particulars of which are as follows: Towards the two War Loans: (1) from the State—First Indian War Loan of 1917, Rs. 4,75,000; Second Indian War Loan of 1918, Rs. 5,00,000; (2) from the subjects of the State, first Indian War Loan of 1917, Rs. 1,92,050; second Indian War Loan of 1918, Rs. 3,17,255; total of investments in War Loans, Rs. 14,84,305. Towards the various war funds: (1) From the State—Imperial War Expenses Fund, through the Political Secretary, Bombay Government, Rs. 2,00,000; Imperial War Relief Fund, through Bombay Branch, Rs. 43,000; Comforts for Wounded Soldiers, through Women's Branches, Rs. 10,000; Comforts for Wounded Soldiers, Rs. 3,000; Motor Ambulance Fleet, Rs. 16,000; Bombay War Sales, Rs. 22,200; Queen Mary's Technical Institute for the Blind, Bombay, Rs. 10,000; H.R.H. Prince of Wales's Hospital at Staines, Rs. 30,000; "Our Day" Funds, Rs. 53,026; Royal Silver Wedding Fund, Rs. 5,000; expenses in connection with recruiting, Rs. 26,307; miscellaneous payments, Rs. 5,162.

From the subjects of the State: Contribution from Dhrangadhra Bhayats to the Imperial War Relief Fund, Rs. 3,000; contribution from ladies of Dhrangadhra towards the comforts of the wounded soldiers, Rs. 2,000; balance of the proceeds of the Dhrangadhra "Our Day" lottery, after distributing cash prizes of Rs. 10,000 to winners, in 1917–18, Rs. 24,000; total of contribution to various war funds, Rs. 4,53,695.

In response to the offer of the black "Waler" horses used by the State troops for services in the war, 41 were selected by the Remount Department and utilized as British cavalry remounts. In addition to this, five large tents, with a total aggregate floor space of 3,436 square feet, were given by the State for use as field hospitals. A large motor charabanc was given on loan for the use of the wounded soldiers' club in Poona.

The period of the Great War is particularly memorable in the history of Dhrangadhra as it witnessed the appreciation of the State Administration by Government in more than one way. On January 1, 1917, His Imperial Majesty the King-Emperor was graciously pleased to confer on His Highness the distinction of a Knight Commandership of the Most Exalted Order of the Star of India. In the beginning of the next year, 1918, in recognition of His Highness' services in connection with the war, His Imperial Majesty the King-Emperor was graciously pleased to confer on His Highness the permanent title of "Maharaja," and, farther, to increase his salute from 11 to 13 guns. The *Gazette of India*, issued on January 1, 1918, also announced that His Imperial Majesty the King-Emperor has appointed Rana Shri Mansinhji S. Jhala, Diwan Saheb of Dhrangadhra, as Companion of the Most Eminent Order of the Indian Empire. The public rejoicings which followed the bestowal of these high distinctions were marked by great enthusiasm and fervour.

As a result of the recruiting efforts of the State, 128 combatant and 102 noncombatant recruits were enlisted from June, 1918, to October in the same year, and a sum of Rs. 24,310 was paid to them as bonuses over and above the continuance of the emoluments of the State servants who joined the Kathiawar Company.

The State of Dhrangadhra *is approximately* 1,167 square miles in extent, but this is exclusive of the area of *that portion* of the Runn of Cutch which belongs to the State. It comprises 151 villages, *many* of which have been founded and populated

THE STATE OF DHRANGADHRA.

1. Halvad Palace from the Lake. 2. Halvad Palace, Inner Court. 3. Balcony, Halvad Palace. 4. View of the Lake, Halvad

THE STATE OF DHRANGADHRA.

1. The Ma Sahib's Palace, Dhrangadhra. 2. City of Dhrangadhra, from Fergusson Bridge. 3. Ranmalsar Lake at Dhrangadhra. 4. The Central Jail, Dhrangadhra.

THE STATE OF DHRANGADHRA

by thrifty settlers since the present Maharana ascended the *gadi*. An additional source of revenue has thus been provided, and the prosperity already enjoyed by these new occupiers is an inducement to the *Durbar* to establish other settlements in uncultivated portions of the State, and thereby bring a considerable quantity of waste land under the plough.

The State also owns *vantas* in certain villages in the Ahmedabad Collectorate of the Bombay Presidency.

A forestry branch was inaugurated in connection with the Revenue Department in the year 1914–15, and it is now in charge of the Revenue Commissioner, who for this duty is styled the Superintendent of State *bids* and forests.

For the protection of order in the State the Durbar maintains Lancers, Artillery, and Police, the Infantry having been merged into the Constabulary immediately after His Highness ascended the *gadi*.

Dhrangadhra is interested in the manufacture of brass and copper vessels, stoneware, coarse cloth, and other goods.

The State owns two cotton-presses and eight ginning factories, four of which are situated in the town of Dhrangadhra, but owing to the shortage of the cotton crops in the year under review only one factory was kept at work.

Turning to the question of revenue it may be said that the gross receipts, in-

THE STATE OF DHRANGADHRA.
MANSAGAR LAKE, WITH MAHARAJA'S PALACE, DHRANGADHRA.

cluding the opening balance of the State, amounted in a recent year to Rs. 46,77,976, while the total expenditure was Rs. 37,69,123.

The census taken in the year 1911 showed that the inhabitants were 79,142 in number, but there has undoubtedly been a considerable increase since that date.

His Highness the Maharana Sahib is the supreme ruling authority, he exercising the full powers of a Chief of a State of the First Class. General administration is conducted, under the supervision of His Highness, by the *Diwan*, who receives aid from the Judicial and Revenue Assistants, and the Private and *Huzur* Secretaries.

The principal crops cultivated during the year 1918–19 were jowari, 42,772 acres; *mug*, 4,622 acres; *til* seeds, 1,925 acres; wheat, 2,646 acres; and cotton, 1,92,102 acres.

The State police force, which is under the close supervision of His Highness the Maharana, comprises 783 men of all ranks, this number including mounted and unmounted men.

A very large trade of a general character is carried on in Dhrangadhra, and during a recent year the principal goods imported consisted of metals, cloth, yarn, hardware, grain, and sugar, the total value of which was Rs. 37,26,634, against Rs. 26,93,401 for the previous 12 months. The chief exports for the same period included cotton, wool, stone, *ghee*, cotton seeds, and hides, amounted to Rs. 1,61,15,902, while for the previous year the value was Rs. 83,24,148.

In addition to the activities of the State in the development of the salt industry

Medical relief is provided by the State at the following hospitals and dispensaries, namely, the Prince of Wales's Hospital at Dhrangadhra, the Prankunverba Zenana Hospital in the same city, the Maconochie Dispensary at Dhrangadhra, the Palace Dispensary, the Baj Raj Ba charitable dispensary at Halvad, Sitapur, Charadva, Tikar, Methan, Umerda, and Ranmalpur.

The original building of the Prince of Wales's Hospital was constructed more than 42 years ago, and it fulfilled all the medical requirements of those days, but His Highness, who is fully alive to the

THE STATE OF DHRANGADHRA.

1. Lady Hardinge Institute, with Jaswantsinhji Library, Dhrangadhra. 2. Prince of Wales's Hospital, Dhrangadhra. 3. Sir Ranjitsinhji Cotton Exchange (under construction). 4. Lal Bungalow, Dhrangadhra. 5. Shri Prankunverba Zenana Hospital, Dhrangadhra.

progress made in Western medical science, recently became convinced that the institution was not up to date in its equipment, and therefore he sanctioned its demolition and the erection of a new and suitable structure. The foundation-stone of the latter was laid by Lieut.-Colonel Horace Pottinger, Acting Agent to the Governor in Kathiawar, on March 24, 1919, and the work is now nearing completion. The inhabitants of Halvad, the second town of importance in the State, have long felt the need of a properly equipped hospital with accommodation for indoor patients, and it is satisfactory to learn that the wishes of the people will soon be fully realized. The proposed building will be named the "Willingdon" Hospital, in order to commemorate Lord Willingdon's Governorship of Bombay.

The total annual expenditure of this department now amounts to about Rs. 30,000.

The Department of Public Instruction is responsible for the maintenance of the following educational appointments, namely, the Sir Ajitsinhji High School at Dhrangadhra, the Bai Saheb Ba Middle School at Halvad, three English schools at Raj Sitapur, Tikar, and Charadva; 49 primary schools for boys and five for girls. Over and above these 59 State schools there are five private academies at Dhrangadhra and Halvad.

The High School at Dhrangadhra teaches up to the full course of study in Standard VII, and prepares students for the school-leaving examination conducted by the joint examination Board of the Bombay University, and the Drawing Examination Board of the Sir Jamsetjee Jejeebhoy School of Art, Bombay.

The Public Works Department, under the supervision of the State Engineer, expended the sum of Rs. 1,79,517 during the past year, and it has recently executed a large number of works of public utility.

The railway line owned by the State is nearly 47 miles in length, and since October 1, 1919, the working of the system has been in the hands of the Bombay-Baroda and Central India Railway Company. The gross earnings of the line for the past year were Rs. 2,15,225, while the net receipts amounted to Rs. 94,014.

The State pays an annual tribute of Rs. 40,671 to the British Government, and Rs. 4,006 as *Jortalbi* to the State of Junagadh.

THE STATE OF JAORA

THE Chiefs of Jaora claim descent from Abdul Majid Khan, an Afghan of the Swati tribe, who crossed the border into India about the middle of the eighteenth century, believing that in this country there were suitable opportunities for acquiring both power and wealth. His grandson, Ghafur Khan, became the representative of the Pindari Chieftain, Amir Khan, at the Court of Holkar, from whom he received, in recognition of his services, the territory now known as the Jaora State. This transfer was confirmed by the British Government about the year 1820, and the Suzerain power at the same time conferred upon Ghafur Khan the title of Nawab. About 20 years later certain powers were conferred by the British Government upon the Nawab of the day, and an agreement was arrived at with regard to the maintenance of troops.

The State was very considerably affected by the rebellious example set by other parts of India during the Mutiny of 1857, but the Ruler at that time, Nawab Ghaus Muhammad Khan, gave abundant proofs of his unswerving loyalty to the Crown by rendering most valuable assistance to the British in quelling disturbances, and in the very difficult matter of restoring quietude among people who had been temporarily enticed from the observance of recognized law. In recognition of these services, many of which were undertaken at great personal risk, the Nawab received merited honours from the British Government. He was succeeded in the year 1865 by his son Muhammad Ismail Khan, a minor, who, in turn, was followed in 1895 by his twelve-years' old son, the present Head of the State, whose title is Major H. H. Fukhruddaula Nawab Sir Mahomed Iftikhar Ali Khan, Sahib Bahadur, Saulat Jung, K.C.I.E. He is entitled to a salute of 13 guns.

The Nawab was born in the year 1883, and his education was received at the Daly College, Indore, and subsequently in his own home under the guidance and tutorship of British officials selected by the Government of India.

The influence which these gentlemen had upon the early life of the young Ruler cannot be over-estimated. They were not merely pedagogues who imposed a circumscribed course of study alone; they moulded the character of their charge; they imbued him with a desire to be associated with the best in men and literature; they inculcated principles tending to a high conception of his future responsibilities as Head of a State, having a population of about 82,000 inhabitants; and they encouraged, at all proper times, his natural love for manly exercises and outdoor sports of various kinds.

The State of Jaora, which is in direct treaty relations with the Government of India, is in the Malwa Political Agency of the Central India States, and is bounded on the north by the States of Indore, Gwalior, and Dewas; on the west by the Gwalior and Dewas States; on the south the Gwalior, Sailana, and Rutlam States; and on the east by the Dewas, Partabgarh, and Banswara States.

The territory has an area of about 570 square miles, and its population is composed of Hindus, Mahomedans, Jains, and others, the first-named being represented by more than 70 per cent. of the aggregate number.

The country does not possess any remarkable physical features, and there are only two rivers of any importance, but it contains some of the richest cotton-growing land in Northern India. A major portion of the area is under cultivation, the principal crops being cotton, wheat, maize, poppies, and *jurar*.

Fifty or sixty years ago the State was in a backward condition as regards industrial occupations of any kind whatsoever, chiefly by reason of a lack of proper communication-roads between the several districts, and an entire absence of trade relationship with other States. It is true that, after British supremacy became an established fact, an organized system of plundering by native marauders had been kept in check, and that some aspirations after a commercial awakening were manifested, but it was the present Nawab who by his sound practical training and his strong personality gave the impetus needed for turning that awakening to good account. Larger areas of land have been tilled; regular survey and settlements made; improvements in all the branches of administration attended to; and foundation stones of prosperity—which is now enjoyed—were substantially laid. One of the chief agencies in the development of the State was the opening of the Rajputana-Malwa Railway, which cuts through the heart of Jaora and connects it with commercial centres of the outside world, thus affording necessary facilities for the transport of agricultural and other products. The natural resources of the country are of a high order, and it is confidently expected that under a pro-

MAJOR H.H. NAWAB SIR MAHOMED IFTIKAR-ALI-KHAN BAHADUR, K.C.I.E., RULER OF JAORA.

THE STATE OF JAORA.

1. State Elephants. 2. The Nawab's Pack of Hounds. 3. The Victoria Club.

THE STATE OF JAORA.

1. The Nawab's Palace. 2. Royal Mausoleum. 3. The State Hospital. 4. The Barr High School.

THE STATE OF JAORA.

1. The Secretariat Building. 2. Minister's Residence.

THE STATE OF JAORA.

1. A Main Street in the City of Jaora. 2. Nawab's Bridge. 3. The Jail.

gressive, intellectual, and wise Ruler the further advancement of the State and its inhabitants is certain to be continued.

The Nawab is President of the State Council, and he is assisted in administration matters by a Vice-President (who is also Chief Secretary to His Highness) and Revenue and Judicial Secretaries.

His Highness is the final authority in each department, frames his own laws, and administers his State with full powers. There are seven districts or *tahsils*, namely, Jaora, Tal, Barauda, Malhargarh, Sanjeet, Nawabganj, and Berkhera, and these are controlled by a *tahsildar*, who is Magistrate of the district and collector of revenue.

Great improvements have been made in the town of Jaora, the capital of the State, which contains several imposing buildings, including a very fine Court House, post and telegraph offices, several schools, two hospitals, and a number of other structures of a public and private character. The town is at an elevation of more than 1,600 feet above the level of the sea, and it has been the official headquarters of the State since the time of the Nawab's ancestor, Ghafur Khan. The inhabitants are about 20,000 in number, Hindus and Mahomedans being represented almost equally in numbers, although the percentage of the former is slightly in excess of the other race.

The truth of the old adage, "*mens sana in sano corpore*," is illustrated forcibly in the life of the Nawab. He is a splendid horseman, a brilliant exponent of polo, and is as clever as he is enthusiastic in his love for manly sport, yet he is still more conspicuous as a Ruler, as his keen intellectual abilities and his determination to regard the welfare of the people as a solemn obligation resting upon him have a remarkable effect upon the State in the direction of reforms and progress.

THE STATE OF JIND

IN respect of its extent and importance, the Jind State stands second in what are known as the three Phulkian States, namely, Patiala, Jind, and Nabha.

The modern State of Jind consists of the three large detached tracts of Sangrur, Jind, and Dadri, constituting three administrative *tahsils*.

The area of the State is 1,268 square miles; its inhabitants were 271,728 in number at the census of 1911; and the gross income of the State is about Rs. 25,00,000 annually.

The climate varies with the locality of each tract, but being in the plains of India the general conditions of the sub-Himalayan area prevail. It is cold during the winter period, and is hot in the summer months. The monsoon is general about July, August, and September, though there is often a shortage of rain in the tracts which lie towards the south, where the desert portions of the Punjab are more nearly approached. The average rainfall of the State is 20 inches, but it is greater in the Sangrur district than fu ther south.

Nearly three-fourths of the population are Hindus, about 10 per cent. are Sikhs, and the remainder are Mahomedans. Sixty-six per cent. of the population live by agriculture. The languages spoken are various dialects of Punjabi, Bangru, Ahirbati, and Hindustani.

The chief exports are wheat, gram, barley, cotton, maize, millet, *ghee*, and *gur*; and the imports are chiefly piece-goods, rice and sugar. The breeding of cattle and camels is carried on extensively, the Jind district being famous for a fine breed of milch buffaloes, and the Dadri *tahsil* for camels. The most important industries are the manufacture of silver and gold ornaments, of wood-work, leather, and country cloth.

Early in the eighteenth century the British were advancing their influence to Delhi, and beyond, while Maharaja Ranjit Singh was consolidating the Punjab and forming the Sikh Government, under which the Phulkian States were establishing themselves on the eastern border.

The British arrived at Delhi in the year 1804. Their influence soon reached Ambala and Ludhiana, and their foremost military stations were quickly extended to Karnal, Ambala, and Ludhiana (on the Sutlej river). During the latter half of the eighteenth century, the Punjab was much disturbed by invasions from the north and west frontiers of India, by successive Mahomedan tribes, while the Moghul Empire appeared to be declining in force and vigour.

The principality of Jind was formally established by Raja Gajpat Singh, the maternal grandfather of Maharaja Ranjit Singh, the "Lion of the Punjab." Raja Gajpat Singh may be considered the first independent Ruler of Jind State. He was the great-grandson of the famous Phul, one of the originators of the Sikh power in the Punjab. Gajpat Singh's influence became so formidable that the title of "Raja" was granted to him and his family by a *farman* of the Emperor Shah Alam in 1772, and from that date the Rulers of Jind have been independent Princes. Raja Gajpat Singh distinguished himself greatly in those days in the wars against the invading Mahomedans, and established himself at Jind, where he erected a large brick fort.

His son and successor, Raja Bhag Singh, was the first of the great Cis-Sutlej Chiefs to seek alliance with the British Government in the earlier years of the nineteenth century (1804). He was associated with General Lake, who wrote to him as his "friend and ally," and in many ways recognized his great influence among the Punjab Chiefs, and acknowledged that that influence was always exercised on the side of the English. When General Ochterlony was in pursuit of the Mahrattas under Jaswant Rao Holkar, Raja Bhag Singh actually held Saharanpur for the British. His influence was mainly used to prevent his nephew, the Maharaja Ranjit Singh, from espousing the cause of the Mahrattas. Until his death, in 1819, Raja Bhag Singh continued to be the firm friend and ally of the East India Company, and to whom he rendered all assistance possible, for which he received many marks of favour and regard. Indeed, he may be said to have been the means of founding many happy relations, which in those days subsisted between the Sikh Chiefs and the British Government. This great Chief, Raja Bhag Singh, died in 1819, and was succeeded by his son, Raja Fateh Singh, who only ruled for a short period, as he died on February 3, 1822, after an uneventful reign, leaving a son, aged only 11 years, named Raja Sangat Singh. This Chief lived until 1834, and died, leaving no issue. He was succeeded by his second cousin, Raja Sarup Singh, who proved a very satisfactory ruler, and Jind was, in his time, one of the best administered States in the Punjab.

During the second Sikh War, in 1849, Raja Sarup Singh, the great-grandfather of the present Ruler, offered to lead his troops in person to Lahore, to join the British army, for which he received the thanks of the Government. This Raja also

LIEUT.-COL. HIS HIGHNESS FARZAND-I-DILBAND, RASIKH-UL-ITIKAD, DAULAT-I-INGLISHIA, RAJA-I-RAJGAN, MAHARAJA SIR RANBIR SINGH, RAJENDRA BAHADUR, G.C.I.E., K.C.S.I., THE PRESENT RULER (SUCCEEDED 1887).

1. LIEUT.-COL. HIS HIGHNESS FARZAND-I-DILBAND, RASIKH-UL-ITIKAD, DAULAT-I-INGLISHIA, RAJA-I-RAJGAN, MAHARAJA SIR RANBIR SINGH, RAJENDRA BAHADUR, G.C.I.E., K.C.S.I., IN UNIFORM.

2. SOME OF THE TROPHIES OF GAME SHOT BY H.H. THE MAHARAJA OF JIND, 1919.

(Photo by Bremner)

offered his troops and personal services in the Mutiny of 1857, and upon its acceptance he rendered signal services to the British, and covered his State with honour. Raja Sarup Singh conducted his troops to Karnal on May 18, 1857, by forced marches, and undertook the defence of the city and cantonment. On June 21st he sent a detachment of his troops to secure the bridge of boats at Baghpat, twenty miles north of Delhi, thus enabling the Meerut force to cross the Jumna and join Sir H. Barnard's column. The Jind force marched in advance of the British Army—the post of honour—when recovering Sambhalka and Rai, securing the road, and collecting supplies for the army. In the battle of Badli Ki Sarai, the Jind troops behaved most gallantly, and were complimented on the field by the Commander-in-Chief, who sent one of the captured guns to the Raja as a present. In the assault of Delhi the Jind troops took a prominent part, scaling the walls side by side with the English. Raja Sarup Singh was the only ruling Prince in India who led his troops in person, and, as a token of gratitude and confidence, the administration of Rohtak was made over to him. In his despatch of September 22, 1857, announcing the fall of Delhi, General Wilson brought "prominently to notice the admirable services performed by the Raja of Jind and his troops, who are said not only to have discharged harassing duties in the constant escort of convoys, but also to have aided the General on more than one occasion in the field, and finally to have participated in the capture and assault of Delhi." The Governor-General, in his Notification of November 5, 1857, declared that the steady support of the Raja of Jind called for the marked thanks of the Government. In recognition of Raja Sarup Singh's services, the Dadri territory, 575 square miles in extent, was conferred on him, thirteen villages of Kularan *Ilaqua* were also ceded in perpetuity, and, as a great mark of honour, the confiscated house of the rebel Shahzada Mirza Abu Bakar, in Delhi, was made over to the Raja. He was also given a *sanad*, dated May 5, 1860, under the hand and seal of the Viceroy, declaring that he and his heirs should for ever exercise full sovereignty over his ancestral and acquired dominions, all feudatories and independants being bound to render obedience to him throughout his dominion. In the *sanad* it was also stated that the British Government "will never demand from the Rulers of Jind any tribute" on account of revenue service or any other pleas, nor receive complaints of any of their subjects.

Raja Sarup Singh, of Mutiny fame, was a magnificent specimen of the Sikh race, tall and strong, and of princely appearance, and in character he was just and honest. Speaking of his services in the field, the Commissary-General, Colonel Thomson, said that "but for the timely supplies furnished by him the quantity of stores would have been insufficient for the troops." He was made a Knight Grand Commander of the Most Exalted Order of the Star of India in September 1863, but before he was invested with the insignia he passed away, on January 26, 1864.

He was succeeded by his son, Raja Raghbir Singh, whose accession to the *gadi* was soon followed by a general revolt among the people of Dadri. This rising was instigated by certain malcontents, who misrepresented the administrative measures introduced by the new Ruler, but it was promptly put down, and peace was restored. His Highness was helpful to the Supreme Government in suppressing the "Kuka" outbreak in 1872. He was made a Knight Grand Commander of the Most Exalted Order of the Star of India in 1876, and a Councillor of the Empire in 1877. A contingent of his army served in the Afghan War (1870–80), and he was ready to assist the Supreme Power with his troops in the Egyptian campaign of 1882, though the Government was not in a position to accept the offer. He died on March 7, 1887. He was an able and sympathetic Ruler, and, under him, Jind improved in many directions. He was a Prince of great taste, and took a keen interest in his administration; he encouraged industries, and did everything in his power to improve agriculture. He was succeeded by his grandson, the present Ruler, who was then only eight years of age, his father, Tikka Balbir Singh, having predeceased Raja Sir Raghbir Singh.

Lieutenant-Colonel His Highness Farzand-i-Dilband, Rasikh-ul-Itikad, Daulat-i-Inglishia, Raja-i-Rajgan, Maharaja Sir Ranbir Singh, Rajendra Bahadur, G.C.I.E., K.C.S.I., Maharaja of Jind State, as has already been stated, succeeded to the *gadi* at the early age of eight years, and, during the period of his minority, a Council of Regency administered the State and watched over his interests. He was invested with full ruling powers on November 10, 1899.

Immediately after his succession he had to face the terrible famine of 1899–1900, when he took prompt and effective measures to relieve the sufferers by opening relief works and poor-houses and by giving relief to the extent of Rs. 2,26,710. As a precaution against further famine, 172 irrigation wells were, with the aid of State grants, sunk in the State, and the famine administration of His Highness was one of which he might well be proud. His Highness has closely followed in the footsteps of his grandfather and great-grandfather, and, under his care, the State has reaped many benefits from various kinds of reforms which have been inaugurated. One of the first things His Highness realized after taking over the reins of administration was that the emoluments of his officials were too low for their respective positions and responsibilities, and, therefore, not compatible with efficiency. He therefore at once ordered suitable increases in salaries and a number of new departments and posts were also established. His Highness separated the Judicial and Executive Departments, and he also created a new post of Accountant-General, the new official being put in charge of all accounts which had previously been submitted to the different Heads of Departments. Another new post was that of Chief Medical Officer, this step being taken with the object of thoroughly reorganizing the Medical and Sanitary Departments, and the marked progress made in this direction, during the present rule, is another evidence of the enlightened interest evinced by His Highness in the genuine welfare of his subjects. The whole State has been adequately provided with hospitals and dispensaries, and the "King-Emperor George V Coronation Wing" has been fitted with ample accommodation for respectable people who wish to remain as indoor patients. Great and systematic efforts have been made for stamping out plague. His Highness is no less anxious to relieve the suffering of dumb creatures than of human beings, and a Veterinary Hospital, built at a cost of Rs. 84,000, is one of the notable institutions of the State. Three Veterinary Assistants are employed, administering relief to hundreds of animals.

The wisdom and efficiency of an administration may be gauged by its educational progress, and not the least among the departments which have undergone a complete overhauling is the Department of Public Instruction. The

1. HIS HIGHNESS RAJA SIR RAGHBIR SINGH, SAHIB BAHADUR OF JIND, G.C.S.I., COUNCILLOR TO HER LATE MAJESTY THE QUEEN EMPRESS. (RULED 1864–87.)

(Photo by Johnston & Hoffman.)

2. HIS HIGHNESS RAJA SIR SARUP SINGH, SAHIB BAHADUR, G.C.S.I., OF JIND, OF MUTINY FAME. (RULED 1837–64.)

3. HIS HIGHNESS RAJA SANJAT SINGH, SAHIB BAHADUR OF JIND. (RULED 1822–34.)

number of schools has been greatly increased, and there are now 2,588 male and female scholars under instruction.

During the reign of His Highness several new State buildings have been erected. These include the High School, with hostel, at Sangrur, the Ranbir Skating Rink, the Lady Minto Ranbir Girls' School, the Female Hospital, the Ranbir Silver Jubilee Orphanage, and the Veterinary Hospital. Among the places of interest, or institutions worthy of a visit, may be mentioned the Durbar Hall, the High School for boys, the Lady Minto Ranbir Girls' School, the Ranbir Rivaz Veterinary Hospital, Ranbir Skating Rink, the State Library and Museum, and the Imperial Service Regimental Lines.

The Police Department has also undergone reorganization and reform, and the expenditure has increased from Rs. 38,000 to Rs. 55,000 per annum, or over 45 per cent.

In order to bring the administration up to date, Executive and Judicial circulars are issued to the Officers of the State, while for the improvement of the criminal law, the provisions of the Indian Penal Code have been introduced in place of the old State criminal law.

During His Highness' reign marked progress has also been made in the administration of civil justice. Cases are promptly decided in Courts, the percentage of the civil and criminal cases decided in the same year being 88 and 98 respectively. The number of the cases for transfer of land has decreased, and the price of land has considerably risen, this giving ample proof of the greater prosperity of the people.

Good progress has been made in the extension of trade and commerce. Efforts have been put forth to increase the means of communication, a number of extensions and improvements in roads have been carried out, and many roads have for the first time been metalled. Formerly there were only two railway lines passing through the State, but in the present reign two other lines, the Ludhiana-Dhuri-Jakhal, and the Jind-Panipat Railways, have been constructed at the cost of the State, jointly with the Malerkotla Durbar, and the Delhi-Umballa-Kalka Railway Company, respectively.

A Court of Wards has been established to protect the interests of minors, and there are at present 151 estates under this Court.

To improve the financial condition of his subjects, His Highness has on different occasions remitted debts and demands of the State amounting to Rs. 3,75,000.

Co-operative Credit Societies were started in the State in 1909, and, during this short period, 65 of these have been established, with a capital of Rs. 1,40,000. Agriculturists are largely benefited by this wholesome system, and this is specially evinced by the fact that many mortgages of farm lands have been redeemed.

His Highness the Maharaja is most devoted to the Royal House of England. Towards the Victoria Memorial Fund, His Highness contributed Rs. 50,000, and at the time of the Coronation Durbar of 1903, His Highness, besides remitting Rs. 2,25,000, representing rents due from his subjects, subscribed Rs. 1,00,000 towards the King Edward Provincial Memorial Fund, which amount is utilized for extending the King Edward Medical College at Lahore. There was also a contribution of Rs. 5,000 towards the All-India Memorial Fund. His Highness attended the Durbar held at Lahore in 1905 in order to meet Their Royal Highnesses the Prince and Princess of Wales. In 1906 His Highness gave a sum of Rs. 25,000, which was equally divided between the Victoria Girls' School at Lahore and the Minto Nursing Association. His Highness was created a Knight Commander of the Most Exalted Order of the Star of India (K.C.S.I.) in 1909, and on the occasion of the Coronation Durbar in 1911 the hereditary distinction of "Maharaja" was conferred on him.

On February 27, 1913, His Highness Maharaja Sir Ranbir Singh completed 25 years' occupancy of the *gadi*, and his Silver Jubilee was celebrated with great *éclat*. On this auspicious occasion His Highness granted several concessions to his people and officials, namely: (1) an increase in the pay of his Imperial Service Regiment; (2) the establishment of an Orphanage at Sangrur; and (3) the introduction of a dignity of "Kursi Nashins." Donations to the *dharamshala* of the Aitchison Chiefs' College, Lahore, and the Temperance Society of Amritsar were also made.

His Highness is very popular with his subjects, and this was marked by the enthusiastic reception and ovation given by the people to His Highness on his State entry on February 24, 1913, and on the occasion of the elephant procession on the 27th of the same month, when his "Silver Jubilee" was celebrated.

The special attention paid by His Highness to his Imperial Service Regiment is quite in keeping with the traditions of loyalty to the British Crown, inherited from his ancestors, whose heroic achievements in upholding the British flag are recorded in history. This State has shown its steady devotion to the Throne from the earliest time of progress of British rule to Delhi and beyond it. The prescribed strength of the regiment was six hundred strong, and the equipment and discipline was so efficient that it was at very short notice mobilized to proceed on active service during the Great War. In order to bring about this state of efficiency several concessions have been granted to the troops by His Highness the present Ruler. At the same time the regiment is proud to have been provided with comfortable barracks, built at a cost of Rs. 3,00,000, and it may safely be said that no State in Northern India has Imperial regimental lines erected in a better manner.

The greatest event of the rule of His Highness remains to be mentioned, namely, the services rendered by the State in support of the Allies in the Great War. When His Highness the Maharaja learned that Britain had declared war against Germany, he at once, by telegram, put the entire resources of his State, and his Imperial Service regiment, at the disposal of His Imperial Majesty the King-Emperor, adding that the regiment was fully equipped with mobilization kit, and ready to move to the front on the shortest notice.

On August 15, 1914, His Highness received a telegram from the Political Agent informing him that the Government of India had thankfully [illegible] the patriotic offer, and that four [illegible] companies of Jind Imperial Service Re[illegible] [illegible] on active service. [illegible] accordingly entrained on September 14, 1914, for field service.

Lieut.-Colonel Baldev Singh (son of Sardar Bahadur Sir Shamsher Singh, K.C.I.E., Chief Minister), who was under training in the Imperial Cadet Corps, Dehra Dun, was immediately called back on mobilization.

By His Highness' order No. 317, dated August 19, 1914, Major-General Natha Singh Bahadur, Commander-in-Chief of the State forces, who volunteered his services for the front, was put in command of the regiment, and Col. Baldev Singh was appointed as Second-in-Command.

On the evening of September 14, 1914, when the regiment, imbued with the spirit of self-sacrifice and devotion, left for the

THE STATE OF JIND.

MOUNTED OFFICERS OF JIND IMPERIAL SERVICE REGIMENT WHO RETURNED FROM THE FRONT WITH THE REGIMENT AFTER THREE AND A QUARTER YEARS' ACTIVE SERVICE IN EAST AFRICA.

1. Lieut.-Gen. Natha Singh, Sardar Bahadur, C.I.E. 2. Lieut.-Col. Baldev Singh, Bahadur, I.C. 3. Major Bihara Singh. 4. Capt. Achra Singh. 5. Capt. Niamat Ali Khan, I.O.M. 6. Capt. Sunder Singh. 7. Lieut. Chanan Singh.

2. WOUNDED OFFICERS AND MEN OF JIND IMPERIAL SERVICE REGIMENT.

1. Lieut.-Gen. Natha Singh, Sardar Bahadur, C.I.E. 2. Capt. Achra Singh. 3. Capt. Niamat Ali Khan, I.O.M. 4. Subedar Harnam Singh, I.O.M. 5. Subedar Kishen Singh. 6. Subedar Bhagwan Singh, I.O.M.

3. WAR TROPHIES CAPTURED FROM THE GERMANS BY JIND IMPERIAL SERVICE REGIMENT IN EAST AFRICA, 1914–17.

4. JIND IMPERIAL SERVICE REGIMENT IN QUARTER COLUMN ON RETURN AFTER THREE AND A QUARTER YEARS' SERVICE IN EAST AFRICA.

THE STATE OF JIND.

1. Ranbir Silver Jubilee Orphanage. 2. Victoria Golden Jubilee Hospital, Sangrur. 3. Dewan Khana (Durbar Hall).

THE STATE OF JIND.

1. Main Entrance to the Durbar Hall (Dewan Khana). 2. Interior of Durbar Hall (Dewan Khana).

front, an enthusiastic scene was witnessed on the platform of the railway station at Sangrur. His Highness the Maharaja and all the officials and other notables, and a large crowd of people were present to say " God speed " to the troops. It was a most pleasant and touching sight to witness the high spirits and cheerfulness of this unit.

His Highness the Maharaja Sahib addressed the regiment in a stirring speech, and Major-General Natha Singh replied on behalf of himself and the regiment under his command, in the Urdu language.

His Highness the Maharaja shook hands with the officers of the regiment, and wished them " God speed," and the band played the Jind national anthem. The regiment, amidst hearty cheers and good wishes of all present, then left for the front. Three loud and hearty cheers were given for the victory of the British arms.

It is a matter for great pride and gratification to the State and its Ruler that the Jind Imperial Service Regiment was the first among the Imperial Service troops to encounter the enemy in this Great War, as will appear from the following :

The Inspector-General Imperial Service troops in his D.O. No. 3,075, dated October 14, 1914, while informing the State of the casualties, wrote : " Jind has the honour of letting the first blood flow for King and Empire amongst the Imperial Service troops."

Again, Lieut.-Colonel B. E. M. Gurdon, C.I.E., D.S.O., Political Agent, Phulkian States, wrote in his letter, dated October 17, 1914 : " I congratulate Your Highness very warmly for the great distinction which has fallen to the lot of your regiment, viz., that of having the honour to be the first Imperial Service unit to engage the enemy beyond the limits of the Indian Empire."

The discipline, manly behaviour, and self-sacrificing spirit of the regiment are borne out by the numerous letters of the General Officers under whom the regiment served, and of the special Service Officers attached to it.

The Government from time to time gave expression to their appreciation of the gallant services of the regiment. His Excellency the Viceroy, in a speech delivered in the Imperial Legislative Council on September 5, 1916, while referring to services of the Imperial Service troops, referred to the congratulations of General Smuts sent to Their Highnesses the Maharajas of Kashmir and Jind. His Excellency the Viceroy also offered, on behalf of himself and his colleagues in the Council, the warmest and most sincere thanks to the Princes named in the speech (of whom His Highness the Maharaja of Jind was one), and of others whose princely gifts and loyal services have been acknowledged on previous occasions.

The regiment was engaged in several encounters, and fought bravely. It had many casualties, as the following figures show : killed in action, 57 ; wounded, 86 (of whom 12 died) ; died of disease, 32 ; making a total of 175.

Adding to 380 combatants and 52 followers who proceeded on field service on September 14, 1914, the number sent as reinforcements in 13 drafts, comprising 712 men (678 combatants, and 34 non-combatants), to fill up the gaps caused by casualties, the total number amounts to 1,144 men sent on service (1,058 combatants, and 86 non-combatants).

The Government having allowed free rations to the Indian army, His Highness the Maharaja Sahib Bahadur was the first among all the Indian Rulers to sanction a similar grant to all combatants (excepting mounted officers). He also gave an increase in the pay of the mounted officers, company officers, non-commissioned officers, and followers, in order to maintain the high level of efficiency of his regiment. His Excellency the Viceroy in his *kharita* of July 23, 1917, thanked His Highness most warmly for the measures taken, and felt assured that they would have the desired effect.

War pensions have been awarded to all the officers and men invalided from the front, sick and wounded who were unfit for further service ; and pensions have been granted to the heirs of those who were killed in action or died on active service, according to the War Pension Regulations of the State, which are nearly the same as those for the Indian army. The regiment had the good fortune to be engaged in several actions, and they earned the admiration of the General Officers Commanding. It is worth mentioning with pride that this unit was honoured with 47 distinctions, as detailed hereafter.

The regiment returned to Sangrur, the capital of the State, after 3½ years' active service in East Africa. They were given a warm reception at the railway station by His Highness the Maharaja, who was accompanied by Mr. L. M. Crump, I.C.S., Political Agent, Phulkian States, Major MacBrayne, Inspecting Officer, Punjab Imperial Service Infantry, and a large number of officials and the general public.

His Highness addressed the officers and men of the regiment in a speech in which he expressed his deep appreciation of their services, and announced the grant of free rations to men, increases of pay, and liberal concessions to officers and non-commissioned officers, and life allowances to those who had received Government distinctions in recognition of the gallant conduct of the regiment.

The following is a list of distinctions conferred on the regiment : one Military Cross ; one Companionship of the Indian Empire ; one First-Class Order of British India, with the title of Sardar Bahadur ; one Second-Class Order of British India, with the title of Bahadur ; five Indian Orders of Merit, Second Class ; nine Indian Distinguished Service Medals ; one Croix-de-Guerre (French Order) ; one St. George Medal, Second Class (Russian Order) ; one St. George Medal, Fourth Class (Russian Order) ; one Cross of St. George, Fourth Class (Russian Order) ; fifteen Meritorious Service Medals, and ten men mentioned in despatches, these making a total of 47 honours.

The following civilians and subjects of the State received titles, noted against their names, from the Government, in recognition of their services rendered in connection with the war : Sardar Bahadur Sardar Shamsher Singh, C.I.E., Chief Minister, received the distinction of a Knight Commandership of the Most Eminent Order of the Indian Empire, Munshi Brij Narain, Judicial Minister, was created Rai Bahadur ; Col. Hargopal Singh, Revenue Minister, was given the title of Sardar Bahadur ; Dr. Behari Lal Dhingra, M.D., M.R.C.S., Chief Medical Officer, gained the Kaiser-i-Hind Medal of the First-Class ; Sardar Dalip Singh, Foreign Minister, was made a Sardar Bahadur ; Lala Ram Gopal, Accountant-General, became a Member of the British Empire ; Lala Shadi Ram, Inspector-General of Police, received the title of Rai Bahadur ; Sardar Bakhtawar Singh, Nazim, became a Sardar Sahib ; Choudhri Ram Dayal, Hon. Magistrate, Sangrur, was given the title of Rai Sahib ; Lala Matu Ram, *Tahsildar*, received a sword of honour ; 28 Government *sanads* were granted ; and five recruiting badges were presented.

In addition to sending his Imperial Service regiment to the front for the cause of the Empire, His Highness gave the

THE STATE OF JIND

following further help in the way of men, money, material, and animals:

The service of all his troops (four companies of Imperial Service infantry) was accepted. Thirteen drafts, comprising 712 men and followers, were sent from time to time as reinforcements.

Recruits to the number of 5,173 were supplied for the Indian army, and 1,150 for the Jind Imperial Service regiment. If the number of men serving in both before the outbreak of war is added the total contribution in men comes to 8,673. The State also supplied 28 drivers and followers for service with General Service wagons in Mesopotamia, and 305 camel and mule drivers.

His Highness the Maharaja made a liberal contribution direct towards the expenses of the war, and to the various funds opened in connection therewith. The following monetary assistance was rendered, Rs. 3,30,000 in cash (in gold and silver coins). Of this sum Rs. 2,00,000 were deposited in the Government Treasury, Ludhiana, on November 6, 1914, a sum of Rs. 1,00,000 was deposited in the same Treasury on April 5, 1917, and a cheque for Rs. 30,000 in favour of the Accountant-General, Punjab, was sent on September 30, 1918. Rs. 75,000 were given for one armoured aeroplane; Rs. 45,000 for one bombing aeroplane for service in Mesopotamia; Rs. 25,050, the cost of three motor ambulance cars; Rs. 13,54,452, the amount expended upon the Jind Imperial Service regiment at the front and depot; Rs. 24,408, the cost of the upkeep of the Imperial remounts; Rs. 30,024, the expenditure towards recruitment for camel and mule drivers supplied by the State (including bonuses); Rs. 50,221, towards the enlistment of recruits and followers; Rs. 540, advanced to the artillery and mule drivers supplied from the local troops for the Indian army for service in Mesopotamia; Rs. 96,151 for extra pay, presents, and *khilats*, awarded to officers and men of the Jind Imperial Service regiment on their return from the field service; Rs. 1,16,921, subscriptions to the various funds; Rs. 11,50,000, towards the first and second Indian War Loans (cash Rs. 8,50,000, by conversion Rs. 3,00,000); and Rs. 5,000, the amount expended in victory celebrations.

The share that the Jind State took in the supply of material for war purposes was quite in keeping with its traditional loyalty, as will appear from the under-mentioned details: Two machine guns; six tents for hospital use in France, of the value of Rs. 2,600; 1,963 *maunds* of *babul* bark, supplied free to the Government harness and saddlery factory, Cawnpore, the cost being Rs. 2,291; 200 pack-camel saddles (*palans*), worth Rs. 1,029; six kitchen tents for the Imperial Service regiment, amounted to Rs. 300.

The Government, having expressed a desire to purchase horses suitable for artillery and *silladar* cavalry, asked the Durbar to afford the necessary facilities for the purchase of the animals. His Highness the Maharaja readily offered to present any number of sound and serviceable horses, without payment, such as might be selected by the Remount Officer, and he assured the Government that every man, animal, Treasury, and in short, everything which he possessed, was at the service of the Empire.

Accordingly 121 horses, selected by the Government Remount Officer as fit for the army, were presented free to the Government.

Similarly, 440 camels and 56 mules were presented free to the Government for service in the army, the total value of all these animals being Rs. 1,09,754, as detailed below:

121 cavalry horses, Rs. 48,000; 440 camels, Rs. 50,114; 56 mules, Rs. 11,640; these making a total of 617 animals.

The share that His Highness and his State has taken in the war has already been related, but it would not be out of place if the total expenditure incurred by the Durbar in supplying money, material, and animals be summarized as follows: contribution in money, Rs. 33,02,767; contribution in material, Rs. 6,220; contribution in animals, Rs. 1,09,754; making a grand total of Rs. 34,18,741.

The total annual gross income of the State is Rs. 25,00,000, and its contribution of Rs. 34,18,741 during the period of the war amounts to the fact that the State made a contribution annually of one-third of its gross income.

In order to meet wastage in the field His Highness the Maharaja firstly increased the strength of the Imperial Service regiment to 800, and then, in response to the appeal of the Prime Minister of England, it rose to 1,600, which is a great undertaking in the way of supply of men and money. With the view of making awards for war services of officials and subjects, and, further, of stimulating enlistment, His Highness the Maharaja held a recruiting Durbar on October 16, 1917. At this Durbar, among others, there were present Mr. L. M. Crump, I.C.S., Political Agent, Phulkian States, and Lieut. R. H. Crump, Assistant Recruiting Officer, Ludhiana. The speakers, while rejoicing at the splendid record of recruitment, urged those present to exert themselves more and more with accelerated efforts. His Highness the Maharaja, expressing his gratification at the result of enlistment, exhorted his people to make "effort and yet greater effort," to use His Excellency the Viceroy's words; and the subjects of the State, through their representatives, tendered assurances of their unflinching devotion to the great cause.

The receipt of the news of the cessation of hostilities and surrender of Germany was received by His Highness the Maharaja, and the booming of the royal salute conveyed the news to every quarter of the town. His Highness the Maharaja issued a *farman* expressing his immense gratification and delight at the victorious and glorious termination of the war. November 13, 1918, was observed as a public holiday, and a gun salute and a *feu de joie* were fired. Thanksgiving prayers were offered by all religious communities in their respective places of worship. Sweets were distributed to the troops and schoolboys, and the poor were fed. The town of Sangrur wore a gala day appearance, and the people gave expression to their joy in various ways. The town was decorated, and excellent arrangements for illumination of the town and regimental lines were made. Religious processions went through the bazars and streets, and were greeted with cheers. Great enthusiasm prevailed. The people from surrounding villages mustered in large numbers, singing and rejoicing, and the Imperial Service troops celebrated the day by holding sports.

Although celebrations had already taken place in the State on November 13, 1918, immediately after the happiest news of the complete victory of the British Government and their allied countries was received in the State, and a holiday had also been observed, yet, in order to partake in the rejoicings with the whole of the Punjab, His Highness the Maharaja ordered the holding of further festivities, and the observance of holiday on the 27th idem. A royal salute of 101 guns was fired in the morning, and military sports were held for the enjoyment of the public at the Parade ground. In the afternoon an elephant procession was formed, to proceed from the main gate of the Durbar Hall, through the principal streets, to the ***Gurdwara Sahib*** (Sikh temple). At this place a thanksgiving service was held. There was very great rejoicing in the city, and much enthusiasm prevailed. In the evening the bazars were illuminated, and fireworks were discharged. Twenty-one prisoners were released in honour of the occasion.

The distinctions gained by the Jind battalion on the battlefield comprised the following: a Commandership of the Indian Empire, granted to General Natha Singh; one Military Cross; two Orders of British India; five Orders of Merit; nine Distinguished Service Medals; 15 Meritorious Service Medals; and four Foreign Medals.

The men of Jind serving in the army were awarded: one Order of British India; three Orders of Merit; 10 Distinguished Service Medals; two Meritorious Service Medals; and two Foreign Decorations.

It would be more fitting if the account of the war services of the State be concluded by giving an extract from the ***kharita***, dated June 30, 1919, from His Excellency the Viceroy to His Highness the Maharaja Sahib Bahadur.

"On behalf of His Majesty the King-Emperor and myself I thank Your Highness most warmly for the staunch support and very substantial aid rendered by the Jind State during the whole period of the war. Your Highness materially assisted with most liberal gifts of money towards the expenses of the war, with ambulance cars, horses, camels, mules, tents for hospital use, and a bomb aeroplane, besides generously contributing to various funds for the provision of comforts for the troops, and for the relief of those who have suffered in the war. Recruiting was stimulated in the State, and the Jind Imperial Service troops rendered valuable service in East Africa, where, by their soldierly qualities and great gallantry, they gained fresh honours, and proved their courage and efficiency throughout the campaign. In these, and in many other varied directions, too numerous to mention in detail here, Your Highness has manifested the depth of your steadfast loyalty and devotion to His Imperial Majesty the King and the British Empire, and has shared in the great struggle for justice and freedom, in which India has so nobly borne her part."

His Highness has a keen eye in detecting men of ability and character, and he has surrounded himself with very able officials, who co-operate with him in every possible way in the work of administration. Sardar Bahadur Sir Shamsher Singh, K.C.I.E., Chief Minister, is the most trusted and loyal official of His Highness, who labours hard for the moral, intellectual, and temporal good of the people. He has the satisfaction of knowing that the resources of the State have greatly increased during his tenure of office, and all the Departments are in smooth working order.

His Highness is a keen sportsman, and fond of shooting big game.

His Highness is entitled to a salute of 15 guns personal, and 13 guns permanent, and is one of the most respected Princes of the Punjab, enjoying the special confidence and appreciation of the Supreme Government. He has proved to be a most capable Ruler, and every movement for the welfare of his people and the advancement of his State has always met with his approval. His sympathetic and kindly disposition has endeared him to the hearts of his subjects. The State has become one of the advanced States of India, under his rule, and keeps itself abreast of the times.

JAGATJIT JUBILEE HALL.

THE STATE OF KAPURTHALA

THIS State lies along the eastern bank of the River Beas, and abuts upon the Hoshiarpur, Ferozepore and Jullundur districts on the north, south, and east respectively.

The area, 652 square miles in extent, consists of three detached portions, the main block covering about three-fourths of the total acreage. The Ruler is also owner of more than thirty villages situated in the districts of Lahore and Amritsar, together with large estates in the Province of Oudh comprising 461,032 acres, the major portion of which was granted by the British Government to the present Maharaja's grandfather in 1857 for conspicuous services rendered during the Sepoy Mutiny.

Of the inhabitants, numbering about 284,070 persons according to the census figures of 1921, nearly 56 per cent. are Mahomedans, 22 per cent. Hindus, while the remainder are Sikhs.

The reigning House of Kapurthala claims to be an offshoot of the Rajput ruling dynasty of Jaisalmer. Owing to the inaccessibility of authentic records, the student of history is perforce deprived of glimpses of the activities and vicissitudes of the family in the remote past. With the dawn of the eighteenth century he would find himself in a position to watch its varying fortunes until he would see its head as the leader of an important branch of the Sikh confederacy popularly known as the Ahluwalia Misal, deriving its name from "Ahlu," a village in the district of Lahore from which the Misal originally sprang, and which is still owned by the Ruler of Kapurthala.

Sadhu Singh, the founder of Ahlu, had four sons, but all that is known of them is that they lived quietly in Lahore. Bhadr Singh, a great-grandson of Sadhu Singh, married the sister of one Bhagu of Tulsi, a shopkeeper of limited means who became an ardent follower of Nawab Kapur Singh, of Fyzulpuria, from whom he received the "Pohl." Bhagu, afterwards known as Bhag Singh, was destined to play an important part in the history of those troubled times when robbers and desperadoes abounded, and when an unquenchable spirit of adventure, born of religious zeal or love of ill-gotten gain, turned constant fighting into an attractive profession. Bhag Singh, who possessed the genius for leadership, soon rose to eminence among his contemporaries. Remaining childless for several years, Bhadr Singh was blessed with a son in 1718. He was named Jassa Singh. The boy lost his father when he was scarcely five years of age. His maternal uncle, Bhag Singh, committed him and his widowed mother to the care of Mai Sundri, wife of Guru Gobind Singh, then living at Delhi. On his reaching the age of 12, Jassa Singh was recalled to the Punjab by Bhadr Singh, and on his departure Mai Sundri is said to have blessed the promising boy and presented him with a silver mace in token of his future greatness. The boy and his mother resided at Jullundur, where they frequently met the Fyzulpuria Chief, Kapur Singh. In the course of one of his visits to Bhag Singh's house the Chief, it is stated, was so struck by the handsome face of the boy that he besought his mother to hand him over to his charge. She acceded to the request, and from that day the Fyzulpuria *Sardar* treated Jassa Singh as his own son. As the boy grew up he was placed in high offices under the protection of the *Sardar*, and soon came to be regarded as a promising leader. He also looked after the affairs of his uncle, Bhag Singh, who was without issue and who subsequently lost his life in a battle with the Moghul troops at Hariana.

On the death of Bhag Singh, the leadership of his confederacy devolved on his nephew Jassa Singh, and with the death of Aurangzeb the Moghul Empire was threatened with rapid decay. Within a decade India seethed with civil strife, kings succeeded kings in a bewilderingly rapid succession, and within the course of a generation the Provinces of Bengal, Oudh, and the Deccan cast off the Moghul yoke and became independent principalities. The sudden rise of the Mahratta power and the hordes of the relentless Nadir Shah accelerated the disintegration of the doomed Empire.

These upheavals afforded an excellent scope for the free play of the martial instincts and political talents of Jassa Singh, whose religious zeal and sanctity had already achieved for him a position of undisputed authority among the Sikhs, so much so that the leading Sikh Chiefs, including Raja Amar Singh of Patiala, deemed it an honour to receive the "Pohl" at his hands. During Nadir Shah's invasion in 1739, Jassa Singh concealed himself in Muktesar, in the district of Ferozepore, but as soon as the invader retraced his steps he reappeared as the leader of a vast host, and built the fort of Dhaliwala, on the River Ravi, which became his headquarters.

In 1743, at the head of a large body of horsemen, he lay in ambush and subsequently attacked Diwan Lakhpat Rai, an official of the Governor of Lahore, while he was on his way from Eminabad in charge of treasure. To this open challenge to his authority the Governor responded by deputing Adina Beg Khan, Governor of Bist Jullundur, to administer a severe lesson. Sardar Jassa Singh and his followers suffered a serious reverse culminating in their retreat beyond the Sutlej. Shortly afterwards Jassa Singh, collecting his scattered forces, reappeared on the banks of the Sutlej and conquered an extensive territory. He was then joined by the Bhangi *Sardars*, Hari Singh and Jhanda Singh, and their combined forces devastated the country by their marauding excursions. Lachmi Narain, a Commander of the Moghul forces, was sent at the head of a large army to punish the recalcitrant *Sardars*, and succeeded in defeating them, Jassa Singh again taking refuge in the hills to the north of the Sutlej.

Zakria Khan, the Governor of the Punjab, died in 1745, and Jassa Singh, finding the central power shaken, descended to the plains, and with the help of other Sirdars raided Kasur. He was not able to accomplish much owing to the severe defeat he and his coadjutors sustained at the hands of Ahmad Shah Abdali near Sirhand in 1747. Soon after Ahmad Shah's departure from India Jassa Singh resumed hostilities against the new Governor of Lahore, Moin-ul-Mulk, commonly known as Mir Manu, and his deputy, Raja Gurdit Mal, who was Governor of Hoshiarpur and Sialkot. Adina Beg Khan, Governor of Jullundur, was attacked by Jassa Singh near Hoshiarpur, but the action remained indecisive. Soon afterwards the army of Salabat Khan, Governor of Amritsar, was repulsed, and he himself was slain, while a large portion of the district of Amritsar was brought under the sway of the *Ahluwalia Misal*.

Sardar Jassa Singh's fame for personal bravery and ability had now become so widespread that the Mahomedan Governors courted his help in settling their domestic quarrels. For instance, he was invited by Mir Manu to expel Shah Niwaz Khan, whom the Delhi Emperor had appointed Governor of Multan. In a stubborn battle which ensued in 1749 the Emperor's nominee was killed and his army defeated. For his labours Jassa Singh was rewarded with a lion's share of the booty as well as high honours and dignities.

In 1753 he defeated Aziz Khan, Commander of the Lahore army, and a couple of years later at Kasur gained a signal victory over Adina Beg Khan, Governor of Jullundur, and succeeded in wresting from his adversary the possession of Fatehabad, a village on the Beas, which has since remained a *Jagir* of the Kapurthala State.

In the same eventful year Nawab Kapur Singh Fyzulpuria died, and Jassa Singh inherited all his influence. Kapur Singh was the first to organize the "*Dal Khalsa*," the army of Sikh theocracy, and on his death-bed handed over to Jassa Singh the historic mace of Guru Govind Singh,[1] hailing him as the leader of the Khalsa. The title of Nawab was subsequently awarded him by the representatives of the Sikh confederacies assembled in a "*Guru Mata*" held at Amritsar about the year 1754, when he was also acknowledged as the successor of the famous Nawab Kapur Singh. In 1756 and 1758 Jassa Singh was in temporary occupation of Lahore, using the mint of the Moghuls to coin his own money, which bore an inscription the substance of which is as follows: "Coined by the Grace of God in the country of Ahmad conquered by Jassa Singh."

In 1761, when two mighty armies were confronting each other on the fateful field of Panipat and the future of India hung in the balance, Jassa Singh, taking advantage of the situation, plundered Sirhind and Dialpur, seized Dogar and Nypal in the district of Ferozepur (where he built small fortresses), and captured Jandiala from Saran Das. In the same year he took Hoshiarpur, Bhiroz and Naraingarh in Amballa, and levied tribute from Rai Ibrahim Bhatti, Chief of Kapurthala. He then marched on Jhang, but failed in his object owing to the stout resistance offered by Inayat Ullah Khan, the Sial Chief.

On the return of Ahmad Shah Durrani to Afghanistan in 1761, the Sikh Chiefs united under the leadership of Jassa Singh and sacked Sirhind, the Governor of Lahore Ubed Khan, being made a prisoner within the walls of the city. Jassa Singh captured Ludhiana, Govindwal, Saliala and Bhopalu, and carried his conquests as far as Tarn Taran in the district of Amritsar.

Sardar Jassa Singh then assisted the Bhangis and Sukerchakias in ejecting Ubed Khan from Gujranwala, and subsequently raided Shikarpore, Raipur, and Mohamedpur lying towards the south of the Province of Jammu. His career of conquest was, however, checked by the rapid onward march of Ahmad Shah Abdali, who was reported to have recovered Lahore and Multan without a struggle. The "*Dal Khalsa*" proposed to give battle, and encamped at Barnala, where a terrific conflict was fought on February 10, 1762, which resulted in a crushing defeat of the Sikhs. The losses on the side of the Khalsa were so great that the battle was termed "*Ghulln-Ghara*," or the "great disaster." Ahmad Shah followed up his victory at Barnala with a hot pursuit of *Sardar* Jassa Singh, who was eventually compelled to retire to the Kangra Hills. After the departure of the Shah Jassa Singh formed a new alliance with the Ramgariah and Kanhia Misals and pillaged Kasur, killing the Pathan Com-

[1] This historic weapon is still reverently preserved in the Akal Bhunga of Darbar Sahib, Amritsar.

HIS HIGHNESS LIEUT.-COL. FARZAND-I-DILBAND RASIKH-UL-ITIQUAD DAULAT-I-INGLISHIA RAJA-I-RAJGAN SHRI MAHARAJA JAGATJIT SINGH, SAHIB BAHADUR, G.C.S.I., MAHARAJA OF KAPURTHALA, IKAUNA, BAUNDI, AND BHITAULI, ETC.

1. THE TIKKA SAHIB OF KAPURTHALA. 2. HIS HIGHNESS AND PRINCES.

manders, Alif Khan, Hassan Khan, and Kamalud Din Khan. The Kasur territory was given to the Bhangi Chiefs, who held it until 1794. The allies, amassing a Ibrahim Bhatti and made the place his permanent headquarters. Kapurthala remains the capital of the Ahluwalia State up to the present day. In 1776 Jassa being a terror to the enemy of the Khalsa in the second half of the eighteenth century, yet he was simple and unostentatious in his habits. At the time of his death he

THE STATE OF KAPURTHALA.
JAGATJIT PALACE.

powerful army of 23,000 men, besieged and destroyed Sirhind, murdering Zen Khan, the Afghan Governor of Ahmad Shah, and his deputy, Lachmi Narain. The conquest of Sirhind led to the subjugation of the whole of the surrounding territory. Jassa Singh proceeded in triumph to Amritsar to pay personal homage at the holy shrine of Guru Ram Das, where he donated a large sum of money towards the reconsecration of the temple desecrated by Ahmad Shah Durrani.

In 1766 Jassa Singh, having combined with the Patiala and Jhind Chiefs, marched southwards, sacking Rewari, Jhajjar and Bhagpat en route, and captured Sayal and Isru from the Kotta Afghans. By these operations he considerably increased his wealth, a portion of which was distributed among his army. Two years later he penetrated into Ghazi-ud-Din-Nagar and Anupshahr, near Delhi, and severely defeated Mirza Sukhan, the Moghul general. Subsequently he conquered Raikot, then in the possession of the Pathans of Barwal, and in 1774 captured Kapurthala from Rai Singh entered into alliance with Jai Singh Kanhia, the Bhangis, and the Sukar-Chakias against the Ramgariahs in order to avenge an attack by the last-named on the Ahluwalias in the previous year. A severe battle ensued in which the Ramgariahs were worsted, and, on the flight of their leader to Hariana, their possessions on the north of the Sutlej fell into the hands of the Ahluwalia Chiefs.

Sardar Jassa Singh died at Amritsar in 1783, and was cremated at the Dera Baba *Attal*, within the precincts of the Golden Temple, where his *smadh* stands by the side of that of his sponsor, Nawab Kapur Singh Fyzulpuria. Jassa Singh was tall, handsome and muscular, and his arms were of unusual length. He was an excellent marksman with the matchlock and bow, and stories are still current of his wonderful physical endurance and horsemanship. He is said to have triumphed over powerful opponents in personal combats with his massive sword,[1] his name possessed enormous wealth and influence. He was liberal in his policy, and, unlike his contemporary co-religionists, tolerant to the Mussalmans, many of whom rose to positions of eminence and trust under him. He constructed at great cost a magnificent reservoir at Anandpur, and distributed alms freely among the *Sodhis* and other religious sects which were numerous in his time. His hospitality was known far and wide.

Jassa Singh died without leaving male issue, and was succeeded by his second cousin, *Sardar* Bhag Singh, who was then thirty-eight years of age, having been born in 1745. His reign of 17 years was comparatively uneventful. He formed an alliance with the Kanheya Chief and led an expedition against Wazir Singh and Bhagwan Singh, *Sardars* of the Nakka country between Gogira and Lahore, while he also attacked the Ramgarhias and Gulab Singh Bhangi. The former had in the meanwhile allied themselves with Raja Sansar Chand of Kangra, and were able to defeat the Ahluwalias under Hamir Singh, who was

[1] This ponderous weapon can still be seen in the State *toshakhana* at Kapurthala.

himself wounded in the conflict. *Sardar* Bhag Singh, in order to retrieve his injured reputation, made preparations on a larger scale, and led his army in person as far as Phagwara, but illness supervened and he was brought back to Kapurthala, where he died in 1801. His mausoleum still exists near the Devi Talab at Kapurthala.

Sardar Bhag Singh was followed by his only surviving son, *Sardar* Fateh Singh, who was born in 1784. The head of the Saker-Chakia Misal, Ranjit Singh, who was eventually destined to be known as "the lion of the Punjab," was then just emerging into prominence. *Sardar* Fateh Singh was also the leader of an important confederacy, and for reasons of expediency both these leaders entered into an offensive and defensive alliance. A treaty of perpetual friendship was signed at Amritsar, and the Chiefs exchanged turbans in token of brotherhood, swearing everlasting goodwill on the sacred *granth* in 1802.

This document stipulated (*inter alia*) that they would lead joint expeditions and divide equally the fruits of conquest. Accordingly, the allied Chiefs attacked the Pathans of Kasur in 1803, but the adventure was unsuccessful, and the Ahluwalia *Sardar* returned to his capital. For a couple of years he confined his activities to consolidating his own territories and introducing an orderly system of government.

In 1805 Jaswant Rao Holkar, of Indore, after being defeated by Lord Lake in his own country, took refuge in the Punjab, and was anxious to form an alliance with the rising Sikh confederacies against the British Government. With that object in view he marched to Amritsar to meet Ranjit Singh and *Sardar* Fateh Singh, and although the former was ready to respond to Holkar's overtures, he was not supported by the Ahluwalia *Sardar*.

A treaty of friendship and amity was signed on January 1, 1806, between the Hon. the East India Company and *Sardar* Ranjit Singh, of Lahore, and *Sardar* Fateh Singh Ahluwalia, by which the two *Sardars* undertook to expel the fugitive Mahratta Chief, who was then approaching Amritsar. The British Government, on the other hand, promised to acknowledge the independence and integrity of their respective territories and to refrain from seizing or sequestrating their possessions or property so long as they remained friendly to the British Power. This is believed to be the first treaty signed between the British Government and any Native State in Northern India. It may not be amiss to mention that, as a mark of esteem and friendship, Lord Lake presented *Sardar* Fateh Singh with a leopard, the *Sardar* returning the compliment by presenting a hawk to the famous general. *Sardar* Fateh Singh remained a staunch friend and ally of Ranjit Singh, and invariably accompanied him on his early expeditions to the north of the Sutlej and Jhang rivers. In 1809 *Sardar* Fateh Singh joined his Lahore ally in the expedition against Kasur, which fell into the hands of the Sikhs after a fierce fight and was thereupon annexed to the Lahore Kingdom.

In 1808 Sir Charles Metcalfe visited Lahore as the plenipotentiary of the British Government, when *Sardar* Fateh Singh, as the foremost ally of the realm, was deputed to receive the distinguished guest. On his part *Sardar* Fateh Singh was sincerely devoted to his Lahore ally, but with the latter the alliance with the Ahluwalia *Sardar* was more or less a business proposition. Sir Charles Metcalfe gauged the character of the two allies in the following terms: "The quiet character

THE STATE OF KAPURTHALA.

THE OLD PALACE (JALAOKHANA).

of Fateh Singh, who was the equal, if not the superior, in rank of power of Ranjit Singh, has yielded to the bold commanding spirit of the other, and he has been the ladder by which Ranjit Singh mounted to greatness." *Sardar* Fateh Singh was present at Amritsar when the treaty between the British Government and the Maharaja was signed in 1809, by which Ranjit Singh agreed not to encroach upon territory on the south of the Sutlej, and the British Government promised to respect the Maharaja's possessions on the north of that river. Ranjit Singh at this period reposed implicit confidence in his friend and ally, so much so that he left *Sardar* Fateh Singh in charge of the administration of his kingdom during his absence from Lahore. Later on, the *Sardar* accompanied the Maharaja on his expedition against Budh Singh, of Jullundur, fought Fateh Khan, the *Wazir* of Kabul, at Haidra in 1813, helped the Maharaja in his Bhinbar, Rajori, and Bhawalpur campaigns, and was present at the arduous siege of Multan in 1818. He was placed in charge of the administration for the second time for two years, when Ranjit Singh was busy conquering Kashmir about the year 1819.

Ranjit Singh's rapacious greed, however, made no exceptions even in the case of his sworn brothers and allies. Assiduously courteous and considerate to *Sardar* Fateh Singh to all appearances, he at heart coveted the Ahluwalia possessions, but the high reputation and popularity *Sardar* Fateh Singh enjoyed in Ranjit Singh's army frustrated the crafty Maharaja's machinations for the time being. *Sardar* Fateh Singh, though steadfast in his attachment to the Lahore Chief, scented danger, and looked for an early opportunity to cast in his lot with the British Government. The Maharaja, however, stole a march over his faithful ally, and in 1825 sent two battalions of the Khalsa army, under *Fajir* Aziz-ud-Din and *Diwan* Anand Ram Pindari, to seize the Kapurthala possessions on the north of the Sutlej. This manœuvre alarmed *Sardar* Fateh Singh, who shifted his headquarters temporarily to Jagraon. The Kapurthala garrison was routed and the Ahluwalia territory was occupied by the Lahore army. Sardar Fateh Singh sought British help, but the Government, though expressing sympathy with the *Sardar's* troubles, declined to interfere in view of the terms of the treaty of 1809. Maharaja Ranjit Singh, however, seemed, for some unknown reason, to have repented of his treacherous action, and expressed an earnest desire for a reconciliation, undertaking to restore the usurped territory and to maintain unbroken amity provided the Ahluwalia *Sardar* returned to his capital. Accordingly, Sardar Fateh Singh reached Kapurthala in 1827, where all his possessions were formally restored to him by a deputation of the Lahore Government. The next occasion on which the Kapurthala State came into direct political touch with the British Government arose in 1817 in connection with the Chiefship of Bairog. The Bairog estate, comprising about a hundred villages, was originally a gift conferred by Nawab Jassa Singh on a dependent named Mirza Singh for his loyal services. In 1810 Maha Singh (grandson of Mirza Singh) declined to obey the orders of the British Government on the ground that he owed allegiance to the Ahluwalia Durbar. Thereupon Sir David Ochterlony asked *Sardar* Fateh Singh to confiscate the estates of this contumacious Chief, and the former accordingly sent a strong force, which defeated the Bhairog Ruler and took possession of his estate.

Maha Singh's conduct was in consequence condoned by the British, and *Sardar* Fateh Singh was advised to restore the estate upon an assurance being given that Bhairog should always acknowledge the supremacy of the Ahluwalia Chief. This episode was followed by another incident known as the "Kotla" case. The small fortress of Kotla, situated in the Cis-Sutlej territories of the Kapurthala State, belonged to a Pathan family represented by Nahang Khan, whose ancestors punctuated with frequent acts of revolt and insubordination. *Sardar* Fateh Singh, in order to put an end to this precarious state of affairs and assert his complete supremacy, attacked Kotla in 1822, occupied the fort and bestowed it upon Balwant Khan, the younger brother of Nahang Khan, who acknowledged the Ahluwalia over-lordship and promised feudal service. This proceeding was resented by the British Political Agent at Amballa, who referred the question to his Government. The latter held that although *Sardar* Fateh Singh had asserted his claim to a fourth share in Kotla in 1813, he had never done anything to protect the interests of the Kotla Chief from the encroachments of the Sikh *Sardars*, which it was incumbent upon him to do. He had further in a letter to Captain Birch in 1815 renounced his claim altogether to Kotla. These acts of omission and commission were put forward by the Government as substantial proofs of annulment of Ahluwalia claims, and the Ahluwalia nominee, Balwant Khan, was subsequently expelled from Kotla and Nahang Khan reinstated in his possessions.

Sardar Fateh Singh continued to enjoy the possession of his territories, both Cis-Sutlej and Trans-Sutlej, without molestation, until 1836, when again the unscrupulous Ranjit Singh broke his sacred vow and confiscated the outlying district of Phagwara. This tract was, however, soon restored, as the Maharaja was fully conscious of the strong sympathy of the British Government towards the Ahluwalia Chief and dreaded interference in favour of the latter. *Sardar* Fateh Singh, however, despite repeated encroachments on his territory and acts of infidelity, remained true to the Lahore Chief. During his reign *Sardar* Fateh Singh enhanced the prestige of his illustrious house and consolidated and even added fresh territory to his State during his *regime*. He constructed many beautiful buildings in Kapurthala. The State temples, which are yet considered to be one of the most magnificent structures in the Punjab, the Kamra Palace, and the Shalamar Gardens bear ample testimony to the architectural taste and refinement of this noble Chief. He died in 1836, after a short illness, and was succeeded by his elder son, Raja Nihal Singh, then a youth of twenty years of age. Maharaja Ranjit Singh, though outwardly sympathizing with the bereaved family, did not acknowledge *Sardar* Nihal Singh as Chief of the Ahluwalia House until he had paid a sum of Rs. 4,00,000 to the Lahore Durbar and had agreed to provide 500 infantry (in addition to 700 cavalry originally supplied), all of which were to be placed at the disposal of the Khalsa kingdom in times of emergency.

Sardar Nihal Singh did not begin his reign under favourable auspices, as at the very outset of his career he met with jealous opposition on the part of his younger brother, Amar Singh, who, in collusion with the intriguing Maharaja of Lahore, endeavoured to oust his elder brother and usurp the *gadi* himself. Amar Singh went so far as to conspire with some desperadoes to take the life of the Raja, who was attacked while leaving the *Zenana* and would have been instantly killed but for the plucky intervention of two loyal attendants who, in defending him, lost their own lives. With the view of putting an end to these family feuds, Raja Nihal Singh, acting on the suggestion of Maharaja Ranjit Singh, provided a *jagir* of Rs. 30,000 per annum for Kanwar Amar Singh in Sultanpur *tahsil*. No improvement in the relations of the two brothers ensued, however,

1. HIS HIGHNESS AND PRINCIPAL OFFICIALS OF THE STATE.
2. HIS HIGHNESS RAJA-I-RAJGAN KHARAK SINGH, SAHIB BAHADUR.

THE STATE OF KAPURTHALA

and secretly encouraged as he was by Ranjit Singh, Amar Singh would certainly have caused further trouble had not the hand of death fallen upon him in 1840.

Raja Nihal Singh's political troubles were ever more serious than his fraternal feuds. When Lord Auckland, Governor-General of India, visited the Punjab in 1838, the Raja was able to render important help in collecting supplies and in aiding the British troops generally on their march to Afghanistan. He also dispatched a contingent to fight at Kabul in 1842, which reached Jallalabad but was not requisitioned for further active service. On the outbreak of the first Sikh War, however, the revolt of his Sikh soldiery made it impossible for him to respond to the British call for help, and forced him to adopt an attitude inconsistent with his personal inclinations and the traditional loyalty of his House. The rebels besieged and even bombarded the Palace and hacked to pieces the Minister, Moulvi Ghulam Mohiud Din, who was credited with having advised his master to abide firmly by his engagements with the British Government. Flushed with this bloody victory at home, the Ahluwalia troops appear to have fought against the British at Aliwal and Buddowal. This deplorable episode led to the confiscation of the Raja's territories south of the Sutlej comprising 451 villages, yielding a yearly revenue of Rs. 5,65,000, while the whole of the estates in the Jullundur Doab were maintained in his independent possession, his service engagements being commuted to a money payment of Rs. 1,31,000 a year. The second Sikh War in 1848 gave Raja Nihal Singh an early opportunity of retrieving the honour and reputation of his House and State. He rendered valuable assistance to the British Government in collecting supplies, and also offered the services of his troops. At the close of the war the Governor-General visited Kapurthala and conferred on him signal marks of distinction. Raja Nihal Singh died in 1852, and was succeeded by his eldest son, Raja Randhir Singh.

Raja Randhir Singh was born in March 1831, and was in his twenty-second year when he succeeded to his princely heritage. At a very early stage in his short but glorious career the Raja was plunged into the throes of protracted litigation which arose out of a will left by his father, the terms of which, if enforced, would have wrecked the very existence of the Kapurthala State as we know it to-day. By this unfortunate document, dated July 11, 1852, Raja Nihal Singh sought to parcel out the State into three parts, the largest portion to be allotted to Raja Randhir Singh and the remainder, yielding an income of Rs. 2,00,000, to be divided equally between his half-brothers, Kanwars Bikrama Singh and Suchet Singh. This dispute was finally settled by the Secretary of State on the basis of a cash allowance of Rs. 60,000 per annum for each of the two brothers, the State itself remaining in the sole possession of the Raja and his heirs and successors.

Thus Raja Randhir Singh may, in a sense, be regarded as the founder of the present Kapurthala State. He succeeded in enhancing its importance and prestige by his splendid services and achievements during the Sepoy Mutiny in 1857. He placed all his resources at the disposal of Government, marched into Jullundur at the head of his troops, consisting of 1,200 infantry, 200 cavalry and 5 guns, guarded the civil station, the Treasury, and the jail, and pursued the rebels. In July 1857 his troops restored order at Hoshiarpur. These signal services evoked a warm acknowledgment from the Government of India. A year's military cash contribution was altogether remitted. *Khilats* of Rs. 15,000 and Rs. 5,000 were conferred on him and his brother Kanwar Bikrama Singh respectively. A salute of 11 guns was assigned to the Raja, who also received the honoured title of "Farzand-i-Dilband Rasikh-ul-Itiqad."

Not content, as it were, with the part played by him in the suppression of the Mutiny nearer home the Raja, in 1858, proceeded to Oudh with his troops, where they participated in six engagements and captured several guns. The Raja was always personally in command of his contingent, and intrepidly faced both danger and fatigue. On the successful conclusion of the operations the Raja and his troops marched back to Kapurthala in March 1859.

For these conspicuous services in Oudh, Raja Randhir Singh was lavishly rewarded. The rich estates of Baundi and Bhitauli, which yielded to Government a yearly revenue of Rs. 1,00,000, were granted to the Raja on *Istimrari* tenure. Kanwar Bikrama Singh likewise received an estate, worth Rs. 45,000 a year, at Ikauna, which was ultimately transferred to the State in exchange for a new *jagir*. The Bari Doab estates, comprising 25 villages in the district of Amritsar and 12 in Lahore, including the village of "Ahlu" and the Naraingarh Garden in the district of Umballa, were restored to the Ruler, the civil and criminal jurisdiction continuing to vest in the British Government. The Ruler of Kapurthala was accorded precedence over all *taluqdars* in Oudh, and to mark his undoubted pre-eminence among them, Government styled him "Raja-i-Rajgan." He was also the happy recipient of the perpetual right of adoption in the case of failure of male issue. On October 17, 1864, Raja-i-Rajgan Randhir Singh was invested with the insignia of the Most Exalted Order of the Star of India at an investiture held specially for the purpose, which was attended by their Highnesses the Maharajas of Kashmir, Patiala, Jhind, and Faridkot, and other ruling Chiefs of the Punjab. The Raja-i-Rajgan was the first Punjab Prince to receive this signal honour from Her Majesty the late Queen Victoria, and the speech in Hindustani of the famous Viceroy, Lord Lawrence, delivered on this occasion is remarkable for the eloquent tribute paid to the great services rendered by the recipient of the title and the high esteem in which he was held by the Imperial Government.

His Highness Raja Randhir Singh had long been contemplating a visit to England with the object of rendering personal homage to the great Queen, and eventually arranged to undertake the trip in March 1870. He was in indifferent health at the time, and alarming symptoms were developed at Bombay just before he sailed. He nevertheless decided to proceed despite medical advice to the contrary, but his condition became hopeless by the time Aden was reached, and he was compelled to tranship to the *Golconda* bound for Bombay, and breathed his last on April 2, 1870, before the conclusion of the voyage. His remains were received at Bombay by his eldest son and successor, Raja Kharak Singh, and some State officials, and conveyed to Nasik, where they were cremated. A magnificent mausoleum and *sarai* mark the last resting-place of this illustrious Ruler of Kapurthala, who possessed in an exquisite blend the qualities of a true soldier and a sagacious and far-seeing statesman. He established a regular system of law in the State, erected buildings of public utility, started Anglo-Vernacular schools, and in many ways improved the amenities of his capital. His Excellency the Viceroy conveyed on the occasion of the Raja-i-Rajgan's untimely demise his condolences in the following terms: "The British Government has lost in him an attached and valued friend, and a Chief who, by a vigorous and progressive administration, set an example to other Rulers.

The valuable services which he rendered to Government in time of trouble and danger will never be forgotten." Raja Kharak Singh, born in 1850, was installed on the *gadi* of the Kapurthala State on May 12, 1870. The Raja commenced his rule by administering his State with great zeal, but symptoms of mental derangement subsequently became apparent, and it was thought advisable to entrust the management of State affairs to a Council of three members. This arrangement did not work well, and a British officer of the Punjab Commission was put in charge of the administration as Superintendent of the State. Raja Kharak Singh did not recover normal health, and died at Dharamsala in 1877, leaving an only son, Maharaja Jagatjit Singh, then a child of five years of age. Maharaja Jagatjit Singh, the present Ruler of Kapurthala, was born on November 24, 1872, and was installed on the *gadi* on October 16, 1877, by Sir Robert Egerton, the Lieutenant-Governor of the Punjab. During his minority the State was managed by a succession of brilliant civilians, who acted as Superintendents, many of whom became in due course heads of Provincial Administrations in India. Among the most prominent of them were Sir Lepel Griffin, K.C.S.I., Sir Mackworth Young, K.C.S.I., and Sir Charles Rivaz, K.C.S.I., Lieutenant-Governors of the Punjab, Sir Frederick Fryer, K.C.S.I., Lieutenant-Governor of Burma, and Sir Denzil Ibbetson, K.C.S.I., Lieutenant-Governor of the Punjab. These Superintendents introduced several desirable reforms which increased the efficiency of the administration and contributed to the general welfare of the people of the State. The young Maharaja was carefully brought up and received a liberal measure of education. At an early age he showed a singular aptitude for the assimilation of new ideas and for acquiring a knowledge of foreign languages. He gained an intimate acquaintance with English and French, both of which he speaks fluently, besides learning Sanskrit, Hindi, Persian, Urdu and Gurmukhi. In 1883 the Maharaja was betrothed to the daughter of Mian Ranjit Singh Gularia of Paprola, a high-caste Rajput, and the ceremony of *Shagun* was performed by Raja Sir Jai Chand, of Lambagraon, another high-caste Rajput Chieftain of the district of Kangra. This alliance publicly recognized the claim of the ruling Ahluwalia family to Rajput origin. The marriage was solemnized with great pomp and *éclat* on April 16, 1886. The wedding party, consisting of representatives of all the important States of the Punjab and nobility of the Province and a large retinue, proceeded all the way from Kapurthala to Paprola. The Lieutenant-Governor of the Punjab participated in the festivities at Kapurthala. The important ceremonies connected with the marriage were conducted by Thakur Mohar Singh, a cousin of the Maharawal of Jaisalmer, who is the head of the senior branch of this ancient House. November 24, 1890, was a red-letter day in the annals of Kapurthala, for it was on this day that the present Ruler, His Highness Maharaja Jagatjit Singh Bahadur, G.C.S.I., G.C.I.E., attained his majority and assumed the government of his State, the formal ceremony being performed by Sir James Lyall, the then Lieutenant-Governor of the Punjab. The occasion was marked by scenes of befitting pomp and public rejoicings throughout the State. His Honour, in a speech at the Durbar, spoke in terms of highest regard and affection of the Prince and his illustrious family, and expressed every confidence as to the future of the State under His Highness' benign and enlightened rule. In the evening a State banquet was held, at which Sir James Lyall, in proposing the Maharaja's health, delivered an eloquent speech, in the course of which he dwelt upon the cordial relations existing between the Ahluwalia State and the British Government, and recounted the brilliant services rendered by His Highness' ancestors at a time of great peril to the Empire. The full titles of the Maharaja, under which he assumed the Rulership, were: His Highness Farzand-i-Dilband Rasikh-ul-Itiqad Daulat-i-Englishia, Raja-i-Rajgan. To these were subsequently added the titles of hereditary Maharaja, G.C.S.I. and G.C.I.E. In addition to these, the Maharaja has also been the recipient of other honours at the hands of British Government from time to time. In December 1890 the Government of India, in order to mark its appreciation of the excellent administration during the present Maharaja's long spell of minority and in recognition of the valuable services rendered during the Afghan War, was pleased to raise the status of the State as regards complimentary *khilats* from Rs. 4,500 to Rs. 6,000. Again, in 1904, the power of passing sentences of death were conferred on His Highness in perpetuity. His Highness from his early youth has been a great believer in the educative value of travelling abroad. He has been all over Europe, America, Egypt, China, Japan and Java. The first of these visits was undertaken in 1893, when His Highness had the honour to be invited as a guest of Queen Victoria on the occasion of the marriage of His Imperial Majesty King George V (then Duke of York). During his various visits His Highness has always been very cordially received by the British Sovereign, and there is hardly a European potentate with whom he cannot claim the privilege of a personal acquaintance. That His Highness enjoys literary fame is amply borne out by the two publications embodying his experiences of foreign travel. These tours, apart from broadening his own mental outlook and invigorating his health, have been of practical value to the State in enabling His Highness to infuse a progressive spirit into his administration. Architecture has been one of His Highness' great hobbies. The most splendid monument of his refined architectural taste is doubtless the New Palace, which might appropriately be described as the Palace of the Versailles of India. This palace, the foundation of which was laid in 1902, occupied seven years in construction and cost Rs. 35,00,000. Among other buildings the most notable are the Courts of Justice, Villa Buona Vista, the Sikh temple and the Jubilee Hall, the Chateau at Mussoorie and the renovated Kapurthala House at Lahore, all of which are the products of His Highness' artistic inspiration. His Highness is blessed with five sons and one daughter. The eldest son, Sri Tikka Paramjit Singh Sahib Bahadur, was born on May 19, 1892, and this happy event was marked by great festivities and rejoicings throughout the State. The upbringing and education of the young Princes was carefully planned and directed by the Maharaja. They were first placed under the tuition of competent English and French governesses and tutors in Kapurthala, and completed their education in Europe.

The Tikka Sahib returned to Kapurthala in 1910, and his marriage with Princess Brinda Mati, a daughter of Kanwar Gambhir Chand, of Jubbal, was solemnized amidst scenes of remarkable splendour and rejoicing on February 2, 1911. The Tikka Rani Sahiba, who, thanks to the foresight of His Highness the Maharaja, had the unique advantage of having been brought up in France, is a highly cultured and accomplished young Princess. A large number of distinguished guests hailing from various parts of India and France contributed by their presence to the grandeur of the occasion. Chief among them were Their Highnesses the Maharajas of Kashmir and Jhalawar, His Highness the Agha

THE STATE OF KAPURTHALA

Khan, the Rajas of Poonch, Lambagraon, Nurpur and Jasuan, His Royal Highness Prince Antoine d'Orleans, and Prince and Princess Amedée de Broglie. The ceremony of *Sehrabandi*, in the great Durbar Hall, was an imposing scene. The *Sehra* was tied round the Tikka Sahib's turban by His Highness the Maharaja of Kashmir. On this occasion numerous loyal and congratulatory addresses were presented to His Highness the Maharaja by several associations and sections of His Highness' subjects, to which the Maharaja made suitable replies. To mark this auspicious occasion His Highness announced that in future primary education would be made free in the State and that *Begar* would be abolished. On the conclusion of the marriage His Highness took a few of his principal European guests to his Oudh estates, where an interesting shooting programme had been arranged.

The marriage of the second son, Maharaj Kumar Mahijit Singh Sahib, who returned to India in 1912 after completing his education, was celebrated in November, 1913, when Kapurthala was again *en fête*. The bride was the daughter of a high-caste Rajput family of Chandpore, in the district of Kangra. The festivities were attended by several prominent people of the Province and by deputations from Kashmir, Baroda, Patiala, Bahawalpore, Rampore and other States. The ceremony of *Sehrabandi* was performed with great pomp in the Durbar Hall, where deputations from other States presented *Tambols* and presents. As on the occasion of Sri Tikka Sahib's wedding, the main feature of the ceremonies, from a spectacular point of view, was the marriage procession consisting of troops and richly-caparisoned elephants bearing the *Granth Sahib*, the Maharaja, the bride and the bridegroom, the distinguished guests, and the leading officials of the State. The festivities concluded with a banquet at the Palace, at which the Commissioner, in a felicitous speech, proposed the health of the young couple. The banquet was followed by a brilliantly successful dance.

His Highness' third son, Maharaj Kumar Amarjit Singh Sahib, returned to Kapurthala in January 1916. He is a Master of Arts of Oxford University, and during the Great War served with the Indian contingent in France. The Maharaj Kumar now enjoys the honorary rank of Captain in the Indian Army.

His Highness has always been a prominent figure at the Imperial Durbars that have taken place in India from time to time. In 1885 he was present at Lord Dufferin's Durbar at Rawalpindi, which was held in honour of Amir Abdur Rehman, of Kabul. His Highness attended both the Coronation Durbars of 1902 and 1911 at Delhi, and on the latter occasion had the honour of being invested with the insignia of a Knight Grand Commander of the Most Exalted Order of the Star of India by His Imperial Majesty the King Emperor in person. It is interesting to recall here that on this very occasion His Highness was made an hereditary Maharaja, and was thus the happy recipient of double honours. In celebration of this auspicious event His Highness held a public Durbar on his return to the capital, at which he made an interesting speech in response to the congratulatory addresses presented by the State officials and others. In the course of his remarks the Maharaja announced various concessions and privileges in commemoration of the event.

The Maharaja was one of the Punjab Princes who took part in the State entry of His Excellency the Viceroy (Lord Hardinge) into the Imperial capital, which was unfortunately marred by the dastardly anarchist attempt made on his life—an outrage that evoked horror and condemnation throughout the length and breadth of this country. On November 24, 1915, His Highness completed 25 years of his benign and enlightened rule. The celebration of this happy consummation was for unavoidable reasons postponed until the following March. The programme of festivities was, owing to the war, simple in character. The poor were fed and the headmen of the villages were entertained. There was a State procession through the gaily decorated streets of the capital as far as the Gurdawara, where a thanksgiving service was held, at which all the guests and the officials of the State were present. To perpetuate the memory of this occasion His Highness laid the foundation of a hall to be called the "Jubilee Memorial Hall." At the State banquet to which 50 people had been invited, the Commissioner of Jullundur, as the principal guest, in a highly complimentary speech proposed the health of His Highness the Maharaja, congratulating him on the highly successful period of 25 years of his rule which had been completed, and expressing the cordial wish of the assembled guests that twenty-five years afterwards, surrounded by prosperous, grateful and devoted subjects, and with the same delightful *joie de vivre* which they saw that day, he would be celebrating his "Golden Jubilee." A Durbar was held the next day at which addresses were presented on behalf of the officials and subjects of the State, to which His Highness made an appropriate reply, in the course of which he said: "I have already expressed my appreciation of the faithfulness that has consistently characterized my subjects, and I feel that I cannot do enough to requite it adequately. However, as a mark of my further confidence and affection for them, I wish to announce that, in order to associate them more intimately with my administration, I propose summoning once a year, probably on the occasion of my birthday Durbar, a selected number of *Zaildars*, *Lambardars*, *Sahukars*, and other representative people from the different *Tahsils*, to meet here in a general assembly, when I can confer with them about general affairs concerning their welfare and when they will also be given an opportunity to submit to me in a proper manner their grievances or other representations; such as are not personal but which touch the interests of the community at large. This is only a rough outline of the proposal, but I hope in due course to elaborate the scheme which I trust, under Divine guidance, may further advance the moral and material progress of my people." Before the close of the same year His Highness was able to inaugurate this Assembly, and the opening ceremony was performed with appropriate solemnity in an extraordinary Durbar, at which His Highness delivered the following address: "Officials and members of the Assembly. You have met here to-day by my command to assist me in the establishment of an institution which, modest though it be in its inception, may in time to come prove to be the forerunner of representative institutions which should in my opinion be the goal of all civilized and progressive communities. It has long been my aim to take measures to associate my subjects more intimately and directly with my Government, but you will realize that political evolution must come slowly and march abreast of the moral and intellectual progress of the times. The consistent loyalty of my people and the strides they have made intellectually, encouraged me to postpone the fulfilment of my fond desire no longer and announce the concession at my Jubilee Durbar.

"You are perhaps aware that the experiment I am embarking on has never been tried in any of the States in Northern India, except Bikaner, and its success or otherwise is bound to react on the prospects

THE STATE OF KAPURTHALA.

1. Gurdwara (Sikh Temple). 2. Hindu Temple.

of its introduction elsewhere. The future development of the institution must depend on your own efforts and on the use you will make of the opportunity now afforded you of operating as the component parts of the administrative machinery of the State. I therefore earnestly enjoin you in your own interests and in those of the Ruler to whom you owe allegiance to approach the performance of the task that has been set you in a spirit of unshaken loyalty, fairness and *pro bono publico*. The strength of your Assembly has for the present been fixed at 50, together with three members representing the three principal religious denominations in my State.

"The elective element has been introduced very cautiously, but with the effluxion of time, and with experience, I hope it may be possible to augment it. You will have noticed that in the allotment of seats I have endeavoured to ensure that all important interests should be represented. My anxiety to place the Assembly on a sound and firm basis will also be gauged from the fact that the nominations have been made with such care as to secure the inclusion of really useful men among my subjects.

"The agenda that has been laid down for your deliberations embrace topics that concern the general welfare of the various classes of my people. Broadly speaking, the questions relate to the existing legislation regarding the settlement of decretal liabilities, measures for the promotion of trade and commerce, and the improvement of communications.

"The fact that you have been asked to consider, discuss, and submit proposals on matters of such importance to myself and my subjects is an earnest of my intention to develop gradually but steadily your connection with the vital problems which confront the administration.

"I anticipate a certain amount of divergence of opinion on one or two items, but I want you to remember that the readiness with which you will sink and adjust your differences for the public weal and unanimously evolve a line of policy for submission to me for my approval, will be regarded as a measure of your fitness to represent the population of the State as a whole rather than a particular class or creed.

"The terms of the solemn obligation that you will presently be called upon to undertake ought also to dictate to you the expediency of following the same course. If I am satisfied with results I propose to extend to you, with effect from the next session, the right of initiating, with my previous approval and subject to proper rules, discussion on matters of general interest which you may consider it necessary to bring to my notice.

"Before concluding this pronouncement I cannot restrain myself from alluding to the colossal struggle in which our great Empire and its powerful allies are at present involved. I may tell you that originally I had a mind to adjourn the inauguration of the Assembly until after the war, but, acting on the doctrine that the business of the world must be transacted even when the booming of guns reverberate from the various corners of the globe, I decided to proceed with the redemption of the promise I had made at my Jubilee Durbar last March.

"Though the end of the war is not yet in sight, the stupendous efforts of our Empire and the allied countries must ere long fructify in unqualified victory.

"You are aware of the part I have so far played with your co-operation in these stirring events, but fresh efforts are needed, particularly in the recruitment of men not only for my own regiment, which has been upholding our splendid traditions in East Africa for the past two years, but also for the British army, whose interests are absolutely identical with ours.

"I take this opportunity therefore of calling on you, members of the Assembly, the representatives of my people, to gird your loins in rendering in this behalf all moral and practical assistance in your power. By doing so you will only be accelerating the triumph of a just cause.

"Members of the Assembly, in extending to you a cordial welcome and in declaring the Assembly open, I devoutly pray that Providence may always guide your labours into channels that will lead to the furtherance of the good of our people and the greater glory of my House and State.

"I invoke His choicest blessings on us all, and formally declare the Assembly of the State to be now open."

During His Highness' reign Kapurthala has received visitors of high rank and Royal birth from time to time. The Marquis of Dufferin and Ava and His Royal Highness Prince Albert Victor of Wales visited Kapurthala in 1887 and 1890 respectively, while the various Lieutenant-Governors of the Punjab have gladly accepted the Maharaja's hospitality during their term of office.

In October 1913 Kapurthala received the honour of a visit from His Excellency Lord Hardinge, Viceroy and Governor-General of India. His Excellency arrived at Kapurthala on the morning of October 15th, and was received at the station by His Highness the Maharaja, the Tikka Sahib and the principal State officials. Soon after His Excellency's arrival at the Palace the Maharaja paid him a formal visit, which was returned in the large Durbar Hall, which was gorgeously decorated and packed with officials and rural and urban gentry. On the following morning His Excellency held a review of the Imperial Service regiment and highly admired the splendid appearance of officers and men. After the review His Excellency performed the opening ceremony of the new grain market called after him, the "Hardinge Gunj," and then inspected the State jewellery. The afternoon was spent on the Beyn river, where the scenery is strikingly reminiscent of old England. The route from the Beyn to the Palace was illumined with blazing torches, and the Tirah memorial, hung with festoons of Chinese lanterns, presented a fairy-like scene. The evening function was the State banquet, to which a large number of guests were invited. In February 1919 His Highness received a visit from His Excellency Lord Chelmsford, Viceroy and Governor-General of India. The arrangements for his reception and entertainment were almost identical with those made on the occasion of Lord Hardinge's visit in 1913. At the banquet His Highness proposed the health of his distinguished guest, and in the course of his speech said: "The free personal exchange of views between the ruling Princes and the high dignitaries of the Government of India on matters of vital import to the States, or of joint concern, rendered possible by the annual conferences at Delhi, the admission of the Princes into the innermost councils of the Empire, and, last but not least, the frank recognition in the Indian Reforms Report, of their historic position in the body politic of India and the regard shown therein for their rights, prerogatives and prestige, are measures which have won for His Excellency Lord Chelmsford the sincere gratitude of us all and will constitute a lasting monument of his far-seeing constructive statesmanship. We are all aware that His Excellency succeeded to the helm of affairs in this country at a most critical epoch in the history of our world-wide Empire. How he steered the ship of State through those momentous and anxious times, with what remarkable success India's vast man-power and material resources were exploited for the service of the common cause, and to what a high pinnacle the fair name of this ancient land has, in consequence, been lifted, are facts too patent to need any emphasis or elaboration from me. Suffice it to say that the Viceregal mantle has never fallen on more worthy shoulders.

"Your Excellency, it is scarcely necessary for me to dwell on the tried loyalty and devotion of my House and State to the Person, Throne and Government of our beloved King-Emperor. To this fact the annals of the Indian Mutiny, the second standing in this very room over five years ago, months before the unsuspecting world received a rude awakening at the hands of the then masters of Germany, in complimenting my Imperial Service troops on their efficiency, almost prophetically observed: 'I am confident that, were the need to arise again for their services in the field, they would acquit themselves worthily and bring fresh honour to their State and to their Ruler.' I rejoice that Lord Hardinge's confidence has been so quickly justified by later events. Directly in shattering the much-vaunted might of the foes of the Empire. It was my fond desire, wholly shared, I believe, by the officers and men themselves, that it might fall to their lot to take part in the epic victories our armies were then achieving on other fronts. Indeed, the unit was thoroughly refitted and was on the eve of departure for Mesopotamia when the sudden *débâcle* of Germany and her Allies terminated hostilities early in November last. Before leaving this theme I cannot omit a thankful acknowledgment of the valuable assistance

THE STATE OF KAPURTHALA.

THE CLUB.

Sikh War, the Afghan Wars of 1877-8, and the Tirah campaign of 1897 bear sufficiently eloquent testimony. But I am naturally reluctant to let this opportunity pass without giving expression to the deep satisfaction I experience in reflecting on the part this State has borne in the war that has only recently been brought to a triumphant conclusion. *Vis-à-vis* with the colossal efforts of our Empire my share would, doubtless, appear like a drop in the ocean. None the less, I shall ever recall with a feeling of pride that in the Empire's hour of need my State and I grudged no sacrifice or endeavour. Your Excellency's distinguished predecessor, on the outbreak of the war I placed the regiment at the disposal of the Imperial Government. It was 600 strong then, and by the time the unit returned home after three and a half years' employment on active service in East Africa, its total strength had risen to 1,000, and subsequently to 1,200. In response to the stirring appeal of the Prime Minister, in May last I offered, as Your Excellency will recollect, to raise the number to 1,600. The manner in which my troops acquitted themselves in the field is known to no one better than Your Excellency, but for me it is enough to realize that in one theatre of war at least they were able to co-operate I have always received from the Inspector-General of the Imperial Service troops, the Inspecting Officer, and the special Service Officers attached to my regiment for the period of the war.

"I do not wish to weary my audience with the details of the other activities of my State in connection with the great crisis, but I would like to mention that we managed to supply nearly 4,000 recruits to the Indian army, and, despite our heavy military commitments, to contribute nearly Rs. 12,00,000 to the various war loans and Rs. 3,00,000 towards the extraordinary expenses of the war.

"Intensely gratifying as this record is

for me, it is now a reminiscence. As to the future, while devoutly hoping that the world will never again witness a repetition of the sanguinary struggle of the past four years and that universal peace may reign for ever, I can confidently assure Your Excellency that should an emergency arise, this State, inspired by its time-honoured traditions, will not fail to rise to the occasion and afford a fresh proof, if indeed such were needed, of its abiding attachment to the Imperial House of Windsor and the Empire.

"Your Excellency, as regards our internal affairs, I propose to confine myself to a few general observations. I have been exercising full ruling powers for more than 28 years, and during this long period I have always essayed to forward the moral, social, and material welfare of my people, whose affection and contentment, upon which I know I can fully rely, I regard as an adequate recompense for my labours. Educational and medical institutions have been provided at convenient centres. Municipalities and local boards, partly elected and partly nominated, administer civic and rural affairs respectively. Free primary education has been introduced at large, and I have lately made it compulsory in selected areas experimentally, while instruction for females has not been neglected. The capital enjoys the benefits of drainage and waterworks schemes, completed on scientific lines at a considerable cost. The income has grown from Rs. 21,00,000 in 1890 to Rs. 35,00,000 at the present time. I am fostering with particular care the movement of agricultural co-operative credit, and with a view to bringing modern methods of cultivation within easy reach of my people, I have recently organized a department of Agriculture and Industries which has commenced its useful career under the guidance of an expert officer whose services Your Excellency's Government have been kind enough to lend to me recently.

"Your Excellency, I trust it will be clear from this outline of some of the broad features of my administration that this State is steadily striving to respond to the spirit of the times."

His Excellency the Viceroy, in the course of his speech in response, said:

"Your Highness has alluded to the war record of the Kapurthala Imperial Service troops, a record of which any State might well be proud. The quality of Your Highness' troops is shown by the long list of distinctions gained by the officers and men of the Kapurthala infantry during three and a half years of arduous campaigning in unhealthy surroundings and a particularly difficult country against a determined and elusive enemy. The regiment was complimented for its excellent work by the General Officer Commanding-in-Chief, East African Expeditionary Force, and several of its officers received various distinctions. Major-General Sardar Pooran Singh was awarded a C.I.E., Colonel Nihal Singh, the officer commanding the regiment, received the 2nd Class of the Order of British India and one Indian Distinguished Medal, ten Meritorious Service Medals and one French Medaille Militaire were won by various non-commissioned officers and men. Not only has the Kapurthala infantry distinguished itself in the manner I have described, but the State has supplied the large number of 4,000 recruits for the ranks of the Indian army at considerable cost. But man-power has not been the only direction in which Kapurthala had helped towards the defeat of the enemies of the British Empire. Your Highness has caused nearly Rs. 12,00,000 to be invested in various war loans, English, Indian and French, and cash contributions have been made on a considerable scale to various charitable and other funds connected with the prosecution of the war.

"In recognition of the services rendered by the Kapurthala State, Your Highness' salute was raised to 13 guns, and the share taken by Your Highness in the results achieved was recognized by the grant of a personal salute of 15 guns and of the rank of Honorary Lieutenant-Colonel in the army. Your Highness' third son, Captain Kanwar Amarjit Singh, also worthily upheld the military traditions of the Kapurthala House by serving in France with the 3rd (Lahore) division, and in recognition of his services received the honorary rank of Captain in the army, while Khan Bahadur Sardar Abdul Hamid, Your Highness' capable Chief Secretary, was made an Officer of the Order of the British Empire for his meritorious services in connection with the war.

"Lord Hardinge, during his visit to Kapurthala in 1913, remarked in terms of appreciation on the able manner in which the administration of the State was conducted, and dwelt on the success of your Highness' efforts in this direction as worthy of all praise. I am glad to learn that the State continues to enjoy the benefits of Your Highness' wise and progressive rule, that the system of administration has earned the gratitude and contentment of your people, and that the finances of the State are in a flourishing and prosperous condition.

"Your Highness has recently given one more proof, though none was needed, of the loyalty of the Kapurthala State to the British Government. During the recent troublous times through which the Punjab passed, as a result of the influx of seditious agitators and returned emigrants, the State co-operated whole-heartedly with the Punjab Government in its efforts to extirpate crime and to bring the guilty to justice. The movements of such of these persons as entered the State were kept under careful surveillance, and the efficiency of the State police was demonstrated by the success which was achieved.

"The success of Your Highness' policy in utilizing local talent in the service of the State has been justified by the results attained. I learn with satisfaction that except for a few technical officers all the officials of the State belong to local families, and that many of them have been educated in Europe at the expense of the State. The heir-apparent devotes himself generally to the service of the State, while Your Highness' second son has been a judicial officer and your third son is now Director of Police and Education.

"Gentlemen, I need say no more to demonstrate the admirable results of the sagacious and far-sighted policy adopted by His Highness in all branches of the administration of his State. I ask you now to drink to the health of our distinguished host, His Highness the Maharaja of Kapurthala, and to the continued prosperity of the Kapurthala State."

Early in March His Honour Sir Michael O'Dwyer paid His Highness his farewell visit. At the State dinner in the evening some interesting speeches were made.

His Highness, in proposing Sir Michael O'Dwyer's health (after some preliminary remarks), said: "Gentlemen, we are all aware that Sir Michael's tenure of office has been of a most strenuous character. Throughout the best part of it the Empire was involved in the greatest war in history. Upon the man-power of this province, aptly described as the 'sword-arm of India,' devolved the brunt of the responsibility for meeting the expanded needs of the Indian army. By its ardent response the Punjab not only led the way but also surpassed its own glorious traditions. Equally earnest was the Punjab in other directions in connection with the war. While His Honour was busy inspiring the activities of the province and mobilizing its resources in a manner so completely

THE STATE OF KAPURTHALA.

1. General View of the City. 2. Samadhs (Tombs) of His Highness's Ancestors. 3. Villa.

effective, he was called upon to face an internal situation of a particularly alarming nature.

"The heavy burdens of His Honour's high office were thus rendered exceptionally onerous. But I am sure the memory of the masterly skill with which he coped with every emergency that arose, and of the success with which he rallied the Punjabis round the common cause, will fill him evermore with profound satisfaction, and that he will look back upon these results as the most signal of the numerous achievements of his long and brilliant career. He will have every right to point with pride to the fact that in contributing to the Empire's splendid triumph the Punjab under his sagacious guidance bore no unworthy share. Speaking for myself and my State, I rejoice to seize this occasion thankfully to acknowledge the regard and consideration His Honour has consistently shown in his official and private dealings with me and the wise counsel and assistance I have never failed to receive from him. In His Honour's time not a single *contretemps* has disturbed the harmonious relations that have subsisted between this State and the Punjab Government and the successive Political Agents across the long space of 28 years during which I have held charge of the destinies of my people, and have endeavoured, according to my lights, to promote their moral and material well-being. Mutual co-operation has been the key-note of our policy. Moreover, here in Kapurthala his *regime* as Lieutenant-Governor will be associated with the higher status and prestige this State and its Ruler have acquired as a consequence of the honours recently conferred by His Imperial Majesty.

"Parting from such a true friend cannot but be a wrench, but all the same we realize that His Honour is leaving us to enjoy a richly-earned relief from the labours of a lifetime in scenes so far removed from the land of his birth."

His Honour Sir Michael O'Dwyer, in his reply, after some complimentary allusions to the Maharaja's hospitality, said: "Just a fortnight ago Your Highness had the honour of entertaining His Excellency the Viceroy, who, in giving the toast of Your Highness' health, dwelt on the distinguished war record of the Kapurthala State army. The record adds another proud chapter to the history of the State which, as far back as 1805, helped to drive the Mahrattas from the north of India, and in so many subsequent campaigns—the second Sikh War, the Mutiny, the Afghan and Tirah Wars—has been prompt to place its resources in men and money at the disposal of the British Government. Immediately on the outbreak of the Great War in August 1914, your Imperial Service troops, 378 strong, were selected as part of the first contingent to proceed on active service, and in September they sailed for East Africa. There they took part, almost as soon as they landed, in the battle of Longido. They sustained for over three years the difficult rôle of garrisoning outposts and patrolling that unhealthy country of wide distances and dense jungles under the command, first, of their stalwart Colonel, Nihal Singh, O.B.I., and then of that distinguished soldier, Major-General S. Pruan Singh Bahadur, C.I.E., who enhanced the fine military reputation which he first earned 20 years ago in the Tirah campaign. His Excellency the Viceroy in his speech paid a generous tribute to the services of the regiment, which received drafts of 300 men to repair the wastage casualties and did not return till the conquest of German East Africa was complete. The roll of honour included 62 deaths, and bears on it the name of the special Service Officer, Major Gordon (whose place was taken up by Major Nicolas, of the Punjab Commission), and of the gallant Subedar Jhaggar Singh. The battalion, which owes much to the training given it by Major MacBrayne and its other Inspecting Officers, was speedily refitted, its strength was increased, and it was keen and ready to take the field again in Palestine or Mesopotamia, when hostilities came to an end. But your Imperial Service troops are only a portion of Kapurthala's contribution in man-power. When war broke out the Kapurthala State was represented in the Indian army by less than 900 men, inclusive of the Imperial Service troops. When the war ended these numbers had been increased to about 5,000 men, or 1 in 30 of the male population exclusive of the extra companies of the Imperial Service troops with which Your Highness had generously raised to bring the strength of the unit to 1,600 men. That is an achievement worthy of the best traditions of the State, which has always prided itself on its devotion to the person and the Throne of His Majesty the King-Emperor, and the value of the State's loyal co-operation was recognized when His Excellency the Viceroy specially invited Your Highness in April last year to be one of the two representatives of the Punjab Princes and Chiefs at the War Conference, at Delhi, and later on to give the Central Recruiting Board the benefit of your practical advice. Your Highness further stimulated the recruiting efforts of the Durbar by entrusting the organization of the war propaganda in the State last year to a Recruiting Board presided over by your third son, Captain Kanwar Amarjit Singh, to whom an honorary King's Commission in the army has been granted in recognition of his services in France and his zeal in developing the man-power of the State. In addition to the 14 distinctions which the Imperial Service troops gained on active service, men of Kapurthala in the Indian army have won an Order of British India, an Order of Merit, four Distinguished Service Medals, and two Foreign Decorations. In every movement to support the war, to relieve the wounded and distressed, and to provide comforts for the troops in the field, Your Highness and your family have been the first to come forward, and Lady O'Dwyer desires me especially to thank Your Highness, your family and people for the constant and generous support given to the Red Cross and comforts funds under her charge. Kapurthala has indeed done its duty nobly, and with Your Highness's permission I will this evening show some recognition by Government of the successful efforts made by the more prominent workers in the common cause. This is the last occasion which I shall have of speaking in a Punjab State, and I take the opportunity of expressing the deep obligations of the Punjab and the Punjab Government to the Punjab States as a body for their magnificent services during the war. In bearing the burdens of the war, in sharing its sacrifices, they have come fully up to the high standard set by the British Punjab and have set a noble example to the States of the Indian Empire. At the close of war, of 4,00,000 Punjabis with the colours, fully 50,000 came from the Punjab States, and their assistance in the matter of money and equipment had been on an even greater scale.

"Those great services were, as Your Highness says, rendered spontaneously from a sense of duty to the King-Emperor, but the Punjab is proud and glad that His Imperial Majesty has graciously signified his appreciation of them by the honours and dignities conferred on Your Highness and your brother Princes and Chiefs.

"But while in recent years the preoccupations of the war have been paramount, Your Highness has not allowed the domestic needs of your people to be neglected, and the annual Administration

THE STATE OF KAPURTHALA.

1. Chateau Kapurthala Mussoorie. 2. Statue of His Highness Raja-i-Rajgan Randhir Singh, Sahib Bahadur, G.C.S.I.

Reports of the State bear witness to the care with which schemes for the improvement of irrigation and agriculture are being studied.

"Kapurthala is second to no State that I know in the efficiency and progressive character of its administration, the prosperity and contentment of its people, and the result for which, after your Highness, so much credit is due to Your Highness' very able Chief Minister, Khan Bahadur Abdul Hamid, O.B.E., is shown in their devotion to the ruling House and their willing co-operation in a crisis such as that which is now happily past. In matters of common interest to Government and the Durbar, such as the repression of the *Ghadr* movement, the suppression of organized crime and the reclamation of the criminal tribes, there has been the most harmonious co-operation with the Punjab Government, and it is a great pleasure to me to hear from Your Highness that in the 28 years during which you have so worthily ruled your State, there has not been a single misunderstanding with the Punjab Government and its Agents, and I am sure that happy state of affairs will continue. Your Highness has wisely associated your sons in the management of State affairs, and the Tikka Sahib especially, in the critical year 1915, gave proof that the confidence is fully deserved. Your Highness, the pleasure of this visit to Your Highness and your State is saddened by the reflection that it is my last, but I shall take away with me very pleasant memories of my official relations and personal friendship with Your Highness. Your Highness, as I have said, is a great traveller. You might well say, like Ulysses :—

For always roaming with an eager heart,
Much have I seen and known, cities of men
And manners, climates, councils, Governments:
Myself not least but honoured of them all.

"For those who know you honour in you not only the capable and progressive Ruler, but the good sportsman, the cultured man of the world, the generous host, and the warm-hearted friend. Gentlemen, I ask you to fill your glasses and to join with me in drinking the health of our host His Highness the Maharaja, and in wishing to him and his State a future even fuller of honours and prosperity than the past."

The fidelity of Kapurthala to the British Raj is beyond question. The present Ruler has fully maintained the glorious traditions of his House in this respect. In 1878-9, on the outbreak of the Afghan War, the State troops, comprising 500 infantry, 100 cavalry, three guns and a hundred artillery, rendered active service on the Bannu frontier under General Watson. The detachment was highly spoken of by the British officers for its discipline and good conduct. In 1897 the Maharaja despatched his Imperial Service regiment (which was formed in 1888) for active service in connection with the Tirah campaign. The regiment received its baptism of fire and gave an excellent account of itself. A detachment of 36 rank and file lost its way at Kurmana, in the Kurrum Valley, and was ambushed by a relentless enemy, but this small force put up a gallant defence against superior odds and preferred heroic death to surrender. On this occasion the Government of India communicated their heartfelt regrets and sympathies to His Highness, who raised near the regimental lines a permanent memorial to the heroism of this ill-fated but gallant little detachment. His Highness was one of the first among the Princes who on the outbreak of the Great War offered to place all their resources at the disposal of the British Government. The Kapurthala Imperial Service regiment was despatched in the middle of September for active service in East Africa, where it remained for nearly four years and did excellent work. His Highness himself visited the battle-front in France in 1915, while his third son, Captain Maharaj Kumar Amarjit Singh Sahib, served with the Indian contingent for more than a year.

It may not be out of place to refer at this point to the State Administration Report (1916-17), which gives in a compact form a complete catalogue of the numerous other services the State rendered with the object of hastening the victory of the British arms. One extra company of 100 men raised as an addition to the regiment; the contributions to the Indian War Relief Fund, Rs. 39,945 (including the subscriptions of State officials and subjects); to the Prince of Wales's Relief Fund, Rs. 7,500; for extra war expenses in 1915, Rs. 1,00,000; for extra expenses of the State regiment in 1916, Rs. 50,000; *Babul* bark supplied free of cost, worth Rs. 3,000; to St. John's Ambulance Fund, Punjab, in 1916, Rs. 500; value of comforts for soldiers in East Africa, Rs. 5,000; value of 12 horses presented; 12 transport drivers provided; Rs. 25,000 paid through the Punjab Government for the purchase of motor ambulances in 1917; Rs. 25,000 paid through the Government of the United Provinces for the purchase of motor ambulances in 1917; 28 mules supplied free of cost; 44 camels supplied free of cost; 16 *Sarwans* maintained at the cost of the State during the war; the strength of the depot of the Imperial Service regiment was nearly doubled, costing roughly Rs. 20,000 annually; free rations to the regimental depot, estimated to cost Rs. 30,000 per annum; double pay to the rank and file of the regiment in the field, and *bhatta* to mounted officers in addition to that granted by Government; to the English War Loan Fund, Rs. 13,00,000; to the Indian War Loan Fund, Rs. 4,00,000 (including subscriptions of State officials and subjects); and to the French War Loan Fund, Rs. 2,50,000. In 1918, in response to the stirring appeal of the British Prime Minister, His Highness offered to raise the strength of his Imperial Service infantry to 1,600 men. For a long period during the Great War the strength of the unit was actually above 1,000. His Highness' final contribution towards this gigantic struggle was his offer, which was accepted, to waive the recovery of a sum of Rs. 4,00,000 payable by the Government of India on account of extra war expenses of the Kapurthala Imperial Service regiment. Since the conclusion of the Great War the regiment has again been on active service in Seistan during the Afghan campaign, and, more recently, has spent six months performing Imperial duties in Mesopotamia. For the numerous services rendered by the State in the Imperial cause since 1914, His Highness has on various occasions received the following honours, namely: a salute of 15 guns, an Honorary Lieutenant-Colonelcy in the army, and the investiture of the insignia of a G.C.I.E. His Highness has not been less mindful of his obligations to his subjects. Realizing the need to modernize the system of administration and bringing it into line with present requirements, His Highness, in 1910, borrowed the services of a capable and an experienced civilian, L. French, Esq., C.I.E., as Chief Minister. Mr. French was in the State for four years, and during that period, under His Highness' orders, reorganized every branch of the administration and introduced many reforms. Efficiency is the key-note of the whole administrative system. The Maharaja habitually takes a large directing share in the transaction of business, and in the work of administration he is assisted by his Chief Minister and a band of capable departmental officers, the majority of whom are local men belonging to old families of tried loyalty. In educational matters particularly, His Highness has always evinced a keen interest from the time of his accession to the present day, and the annual expenditure under this head, which has steadily increased, now exceeds Rs. 1,90,000. The State possesses one college, three high schools, and about 58 primary, secondary and girls' schools. The number of primary schools has risen year by year—in fact the State is pre-eminent in the provision of primary instruction. No fees are charged in the primary department, and free compulsory education has for the first time in the Punjab been established within a limited area as an experimental measure. Agriculture, that all-important factor in the well-being of the mass of the people in this country, has also received its due share of attention. A considerable sum of money is annually spent on the maintenance of an agricultural farm, which has been opened with a view to demonstrate to the general body of cultivators the most up-to-date scientific methods of cultivation. Co-operative credit banks have also been started with a view to ensure the financial independence of the *Zemindars*, and this movement has made a strikingly rapid advance in the State. The banks are now nearly 300 in number, a result which will compare favourably with probably any district in the Punjab. The Medical and Sanitary Department, which is in charge of a European medical officer, is working at a high pitch of efficiency. There is a well-equipped hospital for males and another for females in the capital, while there is a State dispensary at the headquarters of each *tahsil* where free medical relief is afforded. The chief town is provided with a good supply of pure water, together with an efficient system of drainage. The State is, for administrative purposes, divided into five *tahsils*, namely, Kapurthala, Sultanpur, Phagwara, Bholath and Bhunga. The *Tahsildars* have recently been relieved of judicial duties and are in charge of revenue and executive work only. The judicial work is carried on by *Munsiffs*, who have powers to hear civil and revenue cases up to Rs. 1,000 in value. The highest Court of Appeal is the Chief Court, which consists of three judges, but the power of passing sentences of death is vested in His Highness the Maharaja himself. The gross income of the State, including the Oudh estates, is roughly Rs. 37,00,000.

The following crops, mentioned in order of their importance, are grown in the State: wheat, *gram*, maize, cotton and sugar-cane. The three towns of Kapurthala, Phagwara and Sultanpur possess municipalities, the constitution of which has lately been considerably liberalized. His Highness has sanctioned the creation of *Punchayats* for rural areas with power to hear and decide civil cases up to the value of Rs. 100, and in this respect the State may well claim to be ahead of the Punjab and the Punjab States generally. A State Council, with Sri Tikka Sahib as President and the Chief Minister as Vice-President, has recently been formed. This body submits to His Highness its considered opinion on matters of general importance.

His Highness' versatility is not confined to the activities outlined above. He takes an important share in the deliberations of the Princes' Conference (now known as the Princes' Chamber), and his views carry considerable weight and influence with his brother Princes. His contributions to the debates at these gatherings always bear evidence of a robust common sense and a wide knowledge of human affairs. It is interesting to recall that the resolution conveying the united congratulations of the Princes to His Majesty the King-Emperor on the glorious conclusion of the war was moved by His Highness the Maharaja at the Princes Conference in a remarkably eloquent speech

THE STATE OF NABHA

THE STATE OF NABHA.

1. Hira Madal. 2. Pucca Bagh Palace, Nabha.

THE STATE OF NABHA.

1. General View of the City. 2. Kachehrighar (Back View). 3. Civil Hospital, Nabha.

THE STATE OF NABHA.

1. Phul Fort. 2. Amloh Fort. 3. Dhanaula Fort. 4. Bawal Fort.

THE STATE OF NABHA.

1. Jungle Kothi Palace, near Nabha. 2. Dewan Khana. 3. High School, Nabha 4. Kothi Bagh, Nabha.

THE STATE OF NABHA.

1 and 2. Infantry. 3. Cavalry. 4. Artillery.

THE STATE OF NABHA.

1. Copper Hill, near Kanti, Bawal. 2. Military Hospital. 3. Outside View of the Fort Palace, Nabha. 4. Cantonment Barracks, Nabha. 5. Tegh Ginning Factory and Nanak Cotton Press, Nabha.

THE STATE OF NABHA.

1. Samadh (Mausoleum) of His Late Highness Maharaja Hira Singh Ji at Nabha.
2. Group of Samadhs, with Maharaja Jaswant Singh's in the Centre.
3. Bunj (Bastion) Sirepa Sahib, Nabha.
4. Gurdwara, Tibbi Sahib, Nabha.

KOTHA (FORT).

THE STATE OF NAWANAGAR

THE word "Nawanagar," uttered in the presence of educated Indians, who are acquainted with the modern history of their country, will, as a rule, cause them to think of a progressive and prosperous Principality in the Kathiawar peninsula of the Bombay Presidency, and to Englishmen, generally, it may not mean even as much as that. When, however, it is added that its noble and wise Ruler is none other than "Prince Ranji," as he was familiarly, nay, even affectionately called in the Old Country, the liveliest interest will immediately be aroused in the minds of tens of thousands of Britishers in every part of the world, who have witnessed or read about the brilliant performances on the cricket field of a man who is "Prince of a small territory, but king of a great game."

Regarding His Highness's achievements in the field of cricket, it may be observed briefly, that his first appearance for the Sussex County Club was made in 1895, and from that year to 1902 he was at the head of the Sussex batting averages. He was champion batsman for All-England in 1896, and again in 1900, scoring 2,780 runs, with an average of 59.91 ; and he went with Mr. A. J. Stoddart's All-England XI to Australia in 1897–8.

The Maharaja Jam Sahib belongs to the Jadeja tribe of Rajputs of the Lunar race, and it appears that they entered Kathiawar from Cutch, and dispossessed the ancient family of Jethwas (of Porbandar) then established at Ghumli. Several generations later, a descendant, named Jam Rawal, was in possession of extensive possessions in this neighbourhood, and it was he who in 1540 founded the city of Jamnagar. Other territories to the east and west of Nawanagar were obtained by conquest from the Chabadas, the Dedas, and the Vaghelas, and before the death of Jam Rawal in 1562, he had succeeded in consolidating the various districts which had fallen into his hands. There is a lack of authentic chronicles concerning the State for the following 180 years, with this exception, that the Rulers were almost constantly engaged in repelling attacks upon their own territory, or in rendering assistance to neighbouring Chiefs in protecting their possessions.

An important epoch in the political history of Nawanagar seems to have arisen about the year 1743, when Jam Lakhaji ascended the *gadi*. This Ruler married a daughter of the House of Halwad-Dhrangadhra, and when she left the paternal roof for her new home in Nawanagar, her father sent with her a personal attendant, named Mehraman, one of the Khawas, a menial tribe. This man possessed considerable intelligence, and he soon contrived to assume supreme control in the State, the Jam Sahib becoming a mere puppet in his hands. Jam Lakhaji died in 1768, and was succeeded by his

HIS HIGHNESS MAHARAJA JAM SHRI SIR RANJIT-SINHJI, BAHADUR, MAHARAJA JAM SAHIB OF NAWANAGAR.

THE STATE OF NAWANAGAR.

1. Bhavendra Villas Palace, the Residence of H.H. the Maharaja Jam Sahib. 2. Pratap Villas. 3. Guard House, Pratap Villas. 4. Lal Bungalow Palace.

THE STATE OF NAWANAGAR

son. Jam Jasaji, but Mehraman retained the reins of government in his own hands. Jawuba, the queen of Jam Lakhaji, grew alarmed at the increasing power and ambition of Mehraman, and she sought the assistance of her brother, the Ruler of Halwad-Dhrangadhra, for the protection of her minor son against the scarcely veiled aggrandizement of the minister, who now began to administer on his own account the three *mahals* of the State, Amran, Jodiya, and Balambha. But her death was brought about in a violent manner by the ungrateful Khawas, who continued his career of unbridled supremacy until his death in 1800. Jam Jassaji thereupon stepped into his rightful position as Ruler. The successors of Khawas Mehraman continued their acts of turbulence, and began further encroachments upon Nawanagar lands. Nawanagar then sought the assistance of the British Government and the Gaekwar of Baroda, who drove the Khawases from the three mahals. The Amran division was then re-granted on service tenure, but owing to the disregard of such conditions, and the unworthy behaviour of the successive Khawases, the grant of that territory was withdrawn by His Highness the present Jam Sahib. During Jam Jassaji's *regime*, differences had arisen within the State as to the inheritance to be granted to his brother, Sataji, and externally with regard to claims preferred by the States of Baroda, Cutch, and Porbandar, and the questions in dispute were submitted to the British Government for settlement.

In the end, a treaty was entered into in 1807 between Nawanagar and the Paramount Power, and by its provisions, Jam Jassaji, in consideration of receiving British protection, undertook to restore order in the State, to pay tribute regularly, and to refrain from molesting any of the surrounding Principalities.

Almost immediately after this date the cruel practice of female infanticide was prohibited at the instance of the British Resident. Jam Jassaji died in 1814, and was succeeded by his brother, Sataji, who after a short and unimportant reign was followed by Jam Ranmalji, who had been adopted in default of legal male issue.

The State enjoyed a period of peace during this reign, but it was visited by disastrous famines in the year 1834, 1839, and 1846, and the Jam Sahib gained an honoured name for himself by his ceaseless efforts to minimize the sufferings of his unfortunate subjects. With the object of providing work, and the consequent means of subsistence, he constructed the Kotha and Lakhota palaces at Jamnagar, and also excavated a large tank in the vicinity of the city.

Jam Ranmalji died in 1852, and was succeeded by His Highness Sir Shri Vibhaji, whose liberal and wise policy of government commended itself so strongly to the British Government, that in 1862 they granted to him a *sanad* of adoption, whereby in the absence of a direct male heir the Jam was permitted to adopt one without the payment of the customary duty. In 1864 His Highness established civil and criminal Courts of Justice, and also inaugurated several necessary measures of reform, not the least of which was the establishment of a regular system of collection of land revenue. In 1871 His Highness was honoured by a visit from His Excellency Sir Seymour Fitzgerald, Governor of Bombay, who performed the ceremony of opening the waterworks, which had been constructed by the Jam Sahib, and in 1876 he journeyed to Bombay in order to be present on the arrival of His Royal Highness the Prince of Wales, subsequently King Edward VII. In January 1887, His Highness attended the Imperial assemblage at Delhi, on the occasion of the assumption by Her Majesty the late Queen Victoria of the title of Empress of India.

During this visit His Highness was presented with a banner by His Excellency Lord Lytton, the Viceroy and Governor-General of India, and his salute was raised from 11 to 15 guns. In 1878 the insignia of a Knight Commander of the Most Exalted Order of the Star of India was conferred upon His Highness by the Political Agent at Rajkot. Sir Shri Vibhaji was an indefatigable worker for the welfare of his subjects, and it may be mentioned that he abolished the system of "farming out" districts, which afforded ample opportunities for the oppression of *ryots* by wealthy landowners; he codified Laws in force in the State; he formed Departments of Police, Public Works, Medicine, Education, and Municipal administration, and he undertook the construction of works of utility, such as schools, libraries, dispensaries, bridges, and public gardens. In the absence of legitimate male issue, His Highness adopted Kumar Shri Ranjitsinhji (the present Jam Sahib) from the Sarodar family in Kathiawar, in 1878, but subsequently (1882) a son, named Jaswantsinhji, was born, his mother being a Mahomedan lady in the Zenana. This son succeeded to the *gadi* on the death of Jam Shri Vibhaji, in 1895, but he died in the same year at an early age, leaving no heir to succeed him. The claims of Kumar Shri Ranjitsinhji, as the adopted son of His Highness Jam Shri Vibhaji, were, after a period of abeyance, brought on principally by Zenana intrigue during the lifetime of Jam Shri Vibhaji, duly recognized, and he ascended the *gadi* in 1907 as the lawful ruler of Nawanagar.

The present Ruler, Lieut.-Col. His Highness the Maharaja Sir Shri Ranjitsinhji Vibhaji Bahadur, K.C.S.I., G.B.E., Jam Sahib of Nawanagar, was born in September 1872, at Sarodar, in Kathiawar. He received the early portion of his education at the Rajkumar College, Rajkot, but subsequently proceeded to Trinity College at the University of Cambridge, in England. It was here that His Highness found scope for the development of qualities of heart and mind, which made him a *persona grata* with all classes of Englishmen; within the walls of his college, his genial personality and his powers as a *raconteur* gained for him a host of friends; and as a sportsman who "plays the game" in every phase of life he has few equals, and certainly no superiors.

On March 11, 1907, His Highness was installed on the *gadi* by the Hon. Mr. Fitzgerald, Agent to His Excellency the Governor of Bombay, in Kathiawar.

His Highness the Jam Sahib, in replying to the instructive address delivered by the Agent at the installation ceremony, said, *inter alia*: "I am very thankful for the various suggestions you have made as to the different ways in which I can improve my State and its administration. This advice and these suggestions are so rich that I must keep them always before me, and endeavour to act up to them. I know my State and people have suffered much from the scourges mentioned by you, and can only hope that we are now entering upon a better cycle of years. I hope to abide by the traditions of this State, and to maintain an unswerving loyalty to the British throne."

True to the declaration made by His Highness at his installation, the Jam Sahib has laboured unceasingly for the welfare of the large population committed to his care.

The outbreak of the Great War afforded an opportunity for His Highness the Jam Sahib to demonstrate the chivalry of the Rajput, but it also enabled him to manifest his determination to assist Great Britain

THE STATE OF NAWANAGAR.

1. Amar Villas. 2. Vijaya Bhuvan. 3. Badminton House. 4. Cricket Pavilion. 5. New Hospital. 6. Killeshwar Bungalow.

THE STATE OF NAWANAGAR

and her allies in defending right against might, and in securing freedom and justice for all. He approached the Government of India with offers of his personal services, as well as the resources of his State, and he regarded it as a high privilege to be employed on the western front for more than a year, first on the Staff of General Cookson, commanding the 9th Cavalry Division of the Indian Expeditionary Force, and afterwards as A.D.C. to the Commander-in-Chief, Lord French. After his return to India His Highness was invited to join the Staff of Field-Marshal Sir Douglas Haig, but owing to exigencies of State affairs he was very reluctantly unable to accept the honour. Three nephews of His Highness were engaged in the war: Lieut. Kunwar Sahib Savaisinhji was in the African campaign for a period of two years, and was wounded in action; Lieut. Kunwar Sahib Dajiraj served in France for 18 months, and was killed in battle in 1917; and Lieut. Kunwar Sahib Himatsinhji was with the forces in Mesopotamia. The Nawanagar Imperial Service Lancers performed garrison duty at Karachi, and a signalling part of this regiment was attached to Expeditionary Force E. in Egypt. This unit was specially mentioned in despatches for the meritorious manner in which it had carried out its duties. The State Administration Report for the year 1918–19 contains a brief summary of some of the contributions made to various war funds. These included: (*a*) Fourteen motor cars, fully equipped, with eight Indian and two European chauffeurs; (*b*) one ambulance car, with chauffeur, given for use in Bombay; (*c*) six double-poled tents; (*d*) 48 horses; (*e*) a share in the Motor Ambulance Fleet, presented for war services on behalf of Kathiawar, Rs. 28,000; (*f*) cash contributions to various Relief and Red Cross Funds, Rs. 2,10,531; (*g*) contributions for aeroplanes, Rs. 1,00,000; (*h*) contribution to the war, as promised at the Delhi War Conference in April 1918, Rs. 3,00,000; (*i*) gifts and contributions of articles of comfort, flannel and cotton garments, shirts, jerseys, socks, blankets, rugs, sheets, cigarettes, betel-nuts, cloves, books, port and champagne from the Palace cellars, sent to the Women's Branch of the War and Relief Fund, Bombay, Rs. 1,10,000; (*j*) His Highness converted his house at Staines, in England, into a hospital for wounded officers, and shared a considerable portion of the expenditure on maintenance and equipment; the amount spent was about Rs. 4,90,000; (*k*) 50 ponies; (*l*) a few selected camels.

A sum of about Rs. 26,00,000 was invested in War Loans by His Highness and his officials and subjects, not only in Nawanagar, but by others connected with the State who reside in Bombay.

In June 1918 His Highness the Jam Sahib was invited by His Excellency Lord Willingdon, the Governor of Bombay, to attend a war conference in that city, and in moving the principal resolution, His Highness made a very interesting speech, in the course of which he said: "I am not so much a Ruling Prince hailing from a principality in a distant corner of Kathiawar, as a citizen of our Empire—the greatest that history has ever known. We are aware, my Lord, of the terrific struggle which is shaking empires and nations, and devastating God's fair creation, and we realize, I hope, to the full, the stupendous effort that England and the rest of the Empire are making at this moment for the purpose of rendering this world habitable for freemen, and for the peaceful evolution of free and progressive institutions, so dear to humanity as its birthright and its inherent privilege."

An event of outstanding importance in the management of State affairs took place in 1918, when His Highness publicly explained the objects of an Advisory Council which he proposed to establish in Nawanagar.

In 1917 His Imperial Majesty was pleased to grant to His Highness the Jam Sahib the insignia of a Knight Commander of the Most Exalted Order of the Star of India, and in the following year the permanent dynastic salute was raised to 13 guns, His Highness's personal one was declared to be 15 guns, the title of Maharaja was made hereditary, and an honorary commission as Lieut-Col. in His Majesty's forces was granted. On January 1, 1920, His Highness was gazetted a Knight Grand Commander of the British Empire (military), in further recognition of his valuable services during the war.

The State of Nawanagar is situated in the north-western portion of the peninsula of Kathiawar, in the Bombay Presidency, and it is bounded on the north by the Gulf and Runn of Cutch; on the east by the States of Morvi, Rajkot, Dhrol. Gondal, and small *talukas* of Halar Prant; on the south by the Sorath Prant; and on the west by the Okha Runn and the Arabian Sea.

The State is 3,791 square miles in extent, and its sea-board, extending for about 100 miles, gives it the inestimable commercial advantage of having 32 ports and roadsteads, the principal of which are Jodiya, Rozi, Bedi, and Salaya; the last-named possesses such unique natural characteristics, that a great future is most probably in store for it.

The climate is healthy, especially in hilly districts, and areas bordering upon the sea-coast, and the average annual rainfall is about 23 inches. The inhabitants, at the time of the census of 1911, were nearly 3,50,000 in number, comprising 2,76,793 Hindus, 53,000 Mahomedans, 20,050 Jains, and about 300 belonging to various other races.

A large proportion of the inhabitants subsist entirely upon earnings from some form of agricultural or pastoral pursuits, and although His Highness considers no effort too great to make in his zeal for the adoption of improved methods of cultivation, the industry has not yet attained that degree of efficiency which is an absolute essential to commercial prosperity. Experiments have been made from time to time, and suggested improvements have been discussed with His Highness and expert officials, but the inherent apathy of the average Indian, and the ultra-conservatism of the vast majority of the race, have kept cultivators dragging along in the same old ruts, with never so much as a dream of striking out upon new lines. His Highness has laboured incessantly for better tillage, habitable homesteads, the inauguration of a system of corporate existence, and for the spread of agricultural education of a scientific character, but his efforts have not yet met with their deserts.

Kathiawar has for many hundreds of years been noted for its very fine breed of horses, many of which were eagerly claimed by Government Remount Officers, but owing to the laxity of owners with regard to the selection of sires and dams, the type of animal has greatly deteriorated during the past half-century. This defect has been brought home to the minds of Indian Princes and wealthy landowners in the peninsula, and it is reassuring to find that steps are being taken to reproduce size, symmetry, courage, hardihood, and speed, coupled with strength, characteristics which were such prominent features of the old-fashioned Kathi horse.

His Highness the Jam Sahib is keenly alive to the great importance of this matter, and the State now possesses eight

THE STATE OF NAWANAGAR.

1. Jubilee Hall. 2. Railway Station. 3. Bedi Gate. 4. Khamballia Gate. 5. Jail.

THE STATE OF NAWANAGAR.

1. View from Willingdon Crescent. 2. Street Scene, showing Janbai's Masjid. 3. Jumma Masjid. 4. View of Jain Temples.

THE STATE OF NAWANAGAR.

stallions, which are available for stud purposes at the following places, namely, three in the city of Jamnagar, two at the hill paddock at Adhia, and one in each of the Lalpur, Bhanwad, and Kalawad *mahals*. These horses were mated during the past year with 33 mares, 25 of which belonged to the State. There were 37 brood mares in the paddock on March 31, 1918, and two were received from Jamnagar, but the number now stands at 33. The annual cost of maintenance of the paddock is about Rs. 11,700.

A comparatively small amount of work has yet been attempted in the way of conservation and scientific treatment of forest resources, but the duties of preservation are energetically performed by the Forest Officer. His Highness the Jam Sahib is a staunch believer in the protection of forests, but he is not a whit less enthusiastic on the question of afforestation, as he realizes that trees have an immediate bearing upon the productivity of the soil, owing to their influence upon the atmosphere.

The work of opening up parks and pleasure grounds for the benefit of the inhabitants of the State, has proceeded rapidly, under the watchful eye of His Highness, and during the past two or three years numerous gardens have been planted with choice trees and beautiful flowering plants. The Lakhotia gardens have recently been greatly improved by the addition of a fine avenue; and the Tulsidas, Cambridge House, and Vasantvadi gardens are divided into two sections, one of which is reserved for the cultivation of high-class English and indigenous vegetables.

The city of Jamnagar enjoys a time-honoured reputation for its manufacture of extremely beautiful gold and silver brocades, produced in exquisite designs. The factories, in which several hundred looms are constantly plying the most delicate silver and gold threads, and the showrooms, in which the finished articles are exhibited, have always proved to be of the greatest interest to visitors. The major portion of the manufactured articles are disposed of to Calcutta or Bombay merchants. There are 11 factories for the ginning of cotton in the State, and one at Khambhalia, which deals only with the fibre of aloes.

The pearl fisheries of the State constitute an industrial enterprise, capable of great development. There are about 40 oyster rocks in the Gulf of Cutch, lying off the northern coast of Nawanagar, and valuable pearls of various sizes are obtained from these beds. Small ones, known as "Kansara" pearls, are used chiefly in connection with the preparation of medicines.

A very great amount of excellent work of public utility has been completed during the past few years by the Public Works Department. A beautiful palace for His Highness the Jam Sahib is nearing completion, and it is characteristic of His Highness that he, at considerable inconvenience to himself and his household, occupied existing bungalows, and delayed the construction of the palace in order that buildings of a public character, and irrigation, sanitary, and other schemes, might be carried out. Many miles of roads in the city, near the palace, and in the neighbourhood of the numerous *bunders*, have been laid out and metalled, and graceful avenues of trees now adorn the sides of the principal streets.

Much still remains to be done in the matter of reclamation of land, and of harbour improvements, but suitable landing places for passengers have been erected, new beacon lights have been fixed, and the older ones have been thoroughly repaired. The provision of means of irrigation is a most important responsibility placed upon the officials of this Department. The State now possesses four irrigation tanks and 9,532 wells, 327 of which were excavated during the past year.

There were no fewer than 399 vessels owned by subjects of the State at the close of the year 1917–18; four were wrecked or disposed of; 34 new ships were built or purchased; and there are now 429 sea-going craft.

The total value of imports by sea during the past year was Rs. 1,19,89 363, as against Rs. 58 72,866 in the previous 12 months. This substantial increase was accounted for by the high prices of food grains, cotton seed, coco-nuts, tobacco, and other commodities. Exports by sea amounted in value of Rs. 56,13,565, showing an increase of more than 100 per cent. Goods imported by land in the year 1908 9 were of the value of Rs. 7,22,858; ten years later the figures were Rs. 50,28,183; and exports for the same years were respectively Rs. 7,600 and Rs. 7,67,092.

Medical relief is granted in three State hospitals and 11 dispensaries, situated in various districts, and the annual cost of this Department, and of the Veterinary Branch, is about Rs. 81,000.

A concise statement on the subject of education may be given as follows: The Nawanagar State comprises 689 towns and villages; 140 villages are provided with 195 recognized schools, with 16,480 pupils; 46 villages have unrecognized schools; and 70 other villages avail themselves of the privileges afforded by recognized schools in their respective neighbourhoods. Instruction in State schools is imparted free of charge. The higher education of students is encouraged by scholarships of the total annual value of Rs. 3,324, and at the special request of His Highness, a number of these monetary aids have been ear-marked for the study of agriculture, commerce, engineering, and other scientific subjects.

It is particularly gratifying to observe that there are 18 primary schools for girls, in which there are nearly 2,500 pupils, and great anticipations have been formed of the projected Lady Hardinge High School for advanced students, the Department believing that it will act as a great stimulus to the furtherance of higher education among females. A large number of school buildings in the State are of an inferior character, and therefore His Highness the Jam Sahib has generously sanctioned the construction of new premises in the city of Jamnagar, as well as in several districts. Physical drill forms a part of the daily curriculum, and playgrounds and gymnasia have been provided wherever the requisite accommodation is available.

The total annual expenditure upon education in the State amounts to Rs. 1,08,209, the increase of about Rs. 25,000 being due to higher rates of pay to teachers, and to grants made to the same officials during the disastrous famine of the past year.

The Jamnagar State railway from Rajkot junction to Bedi *Bunder*, covering a distance of about 54 miles, was constructed in the year 1897, and the total capital outlay up to the present time is about Rs. 23,50,000. The gross earnings during the past year amounted to Rs. 4,94,48, and the net amount thus received was Rs. 2,73,205, this being an increase of Rs. 96,700 over the amount for 1917–18.

Nawanagar maintains its corps of Imperial Service Lancers, at a strength of 146, including four commissioned officers, and the men are armed with magazine Lee-Enfield carbines, swords, and lances. The services of the squadron were placed at the disposal of the Government during

THE STATE OF NAWANAGAR.

1. View of River Jamnagar. 2. River at Dhunav. 3. Tank at Rozi Bunder. 4. Babada Hill, Killeshwar. 5. Old Fort at Modpar. 6. Shiva Temple at Killeshwar. 7. Type of Bharwad Girls.

THE STATE OF NAWANAGAR.

1. Interior of Jain Temple. 2. Part of Durbargadh Wall, showing Carvings. 3. Pancheswar Clock-tower. 4. View, showing Kotha Lakhota. 5. Bedi Bunder. 6. Lighthouse, Rozi Bunder. 7. Ruins at Ghumli.

the late Great War, and His Excellency the Commander-in-Chief in India, in a special India Army Order, paid a high tribute to the excellent work performed by this unit.

The infantry, comprising 167 men, are employed in guarding State palaces, the jail, and public offices, while a few of them are trained to perform the duties of artillerymen, for firing salutes on special occasions. The duties of the police in Nawanagar have in the past been rendered onerous, owing to the marauding character of the Mianas, Charans, and other turbulent tribes, who not only committed depredations upon neighbouring lands, but defied the authority of State officials. Great credit is due to the Superintendent of Police, who, during the past year, succeeded in capturing the ringleaders, and in restoring peace and order in the several divisions. The force now comprises 837 men of all ranks, but in addition to this number there are 41 employed as police at the principal harbours in the State.

The total revenue from all sources during the past year was Rs. 46,90,387 (of which Rs. 31,70,330 represented the amount derived from land), and although this sum was about Rs. 5,00,000 less than the total receipts of the previous 12 months, it must be borne in mind that a most disastrous famine occurred in the year under report. At the commencement of the year there was a considerable quantity of wheat, rice, and other cereals in the State, but merchants holding considerable supplies began to take advantage of inflated market prices—a natural result of the war—and began to dispose of their stocks to outside purchasers, who were prepared to pay high rates for them. There were, therefore, depleted warehouses and stores when the failure of the monsoon was a sure but sad omen of forthcoming disaster. His Highness quickly realized the unfortunate condition of his subjects, and he at once curtailed the export of food grains ; he reduced the import duty on similar goods, and he made temporary grants of money to the lower grades of civil and military officials. He subsequently opened stores for the sale of grain at exceedingly low rates ; he gave relief to all needy persons, of whatever station in life, by the free distribution of grain, and at the same time fodder was supplied, free of cost, to owners of agricultural stock.

His Highness established relief works, such as the construction of new roads, wells, and bridges, and the expenditure of the State under this head alone was not less than Rs. 6,20,000. Probably the most greatly appreciated assistance prompted by the large-hearted generosity of His Highness the Jam Sahib, was the remission of one-fourth of the total amount assessed upon land, which amounted to Rs. 7.71,455, and the suspension of payment of certain dues of the value of Rs. 6,16,563.

The following amounts are paid annually by the State by way of tribute, namely, Rs. 50,312 to the British Government, Rs. 64,924 to His Highness the Maharaja Gaekwar of Baroda, and Rs. 4,857 to the State of Junagadh.

His Highness the Maharaja Jam Sahib is the supreme administrative authority in the State, and he exercises full civil and criminal powers, the trial of British subjects, however, for penal offences being subject to the consent of the Agent in Kathiawar to the Governor of Bombay.

Jamnagar, the chief city of the State, is situated about 310 miles distant, in a north-westerly direction from Bombay. It is surrounded by a massive wall, having a circuit of nearly four miles, and it is protected by a fort, built in the year 1788. A very large trade is carried on, chiefly in the export of wheat and rice, but, as already mentioned, it has other important industries.

A Municipal Board was established several years ago, and its members have co-operated heartily with State officials in securing greater conformity with modern requirements in the construction of new buildings, in sanitation, the supply of water, and other necessary schemes.

The financial year of 1918-19 opened with a credit balance of Rs. 51,747, and the income for that period amounted to Rs. 73,659. The expenditure reached a sum of Rs. 1,24,808, and therefore the year closed with a balance in hand of nearly Rs 1,200. A considerable increase was noticeable on the debit side of the ledger, but this was due mainly to a virulent attack of influenza.

There are many very fine buildings, including old palaces, and places of recreation and public gardens greatly add to the natural pleasing characteristics of the place.

The inhabitants are nearly 50,000 in number.

THE STATE OF PALANPUR

THIS State in the Palanpur Political Agency of Gujarat, in the Presidency of Bombay, is ruled by Capt. His Highness the Nawab Zubt-tul-mulk Diwan Mahakhan Sir Taley Mahomed Khan Bahadur, K.C.I.E., who is a Yusufzai Lohani Pathan, of Afghan origin. The ancient history of Palanpur is somewhat involved in obscurity, but there seems to be a general agreement among chroniclers in attaching great importance to the tradition that in early days the territory was known by the name of Prahlad Patan, in honour of Prahlad Deo, the brother of a Parmar King of Chandravati. The land subsequently became desolate, and remained so for several generations, until about the year 56 B.C. it was re-populated by Palansi, a Chohan King, who named it after himself.

It may, however, be authoritatively stated that the direct ancestors of His Highness the Nawab lived in Ghor and Khorasan, in Afghanistan, and it is equally clear that they arrived in India in the twelfth century, establishing themselves as traders in the Province of Behar.

The State from the year 1877 until the accession of the present Chief was under the rule of His Highness Zubd-tul-Mulk Diwan Mahakhan Sir Sher Mahomed Khan Bahadur, K.C.I.E., G.C.I.E.

A leading official of the State of Palanpur has recently summed up the high qualifications of the late Nawab in the following terse sentence: "The State owes its present status and prestige more to the sound statesmanship and wise policy of His late Highness than to any other single cause." Sir Sher Mahomed ascended the *gadi* at a time when the revenue did not exceed Rs. 3,00,000, and this amount was subject to various deductions, including substantial sums payable as tribute and expenses to the State of Baroda, but by reason of the excellent administrative genius of His Highness, the gross receipts at the close of the financial period of 1918–19, calculated on the average of the previous five years, was about Rs. 7,63,600.

The question of the development of the agricultural resources of Palanpur received the greatest possible attention from His Highness from the very commencement of his reign, and, mainly through his instrumentality, a vast area of land was brought into cultivation, 68 new villages were established and populated, and 3,000 wells were sunk for irrigation purposes, chiefly with the object of enabling landholders to raise crops in times of drought, and thus avert the horrors of an Indian famine. The system of payment of rents in cash was also introduced, and it is now being rapidly extended in all districts. Arrangements were also made by him for granting loans of money to occupiers, at extremely low rates of interest, for the purpose of assisting them to construct irrigation works, and of purchasing farming implements as well as bullocks. Another great boon conferred by His Highness was the discontinuance of all fees for primary education. Hospitals and dispensaries were erected for the benefit of the people, and the Sher Mahomed Mohtajkhana, or Home of Refuge, was opened for the housing, clothing, and feeding of decrepit, needy, and helpless persons.

The reorganization of the administrative work of the State was effected by the establishment of separate Departments, entitled: Revenue, Finance, Survey, Registration, Education, Medical, Customs, Excise, Opium, Forests, Public Works, Municipal, and Sanitary.

The measures adopted by His late Highness in times of plague epidemics included the evacuation by the people of all dwellings in affected areas, and the construction of temporary houses in other parts of the State, while his lavish expenditure of money in alleviating the hardships of those suffering in times of famine—especially during the terrible one of 1899-1900, was entirely characteristic of his deeply sympathetic nature and his unbounded generosity.

On the outbreak of the Great War, the late Sir Sher Mahomed, with his traditional staunch loyalty and unflinching devotion to the throne and person of His Imperial Majesty the King-Emperor, placed all the resources of the State at the disposal of the British Government, and a sum of about Rs. 2,00,000 was subsequently contributed to various War Funds, in addition to tents, articles of comfort for the troops, and other gifts, which were generously provided by His Highness and his subjects.

The numerous beneficial reforms initiated by the late Nawab, contributed very largely to the economic, intellectual, and material progress of the State, and Palanpur attained the right to be recognized as one of the most enlightened Principalities in the Bombay Presidency.

His Highness the Nawab always paid the greatest attention to the advice tendered to him by the Government, through its Political Agent, and throughout the whole of his career his unswerving loyalty to the Paramount Power was never so much as questioned. His personal habits were simple and unaffected, and he

HIS LATE HIGHNESS ZUBT-TUL-MULK SHREE DEWAN MAHAKHAN NAWAB SIR SHER MAHOMED KHAN, BAHADUR, K.C.I.E., G.C.I.E.

CAPTAIN HIS HIGHNESS ZUBT-TUL-MULK SHREE DEWAN MAHAKHAN TALEY MAHOMED KHAN, NAWAB OF PALANPUR.

was always prepared to extend a sympathetic hearing to any of his subjects.

The wise administration of His Highness, and his devotion to the Throne, was rewarded by his being created a Knight Commander of the Most Eminent Order of the Indian Empire in 1893, and by his being raised to a Knight Grand Commandership of the same Order in the year 1898. In 1911 the title of Nawab was made hereditary, and the customary salute was increased from 11 to 13 guns.

His Highness Sir Sher Mahomed Khan passed away on September 28, 1918, amid universal regret, and in the State Administration Report for 1918–19 it is said of him: "A sagacious Administrator, a loving father, a generous and staunch friend, and a most lovable personality, Nawab Sher Mahomed Khan will long be remembered, and his memory cherished by all who knew him."

His Highness was succeeded by the present Ruler, whose title is Capt. His Highness Zubt-ul-Mulk Shree Diwan Mahakhan Nawab Sir Taley Mahomed Khan Sahib Bahadur, K.C.I.E., who was born on July 7, 1883. His Highness and his younger brother, Amir-ul-Mulk Nawabzada Yavar Husain Khan Bahadur, are, as far as education and high moral training are concerned, typical examples of what may be achieved by noble home influences. The installation ceremony of His Highness on the *gadi* on October 14, 1918, was a most brilliant function, which was attended by all the nobility and leading officials of the State.

His Highness the Nawab Sahib became a member of the Imperial Cadet Corps in 1902, and by the intelligent manner in which he applied himself to his multifarious duties, as well as by his soldierly bearing, he gained the highest opinion of the Government and of the official staff under whom he served. In the following year his capabilities were taxed to the utmost, when a severe outbreak of plague occurred in the capital city. The problem before him was so beset with difficulties that a man of greater age might have been forgiven if he had manifested signs of fear, but it was not so with His Highness, as with remarkable tact, perseverance, and skill in leadership, he threw himself into the fight against the dread enemy, and it is a lasting memorial to his name that his painstaking energies were crowned with complete success.

On the occasion of the visit to India of the Amir of Afghanistan, His Highness was attached to the Staff of Sir Henry MacMahon, who was responsible for all military arrangements.

During the past few years, His Highness the Nawab Sahib has been engaged in the compilation of an authentic historical account of the State of Palanpur and its Rulers. He has taken immense pains to collect ancient chronicles of bards, as well as traditional accounts, relating to the noble deeds of his ancestors, and especially with regard to their profound devotion to the Paramount Power.

The first volume of this important work has already been published, and on completion it will not only be a valuable possession to the author, but it will also be a rich inheritance for the Rulers of future years.

It might be observed here that, owing to the weight of years and enfeebled health, the late Sher Mahomed Khan, in 1912, entrusted the present Nawab with the administration of State affairs, and it is most gratifying to learn that the

AMIR-UL-MULK NAWABZADA YAVAR HUSAIN KHAN BAHADUR, HIS HIGHNESS'S BROTHER.

THE STATE OF PALANPUR.

1. A. M. K. Dehlavi, Barrister-at-Law, Vazir, Palanpur State. 2. G. N. Bhatt, Revenue and Finance Minister, Palanpur State.

latter performed the duties with consummate tact and success, thus securing the love and esteem of the subjects of the State.

His Highness is the supreme authority in the State, but he has a trusty colleague in the duties of administration, one might almost say a partner, in the person of his brother, Nawabzada Yavar Husain, and this close fraternal relationship between a Ruler and his potential successor is probably unique in the history of Indian States.

His Highness succeeded in gaining the affection of the inhabitants of the State during his able conduct of the administration during the life of his late father, but since his accession he has, by just government, progressive ideas, and constant anxiety for their welfare, identified himself still more closely with their highest aspirations.

Europeans as well as Indians, in fact, all who have been brought into contact with His Highness, are charmed with his affable manner, and no doubt is left in their minds that the noble example of his life must act as a stimulus to his subjects in raising them to a higher level, morally, socially, and materially.

His Highness the Nawab has been appointed A.D.C. to His Royal Highness the Prince of Wales during his forthcoming visit to India.

The State of Palanpur covers an area of 1,750 square miles, and it contains the chief town of Palanpur and 516 villages, including four which are in the Mahi Kantha Political Agency, called the Gadhwada villages.

The inhabitants at the census of 1911 were about 225,000 in number, of whom 85 per cent. were Hindus, 10 per cent. Mahomedans, and five per cent. were Jains.

Palanpur is bounded on the north by the States of Jodhpur and Sirohi; on the east by Sirohi, Danta, and the Mahi Kantha Political Agency; on the south by the Baroda districts of Pattan and Kherala; and on the west by Deodar, Tharad, and Kankrej.

The State presents considerable variety in its physical aspects; in the northern and eastern portions, where the Aravali mountains throw out massive spurs, the country is wild and rugged; near the capital town the land rises in numberless sandy hillocks, and the western districts consist of a level plain, covered in many places with low brushwood.

The climate is hot and dry, and when epidemics of disease make their appearance in this part of India, the State of Palanpur rarely seems to escape their visitations. The rainfall is extremely precarious, and the average annual precipitation of about 20 inches was deficient in the year 1918-19 by about eight inches. Droughts are sadly too frequent in Palanpur, and although nearly 5,000 wells have been sunk for irrigation purposes, a dry season involves such a shortage of water in them, that the successful raising of crops is wellnigh impossible.

The total area of land is 11,20,000 acres, nearly one-fourth of which is in the possession of Bhayats and *jagirdars*, the remainder being held by other alienees. The area cultivated during the past year was 3,67,914 acres in extent, the principal crops being wheat, *bajra*, rape-seed, castor-seed, *gram*, and paddy, while the uncultivated portion includes about 99,000 acres of forests, 20,000 acres of *bid* land, 87,000 acres of grazing land, 60,000 acres of culturable land, and 35,000 acres of waste tracts.

The revenue derivable from more than one-half of the occupied land is paid in cash, and while this system is being extended as rapidly as possible, there is still a large area for which rents are assessed according to the number of ploughs in use, or in proportion to the actual quantity of produce.

Special attention is being given by His Highness to the important matter of agricultural development, and an experimental farm has recently been established in the district of Gadha. This has been placed under the management of an expert, who is regularly employed in giving instruction in modern methods of tillage, and in making practical tests of the productivity of various kinds of seeds. A number of experiments have been made in the cultivation of cotton, and many occupiers have been induced to plant selected seed of approved types, which is sold to them at one-half of the usual cost price.

A survey of the forests has not yet been completed, but steps are being taken to protect trees—many of which are exceedingly valuable—and also to increase the quantity of lac, honey, wax, and other by-products.

The total revenue of the Department during the past year amounted to nearly Rs. 30,000, this being about Rs. 10,000 more than the sum obtained in the previous 12 months. Prior to the year 1899-1900, when an exceedingly disastrous famine occurred, the State of Palanpur had a very large number of all kinds of agricultural livestock of a superior character, but owing to the insufficiency of fodder at that time several thousands died from starvation, and the remainder deteriorated so greatly that the *ryots* had the utmost difficulty in tilling their lands. An improvement in the quality of both cattle and horses has, however, been manifested recently, and His Highness is rendering all possible assistance to his subjects in connection with the purchase of suitable stud animals. At the present time there are in the State, approximately, 63,300 bullocks, 56,000 cows, 67,600 young cattle, 1,070 male buffaloes, 38,300 female buffaloes, 32,000 young buffaloes, 600 horses, 1,520 mares, 5,900 asses, and 141,000 sheep and goats.

The inhabitants of Palanpur State are almost entirely devoted to agricultural and pastoral pursuits, and therefore it follows that manufacturing and industrial enterprises have not attained great importance in the production of revenue. Mention should, however, be made of the very fine cloth which is woven by hand-looms in the village of Kamodar, and is exported to Africa, Arabia, Persia, and other distant places, as well as to many cities and towns in India.

A number of Hindu merchants conduct a flourishing trade in precious stones, and a factory has been opened for the manufacture of various articles of brass.

In the year 1878 the Bombay-Baroda and Central India Railway Company desired to construct a line from Gujarat to Northern India, and His Highness the ruling Nawab generously presented that company with a strip of land, 40 miles in length, within the borders of the State, and in 1898 he also gave land, 18 miles in length, which was required for the Palanpur-Deesa railway. The share of dividends due to the State for the past year's working of the last-named section amounted to Rs. 8,263.

Free medical advice and treatment is given to patients at the "Goodfellow" hospital and the Mahajan dispensary, both in the chief city, and also at Deesa and Dhanera, but arrangements are now being made for an extension of such facilities.

His Highness the present Nawab is as enthusiastic on the subject of providing educational privileges for the young as was his late revered father, and his frequent personal visits to schools have been productive of the greatest benefit to

THE STATE OF PALANPUR.

1. Murshad Ali Peer's Roza. 2. The Mausoleums of the Rulers of Palanpur. 3. The Balaram Temple.

THE STATE OF PALANPUR.

1. Kirtisphambha (Pillar of Fame). 2. The Sher Mahomed Mohotzkhana (Poor House).

THE STATE OF PALANPUR.

1. The King Emperor George V Club. 2. The "Good Fellow" Hospital, Palanpur State.

teachers and scholars alike. The teaching institutions include one High School, one Anglo-Vernacular, two for girls, 25 village schools, and others, making a total of 24. There are on the rolls the names of 2,370 pupils, and the daily average attendance is 1,633.

The year which has just closed was a most unfavourable one for the State, owing to the increased cost of living, caused by a partial failure of harvest, and also to a serious outbreak of virulent influenza. These two causes interfered with the educational development of the State, but the results of the year's examination showed that good work had been accomplished. Classes have been formed for the teaching of Science, Agriculture, Drawing, and other subjects, while provision has been made for the physical development of pupils by means of reuglar drills and the establishment of cricket and football clubs.

The High School has not sufficient accommodation to meet present requirements, and therefore His Highness has sanctioned the construction of suitable additions.

The administration of justice is based very largely upon the laws and codes prepared for use in British Indian territories. The *Huzur* Court, presided over by His Highness the Nawab, has power to hear all final appeals; the *Sar Nyayadhish* Court deals with appeals from lower courts, tries civil cases up to Rs. 2,000 in value, and has the powers of a Sessions Judge in criminal matters. There are also Courts for suits of not more than Rs. 150 in value, and First-Class Magistrates' Courts at Palanpur, Vadgam, Deesa, and Dhanera.

The State does not maintain any regular military force, with the exception of a few artillery. It, however, employs 616 men in the police force, 163 of whom are mounted, and the annual cost being about Rs. 90,000.

The financial year of 1918 19 opened with a balance in hand of Rs. 96,631; the gross revenue amounted to Rs. 10,94,660; but after certain deduction had been made the actual revenue was Rs. 9,32,576.

The net expenditure during the same period was Rs. 7,87,806, a sum in excess of the previous year's returns, caused by special expenditure in connection with the Great War, the Public Works Department, and the Political branch.

The State pays an annual sum of Rs. 38,460 in British currency, as tribute to the Gaekwar of Baroda, and the State of Baroda is liable to Palanpur for a yearly sum of Rs. 266, being *jama* in respect of certain villages within its own area.

Palanpur, the capital of the State, is situated on the Bombay-Baroda and Central India railway, and it has a population of 17,220 inhabitants, the majority of whom are Hindus. The city was formerly surrounded by a brick and mortar wall, 17 feet to 20 feet in height, with seven bastioned gateways and several towers, and it had a circumference of about three miles. It is believed that this defensive work was constructed about the middle of the eighteenth century by Diwan Bahadur Khanji, but quite recently this wall has been replaced by one built of stone by the Palanpur Public Works Department. The city contains four Jain temples and a considerable number of mosques, but they do not present any special architectural features. Near to the town are Hindu temples, one of which is said to have been erected about the year 1100; the tombs of former Rulers of Palanpur; and mausoleums, richly ornamented by carvings in Mussulman characters. The city is noted for its manufacture of perfumes, and it has a considerable trade in exporting *ghee*, sesamum, honey, wax, rape-seed, and cotton, and in importing iron, other metals, ivory, groceries, and tobacco.

The city enjoys limited powers of government under the Presidency of Nawabzada Yavar Hussain Khan Sahib, who has recently prepared detailed Regulations to be embodied in a Municipal Act, to be submitted for the consideration of His Highness the Nawab.

THE STATE OF PORBANDAR

PORBANDAR is a first-class State, standing fourth in rank among the Principalities in the Kathiawar Agency, political authority being vested in the Agent subordinate to the Government of the Bombay Presidency.

The Chief belongs to the Jethwa clan of Rajputs, who claim descent from Hanuman, the friend and ally of the great King Rama, and tradition is responsible for the story that the latter Ruler made a grant to Makardhvaj, son of Hanuman, of the district of Shrinagar, the village bearing the same name becoming the first capital, but it is more probable that the Jethwas entered Kathiawar about the end of the ninth century, and that Maurdhvaj, son of Makardhvaj, established himself and his followers at Morbi. It is extremely difficult to trace any really reliable records of the doings of the Jethwas in the peninsula until about the year 1190, when Vikioji, the reigning Chief, was driven out of Morbi and the clan migrated along the coast as far as Nagnath, near the present city of Jamnagar, where they held sway over a considerable area of land, including the islands of Pirotan and Ajad. Shortly afterwards they extended their rule over Shrinagar and Miani, and eventually they founded their famous capital at Ghumli in the Barda Hills.

Rana Bhanji ascended the *gadi* in 1307, and a most romantic incident greatly affecting the future destiny of the present House of Porbandar is given in records of his reign. It appears that he became enamoured of Son Kansari, wife of Rakhayat, and daughter of Dudansi Waghel of Sankodwara, and although she resisted his importunities which had been followed by the death of many Brahmans who had shielded her, she subsequently became *sati* on the funeral pile of her husband. Before the commission of this act she cursed Ghumli, as well as Bhanji, declaring that the capital would become waste land never again to be inhabited.

Six years later Jam Bamanioji of Sindh besieged and completely destroyed the city, thus fulfilling to the letter the prophecy of Son Kansari, and Bhanji fled to Ranpur, making it his headquarters. The present capital, Porbandar, was founded in the reign of Sultanji (1671–99), a prominent chief of the period of Moghul decadence. The first occasion on which the State of Porbandar appealed to the British for assistance was in 1807, when Haloji, the reigning chief, asked for help in the recovery of the fort of Kandorna, which had been fraudulently obtained by the Jam of Nawanagar. Colonel Walker was dispatched to demand its evacuation, but as his request was met with a direct refusal, he marched against it with a body of troops and compelled its surrender to the Rana. Before two years had elapsed Haloji induced the British to aid him in regaining possession of the fort of Chhaya, which had been seized by the Rana's rebellious son Prathiraj, and in view of the fact that effective help was then given, and as, moreover, considerable arrears of tribute were due to the Gaekwar of Baroda, it was agreed that the State should cede to the British Government one-half of the revenue of the port of Porbandar, in consideration of which a loan of Rs. 50,000 was granted by that Government in part satisfaction of the Gaekwar's claims. Under the same agreement, dated December 5, 1809, the State was placed under British protection, and a detachment of 100 soldiers was stationed at the port for the assistance of the Rana. It may be mentioned here that in 1853 the above-mentioned cession to the British of one-half of the revenue of the Port was converted into an annual payment to the Imperial Government of a sum of Rs. 15,000.

Rana Khimoji died in 1831, and was succeeded by his son Bhojraji, who assumed the name of Vikmatji. The latter was a minor, and his mother, Rani Rupaliba, who was appointed Regent, displayed such ability in administering the affairs of the State that outstanding liabilities were liquidated, and surplus money was found for the construction of a temple and tank, which may be seen to-day in the city of Porbandar. At her death in 1841 the reins of government were taken up by the Rana, and considerable progress was made for several years, but in 1866, on the return of the Rana from his pilgrimage to Benares, he found, to his consternation, that, in his absence, his son, Madhavsingh, had been associating with companions who were in the habit of indulging too freely in intoxicating liquor. The death of the son from his excesses in 1869 had a great effect on the Rana, who, in his rage with the faithless Khawas who had been the chief instrument in the ruin of his offspring, caused the man's ears and nose to be cut off as a punishment for his action. When this matter was reported to the British Government, the Rana's first-class ruling powers were withdrawn, and he was permitted to exercise those pertaining to third-class States only.

From this date the Rana led the life of a religious recluse, permitting the affairs of the State to be greatly neglected, and, in 1886, it became necessary for interfer-

H.H. THE MAHARAJA RANA SAHIB NATWARSINHJI BHAVSINHJI, OF PORBANDAR.

ence by the British Government, who appointed Mr. F. S. P. Lely, I.C.S., to carry on the administration.

Under Mr. Lely's careful and energetic guidance great progress ensued. Every department of the State was reorganized, and the revenue system, which was marred by numerous petty exactions, was established on a safe and healthy basis. Good roads and bridges were constructed, and in conjunction with the Gondal State a railway was built from Dhoraji to Porbandar.

Mr. Lely was succeeded in 1890 by Mr. Pandit, who died in 1894. After him, Mr. W. T. Morison, I.C.S., Mr. H. O. Quin, I.C.S., Lieut.-Colonel F. W. Snell, and Lieut.-Colonel L. L. Fenton successively held the post of Administrator, and great improvements in every branch of the State were effected during this long period. Special prominence must be given to the Bhadar irrigation work carried out by the State engineer, Mr. J. J. B. Benson. The main feature consists of a weir and bridge over the Bhadar river near the village of Chikasa, by means of which the waters of the Bhadar are held up in a longitudinal reservoir, the system enabling a large area of cultivated land to be irrigated. Connected with this work are the Gosa Bara *bund* near the village of Tukda, and the wall near the Porbandar railway bridge, constructed with a view to excluding the sea from the Mokul Rann and eventually reclaiming this salt waste and converting it into cultivable land.

In 1899-1900 Porbandar, in common with Kathiawar, suffered severely from famine. By means of relief works, poor houses, and advances to Bhayats and cultivators, the people were saved from starvation, but heavy losses occurred among the cattle, of which it is estimated that at least 50 per cent. died. The most important relief work was the Khambhala tank, in the Barda hills, costing Rs. 1,70,000, from which water can be carried to irrigate the fields of Khambhala, Asiapat, and Bordi.

Rana Vikmatji died in 1900, and was succeeded by his grandson, Bhavsinghji, son of the late Madhavsinghji.

His Highness built the Darya Mahel, a fine palace standing on the seashore, a mile south of Porbandar town. He died in 1908 at the age of 40, and was succeeded by his only son, Natwarsinghji, who was born on June 30, 1901. As His Highness was a minor, Darbar Shri Vajsurvala and Rao Bahadur A. S. Tambe were appointed joint-Administrators. The latter left in 1910 and Mr. K. J. Bakshi took his place. They were followed in 1913 by Major F. de B. Hancock, whose term of administration was marked by great energy in framing or revising departmental rules and regulations. He died in 1916 and Major E. O'Brien was appointed to succeed him.

His Highness the minor Rana entered the Rajkumar College in November, 1911, at the age of 10, and during his last two years at college he won all the important prizes at studies and games. At the end of the spring term of 1918 he crowned a brilliant college career by obtaining the first place in the diploma examination for which candidates from all the Chiefs' colleges in India appear.

His Highness is now (1919) at Porbandar learning the duties of administration. On January 1, 1918, His Highness was granted the title of Maharaja, and his salute was raised from 11 to 13 guns.

The State is bounded on the north by the dominions of the Jam of Nawanagar, on the west and south by the Arabian sea, and on the east by the State of Junagadh. The State has an area of 642¼ square miles, and the inhabitants were, at the census of 1911, about 90,837 in number, the majority of whom are Kanbis, Mers, Sindhis, Sepoys, Brahmins, Luhanas, and Rabaris in the villages, and Banias, Kharwas, and Mahomedans in the capital town.

Porbandar may be described roughly as a plain sloping from the Barda hills to the sea-coast, near which are tracts of marshy land known as *gheds*, formed by rainfall, and while some of these, penetrated by salt water, are capable of producing only grass and reeds, the remainder yield fair crops of rice, gram, *udid*, and *mug*. The largest *ghed*, known as Modhwara, some six miles in length and four miles in breadth, is connected with the sea by the Kindari creek, and it receives the drainage of practically all the streams flowing from the Barda hills. Gangajal, a large fresh-water marsh about two miles in circumference, is situated near the Kindari creek, but unless there is an unusually heavy fall of rain it does not contain water for longer than eight months in the year.

The greater portion of the soil consists of the rich black cotton variety, although the fertile red type is in evidence in many districts, and fully one-half of the whole area is under cultivation, about 60 square miles of which are irrigated. The chief crops are wheat, *juvari*, cotton, gram, rice, castor seeds, sugar-cane, oil-seeds, and tobacco.

The chief imports consist of grain, rice, cloth, sugar, oil, cotton-seed, and timber; while exports include "Porbandar" stone, grain, cotton, and *ghee*. The minor ports of Navibandar, Madhavpur, and Miani have small trade returns.

With regard to industrial enterprises it may be observed that about three miles distant from Ranawao, a railway station 10 miles from Porbandar, are the Adityana quarries in the Barda hills, which yield the famous "Porbandar" stone prized so highly by sculptors and architects alike. This stone is exported in large quantities to Bombay for structural purposes, and the total quantity sent by sea to other places outside the State—including Calcutta, Madras, Karachi, and Rangoon—during the year 1917-18 was 32,420 tons, but this is, of course, exclusive of many hundreds of tons required for the erection of buildings within the State.

In 1894 a railway line was constructed to the quarries with the object of providing greater facilities to merchants, contractors, and others in the prompt delivery of stone from the quarries, and an appointment was made of a quarry superintendent who would interest himself in the extension of the quarries, and in opening up new markets for the stone.

The creeks along the coast yield an excellent supply of fish, such as *vichio*, *palvo*, and turtles and oysters in suitable waters, this industry providing occupation for a considerable number of persons. A large quantity of excellent silk and cotton-cloth is made by hand and a power-loom. Among other enterprises may be mentioned the Indian Cement Company's works, four ginning factories, a saw mill, and a cotton press, but special reference should be made to the immense development which has taken place at the harbour of Porbandar in ship-building.

During the period from March 1, 1917, to the end of October, 1918, 52 vessels of a total registered tonnage of 7,460 were built, the capacity of the individual vessels varying from 37 to 303 tons. Twenty-three more vessels, of an approximate tonnage of 3,405, have since been launched. The last includes a vessel of 584 tons, which is the largest ship ever built at Porbandar.

The Port authorities have from time to time considered proposals for the deepening of the creek and the general improvement of the harbour, and in December, 1917, the Deputy Chief Engineer of the

THE STATE OF PORBANDAR.

1. Raj Mahel (Dariya Mahel). 2. Juri Bungalow. 3. Secretariat (Public Offices). 4. Victoria Jubilee, Madressa.

THE STATE OF PORBANDAR

Bombay Port Trust formulated a scheme which included the building of a breakwater to protect the main entrance channel during the months of April and May when it is subject to the force of very heavy seas. This most important undertaking has been temporarily postponed for financial reasons.

The State was originally joint-owner of the Gondal-Porbandar Railway, 143 miles in length, which was constructed in 1889 by Government agency for the States of Gondal and Porbandar. The line was worked until March 31, 1911, by an Administrative Coalition of the State of Bhavnagar, Gondal, Junagadh, and Porbandar, which was formed for the purpose of working as one undertaking the railways, which, prior to that date, were comprised in the Bhavnagar-Gondal-Junagadh-Porbandar railway system. The coalition ceased to exist on April 1, 1911, from which date the line has been worked jointly, as a separate railway, by the Gondal and Porbandar States. The amount invested by the Porbandar State as its share of the capital is Rs. 24,62,247, and the net earnings for the year ended on March 31, 1918, were Rs. 1,60,089, this amount being an increase of about Rs. 20,000 over the sum realized during the previous 12 months.

On April 1, 1919, the Gondal-Porbandar Railway was partitioned, and the State is now the sole owner of the line from Porbandar to Jam-Jodhpur, in addition to the short lines running to the quarries and Dock estate.

Medical relief at the expense of the State is afforded in five institutions, namely, the Bhavsinghji hospital, built in 1894, and dispensaries at Madhavpur, Ranawao, Bagwadar, and Navibandar. The "Hancock" Memorial Hospital, with accommodation for 20 women indoor patients, was opened in November, 1917, by Mr. E. Maconochie, I.C.S., Agent to the Governor, Kathiawar, but it was not brought into actual use until March 1, 1918.

The State maintains 68 public schools, while there are also 14 private institutions. The pupils on the rolls of the State schools on March 31, 1918, were 4,851 in number, with a daily average attendance of 3,860.

The total amount spent on education during the past year was Rs. 40,528.

The average annual revenue of the State is Rs. 11,75,000; the sum of Rs. 21,202 is paid as tribute to the British Government, in addition to an amount of Rs. 15,000 in commutation of a half-share of the customs revenue of the port of Porbandar. Other payments from the Treasury are Rs. 7,196 as *peshkashi* to the State of Baroda, and Rs. 5,106 as *zortalbi* to the State of Junagadh. The revenue is derived chiefly from land, customs, quarried stone, railways, and stamps.

On January 1, 1918, the Kathiawar customs tariff was abolished, and the Government of Bombay ordered that the ports of the State should thereafter be regarded as British, with British customs rates to take effect from that date.

The State is divided for purposes of administration of revenue into four *mahals*, or districts, namely: Porbandar town, Ranawao, Adwana, and Navibandar, and the chief executive officer of these divisions is a *Mamlatdar*, who is invested with magisterial powers.

The area of land under cultivation in the several *mahals* at the close of the year 1917 was as follows: Ranawao, 45,583 acres; Adwana, 44,198 acres; Navibandar, 50,718 acres; and Porbandar, 272 acres, but these figures do not include 23,215 acres of cultivable land which is still unoccupied, nor of 77,891 acres comprised in alienated villages. The receipts of land revenue under all heads for the financial year 1917–18 amounted to Rs. 9,96,782, as against Rs. 5,82,685 for the previous year. This substantial increase was due very largely to the abnormally high rates of cotton and to the recovery of revenue outstandings.

The Courts of Justice were re-modelled in 1914, and they now comprise four for the disposal of civil actions and six for the administration of criminal laws.

The ruling Chief has power to try persons for capital offences, but in the case of British subjects permission for such procedure must be obtained from the Agent to the Governor of Bombay.

Porbandar, the chief town and seaport of the State, was formerly guarded by a strong wall and fortress, but these were removed during British administration. A brisk trade is carried on with the Konkan and Malabar coasts, the ports of Sind, Baluchistan, the Persian Gulf, Arabia, and East Africa. A lighthouse, 90 feet in height, was erected in 1887, and is equipped with strong dioptric light of the fourth class, which is visible from a distance of 17 miles.

The only municipality in the State is at the capital town, Porbandar, but there are Sanitary Committees at Ranawao, Madhavpur, and Navibandar. The Municipal Board is composed of a President, Vice-President, five official members, and 10 unofficial, who are nominated by the Administrator of the State, and the executive work is carried out by a Managing Committee consisting of three non-official members.

The news of the outbreak of the European War caused some nervousness in the State, and the first noticeable effect was a great depression in trade coupled with a tendency to force the price of certain commodities to an abnormal height. A strong committee was immediately appointed, with full powers to adopt such measures as might be deemed necessary to prevent traders from placing unjust burdens upon the inhabitants.

Special prayers for the success of the Allies were offered in the temples and mosques during the first week in September, 1914, and two enthusiastic public meetings were held in Porbandar, at which the people gave expression to their loyalty in a most unmistakable manner, and at the same time arrangements were made for collections of money in aid of relief funds.

The historic message addressed by His Majesty the King-Emperor to the Princes and people of India was communicated to the minor Chief, and in reporting the fact to the Government of India it was stated that the resources of the State were from that date at the service of the Imperial cause. The Administrator of the State, Major F. De B. Hancock, took an early opportunity of issuing special leaflets dealing with the causes and progress of the war, and the Chief Educational Officer was deputed to undertake a tour throughout the whole State to give lectures, illustrated by maps and diagrams, and to distribute literature bearing upon the all-important struggle in which India, as a component part of the British Empire, was expected to take its share.

The response to the appeal for financial help was very gratifying, and before the end of March, 1915, the contributions on behalf of the minor Rana Sahib included: Rs. 10,000 for the Indian War and Relief Fund (Bombay branch); Rs. 8,000 for an ambulance motor-car; Rs. 1,000 for the Women's Branch of the Imperial Indian War and Relief Fund (Bombay branch); and Rs. 163 for miscellaneous objects.

Private contributions from the inhabitants of the town of Porbandar amounted

THE STATE OF PORBANDAR.

1. Bhavsinhji Hospital. 2. Bhavsinhji High School. 3. Bhavsinhji High School (Extension). 4. Hancock Memorial Hospital for Women. 5. Sudamaji Temple.

THE STATE OF PORBANDAR.

1. Jubilee Waterworks. 2. View of Bundar, showing Custom House. 3. Porbandar Harbour, from Custom House. 4. Street Scene, showing Municipal Offices (Manekchowk). 5. Indian Cement Company Works.

THE STATE OF PORBANDAR.

1. Old Durbargadh at Chhaya. 2. Old Durbargadh in Porbandar Town. 3. The Paddock. 4. Victoria Jubilee Commemoration Hall
5. Porbandar Stone Quarries.

to Rs. 5,003, and the sum of Rs. 447 was collected in the villages.

Several ladies in the State actively engaged in what is essentially women's work, and their labours resulted in the sending of a large number of articles calculated to ameliorate the distressed condition of sick or wounded men. These gifts included blankets, mufflers, socks, mittens, handkerchiefs, sheets, clothing, tobacco, cigarettes, crockery, and other goods.

The following figures show the gifts in cash or kind for the 12 months ending March 31, 1916. Contributions from the State on behalf of the minor Rana Sahib: Rs. 2,000 to the St. John's Ambulance War Hospital; Rs. 1,000 to the Croca Rossa Italiana; Rs. 1,000 to the French Red Cross Society; Rs. 1,000 to the Serbian Red Cross Society; Rs. 500 to the Christmas-pudding Fund of Her Excellency Lady Willingdon; Rs. 5,000, being 10 months' subscriptions to the Women's Branch of the Relief Fund; and Rs. 2,622 to various other agencies. A novel feature was introduced by the Administrator on January 1, 1916, by holding a "Flag Day," when the inaugurator of the movement, the Rana Sahib, and others acted as salesmen, and obtained no less a sum than Rs. 1,594, which was handed over to the St. John's Ambulance Red Cross Fund. Private donations from Porbandar town and several villages yielded Rs. 3,679; the Women's Branch of the Imperial Relief Fund was responsible for Rs. 1,831; and the ladies in the State presented 10,000 *bidis*, khaki cloth and knitting yarn, fleecy vests, Red Cross sheets, towels, flannel, handkerchiefs, soap, tobacco, cigarettes, shoes, and host of other useful articles.

During the following 12 months the State forwarded Rs. 4,000 to the Women's Branch of the Imperial Relief Fund; Rs. 2,000 to the East Indies Naval Station Relief Fund; Rs. 2,000 for monthly subscriptions to the last-named fund, Rs. 200 for Christmas comforts for sailors; Rs. 26,925, being the expenses of salvage operations of the S.S. *Kabul*; Rs. 750 by sale of miniature flags in aid of the East Indian Station Naval Relief Fund; and Rs. 1,670 by private contributions for various relief funds.

The donations for the year ending on March 31, 1918, amounted to Rs. 28,236, made up of Rs. 15,000 to the "Our Day" Fund, Rs. 7,300 to the East Indies Station Naval Fund, and Rs. 2,600 to the Women's Branch of the Imperial Relief Fund, the balance being devoted to various charitable objects or otherwise expended on purchasing necessities for the troops.

Subscriptions to the Indian War Loan of 1917 were as follows: from the Porbandar State, Rs. 2,00,000; from Her Highness the Rani Ramba Saheb, Rs. 5,000; from officials of the State, Rs. 27,400; and from subjects, as far as can be ascertained, Rs. 14,700.

From August 1, 1914, until the end of the war, the contributions on behalf of the minor Chief for war expenses and the various funds connected therewith amounted to Rs. 1,89,177, and private persons contributed Rs. 30,302.

The State subscribed Rs. 5,00,000 to the Indian War Loan of 1918, and officials of the State contributed Rs. 31,600, and private persons, Rs. 46,843.

STREET SCENE.

THE STATE OF RAJPIPLA

THE Rulers of the first-class State of Rajpipla, in the Rewa-Kantha Political Agency, in the Presidency of Bombay, belong to the Gohel clan of Rajputs, who trace their descent from the lunar race of kings, and regard Shalibahan of the Shaka Era as their direct ancestors. Tradition is current to the effect that when Saidawat was King of Ujjain, he had a son named Chokarana, and that the latter, failing to agree with his father concerning certain family matters, took up his residence at Pipla, not far distant from Nandod, the modern capital of the State. His daughter married the Ruler of the Island of Prembar, in the Gulf of Cambay, and it is said that her youngest son, Samar Singhji, succeeded to the Pipla Raj, which had been established by his grandfather. That Ruler appears to have been under the control of the kings of Ahmedabad, but with the extension in Central and Western India of the power of the Moghuls, subsequent Chiefs recognized the supremacy of the Emperor of Delhi. An arrangement had been made, some years previously, which provided that the State should supply 1,000 foot soldiers and 300 horses, but in the seventeenth century the Emperor Akbar agreed to forego this right on payment of a sum of Rs. 35,550. This liability, however, was ignored when the Moghul power was fast declining, and when, as a consequence, it was unable to enforce its claim. The fall of the Moghuls was contemporary with the rise of the Mahrattas, and the latter, encouraged by the success of their arms in many parts of India, soon began to make encroachment upon the territories of Native Chiefs. The State of Rajpipla was not spared, and when the Ruler at that time was in danger of losing his possessions, the British Government found it necessary to interfere in order to prevent the occurrence of such a calamity. Early in the nineteenth century there were two claimants to the *gadi*, and, after full inquiry had been made by the British Government, Verisalji was, in 1821, declared to be the rightful successor. In 1823 he entered into an agreement with the Gaekwar of Baroda, under which the annual tribute payable to that State was fixed at Rs. 65,000, but it was understood that a remission should be made when other conditions considerably reduced the revenue. The Charana Verisalji ruled until the year 1860, when he abdicated in favour of his son, Maharana Gambhir Singhji. For a number of years the State enjoyed peace and prosperity under British protection, but in 1884 it was placed under the direct supervision of a British official, owing to the mismanagement of the Ruler, and it remained under such control until 1897, when the late Chief, His Highness Maharana Shri Sir Chhatrasinhji, K.C.I.E., succeeded to the *gadi*. His Highness was born in the year 1862, and was educated at the Rajkumar College, then under the principalship of the late Mr. Chester Macnaughten. On the conclusion of his College career he travelled in many parts of India, with the object of gaining a practical experience in the duties of administration, and the

CAPTAIN HIS HIGHNESS MAHARANA VIJAYSINHJI, OF RAJPIPLA.

THE STATE OF RAJPIPLA.

Vijay Palace, His Highness's Residence.

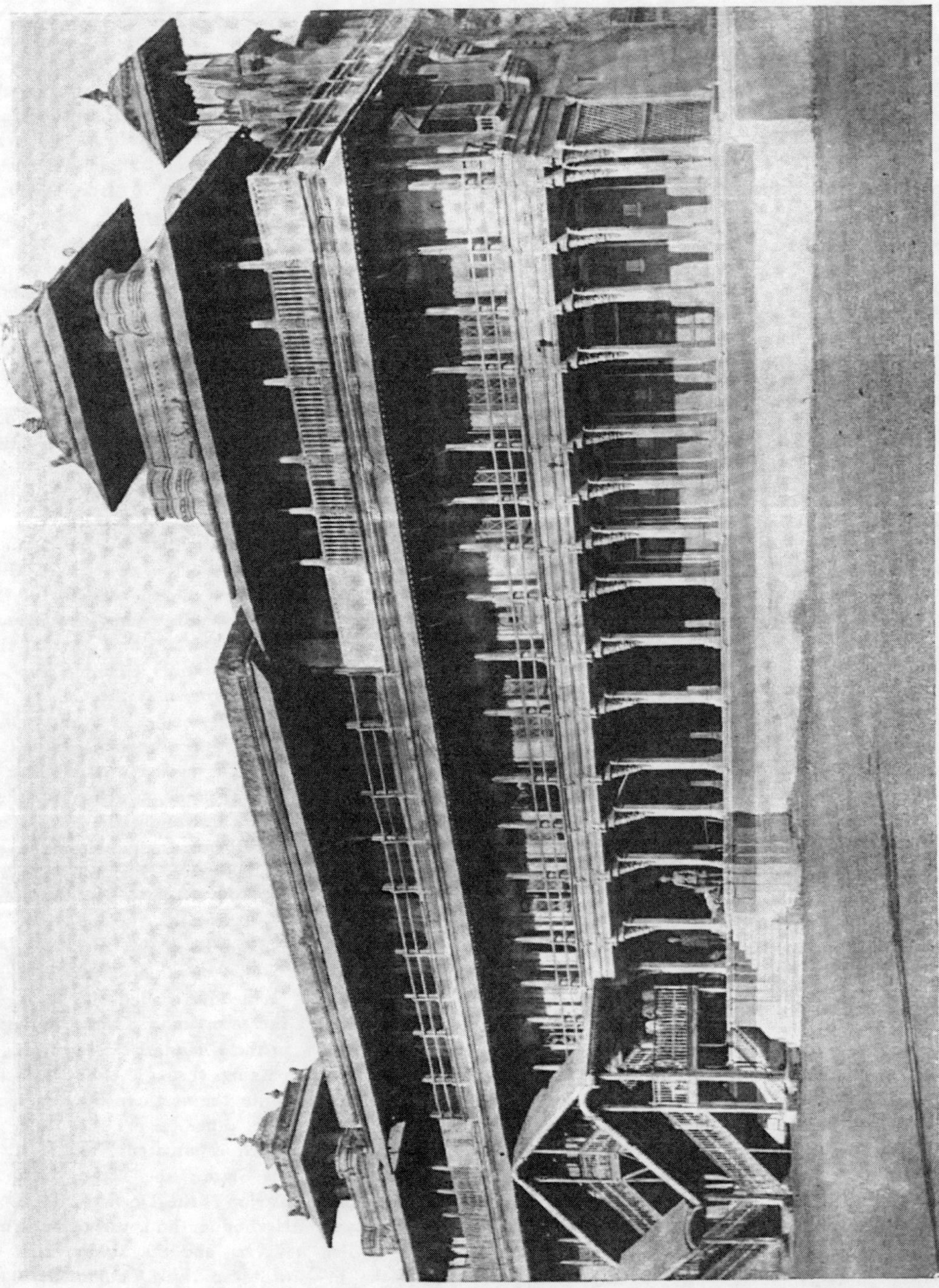

THE STATE OF RAJPIPLA.

THE OLD PALACE.

tour proved to be of the greatest assistance to him, when, as Rajkumar, he was entrusted with duties usually performed by subdivisional officers.

The most important event of the year 1911—12, not only to the State of Rajpipla, nor merely to the vast Indian Empire, but also for the greatest Empire over which floats the Union Jack, was the unique historical visit to Delhi of Their Imperial Majesties the King-Emperor and Queen-Empress, who had arranged to announce their Coronation in London to their loving and devoted feudatories and subjects in India, by whom Their Most Gracious Majesties presence among them will ever be cherished with feelings of the deepest loyalty and gratitude. His Highness had the privilege of paying his homage to Their Gracious Majesties, and he was honoured by having bestowed upon him the distinction of a Knight Commander of the Most Eminent Order of the Indian Empire. Contemporaneously with the brilliant function at Delhi, festivities were held in the capital town of Nandod, and at the headquarters of each of the other five *talu.jas*, and the proceedings included the reading of the Royal proclamation, addresses by prominent officials, and prayers in the various places of worship, while all school children, more than 4,000 in number, were presented with commemorative medals and sweetmeats. A durbar for ladies, under the Presidency of Her Highness the Maharani, was held at the Girls' School at Bhalad, and after the presentation of medals to the girls then present, Her Highness delivered a most suitable address.

His Highness the Maharana Shri Sir Chhatrasinhji, K.C.I.E., died suddenly at Poona on September 26, 1915. He was a most enlightened Ruler, and one imbued with progressive ideas, such as he manifested, could not do other than govern his State with the object of securing the best interests of his subjects, and with an earnest desire to cultivate friendly relations with the Paramount Power and with all neighbouring Chiefs. His death was deeply regretted by a very large circle of friends and admirers, but their grief did not exceed that of his own people, who loved him for the simplicity, sincerity, and honesty of his character.

His Highness was succeeded by his eldest son, Kumar Shri Vijaysinhji, then in the twenty-sixth year of his age, who was invested with full ruling powers on December 10, 1915, by Mr. C. W. M. Hudson, I.C.S., Political Agent at Rewa-Kantha. His Highness received his education at the Rajkumar College, Rajkot, where he distinguished himself by successfully passing the final diploma examination of that Institution, in which he obtained the college medal, and was placed first on the list of candidates. After joining the Imperial Cadet Corps at Dehra Dun, he was no less assiduous in his untiring energy and devotion to duty than he was at College, and he gained a wide experience of men and things, and his mind was broadened by two trips to Europe. His Highness subsequently acquired practical training in administrative work, under the guidance of Mr. R. C. Brown, then Collector of Belgaum, and at a later date—but during the lifetime of his father—he was entrusted with the control of several departments of State. With the object of commemorating his accession to the *gadi*, His Highness contributed liberally to the cause of the allies in the late great war, and he also made concessions to his subjects, which included the remission of all revenue arrears to the end of the year 1909; the establishment of scholarships for boys desiring to study electricity and medicine, and the granting of increased salaries to deserving officials, as well as pensions to the widows of several officials of the State who had died during employment. It was a red-letter day in the annals of the State when Their Excellencies the Governor of Bombay (Lord Willingdon) and Lady Willingdon paid a visit to Rajpipla on February 25, 1917, as this was the first occasion that a Governor of a Presidency had taken the opportunity of coming into personal contact with the Chief, and of ascertaining for himself the manner in which the duties of administration had been performed. In November of the same year His Highness attended the annual conference of Ruling Princes, held at Delhi, and he was satisfied that the discussion at such an important gathering would inevitably tend to the better administration of Indian States, and would necessarily contribute to the good government of India generally.

The State does not pay any tribute to the British Government, but it is liable to the State of Baroda for sums of Rs. 50,000-12-3, and Rs. 10,270, being known respectively as ***ghasdana*** and ***rundh mahal*** payments. The former of these was imposed by the Emperor Akbar, in lieu of a subsidy or troops, which the independent Gohel Chiefs of the State had agreed to furnish, but at the decline of the Mahomedan power, the payment passed to the Gaekwar of Baroda, to whom it is transmitted through the British Government. The ***rundh mahal*** is an allowance made in connection with an exchange of territory, which took place many years ago between the Baroda and Rajpipla States, and in which the latter became possessed of land yielding greater revenue than the former, the difference being made good by cash compensation.

The following payments are received annually by the State, namely, (*a*) from the British Government, a cash allowance of Rs. 12,286 from the treasury of the Broach State, an opium compensation of Rs. 500, and (*b*) from the State of Baroda a cash allowance of Rs. 1,307-6-6.

The State recognized the law of primogeniture with regard to succession to the ***gadi***, and in 1862 a ***sanad*** authorizing adoption was granted by His Excellency the Viceroy, Lord Canning.

The Chief is entitled to a salute of 11 guns.

The State of Rajpipla is bounded almost entirely on the north by the Nerbudda River, on the east by the Chikhli, Raisingpur and Kanti estates of the Khandesh Mehwas, on the south by territory belonging to the State of Baroda, and the Mandvi *taluqa* of the district of Surat, and on the west by the district of Broach. The forests and mountains cover nearly two-thirds of the whole area of the State, two spurs of hills running into the Rajpipla State, known as the Central and Southern ranges, being continuations of the Khandesh Satpura mountains. The highest peaks in the State are in the central range, and some of these are about 2,800 feet above the level of the sea. On a ridge of rock below the peak, known as Devsatra Hill, was formerly situated Juna, or old Rajpipla, the former capital of the State, but this is now an insignificant village, consisting of only a few huts.

The principal river is the Nerbudda (sometimes called the Rewa, from which the term Rewa-Kantha is derived), rising in the Khandesh-Satpura range, and after passing through the Gardeshvar *taluqa*, forms the northern boundary of the State. The other rivers are the Karjan, on which is situated Nandod, the capital of the State; the Tarao, a tributary of the Karjan; the Devnadi, a tributary of the Nerbudda, and the Kim Umravati, the Kaveri, and the Madhuvati. In addition to these rivers, numerous small streams afford good natural drainage, although they are inconvenient for travellers during the monsoon seasons.

THE STATE OF RAJPIPLA.

Civil Hospital.

THE STATE OF RAJPIPLA.

1. Harsiddi Mata Temple. 2. The Clock Tower.

THE STATE OF RAJPIPLA.

1. Old Fort (Lal Darvaza). 2. Member of Bodyguard of H.H. the Maharana.

For the purposes of land revenue administration the State is divided into the following six *taluqas*, namely: Nandod, Bhalod, Jhagadhia, Valia, Gardeshvar and Dedipada, but these are exclusive of the estates of Sagbara and Vadi Mehwas, the two feudatories of the State. Land revenue was originally assessed according to the number of ploughs or pairs of bullocks employed in agricultural work, but the chief objections to this system were that there was no fixity of tenure, and that the *ryot* was at liberty to abandon a piece of land which he had already taken up, and transfer his belongings to another area, which might seem to him to have greater possibilities of development. In recent years, however, the revenue has been fixed upon a survey and settlement scheme, which is based upon correct measurements of land and classification of soils. The total amount of land revenue demanded for the year ending June 30, 1918, was Rs. 8,59,030; the actual collections were Rs. 8,16,312; the sum of Rs. 628 was remitted, and there was an uncollected balance at the end of the year of Rs. 42,090. The fall of rain, which is so essential a factor in arable pursuits, is exceedingly precarious in India, and numerous instances might be given in which it is shown that an excessive precipitation has occurred in a season, and that it has been followed by four or even five years of intense drought, thus making it difficult for cultivators to make a steady income. The annual rainfall in the State usually amounts to about 36 inches, but during the year under review it amounted to 66·29 inches, while in the previous 12 months it was 49·81 inches. The principal crops grown during the year 1917–18, together with the approximate acreage, were as follows: cotton, 62,165; *jowar*, 60,533; rice, 28,065; *bajri*, 17,950; *kodra*, 14,672; Cajan pea, 15,830; sesamum, 4,134; castor seeds, 3,929; pulses, 3,915; *gram*, 4,692; tobacco, 21,495; wheat, 1,357; vegetables and other garden produce, 1,572, and a large quantity of miscellaneous crops making a grand total of 262,849 acres. About 20 years ago the area under cotton was about 32,000 acres; in 1911–12, 97,000 acres were sown with this plant, and there was a steady increase until the year under report, when, owing to an abnormally heavy rainfall, the work of cultivation was rendered exceedingly difficult, and as a consequence the yield was much below the average. The expansion of the area under cotton naturally resulted in a smaller quantity of land being sown with food grains, and this fact doubtless accounted for the increased cost of living. On the other hand, the selling price of cotton has in recent years reached as high a sum as Rs. 150 for 960 maunds of unginned *kapas*. The best soils give a return of nearly 1,000 lb. per acre, while land of inferior quality may be expected to yield about half this quantity. Notwithstanding the unfavourable season above referred to, the Durbar realized that the high prices of cotton and of foodstuffs generally amply compensated cultivators for the deficiency in harvests. There is still considerable shortage of labour, and wages are unusually high, but taking all things into consideration, a vast improvement is noticeable in the condition of the people.

The forests of the State are about 1,517 square miles in extent, but the demarcated area, for working the jungle on scientific lines, is not more than 385 square miles. The principal trees include *khair*, blackwood, teak, *tanachh*, and sandal-wood. The total income of the forest department, during the year under report, was Rs. 1,17,265, while the expenditure for the same period amounted to Rs. 25,279.

The following are the approximate numbers of agricultural livestock in the State; bullocks, including calves, 62 905; cows, including heifers, 61,041; male buffaloes, 1,487; female buffaloes, 2?,145; horses, 720; mares, 689; colts and fillies, 313; asses, 554; and sheep and goats, 36,596. All ploughs in the State are worked by two bullocks, and the number of these implements is nearly 24,000.

With the exception of a small export duty on the produce of *mahua* trees, and a slight octroi duty payable to the Municipality of Nandod, all trade is completely free from taxation. A considerable sum of money changes hands at several annual fairs held at places of pilgrimage. The principal of these are Bahaghor, which is the only place in the State resorted to by Mahomedans; the Duyaniji fair, near Jagadhia, which lasts for several weeks, and a number of sacred places on the banks of the Nerbudda, which are much frequented by Hindu pilgrims from various parts of India.

The only articles of manufacture are mats, baskets, and other articles made from bamboos, *dungari* cloth, and rough wooden trays and other items. The greater portion of the cotton grown in the State is sent to Ankleshwar, where it is mixed and pressed for the Bombay markets; but there are also ginning factories at Nandod, Rajpadi, Umalla, and Partapnagar. The chief exports of the State are cotton, tobacco, timber, bamboos, and other forest produce, castor seeds, sesamum, *mahua* flowers, and *bajri*, *jowar* and other food grains. The principal imports are piece-goods and other similar articles of European manufacture, metal, sugar, molasses, *ghee*, kerosene oil, wheat, and the finer varieties of rice.

The public works department, under the control of the Executive Engineer, expends an annual sum of nearly Rs. 2,50,000 in the construction of and repairs to schools, *dharmsalas*, public offices, dispensaries, tanks, wells and roads; the installation and keeping in order of electric lighting and telephones, and the maintenance of the Nandod waterworks. The department also attends to repairs necessary for the Rajpipla State Railway, which has a gauge of 2 ft. 6 in., is about 39 miles in length, and connects the capital town of Nandod with Ankleshwar station on the Bombay, Baroda and Central India Railway.

The State maintains a civil hospital at Nandod, and a dispensary at the headquarters of each of the remaining five *taluqas*, all of these institutions, with the exception of those at Gardeshvar and Dediapada, having accommodation for indoor patients. The State usually enjoys a healthy climate, but in the year 1917–18 a severe epidemic of plague was introduced into the State, and some of the villages suffered very severely. About 47,000 outdoor patients and 260 ward cases are attended to annually at a cost of Rs. 25,000.

Primary education is free throughout the State for boys and girls of the Rajput, Mahomedan and Kaliparaj communities, but for other pupils a nominal fee of one anna per month is taken. The primary schools, 84 in number, include one for teaching Urdu, and eight others set apart entirely for girls. The English classes, attached to the principal vernacular schools, have been highly appreciated and well attended, there being 227 students in the year under report, as against 129 during the previous 12 months. The High School at Nandod—the only one in the State—teaches up to the Matriculation standard, and the pupils on the register on March 31, 1918, were 350 in number. There is also at Nandod a Sanskrit *Pathshala*, where elementary instructions in literature and in the daily rituals of a Brahmin's life is imparted free of cost. The State maintains a large number of

THE STATE OF RAJPIPLA.

1. Recruit, Rajpipla State. 2. Infantryman, Rajpipla State.

scholarships at Male and Female Training Colleges at Ahmedabad. Further than this, the State provides the following scholarships for higher and technical education, namely, one for the Ahmedabad Technical Schools, two for the Baroda Kalabhavan, three for the Ahmedabad Medical Schools, one for the Agricultural College at Poona, one for the Medical College, Bombay, one for a course of study in Electrical Engineering, and two for the Arts College, Bombay. A special scholarship of the value of £100 a year is given to a son of Kumar Digvijaysinhji (uncle of the present chief) for studying in England. More than 5,200 scholars are now receiving instruction in public institutions in the State, and the annual expenditure of the department of education is about Rs. 61,000.

His Highness the Maharana exercises full judicial powers, excepting in the case of subjects of British birth. In criminal procedure the Sri Nyayadhish is invested with the powers of an assistant Sessions Judge and District Magistrate, while cases beyond his jurisdiction are tried in the *Huzur* Court. Magistrates of the first class hold Courts at Nandod and Jhagadia; the ***Thandars*** of Nandod, Bhalod, Valia and the ***Mahalkari*** of Gardeshvar are Magistrates of the second class, and the ***Mahalkari*** of Dediapada and the *Avil Karkuns* at Valia and Jhagadia are invested with third-class powers. Civil actions are brought before the Sri Nyayadhish, but there are six *Thandar* courts in various *taluqas*. The *Huzur* Court is the only court of appeal.

The State maintains a military force of 148 men, including infantry, bodyguard, irregulars and *sowars*. The total strength of the police is about 230, including 16 mounted men, but these are exclusive of special officers, who are solely employed in connection with the manufacture and sale of liquor.

The gross annual revenue of the State, based on the average of the five years ending March 1, 1918, was Rs. 15,13,758. There were, however, instalments of revenue which had to be postponed owing to the unfavourable season of 1917–18, and if these were properly accounted for, the actual income for the year just mentioned would have been shown as Rs. 21,20,464. During the year a sum of more than Rs. 2,50,000 was added to the Reserve Fund, which then amounted to Rs. 20,59,500.

The inhabitants of the State, according to the census of 1911, were 161,606 in number, but, according to local annual census, held in 1917–18, it was found that the population had increased to 180,777. Aboriginal Bhils and Dhankas form the largest proportion of the people, and the other classes in the order of their numerical importance are Kumbis, Kolis, Rajputs, Brahmins, Banias, Bohras, Machhis and others, including a small number of Parsis.

The State of Rajpipla deserves the highest credit for the magnanimous way in which it laboured in support of the Allies during the late Great War. His Highness the Maharana Sahib took the deepest interest in the proceedings of the Provincial Recruiting Board, in Bombay, of which he was a member, and his efforts to secure men for enlistment met with a marked degree of success. Inducements were offered to the local infantry to join as combatants, and a large number of approved men were eventually sent into the fighting line. The personal generosity of His Highness was manifested early in

THE STATE OF RAJPIPLA.

THE GYMKHANA GROUND AND BUILDINGS.

the war by the gift of an armed aeroplane, costing Rs. 34,000, and by his sending contributions to the extent of Rs. 42,000 to various Relief Funds. "Our Day" celebrations at Nandod resulted in a sum of Rs. 10,000 being placed at the disposal of Her Excellency Lady Willingdon, and an amount of Rs. 5,000 was also despatched at the same time as a contribution to the Silver Wedding Fund of Their Imperial Majesties. In February, 1918, a sum of Rs. 2,00,000 was forwarded by His Highness to His Excellency the Viceroy, to be used in such manner as he might think fit in the successful prosecution of the war, and Rs. 3,000 were given in aid of the Queen Mary Technical School for wounded soldiers; while attending the Provincial War Conference in June, 1918, His Highness announced an annual grant of Rs. 1,00,000 towards the expenses of the struggle. Further than this, the State has invested Rs. 6,00,000 in the four per cent. Government Conversion Loan, Rs. 2,00,000 in bonds of the first War Loan, and similar securities worth Rs. 2,00,000 in the second loan. The contributions of the people of the State to the two loans just mentioned were respectively somewhat more than Rs. 2,00,000 and Rs. 1,00,000.

Nandod, the principal town of the State, was the original capital of Rajpipla, but during Mahomedan invasions the Rajput Ruler of the State was compelled to transfer the seat of government to Juna Rajpipla, or June-Raj (as it is usually called, in order to distinguish it from Nava [new] Rajpipla), which then became the capital, and remained as such until the commencement of the nineteenth century, when Nandod again became the headquarters of the Government. The total income of the Municipality during the year 1917–18 was Rs. 28,135, as against Rs. 8,021 during the previous 12 months. This substantial increase was due principally to the disposal of a large area of *gabham* lands, that is, building sites on the new railway station roads, and also to a larger amount being received for the right to collect octroi duty. The principal public building in the town is the Maharaja Sir Chhatra Sinhji hospital, which was opened in the year 1917, and upon which a sum of Rs. 90,000 was expended in construction work alone. The Victoria Jubilee Library, at Nandod, is maintained entirely as a State institution, and it has been registered, for certain privileges, by the Department of Public Instruction, Bombay. The Durbar also makes an annual grant for the purchase of books and similar purposes. In other ways the State shows itself imbued with the spirit of modern progress.

THE STATE OF RATLAM

RATLAM, an important Rajput State on the border of Rajputana, but actually within the British Political Agency of Malwa in Central India, comprises an area of 871 square miles, and has a population of about 83,000 persons. The boundaries cannot be defined, as they are so greatly intermingled with the State of Sailana, but it may be said, in a general way, that they abut upon the territories of the Jaora and Partabgarh States on the north, Gwalior on the east, Dhar, Kushalgarh and Indore on the south, and Kushalgarh and Banswara on the west.

The State was founded about 1650 by Ratan Singh, a great-grandson of Uda Singh, the first Raja of Jodhpur. The Emperor, Shah Jehan, desiring to place a feudatory Rajput State on the western side of Malwa, conferred special distinctions on Ratan Singh in order to mark his high position. He raised him to the rank of *seh hezari* (Commander of 3,000 horse), and conferred on him the insignia of the *chaur* (Yak's tail), *morchal* (peacock's plumes), *suraj mukhi* (representation of the sun and moon on fans), and *Mahi muratib* (insignia of the fish). These insignia are still preserved and are paraded on great occasions when the Raja appears in full State regalia. The grant of the high honour of the *Mahi muratib*, direct from the Emperor, is an exceptional distinction which no other Chief in Malwa enjoys.

The Maharaja Ratan Singh made Ratlam his capital, and commenced his rule under auspicious circumstances; but in the early portion of 1658 he was requested by the Emperor Shah Jahan to join the Maharaja of Jodhpur in opposing an invading force led by Aurangzeb and Murad, two of the Emperor's own sons. Ratan Singh was killed in the battle which took place near Ujjain on April 20th in that year.

"Of all the deeds of heroism performed on this day, those of Ratan of Ratlam by universal consent are pre-eminent and 'are wreathed into immortal rhyme by the bard' in the Rasa Rao Ratna." So writes Tod in his *Rajasthan* about the heroic founder of the Ratlam State.

Maharaja Ratan Singh was succeeded by his eldest son, Ram Singh, who ruled for 24 years; then by Shiva Singh, who occupied the *gadi* for only two years; and in 1684 Chhatarsal became Chief. The last-named valiantly assisted the Moghul army in many engagements; but in one of the battles his eldest son Hattesingh was slain, and he (Chhatarsal) was so overcome by his loss that he retired into private life after dividing the State between his two surviving sons, Kesri Singh and Pratap Singh, and his grandson Bairisal, son of Hattesingh.

Maharaja Kesri Singh became the Ruler of Ratlam, Pratap Singh received Raoti, and Dhamnode fell to Bairisal. Disputes arose between the recipients, and eventually Bairisal retired to Jaipur, his *jagir* of Dhamnode being joined to Ratlam. The fight between Maharaja Keshri Singh and Pratap Singh of Raoti resulted in the death of the former. His sons, Man Singh and Jey Singh, attacked Pratap Singh in order to avenge their father's death, and killed him at Sagode. Man Singh then mounted the *gadi* of Ratlam, and conferred the *jagir* of Raoti on his younger brother, Jey Singh, from whom the Sailana family is descended.

It was in the time of Man Singh's successor, Prithvi Singh, that the Mahrattas began to overrun the State; and when his son Padam Singh became Raja, he tried to obtain immunity from their incessant incursions by payment of large sums of money. The next Raja of Ratlam, Parbat Singh, finding it impossible to meet Sindhia's exorbitant demands, placed himself at the head of 12,000 Rajputs, including many clansmen who were subjects of other States, and determined to make a last desperate attempt for liberty. Broughton, in his "Letters from a Mahratta Camp," mentions how "Bapu Sindhia experienced a severe mortification in the defeat of the detachment sent against the fort of Ratlam. The garrison sallied out during the night and completely defeated the troops sent against them, with the loss of more than half their numbers and all their guns." Further bloodshed, however, was averted by the opportune appearance of Sir John Malcolm, who in 1819 concluded an agreement with Sindhia, and guaranteed on behalf of the British Government the payment of the tribute due, while Sindhia was to send no troops into the country and was not to interfere in any way in the internal administration or succession. This tribute is now paid to the British Government by virtue of a treaty concluded with Sindhia in 1860. Raja Balwant Singh, reigning Chief at the time of the Indian Mutiny, rendered conspicuous service to the British forces, and in recognition thereof his successor, Bhairov Singh, received a *khilat* and the thanks of the Government.

The next Ruler, Ranjit Singh, succeeded as a minor in 1864, the State remaining under British superintendence until 1880, and, owing to careful management during such period, debts amounting to Rs. 10,00,000 were liquidated, and a sum of about Rs. 6,00,000 was spent in making improvements.

In 1864 an arrangement was made for the cession of land required for railway purposes; in 1881 transit duties on salt

COL. H.H. SIR SAJJAN SINGH BAHADUR, K.C.S.I., RAJA OF RATLAM.

were abolished; and in 1885 the Chief put an end to all transit duties excepting those upon opium.

The State of Ratlam, originally of considerable extent, included, in addition to the present territories, Sailana and Sitamau (each now a separate State), Badnawar (now a district of Dhar State), Dickparawa (now in the Jhalawar and Tonk States), Alote and Gurgachha (now districts of the Dewas State), Titrod (now a portion of Sitamau), Agar, Nahargarh and Kanar (now in Gwalior), Ramguria (now in Jhabua), and the Kotri and Bilara *parganas*. Moreover, the *jagirdars* of Amba (now under Jaora), Kachee Baroda and Multan (both now under Dhar), Baloda (now under Gwalior), and others were also Ratnaut Rathors, descended from younger sons of Ratlam Chiefs, and were subordinate to Ratlam.

The total revenue of the State at that time was about Rs. 5,200,000. Some of these territories were taken from Ratlam in the Mahratta wars, and others were alienated for the support of younger branches of the Ratlam family; but they have since shaken off formal allegiance to Ratlam, with the result that the present State is now 871 square miles in extent, and the revenue is Rs. 10,00,000, including the amount derived from the State feudatories, who are 30 in number, five of them being rated as first class, namely, Pancher, Sarwan, Namli, Amleta, and Sheogarh.

Nearly half the area of the Ratlam State territory is thus granted in *jagirs*, chiefly on service tenure, including Khera in Kushalgarh Chiefship, in the Rajputana Agency, which also pays a tribute annually to the Ratlam Durbar. None of the *Jagirdars* in Malwa are guaranteed in respect of the villages they hold from the Ratlam Durbar. These feudatories are required to maintain a certain number of retainers, who could be called up by the Durbar if necessary for defensive purposes.

Over these *jagirs* the Raja of Ratlam exercises all suzerain rights, such as *sayer* (customs), excise, forests, unclaimed property, treasure trove, and civil and criminal jurisdiction, as well as the escheat of the land in case of a Thakur's death without heirs.

The assertion that the Raja of Ratlam is the principal Rajput leader in Malwa has been called in question at various times; but upon matters relating to the Chiefs of Central India one cannot refer to a more trustworthy authority than the late General Sir John Malcolm, G.C.B., I.A., who was placed by the Marquis of Hastings in the military and political charge of Central India in the year 1818. In his "Memoirs of Central India and Malwa," published in 1823, he says: "Being at the head of a large and powerful family, the Raja of Ratlam has great influence, and can upon emergency call a numerous band of his kindred and clansmen into the field." In another place in the same volume these words occur: "The Rajas of Sitamau, Sailana, Kachee Baroda, and Multan are descendants of Ratan Singh (the founder of the Ratlam State), the elder brother continuing to rule over the town and fine province of Ratlam, and to receive a general obedience and respect from the junior branches." Sir John Malcolm further relates that in 1818, when the State of Ratlam was threatened with an invasion by Bapu Sindhia, the Mahratta Chief, the Raja Parbat Singh, sent a summons to all his relatives and adherents, and although most of them were subjects of other States they deemed the duty of rallying round their Chief paramount to every call and hastened to his relief.

Another matter which has been a bone of contention between the Durbars of Ratlam and other States is the question of levying customs and other dues which arose after the division of territory belonging to Raja Chhatarsal. It is generally admitted that the income from the *sayer* revenue is always deemed a royalty and is never included in land grants made to any *jagirdar*. Until quite recently the *sayer* of Sailana State was collected by Ratlam as a suzerain right, but under the arrangement made by the British Government between the Ratlam and Sailana States in 1887 the Ratlam Durbar agreed to receive annually the sum of Rs. 18,000 from Sailana as compensation for relinquishing its right to levy customs dues in that State.

The Raja of Ratlam is the Head of the Rajputs of Malwa, and important caste questions, concerning even Thakurs' tributary to other Chiefs, are referred to him for decision.

The agricultural industry provides a livelihood for nearly 50 per cent. of the total inhabitants, and the soil, which is of the fertile black cotton variety, found chiefly in districts in the Deccan trap area, yields good crops of cotton, wheat, maize, gram, poppy, and several varieties of indigenous produce. There are not any other industries of importance, but in almost every village one finds handicrafts which either wholly or partially support entire families. The Raja holds a very high opinion as to the value of education in the building up of a State, and his influence has been instrumental in the erection of the Durbar High School, together with more than fifty other institutions of minor pretensions, and it is gratifying to observe that parents are now becoming more greatly impressed with the necessity of obtaining instruction for their children.

The administration of the State is in the hands of His Highness the Raja, who exercises full powers in civil and criminal cases, with the proviso that sentences of death must be confirmed by the Agent to the Governor-General.

The system of "farming out" villages in connection with land revenue which was in practice in former years is now only applied to villages which cannot be managed directly owing to the limited number of cultivators.

The present revenue of *Khalsa* lands is assessed according to the nature of the soil and the possibilities of obtaining sufficient irrigation.

The first settlement for revenue purposes was made in 1867, and ten years later the average annual rates were fixed at Rs. 28 per acre for irrigated land and Rs. 3-13 for those areas which were unable to obtain this boon.

The present Chief, Colonel His Highness Raja Sir Sajjan Singh Bahadur, K.C.S.I., was born in January 1880, and succeeded his father, the late Sir Ranjit Singh, K.C.I.E., in January 1893 while still a minor. He received his education at the Daly College, Indore, and on being invested with full ruling powers in December, 1898, he at once threw himself energetically into the task of making himself thoroughly acquainted with the details of administration in order that he might be able to promote the best interests of the State and his subjects. His Highness is the supreme authority in the State, and is the virtual controlling power of the Judicial, Revenue, Medical, Public Works, Military, Police, Educational and other Departments.

The protection of life and property in the State is entrusted to a regular police force of about 300 men; the army comprises infantry and artillery; and a corps of despatch riders has been maintained for the past nine years. His Highness was the first ruling Chief to join the Imperial Cadet Corps on its constitution towards the close of the year 1901, and in 1903 he attended the Durbar at Delhi in the dual capacity of a ruling Chief and as a member of the newly-formed corps. In 1905 His Highness proceeded to Indore to meet their Royal Highnesses the Prince and

THE STATE OF RATLAM.

1. Ranjit Bilas Palace, Front View. 2. King Edward Memorial Club. 3. Polo Trophies Won by His Highness. 4. Ram Baugh Gardens, Ratlam City.

Princess of Wales (the present King-Emperor and Queen-Empress), and he subsequently visited Calcutta and formed one of the Royal escort. He was further granted a Captaincy in the British Army in February, 1908; in June, 1909, the distinguished honour of being created a K.C.S.I. was conferred upon him; in December, 1911, His Highness was promoted to the honorary rank of Major in His Majesty's Indian Forces; and in July, 1915, his appointment as Hon. A.D.C. was announced in the London Gazette.

The fervent loyalty of His Highness to the Person and Throne of His Majesty the King-Emperor, and his chivalry as a Rajput, caused him to take the earliest opportunity of placing his own services, as well as the resources of the State, at the absolute disposal of the Imperial Government in the Great War, and in March 1915 he left Ratlam for Bombay, where he embarked—with an expeditionary force—for France on the 5th of the following month.

Major-General Sir Douglas Haig, Commander-in-Chief of the British forces in France, in a despatch dated April 30, 1916, mentioned the name of His Highness among those whom he wished to bring to notice for gallant and distinguished conduct in the field.

His Imperial Majesty the King-Emperor was graciously pleased, on the occasion of his birthday in 1916, "to promote Major His Highness Sir Sajjan Singh Bahadur, Raja of Ratlam, in recognition of his very valuable services in connection with the war, from June 3, 1916, inclusive, to be Honorary Lieutenant-Colonel."

On January 1, 1918, His Majesty was pleased to grant to His Highness the Raja of Ratlam the rank of Honorary Colonel in the Army, "for services in connection with the war," and also to sanction a permanent salute of 13 guns.

The following interesting announcement appeared in the London Gazette of April 16, 1918:

"The following are among the decorations and medals awarded by the Allied Powers at various dates to the British forces for distinguished services rendered during the course of the campaign. His Majesty the King has given unrestricted permission in all cases to wear the decorations and medals in question.

"Decorations and medals presented by the President of the French Republic. Legion d'Honneur and Croix d'Officer. Honorary Colonel His Highness Raja Sir Sajjan Singh Bahadur, K.C.S.I., of Ratlam."

His Highness returned to Ratlam on May 29, 1918, having thus spent more than three years in active service in supporting the cause of the Allies.

With characteristic modesty the Raja had expressly desired that his arrival in India should not be marked by any public reception either in Bombay or in Ratlam; but the news of his home-coming spread rapidly, and several ruling Chiefs and Thakurs of Malwa personally visited the State and accorded His Highness a most affectionate greeting.

His Highness the Maharaja of Bikaner, who had been selected by the Government to represent the Indian Rulers at the first Imperial War Conference in London, and who was a delegate to the Peace Conference in Paris, on hearing that His Highness had returned to Ratlam, telegraphed to him as follows: "I have just heard with great pleasure of Your Highness's safe return from the front, on which happy event I offer my heartiest congratulations. Your Highness has indeed nobly upheld the high traditions of our Rathor race. Grateful your kindly telegraphing Your Highness's welfare."

His Excellency the Viceroy and Lady Chelmsford invited His Highness to Viceregal Lodge as their guest, and when there His Excellency Sir Charles Monro, Commander-in-Chief in India, and His Honour Sir Michael O'Dwyer, K.C.S.I., Lieutenant-Governor of the Punjab, and Lady O'Dwyer, gave dinner-parties in his honour.

His Imperial Majesty the King-Emperor forwarded a cablegram from Aldershot, dated June 6, 1918, in which the following sentence occurred: "Hope you are enjoying your well-deserved leave after three years' active service.—GEORGE R.I."

The Durbar, State officials and inhabitants of Ratlam, encouraged by the example set by their honoured Chief, the Raja, in the support given by him to the cause of the Allies, manifested an earnest desire to render such help as was in their power to give, and the following particulars relating thereto will be read with interest.

Immediately after the outbreak of the war in August, 1914, a concentration relief camp was formed at Ratlam for feeding British troops and animals passing through or halting temporarily in the State. A whole-time *Motmid* was appointed by the Durbar to help the Camp Commandant; and two *Sowars*, a State conveyance, and a police guard of six men were placed at his disposal. A bazaar was established at the camp, and telephonic communication was established between it and the city, in order that provisions, fuel, carts and other requisites might be obtained without delay whenever requisitioned by the Commandant. Tents and *chholdaris* were also given for forming post and telegraph offices. The Camp Commandant, with a body of soldiers numbering 100, lived constantly at this camp for about six months, after which period it was broken up.

From the very beginning of the war the higher officials of the State contributed regularly every month 10 per cent. of their salaries to the Imperial Relief Fund, and they continued doing so until the war ended. Their action was followed by some *Jagirdars* and *Sahukars* also. His Excellency the Viceroy was pleased to convey through the Political Agent an expression of his appreciation of the good example thus set, and of his cordial thanks to all thus subscribing to the fund. There were lump sum contributions also, the total collections from the inception of the fund to the end of the war amounting to Rs. 20,472.

For Red Cross objects six single-pole, double-fly tents, 20 by 20 feet, worth Rs. 5,458, were despatched in September, 1915, to the War Gifts Depot, Bombay.

Five ten-bed units and other gifts for British and Indian troops, costing Rs. 1,870 were also sent to the St. John's Ambulance Association, and 4,640 pounds of *gur* (raw cane sugar), the product of the Ratlam Experimental Farm, was sent for Indian troops in France.

As it was difficult to arrange for a regular collection of gifts in kind in this State, a movement for monthly cash subscriptions to the St. John's Ambulance War Fund was started under the patronage of Her Highness the Rani Sahiba of Ratlam, the total collections amounting to Rs. 3,187 to October, 1918.

In December, 1917, the Ratlam Durbar lent the use of His Highness' waiting-rooms at the Ratlam railway station to the military authorities as a rest-house and recreation rooms for British soldiers, and it has paid Rs. 100 per month towards the working expenses of the scheme and the provision of meals for soldiers using the accommodation since February, 1918.

Smaller amounts were contributed to the Prince of Wales's Fund, the Fund for the French sick and wounded, to Queen Mary's technical school for disabled Indian soldiers, to the St. Dunstan's Hostel for blinded soldiers and sailors of the war, and to the "Our Day" Fund.

In April, 1917, the Ratlam Durbar undertook to maintain at Indore two institutions to be called "The Ratlam Durbar's War

THE STATE OF RATLAM.

1. Ratlam City. Bird's-eye View from a Tower of the Central College. 2. Street Scene, Chandni Chowk, Ratlam. 3. Amrit Sagar Lake, Ratlam. 4. Tribeni Bathing Ghat, Ratlam City.

Hospitals," for Indian and British troops, with accommodation for 25 and 20 patients respectively, and it sent a donation of Rs. 3,000 for initial expenditure, and subscribed Rs. 1,000 monthly for more than a year. These hospitals were finally closed in September, 1918, and in communicating this to the Durbar the Political Agent wrote: "I am desired to assure His Highness the Raja that the great use, of which this generous provision of hospital accommodation has proved, is most warmly recognized by the Government of India."

The Durbar also placed a motor-car and a chauffeur at the disposal of invalid British officers at the Roberts Nursing Home at Indore. The Residency Surgeon there wrote that the use of the car was a great boon to the invalids, and on their behalf he thanked His Highness the Raja Sahib for so kindly lending it.

His Highness joined several other Chiefs in the movement for supporting hospital ships, and promised to contribute towards the expense of maintaining the *Loyalty*.

The State subscribed over Rs. 4,00,000 to War Loans, including the conversion of the Durbar's 4 per cent. Government paper of the face value of Rs. 1,10,000, and in 1916 the Durbar had purchased Rs. 5,37,800 worth of new 4 per cent. Conversion Loan.

The Durbar sent 80 recruits, of whom 56 were approved by the Recruiting Officer for Central India, while the Ratlam Despatch Riders served in Egypt.

Some years ago a Political Officer attached to the Government of India, speaking of His Highness, made use of the following remarks: "In His Highness we all recognize the best type of a Rajput gentleman, as high a type as can be found, a thorough sportsman who has never failed to play the game, a capable Ruler who works steadily and unostentatiously for the good of his people, a loyal Chief second to none in devotion to the Crown, and brave soldier who, if occasion arose, would not hesitate to show in the cause of the King-Emperor the same splendid valour of self-sacrifice that won for his great ancestor, Ratan Singh, undying glory on the fatal field of Fatehabad."

Referring to His Highness as a polo player, a well-known critic of the game has said: "He is one of the best 'backs' in the country, always cool, always in his place, and often making magnificent shots." His Highness was captain of the Central India polo team which won a challenge silver cup at the Indore tournament in November, 1910, and in December of the following year he led to victory a team raised by Captain Barrett, A.D.C., at the Coronation polo tournament at Calcutta. On behalf of the winners His Highness had the privilege of receiving from the hands of His Imperial Majesty King George V a handsome gold cup, which is valued as one of the most interesting trophies in the Ratlam Palace.

His Highness is an expert shot with rifle or gun, and it may be mentioned that during the summer of 1912 he visited the jungles of the Rewah State and succeeded in making a record "bag" of 16 tigers and two bears.

His Highness is a born administrator, ruling his people with that sagacity for which he has become so well known, and in a quiet yet effective manner he encourages his people to become workers and not idlers, to cultivate habits of thrift, and to regard education as a stepping-stone to true progress.

Before concluding these notes it may be observed that in consequence of the untimely and lamented death on October 30, 1918, of the late Maharaja of Rewa, Colonel His Highness Sir Venkat Raman Singh Bahadur, G.C.S.I., and owing to the minority of his son and successor, His Highness Raja Gulab Singh, the present Ruler of Ratlam has in deference to the dying wish to that effect of the late Maharaja, and with the approval of the Government of India, taken upon himself the duties of Regent of the Rewa State.

The Rewa State stands second among the eighty Principalities in Central India in point of area, Gwalior being the first. The revenue of Rewa is more than Rs. 50,00,000, and it has valuable mines and extensive forests of considerable density.

As His Highness of Ratlam has to administer his own State while acting as Regent of Rewa, he has formed a Council of Regency to assist him, which will submit to him with their views such important matters as the confirmation of capital sentences, preparation of annual budgets, appointments, dismissals, or suspension of higher officials, initiation and confirmation of any revenue settlement, and other subjects demanding special attention.

His Highness the Maharaja of Alwar, in congratulating the Raja, wrote: "I am sure the fate of the State in your hands will be guided with great ability, and it will be a blessing to the subjects of Rewa to have such a good friend of its late Ruler assisting them."

Further than this, His Highness the Maharaja of Bikaner cabled from Paris to the Regent tendering his hearty congratulations.

It may be added in conclusion that after the termination of the war His Highness was given full plenary jurisdiction, a permanent local salute of 15 guns, and in recognition of war services had the hereditary distinction of Maharaja conferred upon him.

THE STATE OF BARIA

THE State of Baria, in the Bombay Presidency, is bounded on the north by the Rewa Kantha estate of Sanjeli; on the east by the Jhalod and Dohad subdivisions of the Panch Mahals; on the south by the Rewa Kantha State of Chota-Udaipur, of Kathiawada, under the Bhopawar Agency, and the estate of Jambughoda in the Panch Mahals; and on the west by Kalol and Godhra in the Panch Mahals. The Rulers of Baria belong to the Khichi Chauhan clan of Rajputs, and they trace their genealogy from Annal, who, according to mythology, was born out of the *Agni Kund* on Mount Abu in Rajputana.

The official connection of the State with the British appears to have occurred when Mr. C. W. Malet, a representative of the Bombay Government, travelled through Baria on his way to Ujjain in the year 1785, and the friendly relationship then established has been steadily maintained since that date.

The loyalty of the Raja of Baria to the British was conspicuously manifested in 1803, when he entered into an alliance with them and cordially co-operated with their forces under Colonel Murray on their taking possession of the districts in Gujarat belonging to Daulat Rao, Scindia of Gwalior.

The reign of Gangdasji, the ruling prince of that time, was considerably disturbed owing to internal intrigues, and on his death, in 1819, his rightful successor, Prithiraj, was prevented from occupying the *gadi* by Roopji, the Chief Minister, who supported the claims of a Pretender (named Bhimsing, the son of a Bhil). This high-handed action caused the British Government to interfere on behalf of Prithiraj, who was thereupon placed on the throne. The rulership of the latter, which extended for a period of more than 40 years, was marked by conspicuous ability in administration, and by his incessant endeavours to promote the prosperity of the State and the happiness of his subjects. His death in 1864 caused intense grief among the people, by whom he was greatly beloved, and also among a wide circle of friends and acquaintances. He was succeeded by his son, Mansinghji, and as he was then only nine years of age, the administration of the State was placed under the superintendence of the Bombay Government.

The young Prince passed through a successful scholastic career, and his training in general subjects was specially directed with the object of making him thoroughly acquainted with every detail of work in State departments. After being invested with ruling powers in November 1876, Mansinghji at once manifested keen interest in the welfare of his subjects.

The majority of the inhabitants of the State are engaged in arable or pastoral farming, and the Raja, in his desire to stimulate the practice of agriculture in all possible directions, has opened an experimental farm, which has been of the greatest value to the people. The farm, which is about 135 acres in extent, is managed by an expert agriculturist, who gives practical demonstrations in methods of farming, and also makes investigations into such important matters as the classification of soil, selection of seed, manuring, and the sowing and harvesting of crops. Special attention is also given to the adoption of measures for improving the breeds of horses and cattle.

Mansinghji died in February 1908, leaving two sons, Ranjitsinhji and Naharsinhji, and one daughter surviving him. The elder of the sons—the present Ruler—received the early portion of his education at the Rajkumar College at Rajkot, and he eventually proceeded to England, where he completed his studies in one of the principal teaching institutions in that country. Upon his return to India he joined the Imperial Cadet Corps at Dehra Dun, and at a later date he entered upon a course of careful training in administrative work under the able guidance of his father. He ascended the *gadi* on March 21, 1908.

At the installation Durbar, His Highness (*inter alia*) referred to the services rendered by his ancestors from the commencement of the nineteenth century, and their unbroken loyalty to the British Government, and added: "It will be my pride to maintain the traditions of my ancestors in their loyalty and attachment to the British Crown. . . . I shall always regard it as my highest duty to promote the prosperity and well-being of the people whom Providence has been pleased to commit to my charge, and it shall be my ambition rightly to earn their gratitude by a proper discharge of my obligation towards them."

His Highness married a daughter of His Highness Maha Rana Sir Shri Chhatrasinghji, K.C.I.E., of the Rajpipla State, and a son and heir was born on June 9, 1909.

His Highness the Maharawal Saheb and his consort attended the Coronation Durbar ceremony at Delhi in December 1911, where he was presented to Their Imperial Majesties the King-Emperor and Queen-Empress. A special Durbar was held on the same day at Baria, when the Royal Proclamation was read by the

CAPT. H.H. MAHARAWAL SHRI RANJIT SINHJI.

THE STATE OF BARIA.

1. Lieut. K. Nahar Sinhji (His Highness's Brother). 2. Types of Infantry. 3. A Company of Infantry on Parade.

Diwan, with due ceremony, to a large concourse of inhabitants of the State.

Early in the month of August 1914 news was received from the Political Agent that war had broken out between Great Britain and Germany, and His Highness, manifesting the same spirit of devotion to the Throne which had been so characteristically displayed by his predecessors, at once telegraphed a reply in which he placed the services of himself and the State at the disposal of Government. Meetings were held in various parts of the State for the purpose of dispelling unfounded rumours as to the cause of hostilities, and of inducing the inhabitants to contribute to war funds which were then being opened. In December of the same year His Highness received orders to proceed on active service, and at a valedictory meeting of officials, *Sirdars*, and subjects of the State, His Highness gave a most telling address, in the course of which he said : " I am proud to feel that my temporary absence from the State is necessitated in the interests of a noble, righteous, and humane cause which is sure to be triumphant. Patience, prayer, and goodwill must be expected from you who stay at home, while indomitable courage, firm purpose, undaunted bravery, and unflinching faith in Divine justice must be inscribed on the escutcheons of those who go to the front. All of you will be glad to learn that I leave you with an easy heart, since I commit you to the Grace of Heaven and entrust you to the charge of my beloved brother and my worthy veteran Diwan. I am sure on my return I shall find you more happy and prosperous."

His Highness was actively engaged at the front in France and Flanders for several months, and on his return to Bombay he was accorded a most enthusiastic welcome from a large number of distinguished citizens. His Highness signalized his return to Baria by making diligent efforts to support various war funds, not only by personal contributions, but also by collecting sums of money and gifts of articles from his subjects. The monetary assistance rendered under various headings, and the subscriptions to the War Loans, totalled approximately to Rs. 11,16,000, which sum represents an average of about one-third of each year's gross revenue during all the years of the war.

Baria is not a State in which recruits are easily obtainable, but His Highness's personal example and efforts achieved splendid results. Before the close of the year 1918 no fewer than 270 men were recruited for active service, and most of them were combatants. With the object of stimulating enlistment, His Highness had granted liberal concessions to the families of those on service, and had sanctioned the grant of land and pensions to wounded soldiers and to the families of all who were killed.

On the signing of Peace all His Highness's conspicuous services during the war were appreciated by Government, who, in their *Kharita* wrote to the Maharawal Saheb as follows : " On behalf of His Majesty the King-Emperor, His Excellency the Viceroy, and His Excellency the Governor, I am directed to thank you most warmly for the personal assistance and substantial aid rendered by the Baria State during the last four-and-a-half years. In addition to generous contributions in money and material, including an annual gift of Rs. 75,000 towards the expenses of the war, you rendered most valuable services in recruiting, while you yourself took an active part in the military operation as an officer on the staff of General Edwardes, commanding the 7th Indian Cavalry Brigade. You have thus manifested the steadfast loyalty and devotion of the State of Baria to His Imperial Majesty the King and the British Empire, and have shared in the great struggle for justice and freedom in which India has so nobly borne her part."

On the outbreak of hostilities with the Amir of Afghanistan in 1919, His Highness offered his personal services to Government and placed the resources of the State at their disposal. In addition to the generous contributions in money and materials, which included an annual gift of Rs. 5,000 to aid the prosecution of the war, he took part in the campaign as an officer on the staff of General Beynon, commanding the 10th Division.

His Highness, whose full title is Captain Maharawal Shri Ranjitsinghji, enjoys the supreme satisfaction of having witnessed a very marked advance in the prosperity of the State during his beneficent rule of little more than 11 years. He commenced his reign by showing that he held high ideas regarding the responsibilities of a Ruler towards his subjects, and his administration has been so successful that he has in an exceptional degree won the esteem, the heartfelt gratitude, and the sincere love of the people over whose destinies he has been placed.

His Highness is fond of all kinds of sport; he excels in polo, being a clever horseman; and in pig-sticking he has won numerous prizes, including the Gujerat and Salmon cups, as well as the much-coveted Sir Pertab cup.

His Highness is a striking personality, manly in bearing, and regal as a Ruler, yet withal he is one of the most unassuming of the Indian Princes. He undertakes periodical tours in every part of his State, and his direct intercourse with his subjects places him in a position to understand the conditions under which they live. He is always accessible to the people, by whom he is greatly beloved. The domestic life of the family, which includes His Highness's brother, Kumar Shri Naharsinghji, is a model of harmonious concord and perfect happiness.

The independence of the State of Baria has been maintained in spite of much opposition, and few States in the Presidency of Bombay can claim an heredity so illustrious and ancient, and a kingdom so independent. Upon this point one might quote from Bombay State papers (Mahratta series 1785) the words of a report made to Government by Mr. Malet as follows : " Baria is an independent State." Lieutenant-General Sir John Malcolm, in his " Memoirs of Central India " (1824), refers to " the independence of Baria," and Mr. Hamilton, in his " Description of Hindustan " (1820), wrote : " The Baria Principality may be described as one among the few independent States now existing in Hindustan, being not only exempted from the payment of any established tribute, but having a *chouth* upon all neighbouring districts of which it is very tenacious."

As a matter of fact, Baria formerly levied tribute from Sindhia of Gwalior upon his districts of Halol, Dohad, and Kalol, in the Panch Mahals district, but this was commuted, through the intervention of the British Government in 1819, into an annual money payment of Rs. 4,144. Upon the cession of the Panch Mahals to the British under the Treaty of December 1860, the latter undertook to pay the above amount direct to Baria, recouping themselves by deducting the amount of the *chouth* from the tribute which the State of Lunawada paid to Sindhia through them.

The State of Baria has an area of 813 square miles, with 115,201 inhabitants, and for purposes of revenue it is divided into seven *mahals*, namely, Haveli, Randhikpur, Dudhia, Umaria, Dhanpur,

THE STATE OF BARIA.

1. His Highness's Palace. 2. The Old Palace. 3. Guest House. 4. Drawing-room, the Palace.

Sagtala, and Rajgad. The revenue survey of the whole State has been completed, but assessments of rent are fixed annually by the Diwan in order to meet the fluctuating conditions of agriculture. This system has been carried out with such judgment towards the State as well as consideration for occupiers that no coercive measures for recovery of the amounts allocated are necessary. The land revenue for the year 1917–18 amounted to Rs. 1,88,579, and this sum-with the exception of about Rs. 2,363–was paid on demand.

A very large proportion of the population is dependent entirely for a livelihood upon some form of agricultural pursuits, in fact they are averse to taking up any industrial or even labouring work of any kind unless there is a failure of crops owing to an insufficient supply of rain. The possibility of an unfavourable monsoon period is a matter of extreme anxiety to the Durbar, especially as shortages of rain have succeeded each other very frequently in recent years. His Highness, therefore, with characteristic foresight, has recently inaugurated a permanent famine Relief Fund, to which he has generously contributed Rs. 2,00,000. Baria is naturally a very hilly country, and as it is therefore practically impossible to adopt the usual means of irrigation, the Durbar is constructing excellent tanks and wells at State expense.

The breeding and rearing of agricultural livestock receives very careful attention and encouragement. In addition to this, the State is importing first-class bulls which are placed at the free disposal of the *ryots*. In the year 1917–18 the State Administration Report showed the following statistics relating to livestock: 27,765 bullocks, 19,908 cows, 3,810 male buffaloes, 11,005 female buffaloes, 590 horses, 204 mares, 99 colts and fillies, 481 asses, and 17,140 sheep and goats.

Owing to non-demarcation of forest area, it is impossible to give the area under forests, but it may be said that the State is owner of all trees, and in places called " Malwans " felling is absolutely prohibited. The amount derived from the sale of forest produce has for several years been one of the principal items on the credit side of the revenue account, and this sum is obtained chiefly from the annual disposal of teak wood, *mahua* flowers and seeds. Regulations for the preservation of forests have recently been formulated, and the officials, who include an inspector, seven *mahal* rangers, and 27 guards, are doing their utmost to prevent damage being done. The aggregate forest revenue for the year 1917–18 amounted to Rs. 6,49,508, this being Rs. 3,87,881 in excess of the sum obtained during the previous 12 months.

There is almost an entire absence of public industrial concerns; the only enterprise which can be placed under the heading being the Swadeshi Glass Manufacturing Company at Piplod. This concern has, however, met with such success that the factory will doubtless be followed by the erection of others, for which there is ample room in the State. There is an abundance of first-class quartz in the neighbourhood, and liberal concessions are made by the Durbar with the object of encouraging the development of this industry. Baria is rich in minerals, especially marble and stone suitable for building purposes, and quite recently a prospecting licence has been granted to a firm in Bombay. Important results are expected in the near future.

Civil and criminal justice is administered in accordance with British Indian Enactments and local laws and rules, and the spirit rather than the actual letter of the law is followed.

The Courts administering justice in the State, dealing with civil as well as criminal matters, are: The *Huzur* Court, presided over by the Ruling Prince, in which final appeals and revisions of verdicts are heard; the Diwan's Court, which exercises the powers of a Court of Sessions in criminal cases and hears civil suits; the Naib-Diwan's Court, which exercises criminal jurisdiction of a First-class and District Magistrate, and civil jurisdiction of trying civil suits of a value not exceeding Rs. 1,000; and the *Nyavadhisha* Court, which exercises powers of Magistrates of the Second Class, and deals with Small Causes Court suits.

The police force for the protection of the State consists of 107 constables armed with muzzle-loading guns, 60 unarmed men, 18 head constables, seven sub-inspectors, and one superintendent. For the further protection of the State there are 24 cavalry and 101 infantry. The former are employed as a bodyguard for His Highness, and the latter are responsible for the safety of the palace. The Commanding Officer of the forces—Kumar Shri Naharsinghji deserves all praise for the admirable discipline manifested by his men, and earned the thanks of the Government of India for his valuable work in obtaining suitable recruits during the late war work which was recognized by the conference upon him of the Royal Commission of a Lieutenancy in the British Army.

When His Highness ascended the *gadi* in 1908 the only provision for affording medical relief to the people was a solitary dispensary at Devgad-Baria. Mr. Harilal M. Parekh, the late Dewan, presented to the State a new building for the purpose, which was opened about five years ago. The Durbar proposes to erect a hospital, which will be a model of its kind as regards general internal arrangements and scientific, surgical, and other accessories. In the year 1914 Kumar Shri Naharsinghji, the brother of His Highness, generously gave a building for a fully-equipped hospital for the use of women and children of the State. These two institutions are under the direct management of the State Medical Officer, who is assisted by a junior surgeon and a midwife. Dispensaries have been opened at Dudhia and Rajgadh, and arrangements are now in progress for the establishment of five others in other *mahals* of the State.

The firm belief of His Highness in education as the only foundation upon which the social and moral status of the people can be raised has been manifested by granting free education in the English and Gujerathi schools, and by the opening of several schools in various parts of the State. The capital has a full-fledged High School, preparing students for the University Entrance Examination. There is also a hostel attached to it.

Baria is exceedingly fortunate in having for its Ruler one who is so enthusiastic in his desire to promote the welfare of his subjects, that at the time of his accession he issued a *firman* making all primary and secondary education absolutely free of all cost. With the object of encouraging the study of the English language, His Highness founded scholarships for pupils attending Government High Schools in British Districts, and at the same time he started an English Middle School at Devgad-Baria, this being the first step towards the establishment of a system of higher education in Baria. This teaching institution has prospered greatly, and as remarked above, has developed into a full High School. The premises now occupied will very shortly be superseded by a palatial structure, which is to be erected at a cost of Rs. 75,000. The staff consists of a Head Master, obtained from the

THE STATE OF BARIA.

1. Ranjit Sinhji Club. 2. Mansarover Tank and Landscape at Devgad Baria. 3. Picturesque Road on Devgad Hill.

Bombay Government Educational Department, and a number of graduate teachers. His Highness has also arranged for endowments for scholarships for collegiate training, and as a result of this action one student of the " potter " caste has become a Bachelor of Law, and a Rajput scholar has qualified as a Bachelor of Medicine and Surgery. The year 1917–18 was an important one in the educational annals of Baria from the fact that the control of teaching institutions was transferred. to the State officials. This change, by a happy coincidence, synchronized with the ceremony of laying the foundation stone of the new High School building, and also with the establishment of a permanent Estate Educational Fund for the purpose of providing well-constructed schools, supplied with sanitary and other modern requirements.

His Highness most generously started this fund with a donation of Rs. 50,000. The whole burden of expenditure upon educational matters is borne by the State revenues. His Highness makes an annual grant to the " Pellen " school boarding-house at Godhra. There are two libraries and reading-rooms at Devgad-Baria, namely, the Native General Library and the Mansinghji Library and reading-room (located in the Town Hall), and these popular institutions are almost entirely maintained at the cost of the State.

The State is traversed by the main line of the Bombay-Baroda and Central India Railway, which passes almost midway from the western extremity of the State to its eastern boundary. The South-western part of the State is crossed by the Champaner-Shivrajpur Light Railway. The State has under contemplation the construction of a line in the southern parts of the territory, so as to bring them closer to the main line at Godhra. There are good metalled roads throughout the State, the longest being from Sagtala in a northerly direction to Randhikpur, measuring a total length of about 35 miles.

The gross revenue of Baria for the year 1917–18 amounted to about Rs. 11,40,000.

The State does not pay any tribute to the British Government nor to any other State.

The principal villages in Baria are connected by telephone, and a complete system of electric lighting has been installed in the capital town, which is eight miles distant from Piplod station on the main line of the Bombay-Baroda and Central India Railway.

THE STATE OF BARWANI

INCLUDED within the political charge of the Southern States Agency of Central India, and lying within the mountainous area formed by the Vindhyan and Satpura ranges, the State of Barwani falls naturally into three divisions, of which the northern, or Narbada, and the eastern, or Jalgone, sections are composed chiefly of a large fertile alluvial plain, while the Satpura portion is distinctly hilly in character. It is situated near the left bank of the river Narbada, and is bounded on the north by the States of Gwalior, Dhar, and Indore; on the north-west by the Ali-Rajpur State; on the east by a portion of Indore; and on the south and west by the Khandesh district of the Bombay Presidency. The State is 1,178 square miles in extent, and at the census of 1911 there were 108,583 inhabitants.

More than one-half of the total area is covered by luxuriant forest, and about one-fourth is under cultivation, the principal crops being cotton, wheat, gram, *jowar*, and maize.

The acreage devoted to the growing of cotton is increasing, and with the object of improving the quality of the yield the Durbar has been distributing various kinds of selected seed for experimental work.

The area under *kharif* and *rabi* crops respectively during the year 1916–17 was 214,936 acres and 34,207 acres. The necessity for the development of agriculture according to modern scientific methods is so thoroughly appreciated by His Highness the Rana that the State has sent two pupils to undergo a course of training at the Agricultural College at Cawnpore, and it is anticipated that *ryots* will derive much assistance from the advice and practical demonstration work of these students, who will commence their duties in the State during the present year, 1918.

A certain quantity of land was set apart in 1912–13 as a cattle-breeding farm, the main object being the revival of the Nimari stock, which are noted for size and strength, and recently the Durbar has distributed a number of young stud bulls of this noted breed in each of the five *perganas*. The State employs two veterinary surgeons, one of whom is attached to the Palace stables and the other to the Revenue Department.

The main reason for the almost entire absence of manufacturing or industrial concerns within the State, and the impracticability of developing trade with outside districts, lies in the fact that Barwani is not less than 80 miles distant from a railway, the nearest station being Mhow on the Bombay-Baroda and Central India system. There are, however, eight ginning factories at work, and it is hoped that as the production of cotton is increased in quantity there may be a necessity for several more of these industrial enterprises.

The State has provided nine hospitals and dispensaries, which are in charge of a head surgeon, four male and one female assistant surgeons, 17 compounders, and one fully-trained nurse.

For administrative purposes the State is divided into four divisions, namely, Rajpur, Anjar, Silawad, and Pansemal, but His Highness the Rana exercises full authority in all matters.

Barwani, the capital town, is pleasantly situated near the river Narbada, and it is believed to have been founded in the seventeenth century. Near to Barwani are several places of interest, including a *kapila sangam*, where, according to the Rewa Chand, Barkundan, King of Ajodhya, performed a great sacrifice; a famous place of pilgrimage for Jains named Bawangaja; and a number of temples, some of which evidently belong to the twelfth or thirteenth century. With the object of preventing the people of Barwani from falling into the hands of unscrupulous money-lenders, His Highness consented to the establishment of a State Bank in the year 1914–15, which was placed in charge of a competent official under the direct supervision of the Durbar.

The gross revenue of the State, based on the average of the past five years, is approximately Rs. 6,50,000, but the Durbar does not pay tribute to the Government or any other State, although it contributes Rs. 3,389 towards the maintenance of the Malwa Bhil Corps.

His Highness the Rana belongs to the famous Sisodia clan of Rajputs, and he traces descent from Sri Rama of the Ramayana.

Rana Indrajit occupied the *gadi* from 1880 to his death in 1894, when he was succeeded by his son, Ranjit Singhji, the present Ruler, whose full title is Captain His Highness Sir Rana Ranjit Singhji, K.C.I.E. His Highness was then only six years of age, and the State was accordingly placed under the supervision of the Political Agent, while the young Chief commenced his educational career at the Rajkumar College at Indore, and subsequently completed it at the Mayo College, Ajmer.

On January 12, 1910, His Highness was invested with full powers of administration, and during the short period of

1. SAGAR VILAS PALACE.
2. CAPTAIN HIS HIGHNESS SIR RANA RANJIT SINGHJI BAHADUR, K.C.I.E.
3. HIS HIGHNESS AND STATE OFFICERS.

THE STATE OF BARWANI.

1. Indra Bhawan Palace. 2. Dharam Bungalow. 3. Bird's-eye View of Barwani City. 4. Ranjit Club.
5. Bawangaza Temples.

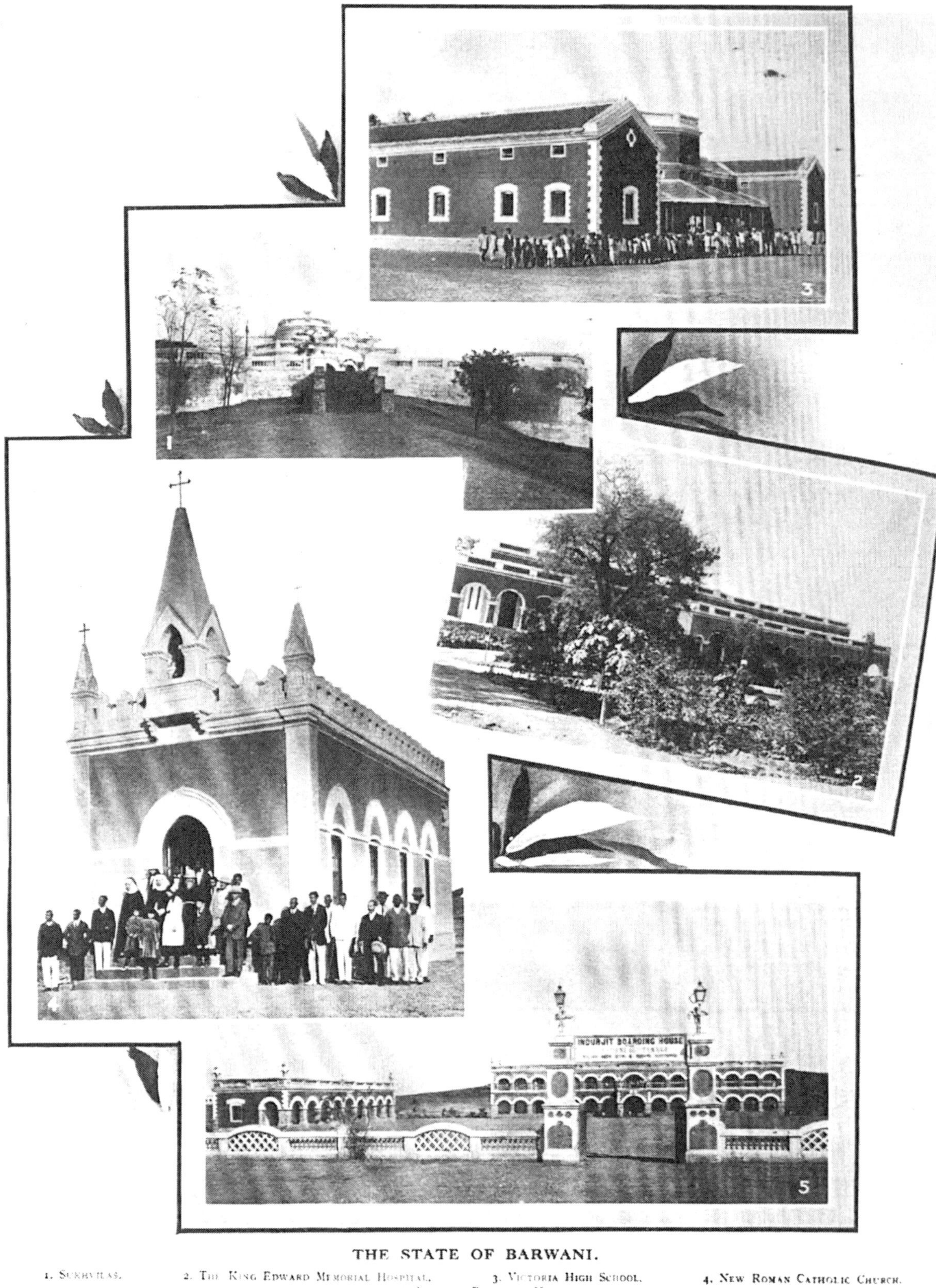

THE STATE OF BARWANI.

1. Sukhvilas. 2. The King Edward Memorial Hospital. 3. Victoria High School. 4. New Roman Catholic Church. 5. Indrajit Boarding House.

eight years has manifested conspicuous ability in guiding the affairs of the State. Among numerous instances of his efforts to promote reforms it may be mentioned that the whole of the area of land under the control of the Revenue Department, with the exception of some hilly portions of the Satpura region and the newly acquired villages from the Forest Department in the Jalgone district, has been surveyed and assessed; considerable improvement has been effected in the discipline of the police force; numerous public works have been carried out, such as the construction of tanks, wells, roads, and bridges; and many buildings have been erected for State officials. His Highness has already endeared himself to his subjects by the warm interest taken by him in their welfare, and it is his chief desire to earn for himself a reputation worthy of the race to which he belongs.

The Rana is a keen supporter of outdoor and indoor sports of all kinds, and his desire to stimulate a love for healthy games and contests among his subjects has prompted him to erect a club-house at Barwani for their benefit. His Highness is thoroughly loyal to the Throne, and his desire to help the cause of the Allies is shown by his going to France and taking part in the actual fighting, and also bearing the annual cost of the maintenance of 50 beds for sick and wounded soldiers at the King Edward Hospital at Indore, and by his substantial monthly contribution to the Chief Guest House Hospital at the same place, and other donations from time to time.

A large sum raised by means of a war lottery has been forwarded to the Political Agent in the Southern States of Central India for various army funds, and War Loan bonds to the value of Rs. 150,000 have been purchased on behalf of the State and its inhabitants.

His Highness was present at the Coronation Durbar at Delhi in 1911, and his salute of nine guns was then raised to 11 in number.

THE STATE OF BIJAWAR

HIS Highness the Sawai Maharaja, Sir Sawant Singh Bahadur, K.C.I.E., is the present Ruling Chief of Bijawar, a *sanad* State in the Bundelkhand Political Agency, the latter being under the Political Agency of the Central India States. The Maharaja is a Bundela (Vindhyela) Rajput claiming to be a descendant of the Gaharwar family of Benares who, it is alleged, were at one time possessors of all the territory in this region, with Benares and Mahoba as its chief centres. The Bundelas were, about the year 600, driven from their holdings by the Pawar Rajputs, and it was not until the fifteenth century that some of their descendants returned to the original home. About the end of the seventeenth century the territory now forming the Bijawar State fell into the hands of the Maharaja Chhatarsal of Panna, and when the possessions of this Ruler were divided at his death Bijawar was transferred to his brother's son, Narayan Das, in return for gallant services rendered. The latter and his successors held the grant of Bijawar until the year 1780 when, with a rent-roll of about Rs. 6,00,000, it passed to Sawai Duvan Birsingh Deo, a son of Jagatraj. The latter extended his area of land very considerably prior to his death in 1793, when he was killed in battle in opposing the invasion of Bundelkhand by Ali Bahadur.

His eldest son, Dhokal Singh, had predeceased his father, and therefore the second, Kesri Singh, was permitted by the conqueror to remain in possession on his entering into engagements of fidelity and allegiance. This Chief was on the *gadi* when the British Government obtained supremacy in Bundelkhand, and he immediately acknowledged the new power, but a *sanad* was not granted to him on account of certain complicated disputes with the Raja Bijai Bahadur of Charkhari and with Kunwar Sone Shah of Chhatarpur regarding a number of villages and *perganas*. Kesri Singh died in December 1810, and as the difficulties just referred to had been settled a *sanad* was in the following year handed to Ratan Singh, his eldest son, who died in 1832 without male issue. Serious disputes arose as to a successor, as the late Chief's brother-in-law attempted to usurp the *Raj*, while the *Thakurs* and State officials supported Lachman Singh, the son of Ratan Singh's brother, Khet Singh. The rivalry between the two parties led to fighting in which Zalim Singh, the pretender, was killed, and thereupon Lachman Singh was recognized by the Government of India. This Chief ruled until 1847 and was succeeded by his minor son Bhan Partab Singh, while the Regency was entrusted to the widow of Khet Singh, his grandfather, although the greatest portion of the responsibility for administration was undertaken by the Regent's youngest daughter, Nanne Raja. The latter manifested the most conspicuous ability in assisting the English to drive the Nawab of Banda's rebel army from Kabrai, in the district of Hamirpur, and in recognition of these services the minor Raja first received a *khilat* and an hereditary salute of eleven guns; in 1862 he was granted the right of adoption; in 1866 the title of Maharaja was conferred upon him; in the following year he was formally invested by *sanad*, under certain conditions, with supreme criminal jurisdiction within his State; and at the Delhi Assemblage of 1877 his title of Maharaja was amplified by the addition of "Sawai."

Bhan Partab Singh's administration was, owing to various causes, unsatisfactory, and in 1887 the State was placed under the management of officers appointed by the British Government. Bhan Partab had no issue, and was not on friendly terms with his nearest relatives; therefore he adopted in 1899 Sawai Maharaja Sawant Singh Bahadur, second son of His Highness the Maharaja of Orchha, who succeeded in 1899. Disputes once more arose owing to a claim made by a descendant of Bir Singh Deo, the founder of the State, who was supported by many of the principal *Thakurs* and *Jagirdars*, but the Government recognized the adoption already made, and the Sawai Maharaja was at the age of twenty-three installed on the *gadi* of his adoptive father on June 26, 1900.

The State—covering an area of 973 square miles—is situated in the low-lying natural portion of Central India between 24 and 25 degrees of north latitude and between 79 and 81 degrees of east longitude. It is divided into two unequal blocks by the northernmost range of the Vindhyan hills, running in a south-westerly direction, at the foot of which is the capital town of Bijawar.

The State has a forest area of very considerable extent, but the timber was in past years ruthlessly depleted by inhabitants who indiscriminately felled large numbers of the finest trees for the smelting of iron, an industry which was successfully carried on until imports from Europe rendered it unprofitable. The forests in the State are estimated to be about 270,000 acres in extent.

The population of the State, according to the census of 1911, was 125,202 in number, giving a mean density of 129 persons to the square mile. About 96 per cent. of the people are Hindus, the most important castes and tribes being Brahmans, 11 per cent.; Chamars, 16 per cent.; Lodhi, 7 per cent.; Rajput, 6 per cent.; and Dhimars,

1. H.H. SAWAI MAHARAJA BHAN PARTAB SINGH, THE LATE MAHARAJA.
2. H.H. SAWAI MAHARAJA SIR SAWANT SINGH BAHADUR, K.C.I.E., MAHARAJA OF BIJAWAR.
3. SHRI MAHARAJ KUMAR JAGDISH SINGH, THE HEIR-APPARENT.

THE STATE OF BIJAWAR.

1. The Palace from the West. 2. The Durbar Hall. 3. Trophies of Game Shot by H.H. the Maharaja

THE STATE OF BIJAWAR.

1. The Palace from the East. 2. The Janki Niwas Temple. 3. The Ram Niwas Temple. 4. Bhiakund Lake. 5. The Sadar Gate of the Fort.

THE STATE OF BIJAWAR.

1. General View of Bijawar City. 2. Bara Bagh Cenotaphs. 3. The Bazar Street, Bijawar. 4. The Shikas Gat at Pathar.

THE STATE OF BIJAWAR

4 per cent., and occupations are distributed in four main divisions, namely, agriculture, 78 per cent.; industries, 12 per cent.; trades, 6 per cent.; and professions, one per cent.; while the remainder consist of labourers of various kinds.

The agricultural industry plays an important part in the Bundelkhand States generally, and in Bijawar in particular, since nearly 80 per cent. of the people are dependent upon it for a livelihood.

The principal sums in the revenue account are derived from land, excise, and customs duties, and in a statement of accounts for the year 1916–17 issued by the Diwan of the State it is observed that the receipts from all sources amounted to Rs. 348,752, and the expenditure was Rs. 3,34,772.

There are seven courts exercising jurisdiction in civil and criminal justice, namely, the Chief Court, the Durbar Court, the Nizamat, and four Courts presided over by *tahsildars*.

His Highness is at the head of administration, and he is assisted by his Diwan, Shri Ram Naib Rai Sahib, the principal Executive Officer, while there are separate departments known as Revenue, Judicial, Police, Forests, and Public Works.

A definite system of education may be said to have been started when the first public school was opened at Bijawar in 1864, and considerable advance has been made since that date, notwithstanding the fact that the people manifest little or no desire to avail themselves of the opportunity afforded for securing instruction for their children.

Full administrative powers in the State were granted to His Highness the Maharaja in the year 1905.

On November 16, 1905, His Highness the Maharaja had the honour of attending a Durbar held at Indore by Their Royal Highnesses the Prince and Princess of Wales (their present Majesties the King-Emperor and Queen-Empress), when he was present at the various functions which had been arranged.

The most important event, however, was the Imperial Durbar at Delhi in December, 1911, which their Majesties the King-Emperor George V and the Queen-Empress attended with the object of commemorating the Coronation ceremony which took place at Westminster Abbey on June 22 previously. His Highness the Maharaja gladly responded to the invitation to be present on so auspicious an occasion, and arrived at Delhi on December 2, whence he was conducted to his camp on the Coronation road. On the morning of the 7th, His Highness proceeded to the pavilion where all the Ruling Chiefs were subsequently presented and rendered homage to Their Imperial Majesties. A reception was held by His Majesty the King-Emperor on the morning of the 9th, and this visit was returned on the same day by His Excellency the Governor-General (Lord Curzon), who conversed with the Maharaja on various topics connected with State affairs.

At the investiture held on December 12 His Highness the Maharaja was honoured by receiving from the hand of His Majesty the King-Emperor the Riband, Badge, and Star of a Knight-Commander of the Most Eminent Order of the Indian Empire. On the 16th, the closing day of the visit of Their Imperial Majesties to Delhi, all Ruling Chiefs who had been present at the Durbar were commanded to appear in the Audience Chamber of the Royal Camp, where each was presented with a gold medal in commemoration of the occasion.

In November 1912 His Highness was invited to attend at Indore on the opening of the new buildings of the Daly College by His Excellency the Viceroy and Governor-General, and he formed one of the Viceregal procession to the beautiful spacious College Hall and the dais at the further end. A visit paid by the Maharaja to His Excellency at the Residency was subsequently returned, when the customary ceremonies were observed, while a *bhil* dance, a garden party, and a State banquet were included in the festivities.

Since His Highness assumed control of the State he has interested himself deeply in the working of each department and with all details of administration; he has initiated many schemes of social reform; land tenure has been revised; forestry has been placed upon a satisfactory working basis under the supervision of an experienced officer lent by the Government of India; and he has succeeded in carrying out the injunction of the Political Agent of Bundelkhand on the occasion of his being invested with full administrative powers, namely, "to earn for himself a place among the pillars of that Empire to which his ancestors pledged their loyalty nearly a hundred years ago."

THE STATE OF CAMBAY

UNDER the political agency of Kaira, in the Bombay Presidency, and at the head of the gulf of the same name is the prosperous little State of Cambay, which has an area of 350 square miles, and a population of about 73,000 inhabitants, who reside in the chief town, Cambay, and 88 villages. It is bounded on the north by the Matar *taluq* of the British district of Kaira, on the east by Borsad in the same district, and by Petlad in the State of Baroda, on the south by the Gulf of Cambay, and on the west by the river Subarmati.

The surface of the land is a gently undulating plain of fertile soil interspersed with groves of trees especially in the vicinity of villages. The climate is suitable for the cultivation of a variety of crops, and although the annual rainfall occasionally exceeds 34 inches, it is only rarely that serious losses occur by reason of the severity of storms; while, on the other hand, the evils arising from drought which are occasionally experienced, are to some extent minimized by tanks and wells, and by the rivers Mahi and Sabarmati which flow on either side of the State.

The agricultural stock comprise 14,625 bullocks, 9,639 cows, 1,462 male buffaloes, 17,536 female buffaloes, 255 horses, 162 mares, 35 colts and fillies, 895 asses, and 5,443 sheep and goats.

Communications by rail, road, or sea, not only within its own borders, but beyond its confines, are of incalculable advantage to a Province or State in the development of its industrial resources, and in this respect Cambay is in a somewhat fortunate position. It has about six miles of good metalled roads, and several fair-weather roads, connecting it with important towns, and although its coasting trade is diminishing in volume and does not exceed Rs. 6.00,000 in value per annum, it has an advantage in the Cambay-Petlad railway, which connects the chief town with Anand on the system of the Bombay-Baroda and Central India Railway Company. The Anand-Tarapur section, 22 miles in length, is the property of and is maintained and worked by the latter Company, while the line from Tarapur to Cambay, 12½ miles in length, belongs to the Cambay Durbar, which provides all funds, chargeable to capital account, but it is managed, maintained, and worked by the same Company as the other section.

The chief manufactures in the State are cotton and silk fabrics, cloth, salt, carpets, and embroidery, while the brisk trade carried on in normal times in agate and cornelian stones has suffered much owing to the Great War. There are also 3,210 handlooms at work, which give employment to 6,189 persons. The most important industrial concern is "The Nawab of Cambay Mills Co., Ltd.," whose premises are fitted with 17,106 spindles and 264 looms, and of which Messrs. Maganlal Harilal & Co., of Bombay, are agents, secretaries, and treasurers.

The expenditure of the Public Works Department controlled by the State engineer, for the year 1917–18, under the headings of "State Funds" and "Local Funds," was Rs. 1,61,430, but a few remarks may be made with regard to some of the items in the account. For example, the sum of Rs. 64,854 put down as payments for buildings, includes Rs. 45,278 for a new bungalow, stables, and outhouses for the Administrator; nearly Rs. 13,000 for new schools and extensions to the main vernacular teaching institution; and Rs. 2,000 for quarters for the State Engineer. The construction of tanks and wells is one of the most reproductive of all works, since it tends to the cultivation of a larger area of land, and therefore the sum of Rs. 24,324 disbursed is not by any means excessive. During the year just mentioned, Rs. 13,890 were spent on the Kenewal tank in Valli, Rs. 7,185 on improvements to the Alang Channel, Rs. 1,695 on the Vank tank at Daloli, and Rs. 1,552 on the Mehmedabad tank. The value of the Kenewal tank has been enhanced by the opening up of new distributary channels, and it is anticipated that as a result a considerable area of waste land will be converted into profitable gardens. The Alang channel—upon which Rs. 10.000 have been expended already—has been repaired and improved over a distance of seven miles from the northern boundary of the State, and with a "feeder" of a mile in length it is of material assistance in filling the Kenewal tank.

The police force, of 221 men, comprises 62 carrying arms, 19 *sowars*, and 140 foot constables. These are exclusive of 383 village policemen, who are remunerated partly by cash payments and partly by grants of land.

Criminal jurisdiction is dispensed according to laws based upon the code adopted generally in British Indian territories, and cases are heard by the Magistrate, First Class, the Nyayadhish, and in the Sessions Court.

The prisoners in the Central jail at Cambay are employed in weaving carpets

HIS HIGHNESS NAZAM-UD-DAULA MUMTAZ-UL-MULK MOMIN-KHAN BAHADUR DILAVERJANG, NAWAB HUSSAIN YAVAR-KHAN BAHADUR.

and other articles with fly shuttle and other improved looms, and also in grinding corn. They are occasionally lent to the Public Works Department for outdoor work under police guards.

Civil suits are adjudicated upon in the Courts of the Nyayadhish, the Sar Nyayadhish, and in the Sardars' Court while final appeals are heard by the Administrator. The village *panchayat* system, on the hearing of minor civil as well as criminal cases, is found to work satisfactorily in Cambay, as it relieves the ordinary Courts of a great amount of petty work, and saves the people from the expenditure of large sums of money in litigation.

The educational establishments maintained by the State are 43 in number, and there are, in addition, 14 private schools.

Medical relief, including medicine, is dispensed free of cost at the Kennedy hospital, the Bibi Bahu Begam Saheb dispensary, and the Diamond Jubilee Zenana hospital at Cambay, and at the Tarapur and Varasda dispensaries, and at the Veterinary dispensary at the chief town.

During the year 1917 18 about 44,800 persons were treated in the hospitals and dispensaries, while more than 7,000 animals were attended to by the veterinary officer, and the total annual cost of the maintenance of the above-named six institutions is about Rs. 14,000.

In connection with the administration of land, the fixed revenue for the past year was Rs. 2,99,188, and the miscellaneous land revenue amounted to Rs. 51,671, making a total of Rs. 3,50,859. Out of the 17,795 acres of waste land 11,490 acres are capable of cultivation, and the easiest terms possible are being offered with the object of inducing subjects of the State to become occupiers and cultivators.

The municipal administration of the town of Cambay was originally carried on by a Board of nominated members, but the elective system has been lately adopted, and it is believed that this innovation will induce the inhabitants to take a greater personal interest in the local government of the place in which they reside.

The history of the State of Cambay is in a great degree the history of its chief town, which was formerly one of the principal seaports on the western coast of India.

The Portuguese plundered the town in 1538, and the whole territory now forming the State of Cambay was in the utmost disorder when it came under the sway of the Emperor Akbar (1556–1605). The fine harbour, in which a large number of ships could be accommodated, shortly afterwards became silted up, and as a consequence a large proportion of the trade of the port gradually drifted to Surat. The British established themselves at Cambay in 1616, and in the following year the Portuguese built factories; but on the death of the Emperor Aurangzeb, in 1707, the town and surrounding districts were overrun by the Mahrattas, who exacted large sums of money from the people.

Cambay appears to have been founded as a separate State about the year 1730, by Momin Khan, the penultimate Governor of Gujarat, who placed his son-in-law, Nizam Khan, in charge of it. After the death of Momin Khan, in 1742, his son Muftakhir, or Momin Khan II, compassed the death of his brother-in-law and assumed government of the State. British control of Cambay took place in 1802, after the treaty of Bassein, during the Rulership of Fateh Ali Khan, whose successor, Bandeh Ali Khan, was the uncle of Hussain Yavar Khan, father of the late Nawab, His Highness Najib-ud-Daula, Mumtaz-ul Mulk, Jafar Ali Khan Hussain Yavar Khan Sahib Bahadur.

His Highness ascended the *gadi* on April 25, 1880, and was duly invested with full ruling powers.

May 16, 1911, stands out clearly as a red-letter day as the date of the birth of a son and heir to His Highness the Nawab, to whom the name of Prince Hussain Yavar Khan was given.

It was with the greatest pleasure that His Highness accepted the invitation of the Bombay Government to attend the Coronation Durbar of their Imperial Majesties, the King-Emperor and Queen-Empress, at Delhi, in December 1911, and he had the honour of attending all the functions and ceremonies which were held on that occasion.

Occasions for sadness and mourning are curiously intermingled not only in individual life, but also in the history of nations, and scarcely had the boom of guns connected with the birth of an heir and the Coronation of their Imperial Majesties died away, before the people of the State were plunged into the deepest distress at the death of their beloved Ruler, who passed away on January 21, 1915, at the age of 67.

One of the leading State officials wrote concerning him, that " the welfare of the people was very dear to his heart, and he had a forgiving disposition even towards those who had seriously wronged him.

" Though a very shy and retiring man of the simplest habits, he had endeared himself to all his subjects.

" The deep and respectful sorrow which men and women, young and old, displayed at his funeral was most touching."

His Highness was succeeded by his only son, Nazam-ud-Daula Mumtaz-ul-Mulk Momin Khan Bahadur Dilaverjang Nawab Hussain Yavar Khan Bahadur, who has commenced a collegiate course of study at Rajkot. He has already won high praise from his teachers, and is very popular with his fellow-students at the College.

His Highness the late Nawab, as well as the officials and subjects of the State, were considerably perturbed by the news of the unfortunate outbreak of hostilities in Europe in 1914, and in December of that year His Highness convened a public meeting of the Mahomedans of Cambay, at which the leaders and members of the community generally were present in large numbers. The circumstances leading to the misguided intervention of Turkey against England, her own Ally and confederate in arms of former years, was fully explained, and the meeting was unanimous in its expression of loyalty to His Majesty the King-Emperor and the British *Raj*.

A public meeting of the residents of the town was held, and a committee was formed to raise subscriptions for the War Fund. In the Zenana Durbar a meeting of ladies was held for the same purpose. The subscriptions amounted to Rs. 9,871-5-9. His Highness the late Nawab gave Rs. 5,000 more, and H.H. Bibi Sikandar Jahan Begam contributed Rs. 1,000 from her private purse, making a grand total of Rs. 15,871-5-9. The " Nawab " launch (which costs about Rs. 110 a month for upkeep), was lent to Government for war purposes in August 1914.

Throughout the year 1915–16 the State of Cambay and its people adhered to their determination to support the cause of the Allies to the utmost possible extent, and among the many contributions may be mentioned a sum of Rs. 4,000 presented by the Durbar to the Imperial War Relief Fund, and an amount of Rs. 1,000 to the Women's Branch of that fund established by Her Excellency Lady Willingdon, wife of His Excellency the Governor of Bombay.

THE STATE OF CAMBAY.

1. The Narieli Bag Bungalow. 2. The Law Courts. 3. A Jain Temple. 4. The Three Gates Clock Tower.

THE STATE OF CAMBAY.

1. THE KOTHI—EAST INDIA COMPANY'S BUILDING (BUILT IN A.D. 1613). 2. THE JUMMA MASJID. 3. THE WATERWORKS (SHOWING PART OF NARESHWAR TANK). 4. THE NAWAB OF CAMBAY SPINNING AND WEAVING MILL.

THE STATE OF CAMBAY.

1. The Bibi Bahu Begum Sahib Free Dispensary. 2. The Cambay High School. 3. The Bodyguard of H.H. the Nawab. 4. Working on Agate Stones.

In the following year the State contributed Rs. 5,000 to the Women's Branch of the Bombay War Relief Fund, Rs. 500 to the Belgian Relief Fund, a similar sum to the "Lord Kitchener" Memorial Fund, and other amounts to various other objects in support of the British Arms. It also purchased bonds to the value of £6,500 in the English War issue, as well as of Rs. 50,000 in Indian securities, and at the end of June, 1917, the people of Cambay had placed Rs. 25,400 in War Loans, Rs. 62,900 in War Bonds, and Rs. 62,040 in postal certificates, making a grand total of Rs. 1,50.340.

During the year ending May 31, 1918, the State contributed Rs. 2,000 for the purchase of recreation tents for troops in Mesopotamia; Rs. 2,000 to Queen Mary's Technical School for disabled Indian soldiers; Rs. 1,000 to the "Our Day" fund of Cambay, and Rs. 1,263 to the Anand Recruiting Depot, together with other sums. Investments to the extent of Rs. 1,00,000 were taken by the State in the Second Indian War Loan Fund, and Rs. 1,58,000 were promised by His Highness' subjects for the same purpose.

Valuable assistance has been rendered by State officials in the way of obtaining recruits, and with the object of encouraging enlistment a larger bonus than was originally proposed was offered to suitable individuals.

The result was satisfactory, as a considerable number of men went into training preparatory to their being sent to join selected units.

THE STATE OF CHAMBA

CHAMBA, one of the independent hill States under the control of the Government of the Province of the Punjab, is situated in the Himalaya mountains, and it is bounded on the north-west and west by the State of Jammu and Kashmir, on the north-east and east by Ladakh, British Lahul, and Bara Bangahal, and on the south-east and south by the districts of Kangra and Gurdaspur.

Historians are entirely in the dark as far as authentic records are concerned with regard to the original inhabitants of the extensive mountainous region of the Himalayas, of which the State of Chamba is a portion, but tradition leads one to suppose that they were low-caste tribes who migrated from the plains, and that by the fusion of races which accompanies intermarriages they now exhibit distinct features of the Aryans, and also make use of dialects of the Aryan family. In tracing the history of the State the chief sources of authority are the genealogical roll of the Rajas, epigraphical records, and popular tradition which has been of immense service to chroniclers in throwing light upon past events.

The Rajas of Chamba belong to the Suryavansi line of Rajputs, and their genealogical record commences with Vishnu, or Narayana, Rama, the hero of the "Ramayana," being sixty-third in order of descent. The family is an ancient one, as it is said to have been founded by Maru, a religious devotee, who subsequently acquired a considerable area of territory by conquering a number of petty Chiefs in the valley of the Upper Ganges river.

Maru had three sons; the eldest of them entered into possession of the ancestral home, and the second was established by his father in the mountains near Kashmir, while the third received as his share certain territory in the valley of the Ravi river, which was formed into a new State with the town of Brahmaputra (now Brahmaur) as its capital. This event is believed to have taken place about the year 550. Raja Aditya (620) was the first Ruler to assume the title or suffix of "Varma," this being a Sanskrit word meaning "armour," or "coat of mail," and when following the ordinary name it signifies "protected by."

One of the most notable of the early Rulers was Sahilla Varma, who ascended the *gadi* in the year 920. One of the first acts of this Chief was to bring under his sway all the petty Ranas who held territory in the lower portion of the River Ravi, and to found a town named Chamba after his daughter Champavati.

The land upon which this new capital was built had been assigned by one of the Ranas to a family of Kanwan Brahmans, and as the Raja did not wish to dispossess them he made an arrangement whereby, "in recognition of their proprietary rights, eight *chaklis*—Chamba copper coins—were promised in perpetuity on the occasion of every marriage in the town." The land was then given up, and the condition has been observed to this day. Sahila Varma erected the temple known as Champavati, or Chamasni, as a memorial to his daughter, who is worshipped there as a goddess. Several other temples were constructed by this Raja in Chamba, the oldest being Chandragupta and Kameshwara, built for two idols of Siva. Raja Sahila Varma was the hero in many battles, and his courage never flagged, but on the approach of old age he abdicated in favour of his eldest son Yugakar, while he himself retired to Brahmapura, the home of his early days, where he dwelt as a recluse in the company of a number of holy men. The accession of Raja Yugakar Varma did not cause any departure from the settled practices of the previous reign, but interest to-day is centred in a deed of gift, inscribed on a copper plate (still in existence) granted about ten years after his succession to the *gadi*. The deed, bearing the names of the Raja and his father and mother, conveyed certain land to the Narsingh temple at Brahmapura. Little is known of the history of Rajas Vidagdha, Dadaka, Vichitar, and Dhairya, beyond that which is gleaned from copper-plate deeds which are still in possession of the Chamba Durbar.

The State underwent many vicissitudes in the course of centuries, but it is possible to trace its succession of Rulers with fair accuracy from records and inscriptions on copper plates and coins which still exist. In the Moghul period disaster overtook the Chamba State when Jagat Singh, the Chief of Nurpur, treacherously murdered Janardan, the reigning prince, and occupied his palace. During the hostilities Janardan's Rani gave birth to a son, and the child, who was named Prithvi Singh, was secretly carried away to Mandi, where he remained until he grew up to manhood. The young prince, on reaching manhood, patiently awaited an opportunity to recover Chamba, and in 1641, when Jagat Singh was in serious trouble with the Emperor Shah Jahan, he obtained money and troops from the Rajas of Mandi and Suket, and, passing through Kulu, he crossed the Chessi Pass into the northern portion of Chamba, and continued fighting his way until he captured the capital town and expelled all Nurpur officials from the State. This recovery of Chamba

HIS HIGHNESS RAJA RAMA SINGH.

THE STATE OF CHAMBA

occurred in 1641, and in December of that year Prithvi Singh was ordered to attend the Imperial Court, then at Lahore, in order to pay his respects to the Emperor. In consolidating his kingdom the Raja displaced several Ranas in the Pangi valley, and appointed his own officials, thus bringing the country under the direct control of Chamba. Prithvi Singh was on several occasions received with much favour at Delhi by the Emperor Shah Jahan, and the treasure-house at Chamba now contains inlaid daggers and magnificent jewelled ornaments presented to him by the Emperor. Raja Chatar Singh, who succeeded in 1664, is famous in history as the Ruler who refused to obey an order of the Emperor, Aurangzeb, for the demolition of all Hindu temples, and in defiance of the edict he directed that a gilt pinnacle should be placed on each of the shrines. The next succeeding Rulers were Udai Singh, Uggar Singh, Dalel Singh, and Ummed Singh, who ascended the *gadi* in 1748 just at the time when the Moghul Empire was on the verge of downfall, when the Emperor's Viceroys were assuming independence, and establishing themselves as Rulers in various parts of the country, and when the Mahrattas and Afghans were commencing their struggle for supremacy in India. This upheaval among superior powers gave to the Hill Chiefs the opportunity of throwing off their allegiance and of recovering territory which had been taken from them.

Moghul control entirely ceased about the year 1750, when the Province of the Punjab, including the Hill States, passed into the hands of the Afghan conqueror, Ahmed Shah Durrani. Afghan rule was merely nominal over the Hill States, and they practically enjoyed independence until about 10 years later, when they came under the influence of the Sikhs.

Ummed Singh died in 1764, and during the reigns of his successors, Raj Singh and Jit Singh, the Chamba forces were almost continually engaged in warfare, chiefly with Kangra, whose ruler, Sansar Chand, arrogated to himself superior authority over all of the Hill States, and even compelled their Chiefs to attend his Courts and furnish him with auxiliary forces during his expeditions. His ambition appeared to be insatiable, and for more than 20 years he ruled despotically, but when he attempted to recover some of his ancestral possessions on the plains he was in 1803-04 driven back by the famous Ranjit Singh, who was at that time a power to be reckoned with in the Punjab. The first important event in the history of the State after the accession of Charat Singh (1808) was a threatened invasion by the Sikhs under Maharaja Ranjit Singh, who had just previously made tributaries of Jasrota and Basohli in the Jammu Hills, and was then marching towards Chamba, but he was persuaded to retire by the gift to him of most valuable presents. Towards the close of the eighteenth century troubles of a family nature had occurred in the small State of Bhadrawah, which had for many years been tributary to Chamba, and about the year 1810 the ruling Chief was driven from his territory without leaving behind him a direct heir.

Pahar Chand succeeded to the *gadi*, and in 1820 he declined to continue the annual payment. The Wazir of Chamba failed in an attempt to punish the offending Raja, but in 1821, with the aid of Ranjit Singh, he captured the fort and annexed the State, placing Chamba officials in direct control of its affairs. In the same year Desa Singh, the first Sikh Governor of Kangra, acting under the orders of Maharaja Ranjit Singh, laid claim to Rihlu, an important division of Chamba, and actually began to attack the fort of the same name. The Wazir, Nathu, gave instructions that the siege was to be held in check while he went to Lahore in order to have a conference with Ranjit Singh, but the Queen-Mother, fearing the consequences of further resistance, directed the fort to be surrendered to the Sikhs, and thus Rihlu was lost to Chamba for ever. Nathu's mission failed with regard to the restoration of Rihlu, but it was successful in ridding the State of the yearly tribute of Rs. 30,000.

Raja Charat Singh died in 1844, and was succeeded by his eldest son, Sri Singh, the administration of the State being vested in his mother.

The strong personality of Maharaja Ranjit Singh kept down the forces of disorder latent in the Punjab, but on his death a crisis occurred which resulted in the first Sikh War. On its conclusion a treaty of peace was arranged, which provided for "the transfer to the British Government in perpetual sovereignty of the Jalandhar Doab and the hill country between the Beas and Sutlej rivers." Further negotiations regarding the settlement of the country took place from time to time, and in April, 1848, a *sanad* was granted to Raja Sri Singh, conferring the territory of Chamba upon him, and in 1862 the right of adoption on the failure of direct heirs was granted.

The State was loyal to the core to the British Government during the Sepoy Mutiny of 1857, and most efficient service was rendered in providing troops for guarding the borders of disaffected areas. During the time of Raja Sri Singh the Government of India arranged with the State authorities for the acquisition of certain plateaux, upon which it was proposed to erect a sanatorium, and in consideration of the grants of land made then, as well as at later dates, the annual tribute payable by Chamba was reduced to Rs. 3,800. The health resort which was erected was named Dalhousie. The administration of the State must have been inefficiently controlled during the minority of Raja Sri Singh, as he discovered, after attaining his majority, that he was unequal to the task of dealing with the disorder into which affairs had fallen. The revenue had decreased to about Rs. 1,00,000 annually, heavy debts had been incurred, and the authority of his officials had been usurped by men of the State of Suket, who had arrived in Chamba with the Princess who had become the wife of Sri Singh. In 1862, therefore, the Raja asked the Punjab Government to appoint a British official as Superintendent of the State, and on January 1, 1863, Major (now Major-General) Blair Reid assumed full control.

This was the commencement of a brighter era for Chamba; drastic reforms were carried out in every Department of State, useless servants and self-imposed dependants at the Court were summarily dismissed, debts were paid, and the State finances were placed on a sound basis.

The development of the internal resources of the State next claimed the attention of the Superintendent, and by the organization of a Public Works Department he was enabled to construct good roads in place of the mere cattle tracks which obtained in that mountainous region.

In 1863 a post office was opened in the capital, and a daily mail service was established and maintained with Dalhousie at the cost of the State. Educational work was commenced in the same year by the opening of a primary school, and the foundation of the present High School was laid. The efficiency of British control was manifested in an increase of revenue resulting from security of tenure, the extension of the cultivated area, and the enhanced prices of agricultural and other produce.

Raja Sri Singh died while these reforms were in progress, his life being terminated by a short illness in 1870, while in the thirty-second year of his age.

In the absence of a direct heir Mian Gopal Singh was, by virtue of the *sanad* of 1848, declared the rightful successor, and an order directing his recognition as Raja was notified on October 25, 1870. A Political

THE STATE OF CHAMBA.

1. His Highness Raja Ram Singh with his Officials. 2. The Lieut.-Governor and the Raja on the way to the Durbar Hall. 3. His Highness seated on the Masnad, with His Honour on the Right. 4. The Lieut.-Governor and the Raja returning from the Durbar Hall after the Installation Ceremony.

THE STATE OF CHAMBA.

1. View from the Residency. 2. The Town from the South-east. 3. The Town Looking North. 4. Khajiar Temples and Lakes. 5. Suspension Bridge, Chamba. 6. The Town of Chamba.

Officer was retained as Superintendent, and reforms already initiated were continued under this *régime*. Gopal Singh cared little for the responsibilities of his position, and in 1873 he abdicated in favour of his eldest son, Sham Singh, then seven years of age, suitable provision was made for the education of the young Chief, and the State was again placed in charge of a Political Officer.

Sir Henry Davies, Lieutenant-Governor of the Punjab, paid a visit to Chamba in April 1874, in March of the following year the Raja was present at the Imperial Durbar held at Delhi, in 1876 he visited Lahore with other Punjab Chiefs, in order to bid welcome to His Royal Highness the Prince of Wales, and in January 1877 he took part in the Grand Ceremonial Durbar at Delhi on the occasion of the assumption by Her late Majesty Queen Victoria of the title of Empress of India.

His Highness the Raja was married in 1883 to a granddaughter of His Highness the Maharaja of Jammu and Kashmir, and in the following year to a cousin of the Raja of Sirmur. After being thoroughly instructed in the duties of government His Highness was in October, 1884, invested with full ruling powers by Colonel C. A. McMahon, Commissioner of Lahore, but the actual withdrawal of the Political Superintendent did not take place until November 1885. His Highness keenly supervised the working of each State Department, and his zeal in work elicited from the Commissioner a flattering report at the close of the year 1886. In 1887 postal arrangements were made with the Imperial Service, and branch offices were opened in several of the most important places; the Judicial Department was organized according to British models, subject to necessary local requirements; the renovation of the Raja's palace was carried out; public buildings, including a new court house, hospital, and jail were constructed; and an old wire suspension bridge over the River Ravi was replaced by a substantial one of iron at a cost of nearly Rs. 1,00,000. In January, 1898, the Raja's brother, Mian Bhuri Singh, who had for some time acted as Private Secretary to His Highness, was appointed Wazir, and it was generally felt that no more suitable selection could have been made, as the brothers were greatly attached to each other, and the duties of administration had been shared between them in previous years.

Chamba had the honour in September, 1900, of receiving as guests His Excellency the Viceroy of India and Lady Curzon, and in November of the following year His Honour Sir Mackworth Young, Lieutenant-Governor of the Punjab, included the State in his cold-weather tour.

His Highness the Raja was prostrated by serious illness in September, 1902, and although he was partially restored to health after more than a year's medical treatment, he found that his strength was insufficient for the arduous duties of Rulership. He therefore begged that the Government would consent to his abdication in favour of his brother, Mian Bhuri Singh, to whom reference has already been made. The Government deeply regretted the necessity for the request, but acceptance of the proposal was in January, 1904, notified in open Durbar by the Hon. Mr. A. Anderson, C.I.E., Commissioner of Lahore. The actual installation ceremony was performed on May 12, 1904, by His Honour Sir Charles Rivaz, K.C.S.I., Lieutenant-Governor of the Punjab.

Raja Sir Bhuri Singh's successful administration of the State earned for him the approbation of Government, and he was honoured by being created a Knight Commander of the Most Exalted Order of the Star of India, as well as a Knight Commander of the Most Eminent Order of the Indian Empire.

He died in September, 1919, and was succeeded by his elder son, His Highness Raja Rama Singh, the present Ruler, who appointed his younger brother, Mian Kesri Singh, as the Wazir of the State. The formal installation on the *gadi* of His Highness Raja Rama Singh was performed by His Honour the Lieutenant-Governor of the Punjab in a Durbar held at Chamba on April 24, 1920.

Since his accession His Highness has been assiduous in promoting measures for the welfare of his subjects, and it might be said that he has devoted special attention to improving the means of communication in the State, to the provision of additional educational facilities, and the extension of the postal service system, which has already been established.

During the late Great War the State of Chamba responded heartily to the call for assistance on behalf of the Allies, and from a statement recently published by the Durbar the following items relating to gifts of money and other help are extracted: Recruits supplied by the State were 232 in number, and 267 others were enlisted by the Recruiting Officer; contributions to war expenses, Rs. 1,50,000; maintenance of the Chamba Company, Rs. 53,634; amount paid to the Punjab aeroplane fund, Rs. 31,000; subscriptions to War Loan Fund, Rs. 3,79,200; postal cash certificates purchased of the value of Rs. 4,400; contributed to the Imperial Relief Fund, Rs. 27,450; to the Prince of Wales's Fund, £100; and to the "Our Day" Fund, Rs. 5,056-12-3. The State also lent one "Standard" car to the General Officer Commanding, Secunderabad, as well as generators for the Lahore Cantonment war hospital, and presented 18 Australian horses, potatoes to soldiers at Dalhousie and rations to Gurkhas at Bakloh.

The State of Chamba, 3,216 miles in extent, is in shape much like a rough and irregular oblong, tapering towards the north, and within this area are comprised a portion of the Beas valley; a section of the Ravi valley, which is the Chamba valley proper; and a similar section of the Chenab valley, called Pangi and Chamba-Lahul. The whole of the territory is exceedingly mountainous with altitudes ranging from 2,000 to 21,000 feet, while the inhabited portions reach an elevation of 10,000 feet. The most striking geographical feature is that, within the State, the Himalaya mountains present three well-defined snowy parallel ranges lying from 30 to 40 miles apart. One of these—that which is nearest to the plains—is called the Outer Himalayas, and it separates the basins of the Beas and Ravi rivers; the second range is the Mid-Himalayas, which forms the watershed between the Ravi and Chenab rivers; and the third, known as the Inner Himalayas, is situated between the Chenab and Indus rivers.

It is impossible in these brief notes to give anything like an adequate description of the magnificence of the scenery presented by the endless variety of forest-clad slopes, of highly-cultivated valleys, and of the rich carpets of flowers of every hue, while towering over all are mighty pinnacles of rock, rearing themselves to altitudes of 19,000 and 20,000 feet, and standing amid vast fields of glittering glaciers and untrodden snow.

The Ravi is the principal river in the State, and in conjunction with its numerous tributaries, it drains the whole of the Chamba valley proper. Its largest off-shoot is the Siul, which receives the surplus water of the north-western portion of the State. The Chenab, another large river, rising near the summit of the Bara Lacha Pass in British Lahul in two separate heads known as Chandra and Bhaga, which unite at Tandi, is noted for the peculiar grey colour of its waters, a phenomenon caused by the melting of snow in the defiles of the upper elevations of the mountains.

In a country like Chamba, with such varying elevations, one must necessarily be

THE STATE OF CHAMBA.

1. Temples, Chamba. 2. The Gaddis. 3. The Pangwala. 4. The Lahoulis.

prepared for a similar diversity in its fauna, flora, and general products. The flora has not yet been fully classified, but its specimens range from arctic to tropical types, trees and plants of purely European origin being in the minority. At a higher elevation than 6,000 feet there may be seen different kinds of pine, fir, holm-oak, flowering-chestnut, maple, holly, elm, yew, walnut, and other trees of a similar kind. Chamba is especially rich in non-flowering plants, no fewer than 132 species, with varieties, being collected and identified by Mr. J. C. McDonell, of the Imperial Forest Service, during investigations made a few years ago. The fauna of Chamba is as varied as its climate. Upon the higher ranges, near the snow-line, the hunter may meet with the ounce, or snow leopard, the ibex, marmot, ermine weasel, and the hill fox; lower elevations are inhabited by red bear and musk deer; and still lower down the slopes sport may be obtained with black bear, leopard, jackal, barking deer, and wild pig. Ornithologists have observed nearly 300 species of birds, including pheasant, partridge, peacock, grey quail, woodcock, snipe, pigeon, and wild geese and ducks. Numerous specimens of birds of prey are met with in Chamba, one of the most common being the great Lammer geyer, which measures 9 feet across the wings. Four types of vultures inhabit the plains, and throughout the greater portion of the State one may notice the golden eagle, falcon, sparrowhawk, crested and serpent eagle, buzzard, kite, and owl.

The inhabitants of the State, about 137,000 in number, belong to various castes, the principal of which are the Rathis, Halis, Brahmaur, Gaddis, Thakurs, and Rajputs. It is said that Hinduism in Chamba has undergone very little change for many centuries, but this is not so surprising as it might at first seem to be, owing to the fact that the mountainous nature of the country has rendered it almost impossible for the inhabitants to have any social intercourse or commercial dealings with the outside world, and therefore the habits and customs of the people are practically the same as they were when the State was founded.

In turning to consider the agricultural industry, it will at once be apparent that it must necessarily be of a very different character from the practice which prevails in countries which are not broken up by endless chains of mountains. Terraced fields, such as are common in Switzerland, are familiar sights in Chamba, and one must admire the patience and perseverance displayed by occupiers in the preparation of the soil in such disadvantageous positions.

The principal crops are maize (the staple product and food of the people), rice, wheat, barley, *bajra*, potatoes, peas, and *bhang*. Cultivation, although primitive in character, is usually well performed, and excellent crops are the rule rather than the exception, but the owner's profits are seriously reduced by the large amount necessary to be expended in guarding the fields at night against the ravages of bears, wild pig, and jackals.

A considerable portion of Chamba is particularly suitable for the growth of fruit, and some of the finest English varieties are now sent to market. Included in the orchard products are apricots, walnuts, black and red currants, raspberries, strawberries, *mango*, and other kinds of fruit.

Sheep are kept by nearly every occupier of land in Chamba, and blankets, shawls, and wearing apparel of superior quality are manufactured from the wool. There is a very large area of excellent pasturage upon State land, and flock-owners are not slow in availing themselves of the grazing privileges afforded.

The tribe known by the name of Gaddis are migratory pastoralists, and during their wanderings their flocks are in great request by arable farmers, who afford safe shelter for the sake of their manure, which is so invaluable in the production of good crops. The ponies of Lahul are small but remarkably sturdy animals, while for travelling the zigzag and sometimes precipitous mountain tracks they appear to be as nimble and as sure-footed as goats. Cattle are generally small in size, yielding only a small quantity of milk, but attempts are being made to improve the breeds by the importation of suitable animals from Great Britain.

The original method of fixing the revenue derivable from land was by dividing the total produce equally between the landlord and the tenant, but this practice was modified some years ago by a fixed quantity of the yield being handed over by the occupier in unfavourable as well as good years. Even this plan, however, was not free from serious objection, and annual cash rents are now becoming general.

The control of the reserved forests in Chamba was in the year 1864 vested in the British Forest Department, and the area formed one of the Punjab forest divisions. In 1908 the Government restored the management to His Highness the Raja, and from that date the whole area has been divided into two classes, known as "reserved" and "unclassed" forests. The reserved portion is about 100,000 acres in extent, while the area of the remainder is estimated at 65,000 acres.

The mountain ranges in Chamba are rich in minerals, but exploitation has not yet been carried on according to any definite system or plan.

Iron ore is found in several districts, but the cost of working has been proved to be too great for smelting and foundry works to compete with imported iron goods. Mica exists in Pangi and other divisions, and the workings of an old copper mine may be seen in the Hul *pergana*. The most profitable minerals to-day are slates, limestone, gypsum, and clay, the last-named being in great demand by the inhabitants, who make all the pottery ware and domestic articles required by the inhabitants of the State.

Manufactures are confined almost entirely to goods and articles required for the use of the people themselves.

The means of communication are perhaps almost as good as one could expect, considering the wild and rugged nature of the country. The only metalled highway within the area of the State is the *tonga* and cart road from Pathankot to Dalhousie, which is 80 feet in width, but these are nearly 350 miles of unmetalled roads, having an average breadth of four feet.

The State is divided for administrative purposes into five *wizarats*, namely, Chamba, Churah, Pangi, Brahmaur, and Bhattiyat. The civil and criminal Courts of Justice are situated in the capital, but during the summer months the Raja sends all or any of the judges and magistrates to hear suits and try cases in the several districts, which are allowed to accumulate until the days fixed for hearing. The Indian Penal Code and the codes of Civil and Criminal Procedure are in force in the State.

There are not any Imperial Service troops in Chamba, but the State maintains an army of about 300 men, who are most satisfactorily housed in three sets of barracks. His Highness evinces the greatest interest in the discipline as well as the welfare of the troops, who are recruited principally from Rathis, Rajputs, and Brahmans. The State does not possess any artillery, but there is a small cavalry regiment, whose duties consist chiefly in acting as bodyguard to the Chief.

The literary tastes of His Highness and his insistence upon the necessity for the acquisition of learning have been abundantly exemplified by his readiness to erect suitable schools, by seeing that they are staffed by trained teachers of recognized ability, and

THE STATE OF CHAMBA.

1. Shooting Box, Mangli. 2. The Sach Pass (14,300 feet). 3. Kilar, Pangi. 4. Pangwalas in the Fields. 5. Encamping Ground, Dharwas. 6. The Ibex Ground.

THE STATE OF CHAMBA.

1. KHAJIAR. 2. CHURAH LADIES. 3. THE JHOOLA BRIDGE. 4. TISSA, CHAMBA STATE. 5. DANCE BY CHURAH WOMEN.

by having them equipped with modern aids to teaching. One of the most satisfactory features of educational work in Chamba is the existence of a considerable number of schools set apart for instruction being given to girls, for whom the curriculum now includes sewing, knitting, and embroidery work. There are two English schools for boys at Chamba, and the State girls' school is held in the Rang Mahal.

The State Medical Department was established in the year 1866, when a hospital was opened under Dr. Elmslie, of the Kashmir Medical Mission, in connection with the Chamba State. The chief medical institution in the capital at the present time is the "Sham Singh" Hospital, which was built in 1891, and in addition to an out-patient department there is accommodation for 40 in-patients.

The building has a first-class equipment of up-to-date surgical instruments and scientific appliances. The staff consists of the State surgeon, assistant surgeons, dressers, compounders, and ordinary servants.

There is also a dispensary at Tisa, the headquarters of the Churah *wizarat*, opened in 1881, which is in charge of a qualified hospital assistant. The State also maintains a leper asylum, which was inaugurated by the Mission to lepers in 1876, and was taken over by the State in 1881. The Durbar is indebted to the Church of Scotland Mission in Chamba, which organizes extensive medical missionary tours annually throughout the State, which have been of incalculable benefit to persons resident in outlying portions of the territory.

Chamba, the capital, and the only town in the principality, is picturesquely situated on a plateau on the right bank of the River Ravi, near its junction with the Saho. It is 50 miles distant from Shahpur, 18 miles from the hill sanatorium of Dalhousie, and 70 miles (*via* Dalhousie) from Pathankot, the nearest station, which is on the North-Western Railway Company's system. The city presents an exceedingly pretty picture to the traveller, as it is built on two elevated terraces, the palace of His Highness the Raja being conspicuous on the upper one, and the *chaugan*, or public promenade, as well as the State Departmental offices being the chief features of the lower one. The fine bungalow at the southern end of the *chaugan* was constructed for the use of Political Officials who resided there—when it was known as the Residency—during the years of British control between 1863–85, but it now serves the purposes of a guest-house.

The palace of His Highness is arranged in two blocks, the northern portion containing the Durbar halls and private apartments of the Chief. The greater part of the present building was constructed by the late Raja, but a wing in the north-west corner has been standing since the *regime* of Raja Ummed Singh (1748–64). The residence, beautifully furnished in European style, usually occupied by the present Raja, abuts upon the southern walls of the palace just referred to. The chief buildings in the city are the Rang Mahal, or old palace, the "Sham Singh" Hospital, the "Bhuri Singh" Museum, the dwelling-houses of a considerable number of inhabitants of high caste, and the club.

THE STATE OF CHARKHARI

THIS State in Central India, in the direct charge of the Bundelkhand Political Agency, is about 879 square miles in extent.

The Rulers of the State are connected by descent with a noted family of Bundela Rajputs, who gained considerable popularity early in the thirteenth century.

It appears that the great Chhatarsal, who was the Ruler of the State of Panna about the year 1732, divided his territories into several portions, one of which fell to his second son, Jagat Raj. In 1764 Pahar Singh, a son of Jagat Raj, acquired control over the whole area, and in 1764 he assigned the Charkhari portion to his nephew, Khuman Singh, who was thereupon installed as Chief. Difficulties arose a few years later owing to disputes with the Rulers of other States, but Bijai Bahadur, the occupant of the *gadi* in 1804, submitted to the authority of the British Government and was confirmed in his possession of the Charkhari Principality. Ratan Singh was Chief during the time of the Sepoy Mutiny, and in recognition of his sterling loyalty to the British, the Government bestowed upon him a grant of land in perpetuity, and an hereditary salute of 11 guns.

The next Ruler, Jai Singh Deo, held the reins of office for a period of six years (1874–80), and the powers with which he had been invested were withdrawn owing to his incapacity to carry out his duties. Malkhan Singh, a minor, was adopted as his successor, and the administrative work of the State was admirably performed by the young Prince's father, Diwan Jujhar Singh Ju Deo, C.I.E. His Highness the Maharaja was honoured in 1902 by having conferred upon him the insignia of a Knight Commander of the Most Eminent Order of the Indian Empire. He died without issue in 1908 and was succeeded by his father, to whom reference has already been made.

Maharaja Jujhar Singh Ju Deo was created a Companion of the Indian Empire in 1895, and in 1911 His Imperial Majesty the King-Emperor raised him to the dignity of a Knight-Commander of the same order. He died in 1914 and was succeeded by his younger brother, Rao Bahadur Diwan Ganga Singh Ju Deo, with his title as His Highness Maharajadhiraja Sipahdar-ul-Mulk Ganga Singh Ju Deo Bahadur.

His Highness is an exceptionally capable head of the State, and not only during the lifetime of his predecessor but also since he ascended the *gadi*, he has successfully carried through a large number of reforms in every Department of the State. The Maharaja was created a Commander of the Indian Empire in 1895 and in 1911 His Imperial Majesty the King-Emperor raised him to the dignity of a Knight-Commander of the same Order. He died in 1914.

The census of 1911 showed that there were about 132,500 persons in the State, and that more than 90 per cent. of these were Hindus.

The practice of agriculture, the chief industry in the State, is carried on with a varying measure of success owing to the irregularity of rainfall. The average annual area under cultivation is about 160,000 acres, the chief crops being *jowar*, cotton, wheat, *gram*, *til*, linseed, and a mixture of barley and *gram*.

There is an Imperial post and telegraph office at Charkhari (usually referred to as Maharajnagar), the capital town, and the State has its own head and branch post offices in various parts of the territory.

All State letters are carried free, the stamps bearing an emblem of two crossed swords as well as having the words "Charkhari State" printed thereon.

Medical relief is granted in the State hospital and dispensary at the chief town, the medical officer attending annually to nearly 9,000 and 120 outdoor and indoor patients respectively. Medicines and other necessities are obtained from a first-class London house through the office of the Bundelkhand Agency surgeon, who pays periodical visits to the State hospital

Education is imparted in the High School, at Maharajnagar, which is affiliated to the Allahabad University up to the matriculation examination; in a school for cadets; in one school for girls; and in six Hindi vernacular schools in the villages of Jujharnagar, Chandla, Mahewa, Isanagar, Riwai, and Barauli. There is also an Arts school, situated in Rayanpur, in which boys are trained in knitting carpets, *puggarees*, and other articles, and in making muslin embroidery.

The State is divided into five *tahsils*, namely, Malkhanpur, comprising 87 villages; Satwara, 92 villages; Balrampur, 42 villages; Isanagar, 59 villages; and Ranipur Maira, 26 villages.

A few diamond mines, some of which are worked by the State, are found in the *tahsil* of Ranipur Maira.

The civil and criminal codes in force in British territory are, with slight modifications, followed in the Judicial Courts of the State. Sentences of transportation or of death must be confirmed by the Agent of the Governor-General.

Charkhari, or Maharajnagar, is a picturesque little town of about 10,000 inhabitants, situated about nine miles distant from Mahoba, a station on the Jhansi-Manikpur section of the Great Indian Peninsula Railway.

The annual revenue of the State amounts to about Rs. 6,00,000.

1. MAHARAJA DHIRAJA SIPAHDAR-UL-MULK GANGA SINGH, JU DEO BAHADUR, THE LATE CHIEF.
2. MAHARAJA DHIRAJA SIPAHDAR-UL-MULK ARMARDAN SINGH, JU DEO BAHADUR, THE PRESENT CHIEF.
3. RAO BHAU PRATAP SINGH JU DEO BAHADUR, REGENT, COUNCIL OF REGENCY.

THE STATE OF CHHATARPUR

THE State of Chhatarpur, in the Bundelkhand Political Agency of Central India, having its own laws, police, and military forces, is bounded on the north by the Charkhari State and the district of Hamirpur in the United Provinces; on the east by the Charkhari, Ajaigarh and Panna States, and the River Ken; on the south by the Panna and Bijawar States; and on the west by the Bijawar and Charkhari States. It has a total area of 1,130 square miles, and its extreme length from north to south is about 60 miles, while its greatest breadth is 45 miles. The State consists almost entirely of a level plain at an elevation of about 600 feet, although in the Deora *pergana* there are hills connected with the Vindhya range which are 1,600 feet above the level of the sea. The principal river is the Ken, which flows for several miles along the eastern border of the State and gives birth to a considerable number of rivulets along its course, while its tributaries, the Urmal and Katne, are flowing streams during the greater portion of the year. The nearest railway stations to Chhatarpur, the principal town, are Harpalpur and Mahoba, on the Jhansi-Manikpur section of the Great Indian Peninsula Railway, each of which is 34 miles distant from the town of Chhatarpur.

The principal exports of the State are *glue, til*, betel leaves, country soap, shellac, brass-ware, mahua leaves, fruit, and gum, while imports include piece-goods, metals, groceries, salt, sugar, tobacco, kerosine oil, hardware, and rice.

The State comprises 323 villages divided into four *tahsils*, namely, Chhatarpur, Rajnagar, Laundi, and Deora, but there are two outlying villages, Ramgarh and Phutera, which are respectively under the *tahsildars* of Chhatarpur and Deora. The total revenue from land, forests, excise, and other sources amounts to about Rs. 5,50,000 annually.

Forests cover a total area of about 86,000 acres, and they are in charge of a competent officer who is assisted by about eighty rangers and guards. Deposits of iron ore and other minerals are found in the State, and it is believed that diamonds and other precious stones may be discovered, but until a thorough geological survey has been made the wealth of these resources cannot be estimated.

The greatest credit is due to the Maharaja and the Officials of the State for the vigorous methods adopted for bringing the educational system into a condition of efficiency. Instruction is practically free, and is partially compulsory, although a small cess is levied upon the people. The total number of scholars is about 1,900, equivalent to 7·33 per cent. of those within the school-going age limit.

The inhabitants in the State are about 1,79,940 in number, and the most important castes are Chamars, Brahmans, and Kachhis, who collectively represent nearly 40 per cent. of the total population.

Chhatarpur was a portion of the Panna State until the time of Maharaja Hindupati, who nominated his second son as his successor to the exclusion of his eldest son Sarnet Singh, who thereupon retired to his *jagir*, the *pergana* of Laundi. After the death of the last-named Prince in the year 1785, Kunwar Sone Shah, a relative, entered into possession of the *jagir*, and defeated the forces of Panna and considerably enlarged his boundaries by military successes. In 1806 he was confirmed in his possessions by the British Government. Raja Pratap Singh Bahadur, the eldest son of Sone Shah, succeeded on the death of the latter in 1816, and in the following year he was duly recognized by a *sanad*. Pratap Singh died without issue, and the State was escheated to the British Government, but his adopted son Jagat Raj was confirmed in succession in 1854 in consideration of the staunch loyalty of the family. From 1854 to 1863 the State was administered by Pratap Singh's second Rani, while it was under British control from 1863 to 1867, when Jagat Raj attained the age of 21 years and was given powers of administration. He, however, died within five months leaving an infant child, the present Chief, the Maharaja Vishwanath Singh Bahadur, who was born on August 29, 1866. The young Prince was educated at the Rajkumar College, Nowgong, and subsequently was placed under the tutorship of Mr. (afterwards Sir) Theodore Morison. The State came under British superintendence in 1867, and continued so until 1887 when the young Ruler was endowed with full powers. His Highness was married in 1883 to the daughter of His Highness the Maharaja Sir Pratap Singh Bahadur, G.C.S.I., G.C.I.E., of Orchha but there is no issue of the marriage. The Maharaja is a thoroughly enlightened Chief, possessing great scholarly attainments and he is so strongly convinced that education is one of the main foundations of prosperity that he has made this question one of the leading features in his administration. His Highness is a progressive Ruler, ceaselessly inaugurating schemes for the material benefit of the State and its people, and his personal efforts, ably supported by his Minister, have been attended with most satisfactory results. He holds the hereditary titles of His Highness and Raja Bahadur

THE STATE OF CHHATARPUR.

1. Front View of the Palace. 2. Interior of the Durbar Hall. 3. The Guest House. 4. Interior of the Guest House. 5. Khandaria Mahadeva's Temple.

and the personal one of Maharaja, while he is entitled to a salute of 11 guns.

The Coronation Durbar held at Delhi in December 1911 will ever be remembered by His Highness as a day upon which he had the honour of being received in audience by His Majesty the King-Emperor.

The Maharaja arrived by special train at the Kingsway station at Delhi with a following of about 300 persons, including their Highnesses the Maharani and the Dowager Maharani, the Diwan and other Officials of the State and was received by two European military officers on behalf of the Government of India. His Highness took part in the Royal procession preceding the Durbar, which was attended by the Maharaja and 16 of his followers, while their Highnesses the Maharani and Dowager Maharani had the honour of a special *purdah* interview with Her Most Gracious Majesty the Queen-Empress. The Maharaja was decorated with a gold medal on this occasion, while silver medals were presented to several of his officials.

The exceedingly attractive scenery in practically every portion of Chhatarpur renders it the most beautiful State in the Bundelkhand Agency, and in this connection Satdhara and Jatashanker in the Deora *pergana*, and the Ken waterfall at Raneh 33 miles from the town of Chhatarpur are especially worthy of notice.

THE PALACE GARDENS.

THE STATE OF FARIDKOT

FARIDKOT, one of the Sikh States in the Bahawalpur Political Agency under the superintendence of the Government of the Punjab, is practically surrounded by the State of Ferozepore, with the exception of a strip of land on its southern border which abuts upon the native State of Patiala.

The ruling family of Faridkot was founded during the reign of the Emperor Akbar by a Chief named Shalan (ruling over territory including the present State of Faridkot), who belonged to the Brar clan of Rajputs, and was descended from the famous Ruler, Dul, son of Brar, whose younger brother, Paor, founded the Phulkian Houses of Jind, Patiala and Nabha. They are known as Brar Jat Sikhs, although they were originally Rajputs of Jaisalmer.

Chaudhri Kapura, eleventh in descent from Dul, built the town of Kotkapura and made it his capital, but his grandson, Sardar Hamir Singh, transferred the seat of government of Faridkot.

In the year 1809, when Sardar Gulab Singh, great-grandson of Sardar Hamir Singh, was Chief, the Maharaja Ranjit Singh of Lahore threw the whole weight of his army against the fort of Faridkot, and eventually succeeded in capturing it; but this action appeared to the British Government to be so unjust that they intervened and compelled its restoration.

There were numerous family quarrels on the question of succession after the death of Gulab Singh, and in 1827 the British authorities recognized the claim of his younger brother, Sardar Pahar Singh. The new Chief, who was an exceedingly able Ruler, made such improvements in his possession that the annual revenue was considerably increased in value.

During the Sikh War of 1840 he threw in his lot with the British, and assisted them to the utmost of his resources by supplying means of transport, provisions and other necessaries for the army.

The title of Raja was conferred upon him in recognition of these services, and as further reward he was granted a considerable portion of confiscated territory, including the ancestral estate of Kotkapura and a number of villages lying on the southern side of Faridkot.

Upon his death in 1849 he was succeeded by his son Raja Wazir Singh, who followed in his father's footsteps by proving himself to be a most liberal-minded Ruler, and one who, in accordance with the traditions of his House, remained faithful to the British during the second Sikh War, as well as throughout the Sepoy Mutiny of 1857. In the latter cause he rendered conspicuous aid by guarding the ferries on the River Sutlej, thus preventing the crossing of rebels from one district to another. He gained further distinction by sending a squadron of cavalry and two guns against the notorious rebel, Sham Dass, whom he defeated with great loss and the destruction of his stronghold. In acknowledgment of the Raja's services he was given the honorary title of Barar Bans Raja Sahib Bahadur, and was accorded a salute of 11 guns.

HIS HIGHNESS RAJA HAR INDER SINGH, BAHADUR, BARAR-BANS, FARZAND-I-SAADAT-I-NISHAN-I-HAZRAT-I-KAISAR-I-HIND, CHIEF OF FARIDKOT.

HIS LATE HIGHNESS, MAJOR MAHARAJA BRIJ INDER SINGH, BAHADUR, BRAR BANS FARZAND-I-SAADAT-I-NISHAN-I-HAZRAT-I-KAISAR-I-HIND.

1. KANWAR MANJIT INDER SINGH, BAHADUR. 2. GROUP OF STATE OFFICIALS.

THE STATE OF FARIDKOT.

1. The Mubarak Mahal Palace. 2. The Raj Mahal Palace.

THE STATE OF FARIDKOT.
THE ELEPHANT "MOTI."

After a reign marked by the inauguration of many measures of reform, he died in 1875, and was succeeded by his son, Raja Bikram Singh, a highly-educated Chief, conversant with many languages, and an enlightened and capable Ruler. It is recorded that he obtained the assistance of British officials with the view of raising the standard of administration, he undertook fixed settlement of land, and he erected a number of Sikh temples in addition to several handsome buildings in Faridkot. During the second Afghan War he furnished a contingent of 250 horse and foot soldiers, and as a reward for his loyalty and the progressive nature of his Rulership he was honoured by the British Government with the bestowal of the hereditary titles of Farzand-i-Saadat Nishan-i-Hazrat Kaisar-i-Hind Barar Bans.

Upon his death in 1898 he was succeeded by his elder son Raja Balbir Singh, who died after a most promising but unfortunately short reign of only eight years' duration. Shortly after the Raja's accession to the *gadi* the terrible famine of 1899 occurred, and this event, which caused such widespread mortality and desolation in Northern and Western India, revealed the deeply sympathetic nature of His Highness, who gave liberally of his own personal resources, as well as those of the State, in order to administer relief to the stricken people. He started works of a public character, and paid generously for all labour performed, and he further procured food-grain from other districts and sold it at a reduced price. The Raja had inherited natural ability to rule, and although he safeguarded the dignity of his position he administered the State in such a manner that his subjects might have an opportunity of raising themselves from the desperate condition into which the famine had brought them. His Highness erected a number of important buildings at Faridkot, such as cantonments for his company of sappers, a clock tower as a memorial to Her Majesty the late Queen-Empress Victoria, and the Raj Mahal Palace, while he offered the services of his Imperial sappers for employment with the Tibet Mission in 1904. He died in 1906 without leaving direct issue, but during his lifetime he had adopted his nephew the late Chief, His Highness Farzand-i-Saadat Nishan-i-Hazrat Kaisar-i-Hind Barar Bans, Major Maharaja Brij Indar Singh Sahib Bahadur, who was born on October 26, 1896.

The administration of the State was placed in the hands of a Council of Regency under the Presidency of Sardar Bahadur Sardar Dayal Singh Man, who was connected with a well-known family of Sikh Chiefs. His Highness was sent for his educational career to the Aitchison College for sons of Punjab Chiefs at Lahore, where he greatly distinguished himself by the thorough manner in which he prosecuted his studies, by his subsequent success in winning the "Godley" medal for the best essay written by College students, and by his being the first Ruling Prince of the Punjab to pass the diploma examination in that institution.

After leaving Lahore His Highness commenced a course of systematic training in the duties of administration, his instructors being two highly-qualified members of the Punjab Civil Service who were specially selected for the purpose. He made such progress in this branch of learning that the highest hopes of him were entertained.

It subsequently became apparent that the administration of the State by the Regency Council was being hopelessly mismanaged, and in the year 1914 it was abolished in favour of the appointment of Rai Bahadur Ganga Sahai, M.A., as Superintendent of the State.

Since the change in management took place the Superintendent and his colleagues have been fortunate in having the full

THE STATE OF FARIDKOT.

1. The Fort Gate. 2. An Avenue in the Durbar Ganj Gardens.

THE STATE OF FARIDKOT.

1. The Durbar Ganj. 2. Sappers and Miners.

THE STATE OF FARIDKOT

sympathy of His Honour Sir Michael Francis O'Dwyer, K.C.S.I., the late Lieutenant-Governor of the Punjab, who on several occasions deputed competent officials of the Punjab Government to assist in the thorough reorganization of every State department.

Improvements and reforms were effected, abuses were eliminated, complicated points were settled, and the whole structure of administration was rebuilt on a sound foundation.

His Highness the Maharaja was married in 1912 to the daughter of Sardar Jiwan Singh of Shahzadpur, the nuptials being accompanied by grand ceremonials performed in the presence of the Lieutenant-Governor of the Punjab and other distinguished guests.

His Highness appointed, upon being invested with full ruling powers in November 1911, a Revenue Secretary, who was charged with the control of the following departments, namely, Judicial, Revenue, Police, Education, Medical, Financial, and State Farm and Gardens; and a House Secretary responsible for the departments dealing with Foreign and Political business, the Army, Stables, Guests, the Municipality, *Toshi Khana* (or Household Supplies) and Public Works; but His Highness exercised personal supervision over every branch of work.

It was a sad day, not only in the State but also in many parts of India, when it was announced that His Highness the Maharaja succumbed on December 23, 1918, to an attack of influenza, which he had borne with great patience and fortitude. He was an intelligent young Ruler of only 22 years of age, and had endeared himself to all who knew him, besides giving great hopes of being a worthy and capable administrator. There is no doubt that had his life been spared the State would have been greatly improved under his wise rulership, and the interests and happiness of his people would have been his first consideration. He left two sons, aged four and three respectively, the elder and successor, Harindar Singh, being at present under the guardianship of his mother, Her Highness the Maharani. The State is being administered during minority by the before-mentioned Superintendent under the supervision of the Government of the Punjab.

When the dark cloud of war stretched over a considerable portion of the whole world in 1914 His Highness the Maharaja placed all the resources of his State at the disposal of His Majesty's Government, and a contingent of 184 Imperial Service Sappers left Faridkot on October 10, 1914, in support of the Allies. Reinforcements were subsequently despatched on no fewer than 12 occasions, the additions being 260 in number, and the State also furnished 401 *Sarwans* and muleteers, together with 11 trained mule-drivers.

The Sappers rendered excellent service at the front, gaining the highest praise from their British officers for gallantry as well as discipline.

The men returned to Faridkot in February, 1918, with 29 decorations for distinguished conduct.

The contributions in money, materials, camels, mules, comforts for troops, and equipment forwarded by the Durbar from the commencement of the War to September 15, 1918, amounted in value to nearly Rs. 20,00,000, and among the items are: Rs. 50,000 to the Imperial Indian Relief Fund; Rs. 25,000 to His Royal Highness the Prince of Wales's Fund; Rs. 75,000 to the Punjab Aeroplane Fleet Fund; Rs. 10,000 to the St. John's Ambulance Red Cross Fund; Rs. 36,000, the purchase price of four motor ambulances; Rs. 40,000 for comforts of soldiers of the Mesopotamia Force; Rs. 6,17,500 cash invested in war loans; and Rs. 4,00,000 invested by officials of the State and private persons in post-office cash certificates, costing about Rs. 17,000; and 48 camels and 27 mules of the value of Rs. 14,000; in addition to a large quantity of clothing, books and other necessaries.

The Durbar gave every encouragement to men to enlist by offering a bonus of Rs. 50 to each man who joined the Faridkot Imperial Service Sappers Company; relief was granted from the State branch of the Imperial Indian Relief Fund (on the same scale as that adopted for men and their families in the Indian Army) in case of casualties and wounds; arrangements were made for the employment of pensioned or discharged wounded or invalided soldiers; civil suits commenced against sappers were postponed until their return to India; prompt assistance was given by State officials to distressed families of men at the front; and generous provision was made whereby all who had in any way suffered through the existence of the war might be placed beyond the reach of cares commonly attendant upon unemployment.

The State of Faridkot, 643 square miles in extent, is naturally divided into two distinct parts, but the fertility of the soil is of a comparatively low order excepting in those tracts which are irrigated from the Sirhind Canal. The climate is generally dry and healthy, and although the rainfall is so slight the land in many districts usually absorbs sufficient water for the cultivation of a number of crops usually grown in the Punjab, the principal ones being wheat, barley, *gram*, *jowar*, fodder crops, and maize.

The Durbar in 1911 established an experimental farm in the State for the purpose of improving the conditions of agriculture by sowing selected seed for valuable crops such as wheat, cotton, sugar-cane, and others which are suitable to the prevailing conditions. The farm is managed by a Superintendent (a graduate of the Lyallpur Agriculture College), who gives practical demonstrations to *Zemindars* on this important subject, and upon the use of modern types of agricultural machinery.

The estate is 119 acres in extent, 60 acres of which are reserved for growing crops and 59 acres for the cultivation of various kinds of fruit trees.

Civil and criminal justice is administered in several Courts in accordance with the enactments commonly in force in British India.

One may justly conclude that the instruction given in schools is of a very satisfactory kind when it is noticed that in 1913 the percentage of High School pupils who passed the University Matriculation Examination was 33, and that in 1916 no fewer than 93 per cent. of the entries were successful. The State has recently provided classes for the teaching of science, manual exercises, carpentry, and the use of metals. There are about 50 primary schools in the State, but the attendance is not very satisfactory, a condition which is attributed by the Director of Public Instruction to the indifference of the people, as "they prefer their boys to work on the land."

An annual sum of more than Rs. 30,000 is, however, being expended by the Durbar in this department, and as the status of teachers has been raised it is confidently expected that more favourable reports will soon be forthcoming.

THE STATE OF JANJIRA

THIS exceedingly pretty State, with a sea-coast some 40 miles in length and hill ranges or mountainous spurs running parallel with the litoral, is included in the Kolaba Political Agency of the Konkan on the western shores of the Bombay Presidency.

The Rulers of Janjira, who hold the title of Nawab, have sprung from an Abyssinian family of the Suni branch of Mahomedans, and the particulars of their early settlement in the State are so strange and yet so interesting that no apology is needed for relating the facts as given by so reliable an authority as the *Imperial Gazetteer.* "About the year 1489 an Abyssinian in the service of the Nizam Shahi Kings of Ahmednagar, disguised as a merchant, obtained permission from Ram Patel, the Koli Captain then holding the island, to convey from ships to the shore a consignment of 300 boxes. Each of these cases contained a soldier, and by this means the Abyssinians became possessed of the island of Janjira as well as the forts of Rajpuri."

The territory was at a later date subject to the kings of Bijapur, but when the Mahrattas attained greater power and were trying to take Janjira the Sidis (as the ruling race came to be described) in 1670 transferred their allegiance to Aurangzeb, the Moghul Emperor who conferred the title of Nawab upon the Chief. The history of Janjira is singular in this respect, namely, that the State was the only one in Western India which successfully resisted the repeated attacks of the Mahrattas. It was, on several occasions, assaulted by Sivaji, who had gone so far as to make it a point of honour to secure its conquest, but it remained unscathed, and even in 1683, when Sambhaji constructed a mole to connect it with the mainland and thus facilitate the movement of his army, its opposition was successful. Early in the eighteenth century the Peshwa marched against Janjira, but he was no more fortunate than previous invaders, and even when the Mahrattas were superseded in the Konkan by the British, the latter did not interfere with the internal affairs of the State.

Janjira was practically independent until 1868, when the maladministration of the Nawab Sidi Ibrahim Khan, especially with regard to police and criminal judicial matters, compelled the British to place those departments in charge of a Political Agent. On his death full powers were restored to his son, the present Nawab. His powers in revenue and civil matters are unlimited and also in criminal, except that British India subjects charged with capital offences committed in the State, cannot be tried without the previous sanction of the Political Agent.

The present Ruler, His Highness Sir Sidi Ahmad Khan Sidi Ibrahim Khan, K.C.I.E., G.C.I.E., succeeded to the *gadi* in 1879 and was invested with full ruling powers in 1883. The Prince was educated at the Rajkumar College, Rajkot, and his accomplishments are of a high character, including a good knowledge of the English, Marathi, Persian, Gujarati and Urdu tongues. Prior to taking over the responsibilities of his position as Nawab, His Highness was thoroughly grounded in the practical work of each State Department under the guidance of the Political Agent, and the steady social and material progress made under his administration is due to his intellectual abilities, and his deep sympathies with the legitimate aspirations of the inhabitants.

The theoretical knowledge of the principles of good government obtained by [illegible] in earlier years has proved to be an exc[illegible] foundation for the structure of practical [illegible] beneficial rule for which he has earn[illegible] justifiable reputation. Intensely fon[illegible] good literature, His Highness has [illegible] fested an earnest desire that his people and their children should enjoy facilities for the acquisition of learning, and his solicitude for the poor and suffering [illegible] led him to establish dispensaries at [illegible] suitable relief can be given. The Sup[illegible] Government was in 1895 pleased to recog[illegible] the admirable rule of His Highness by con-ferring upon him the distinction of a Kn[illegible] Commandership of the Most Eminent [illegible] of the Indian Empire; at a subseq[illegible] date his salute was increased from [illegible] guns to 11; and in 1900 he was cre[illegible] a Knight Grand Commander of the [illegible] Order. In January, 1918, the salute [illegible] raised to 13 guns personal for his war [illegible] vices, and in 1921 it was made perm[illegible] within the State.

In the year 1908 the Nawab and [illegible] Begum Sahiba proceeded to England [illegible] during their visit to London they had [illegible] honour of a private interview with [illegible] Majesty the late King-Emperor Edward [illegible] and they also enjoyed the hospitality [illegible] Lord Morley, Lord Lamington, a form[illegible] Governor of Bombay, and other distinguish[illegible] persons. After spending a short time [illegible] Paris, Switzerland and Vienna the pa[illegible] reached Constantinople. His Majesty [illegible] Sultan conferred upon His Highness [illegible] Nawab the Order of the first class of Osm[illegible] and the Order of Shafakat Nishan upon [illegible] Highness.

His Highness the Nawab Saheb has only one son, the heir-apparent, Sidi Mahomed. He is now in his seventh year, and has made considerable progress in Urdu.

HIS HIGHNESS SIR SIDI AHMAD KHAN, G.C.I.E., NAWAB SAHIB OF JANJIRA.

THE STATE OF JANJIRA.

1. Baksi Sahib Mohamed Khan (Heir-Apparent). 2. State Officers. 3. His Highness's Palace. 4. The Palace from the Hill.

THE STATE OF JANJIRA.

1. The Palace from the Hill. 2. Durbar Hall, Janjira. 3. Guest House, Janjira. 4. The Garmbi Waterworks.

THE STATE OF JANJIRA.

1. The Rajpuri Jumma Mosque. 2. Kairat Khan Magbira, Khokari. 3. Yakoot Khan Magbira, Khokari. 4. Soorul Khan Magbira, Khokari.

THE STATE OF JANJIRA.

1. Janjira Fort from Rajpuri. 2. Janjira Fort Looking West. 3. View of Mhasla Creek from Khokari. 4. The Fort from Janjira. 5. The Cannon, "Kalalbangdi," Janjira Fort.

The State of Janjira, having an area of 324 square miles, is bounded on the north by the Kundalika or Roha creek in the district of Kolaba, on the east by the Roha and Mangaon *talukas* of the same district, on the south by the Bankot creek in the district of Ratnagiri, and on the west by the Arabian sea. Some historians give to Janjira the name of " Habsan," or " African's land," but it is generally believed that Janjira is a corruption of the Arabic word " jazira," signifying " an island." Situated about half-way between the northern and southern extreme points of the coast-line is the Rajpuri Gulf, which divides Janjira into two almost equal portions. The surface of the State is covered with spurs and ranges of hills averaging 1,000 feet in height, and the majority of these fringe the numerous arms of the sea, while the sides of the hills are thickly wooded excepting where pasture or cultivated lands may be seen. Fine palm groves nearly two miles in breadth adorn the mouths of the creeks, behind them are salt marshes and bushes of mangroves, and still further inland are the fertile rice fields of the valleys.

The principal creeks and backwaters in the State are: Mandla-Borlai, Nandgaon, Murad, Rajpuri, Panchaitan, and Srivardhan, and with the exception of Rajpuri the entrances to these inlets are dangerous owing to the presence of rocks or shoals. During the rainy season, however, vessels of not more than a ton and a half burden can sail for a considerable distance up the streams, although the latter do not exceed six miles in length.

The inhabitants of the State are about 89,000 in number, of whom 82 per cent. are Hindus, and 17 per cent. are Mahomedans while the chief castes are Agris, Kolis, Kunbis, Mahars, Brahmans and Prabhus. The Kataris and other hill tribes make their homes in the forests.

With the exception of the fertile land on the plains upon which rice is largely cultivated, and a number of sandy tracts near the sea-coast, the soil consists of the red, stony type which is common to the greater portion of the Konkan territory. The area under cultivation is about 45 square miles in extent, and the principal crops are rice, coco-nuts and betel-nuts. The luxuriant plantations of nuts fringing the sea-shore are of great economic value to the State, and an excellent market is found for them in the city of Bombay.

The valuable forests of the State were about 15 years ago brought under a regular system of control, such as is adopted in British Indian districts, and the whole area is now rigidly protected under the supervision of qualified officials. The trees include teak (which is plentiful), *sal*, *sisu*, and bamboo.

The general administration of the State is carried on by the Diwan, under the orders of His Highness the Nawab. The Judicial Department has been well organized.

Janjira, the capital of the State, 44 miles distant from Bombay, presents a most charming appearance from the sea with its comfortable-looking dwelling-houses occupied by well-to-do traders and fishermen, and its walls rising abruptly to a height of 50 feet surmounted by battlements and loopholes and ten guns fixed on the bastions. The seat of government has now been removed to Murud, a small town on the coast. The fringe of palm trees extending about a mile and a half along the coast gives a very picturesque appearance. Behind it can be seen the roofs of Government and private buildings. The palace of the Nawab is situated on a small spur to the north-west of the town.

About two miles to the west of the fort is the Nanwell headland, upon which there stands a lighthouse, 150 feet in height, exhibiting a dioptric light as a warning against the dangerous sunken reef known as the " Chorkassa."

JAFARABAD

THIS small State, 53 square miles in extent, in the Kathiawar Political Agency, is a dependency of the Nawabs of Janjira.

When the Moghul power was waning in Kathiawar early in the eighteenth century, Jafarabad was practically independent under the rule of its *Thanadars*, but when the latter, assisted by the Mahomedan garrison and local tribes, entered upon a course of piracy seriously affecting the shipping trade of Surat, Sidi Hilal of the House of Janjira (then residing at Surat) attacked the plunderers, destroyed their ships and imprisoned a number of the crews. Sidi Hilal imposed a heavy fine upon the *Thanadars*, but as they were unable to pay the amount, they sold the territory to him. Owing to continued anarchy Sidi Hilal was unable to retain and protect the State, and he therefore in 1762 transferred it to the then Nawab of Janjira.

THE STATE OF JHABUA

THE State of Jhabua, with an area of 1,336 square miles, is one of the group of States known as the Southern States of Central India, and lies between latitude 22°28 and 23°14 north and longitude 74°20 and 75°19 east. It is situated in the mountainous region of Malwa Plateau known as Rath, and is bounded on the north by the Kushalgarh State of Rajputana Agency and the State of Sailana ; on the east by the States of Dhar and Gwalior ; on the south by the States of Ali-Rajpur, Jobat and Dhar, and on the west by the Panch Mahals district of the Bombay Presidency. The climate throughout the State is subject to greater extremes than are generally met with in the more open land of the Malwa Plateau.

The State is very largely comprised of hilly and forest-clad tracts containing valuable timber trees, such as teak and blackwood, and series of thick-jungled ridges generally run from north and south, along which flow several streams to join the Anas, a tributary of the Mahi. The population of the State, according to the census of 1921, is 123,932 souls, to which number the Bhils contribute very largely. As is characteristic of India as a whole, a very large majority live by agriculture, employing implements of a venerable antiquity. Generally speaking, the soil is of moderate fertility, though patches of rich lands are met with in the valleys with an average rainfall of 30 inches. The State produces rice, poppy, cotton, wheat, barley, maize (Macca) being the principal crop.

The Rulers of Jhabua are Rathor Rajputs, being descended from Bir Singh, fifth son of Jodh Singh, commonly known as Jodha, the founder of the principal Rathor State of Jodhpur in Rajputana. Bir Singh was granted Riya in fief, where he died in 1495, and was succeeded by his son Suyaji (1495–1522), who received Bhinai, in the Ajmer district, in 1497. After Jaswant Singh (1522–48), and Ram Singh (1548–67), Bhimanji came to the *gadi* in 1567. Bhimanji distinguished himself in several of Akbar's campaigns, and in recognition of his meritorious services and splendid gallantry, received 52 districts in Malwa from the Emperor ; on the death of Bhimanji Kesho Das, the founder of the State, succeeded him in 1584.

Kesho Das, who in 1572 had been attached to the staff of Prince Salim, won his spurs in the Bengal campaign of 1584. On Salim's accession to the throne, Kesho Das was entrusted with the difficult task of subduing the organized plundering bands under Jhabbu Naik, Thana Naik, and Lakha Naik, who infested the south-western districts of Malwa, and had brutally murdered the son of the Guzerat Governor. Kesho Das was wholly successful and came into possession of their territory, which included Jhabua, Thandla, Bhagore, and Ramgarh, and the Emperor, in appreciation of his services, invested him with the insignia of Royalty in 1607. Kesho Das, however, did not long survive to enjoy his glories and honours, but died the same year, being poisoned by his son and successor, Karan Singh. This dastardly patricide threw the whole State into confusion, and in general terms it may be said that disturbances continued with more or less virulence throughout the whole of the seventeenth century.

In the twenties of the next century the Marathas began to invade the country, and Jhabua experienced the most critical times in its history under their ambitious aggressions. After several vicissitudes of fortune, the dawn of a more peaceful and promising era was ushered when the Settlement of Malwa was entrusted to Sir John Malcolm.

After Kesho Das, Karan Singh (1607–10), Mah Singh (1610–77), Kushal Singh (1677–1723), Anup Singh (1723–27), Sheo Singh (1727–58), Bahadur Singh (1758–70), Bhim Singh (1770–1829), Pratap Singh (1829–32), Ratan Singh (1832–40), came to the *gadi.* Raja Gopal Singh, who came to the *gadi* in 1840, though only 17 years of age, rendered good assistance to the British Government during the Sepoy Mutiny, and in spite of the demand for their surrender, made by the local Arab faction, afforded protection to the fugitives from Bhopawar in his own palace. In recognition of his services he was presented with a *khilat* of Rs. 12,500, and the State contribution towards the maintenance of the Malwa Bhil corps was considerably reduced. In a *kharita* His Excellency the Viceroy and Governor-General, Lord Canning, acknowledged the good services rendered by the State, which are always gratefully remembered by the Government of India. Raja Gopal Singh died in 1895, and was succeeded by his adopted son, the present ruler, His Highness Raja Udai Singh Bahadur, who was invested with full powers in 1898. The State enjoys a salute of 11 guns, and the Ruler is a Member of the Chamber of Princes, and is entitled to be received in a separate Durbar by His Excellency the Viceroy and Governor-General of India. His Highness

1. H.H. THE LATE RAJA GOPAL SINGHJI SAHIB BAHADUR, OF JHABUA.
2. HIS HIGHNESS RAJA UDAISINHJI, SAHIB BAHADUR, OF JHABUA.
3. HIS HIGHNESS RAJA UDAISINHJI ON HORSEBACK.

THE STATE OF JHABUA.

1. Deodi Palace, and portion of another Palace under Construction. 2. The Palace from a Hillock. 3. The Palace from the State Guest House. 4. Durbar and Huzar Offices, Jhabua.

THE STATE OF JHABUA.

1. Pili Kothi. 2. State Temple of Govardhan Nathji. 3. Jain Temple, Jhabua. 4. Victoria Memorial Hospital, Jhabua. 5. Jhabua Town. 6. Market in Jhabua.

was invited, and attended, the Grand Durbar held by His Royal Highness the Prince of Wales (now H.M. the King-Emperor) at Indore in 1905.

During the reign of the present ruler much improvement has taken place. Revenue has considerably increased; regular Courts of Justice administering British India law, except when it is modified by special circulars, have been opened; hospitals, schools, roads, bridges and inns have been constructed. A decennial land revenue settlement has been effected, and Excise administration is based on the Madras system, which has proved highly beneficial to the State. Municipal and Panchayet Boards have been established throughout the State to vigilantly look into matters of public health and convenience, and Customs rules and tariffs have been prepared in the interest of the public, and this will afford facilities for trade to flourish.

For purposes of Revenue administration the State is divided into four *tahsils*, viz., Jhabua, Ranapur, Thandla and Rambhapur, each being under a *tahsildar*, while first-class Magistrate and District and Sessions Judges have their Courts in the capital.

Land revenue is paid in cash through the *tahsildars* to the Treasury. Nearly 70 per cent. of the cultivated area is held in *jagir* by Umraos, who number eighteen, and pay tribute to the State as a mark of the subordination.

Jhabua enjoys the advantage of having within its borders the railway stations of Nahargarh, Meghnagar, Udaigarh, Bajrangarh, Amargarh and Bhairongarh, all of which are on the Rutlam-Godhra branch of the Bombay, Baroda and Central India system. British Post Offices have been opened at several places in the State, whilst there is a telegraph office at Jhabua. The official language is Hindi, in which all State records are kept.

The State and its people remained devoted and loyal to the Supreme Government during the world-wide European War of 1914–18, and contributed in different ways. Recruits and horses were also supplied.

THE STATE OF JHALAWAR

JHALAWAR is a State in the Kotah-Jhalawar Political Agency of Rajputana, and has an area of 808 square miles and a population of 96,198 persons. It consists of two detached parts, the main one being bounded on the north, north-east, and north-west by the State of Kotah; on the east by the Indore and Gwalior States; on the south by the State of Dewas; and on the west by the States of Sitamau and Gwalior; while the second portion, a very small tract known as Kirpapur, lies between the outlying districts of Gwalior and Mewar.

The Ruling family belong to the Jhala clan of Rajputs, but the existence of the State as a separate Principality is of comparatively recent origin.

The greater portion of the State consists of an undulating plain of productive soil, but in the southern and south-western districts there are a number of small ranges of hills from which flow several streams of water, while the principal crops are wheat, cotton, maize, oil-seeds, and *jowar*. The chief exports, according to statistics published in the State, are grain, cotton, hides, oil-seeds, *ghee*, oil, and opium; and the imports include grains (including rice), groceries, *gur*, tobacco, oil-seeds, *ghee*, iron, cloth, and metals. Manufacturing and industrial enterprises are not of great importance, those chiefly engaged in being the making of utensils of brass and other metals, cotton goods, knives, and other articles of household requirements. Prisoners in the Central Jail manufacture very fine carpets, rugs, shikari cloth, and also work a printing press.

The State is now working a flour mill at Jhalrapatan, and it is anticipated that it will soon be patronized by the general public to a far greater extent than at present. The machinery, which is of modern manufacture, is driven by a 20 h.p. crude oil-engine, and it is capable of grinding wheat at the rate of four *maunds* an hour.

The majority of the people devote a considerable portion of their time to work upon the land, and His Highness the Maharaj Rana has evinced his practical interest in the development of the science of agriculture and boring wells by appointing a diplomaed student of the Agricultural College, Lyalpur, to conduct experiments and give practical demonstrations in farming for the benefit of the ryots. He has, further, arranged for the holding of an annual agri-horticultural exhibition, at which prizes are awarded for the encouragement of his subjects in the cultivation of a greater number of varieties, and better qualities of cereals, fruits, and flowers. Another diplomaed student (a graduate of the State, trained at Allahabad) has been placed in charge of a newly-started poultry farm.

The following is a list of the different kinds of livestock in the State: bullocks, 18,101; cows, 68,360; buffaloes, 21,000; mares, 1,250; colts and fillies, 650; asses, 930; and goats and sheep, 26,140. The total forest area is about 4,230 acres in extent, and although an abundance of firewood is produced there are comparatively few timber trees of importance.

The mining department has recently issued a report upon the mineral resources of the State, and it is stated therein that copper ore is found near Chhaoni; laterite, containing large quantities of alumina, suitable for the manufacture of aluminium and its salts, is obtainable in immense quantities in several *tahsils*; dolomite clay, strongly impregnated with magnesium, pottery clay, and bauxite may be recovered in the north-western parts of Jhalawar; limestone for the manufacture of Portland and hydraulic lime; quartz in a very pure state for the making of glass; agate which can be converted into mortars and fancy articles; and sandstone of the first quality are abundant near Chhaoni. Negotiations regarding prospecting work in copper and aluminium deposits have been concluded with a Bombay firm, and profitable results are anticipated.

About five miles distant from Jhalrapatan are the celebrated Chandrawati ruins with their characteristic massive pillars with deeply-engraved carvings, which evidently belong to about the seventh century.

A considerable variety of large and small game is found in Jhalawar, and excellent sport is provided on State and other occasions. The list includes: tigers, which are occasionally met with in forests near Jhalrapatan; leopards and wild pig are fairly common in all districts; sambhur, chital, and nilghai frequent a few suitable localities in limited numbers, and antelope and ravine deer are found on the plains.

The main portion of the State is divided for revenue purposes into six *tahsils*, and the isolated tract of Kirpapur is under the supervision of a manager who has certain executive powers vested in him. *Tahsildar*

H.H. THE MAHARAJ RANA SIR BHAWANI SINGH BAHADUR, K.C.S.I.

THE STATE OF JHALAWAR.

1. Maharaj Kumar Rajendra Singh Bahadur. 2. Members of the State Council. 3. Madan Vilas Palace. 4. Kemball Library.

THE STATE OF JHALAWAR.

1. Prithvi Vilas Palace. 2. Drawing-room, Prithvi Vilas Palace. 3. Library, Prithvi Vilas Palace. 4. The Garh Palace.

Courts of Justice can pass sentences of imprisonment up to one month's duration in criminal matters, and can deal with civil cases up to Rs. 100 in value; Magistrates' Courts have power to imprison for two years; the *Adalat Dewani* has jurisdiction in claims not exceeding Rs. 5,000; and the Appellate Court can pass any sentence allowed by law or try civil cases of the value of more than Rs. 5,000, but sentences of death must be confirmed by His Highness. The total length of metalled and fair-weather roads in Jhalawar is 64 miles and 77 miles respectively, and the State expends a considerable amount of money annually in the maintenance of these, in the construction of new means of communication, and in other public works of a general character. The Nagda-Muttra railway traverses the entire length of the State, and it has been of the utmost value in facilitating trading relationship with various places in India.

As an enthusiastic supporter of education, His Highness the Maharaj Rana is not excelled by any other Ruling Chief in India.

Instruction is quite free of cost to parents, and books, slates, and other necessaries are supplied *gratis* to pupils who cannot afford to pay for them. The Durbar High School at Jhalrapatan (the capital) is affiliated to the University of Allahabad, and the teaching staff comprises a trained graduate head master, six assistants, two science masters, and others. Excellent progress is being made with regard to education for females, which is given in six schools set apart for the purpose, and it may be added that needlework forms part of the curriculum in each of these. There are now 43 schools in the State, exclusive of two which are entirely supported by the State Temple at Patan. There are about 2,200 names of pupils on the rolls, and the average daily attendance reaches the excellent total of 1,625 scholars. A High School is shortly to be started at Patan, and a fine building for it is under construction. Another building is to be undertaken at Patan for a Girls' School.

The administration of the State is in the hands of His Highness, who is assisted by a Council of five members, which was formed in the year 1914, but a member for commerce has lately been added.

The gross annual revenue of the State, excluding *jagir* and *muafi* lands, based on the average of the past five years, is nearly Rs. 5,50,000, and a yearly tribute of Rs. 30,000 is paid to the Imperial Government.

His Highness the Maharaj Rana Sir Bhawani Singh Bahadur, K.C.S.I., was born on September 4, 1874, and was educated at the Mayo College, Ajmer, where he greatly distinguished himself equally as well in general athletics as he did in class-work. He was installed on the *gadi* on February 6, 1899, being at the same time invested with full powers of administration by Sir Arthur Martindale, then Agent to the Governor-General in Rajputana.

He had barely succeeded to the Chiefship, when he was confronted with one of those terrible famines which have on various occasions caused the death of many thousands of persons in India, but, young as he was, he faced difficulties boldly and manifested his deep sympathy with his subjects by starting relief works and by importing large quantities of grain foods for sale to the inhabitants at much lower prices than current market rates. His Highness also granted remissions of arrears of rents to *ryots* to the amount of Rs. 3,64,627.

"Progress" and "reform" have been watchwords with the Maharaj Rana throughout the whole of his career, and he has ceaselessly endeavoured to inaugurate or support measures for the development of the social and material welfare of his people.

As an illustration of this it may be said that His Highness has introduced into the Jhalawar State the adoption of Imperial Postal unity, British currency and weights, and the *Nagri* script in State Courts and departments; while he has remitted a number of petty *cesses* which were intolerable to his subjects.

His Highness is indefatigable in his efforts to promote the best interests of the State in agricultural, horticultural, and industrial enterprises, but he excels as an educationalist, he himself being a profound student rejoicing especially in standard works on science, State administration, education, and other kindred subjects. Apart from his private library, recognized as one of the finest in India, His Highness has established the "Kemball" library, which contains a very fine selection of volumes by famous writers.

The Maharaj Rana is conversant with the details of work in each department, and he constantly discusses matters of importance with his officials in order that just and wise decisions may tend to the advancement of the interests of the State.

His Highness is a member of the leading literary and scientific institutions of Great Britain, as well as of La Société d'Astronomique de France, and he is Vice-President of the Astronomical Society of India, the International Arbitration and Peace Association, and the National Indian Association.

In April, 1904, he left India for a tour of nine months in Europe, visiting London and other cities in England, as well as others on the Continent, and the experience gained by coming in contact with "men of light and leading" has been of the greatest assistance to him in his control of State affairs. He was received in audience by His late Majesty King Edward VII, and the cordiality then extended to him greatly strengthened that loyalty to the Throne which had previously been implanted within him. A second visit to England was undertaken in 1912, when one of His Highness' most cherished experiences was his reception by His Majesty the present King-Emperor, George V.

His Highness married the daughter of the Maharaja Durjan Salji of Kherli in the State of Kotah, and the heir apparent, Maharaj Kumar Rajendra Singh Bahadur, was born on July 15, 1900, and is now being educated at the Mayo College, Ajmer. The Maharaj Rana is entitled to a salute of 11 guns.

A few words may now be added concerning some memorable events which have occurred during the past two or three years in connection with the Jhalawar State.

The steady improvement made in the cause of education, mainly through the fostering care of His Highness, made the need of a hostel for students more and more keenly felt, and eventually a handsome building was erected at Jhalrapatan, the structure containing, in addition to reading, class, and other rooms, a number of dormitories, bedrooms, and baths, the majority of which are fitted with electric lights and fans, the power being obtained from the current generated at the palace. The building—named the "Parmanand" hostel—was opened on December 26, 1915, by a friend and guest of His Highness, namely, Mr. W. G. Howard Gritten, M.A. (Oxon.), Barrister-at-Law.

The intense interest of His Highness in the cause of education—particularly for the mothers of future generations—has

THE STATE OF JHALAWAR.

1. Colvin Girls' School. 2. Durbar High School. 3. Hospital (Chhaoni). 4. Temple.

THE STATE OF JHALAWAR.

1. Panoramic View of Jhalrapatan (Chhaoni). 2. Parmanand Hostel. 3. General View of Jhalrapatan City. 4. Chandravati. 5. Fort near Jhalrapatan.

already been noticed, and in 1910, when the number of girls attending the Chhaoni School had risen to about 100, it was felt that a much larger building of an improved character was essential. The Maharaj Rana selected a suitable site and suggested designs for the structure, which eventually cost no less than Rs. 33,000. The institution is double-storeyed, comprising 4 rooms 19 feet by 18 feet, and one large central hall with verandahs on two sides. The hall of the lower storey is 41 feet by 23 feet, and that of the upper storey is 30 feet by 23 feet, while there is ample accommodation for 300 girls.

The opening ceremony was performed on February 9, 1917, by the Hon. Sir Elliott Graham Colvin, K.C.S.I., Agent to the Governor - General in Rajputana.

Medical relief is free throughout the State, which has now seven hospitals. Under the philanthropic influence of His Highness, the rich bankers of Patan, Seth Binodi Ram Balchand, are building the " Balchand Hospital " for the benefit of the public.

Municipal Government on a limited scale has been granted to the towns Jhalrapatan and Chhaoni, and there are also district councils at the headquarters of each *tahsil*. The members consist of officials, bankers, merchants, and other persons of influence, and they concern themselves chiefly with general conservancy, lighting, and other kindred matters.

The capital of Jhalawar is divided between two towns, namely, Jhalrapatan City and Jhalrapatan Camp, commonly known by the name of Chhaoni, and situated at a distance of four miles from Jhalrapatan City. The former of these (the name Jhalrapatan signifying " city of bells ") is of ancient origin, but it is still a trading centre of considerable importance, and the latter was founded by Raj Rana Zalim Singh as a cantonment, but it has gradually grown into a large town.

The nearest railway-station is Shrichhatrapur, on the Bombay-Baroda-Delhi main line.

THE STATE OF MALER-KOTLA.

1. The Dak Bungalow, Maler-Kotla (adjoining Railway Station). 2. Bird's-eye View of the City from Top of Diwan Khana. 3. A Corner View of the Civil Hospital, Maler-Kotla City.

THE STATE OF MALER-KOTLA

MALER-KOTLA, a Mahomedan Pathan State, belonging to the group known as the Cis-Sutlej States, is attached to the Bahawalpur Political Agency, under the Government of the Punjab. Its Rulers are of Afghan descent, belonging to the Sherwani family. Their ancestor, Shaikh Sadr-ud-Din, travelled from Kabul to Delhi about the end of the fifteenth century, and he married a daughter of the then reigning Afghan Emperor of India, who granted to the bride as dowry a considerable portion of the old Province of Sirhind. Five generations later Maler-Kotla was ruled by Bayazid Khan, who in 1657 received from the Emperor Alamgir the title of Nawab. On the decline of the Moghul Empire, owing to the increasing power of the Mahrattas, Maler-Kotla, together with other States in the Punjab, obtained independence. About the year 1730 the ruling Nawab, Jamal Khan, assisted the Imperial forces against the Sikh Chief of Patiala, and some 30 years later he allied himself with the troops of Ahmad Shah Durrani, in opposition to several Sikh Rulers of the Punjab. This action on the part of the Nawab led to a serious quarrel between the Houses of Maler-Kotla and of several neighbouring Sikh States, but especially of Patiala. Nawab Bhikan Khan, the son of Jamal Khan, through whom the estrangement referred to was caused, was deprived of much of his power and a considerable portion of his territories during the numerous attacks of the Sikhs, and he was eventually compelled to enter into a treaty with them. Patiala and other Sikh States bordering upon Nabha became friendly to the latter, and, in fact, they loyally helped one another with troops whenever an occasion arose for repelling invaders. In 1787, for example, the Chief of Patiala assisted the Nawab of Maler-Kotla in regaining possession of certain villages which the Sardar of Bhadaur had unlawfully seized. Seven years later the State was invaded by Badi Sahib Sinh, who defeated the Nawab's army and besieged the capital, but when news of the disaster reached Patiala, the Ruler of that State hastened to the help of the Nawab, and forced the invader to cross the Sutlej, and to return to his own country. The Nawab threw in his lot with the British in the campaign conducted by General Lake against the Mahrattas, who had been in the ascendant for the previous 20 years.

The famous Maharaja Ranjit Singh, of Lahore, conquered Faridkot in 1808, and then, marching to Maler-Kotla he, in spite of a protest made by Mr. Metcalfe, British Envoy in the camp of the invader, demanded from the Nawab the sum of Rs. 1,55,000. This led to stern interference on the part of the British, who

MAJOR HIS HIGHNESS NAWAB SIR MOHAMMAD AHMAD ALI KHAN BAHADUR, K.C.S.I., RULER OF MALER-KOTLA, IN CIVIL DRESS.

MAJOR HIS HIGHNESS NAWAB SIR MOHAMMAD AHMAD ALI KHAN BAHADUR, K.C.S.I., RULER OF MALER-KOTLA, IN MILITARY UNIFORM.

THE STATE OF MALER-KOTLA.

1. Principal Officials of the State.

From left to right—Brig.-Gen. Mohamad Bakhsh Khan Bahadur (Diwan); Brig.-Gen. Sardar Mehr Mohamad Khan Bahadur (Officer Commanding State Forces); Khan Bahadur Syed Abdullah, B.A. (Foreign and Home Minister); Mirza Ijaz Husain, B.A. (Chief Judge).

Standing—Lala Ramji Dass, B.A., LL.B. (Judge, Chief Court); Lala Sawan Ram (Bakhshi); Syed Mohammad Husain (Private Secretary).

2. An A.D.C. to His Highness the Nawab (Captain Abdul Hamid). 3. Some of the Military Officers of the State Forces.

4. Types of State Forces (State Lancers, Horse Artillery, and I.S. Sappers). 5. The State Coach.

THE STATE OF MALER-KOTLA.

1. Moti Bazar, Maler-Kotla. 2. Ahmadganj Grain Market, Maler-Kotla City. 3. The Chowk Bazar, Maler-Kotla City
4. The Tal Katora Bazar, Maler-Kotla City. 5. Interior View of Ahmadgarh Town (Thirteen Miles North of Maler-Kotla City).

THE STATE OF MALER-KOTLA.

1. The Mubarik Manzil Palace (under Alterations). 2. A Corner of the Palace Gardens. 3. The Diwan Khana Palace in Qila Moalla, in the City. 4. The Guest-House. 5. Maler-Kotla Railway Station.

THE STATE OF MALER-KOTLA.

1. The Sarai and Dhabi Gate, Maler-Kotla City. 2. The Juma Masjid, Maler-Kotla City. 3. The Sikh Gurdawara, Maler-Kotla City. 4. The Hindu Jain Temple, Maler-Kotla City. 5. The Main Gate, Rahmatgarh Fort. 6. Delhi Gate.

THE STATE OF MALER-KOTLA

ordered troops to be despatched under the command of Col. Ochterlony, for the purpose of assisting the Nawab. At the same time the Government sent an ultimatum to Ranjit Singh declaring the "Cis-Sutlej States to be under British protection." Col. Ochterlony prevented further encroachments by Ranjit Singh, and after strengthening the position of the Nawab on the *gadi*, Mr. Metcalfe, in April, 1809, secured the signature of Ranjit Singh to a treaty, which affirmed the dependence of the Cis-Sutlej States upon the British Government.

In 1862 a *sanad*, conferring certain rights and privileges, was granted, and on the death of Nawab Sijandar Ali Khan in 1871, without leaving issue, the power to adopt a successor was utilized in the selection of Mahomed Ibrahim Ali Khan Bahadur, the late Nawab, who was born in 1857. His Highness attended the Imperial Assemblage at Delhi on January 1, 1877, when His Excellency Lord Lytton, the Viceroy of India at the time, proclaimed the assumption by Her Majesty the late Queen Victoria of the title of "Empress of India."

The Nawab subsequently manifested signs of mental trouble, and the administration of the State was handed-over to Sahibzada Ahmad Ali Khan, the heir-apparent, who succeeded to the *gadi* on the death of his father in 1908.

His Highness the Nawab, Sir Ahmad Ali Khan Bahadur, K.C.S.I., was born in 1881, and was educated at the Aitchison Chief's College, Lahore. He was a guest at the Coronation Durbar in 1903; he proceeded to Lahore in 1906 to meet Their Royal Highnesses the Prince and Princess of Wales (now King George and Queen Mary); in 1909 His Highness was formally invested with full ruling powers, and in 1911 he went to Delhi to participate in the various functions in connection with the Coronation ceremonies of Their Imperial Majesties, the present King-Emperor and Queen Empress. His Highness was in June, 1915, the recipient of the distinguished honour of being created a Knight Commander of the Most Exalted Order of the Star of India.

The State of Maler-Kotla, 167 square miles in extent, consists of a level plain of unbroken surface, excepting that in many portions there are sand-drifts, which occasionally assume the form of ridges. It is bounded on the north by the district of Ludhiana, in the Jullundur Division of the Punjab, and in all other directions by the State of Patiala, and a few villages belonging to the State of Nabha.

The principal products are cotton, sugar, aniseed, garlic, tobacco and *gram*, and the chief exports are grain of various kinds, paper and survey instruments, which are manufactured in the capital town.

The State maintains a contingent of Imperial Service Sappers and Miners, infantry and artillery, and the first-named of these was employed on active service in the Tirah Campaign of 1897–8, and in the China Expedition of 1900-01.

There are not many rivers in the State, but two branches of the Sirhind canal pass through the State, although these are not yet used for irrigation purposes. Considerable attention is given to the question of education, and good progress has been made, especially in primary instruction. Several schools have been opened in various parts of the State, and there is a High School at Maler-Kotla and a middle school at Amadgarh.

The Nawab receives from the Government of India the annual sum of Rs. 2,500, by way of compensation for loss of revenue, owing to the abolition of customs duties, and the yearly income of the State is about Rs. 12,00,000.

The chief town of Maler-Kotla is divided into two portions, Maler, the older part, being built by Sadr-ud-Din, the founder of the family, in 1466, while Kotla owes its origin to Nawab Bayazid in the year 1656. The principal buildings are the residence of His Highness the Nawab, a hospital, the High School, and a fine court-house. A very large trade in grain is carried on, and other industries include factories for ginning and pressing cotton, the making of ice, survey instruments, and paper, and for the manufacture of flour.

The town is situated about 30 miles distant in a southwardly direction from Ludhiana, and it is 50 miles to the north of Ambala, while its inhabitants at the census of 1911 were nearly 30,000 in number.

THE STATE OF MANDI.

1. Drang Salt Quarry. 2. The Palace from across Seri Tank.

THE STATE OF MANDI

MANDI, a State some 1,200 square miles in extent, lying on the upper reaches of the Beas river, is under the political superintendence of the Commissioner of Jullundur, representing the Government of the Punjab. The territory is bounded on the north and west by the district of Kangra, on the east by Kulu, and on the south by the State of Suket. The name of the State, "Mandi," is a Hindi word signifying "market," although some writers have connected it with the Sanskrit "Mandapika," meaning "an open hall, or shed." It appears that Mandi was in early days, and still is, an important centre of trade on the main route from Yarkand and Ladakh to Hoshiarpur and the plains, the earliest mention of the town being in an inscription at the Trilok Nath temple in old Mandi, which is dated in the year 1520.

The Rajas of Mandi are Rajputs of the Chandra Bansi clan, and therefore they claim descent from the Pandavas of the *Mahabharata*. It is traditionally asserted that the progenitors of the line ruled in Indraprastha (Delhi) for more than 1,500 years until one Khemraj—the last ruler of the early dynasty—was driven out by his *Wazir*, Bisarp, who then usurped the throne. Khemraj having lost the kingdom of Indraprastha, fled eastward and settled in Bengal about the middle of the tenth century, where thirteen of his successors are said to have ruled for 350 years. The ruling Chiefs adopted the patronymic "Sen," while the younger members of the family took the name of "Singh." One of the most illustrious Rulers of this Sena dynasty was Lakshman Sen, who, it is said, extended his conquests to Kanauj, Nepal, and Orissa. After founding Gaur, in Malda, he made it his seat of government, and styled it Lakshmanpore, after himself.

A descendant, Balala Sen, selected Nadia as his capital, and it remained the chief seat of the Sena dynasty until Sur Sen was expelled from his territory about the end of the twelfth century by a general of Kutb-ud-din, the first slave king of Delhi. This Ruler went into exile at Allahabad, where he died, while his son, Rup Sen, with other members of the family, removed to Rupar in the district of Ambala. The Mahomedans attacked Rupar in the year 1210, and Rup Sen lost his life in one of the ensuing battles. His three sons fled to the neighbouring hills and established themselves in separate Principalities, Bir Sen becoming Chief of the Suket State, Giri Sen of Keonthal, and Hamir Sen of Kishtwar. The four families (including Mandi) descended from Rup Sen and his sons still recognize a common origin from the Gaur dynasty in Bengal.

Early in the fourteenth century, when Sahu Sen was Ruler of Suket, his younger brother, Bahu Sen, quarrelled with the Raja and left the State, eventually estab-

H.H. RAJA JOGENDRA SEN.

lishing himself in Manglaur, in Kulu. Several generations of Bahu Sen's successors ruled and became powerful in the newly-acquired territory, and an incident in the life of a descendant, named Karanchan Sen, led to the separation of Mandi as a distinct Principality among the hill States of Northern India. Karanchan Sen, it appears, was at war with the Kulu Raja, and when he was killed in battle his Rani, a daughter of the Chief of Seokot in Mandi, was compelled to seek refuge in flight. Becoming utterly exhausted by wandering in the dense jungle in which she had completely lost her way, she fell to the ground under the branches of a *ban*, or oak tree. A son was born to her during the dark hours of the night, and some followers of the Raja of Seokot discovered the mother and child early on the following day and carefully removed them to the home of the Rani's father. The Raja had no male heir, and therefore he adopted his grandson as his successor. The boy was named Ban, or Bana, on account of the strange circumstances attending his birth, and in due time he became Raja of Seokot. Bana Sen greatly enlarged his possessions, and built a new residence for himself at Bhiuli, about four miles distant from the present town of Mandi, as well as the temple of Parasar Deo. He died about the year 1304.

Kalian Sen, his son and successor, acquired territory on the bank of the River Beas, called Batahuli, opposite to Mandi, where he constructed a palace, the ruins of which are still in existence.

The capital of the State, built on this newly-acquired territory, remained the headquarters of the State until the founding of the new one at Mandi. From this date the work of territorial extension progressed rapidly. The Rana of Kelti was subdued; the country around Chahti and Sanor being annexed, and the Rana of Sagrur was killed and his territory seized. Kalian Sen died in the year 1332, and was succeeded by his son Hira Sen. During his reign the district of Kanhwal was added to the State, but the Raja was, in 1360, killed by the Rana of Gandharb. He was followed by his brother Dharitri Sen. Conquest of other territory continued under this Raja, as well as his three successors, named respectively Narindar Sen (1416), Harjai Sen (1444), and Dilawar Sen (1472).

The small estates of subjugated Ranas and Thakurs were brought under one head, and became more or less subject to the central authority at old Mandi.

Consolidation of these separate areas took place in the year 1500, during the administration of Ajbar Sen, an intelligent and wise ruler, who in 1527 founded the present town of Mandi and made it his capital. Chatar Sen succeeded in 1534, but there is nothing of note recorded concerning him excepting that he built the Lakargarh fortress in ths district of Kalar. His death in 1554 brought his son, Sahib Sen, to the *gadi*.

Narayan Sen (1575) subdued the Ranae (or petty Chiefs) of Ner, Pandoh, and Chuhar, and acquired several districts from them as well as from the Raja of Suket; and he also built the fort of Narayangarh. Narayan Sen died in 1595, and was followed by his son, Kesab Sen, of whom nothing much is known.

Raja Suraj Sen became the occupant of the *gadi* in the year 1637, and he signalized his accession to power by making attacks upon neighbouring States with the view of extending his possessions. When the Raja of Bhangal was pressed by the troops of Suraj Sen he obtained the assistance of the Raja of Kulu, and the combined forces inflicted a defeat upon the invader. The Kulu army overran Mandi, and seized the salt mines of Guma and Drang, which yielded the greater portion of the revenue of the State. Suraj Sen was therefore compelled to sue for peace and to pay the expenses of the war before he could obtain restoration of the valuable assets which had been taken from him. Subsequently to this date Suraj Sen was more successful in his invasions, and a considerable area of territory was added to the State. Shortly before his death Suraj Sen sent a messenger to summon his brother Shiam Sen with the object of openly appointing him as his successor. After the new Raja's accession in 1664 he went to the assistance of the Kahlur (Bilaspur) State, which was in grave danger owing to the advance of the Moghul forces, and it is recorded that grants of land were subsequently made by the Raja to the families of all who had fallen in the campaign in return for the services rendered by them. He completely routed the Suket Chief, and Lohara was then annexed to Mandi. His term of office is memorable chiefly, however, by the construction of the celebrated Shiama Kali temple on a hill adjoining the town of Mandi, at an elevation of about 3,000 feet above the level of the sea.

Gur Sen (1679), son of the previous Raja, acquired several neighbouring districts by conquest, but he died about five years after his accession. Sidh Sen (1684) was a great warrior, and added a very large area of territory to the State, obtained chiefly at the expense of Kulu, Suket, and Bangahal. The *Wazir* of the State in the early part of this *regime* was Mian Jippa, a man of unusual ability. He held full administrative charge, and among many important progressive measures inaugurated by him was the introduction of the revenue system, which remained in force in Mandi until the recent Land Revenue Settlement was effected in 1917.

Sidh Sen treacherously murdered his son-in-law, Raja Prithi Pal of Bhangal, while he was on a visit to Mandi, made ostensibly for the purpose of obtaining his consent to assist Mandi to annex other territory. The body of the unfortunate Raja was burned, but his head was buried in front of the palace on the spot now marked by a pillar in the middle of a tank. At the top of the pillar is an aperture, in which a light is still kept burning every evening. Sidh's Sen reign is said to have continued for more than 40 years, and the Raja, who has been described as a giant, is supposed to have reached the age of 100 years. Shiv Jawala Sen is mentioned as having been the next Raja, but the balance of evidence seems to denote that he was co-ruler with his father during the latter part of his life.

A story is related in Mandi that during Raja Sidh Sen's absence from his capital both the Ranis of Shiv Jawala Sen gave birth to sons; as the news of Shamsher Sen's birth was the first to reach the Raja he was declared to be the elder of the two infants. Strife having arisen between the Ranis the Raja ordered a sword and a bag of dust to be placed where the children were playing. Shamsher Sen at once scrambled and caught hold of the sword, while the other showed his preference for the dust. Thereupon the Raja again declared Shamsher Sen to be the elder, and he gave the name of Dhur Jatiya, or "dust eater," to the other one.

Shamsher Sen succeeded to the *gadi* in 1727, when only five years of age, and during his minority the State was administered by Mian Juppu, who was also responsible for the education of the young Chief.

Shamsher Sen died in 1781, and was succeeded by Surma Sen, who at the commencement of his rule determined that the Mians, his kinsmen in the State, should not appropriate to themselves positions to which they had no right (as they had been doing for many years past), and this firm attitude of the Raja had a most wholesome effect upon them. The Raja died in 1788, leaving a son and heir, Ishwari Sen, then a boy of only four years of age. During the period of minority the fortunes of the State were brought to the lowest ebb owing chiefly to the action of the Mians, who, freed from the

THE STATE OF MANDI

1. General Vizw of Mandi Town from the North-west. 2. The Ghauhya Bazar, Mandi. 3. H.H. Raja Sir Bajia Sen, K.C.S.I. 4. H.H. Raja Bhawani Sen. 5. His Highness and Officials.

strong hand of Surma Sen, again endeavoured to usurp power for themselves. The minister realizing the danger in which he stood, appealed for help from Raja Sansar Chand of Kangra, who was glad to have the opportunity of entering the State with his troops, but instead of rendering assistance he, in 1792, plundered the capital town. Local chronicles assert "Ishwari Sen was captured and carried off to Kangra; the rich district of Hatli was handed over to Suket, Chohar was allotted to Kulu; and Anantpur was retained by the victor, while the State thus impoverished was ordered to pay an annual tribute of Rs. 1,00,000."

Raja Ishwari Sen was transferred to Sansar Chand's Court, where he was detained as a prisoner for about 12 years. Robbed of some of its richest districts, and burdened with heavy tributary debt, the State of Mandi struggled with little or no success against the catastrophe which had fallen upon it.

Ultimately the imprisoned Ishwari Sen was liberated by a Gurkha force, who restored him to his territory. Sansar Chand soon afterwards found himself in a perilous position owing to pressure by the Gurkhas, and he begged Ranjit Singh, the Ruler of the Punjab, to help him. The latter agreed to the proposals made to him, and his large army in May 1809 put the Gurkhas to flight and drove them across the Sutlej. This aid was, however, a costly affair, as Kangra and the other Hill States, which had been brought under Gurkha domination, became tributary to the Punjabi leader. Sardar Desa Singh Majithia was appointed by Ranjit Singh to be *Nazim* or Superintendent of all the Hill States. Ishwari Sen recovered his lost districts, but he was required to pay an annual tribute of Rs. 30,000. This sum was in 1815 increased to Rs. 1,00,000, but two years later the amount was, "by judicious bribery," reduced to Rs. 50,000.

Raja Ishwari Sen died in 1826 without leaving lawful male issue, and Zalim Sen, brother of the late Chief, ascended the *gadi* on condition that he paid to Lahore the sum of Rs. 1,00,000 as succession duty and the increased annual tribute, which at that time stood at Rs. 75,000. Zalim Sen passed away in 1839, but some years previously he had entrusted the administration to his nephew, Balbir Sen, one of the younger sons of Ishwari Sen by a concubine. Maharaja Ranjit Singh died in the month of June 1839, and the Sikh troops formerly under his control began to chafe against the state of inaction into which they were thrown.

Mandi had not broken faith with the court at Lahore, yet it was decided to send an army against the State, which was occupied by troops under General Ventura. After subduing the country, General Ventura returned to Lahore, leaving a small Sikh force at Mandi under a young English adventurer, who had been in the service of the Sikhs.

Sher Singh became Maharaja of Lahore in January 1841, and the Rulers of the Hill States found in him a man who, recognizing that they had been subjected to a considerable amount of tyranny, began to manifest a desire to relieve them of the yoke with which they were burdened. Raja Balbir Sen, who had been imprisoned on the conquest of the State, was liberated, and in 1846 a treaty was concluded between the British Government and the Sikh Durbar, under which provision was made for the cession in perpetuity to the former of "the whole of the Doab between the Sutlej and Beas rivers." This area included Mandi, which was then placed under the control of the Commissioner of Jullundur. The Raja was therefore confirmed in his possessions, and in October 1840 a *sanad* was granted to him defining his rights and obligations. By virtue of this document the suzerainty of Mandi State was finally transferred from the Sikh to the British Government.

The death of Balbir Sen occurred in 1851, and he left three sons, the oldest of whom, Bijai, was only four years of age. A Council of Regency was appointed under the presidency of Wazir Gosaon, a man of unusual ability and experience, who subsequently became sole Regent. For several years the State enjoyed considerable prosperity, but in the year 1868 it was discovered that the education of the young Prince had been greatly neglected, and an official of the Educational Department of the Punjab Government was appointed to give the necessary training to the young Ruler. In 1863 the Government granted the Raja a salute of 11 guns, and in October 1866, having attained his majority, he was formally invested by Sir Douglas Forsyth with the powers of a ruling Prince.

The Raja, upon taking up the administration, began the construction of a school, hospital, post office, roads, and other works of public utility, but the bright future anticipated for the State was not realized, as the Raja developed a vacillating disposition, and trusted to men whose object in life appeared to be the furtherance of their own aims.

The general administration fell into the greatest confusion, and in 1870 the British Government found it necessary to interfere by appointing Mr. E. Harrison, B.C.S., as Adviser to the Raja. This step proved to be most advantageous for the State, as long-promised reforms were introduced, abuses were corrected, and the various departments of the State were thoroughly reorganized.

His Excellency Lord Mayo, Viceroy of India, visited Mandi in October 1871, and a grand Durbar was held, at which the principal State officials, *Zamindars*, and others were present.

In 1874 the Raja was assisted in administration by his brother, Mian Pradhan Singh, who won the highest esteem of the inhabitants by his untiring efforts for their welfare, but he was unfortunately removed by death in the following year. He was succeeded by Mian Uttam Singh, who died in 1888, and was succeeded by Jowahir Lal. The latter's appointment caused discontent, and on the Raja's application a British official was lent to the State to supervise the administration.

The Raja was present at the Proclamation Durbar at Delhi in January 1877, and with the view of commemorating the event he built the fine Victoria suspension bridge over the Beas near Mandi at a cost of Rs. 1,00,000. The Public Works Department was about this date busily engaged in the construction of necessary new roads, including one between Mandi and Kulu, over the Dulchi Pass, a distance of 31 miles (together with a suspension bridge over the Uhl River); one from Baijnath to Mandi; and another from Mandi to Bhamla, 25 miles in length. In 1884 the two daughters of the Raja were married to the heir-apparent of Bashahr, when the sum of Rs. 2,77,000 was expended in connection with the festivities; but this included an amount of Rs. 60,000 raised by the people in accordance with the usual custom. The period between the years 1894 and 1900 was unfortunate for Mandi, as the Raja lost two sons, both of whom died in infancy.

The remaining years of Bjiai Sen's life were uneventful, although several changes were made in the control of some of the principal departmental offices. The Raja died in 1902, just three weeks before an announcement was made that, in recognition of his good government, it had been proposed to invest him with the insignia of a K.C.S.I., on the occasion of the accession of His Majesty the late King Edward VII.

In default of legitimate heirs, Bhawani Singh was recognized as successor by the British Government, and he was formally installed at Mandi in November 1903 by His Honour Sir Charles Rivaz, Lieutenant-Governor of the Punjab. The young Raja remained for several years at the Chiefs' College in Lahore, while the administration of the State was entrusted to Mr. Millar, I.C.S.

THE STATE OF MANDI.

1. The Uhl River, near Jhatingri. 2. Parasar Deo Temple. 3. The Barsela Stones of the Rajas, Mandi. 4. Gateway leading to the Dam-dama. 5. Jhatingri.

THE STATE OF MANDI.

1. The Shivratri Fair, Mandi (Madho Rao returning to the Palace). 2. Shivratri Fair in the Time of H.H. Raja Ishwari Sen, 1789-1826. 3 and 5. The Shivratri Fair, Mandi. 4. A Wrestling Match.

THE STATE OF MANDI

The Raja completed his studies at college and returned to Mandi in April 1904. An exceedingly severe earthquake occurred in April 1905, and the Raja and Mr. Millar, who were at the time staying at the *dak* bungalow at Palampur, were in imminent peril of losing their lives by falling *débris*, from which they were with difficulty extricated. A very great amount of damage was caused in Mandi, as from the Baijnath border to the town of Mandi only the village of Aiju was left intact.

The town of Mandi was almost ruined, the salt mines at Guma were rendered almost useless, roads and bridges were impassable, and there was general devastation of buildings and other property. It was estimated that the damage done in the State amounted to a sum of fully Rs. 10,00,000. The Durbar acted with great liberality in granting loans of money and grain to thousands of sufferers, and timber was given for the construction of new homesteads. It is believed that more than 1,500 persons lost their lives.

The Raja was invested with full ruling powers by Mr. H. A. Anderson, C.S.I., on October 7, 1905.

The work of repairing and restoring buildings had been commenced as early as possible after the earthquake, and in 1906 a new Durbar Hall was erected at a cost of Rs. 30,000, and the town of Mandi was lighted by electricity, the amount expended on installation being Rs. 20,000.

His Honour Sir Louis Dane, K.C.S.I., Lieutenant-Governor of the Punjab, paid a short visit to Mandi in 1908, and he expressed his satisfaction at the manner in which the State was being administered.

Disturbances broke out in Mandi early in the year 1909 owing to allegations of oppression made by occupiers of land against certain State officials. The agitation became a riot, which was not suppressed until British officials, at the head of an armed force, appeared on the scene.

Raja Bhawani Sen was present at the Coronation Durbar held at Delhi in December 1911, but he was attacked by illness shortly after his return to Mandi, and universal grief was manifested at his untimely death in February 1912.

In the absence of a direct heir the Government selected Mian Jogendra Singh, the nearest male relative of the late Raja, to succeed to the *gadi*, and he was formally installed as Raja Jogendra Sen by His Honour Sir Louis Dane, K.C.S.I., on April 28, 1913. The young Prince was at that time little more than eight years of age, and Mr. Gordon Walker was appointed Superintendent of the State and Settlement Officer.

The services of Mr. H. L. Wright, an officer of the Indian Forest Department, were lent to the State from May 1914 to November 1917 for the purpose of carrying out a Forest Settlement Scheme, and of formulating a working plan for future years.

In October 1916 the young Raja entered the Chiefs' College at Lahore as a day-boarder, he is residing in that city under the charge of his tutor, Mr. T. P. Gillmore, and his Brahmin instructor, Pandit Brij Bihusi Lal.

Mr. H. W. Emerson, I.C.S., who succeeded Mr. Walker as Superintendent and Settlement Officer in March 1915, left the State at the end of June 1917 on the virtual conclusion of the Regular Settlement, and he was succeeded as Superintendent by Mr. J. R. S. Parsons, I.C.S. The latter left the State in May 1920, and was succeeded by Pandit Maharaj Kishan, M.B.E.

The State of Mandi presents a great variety of physical aspects, prominent among which are its two huge parallel ranges of mountains running from the north-west in a south-easterly direction, its numerous rivers, and its boundless extent of forests.

The Ghogar-ki-Dhar range, the most important of all, enters the State near the centre of its northern boundary.

A considerable portion is well wooded and abounds in large game, while an extensive area comprises land usually classed as "fertile." The Nargu range, varying from 9,000 feet to 12,000 feet in height, is covered with useful timber trees, such as pine, walnut, box, chestnut, *deodar*, and other species.

The principal river, the Beas, drains nearly the entire area of the State, and its numerous tributaries are largely used for purposes of irrigation.

The State has a population of about 185,000 persons, of whom 98 per cent. are Hindus, the remainder comprising Mahomedans and Buddhists.

The practice of agriculture claims the attention of 75 per cent. of the people, and it is evident that many occupiers have acquired a good knowledge of many of the primary principles of sound cultivation. A large proportion of the land is so hilly that it almost defies cultivation, yet it is a common sight to witness numerous embankments which have resulted in as many as 50 or 60 fields being ranged one above another in the side of a hill.

The principal crops are rice, maize, millets, wheat, barley, potatoes, tobacco, sugar-cane, and cotton. The growing of tea was introduced about half a century ago, and at the present time there are several flourishing gardens on the borders of Bir Bangahal, where the climate is suitable.

The whole of the State abounds in mineral wealth, but the difficulties in the way of mining are almost insuperable owing to the insufficiency of railway and other means of communication. Iron, the most widely distributed metal, is found in Saraj, Nachan, Pandoh Chohar, and Sanor in the form of crystals of magnetic oxide of iron. A little gold is obtained from the bed of the Son, a tributary of the Beas river; several slate quarries are being worked, and the salt mines yield about one-third of the total revenue.

The trade of Mandi, in the exportation of agricultural produce, chiefly wheat, rice, *ghee*, timber, and potatoes, is an exceedingly valuable one, and a considerable increase in volume has been apparent since the Durbar undertook the construction of new roads. Timber is floated down the Beas river and collected at Wazir Bular and Doraha for sale; wheat, rice, and other cereals are carried on camels from Hatli and Suranga to the markets of Hoshiarpur and Palampur; and salt is sent in large quantities to Kangra and other hill States.

The State is divided into four *tahsils* for revenue purposes, but the whole of the judicial work was formerly performed at the capital town, although it is now decentralized by the establishment of *tahsils* outside the headquarters of the State.

In general administrative duties the Raja is assisted by the *Wazir*, who is invested with the highest executive and judicial powers. The work controlled by this official is of an onerous and responsible character, but it should be observed that every appeal or revision decided by him may be taken to the Court of His Highness the Raja. The administration of the land revenue system is in the hands of the *Wazir* and his *tahsildars*, who exercise judicial functions, and are also revenue officers. There are in addition a sub-Judge, a Treasury officer, with powers of a first-class magistrate and munsiff, and a second-class munsiff and magistrate.

His Highness the Raja is sole proprietor of all land in the State, and occupants have no right to sell or mortgage their lands, although under certain circumstances they may give up possession of the produce of their fields for any term not exceeding 15 years.

There are 27 schools in the State, including an Anglo-Vernacular High School at Mandi, which has an efficient staff of teachers.

The principal medical institution is the King Edward VII Hospital at Mandi, but a *zenana* hospital at Mandi and a dispensary at Chauntra have also been started, while provision is also made for affording medical relief by means of dispensaries.

THE STATE OF MORVI

SITUATED in the Kathiawar Political Agency in the Bombay Presidency is the First Class State of Morvi, enjoying plenary powers. Geographically, it lies in the Machhukantha division in the northern portion of Kathiawar, while its ***mahal*** of Adhoi is in the Wagad district of the peninsula of Cutch. The capital town, of the same name as the State, stands on the banks of the Machhu river, from the east bank of which the view of the stream and the city is most picturesque.

Morvi was, until the fifteenth century, ruled over by the Jethwa Rajputs, from whom it passed to the sway of the Sultans of Ahmedabad. On the surrender of Sultan Muzaffar to the Moghul Emperor Khengarji, the Chief of Cutch, was rewarded for his services by a grant of the district of Morvi and the title of Rao—a designation which is held by the Rulers of Cutch to this day. In Rao Raidhanji's reign an army from Ahmedabad attacked Morvi, and his son, Rawaji, the direct ancestor of the Morvi House, boldly undertook the enterprise of expelling the enemy. For his exertions in rescuing Morvi he obtained it as a gift from his father in 1675–6.

His Highness Sir Waghji Rawaji Bahadur, G.C.I.E., Maharaja Thakore Saheb, the present Ruler of Morvi, is a direct descendant of that Rawaji who distinguished himself so greatly in the time of his father, Aliyaji. He belongs to the Jadeja clan of Rajputs, and to the same family as the Rao of Cutch and the Jam of Nawanagar, being, however, senior in descent to both of them.

His Highness, who worthily upholds the traditions of the Rajput race, is eighth in descent from Rawaji, the founder of the State, and third in the line of succession from the illustrious Jiyaji, the Thakore who rendered conspicuous services to the British in their operations in Kathiawar at the beginning of the eighteenth century. The Thakore Saheb was born in April 1858, and succeeded to the ***gadi*** in February 1870. Being then a minor, the affairs of the State were carried on by a joint Administration, consisting of Rao Bahadur Shambhuprasad Laxmilal, a trusted officer of the British Government, and Azam Jhunjhabhai Sakhidas, ***Karbhari*** of the late Thakore Saheb Shri Rawaji. In the same year a college for the education of Rajkumars (the first of its kind in India) was opened at Rajkot, with Mr. Chester Macnaghten as Principal, and His Highness was among the first to join the College, where he received instruction for six years. On leaving Rajkot in 1876, he offered the sum of Rs. 30,000 to his ***Alma Mater*** as a donation to the Endowment Fund of the College, the only other contribution being from His Highness Maharaja Takhtasinhji of Bhavnagar. The Government, in accepting the gift, were pleased to inform the Administrators that they observed with pleasure the appreciation by the Thakore Saheb of the benefit he had derived from his education at the College. In commemoration of his visit to India in 1875, His Royal Highness the Prince of Wales was pleased to send to the Thakore Saheb a silver medal, and further to accept a present of a gold fish, ***Uttardan***, in a silver casket, from the Thakore Saheb in return. In 1878, though then a minor, His Highness was invited to attend the Delhi Imperial Assemblage, as a Ruling Chief, on the occasion of the assumption by Her Majesty of the title of "Empress of India." After finishing his education at the Rajkumar College, the young Thakore Saheb undertook a tour in India, being accompanied by Capt. Humfrey and Mr. Jamshedji Unwalla, M.A. In 1877, on returning from his trip, he was associated as joint Administrator with Rao Bahadur Shambhuprasad. After fifteen months' experience with such an able and zealous officer as the Rao Bahadur as his guide and instructor, the Thakore Saheb assumed sole charge on January 1, 1879.

Immediately on taking sole charge, the Thakore Saheb turned his attention, among other things, to works of public utility. First and foremost was a bridge across the Machhu river. It was a deep river, about 1,000 feet in width, with steep banks cut up by ***nullahs***, and was very difficult to cross. In times of floods, people travelling to Morvi had to wait for several days on the other side before the water became fordable. The foundation stone of the structure was laid by His Excellency Sir Richard Temple, Governor of Bombay, in 1879, and the opening ceremony was performed by his successor, Sir James Fergusson. The bridge, with its parapets adorned with equestrian statues, is one of the largest and handsomest in Kathiawar, and it is 1,150 feet in length, including abutments. It has cost Rs. 3,27,000.

His Highness the Thakore Saheb next devoted his attention to making railway connections, linking up the terminus of the Bombay-Baroda and Central India Railway at Wadhwan with his capital as well as with Rajkot, the headquarters of the British Political Agency.

In 1883 His Highness paid his first visit to England, and while there he pur-

HIS HIGHNESS SIR WAGHJI BAHADUR, G.C.I.E., THAKORE SAHIB OF MORVI.

chased rolling stock and rails, 65 miles in length, for extensions to Morvi, but the consignment had scarcely arrived in the harbour at Bombay when, owing to the urgent need of the Government of India for such goods in connection with military activities, His Highness the Thakore Saheb, staunch in his loyalty to the Throne, generously placed the whole of the materials at the immediate disposal of the Government.

In 1884–5 a fresh stock of rails and rolling stock was ordered, and a railway from Wadhwan to Dolia, and thence to Wankaner, was opened for traffic in 1886, and to Morvi in 1887, a total distance of 66 miles, the whole cost being borne by the Morvi State.

Side by side with the improvement of communications, His Highness turned his attention to the improvement and expansion of the capital town. The years 1882-7 were devoted to the laying out and widening of the bazar, which is now a splendid row of artistic buildings, erected on each side of a broad street, and extending from the palace to the Nagar gate. To complete the work, a magnificent tower has been constructed in the heart of the bazar, where the Superintendent of Police has his office.

At the same time was commenced the laying out of the land on the opposite side of the Machhu river, where there are now a number of fine buildings of a residential character, as well as those connected with the State administration and industries. In order to obtain easy crossing of the river His Highness has thrown a suspension bridge over the Machhu, thus connecting the City Palace and the Nazar Baugh. This is one of the wonders of Morvi, and is one of the largest in India, being over 600 feet in length, resting on strong knitted iron cords, supported over pulleys by two towers.

In February 1887, Morvi was raised to a State of the First Class. In the same month His Highness the Thakore Saheb proceeded to England as a representative of the Kathiawar Chiefs, to present a congratulatory address to Her Majesty the late Queen-Empress Victoria, on the occasion of the fiftieth year of her reign. It was during this visit that His Highness was appointed a Knight Commander of the Most Eminent Order of the Indian Empire, and he received the insignia of the Order from the hands of Her Majesty herself. In commemoration of the event there are in Morvi the Jubilee grain market, the Jubilee fountain, and the Jubilee bridge over the Dhutari river.

While in England in 1887, His Highness, who had early imbibed a passion for a knowledge of mechanical science, visited the Manchester Exhibition, and also travelled to America. It is interesting to note that during this trip His Highness purchased lands in Manitoba (Canada), near the lakes.

In the year 1889 His Excellency Lord Reay (then Governor of Bombay) paid a visit to Morvi. On being requested to lay the foundation stone of the Ba Shri Vakhtuba Charitable High School, His Excellency in the course of his speech strongly eulogized the progressive rule of the Thakore Saheb.

In 1889 the Morvi Railway was further extended from Wankaner to Rajkot, a distance of 25 miles, thus bringing the Kathiawar Political Agency within reach of the Presidency town.

In the year 1888-9, cultivators were given the right of permanent occupancy, and measures were adopted with the object of preventing the adulteration of cotton. In the same year a tramway was opened in Morvi, and in 1891 its extension to the Port of Wawania—a distance of 25 miles—was opened for traffic, thus linking up the railway system with the sea.

In 1890 His Royal Highness the Duke of Connaught graced Morvi with a visit.

The deep interest taken by His Highness in the welfare of his subjects, and especially by finding employment for them in the carrying out of public works of utility was commented on by His Excellency Lord Harris, Governor of Bombay, when at Morvi in 1892.

In 1893 His Highness undertook his third trip to England. During his sojourn there he visited America again, and attended the Chicago Exhibition. In the same year a cotton spinning and weaving mill was opened in Morvi, and a tramway from Morvi to the Tankara *mahal* in the south—a distance of 14 miles—was opened for traffic. In the next year a branch line was constructed to Maliya.

His Highness the Thakore Saheb paid his fourth visit to England in the year 1897, in order to obtain medical advice and treatment. While there he took part in the celebrations held in honour of the Diamond Jubilee of the reign of Her Majesty the late Queen Victoria, and it was during this visit that he was appointed a Knight Grand Commander of the Most Eminent Order of the Indian Empire. His Highness was graciously accorded an interview by Her Majesty, who received him cordially, and personally invested him with the insignia of the Order. As a memento of the occasion the Queen-Empress was graciously pleased to present His Highness with a marble bust of herself.

In the year 1899–1900 Kathiawar was visited by a terrible famine, the like of which had not been seen for almost a hundred years, but His Highness quickly recognized that a crisis was at hand, and prepared to face the problems. When the prospect of rain was passing away, he sent his officers through all his villages to take a complete census of the population, with the view of ascertaining the different classes and conditions of people, as well as the number of those requiring assistance. Grain was imported from Bombay, Karachi, Muttra, Agra, Fyzabad, and Bhavnagar, and import duty on grain was remitted in order to encourage private enterprise. Desirous of obtaining a thorough grasp of the situation, the Thakore Saheb himself visited every village, and studied the requirements of the inhabitants. Cultivators were presented with grain as early as June, and the digging of wells was started, so that by means of irrigation it might be possible to grow fodder for the saving of the cattle. A sum of Rs. 3,00,000, sanctioned by the Thakore Saheb for this help, was expended by the Durbar. For the maintenance of cattle, every cultivator had a monthly allowance of four *maunds* of grain per plough, so that, given enough food for themselves and their families, they could devote their energies to the irrigation of fodder crops, and thus save their livestock. The labouring classes obtained relief through employment in the sinking of wells, those residing on the coast-line got their livelihood from mangroves, some were employed in filling up *nullahs*, thousands were engaged on the railway, and lastly, the construction of the Paneli waterworks provided occupation for a considerable number of labourers and artisans. Poor houses in the town, with branches in districts, were opened for those unable to work, and the infirm who could not walk were conveyed by the three tramways, two in the north —Wawania and Jetpur—and one in the south—Tankara. Every official in State employ, and, in fact, every inhabitant, was held responsible for taking to places of relief any person found suffering from sickness or scarcity of food. The State has a network of telephone communica-

THE STATE OF MORVI.

1. Mani Mandir. 2. Palace in the City.

tions, and cases of sickness caused through privation were promptly reported with all particulars to headquarters. Lastly, the "shabby genteel," whose poverty was more distressing than that of any other class, were helped in their own homes. A meeting of the heads of communities was called, and Rs. 10,000 were subscribed on the spot, to which His Highness added Rs. 15,000. In one poorhouse 750 people of both sexes were housed, fed, and medically treated, and in another 400 orphan children were housed, clothed, fed, and instructed, while the hospital was used for the treatment of those suffering from the effects of privation and improper food. These poorhouses and hospitals were visited by His Highness every day in order that he might see for himself that the inmates were properly looked after. About 1,200 to 1,300 persons from other States also received employment. Such in brief were His Highness' efforts in the year of famine to relieve distress.

In 1899 the Morvi State was confronted with another difficulty. In order to have uniformity of gauge between Northern India and the Kathiawar railway systems, the Bombay-Baroda and Central India Railway Company undertook the conversion of the permanent way, from broad to metre-gauge, of the line between Viramgam and Wadhwan, and the Morvi State also consented to change its narrow gauge to metre width. Col. Hunter, then Political Agent, desired that there should be one management, and that His Highness should surrender his separate control as a condition precedent to conversion by him. His Highness' management of the line had been efficient, and has been described by successive Government Consulting Engineers and Inspectors, every half-year, without exception, in such terms as "a very great success," "in excellent order," "wonderfully well kept up," "successful management," and "well and economically managed line." The interests of other sections were antagonistic to the Morvi railway, and therefore His Highness was unable to consent to the surrender of his management. The Political Agent thereupon started another parallel and competitive line, between the same points, Wadhwan and Rajkot, via Chotila, and proposed to deprive the Morvi railway of the Wadhwan-Dola section. Earthworks were at once commenced, and in spite of repeated protests the work was pushed on rapidly. Fortunately, however, His Excellency Lord Curzon, then Viceroy, visited Kathiawar, and having ridden over the line for 30 miles with His Highness, he saw the situation, and ordered suspension of the work. It was decided that His Highness should convert the line, and that he should be the sole owner of it, and on the question of management Lord Curzon assured His Highness "of the fullest and most careful consideration." His Excellency realized the value of vested interests, as well as the inequity of allowing the competitive parallel line, and he appreciated what a shock it would be to railway enterprise, and to the faith with which it was undertaken. Morvi's troubles were not over, however, as Col. Hunter prevailed upon Sir Arthur Trevor to adopt the via Chotila alignment on which he had started, and for which he had made advances from certain funds held by the Agency, as neither Sayla nor Wadhwan would finance the undertaking. Although the Tikar alignment was the proper one, the Sayla route was forced upon Morvi, and Rs. 90,000 were recovered from the Durbar to recoup the advances made from the Agency funds. The Consulting Engineer, the Bombay Government, and the Government of India, approved of the Tikar route, which was then adopted, and it was Lord Curzon again who ordered a refund to Morvi from the Imperial Treasury of the money taken from the State. Before leaving India His Excellency Lord Curzon assured His Highness that "he was very hopeful that it might be found possible to meet His Highness the Thakore Saheb's views in the matter, and to retain his keen personal interest in the management of the line which His Highness showed so much interest in building and so much public spirit in converting." Eventually the question of management was decided in His Highness' favour. The States of Bhavnagar, Junagadh, and Jamnagar favoured separate management, and Sir T. Wynne, President of the Railway Board, adopted that as the only solution of providing for conflicting interests.

The Paneli Water-works, undertaken in 1898 9 to help irrigation and to give good drinking water to the capital, were opened in 1901. The State expended a sum of Rs. 7,00,000 upon the undertaking.

In 1903 His Highness undertook his first district tour, in order to look into the condition of the people after the dire famine of 1899-1900 and the partial one of 1901 2. His Highness visited and encamped at every village, saw for himself the condition of every cultivator, his dependence on or independence of the *Saukar*, the extent of the land cultivated, the adequacy or inadequacy of his live stock for the soil he tilled, the quality of land under cultivation, and the disposal of the waste land, if any. For a number of years His Highness held the revenue portfolio, personally inquiring into difficult subjects, listening to cultivators, and sitting far into the night disposing of their petitions. An extended tour of the districts was again made in 1906, and the practical result of all this care on the part of His Highness has been a contented and prosperous peasantry.

At the end of the British Administration there were no properly made roads, but at the present day there are excellent highways, connecting village with village, and extending over five hundred miles. It is customary for His Highness to make motor tours into the various districts with the object of coming into personal touch with the people, and of dealing with their grievances.

In the year 1903-4 the people of Morvi celebrated, amid great rejoicings, the Silver Jubilee of His Highness' reign, he having taken sole charge of the State in 1879. In order to commemorate the event they decided to erect a fine equestrian statue of His Highness in bronze, and it now adorns the open *chok* on the eastern side of the Machhu bridge, while the marble statue of Lord Reay is an attraction on the opposite side.

In the year 1905 the narrow-gauge railway from Rajkot to Wadhwan was converted into a metre-gauge line, the cost of the work, amounting to more than Rs. 20,00,000, being borne by the State.

In the year 1906 His Highness made an extensive tour in India, visiting a large number of important places, and he subsequently undertook a pilgrimage to Badri Narayan, where 600 miles of his journey were covered in walking.

The Secretariat offices in Morvi, situated in a fine structure known as "Hill" buildings, were opened in the year 1907 8 by Mr. (now Sir Claud) Hill, late Member of the Supreme Council, Delhi.

All the offices in the Secretariat are provided with up-to-date conveniences, and are fitted with telephones, electric lights and fans, there being 30 telephone connections in the building, which greatly facilitate the transaction of business.

The years 1911-2 and 1915-16 were again famine years, and adequate measures were adopted for the relief of distress

THE STATE OF MORVI.

1. His Highness's Statue. 2. Entrance to Nazar Bagh Palace. 3. Nazar Bagh Palace.

THE STATE OF MORVI.

1. Bazar View from Tower, looking towards Darbargadh. 2. Grand Chowk Tower. 3. Hill Buildings.

THE STATE OF MORVI.

1. Guest-House. 2. Tramway Station. 3. Ba Shree Vaktuba High School.

among all classes of people, as in the year 1899-1900. In both these years the entire *Khatabandi*--annual assessments payable by the cultivators -was wholly remitted.

The administration of law and order is well carried out, and although the borders of the State are inhabited by a most criminal and turbulent tribe—the Mianas, who are notorious outlaws and marauders--the people of Morvi, through the vigilance of its police, enjoy perfect immunity. In the words of Mr. Chester Macnaghten, " His Highness the Thakore Saheb has, by his railway, afforded to the public one of the best safeguards against outlawry and highwaymen," and it may be added that His Highness has rendered the whole State immune from serious crime, such as dacoity or highway robbery. The last outlaws met their fate when Capt. Gordon, assisted by the Morvi police, practically annihilated them at Karadia.

It may here be mentioned that of the taxes which existed at the end of the British administration, some were abolished in 1899, and the remainder at a later date, with the result that there is not a single tax on any of the population in the whole State.

From the very commencement of the Great War in 1914, to its conclusion in 1918, the Chief of Morvi, his officials, and the subjects of the State generally, made every effort to render aid to the Allies by contributions of money and materials, and by subscriptions to War Loan Funds.

The news of the cessation of hostilities near the close of the year 1918 was hailed with delight throughout the whole State. Thanksgiving services were held in places of worship, a salute of guns was fired, a parade of troops was held, and the occasion was marked by public rejoicings of such a character that the ushering in of peace, after the long and hideous struggle, will live long in the minds of the people. The celebrations were on even a more elaborate scale in December 1919.

The following particulars have been extracted from an account of the assistance given by the State for war purposes: Rs. 15,000 to the Bombay Presidency War and Relief Fund; two motor ambulance cars, to seat five and 23 persons respectively, of the value of Rs. 25,000; two motor ambulance cars, presented to His Majesty the King-Empe or for the use of the Indian Expeditionary Force in France; four tents for field hospitals in France; a metre-gauge engine, worth Rs. 43,000, to the Government of India; the State workshops were placed at the disposal of Government for the manufacture of base plates for shells (in combination with the railway workshops, Ajmer); from August 1915 to the end of the war a contribution of Rs. 20 per month was made to the Rajkot tailoring fund; Rs. 29,000 were contributed in purchases at the Great War sale, held in December 1916; one race-horse, worth Rs. 2,000, was presented in aid of Her Excellency Lady Chelmsford's lucky bag; Rs. 7,000 were spent at the Exhibition held by Her Excellency Lady Willingdon in Bombay in 1917; Rs. 2,000 were given to the Matheran lucky bag; Rs. 11,500 spent at the Rajkot "Our Day" celebrations; Rs. 1,000, purchase by the State of 1,000 tickets in the Rajkot lucky bag; Rs. 2,000 sent to the Bombay Women's Branch; Rs. 500 for fifty St. Raphael tickets; Rs. 500 for fifty tickets in the Western Indian Turf Club lottery in aid of the War Loan; Rs. 150 to the East India Station Naval Fund; two cavalry horses, each worth Rs. 1,000; Rs. 1,000 to the Recruiting Fund of the Kathiawar Company under formation; offer of four tents for the use of the abovementioned Company; at the request of the Agent to the Governor and the Commanding Officer, 125 Napier rifles; the State bungalow and outhouses at Rajkot were placed at the disposal of the military authorities; Rs. 2,000, given to the pageant held at Poona on September 18, 1918; Rs. 250, in aid of the Annandale Club, sent through Lady Hill; Rs. 200 to the Seamen's Institute; and Rs. 3,101 to Their Imperial Majesty's Silver Wedding Fund. The total contributions by the State to English and Indian War Loan Funds amounted to Rs. 50,32,000.

The State is 91 square miles in extent, less the territory transferred to Cutch in the exchange settlement of 1900, and it comprises 147 villages, the inhabitants according to the census of 1911, being 90,230 in number. The major portion of the State consists of a comparatively flat plain, hills being rarely seen, and the soil is, generally speaking, fertile in character, and suitable for the cultivation of cotton of a superior type.

The State maintains horticultural gardens at Morvi, Tankara, Adhoi, and other places, and nearly 800 young trees of various kinds were supplied from them for plantation purposes.

In the year 1906 a State Agricultural Bank was opened, and in addition to the very great financial assistance given by it to depositors during the famines of 1911-12 and 1915-16, the success of the institution is shown by the fact that there is at the present time a sum of more than Rs. 5,00,000 standing to the credit of investors.

The State workshops are exceedingly well equipped with plant and machinery, and in normal times they are employed in the manufacture of railway materials, agricultural implements, artistic furniture, and other necessaries, while they have also served as a training school for youths who have an aptitude for mechanical work. These works, in conjunction with those of the Bombay-Baroda and Central India Railway Company at Ajmer, were engaged from 1914 until the end of the year 1916 in making munitions of war, chiefly plates for shells.

All materials required for railway purposes, including the casting of iron and brass fittings, and the construction of rolling stock, are supplied by these shops, which also furnish electric power for the lighting of the palace, departmental offices, the guest-house, and other buildings in the town of Morvi. These workshops have been the means of preparing many poor boys to become fitters, drivers, and artisans, who now earn a good livelihood within the State and abroad. The credit of having produced a railway manager, a traffic superintendent, a resident engineer, a locomotive superintendent, and station masters, all of them Morvi men, belongs to His Highness.

The principal industrial enterprises are the manufacture of cotton fabrics, metal utensils, carved and inlaid ivory, fine gold thread, and gold, silver, and jewelled ornaments. With the object of inaugurating new commercial enterprises, His Highness the Thakore Saheb, in the year 1909, established an industrial and experimental department, in which he has expended a sum of Rs. 1,00,000 in carrying out experiments in pottery, glassware, and stoneware.

The construction of works of public utility has been a marked feature of the administration of His Highness the Thakore Saheb, and since his assumption of the reins of government the sum of more than Rs. 20,000,000 has been expended under this heading. The following are some of the more important undertakings, namely: Railway, Rajkot to Wadhwan and Wankaner to Morvi, 92 miles, costing Rs. 55,00,000; tramways, 66 miles, Morvi-Navlakhia, 30 miles; Morvi-Wawania; Morvi-Tankara, 14

THE STATE OF MORVI.

1. SUSPENSION BRIDGE. 2. BRIDGE VIEW FROM HILL BUILDINGS.

miles; Morvi-Jetpur-Khakhrechi road, 22 miles, Rs. 11,00,000; Waterworks, Rs. 7,00,000; Navlakhi Bundar road and wharf, Rs. 5,00,000; River face-wall, Rs. 4,00,000; High School, Rs. 40,000; Asylum, Rs. 25,000; Electric plant, Rs. 1,00,000; Clock Tower, Rs. 60,000; Grain market, Rs. 25,000; Agricultural plant, Rs. 1,00,000; Suspension Bridge, Rs. 50,000; Widening bazar, Rs. 4,00,000; Telephones (about 100 connections), Rs. 1,00,000; District roads, Rs. 6,00,000; Workshops (excluding machinery), Rs. 25,000; Patel House, Rs. 35,000; a Crematorium, Rs. 30,000; Jail, Rs. 40,000; Native Guest-house, Rs. 35,000; Bridges, Rs. 1,00,000; and the Hill Buildings (Secretariat), Rs. 2,50,000.

The "Mani Mandir," which is nearing completion, and which has so far cost more than Rs. 12,00,000, is also one of the wonders of Morvi, and in point of style and architecture it will rank as one of the finest on this side of India.

The trading activities of the inhabitants of the State are greatly facilitated by the Morvi State Railway and the network of tramway lines which connect the capital town with various commercial centres, and cotton ginning, pressing, and other factories. One of the tramway sections is laid from Morvi town to the seaport of Navlakhi, whence consignments of goods may be shipped by steam launches to neighbouring ports. Other tramways extend from Morvi Railway Station to Wawania, 23 miles in length; to Jetpur, 16 miles, and thence to Khakhrechi road. The Navlakhi and Jetpur sections are connected with outside agencies, by which means goods can be booked through to stations on the principal Indian railways. These out-stations are at the port of Navlakhi, Wawania, Jetpur, and Tankara, and passengers can be booked through from them to Bombay. The total capital outlay of the whole tramway system is Rs. 10,72,655.

The Morvi Railway is about 93 miles in length, and the gross earnings for the past year were Rs. 14,44,127, while the working expenses amounted to Rs. 4,17,637, thus leaving a net profit of Rs. 10,26,490, which gives a dividend of 19·16 upon the invested capital. The total value of all kinds of goods imported into Morvi during the past revenue year was Rs. 25,07,403, while exports amounted to Rs. 70,04,729.

For the preservation of law and order the State is patrolled by 642 police of all grades. The head of the Department is the Superintendent, who is assisted by a city *Fouzdar*, divisional officers, and others of lower rank. The force consists of 131 regular police, 29 mounted men, and 482 irregular police, including village constables, Arabs, and Makranis.

The following tribunals have been established for the administration of criminal justice, namely: Four Magistrates' Courts, one of which at Morvi exercises powers of the first class; the *Sir Nyayadhish* Court, the *Diwani Nyayadhish* Court; the Small Cause Court and the *Nyayadhish* Courts at Adhoi, and in the northern and southern divisions. The *Huzur* Court is the highest authority of appeal in the State, and it also exercises powers of revision and reference.

There is a central jail at Morvi, together with a lockup at the district headquarters of Tankara, Derala, and Adhoi.

The gross revenue receipts for the financial year ending September 30, 1918, were respectively, Rs. 13,63,475 and Rs. 5,33,822. The State pays an annual tribute of Rs. 9,263 to the British Government, Rs. 49,209 as *Peshkashi* to the State of Baroda, and Rs. 3,093 as *Zortalbi* to the State of Junagadh.

The institutions maintained by the State for affording medical relief are eight in number, comprising an asylum and hospital at the capital town, and six dispensaries at important district centres.

The installation of a telephone system throughout the length and breadth of the State has been a great boon to the State and the people. Besides facilitating administration generally, they help the district police in reporting cases of accidents and of serious illness, and thanks to the fine network of public roads and the free use of motor-cars provided by the State, medical officers are able to avoid delay in attending patients.

Education for the young was made compulsory several years ago, but quite recently the Durbar, realizing that this hard and fast rule entails some hardships, especially among the agricultural community who frequently found it necessary to employ their children in cultivated fields, withdrew the order of compulsion for one year, and made the question of attendance at schools a purely voluntary one. The State now maintains 34 primary schools, in which there are enrolled the names of 1,385 pupils, with an average daily attendance of 1,083, while 221 girls are being educated in two separate institutions.

The principal library and reading-room maintained by the State is situated in the Hill Building (in which all State Departmental Officers are located), in Morvi, and it is well stocked with valuable literary works, newspapers, periodicals, and magazines. There is also a library attached to the State Engineer's office, which contains a unique collection of more than 2,200 selected volumes of treatises on science, technology, engineering, and other subjects, which is valued at fully Rs. 12,000.

The State printing press is employed in printing and publishing the official gazette of Morvi, and in executing miscellaneous work for the public offices and for private individuals. The net earnings for the past year were Rs. 5,344.

The four Municipalities in the State are at Morvi, Tankara, Wawania, and Adhoi, and these are maintained by the Durbar, the total expenditure for the year 1918–19 being Rs. 3,887.

THE NEW FORT PALACE, FROM THE BAZAAR.

THE STATE OF NARSINGARH

THE mediatized Chiefship of Narsingarh, in the Bhopal Political Agency in Central India, is situated in that part of the Malwa Plateau known as Umatwara, designated thus after the Umat clan of Rajputs, to which the Rulers of the State belong.

The boundaries of the State are well-nigh indistinguishably intermingled with the brother State of Rajgarh, but, in a general way, it may be said to be bordered on the north by the States of Indore, Khilchipur and Rajgarh, on the east by the State of Bhopal, on the west by the States of Gwalior and Dewas, and on the south by Bhopal and Gwalior.

Narsingarh is also historically connected with Rajgarh, as the Chiefs of both States are descended from Dudaji, younger brother and Prime Minister of Udaji, who was Chief of Rajgarh during the early part of the 17th century. About the year 1660, Rawat Mohan Singh, a minor, succeeded to the Rajgarh *gadi*, and the administration of the State was entrusted to his cousin, Diwan Ajab Singh, the latter being subsequently superseded by his son, Paras Ram. Differences soon afterwards arose between the partisans of the Rawat and those of his Minister, and in 1668 an arrangement was made for a kind of joint rule over the State by the two branches of the family. This arrangement succeeded for a time, but in 1681 an actual division of territory took place, and Paras Ram, leaving Patan, his former residence, founded the town and State of Narsingarh.

Existing records do not relate anything of great importance connected with the State until the year 1819, when Subhag Singh, the Ruler at that time, became mentally afflicted. The management of Narsingarh was placed in the hands of the heir-apparent, Chain Singh, who subsequently quarrelled with the Political Agent, and attacked the British forces at Sehore, when he was killed in an engagement with them. Subhag Singh, having recovered in health, was again entrusted with the rulership, and upon his death he was succeeded by Hanwant Singh, who, in 1872, was honoured by the bestowal of the hereditary title of Raja, with a salute of 11 guns. He died in 1873, and a claim for succession duty from Pratap Singh, the heir to the *gadi*, made by the Holkar of Indore, was disallowed by the British Government. In 1880 this Chief abolished duties upon salt carried through the State in return for an annual payment of Rs. 618. Four years later consigners were relieved of the payment of all transit duties excepting that on opium, and in further proof of the Raja's desire to encourage the growth of commercial and industrial enterprises, and to facilitate the transport of merchandize, he contributed Rs. 56,000 towards the construction of a new road between Sehore and Biaora. Pratap Singh attended the Durbar held at Sehore simultaneously with the Imperial Assemblage at Delhi in 1877. He was the first Rajput Chief

HIS HIGHNESS RAJA SIR ARJUN SINGHJI SAHIB BAHADUR, K.C.I.E., OF NARSINGARH (PRESENT CHIEF).

THE STATE OF NARSINGARH.

1. Sri Maharaj Kumar Vikram Singhji, Sahib Bahadur (Heir-Apparent). 2. Khan Bahadur Munshi Enayat Hussain, Khan Sahib (Diwan). 3. Group of Chhatris of the late Chiefs of Narsingarh. 4. The Arjun Kiwas Palace.

to cross the black water and proceed to England, which he visited in 1887. In England he had the unique honour of an audience with Her Majesty Queen Victoria of sacred memory. The University of Edinburgh conferred upon him the Honorary Degree of D.C.L. Pratap Singh died without male issue in 1890, and was succeeded by his uncle, Raja Mahtab Singh. When Raja Mahtab Singh also died without issue in 1896, the British Government selected the present Ruler, Arjun Singh of the Bhatkhera Thakur's family, as the next occupant of the *gadi*. The full title of the present Chief is His Highness Raja Sir Arjunsingh Sahib Bahadur, K.C.I.E.

His Highness, born in January, 1887, was educated at the Daly College at Indore, and subsequently at the Mayo College, Ajmere, and the Imperial Cadet Corps at Dehradun. During the period of minority the State was managed by Superintendents under the di e.t cont:ol of the Political Agents.

His Highness belongs to the clan of Umat Rajputs, who are a branch of the illustrious Parmars, the former Lords of Malwa, and he is related by marriage to the ruling houses of Jodhpur, Sailana, Khetri (Jaipur), and Indargarh (Kotah). He was invested with full ruling powers in 1909 by Sir Hugh Daly, who referred in his speech to the development of the State which had taken place since the death of the previous Chief, more specially with regard to the liquidation of debts and the accumulation of a substantial Treasury reserve. The surplus thus acquired enabled the Durbar to assuage the sufferings of the people of Narsingarh during the great famine of 1899 1900 without borrowing money, notwithstanding the fact that more than a million persons were relieved at a cost exceeding Rs. 1,00,000. At the initiative of His Highness metalled roads have been constructed along the principal routes of communication, the various State Departments have been re-organized, the land revenue settlement has been extended to all *jagirs* in Narsingarh, modern systems of revenue accounts have been adopted, a State Bank, Panchayats, Co-operative Societies and Grain Co-operative Stores, from which advances of money and seed-grain may be obtained, have been established, and large sums of money have been expended on public works. There has been a large increase in forest receipts, Excise and Customs; and medical relief and the provision of educational facilities have received sympathetic attention from His Highness.

The enlightened administration of His Highness, the Raja Sahib, was recognized by His Majesty the King-Emperor in 1916, when the distinction of a Knight Commandership of the Most Eminent Order of the Indian Empire was conferred upon him.

In January, 1917, the Hon. Mr. O. V. Bosanquet, C.S.I., C.I.E., I.C.S., the Agent to the Governor-General in Central India, paid a visit to Narsingarh for the purpose of decorating His Highness with the insignia of the high order to which reference has just been made.

A grand Durbar was held in the Arjun Niwas Palace, and after Mr. Bosanquet had affixed the ribbon, badge, and star upon His Highness, the former gave an interesting address, which commenced as follows:

"I voice the feelings of this assembly in offering our sincere congratulations on the honour which His Gracious Majesty the King-Emperor has been pleased to bestow upon Your Highness. It is a recognition of Your Highness' steadfast loyalty to His Imperial Majesty the King-Emperor, and of your capable administration of your State and regard for the welfare of your subjects." The speaker then gave a *résumé* of the beneficent measures inaugurated by His Highness, and concluded by saying:

"All these improvements are well-known in Narsingarh, but I refer to them here as a part of the reasons which have led to the grant of the decoration, on which we all congratulate Your Highness. May you live long to enjoy it, and to continue to promote the welfare of your people."

On the conclusion of this ceremony Mr. Bosanquet handed to His Highness the Kaisar-i-Hind Gold Medal, conferred upon Her Highness the Sani Sahiba in the New Year's honours list of 1916, and he remarked: "The services thus recognized by His Majesty have won for Her Highness the gratitude of the people of Narsingarh. To mention only a few, it was at her suggestion, on the birth of her first son, that Your Highness established the Vikram Hospital for Pardanashin patients and children with the funds subscribed by the public to commemorate that happy event. The good work which it does is largely due to Her Highness's support, for she provides the lady doctor in charge, and takes a personal share in the management, besides contributing from her own purse to its equipment and upkeep. The institution completes the scheme of medical relief inaugurated by Her Highness the Maharani Bhatianiji, who founded the Mahtab Hospital opened in 1908. Having enjoyed a liberal education herself, Her Highness the Rani Sahiba has placed similar advantages within the reach of the girls of the State by founding and supporting the Shiv Kumari Girls' School, which, when last I heard, had an attendance of over 100 girls. Her Highness could have devised no better means than those two Institutions for promoting the welfare of the women of the Narsingarh State, and their benefits will, I know, be more and more appreciated as time goes on.

"We heartily congratulate Her Highness on the distinction by which His Majesty has recognized her achievements."

The Agent to the Governor-General then presented the usual *sanad* and badge of the title of Khan Bahadur, which had been bestowed upon Munshi Enayat Hussain, the Dewan of the Narsingarh State, and in a few words of congratulation, he said: "I take this opportunity to present to your new Dewan Khan Sahib Munshi Enayat Hussain the *sanad* and badge of the title which was conferred on him last year. He comes of a family which, though belonging to the United Provinces, has been connected with the Central India Agency for three generations. His father was Superintendent of Sehore for many years, and he himself has served the Agency well during the period of over 20 years, of which seven were spent as Superintendent of Minor Estates in the Southern States Agency, and five as Attaché to the Agent to the Governor-General. I feel sure that his experience, ability and integri y will fully justify Your Highness's selection of him as your Dewan, and that Your Highness will be able to repose complete confidence in him."

In the evening of the same day Her Highness, the Rani Sahiba, gave a garden party in the grounds of the Palace, which was attended by all the distinguished guests who had been present at the Durbar, and at a later hour the same gentlemen accepted the hospitality of His Highness at a State dinner.

Another important function in the same year, on September 5th, was the presentation of an address to His Highness the Raja Sahib by the Members

THE STATE OF NARSINGARH.

1. The Guest-house. 2. King Edward Memorial Market. 3. Victoria High School. 4. General View of Narsingarh Town from the adjoining Hills. 5. The King George Club.

of the King George Club at Narsingarh, in order to commemorate the honour of the bestowal of the title of K.C.I.E. upon the Chief.' The words of the address convey such a deep sense of the high respect in which His Highness is held by his subjects, that a few sentences may be quoted here: "Your Highness has so endeared yourself to all your subjects, high and low, by innumerable qualities of head and heart, by your genuine sympathy in their joys and sorrows, by your keen anxiety to see evenhanded justice dealt to all of them, and by your sincere desire for, and ever-vigilant watchfulness over, their welfare and interests that they have an innate pleasure in seeing Your Highness honoured by this well-deserved distinction, and it is no wonder that they all vie with one another in giving expression to their natural feelings. We, the Members of the King George Club, fully share these feelings of the whole populace, and though a little belated in our expression of them in a formal manner, we assure Your Highness that, in the sincerity and earnestness of our express, we are behind none of them.

"Your Highness, as Members of the King George Club, we have the special privilege and honour of enjoying Your Highness' society on evenings at the Club, when Your Highness condescends to put aside all regal authority and Court formalities, and freely mixes with us in our games and pastimes. We also have the honour of possessing in Your Highness a most talented and sympathetic Patron and President of the Club. We therefore look upon this honour and distinction, which the benign British Government has conferred upon Your Highness, as an honour done to the Club, and we feel the prouder."

His Highness has one son, Maharaj Kumar Vikram Singh, the heir apparent, and three little Princesses. Maharaj Kumar Vikram Singh, the heir apparent, was born in 1908, and is now in the 12th year of his age. He is studying at the Daly College, Indore, which institution he joined in 1920. He is making good progress in his studies and takes a keen interest in games. The Princesses are very young, and are studying at home with a governess, a tutor, and a Pandit.

The State does not pay any tribute to the British Government, but it recognizes its liability for an annual sum of Rs. 85,000, Salim Shahi coin, to the State of Indore, which is discharged through the medium of the British Government. This liability was occasioned during the 18th century, on the subjugation of Narsingarh by the Mahrathas, when the Raja was compelled to agree to this payment in order to preserve his independence. At the time of the settlement of Malwa, by Sir John Malcolm in 1818, an arrangement was entered into between the Chief of Narsingarh and the Rulers of Indore, Gwalior and Dewas, by which regular instalments were guaranteed to Holkar, and in which acknowledgment of the receipt by Narsingarh of two cash grants of Rs. 1,200 and Rs. 5,102 from Gwalior and Dewas respectively in settlement of certain claims on the Shujalpur and Sarangpur perganas of the State now under notice.

The State of Narsingarh is 734 square miles in extent, and its inhabitants, 110,000 in number, comprise Hindus, 90 per cent. of the total population, Animists (of whom nearly one half are Bhils 5 per cent., and Mahomedans 4 per cent., while the chief castes are Brahmans, Rajputs, Chamars and Balais.

The four administrative divisions of the State are Narsingarh, Pachore, Khujnere, and Chhapihera, and each of these is placed under a *tahsildar*, who is collector of revenue, and is also invested with magisterial powers.

The State is also proprietor of all lands, villages being leased to farmers, who are responsible for the assessed revenue of their individual holdings, all rates being fixed according to the quality of the soil, but with an additional amount where irrigation is carried out. The area under actual cultivation in 1916–17 was 143,485 acres, and the revenue demand for that period was Rs. 4,35,382. It may be observed here that it is obvious that occupiers are intelligent and capable cultivators, as the actual annual collections for the past few years have averaged from 97 per cent. to 99 per cent. of the assessments. The culturable soil consists largely of the fertile black type, and the principal crops are jowar, sown on 141 square miles of the total area, cotton 27 square miles, wheat 20 square miles, maize 17 square miles, gram 14 square miles, and poppy 8 square miles.

Narsingarh forests are 141 square miles in extent, and the whole area is classed as "reserved." Diligent efforts are being made by the conservator to maintain the value of the forests and tracts, in which coppice shoots are grown from felled trees, and nurseries, where suitable seeds are sown for subsequent transplantation purposes, are securely closed against grazing cattle.

Commercial enterprises have never been of great importance in the State, and the disastrous war of 1914–18 caused such an increase in the cost of imported goods, that general trading has been brought to a low standard. A few home industries, such as the weaving of coarse cloth and the making of ordinary household goods, give employment to a few persons, but there are not any manufactures worth mentioning. Cotton ginning factories have been established at Pachore, Khujnere and Narsingarh, and they usually deal with from 15,000 to 18,000 maunds (maund = 80 lb.) of cotton annually.

The transactions of the State Bank amounted in 1916–17 to Rs. 5,78,492, and a net profit of Rs. 11,955 enabled the management to pay a dividend at the rate of 15 per cent.

The Public Works Department, under the control of the State Engineer, expends from Rs. 50,000 to Rs. 60,000 annually, but this sum naturally varies according to the quantity of new constructive work carried out. Taking a recent year, by way of example, State Administration Reports show that new buildings necessitated an expenditure of nearly Rs. 26,000, repairs to others cost Rs. 6,800, the sum of about Rs. 6,000 was spent upon roads, repairs of wells, and tanks cost Rs. 800, and improvements and establishment charges amounted to Rs. 7,000.

Although Narsingarh has, in common with other States in India, been prejudicially affected by the 'a e general dislocation of commercial activities, it has a considerable trade in exports, as the following figures will show. In a recent year the grain consigned from the State amounted in value to about Rs. 12,000, ghee to Rs. 2,000, raw and cleaned cotton to Rs. 12,340; cattle to nearly Rs. 16,000, and miscellaneous goods to Rs. 3,000. The imports during the same period included cloth worth Rs. 3,000, salt, Rs. 1,250; sular, Rs. 1,000; and other merchandise, Rs. 5,400.

The State possesses a distillery as well as a factory for making opium tablets at Narsingarh, and these are stocked in warehouses, whence they are despatched to the headquarters of each *tahsil* for sale in the surrounding districts.

His Highness, the Raja, is invested with full powers in general revenue, and judicial and in criminal matters, but in the last-named his jurisdiction is limited only so far that applications for mercy in cases

THE STATE OF NARSINGARH.

1. Entrance Gate to the Town of Narsingarh. 2. The Old Fort Palace from Parasran Sagar. 3. The State Courts.

where the punishment inflicted is death, transportation, or imprisonment for life, lies to the Hon. the Agent to the Governor-General in Central India. The tribunals for trying penal offences are the Ijilas Khas, the Dewan's Court, which is the Sessions Court, the Nizam's or First-Class Magistrate's Court, the Courts of the City Magistrate, and the four *tahsildars* with powers of Magistrates of the Second Class, and the Courts of the Chief Officers of the Forest and Excise Departments respectively. The Civil Courts are those presided over by the Dewan, the Nizam, the City Magistrate, and the *tahsildars*. The Central Jail at Narsingarh is under the supervision of the State Surgeon, and there are three others, together with five temporary detention buildings, in various parts of the State. Prisoners are usefully employed in weaving coarse cloth and making carpets, durries, blankets, tape and towels.

The strength of the Police Force is 261 men, and the proportion to the area and population of the State is one constable to 3 square miles and 421 persons. The annual expenditure of the Department is about Rs. 22,000.

Narsingarh is comparatively free from offences of a heinous character, and it is noted that about one-third of the finger impressions taken are those of Moghias, a settled criminal tribe, while the remainder are connected with wandering tribes.

The Military Forces of the State comprise 38 cavalry, 21 artillery, 90 infantry, 15 camel sowars, 173 irregulars and 16 attendants. The annual cost of this Service is about Rs. 36,000.

In connection with the medical supervision of Narsingarh, the attention of the professional staff was recently drawn to the fact that certain diseases, such as those of the respiratory and digestive organs and malaria, were still causing a high percentage of the annual mortality, and in spite of the difficulties experienced in preventing the introduction of ailments from outside, and of those caused by the indifferences of the people on the question of segregation of patients, the State Surgeon and his assistants have been most successful in their campaign.

Patients are received for treatment in three medical institutions, namely, the Mahtab and Vikram Female Hospitals at Narsingarh, and the Shiv Kumari Hospital at Khujnere, while attention is given to outdoor cases at the dispensaries of Pachore and Chhapihera.

His Highness the Raja is indefatigable in his efforts to encourage his subjects to give their children such education as will enable them to become honoured citizens of Narsingarh, or of any other places where they make their homes.

At the present time there are about 1,100 pupils receiving instruction in 18 teaching institutions, one of which is a High School teaching up to the Matric standard. This readiness to help in every possible way was acknowledged by the Agent to the Governor-General in Central India, in a speech delivered by him on January 8, 1917, when the following words were uttered :

" Fate unfortunately prevented Your Highness from serving His Majesty in the field, but you placed the resources of your State at the disposal of the British Government, and have assisted towards the cost of the War to the full extent of your capacity."

A list of donations in money and other gifts, contributed by Their Highnesses

THE MAHTAB MALE HOSPITAL.

the Raja Sahib Bahadur and Maharani Jodhpuriji Sahiba, was published in the State Administration Report for the year 1916–17, and a copy thereof is here set forth.

To the Imperial Indian Relief Fund, Rs. 33,000; St. John's Ambulance Fund, Rs. 500; the Prince of Wales's Fund, Rs. 8,000; the Imperial Relief Fund, Rs. 500; the Khaki Fund, Rs. 500; for the relief of wounded sepoys in the war, Rs. 500; to the Lord Kitchener Fund, Rs. 500; donation to relieve the Prisoners of War in Germany, Rs. 75; the Officer's Family Fund, Rs. 10,000; for relief of helpless persons in Belgium, Rs. 100; War Loan Fund, Rs. 1,74,000; Our Day collections, Rs. 5,925; to His Excellency the Viceroy's War Gifts Fund, Rs. 7,500; to the Imperial Relief Fund (Red Cross), Rs. 1,080; subscription towards the Sehore War Bulletine, Rs. 630; two complete tents, and gift of one hundred sleeping suits presented by Her Highness Maharani Jodhpuriji Sahiba of Narsingarh.

The town of Narsingarh, the Capital of the State, is most picturesquely situated on the edge of an artificial lake, about 1,650 feet above the level of the sea, while towering above it is the old fort, several palaces, temples, and other interesting buildings.

The town was founded by Paras Ram, the first Chief of Narsingarh, in the year 1681, and it is constructed on the site of an old village named Toplia Mahadeo.

The town was constituted a municipality a few years ago, and the Commissioners have been most energetic in making improvements, in order that its general appearance may harmonize more completely with the natural pleasing aspects of its situation. Several roads have been widened, the platforms of wells, as well as drains, have been made of masonry, with the object of carrying away overflow of water which formerly tended to keep thoroughfares in a muddy condition, and persons who contemplate building homes or places of business, are now required to submit plans of the same with the view of securing improved hygienic and sanitary conditions.

The King Edward Memorial Market has recently been transferred from its old site outside the town to a place more suitable for the purpose by the Public Works Department, at a cost of Rs. 5,000, and its position in a busy portion of the town is not the least of its many advantages. The site of the mausoleums of the old Chiefs of Narsingarh, which lay desolate and dirty in the heart of the town, has been improved, and they now are the central feature of a beautiful garden, where it is a pleasure to walk about.

His Highness's desire to be of service to his subjects was further demonstrated by the provision of a commodious club building with spacious grounds for the recreation of the people of the capital. The work in the provision of which the able and energetic Dewan Munshi Enayat Hussain co-operated, and for which the inhabitants of the town were duly grateful, is known as the Shri Arjun Club.

Unfortunately a constitutional ailment, which grew in severity with the advance of years, and in due course practically disabled His Highness, necessitated a reconsideration by the Raja Sahib of his position as head of the State, and in November, 1920, he decided upon retirement from active work. Subsequently, His Highness established a Council of Regency, with Her Highness Rani Jodhpuriji Sahiba, his beloved and able consort, as the Regent, the Political Agent in Bhopal as the President, Dewan Khan Bahadur Munshi Enayat Hussein as the Vice-President, and two ordinary members and one consultative member to complete the Council. Her Highness the Rani Sahiba's solicitude for the welfare of her people in the early stage of her regency induced her to cause special attention to be given to the question of *begár* (forced labour) in the State, and following the appointment of a special committee of inquiry a satisfactory solution of the problem was reached, much to the relief and gratification of the poorer classes of the people.

Narsingarh is 44 miles from Sehore Station, on the Bhopal-Ujjain branch of the G.I.P. Railway.

HIS HIGHNESS, WITH RETAINERS AND STAFF READY FOR A PROCESSION.

THE STATE OF PANNA

SITUATED in the Bundelkhand Political Charge of the Central India Agency is the *sanad* State of Panna, which is bounded on the north by the district of Banda and the States of Ajaigarh and Bhausaunda; on the east by the States of Kothi, Nagod and Ajaigarh; on the south by the districts of Jubbulpore and Damoh; and on the west by the States of Chhatarpur, Charkhari and Bijawar. The history of Panna as an independent Principality dates from the time of the founder of the State, Maharaja Chhatarsal, who was the son of Champat Rai, a brave prince greatly distinguished in the wars with the Moghuls in the early part of the seventeenth century.

Maharaja Chhatarsal was only about thirteen years of age on his father's death in 1662. On reaching manhood he entered upon a military career which left him, on the death of the Emperor Aurungzeb in 1707, the Ruler of possessions which extended from the Betwa to the Tons rivers and from the Jumna nearly as far as Jubbulpore.

Maharaja Chhatarsal died in 1732 when 80 years of age, and his cenotaph may be seen on the road to Nowgong in the village of Mau, in the State of Chhatarpur. His descendants are now in possession of, in addition to Panna, Ajaigarh, Charkhari, Jaso, Bijawar, Jigni, Lugasi, and Sarila.

Chhatarsal's eldest son, Hirde Shah, succeeded to the *gadi* of Panna, which dates its existence as a separate Chiefship from that year. The history of the State during the eighteenth century was of an extremely chequered description. Bundelkhand was one of the storm-centres in the period of Moghul decadence, and there was continual fighting in the efforts made by contending forces to secure supremacy. Ultimately the country was reduced to a state of anarchy, the Mahratta power being mainly in the ascendant. The British operations in Bundelkhand at the close of the century gave a new turn to events, and on the conclusion of the Treaty of Bassein the whole of the Mahratta Peshwa's possessions in that region were placed under British rule.

British supremacy was firmly established in 1803, when Kishor Singh, nominally ruling at Panna, was in reality an exile. He was, however, granted *sanads* of confirmation in 1807 and 1811. His oppressive government caused British intervention on several occasions, and in 1834 he was deposed, his son Harbans Rai being installed as Regent.

Kishor Singh died in the same year and Harbans Rai succeeded to the *gadi*, but his Rulership was devoid of events of great importance, and he died, without leaving issue, in 1849. Although Nirpat Singh was the legal successor of the previous Ruler, the Government refused to recognize him as such, until he had abolished the practice of *sati* throughout his territories.

After being invested with ruling powers Nirpat Singh manifested great ability as an administrator. His strong support of the British during the Sepoy Mutiny of

H.H. MAHENDRA MAHARAJA YADVENDRA SINGH SAHIB BAHADUR.

THE STATE OF PANNA.

1. Raja Bahadur Narendra Singh Sahib, Heir-Apparent. 2. Interior of Durbar Hall, showing Throne.

THE STATE OF PANNA.

1. Raj Mander—An Old Palace. 2. Nahendra Bhuwan—His Highness's Palace. 3. New Kothi.

THE STATE OF PANNA.

1. Town View. 2. Club 3. Guest House. 4. Bird's-eye View of Panna Town

THE STATE OF PANNA.

1. Lake View—Dewan's Residence. 2. Lakshamipur Palace. 3. Rani Bagh—Residence of His Highness's Mother.
4. Kerban—A Shooting-box Two and a Half Miles from the Capital.

THE STATE OF PANNA.

1. Cenotaphs of the Old Rulers of Panna State, in Nazar Bagh. 2. Shri Badeoji's Temple. 3. Shri Jugalkishorji's Temple. 4. Saint Pran Nathje's Temple.

THE STATE OF PANNA.

1. Workshops. 2. Jail. 3. Sardar Boarding Quarters. 4. Hospital. 5. High School.

1857 was most commendable, and in recognition of his services the Government rewarded him with a *khilat* of the value of Rs. 20,000 together with a grant of the *pergana* of Simaria. In 1862 a *sanad* of adoption was granted to him, and in 1869 he was given the personal title of Mahendra which was made hereditary in the ruling House of Panna in 1875.

The Maharaja died in 1870, and was succeeded on the *gadi* by Maharaja Rudra Pratap, who in 1875 had the honour of receiving from the hands of His Royal Highness the Prince of Wales (afterwards King Edward VII) the insignia of a Knight Commander of the Most Exalted Order of the Star of India. His Highness was a guest at the Imperial Assemblage at Delhi in 1877, and in commemoration of the event, he was granted as a personal honour an addition of two guns to his salute, and he was also presented with a banner and medal. The Maharaja died without issue in 1893, and his brother, Maharaja Lokpal Singh, succeeded to the *gadi*. The only event claiming notice during this *regime* was the terrible famine of 1897, in which His Highness laboured incessantly in establishing relief works, in distributing food-grains, money, and other necessities, and in numerous other ways calculated to relieve the dire distress of his suffering subjects. His Highness died in 1897 and the reins of Government devolved upon his son, Madho Singh, who was deposed in 1902.

The successor to the *gadi* was the present Prince, whose title is His Highness the Maharaja Mahendra Yadvendra Singh Bahadur, Maharaja of Panna. His Highness was born in January, 1893, and during his minority the State was administered by a Diwan and Council, under the direction of the Political Agent. The young Prince spent ten years of profitable study at the Mayo College, Ajmer, and he subsequently undertook a course of training in the Imperial Cadet Corps.

His Highness was married in December, 1912, to the only daughter of the late Maharaja Sir Bhav Singhji, of Bhavnagar. The ceremony as well as the festivities were conducted with all the pomp and splendour for which the East is justly famous, and the large gathering comprised ruling Princes and notabilities of a number of Indian States, in addition to several European guests.

THE STATE OF PANNA.
STATE TROOPS ON PARADE.

The State suffered severely from famine during the years 1905-06, 1907-08, and 1913-14, and too high praise cannot be given to the administration for the strenuous efforts made at tremendous cost to alleviate the poverty and sufferings of the people.

His Highness was invested with full ruling powers on February 4, 1915.

His Highness quickly realized the responsibilities of the high position to which he had been inducted, and he forthwith made a careful investigation into the working of each Department of State and introduced many measures of reform in administration, which have already been productive of great good for the general welfare of his subjects. Full hereditary powers to try all criminal cases were granted to the State on March 1, 1921.

The heir-apparent, Raja Bahadur Narendra Singh Ju Dev, was born in the year 1915, and a second Prince, Pushpende Singh Ju Dev, was born on October 25, 1916.

The State of Panna, 2,596 square miles in extent, consists of seven *tahsils*, or divisions, but they do not form one distinct block, but are detached and occasionally separated by considerable distances. The *tahsils* of Panna, Pawai, and Mahodra, form a fairly compact area; Malahra lies to the south-west of this block; Aktohan is wholly in the district of Banda; Dharampur is on the south side of Banda; and Birsingpur, to the east, is near to the States of Kothi and Sohawal.

One part of the State, along the line of the Panna range, is hilly in character and covered almost entirely by dense forests, while the other section, known as the Haveli valley, is a level alluvial plain.

Diamonds are the most valuable of all the minerals found in the State, but first-class building stone is found practically all over the hilly portion, especially in the Upper Kaimur and Upper Bhander. Two kinds of iron ore, classed as lateritic and heomatitic, are plentiful, but the manufacture of the substance into a commercial commodity has been reduced to a minimum owing to severe competition of imported iron, a first-class grade of yellow and some red ochre are found in Birsingpur.

The inhabitants of the State, 228,880 in number at the census of 1911, comprise people of various castes, the following being the most important, namely: Brahmans, 12 per cent.; Chamars, 11 per cent.; Lodhis, 8 per cent.; Ahirs and Kurmis, 7 per cent.; Kachhis, 5 per cent.; and Rajputi, 4 per cent. of the total.

Classified according to religious creeds, it is shown that 90 per cent. of the population are Hindus, 6 per cent. are Animists, and 3 per cent. are Mahomedans, the remainder consisting of Jains, Sikhs and Christians.

For administrative purposes the State is divided into the following seven *tahsils*, namely, Panna, with an area of about 619 square miles with a sub-tahsil of Singpur; Pawai, 570 square miles with sub-tahsils of Shahnagar and Amangunj; Semaria with a sub-tahsil of Raipura and Buxwaho with a sub-tahsil of Malahra, 487 square miles; Birsingpur, 135 square miles; Dharampur, 93 square miles; and Aktohan, 31 square miles. The Chief exercises final and absolute control in all general questions connected with the administration. He is the final authority of appeal in civil and criminal cases.

THE STATE OF PANNA.

1. Dharam Sagar Tank. 2. Lokpal Sagar Tank. 3. The Palace of Maharaja Hirdeshah at Mhow. 4. The Ruins of an Old Fort at Mhow.

THE STATE OF PANNA.

1. Shri Jagdishji's Temple. 2. Cenotaph of the Founder of the State.

THE STATE OF PANNA.

1. Diamond Mines as worked at present. 2. Pandwa Falls. 3. View of Biskamgank Ghauts. 4. View of Ken Ghauts.

The principal executive officer is the Diwan, who controls the working of all Departments and is the highest court of appeal in revenue matters. The *Tahsildars* in charge of the seven divisions are assistant revenue officers exercising magisterial powers as well as authority to dispose of civil actions up to Rs. 50 in value.

A survey of land for revenue purposes was made in the year 1908, and a settlement of assessment carried out by a British official is now the basis upon which collections are made. Rents were formerly paid upon valuations of seed sown, or upon calculations of the probable results of harvest, but this method proved to be so unsatisfactory that cash rents have now been substituted which are based upon a correctly ascertained average, and proportioned to classes of soil.

Tenures are of two kinds, namely, (*a*) lands directly managed by the Durbar; and (*b*) alienated land held by *jagirdars* and others. Occupiers may avail themselves of the right of inheritance, but they are not allowed to transfer their holdings, and occupancy rents may not be increased during the term of settlement.

The soils of the State are only moderately fertile excepting in the Haveli Valley comprising the *tahsils* of Pawai, Simaria, Singhpur, Buxwaho, and Birsingpur, and a portion of Panna where excellent crops of various kinds are cultivated without the aid of irrigation.

Agricultural occupations are followed by more than 60 per cent. of the inhabitants, the most successful cultivators being Lodhis, Kurmis, Kachhis, and Talis.

Rich and extensive forests of varying density occur in every part of the State, excepting in the Haveli country, and there are also large tracts of scrub jungles. The area actually covered by forests is about 1,800 square miles in extent, and the principal trees include teak, bamboo, mango and *khair*, although there are many others of the usual Central India type.

It is not quite twenty years since the administration of forests was placed on a sound working basis, and a fully-qualified Conservator — with several Assistants—is now employed in protecting existing trees, in rearing and transplanting saplings, in forming fire-belts, and in the thousand and one other duties which are necessary for this extremely valuable portion of the State. The revenue derived from forests in the year 1907, when systematic forestry was commenced, was about Rs. 30,000, but owing to proper management the receipts have now reached a much larger figure.

THE STATE OF PANNA.
STATE ELEPHANT.

Reference has already been made to the diamonds found in the neighbourhood of the capital town, but a few further particulars extracted from the Panna State Gazetteer may be added. "From a crystallographic point of view the Panna diamonds are modifications of the hexakis-octahedron. The crystals are ordinarily remarkably perfect, the surface beautifully smooth, and the colour a brilliant white seldom seen in South African specimens, or of a blue-grey colour never seen in them. An exquisite pale sea-green stone, called *banspat*, or bamboo leaf, is found, which, however, becomes white when cut; they are rare. Of 235 stones examined, 71 per cent. were pure white." The Panna mines have been well known since the early portion of the eighteenth century, and modern history says that they were first worked about the year 1740, but it is generally believed that they were in existence long before that time, although not systematically worked. It is said that the State about the year 1750 derived as much as Rs. 4,00,000 annually from the sale of diamonds, but the receipts do not now exceed the sum of Rs. 10,000. One stone taken from the mines, weighing about 100 carats, is in the possession of the present Ruler.

The chief exports are grain, timber, building stone and diamonds, while imports include piece-goods, sugar, salt, kerosene oil and spices. The principal market towns are Panna, Birsingpur, Raipura, Malahra, Pawai, Simaria, Singhpur, Amanganj, and Mahodra, but a considerable quantity of merchandise changes hands at weekly sales in several of the larger villages.

The principal trade routes are along the metalled roads to Sutna, E.I. Railway, and Nowgong and thence to the Harpalpur station on the Jhansi-Manikpur section of the Great Indian Peninsula Railway to Banda.

Not many years ago educational facilities were obtainable only at one State school—English and vernacular—and a small number of private institutions, but there are now more than 50 schools, 11 of which are aided by the Durbar. A Sardars' boarding-house has been established at Panna with the object of encouraging *jagirdars* to place their sons under tuition. The Durbar at present bears the entire expenses of the boys, of whom about 50 are in residence.

THE STATE OF RADHANPUR

SITUATED in the southern portion of the Palanpur Political Agency in the north of Gujrat, under the Government of Bombay, is the first-class Mahomedan State of Radhanpur, which has an area of 1,150 square miles, with a population of 65,567 inhabitants, who reside in three towns and 171 villages.

The Nawabs of Radhanpur belong to the famous Babi family, that cast its fortunes in with the Moghuls. They came to India with Humayun, the second Moghul Emperor, whom the family regard as their first Indian patron. Usmankhan was the first to accompany Humayun, but the family acquired official positions and landed property in the time of Shah Jahan. Bahadurkhan Babi, the son of Usmankhan Babi, was for signal services rendered to the Emperor, appointed *Foujdar* of Tharad, which is now a separate State in the north-west portion of the Palanpur Agency. The Babis thus began to acquire distinction in the neighbourhood of the district that eventually was to be their own. On the break up of the Moghul power representatives of the family created for themselves an independent position in this part of Gujrat and in July, 1820, the reigning Nawab of Radhanpur (Sherkhan) concluded an agreement with the British by which he undertook not to harbour robbers, marauders, or any other enemies of the Supreme Government, and bound himself to assist British troops with all his available forces. He further agreed to pay an annual tribute in proportion to his means as the Government might direct. Payment under the last-named clause was made at the rate of Rs. 17,000 per annum until July, 1825, when the tribute was entirely remitted, and has not since that date been reimposed.

Nawab Sherkhan died in 1825, and was followed by his son, Zorawar Khan, then three years of age. During the period of minority the State was administered by Sardar Bibi, a widow of the recently deceased Nawab. Zorawar Khan was invested with full ruling powers on attaining his majority in the year 1837. He proved to be a wise and clever Ruler, devoted to the welfare of his people, encouraging the spread of education, and interesting himself deeply in the inauguration of measures of reform and progress. He beautified the town of Radhanpur by making a number of fine public gardens, provided the inhabitants with a plentiful supply of good water, and introduced numerous improvements in the management of State departments. A *sanad* of adoption according to Mahomedan law was granted to the Nawab in 1862.

One of the most important transactions completed by the Nawab was the surrender to the British of the monopoly for the manufacture of salt in the State in return for an annual payment of Rs. 11,048.

Zorawar Khan died in October, 1874, and was succeeded by his eldest son, Nawab Bismillah Khan, who was 32 years of age at the time. In honour of the Golden Jubilee of the reign of Her Majesty the late Queen-Empress Victoria, the Nawab erected the "Victoria Jubilee Institute," and also abolished all transit dues in the State, which were then realizing about Rs. 1,00,000 annually. The "Bismillah" Government Printing Press was started about the same time, and among other important works carried out upon the initiation of the Nawab were the erection of a fine clock tower in Radhanpur in commemoration of the Governorship of Bombay by Lord Harris, and the construction of the "Scott" canal (nine miles in length) and a central jail. The Nawab Bismillah Khan died in December, 1895, after a most successful rule of 21 years, and was succeeded by his eldest minor son, Mahomed Sherkhanji, the administration of the State being placed in the hands of British officials. During this period, which continued for about 12 years, many improvements in the work of the several departments were effected, and by good management the State enjoyed peace and prosperity. His Highness and his brother Jalaludinkhanji were educated at the Rajkumar College in Rajkot, where their diligent studies earned for them a large number of awards. The elder of the two brothers, the heir to the *gadi*, was, even in those days, a fine horseman and athlete, and among successes gained by him in the world of sport were the "Gordon" athletic medal and the "Ranjitsinghji" challenge cup.

Shortly after leaving college His Highness made an extended tour in Europe under the guidance of Dr. John Pollen, C.I.E., LL.D., and on his return he proceeded to Mecca in order to obtain *haj*, he thereafter being styled "Haji." Famine was rampant in the State between the years 1899 and 1903, and the excessive strain upon the treasury made it incumbent upon the Durbar to obtain loans from Government to the amount of Rs. 6,90,000. The several Administrators from 1903 to 1907 had no easy task to maintain efficiency in the management of State affairs, while at the same time they did all in their power to repay the sums borrowed from the Government, but when His Highness Mahomed Sherkhanji was endowed with full ruling powers, on April 13, 1907, he succeeded to a State

THE STATE OF RADHANPUR.

1. General View, Dasera Races, Radhanpur. 2. Snapshot at Races. 3. Cutchery Buildings. 4. Durbar Buildings from the River.

THE STATE OF RADHANPUR.

1. Fate-a-Kot Bungalow. 2. Durbar Buildings. 3. Wodehouse Club. 4. Lall Bagh Bungalow.

which was not only clear of debt, but which had a working balance (including a credit amount in the Bank of Bombay) of nearly Rs. 2,00,000.

His Highness at once threw himself heartily into the responsibilities of his high position; he introduced free education into the State, and made himself popular with his subjects by conducting personal investigations into their grievances, while he secured the devotion of the Hindus in the State by prohibiting the slaughter of cows.

Owing to an alarming illness His Highness the Nawab sailed for England, via Colombo, in April, 1908, where he placed himself under the care of Sir Victor Horsley, the eminent consulting physician and surgeon in London. Early in the year 1909 a report was received by the Durbar that His Highness was permanently incapacitated from the duties of administration, and the Government thereupon appointed Mr. A. O. Korrishi as Administrator.

On March 1, 1910, the sorrowful news was received by cable that His Highness had passed away while at sea on February 25th, and arrangements were at once made for the performance of the necessary ceremonials.

His brother and successor, His Highness the Nawab Sahib Shri Jalaludin-khanji Sahib (the present Ruler) was still a minor, but on certain representations being made, His Highness left the Rajkumar College and became associated with Mr. Monteath, I.C.S., from whom he obtained instruction in the management of the State, and in making himself acquainted with the work of the officials of each department. He was accompanied by Mr. Monteath in a tour over the greater portion of India, and the experience then gained has been of incalculable benefit to him in his subsequent administration.

His Highness having attained his majority, a Durbar was held at Radhanpur on November 27, 1910, by Colonel H. D. Merewether, Political Agent, Palanpur, who invested the Prince with full ruling powers.

The marriage ceremony of His Highness the Nawab was performed amid great rejoicing on June 20, 1911, the numerous guests including several ruling Princes, representatives from Baroda and other important States in the Bombay Presidency, and a large gathering of State officials and friends.

On November 29th His Highness the Nawab, accompanied by his Adviser, Mr. Monteath, Sardars, and State officials, left Radhanpur for Delhi in order to take part in the Coronation Durbar to be held in the month of December. His Highness was present at the entry of Their Imperial Majesties into Delhi. He attended the Royal Durbar, and was a guest at the State dinner and reception. The event was celebrated in Radhanpur by the closing of business houses and schools, by the distribution of medals to children and sweetmeats to the poor, and by illuminations and fireworks in the capital town.

His Highness the Nawab is a most capable and energetic Ruler, devoting a considerable portion of his time to the transaction of business connected with the State.

His Highness is a good all-round sportsman, but he may be said to excel in polo and pig-sticking, having won the Gujrat cup for securing the greatest number of boars in a competition open to British military officers and others held at Bhandu in the year 1911.

His Highness the Nawab is entitled to a salute of 11 guns.

The State of Radhanpur, which is roughly square in shape, comprises an area of 1,150 square miles, and has a population of about 65,000 inhabitants. It is bounded on the north by Bhabhar and Terwada; on the east by Terwada, Kankrej, and the district of Patan in Baroda; on the south by Vanod, Dasada, and Jhinjuvada; and on the west by the Runn of Cutch and Warahi.

The surface of the land is practically an open plain, unrelieved by hills, and without forests, although a few plantations have been reared in various parts of the State. There are only three rivers of any importance, namely, the Banas, Sarasvati, and Rupen, but there are many fine tanks which contain water throughout the year, and a large number of wells, which are the chief source from which irrigation for crops is obtained. One of the tanks, situated at Waghel, and probably the finest in Gujrat, was constructed by the Waghela Rajputs and is still in a good state of preservation.

Although a considerable amount of trade is carried on in the State, there is no doubt that the absence of railway facilities is a very serious obstacle to expansion, and the necessity for the construction of lines connecting Radhanpur with neighbouring districts is being urged upon the attention of the Government and the Railway Board. The majority of the people are engaged in various forms of agricultural pursuits, although a large number are employed in cotton-ginning factories at Sami, Lolada, and Munjpur.

Experiments made in Radhanpur with a view to the manufacture of sugar from date palms have given abundant promise of good results, and, as a consequence, the people have been encouraged to plant a large number of trees and thus render practical assistance to the State in building up a new and profitable industry.

A considerable trade of a general character is carried on in Radhanpur, Sami, and Munjpur, and although the capital town is 34 miles distant from the nearest railway station the exports for the past year amounted in value to Rs. 5,25,928, and the imports to Rs. 5,43,683.

An agricultural show inaugurated in 1914 by His Highness is held annually, and the State maintains three well-bred stallions for the encouragement of those who seek to restore the great reputation formerly held by Kathiawar horses.

The State maintains 26 schools, including the High School at Radhanpur, which, in July, 1914, was placed on the list of schools recognized by the University of Bombay. There are 1,277 pupils on the rolls.

The spirit of British laws and Acts in force in British India is usually followed in all the Courts in Radhanpur.

The State contains 469,451 acres of land, 40,789 acres of which are unculturable. The area under occupation is divided into two classes, namely: (a) the State portion of village lands, comprising 162,264 acres under actual occupation, and 33,736 acres of waste land; and (b) rent-free land allotted to village servants, consisting of 47,348 under tillage, and 19,057 acres still uncultivated. Further than this, there are 21 villages containing 45,206 acres of cultivated and culturable waste land, which are occupied collaterally by families, or are grants in consideration of past services.

Customs duties are levied in the State on the export and import of certain specified goods, and the amount realized in 1917–18 was Rs. 1,26,689, an increase of more than Rs. 93,000 over the sum recovered during the previous year, owing chiefly to the excellency of the winter crops.

The gross receipts of the State for the past year amounted to Rs. 6,91,831, this sum being larger than in former years, owing chiefly to higher prices being

THE STATE OF RADHANPUR.

1 and 2. Exhibition of Cattle. 3. Camels. 4. Exhibition of Horses.

obtained by the sale of opium, and the recovery of outstanding arrears of revenue upon land. The expenditure side of the balance-sheet showed a total of Rs. 6,90,176, but these figures include Rs. 27.000 paid in purchase of War Bonds.

The Mahomedan Rulers of Radhanpur have always been conspicuous for their loyalty to the British Throne, and on the outbreak of the European War His Highness the Nawab Sahib placed all the resources of his State at the absolute disposal of the Government, and he expressed a desire that he might be allowed to fight side by side with the Allies. A public meeting was held on August 20, 1914, and His Highness, in the course of an excellent address, explained the reasons which compelled the British Government to take up arms, and he concluded by urging all his subjects to assist to the utmost of their ability those who were engaged in the field against Prussian militarism. Contribution lists were opened, and in less than six months the sum of Rs. 19,900 was forwarded to the Bombay Branch of the Imperial War Relief Fund.

Although the ambition of His Highness the Nawab to be allowed to go to the front was not realized, he nevertheless continued to keep his people well informed as to the progress of events on the Continent of Europe and in other parts of the world over which the war cloud hung, and he arranged for a series of lectures bearing upon the great struggle to be delivered in various places in the State.

During the year 1915–16 the sum of Rs. 4,000 was remitted to the Women's Branch of the War Relief Fund. In the following year public meetings were held with the object of encouraging the subjects of the State to contribute liberally to War Funds, but particularly with regard to the Indian War Loan, and it was not long before the Durbar was able to report that Rs. 70,000 had been subscribed for this purpose. Contributions as follows were also raised: Rs. 500 towards war sales; Rs. 500 for Lord Kitchener's Memorial Fund; Rs. 4,500 for the Women's Branch of the Relief Fund; Rs. 6,000 for the War Fund of the "Willingdon" Sports Club, Bombay, and Rs. 1,000 for the relief of Belgian children; while two bulls and a panther were presented to a war sale and fête at Ahmedabad.

Radhanpur, in common with other towns and cities in India, held an "Our Day" celebration, and on December 11 and 12, 1917, attractive events, including boating on the tank, wrestling, racing, and other sports, together with cinematograph performances, were held. His Highness made a personal appeal to the citizens to render all assistance in their power in order to ensure success, and the results proved that the request had not been made in vain. The sum of Rs. 2,117 was collected from the public, and an amount of Rs. 2,045 was added from the State Treasury.

During the year ended March 31, 1918, the State contributed Rs. 1,000 to Queen Mary's Technical School for disabled Indian soldiers: Rs. 2,500 towards the fund for a banquet given at Delhi in honour of the safe arrival of the Indian delegates from the War Conference; Rs. 500 to the fund of the "Willingdon" Sports Club; and Rs. 2,000 to the fund for relief of disabled naval and military officers.

His Highness the Nawab was persistent in his efforts to secure recruits for the army, and he offered liberal concessions and special grants to all who would present themselves for enlistment.

RAIGARH STATE

RAIGARH is one of the fifteen Feudatory States subordinate to the Government of the Central Provinces, the relations being controlled by a Political Agent.

The family of the present Chief is descended from the ancient Gond Kingdom of Chanda. The founder of the State, Madan Singh, was born at Wairagarh in the district of Chanda, but he afterwards removed to Bunga, a village situated within the territory now comprised. Tradition is silent as to the nature of subsequent occurrences which rendered it necessary that Madan Singh should remove from Bunga to Raigarhh where he made a home for himself, but the fact remains that it is generally believed in the locality that he never afterwards paid a visit to that village. Further than that, each succeeding generation has avoided Bunga, and to-day the family observe the same custom under the belief that any violation of it would certainly be followed by the death of one of its members as the result of the divine vengeance of their goddess, which is enshrined in the village.

Madan Singh, as ruling Chief, was followed in succession by Takhat Singh, Beth Singh, Drip Singh, and Jujhar Singh, who entered into a subsidiary treaty with the Honourable the East India Company in the year 1800 on the annexation by the Mahrattas of Sambalpur, of which Raigarh had formerly been a tributary.

One clause in the agreement just referred to provided for the cession by Jujhar Singh of the *pergana* of Padampur, which had been granted to him by the Rani of Sambalpur.

This Chief was on his death succeeded by his eldest son, Deonath Singh, who proved himself to be a most capable Ruler, but who was more particularly distinguished by his readiness to aid in suppressing opposition to the good government of the paramount power.

The first opportunity afforded to Deonath Singh for manifesting his loyalty occurred in 1833, when he crushed a rebellion instigated against the British by Raja Ajit Singh of Bargarh, and the *zemindary* of that principality was conferred upon him in recognition of his valuable services.

During the Mutiny of 1857 he displayed great activity and no little skill as a leader of troops in assisting to capture the followers of the rebels, Sundar Sai of Sambalpur and Sheoraj Singh of Udaipur.

Deonath Singh died in the year 1865, and was succeeded by his eldest son, Raja Ghansgram Singh, who in the same year received a *sanad* of adoption, and in 1867 was honoured by the grant of another document, which defined his status as a Feudatory Chief.

Owing to maladministration the management of the State was taken over by the British Government in 1885, and five years later, when Ghansgram Singh died, his son Bhup Deo Singh became Raja, but the Government retained control of Raigarh, and did not grant him the full powers of a Feudatory Chief until the year 1895.

Raja Bahadur Bhup Singh died in March 1917, and was followed by his eldest son, Lal Natwan Singh, the present Chief, who was born in the year 1891. The British Government in 1918 again assumed management of the State, and appointed Rai Sahib Umrao Singh, Extra-Assistant Commissioner, as Administrator. This official has already proved his qualifications for his important position, and it is confidently expected that the State will continue to make good progress under his capable supervision.

The State of Raigarh, with an area of 1,486 square miles, and a population of about 218,860 persons, has an elevation of 773 feet above sea-level in the southern portion, and it rises to fully 1,250 feet along the northern border.

The surface is, generally, of a hilly character, especially in the north, where the heights are covered with dense forests, but the Chawardal range of mountains, with peaks rising to nearly 2,700 feet, traverses the whole of the State from west to east.

The Mahanadi river, which forms the boundary between Raigarh and the State of Sarangarh, receives nearly all the drainage of the whole area of the State, and in various places along its course it forms valuable alluvial deposits, which yield excellent crops of rice, sugar-cane, tobacco, and vegetables.

Forests cover about 46 per cent. of the total acreage, and the principal trees are *sal* (*Shorea Robusta*), *saj*, *rohua* (the bark of which is valuable for tanning and dyeing purposes), *mahua*, pipal, tamarind, and mango.

The mineral resources of the State have not yet been developed to any appreciable extent, but there are fair deposits of coal, iron, mica, and limestone.

In the year 1890 the Chief transferred to the British Government a certain quantity of land required for an extension of the Bengal-Nagpur system, and this line now traverses the southern portion of the State for a distance of 35 miles, in the course of which length there are four stations, namely, Raigarh, Naharpali, Khussia, and Jamgaon.

The State has increased greatly in commercial importance since the opening of the

1. THE LATE RAJA BAHADUR BHUP DEO SINGH, FEUDATORY CHIEF, RAIGARH STATE.
2. RAJA NATWAN SINGH, THE PRESENT FEUDATORY CHIEF, WITH HIS YOUNGER BROTHER, LAL CHAKRADHAR SINGH.
3. CHAKRADHAR MOTI MAHAL AND GEORGE TOWN HALL.
4. GEORGE GUEST-HOUSE. 5. SUMMER RESIDENCE OF THE FEUDATORY CHIEF.

THE STATE OF RAIGARH.

1. Main Street, Raigarh Town. 2. Court-house, High School, Administrator's Bungalow, and other State Buildings, with Maidan in Foreground. 3. River Kelo, with Bathing-ghats.

railway, and a very large trade is carried on in the sale and transport of farm produce, especially rice, which is the principal crop.

The State maintains 28 schools, three of which are for the training of girls, and the scholars on the rolls are 3,000 in number.

The State is divided into the three *perganas* of Raigarh, Bargarh, and Taumar; the gross revenue, based upon an average of the past five years, is Rs. 2,33,506; and the annual income calculated on the same basis is Rs. 2,05,411.

The word Raigarh is derived from *rai*, a species of thorny tree, and *garh*, signifying a fort.

Though the State has undergone many vicissitudes it is now progressing on the right lines, and its future is assured.

THE STATE OF SAILANA

HISTORIANS have always been confronted with immense difficulties in compiling chronological events connected with the history of ruling Chiefs in India, partly by reason of the rise and subsequent overthrow of dynasties either by conquest or by the natural process of decay, and partly owing to the struggle for supremacy and the consequent acquisition or loss of territory. Thus vast areas have been divided into several portions in order to satisfy the claims of supporters, and Princes of noble houses have become separate owners of States individually or collectively, and in numberless instances these divisions have again been split up or have been merged in the possessions of large Powers. This process of exchange has been going on for many hundreds of years during the numberless conflicts which have been waged, but since the Mutiny of 1857 alterations of boundaries have been caused mainly by the various Governments for administrative purposes, or by agreements, or even disagreements among ruling Chiefs.

The State of Sailana, in the Malwa Political Agency of the Central India States, is a case in point.

Its history is very closely interwoven with that of the adjoining State of Rutlam, and further evidence of the relationship existing between the two is found in the fact that the Rulers of each are Rathor Rajputs, and have a common ancestry with the Maharajas of Jodhpur.

In order to understand clearly the origin of the Sailana State it is necessary to refer to events which belong to Jodhpur records.

The statement which follows gives the history of past occurrences as it is accepted in Sailana.

Towards the close of the sixteenth century the Rathor Ruler of Jodhpur—which had previously been an independent Principality—admitted suzerainty under the Moghul Emperor, Akbar, and several of his sons thereupon founded States on their own account in north-western India. One of them, Mahesh-dassji, rendered exceedingly valuable services to the Emperor Shah Jehan in Afghanistan and elsewhere, and in return for these services he was rewarded with grants of land in several districts. The Emperor, with a further desire to recognize the help of his colleague in battles, honoured Mahesh Dassji's son, Ratan Singhji, by requiring his attendance at the Royal Palace in Delhi. This young Prince was barely out of his teens when the whole course of his life was changed by entirely unforeseen circumstances. Happening to be in the streets of Delhi, his attention was attracted by a mad elephant, which had broken loose from its quarters and threatened death to all in its headlong career. The Prince was no coward, however, for he boldly attacked the beast, and wounded it sufficiently to prevent it from doing any damage. This heroic deed was greatly applauded by the Emperor, who granted to the youth a rich tract of country comprising 12 large districts in Malwa, which yielded an annual income of Rs. 53,00,000. Shortly after that date Shah Jahan was in danger of being dethroned by his two sons Aurangzeb and Murad, who, at the head of a large army, had presented themselves at Court with the ostensible object of paying a filial visit to their father, who was then seriously unwell.

The plot was revealed to the Emperor, who ordered the Maharaja Jeswant Singhji of Jodhpur, the Raja of Kotah, and Raja Ratan Singhji of Ratlam, to oppose the invading forces, and in the great battle which ensued Ratan Singhji was fatally wounded. The Raja was succeeded by his son, Ram Singhji, who founded the city of Ratlam, and who died while fighting, after a prosperous reign of 24 years. Shiv Singhji succeeded, and on his death, without issue, the State was seized by Keshao Dasjji, another natural son of Ram Singhji, although his claim was strenuously opposed by the nobles of the State. Keshao Dasjji incurred the displeasure of the Emperor Aurangzeb, who deposed him in favour of Chhatrasalji, a surviving son of Ratan Singhji, who had valiantly assisted the Moghul army at Bijapur, Golconda, and other places. Chhatrasalji then ascended the *gadi* of Ratlam, but in A.D. 1709 he joined the Imperial army in an expedition to the Deccan, where his eldest son, Hate Singhji, was killed. This disaster had such an overwhelming effect upon Chhatrasalji that he voluntarily gave up all his powers and honours, and entered upon the life of a recluse at Ujjain. He was succeeded by his second son, Kesri Singhji, but his territories, together with the right of levying customs duties, were apportioned in three equal parts, with insignia, to his two sons, Kesri Singhji and Partab Singhji, and his grandson, Bairisalji, the rightful heir, with equal rights and privileges. In the division which subsequently took place, Raoti (the present Sailana State) was handed over to Partab

THE STATE OF SAILANA.

1. Jeswant Nivas Palace. 2. Jeswant Nivas Palace (Back View).

3. H.H. Raja Sahib Sir Jeswant Singhji Bahadur, K.C.I.E., of Sailana State.

THE STATE OF SAILANA.

1. Kedar Nath Cave Temple 2. Ganeshi Dorhi and Rang Mahal Palace. 3. Govind Kund. 4. Back View of the Castle 5. View of the Castle.

Singhji: Bairisalji received Dhamnod: and Ratlam, which was his by right, was seized by Kesri Singhji. Bairisalji, however, was forced to relinquish his share, leaving it to Kesri Singhji, while he himself proceeded to the Jaipur Court, where his sister was married to the Maharaja Sawai Madho Singhji Bahadur. Ill-feeling sprang up between the brothers, as Partab Singhji demanded one-half of the territory given up by Bairisalji, but this claim was strongly opposed by Kesri Singhji, and the latter was killed by his brother, who assumed control of Ratlam, in addition to Raoti. Prior to that time, however, Partab Singhji—who had no male issue—had adopted Jai Singhji, the younger son of Kesri Singhji, and the young Prince thereupon fled from Ratlam, and collected an army, with which he marched against the State which he had recently left. The forces of Partab Singhji were utterly routed, and the latter was killed by Jai Singhji in a single-handed conflict.

Jai Singhji entered Ratlam with due ceremony, but one of his first acts was the recognition that his elder brother, Man Singhji, then at Delhi, was the rightful heir to the *gadi*, by sending to him an invitation to return to Ratlam, in order that he might reign in the place of their father. Man Singhji acceded to the request, and was duly installed with great pomp.

It should be stated here that events connected with the incidents just mentioned have been incorrectly stated by certain historians, but the authenticity of the present narrative is proved by indisputable documents, including a *kafiyat* of Ratlam submitted to the Central India Agency, the book of Lalji Kulguru, common chronologer of the Rathors, and Raja Laxman Singhji's " Narak Vachan."

Raja Jai Singhji then transferred his capital from Raoti to Sailana, and the State was from that time known by this name. This Raja was as valiant in battle as he was capable in administrative affairs, and when his elder brother offered to share with him the division of Dhamnod he replied that he " would rather conquer fresh States by force of arms than accept territory that had already caused so much dissension in the family." Shortly after this time his prowess was put to the test, owing to serious differences with the Ruler of the State of Jhabua, but these were eventually settled. A significant trait of the character of Jai Singhji is worthy of notice at this juncture.

Several years after this conflict had taken place the vanquished Chief of Jhabua appeared before the Raja, and, laying down his sword, remarked in bitter tones, " A mad elephant destroys its own army," these words signifying that Jai Singhji's thirst for military glory had only resulted in the ruin of a kinsman, therefore weakening the power of the Rathor Rajputs in general. The Chief continued, " If you are bent upon the acquisition of new territory it would have been a finer thing to have assailed other States with my help." Jai Singhji had a noble heart, and these words made a remarkable impression upon him, and they struck the right chord, so much so that he at once reinstated his former opponent as Ruler of Jhabua. The Ruler died at the age of 61 years, having, during his reign, fought no fewer than 22 battles.

Devi Singhji, his eldest son, had predeceased his father, without leaving issue, and as the second son, Daulat Singhji, was mentally unfit to occupy the *gadi*, the third of the family, Jaswant Singhji, became Raja, but his pacific rule lasted for only 14 years. He was succeeded by Ajab Singhji, fourth son of Jai Singhji, who went to an early grave owing to his extravagances in living, and was followed in the Rajaship by his son, Mokham Singhji, who is reported to have been " a weak Ruler, distinguished by an inordinate partiality for elephants, which in his stables displaced horses to a great extent." The Mahrattas were at that time ravaging the Central India States, and Mokham Singhji, being powerless to defend his country against such powerful enemies, agreed to pay to the Maharaja Sindhia of Gwalior an annual tribute of *Salim Shahi*, Rs. 40,000. He subsequently handed over the control of the State to his son, Lakshman Singhji, who took measures to overthrow the yoke of the Mahrattas. Sailana — with other neighbouring States—was occupied by Sindhia's hordes, who pillaged and destroyed on all sides, but in January, 1819, Lakshman Singhji approached the British Government, who, through the mediation of General Sir John Malcolm, arranged a settlement, whereby Sailana and other States were saved from their common enemy.

An agreement was also entered into whereby the tribute was secured to Sindhia, Maharaja of Gwalior, who, on his part, undertook never to interfere with the internal administration of the State of Sailana. Lakshman Singhji was a Ruler of whom any subjects might be proud: he was valiant in battle, keenly intellectual, and withal of such an amiable disposition that he endeared himself to all with whom he came in contact. His assistance was on one occasion sought in connection with the succession to the Ratlam *gadi*, and the action taken by him, although generally approved, caused a disappointed Rani to instigate three attempts upon his life. The Raja had a long and glorious rule, and his name is to this day cherished by the inhabitants of Sailana. His son, Ratan Singhji, ruled in a feeble manner for 18 months, when his uncle, Nahar Singhji, succeeded. When the division of estates took place on the death of Chhatrasalji, they were apportioned, as already mentioned, in three equal parts, but as Ratlam was the only commercial city the Customs collection could not be divided, but was made conjointly, and the sum thus received was divided into three equal parts. Ratan Singhji was a weak administrator, and left the management of the State almost entirely in the hands of his Minister, who adopted the unsatisfactory policy of *laissez-faire*. The State suffered considerably in consequence, and particularly with regard to the *sayer*, or customs dues, which were reduced from one-third to seven per cent., although Sailana continued to pay the *sushi kharch* and the other expenses at the rate of one-third.

A more enlightened Ruler followed in the person of Takhat Singhji, but he, unfortunately, gave way to excessive drinking, and died at the early age of 26 years, after a rule of nine years. One beneficial action of his, however, was the stoppage of the practice of killing buffaloes at the Dashera festival, and a copper plate was affixed to a main gateway forbidding the revival of this custom. He left an only son, Duleh Singhji, who succeeded when ten years of age, and a Regency Council, with Basahib Nath Kanwarji, his great-grandmother, at its head. She was an exceedingly wise and clever woman, and accomplished much good in the State. During the Mutiny of 1857, which occurred in his time, the State manifested its loyalty to the Throne by sending troops against the rebels at Mandasor, and in consideration of these valuable services to the British Government, the Viceroy, Lord Canning, sent a *kharita* to the Raja, and also conferred a *khilat* upon him. In the year 1864 the Government of India took steps to secure railway facilities for the State, and in 1891 an agreement was

THE STATE OF SAILANA.

1. Dwarkadhish Temple. 2. Old Palace. 3. Surajpole Gate. 4. Gagan Darwaja. 5. Moti Bungalow. 6. Kirtisthambha.

entered into by which the State renounced all rights of jurisdiction over lands required for the Bombay-Baroda and Central India Railway line. Since that date a portion of the Rajputana-Malwa system has also been laid within the boundaries of Sailana. The Raja unfortunately contracted the habit of over-indulgence in liquor during the latter part of his life, and the administration of affairs being left in the hands of incapable Ministers, the resources of the State became greatly impoverished. Eleven years before his death, which occurred in October, 1895, Duleh Singhji, in default of male issue, had adopted Jeswant Singhji, eldest son of the late Maharaj Bhawani Singhji, of Semlia.

His Highness, whose title is Raja Sahib Sir Jeswant Singhji Bahadur, K.C.I.E., was born in September, 1864, and was carefully instructed by his father in the vernacular and Sanskrit tongues, but he afterwards received an excellent education in general English subjects and in Persian at the Residency Rajkumar College at Indore, now known as the Daly College, and later he studied Vedant philosophy, with six systems of orthodox philosophies and politics. Jeswant Singhji had, prior to the death of Duleh Singhji, taken a keen interest in State affairs, his chief aim in life being to acquit himself as a thoroughly competent and wise Ruler. He succeeded to the *gadi* on December 24, 1895, the installation ceremony being conducted by the late Sir David Barr, Agent to the Governor-General in Central India. Adoption *nazrana* was paid on this occasion to the British Government, but it was remitted for ever by His Imperial Majesty King George V at the Coronation Durbar in 1911.

It has already been mentioned that the ineptitude of Duleh Singhji caused State affairs to become greatly embarrassed, therefore when His Highness assumed the reins of government, he forthwith took energetic steps to rescue them from the chaos into which they had been plunged. The unsatisfactory financial condition of Sailana was vigorously taken in hand, and in a comparatively short space of time accumulated liabilities—some of more than one hundred years' standing—were discharged.

Reforms were inaugurated with tact, some of the most important being the organization of the State police, the establishment of permanent Courts of Justice, and the placing of each Department of State upon an efficient and economical basis.

In appreciation of these and other services, and especially those rendered during the terrible famine in 1900, the British Government conferred upon the Raja the Kaiser-i-Hind medal of the first class, and in 1904 he was created a Knight Commander of the Order of the Indian Empire, and was decorated with the insignia by His Royal Highness the Prince of Wales (now the King-Emperor) at Indore. In the same year the Viceroy, Lord Curzon, held a Conference, with the object of reorganizing the Mayo College, and His Highness was selected as a representative. The Raja has subsequently become a permanent member of the Council of that institution, as well as of the Daly College.

Numerous other progressive measures for the benefit of the State were undertaken, and not the least important of these were the founding of hospitals and schools for both sexes, the construction of magnificent palaces and temples, the making of roads and gardens, the sinking of wells, the planting of thousands of mango trees, the widening and lighting of public streets, and the improvement of sanitary conditions.

Among the principal structural works initiated by His Highness are the temples of Kalha Mata and Govind Deoji; a school; the grand palace called Jeswant Nivas, built at a cost of Rs. 2,00,000, famous for its marble pillars and for having the largest arch hall in Central India; Rang Mahal, with arch and clock-tower; Kirti Sthamb; *risala* lines; Kulkar Khana; Maleni bridge; a great clock arch-gate, and many others. The reconstruction of the fort and the well of Govind Kund was instigated by the Raja, the well being in memory of his late Rani, Govind Kunwar Kachwaiji, of Machhand. Since the death of the Rani, which was a terrible blow to His Highness, the latter has always worn mourning, and does not appear at State ceremonials. The deep interest taken by the Raja is exemplified by the establishment of a library and club in the chief town of Sailana, and the grant of Royal patronage was of the greatest possible assistance in the establishment of the Sailana Bank, which is now in a flourishing condition.

His Highness possesses all the qualifications of a successful Ruler; he has a keen and well-trained intellect, a well-balanced mind, a fearless spirit, and, although of a kindly disposition, he is stern in the repression of evil of any kind. His numerous projects for the betterment of his people have had the most beneficial results, and have marked him as an enlightened Ruler of the most progressive type.

His Highness is a staunch advocate of temperance and vegetarianism, and his munificent gifts to charities, or the deserving poor, are bestowed freely, yet with wise caution. He is, moreover, a thoroughly good sportsman, and enjoys shooting large game, but his natural kindness of heart makes him regard with strong disapproval the indiscriminate slaughter of small birds.

The Raja received an invitation from His Excellency Lord Hardinge, of Penshurst, Viceroy of India, to attend the Delhi Coronation Durbar in 1911, and he was presented with the Coronation medal and photographs, with autograph signatures, of Their Majesties the King-Emperor and Queen-Empress. His Diwan, Pandit Rajkishen, was the recipient of the title of Rao Sahib, and his two younger sons, Maharaj Kunwar Mandhata Singhji and Ramchandra Singhji, had the honour of being appointed pages to Her Majesty, who conferred upon them diamond badges as marks of honour.

His Highness has five surviving sons and three daughters, the former receiving their education at the Mayo College, Ajmer. The heir-apparent is the Maharaj Kunwar Dalip Singhji.

The State of Sailana is a first-class State of the Malwa Political Agency, and it has an area of 450 square miles, and a population of nearly 29,000 inhabitants. The revenue amounts to about Rs. 5,00,000 per annum, and a tribute of Rs. 21,000 is paid to the Government of India. The military force comprises [illegible] cavalry and 400 infantry, and His Highness is entitled to a salute of 11 guns.

Sailana, the chief town, is situated on the Western Malwa plateau, 1,847 feet above the level of the sea, and is ten miles distant from Namli station, on the Rajputana-Malwa Railway.

THE STATE OF SIRMOOR

HINDUS were always reluctant to put down in black and while the history of their own times or of those of their predecessors, and this is doubtless the reason why there is not a single book which does full justice to the subject in its relation to the whole of India. It need not, therefore, occasion surprise that it is difficult to discover any systematic chronicles of the past relating to such a remote hill State as Sirmoor, but such information as could be gathered from various sources is briefly narrated below :

The word Sirmoor, or rather Sarmour, as it is generally pronounced by the natives, is derived from two words, Sar (head), maur (crown), and thus it means literally "a crown for the head." Probably this State was called by this name on account of its being formerly at the head of all other hill States in the Punjab, some of which were actually feudatory to it. There is yet another reason which may account for this appellation. Raja Bland, son of Salbahan I, the Rawal of Jaisalmer, had a son who bore the name of Sarmaur, and it is therefore probable that this prince, who was a cousin of Raja Rasalu, the founder of this State, gave the name of Sarmaur to the capital city of his kingdom.

The State is bounded on the north by the Jubbal and Balsan States ; on the east by the district of Dehra Dun, which is separated from it by the river Jumna and its tributary, the Tons ; on the north-west by the Patiala and Keonthal States ; and on the south-west by the district of Ambala and the State of Kalsia. Sirmoor lies in the southern Himalayas, and its area is 1,160 square miles in extent, while the inhabitants, according to the census of 1911, were 138,523 in number.

The country is for the most part hilly, excepting at Kiarda Dun, which is on the western side of the Jumna, and is situated between the Sewalik and Himalayas ranges. The city of Nahan has been the capital of the State for the past 300 years.

Sirmoor is naturally divided into three parts, namely, the northern, the interior, and the southern, and the climate and products of these areas vary greatly from one another.

1. The Northern portion is separated from the remainder of the country by the river Giri, and is, therefore, called the Trans-Giri territory. The climate of this part is very cold and invigorating, as the fall of snow during the winter months is not an infrequent occurrence. The *kharif* harvest is generally better than the *rabi* one. The people are stoutly built and simple-minded, though somewhat stubborn in disposition.

2. The interior, that is the country lying between the Giri and the Markanda rivers, comprises the heights of Sain, Dharti, and Khols. The climate is mild, and both harvests generally yield fair crops.

3. The Southern part, or the country which is known as "Dun," lies between the Markanda and the Jumna. The climate is warm, and the harvests are generally good, especially the *rabi* one.

There are four chains of mountains in the State, which are known as Dhars. Chur Dhar rises to an altitude of 11,982 feet above the level of the sea, and is situated in the Northern part ; Dhar Sain and Dharti are in the interior ; and the Dhar of Laya Devi is in the south.

The chief rivers, including streams, are the Jumna, Giri, Tons, Jalal, Markanda, and Bata ; the first three of these are great highways for the floatage of timber. The Giri and its tributary, the Jalal, are preserved for fishing.

The lake of Rainka, situated in the northern area, between two mountains, is a mile and a half in length, while the breadth is only 1,100 feet. It is a place of pilgrimage for Hindus, and near to it are the hill of the sage Jamdigan, and a small pond, called Parsram's Tal. To the south may be seen the temple of Paras Ram, the son of Jamdigan, and his wife, Rainka, and in honour of these three a fair is held annually at Rainka in the month of November.

The people speak different dialects, according to the territorial division of the State inhabited by them, and thus there are three types of language, namely, Urdu, Hindi, mixed Pahari, and Sirmauri. The manner of living also differs greatly. Marriage and funeral rites are more or less observed in accordance with the Dharamshastra of Manu.

The hills in Sirmoor are rich in mineral ores ; magnetic ore is found at Chehta, about 20 miles distant from Nahan ; copper exists at Chandni ; alum at Narag ; and mines of marble and mica are met with in Jaghar and Nahra Dhar. Pure gold, though not in large quantities, is found in the sands of various streams, and limestone is fairly abundant throughout the State.

A considerable quantity of iron ore was mined fully half a century ago, and in 1867 the State erected a foundry, but as the returns from the undertaking were

LIEUT.-COL. H.H. MAHARAJA SIR AMAR PRAKASH BAHADUR, K.C.S.I.

1. H.H. MAHARAJA SIR SHAMSHER PRAKASH BAHADUR, G.C.S.I.
2. H.H. MAHARAJA SIR SURENDRA BIKRAM PRAKASH BAHADUR, K.C.S.I.

not satisfactory, the premises are now employed in the manufacture of a large number of mills for crushing sugar-cane, and wheat and other cereals.

Sirmoor is exceedingly rich in vegetation, which varies in character according to the temperate or tropical zone in which it is grown. About two-thirds of the whole area of the State are covered with forests, which, in some instances, are found in connected tracts many miles in length. For example, there is one compact belt 20 miles in length, and from three to five miles in breadth, which consists almost entirely of oak trees, although there is a considerable quantity of silver fir. Among the other species which are common in this well-wooded State, are *sal* (*Shorea robusta*), Himalayan spruce, birch, yew, and blue pine (*Pinus excelsa*), together with a large number of others of economic value, which yield gums, dyes, edible fruits, and medicines.

In the first quarter of the nineteenth century the State played a prominent part in the operations conducted by the British against Nepal. By a treaty concluded in 1815 between the British and the Nepalese the latter were excluded from Sirmoor, and Prince Fateh Prakash, the young son of a deposed Rajah, was placed upon the *gadi*. This Chief continued to administer the State until 1827, under the Regency of his mother, Rani Guleri, an able and prudent woman. In that year the British Government invested the Raja with full ruling powers, and he forthwith turned his attention towards the removal of the defects which had led to the decline of the State. By his wise administration peace and order were restored in his territory, but he also introduced several financial and other much-needed reforms. In 1838 he offered his help in connection with the first Afghan war, for which he received in return the thanks of the Government. In 1845 he sent an army to help the British Government against the Sikhs in the Punjab, and thus again he proved his fealty to the cause of the British Empire.

The Raja was succeeded by his son, Raghubir Prakash, who was a very simple-minded Chief, and the next Raja was his son, the illustrious Sir Shamsher Prakash, who ascended the *gadi* at the early age of 10. During his minority the administration of the State was carried on by his uncle, Kanwar Surjan Singh. From the first onset in his career Shamsher Prakash was a promising Prince, and his personal appearance and habits prepossessed those who came into contact with him. His knowledge of Persian and English was by no means considerable, but he had acquired all the qualities which a Ruling Chief ought to possess.

In 1857, when the Sepoy Mutiny broke out in India, he showed his desire to render help to the English by sending a contingent to Simla, that it might be employed in quelling the insurrection. After being invested with full ruling powers, he travelled throughout India, making himself acquainted with the most successful forms of administration, his desire being to govern his subjects in an enlightened manner. On his return he gradually established police, judicial, and revenue Courts, District and Municipal Boards, a Public Works Department, School, Dispensaries, and Post and Telegraphic offices. He constructed roads, erected *dak* bungalows, provided work for regular land settlements, and preserved forests and worked them on scientific principles. At Nahan proper he established an ironfoundry, in which mills for crushing sugar-cane and grinding corn are manufactured, and subsequently sold throughout India. In short, a new era of progress and reform in the State commenced with his reign. He was always faithful to the cause of the British Government, and in recognition of his services during the Mutiny, he was given a *khilat takhira* (a robe of honour), and became entitled to a salute of seven guns, which were increased to 11 in 1867. During the Viceroyalty of Lord Lytton he was appointed a member of the Imperial Legislative Council, and in 1876 he received the distinction of a Knight Commandership of the Exalted Order of the Star of India. In 1880 he sent a Sirmoor Corps to the assistance of the British Government in the third Afghan war, and in recognition of this the Sirmoor Durbar was granted the honour of being entitled to return visits by His Excellency the Viceroy. In 1886 he was made Knight Grand Commander of the Order of the Star of India. In 1889 he raised an Imperial Service Corps in Sirmoor, which was afterwards converted into a company of Sappers and Miners, who rendered invaluable help to the Government during the Tirah expedition, under the command of his younger son, Raj Kumar Bir Bikram Singh Sahib. In recognition of his meritorious services, the Raj Kumar was invested by the Government with the title of C.I.E., and was subsequently made C.S.I., and a Lieutenant-Colonel. Sir Shamsher's reign of more than forty-two years was distinguished by most remarkable devotion to the welfare of the State and his subjects. He was incessant in his endeavours to inaugurate measures of reform, and there was widespread grief in Sirmoor when his death, hastened by the wear and tear of a strenuous life, occurred in October 1898.

Sir Shamsher Prakash was succeeded by his son, Sir Surendra Bikram Prakash, a man of fine physical features, hard-working, intelligent, persevering, a strict disciplinarian, yet the embodiment of kindliness, of keen statesmanlike capabilities, and a devotee of cleanliness. As with his father, his knowledge of Persian and English was not profound, but during the reign of his father he had acquired all the requisites for a Ruling Chief. His practically-minded father arranged for him to become acquainted with the ordinary duties of State management, and for several years he discharged the duties of a Magistrate and Collector; in fact, he afterwards, as Regent, assumed full administrative control during the last two years of his father's life, on account of the illness of the latter. This gave him practical experience in administrative work, Civil and Criminal law, and Revenue affairs, and on his accession he removed the defects noticed in the working of the Courts and offices, modelling them after the plan of those in the British Government. With a special taste for law (legislation), he introduced several local measures of a beneficent character, including an Act prohibiting children from smoking. He was passionately devoted to the well-being of his subjects, and always strove to protect them against oppression and tyranny. In order to safeguard them against the dread disease of plague, he established quarantine posts at various places, and framed regulations regarding its prevention, which are still in force in the State. He inaugurated a scheme for the supply of water to the town of Nahan, where its scarcity was greatly felt, and for the recreation of his Indian officials he established a club which still exists, and is known after his name as the "Surendra Club." He effectively checked bribery in the State; he raised the Judicial Courts to a high standard of excellence; for the convenience of passengers he arranged a mail *tonga* service between Barara (on the North-Western Railway) and Nahan; and in short, he devoted himself to the ad-

THE STATE OF SIRMOOR.

1. Tikka Raj Rajendra Singh, Sahib Bahadur. 2 and 3. Palace. 4. Shamsher Villa (Exterior). 5. Shamsher Villa (Interior).

THE STATE OF SIRMOOR.

1. Panorama of the City. 2. Boys' High School. 3. Girls' School. 4. European Guest-house. 5. Birbam Castle.

THE STATE OF SIRMOOR.

1. Jagannath Temple. 2. Amar Boarding House. 3. Foundry. 4 and 5. Cemetery at Pucca Tank. 6. Kalisthan Temple.

THE STATE OF SIRMOOR.

1. Lytton Memorial. 2. Surendra Waterworks Reservoir. 3. Victoria Diamond Jubilee Hospital. 4. Ranital Garden. 5. Mosque and Katcha Tank. 6. Temple of Paras Ram.

THE STATE OF SIRMOOR.

1. Chowgan (Sports Ground). 2. Shamsher and Surendra Clubs, and Govind Singh's Temple. 3. Shamsher Zenana Hospital. 4. Shamsherpur Lines (Cantonment). 5. Raiska Lake. 6. View of Paonta.

ministration of the State with untiring energy. His loyalty to the Supreme Government was never doubted. In 1900 he offered to the British Government 20,000 pounds of tea in connection with the Boer War in South Africa, and on the termination of hostilities and the capture of Pretoria, he organized public rejoicings in the State. At a later date he detailed the Sirmoor Sappers to Kohat Khushalgarh, in order to assist the Government in connection with the extension of the railway line at that place, the corps discharging its duties for a year with admirable zeal and earnestness. In 1901 he was made a Knight Commander of the Most Exalted Order of the Star of India, in recognition of his commendable administration and thorough loyalty to the Government, and in 1902 he was made a member of the Imperial Legislative Council.

After the death of Sir Surendra Bikram Prakash, his son, Sir Amar Prakash Bahadur, K.C.S.I., the present Maharaja, was duly installed on the *gadi*. He, too, possesses a stately figure, is passionately devoted to the welfare of his subjects, and is very kindly disposed towards them. Under competent tutelage he gained a sufficient knowledge of the English and Persian languages, and after acquiring a good education in literary matters he made himself practically acquainted with the working of Judicial and Criminal Courts during the lifetime of his father. He also ably performed the work of the State during his father's illness, and thus acquired the administrative talents desirable in a Ruling Chief. Since his accession to the *gadi* he has admirably discharged the heavy and multifarious duties and responsibilities attached to his high rank, and while his work in this direction is being most zealously performed, he has embraced every opportunity of inaugurating reforms calculated to promote the welfare and prosperity of his subjects, one of the most important of these being the grant of free primary education throughout the State, in commemoration of his installation. He also, at great cost, provided a stately building as a hostel for the students, and he carried through the project of his father for the construction of waterworks, and supplied the town of Nahan with water, at considerable expense to the State.

In common with his father, he is untiring in his efforts to govern his State on the lines of the British Government, and by reason of his excellent management, and goodwill towards his subjects, he is much admired and loved by them. The internal administration of the State is, therefore, admirably carried out in Sirmoor, owing chiefly to the personal interest taken by the Maharaja in its affairs. The Supreme Government have not hesitated to recognize his intelligent administrative abilities, as in 1915 he received the distinction of the title of K.C.S.I., and in 1918 the personal rank of Lieutenant-Colonel and the hereditary title of Maharaja were bestowed upon him.

In 1910 His Highness married the daughter of His Excellency Maharaja Deb Shamsher Jung Bahadur, ex-Prime Minister of Nepal, and four years later an heir was born, to whom was given the name of Raj Rajendra Singh. Her Highness the Maharani, who is well educated in English, is an accomplished lady and a wise consort, and at the time of the Delhi Durbar in 1911 she had the honour of being presented to Her Majesty the Queen-Empress.

Following in the footsteps of his forefathers, the Maharaja is thoroughly faithful to the cause of the British Empire, and in 1914 His Highness manifested this spirit of loyalty by offering to the Government his personal services, in addition to the resources of his State, in connection with the Great War. In 1914 he sent the Sirmoor Sappers and Miners to Mesopotamia to help the Government, and when this corps was, with other troops of the Government, besieged and taken prisoners at Kut, in the loyal and heroic discharge of their duty, a second corps was organized and sent on active service to the same country.

In addition to the above, the Maharaja has given ample proof of his faithfulness to the Government by making various gifts of money and material from time to time, which are mentioned in the accompanying list.

The following statement shows the contributions made by the Sirmoor Durbar towards the late Great War in men, money, and materials.

In the first place an offer was made of the personal services of His Highness; also of a company of Sappers and Miners; and of the State Infantry. Secondly, financial aid given included £50 to the British Ambulance Fund, London; Rs. 10,000 towards the Imperial Indian Relief Fund; Rs. 21,500 towards the Imperial Indian Relief Fund, given by State officials, residents, and Her Highness the Maharani; Rs. 500 towards the Young Men's Christian Association Fund; Rs. 8,750, as the cost of 25 horses not accepted by the Government; Rs. 2,000, being subscription towards the maintenance of 2½ unit beds for the wounded at Dehra Dun; Rs. 500 to the Princes' "Kitchener" Memorial Fund; Rs. 100 to Lady Munro's "Monster Lucky Bag," Simla; Rs. 4,00,000 offered to the War Loan Fund, out of which Rs. 2,00,000 with due interest, were accepted by the Government; Rs. 1,542 for the upkeep of the 2½ 10-bed units for the wounded at Dehra Dun, to the end of March 1918; Rs. 200 towards the "Ambala Lucky Bag"; Rs. 1,000 towards the "Lahore Lucky Bag"; Rs. 2,000 towards the "Our Day" celebrations; Rs. 500 by Her Highness the Maharani Sahiba towards the "Our Day" sports; Rs. 5,000 for the upkeep of 2½ 10-bed hospital units for the wounded in India; Rs. 100 as donation towards the Grand Fancy Fair and Fête at Ambala; £10 to Mlle. A. Rousseau, London, for "Œuvre du Vêtements des Soldats," Belges; Rs. 30 towards the Red Cross Fund, Geneva, by Her Highness the Maharani Sahiba; Rs. 100 towards the Young Men's Christian Association, Cawnpore; Rs. 91,830, subscribed by the State officials and subjects, towards the first War Loan; Rs. 2,518-12-3 towards "Our Day" Fund, by State officials and residents; Rs. 25,000 towards the War Loan, by the Kowlagarh and Annfield Tea Estates, Dehra Dun; Rs. 10,000 towards the second Imperial Indian Relief Fund, by His Highness the Maharaja. Thirdly, materials and goods contributed comprised 25,000 lb. of tea for the use of Expeditionary Forces; cigarettes, to the value of Rs. 1,000, for the use of the 1st Battalion 2nd Gurkha Rifles; 12 tents, eight 560 square feet each, and four 912 square feet each (only six of these were delivered at Bombay, measuring 560 square feet each); one motor ambulance car, to the value of Rs. 9,000; one bungalow at Kowlagarh Tea Estate, Dehra Dun, lent for hospital use; five lathes lent; Bantony and Bantony Cottage, Simla, lent for the Military Works Office until the end of the war; bought 50 copies of the Hindi translation of the book entitled "The Life of Field-Marshal Earl Kitchener of Khartoum, K.G.," for Rs. 150, which will go to the War Fund.

THE STATE OF SITAMAU

THE Chiefs of Sitamau, one of the mediatized States in the Malwa Political charge of the Central India Agency, are descendants of the Rathor Rajputs represented to-day by the Rulers of Jodhpur, Bikaner, Kishangarh, Idar, Ratlam, Sailana and Jhabua. During the sixteenth century Maharaja Udai Singhji, Ruler of Jodhpur, accepted the suzerainty of the Moghul Emperor Akbar, and his sons, upon leaving the paternal home, established States for themselves in adjoining territory. One of these had a grandson named Ratan Singhji, who by personal bravery found favour with the Delhi Emperor, from whom he received a grant of 12 extensive districts in Malwa. Ratan Singhji was killed in battle at Fatehabad, near Ujjain, in the year 1658, and the line of succession was continued by Maharaja Ram Singhji and Maharaja Shiv Singhji, to Maharaja Keshao Dasji, a son of Ram Singhji, who was deposed by the Moghul Court on the ground that he, in the capacity of Ruling Chief, was morally responsible for the murder of a tax collector sent by the Emperor of Delhi. Having been thus deprived of his lands, he retired to the Imperial city; and after a residence there of several years, obtained from the Emperor a grant of Khalsa territory, of which the present State of Sitamau is a portion, and he selected the town of the same name as his capital. The Raja died in 1743, and was succeeded by his son Maharaja Gaj Singhji Sahib, during whose reign the Mahrattas made so many continuous raids in Malwa that, with the view of obtaining better protection, he made his headquarters at Laduna instead of Sitamau.

During the occupancy of the *gadi* by his grandson Raja Raj Singhji Sahib, who was born in 1783, the Mahratta generals Sindhia and Holkar continued to lay waste the districts over which they swarmed, and the pillaging was at its highest point in 1820, when the British, through Sir John Malcolm, intervened, and secured an agreement under which Raja Raj Singhji was confirmed in the possession of Sitamau on his covenanting to pay an annual tribute of Rs. 60,000 Shah Alam Shahi to the State of Gwalior, whose Ruler, in return, gave an undertaking that he would not interfere in any way with the management of Sitamau or with the question of succession to the *gadi*, nor would he make use of troops in order to compel payment of the above-mentioned tribute. It should be mentioned that the Maharaj Kumar Ratan Singhji, son of Raj Singhji, subsequently succeeded through the intervention of British officers in obtaining a reduction of Rs. 5,000 from the amount originally fixed to be paid by Sitamau, leaving a balance of Rs. 55,000 Salim Shahi as the payment due to Gwalior. This was further converted into Rs. 27,500 (British coin) by virtue of an award confirmed by the Government of India.

After terms of peace had been arranged the Raja and his officials made the best use of their opportunities for promoting the welfare of the State, and the name of this Chief is revered to-day as that of a capable administrator, a father of his people, and a liberal contributor to charitable institutions. In his time, which terminated about the year 1867, he removed his capital from Laduna back to Sitamau.

On the death of His Highness Raja Bhawani Singhji Sahib the Maharaja Sindhia of Gwalior protested that he was entitled to be consulted with regard to the succession of Rulers, and he also claimed *nazarana* dues when the *gadi* devolved upon His Highness Raja Bahadur Singhji Sahib. The matter was submitted for the decision of the Imperial authorities, who ruled that Sitamau was a mediatized State belonging to the first class, and therefore Gwalior had no right to raise any objection upon the question of succession, and that *nazarana* was payable only to the British Government.

During the time of His Highness Raja Shardul Singhji Sahib (1899–1900) the State was visited by a famine of unprecedented severity, which so disastrously affected its finances that a debt of Rs. 1,25,000 was incurred in affording relief.

Raja Shardul Singhji died without issue in 1900, and the present Chief, His Highness Raja Sir Ram Singhji Sahib Bahadur, K.C.I.E., second son of Thakur Dalel Singhji Sahib of Kachi-Baroda, was selected by the Government of India to succeed to the *gadi*.

His Highness the Raja is at the head of the administration of affairs, and the ability manifested by him as a Ruler is only what one would expect from a man who from early days has by study and training fitted himself for the onerous responsibilities of his high position. He was educated at the Daly College at Indore, where he greatly distinguished himself during a course of study extending over a period of about seven years. The Raja did not, however, imagine that his education was completed when he left College; far from it, as he spent a considerable time in making himself acquainted, under the capable tuition of Sir Michael O'Dwyer, then Settlement Officer at Bharatpur, with the intricacies of land tenures, revenue, and other matters connected with the management of estates. His Highness is of opinion that a person

1. H.H. RAJA SAHIB SIR RAM SINGHJI, K.C.I.E., RULER OF SITAMAU STATE.
2. THE RAJKUMAR SAHIBS.

Reading from Right—Rajkumar Sahib Raghubir Singhji, Rajkumar Sahib Govind Singhji, Rajkumar Sahib Raghunath Singhji.

THE STATE OF SITAMAU.

1. Sitamau from the Mandsaur Road. 2 Bazar Street Scene, Sitamau. 4. Bird's-eye View of Sitamau from the Hospital.

THE STATE OF SITAMAU.

1. The Ramniwas Kothi. 2. The Laduna Palace and Tank. 3. Sitamau Fort: The Hagore Gate. 4. Temple of Mahadeo at Kodiazar.

can never know too much, and therefore he not only spends a large portion of his spare time in literary pursuits, but he is tireless in his endeavours to instil into his people a genuine desire for instruction to be given to their children. But the Chief is a man of action, and he had given practical effect to his theories by establishing schools in various places in the State, the two principal ones being an Anglo-Vernacular Institute teaching up to the English fifth standard at the capital Sitamau, and a flourishing vernacular one at Laduna, which is about 1½ miles distant, besides the vernacular schools at Bhagore and Titrod.

His Highness was invested with full ruling powers in February, 1905, and his wise administration has stamped him as a man worthy in every way to be a leader among his subjects. He has full powers in all revenue, civil, judicial and general administration matters, and in the criminal cases the only restriction on his authority is that all sentences of death, transportation for life, or imprisonment for life must be confirmed by the Agent to the Governor-General, Central India. The Raja has been married three times, having lost two wives. The present Rani is the granddaughter of the Thakur of Marauli, in the Udaipur State. His Highness has three sons and two daughters.

The Raja was presented to their Royal Highnesses the Prince and Princess of Wales on their visit to Indore in 1905, and at the Coronation Durbar at Delhi in 1911 he received from His Majesty the King-Emperor the insignia of a Knight Commander of the Most Eminent Order of the Indian Empire, while he is entitled to a hereditary salute of 11 guns.

The State of Sitamau is bounded on the north by the Indore and Gwalior States, on the south by Jaora and Dewas, on the east by the Jhalawar State of the Rajputana Agency, and on the west by the State of Gwalior. It has an area of about 185 square miles, and it has a population of nearly 26,484 inhabitants (according to the census of 1911). The gross income of the State is Rs. 3,50,000, including alienated *jagirs*. The greater portion of the land consists of undulating plains, characteristic of the Malwa Country although in several parts there are a number of low hills with masses of irregularly-shaped boulders, and the soil, chiefly of the black cotton variety, is generally of a fertile character. The principal crops consist of different kinds, including *jowar*, maize, *tuar*, wheat, gram, and barley, while oil-seeds, *til*, fibres, hemp, cotton, tobacco, and poppy are also grown. Methods of tillage are practically the same as they were a hundred years ago, but the people have shown that they are willing to follow other systems when their value has been demonstrated.

The opening of the Rajputana-Malwa Railway a few years ago caused a very considerable expansion of trade and commerce throughout the State, and a good metalled road 13 miles in length, constructed by the Gwalior State between Mandsaur, the nearest station, and the chief town, has greatly facilitated the transport of goods.

The State is divided for administrative purposes into three *tahsils*, Sitamau, Bhagor, and Titrod, and each of these is under the control of an official who is Collector of Revenue and Magistrate in his own district.

Sitamau, the capital town, is believed to have been founded by a Mina Chief named Sataji about the year 1645, and it is surrounded by a wall, with seven gates, which was commenced by Keshao Dassji and completed by Raja Raj Singhji about a century afterwards.

The whole of the administration is carried on directly by His Highness.

The Diwan is the Executive Officer, the whole administration consisting of the following departments: (1) Judicial; (2) Revenue; (3) Survey and Settlement; (4) Excise; (5) Opium; (6) Public Works; (7) Forest; (8) Police; (9) Household; (10) Risala; (11) Stables.

THE STATE OF TEHRI-GARHWAL

THIS State, under the political superintendence of the Government of the United Provinces of Agra and Oudh, is bounded on the north by the States of Rawin and Bashahr in the Punjab, and also by Tibet ; on the east and south by the district of Garhwal ; and on the west by Dehra Dun.

Many generations ago the territory known as Tehri, and the district of Garhwal, were jointly governed by Rulers as a separate unit, and the control of that dynasty was maintained until the early part of the nineteenth century, when Parduman Shah, the last Raja of the whole tract, was killed in battle when fighting against the Gurkhas. Northern India was about that time darkened by the black clouds of war, and there were few attempts on the part of Rulers to consolidate their possessions owing to a wholesome fear that any marked activities on their part might produce disastrous results for them.

At the close of the Nepalese War in 1815, however, Raja Sudarshan Shah, son of Parduman Shah, received from the British a grant of the present State of Tehri. The Raja gained the highest praise from the Government of India for the very efficient services rendered by him during the Sepoy Mutiny of 1857, and it should be borne in mind that the arduous duties performed by the Chief and his troops were made a thousand times more difficult owing to the exceedingly rugged and mountainous character of the country in which the operations took place.

Raja Sudarshan Shah died in 1859, without leaving lawful issue, and although the State should have in these circumstances lapsed to the Supreme Government, in accordance with a treaty then in existence, the British consented to the succession of Bhawani Shah.

The new Raja was duly installed on the *gadi*, and he was shortly afterwards presented with a *sanad*, conferring upon him the right of adoption. Upon the death of Raja Bhawani Shah, in 1872, he was followed by his son, Pratap Singh, and then, in 1887, by His Highness Raja Kirti Shah, who was invested with full ruling powers in 1894, and was subsequently created a Knight Commander of the Most Exalted Order of the Star of India.

The State, which is entirely situated in what is generally known as the region of the Himalayas, consists of irregular series of rugged ridges with numberless spurs interspersed with narrow valleys. The majority of these ridges, which run in north-easterly and south-westerly directions, seem to spring from lofty peaks on the borders of Tibet, which attain heights ranging from 20,000 to 23,000 feet.

It is interesting that the sources of those two mighty rivers, the Ganges and Jumna, have their sources in this State. The former of these emerges from a glacier named Gaumakh, at an elevation of more than 13,500 feet above the level of the sea. At the commencement of its course it is known as the Bhagirathi, and after flowing for a considerable distance in a south-westerly, and then in a south-easterly direction, it joins the Alaknanda at Devaprayag, where the two streams, having united, are then called the Ganges.

In a territory with such varying elevations as there are in Tehri, one will expect to find an equally great diversity in the flora with which it abounds. Beautiful trees and plants of the sub-tropical type grow in rich profusion on the outer ranges of low hills, while the choicest Alpine flowers provide natural decoration for the rugged heights in the north.

The fauna belong to those species which are usually met with in Himalayan regions. Tigers frequent the northern portion of the State ; leopards are fairly common in the west ; and black bear and wild dogs inhabit the lower slopes of ranges, while the *sambhur*, spotted and barking deer, and several species of wild goats, are always in evidence.

The State, which is 4,200 square miles in extent, contains about 2,450 villages, and the capital town, Tehri, which is the only place of importance. More than 98 per cent. of the inhabitants are Hindus, and the principal castes include Rajputs, Brahmans and Doms. About 88 per cent. of the people are engaged in agricultural pursuits, the method of cultivation of land being similar to the practice prevailing in the British districts of Garhwal and Almora.

The chief crops are rice, potatoes, small millets and wheat, while a few tea gardens may be observed in western districts.

The forests of Tehri, which are 141 square miles in extent, contain a large number of well-grown trees of great value in respect of their timber-producing capabilities. Among these are *deodar, sal, char*, and various kinds of oak and pine, while boxwood, which is plentiful in the north, has not yet been felled in large quantities. The administration of State forests was organized in 1884, upon the lines of management customary in British India territories.

The State is practically isolated from

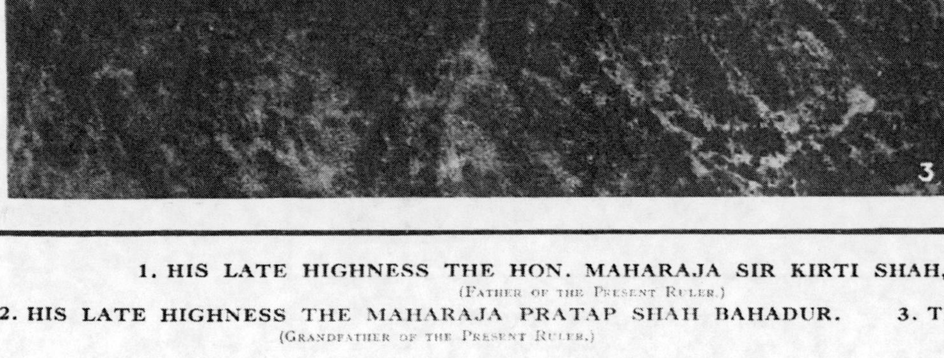

1. HIS LATE HIGHNESS THE HON. MAHARAJA SIR KIRTI SHAH, K.C.S.I.
(Father of the Present Ruler.)

2. HIS LATE HIGHNESS THE MAHARAJA PRATAP SHAH BAHADUR.
(Grandfather of the Present Ruler.)

3. THE PALACE, TEHRI.

THE STATE OF TEHRI-GARHWAL.

1. The Bhagirathi and Bhilangana Sangam. 2. The Ganges Bridge and River. 3. Shri Badri Nath Temple.

THE STATE OF TEHRI-GARHWAL.

1. The European Guest-house at Simlasu Gardens. 2. Gol Kothi (at Simlasu Garden). 3. The Ranibag Palace.

THE STATE OF TEHRI-GARHWAL.

1. The Hewett Sanskrit Pathshala. 2. The Campbell Boarding House. 3. The Clock Tower. 4. The Chief Court.

THE STATE OF TEHRI-GARHWAL.

1. Pratap High School. 2. General View of Tehri Town. 3. The Old Durbar.

the chief commercial towns of India, and therefore it is not difficult to understand that it is not a manufacturing centre. It has about 260 miles of so-called roads, but as these are not suitable for wheeled traffic, the transport of merchandise is carried on exclusively by means of pack animals or coolies, with this exception, however, that timber is rafted down rivers to various depôts. A few of the inhabitants find employment in weaving blankets and the tanning of leather, but beyond these the industries are confined to the making of purely household goods.

The exports from Tehri comprise timber, other forest produce, *ghee*, rice and potatoes; and its imports include piece-goods, sugar, salt, iron and brass vessels, spices and oils.

The Rajas of Tehri exercise full ruling powers within the borders of the State, but the principality is under the political superintendence of the Government of the United Provinces, its representative at the present time being the Commissioner of Kumaun. An official, styled a Wazir, is at the head of the executive authority, and he possesses powers of a Magistrate of the first class; Deputy Collectors are second-class Magistrates; and revenue cases are disposed of by *tahsildars*, while magistrates of the third class are stationed at Devaprayag and Kirtinagar. The inhabitants of Tehri are singularly free from participation in crime, and this circumstance is attributed by police officials to the fact that the people are contented with their lot; that they cannot, owing to geographical reasons, intermingle with crowds in large cities, and that they have little inclination to run risks of punishment for the sake of trifling gains. Civil suits are heard by the Deputy Commissioners and by two other judges, while all appeals are placed before the Raja who, however, occasionally transfers them for decision by the Wazir or a Magistrate of the first class.

In assessing revenue upon land, the Durbar makes a distinction between areas which are irrigated and those tracts which are not watered by artificial means; and the latter portion is again placed in four classes, according to quality of soil and propinquity to villages. Separate rates, fixed after inspection of the land, are then placed upon the several holdings, and they remain in force for a number of years.

Miscellaneous items of revenue include licence fees upon the sale of country liquor and certain drugs, as well as tolls charged to pilgrims who visit Gangotri (a sacred place near the source of the Ganges), and carry away with them water from the venerated river.

The State maintains a small infantry force of about one hundred and twenty men, as well as a few artillery, whose duties consist in the firing of salutes on special occasions. Detachments of police are stationed at Tehri, Kirtinagar and Devaprayag, while similar duties are performed in other parts of the State by the headmen of villages.

The town of Tehri, the headquarters of the State, is situated upon a tongue of land three-quarters of a mile in length and half a mile in width, at the junction of the Bhagirathi and Bhalong rivers, and at an elevation of 2,278 feet above the level of the sea.

Tehri was only an insignificant village in 1815, when Raja Sudarshan Shah took up his residence there, but it now contains many fine buildings, including the Raja's palace, Courts of Justice, State offices, schools, one hospital and a jail. The bazar is built in the bed of an old river, which divides the town into two portions. The Durbar offices, dispensary and other structures, occupy a site on the south side, members of the ruling family reside in houses on a ridge on the north, and at a higher altitude stands the palace of the Chief, from which a commanding view of the surrounding country is obtained. Several temples, as well as *dharamsalas* for pilgrims, have been erected by various Rulers.

Tehri is an important commercial centre for the disposal of agricultural produce grown upon the plains.

The summer residence of the Raja is at Pratapnagar, on the summit of a hill 8,000 feet in height, and about nine miles distant from Tehri.

Jamnotri is famous for its temple on the western flank of the great peak of Bandarpunch (30,731 feet), which has been constructed upon ground at an elevation of nearly 11,000 feet above the level of the sea, and four miles below the glacier, from which the Jumna river issues forth.

The temple is a small wooden edifice, containing an image of the goddess Jumna. In close proximity to the shrine are some springs, from which water flows continuously at a temperature of 194 degrees Fahrenheit.

Gangotri has a mountain temple, situated at an elevation of 10,319 feet, on the right bank of the Bhagirathi river, and about eight miles distant from the source of the Ganges in the Gaumukh glacier. The temple, which is only 20 feet in height, possesses images of several mythological personages.

A large number of pilgrims journey to Gangotri during the summer months, and many of them obtain flasks of sacred water, sealed up by officiating priests, and convey them to the plains, where they are highly prized.

THE STATE OF BANSDA

BANSDA is a second-class State, some 215 square miles in extent, in the Surat Political Agency in the Bombay Presidency.

The rulers of Bansda belong to the Kshatriya clan of Rajputs and are descended from the lunar race of which the most prominent figure was the great Sri Krishna. The family also include among their ancestors the brave Solankis who, prior to the fifteenth century, were the most powerful chiefs in the whole of Gujarat. When they appeared to be enjoying peaceable possession of their territories three princes, brothers in direct lineage from Dhavaldeo, a noted Rajput king whose headquarters were at Dholka, were attacked by the Mahomedan Sultan of Ahmedabad, and although they fought desperately, with the greatest valour, in defence of their strongholds, they were driven from their territory.

One of the trio found a new home at Sagwada, another established himself in distant regions, and the third took possession of Bansda. Ancient Bansda seems to have extended originally as far as the sea-coast, and the area now known as the State of Bansda must have been in a prosperous condition if one may judge from the ruins of old forts, temples, and well-built reservoirs which may now be seen in the vicinity of the capital town.

The history of the Solankis in Gujarat connected with the Bansda family about this period is not perfectly clear, but it is well-established that Muldeoji Solanki was Ruler of Bansda during the early portion of the sixteenth century, and that he is regarded as the actual founder of the State as it is known to-day.

This Chief was followed in succession by Khandhaldeoji, Baldeoji, Karandeoji, Udayasinhji, Molkaranji, Udayasinghji II, Veersinhji, Bhanji and Gulabsinhji, during whose reign the Gaekwar established his influence as a Suzerain power in Gujarat. On the death of Gulabsinhji in 1753, without leaving issue, the Chief Minister secured the throne for Udayasinhji, a cousin of the deceased Ruler. Some opposition was manifested towards this proceeding, but when the matter was placed before the Court of the Peshwa, who had then gained ascendancy in Gujarat, the selection of Udayasinhji was confirmed.

Veersinhji became Ruler in 1780. He shifted his capital from Navanagar to Bansda, where besides the courts of justice he built the large temples of Visheshwar Mahadev, Veerbhadra Hanuman, and Vijaydata Mata, all of which are still in existence. During the regime of Rayasinhji negotiations were opened which led to the signing in December, 1802, of the treaty of Bassein, under which the Political supervision of Bansda passed into the hands of the British. Rayasinhji was succeeded in 1815 by a distant cousin named Udayasinhji, whom he had adopted some years previously.

He died after reigning for about 14 years, and his widow, with the sanction of the British Government, adopted Hamirsinhji, a child not then two years of age. Hamirsinhji was entrusted with full ruling powers in 1852, and six years later he made an agreement with the British Government by which he undertook to pay annually a sum of Rs. 1,500 as *chouth* in lieu of a share in transit duties which the British Government arranged to forego.

Raja Hamirsinhji died in the year 1861, and the succession to the *gadi* fell to the lot of Maharaul Gulabsinhji, a distant cousin of the previous Ruler.

In 1862 a *sanad* was granted to the Raja and his descendants guaranteeing to them the right of adoption in the event of failure of male issue.

Raja Gulabsinhji passed away in 1876, and was succeeded by his only son, Kumar Sri Pratapsinhji, then eleven years of age; the management of the State being handed over to a British official as Administrator.

During the minority of the young Prince —who, by the way, was educated at the Rajkumar College at Rajkot—Her Majesty the late Queen Victoria was proclaimed Empress of India, and on the occasion of the first Imperial Durbar held at Delhi on January 1, 1877, a personal salute of nine guns was granted to the Raja, to which was added a present of a banner to commemorate such an important event.

The Raja was invested with full ruling powers in the year 1885, and on taking up the reins of government he showed that he was well qualified for the high position to which he had been called.

By observation and study of advanced progressive States in India the Raja introduced measuers which he believed would tend to the prosperity of the State and the well-being of the inhabitants. Land was for the first time surveyed for revenue purposes, and cash assessments were introduced in place of the primitive and most unsatisfactory method of payment of rent by handing over a certain proportion of the produce of each harvest. Primary as well as secondary education was made free of all cost; vernacular schools for boys were opened at Bansda, and a considerable number ot village schools were established. Attention was also given to the importance of affording medical relief, and the Raja founded a hospital at the chief town in honour of his mother, Ratan Kunverba.

His Highness Raja Pratapsinhji completed 25 years of his successful rulership in the

MAHARAUL SHRI INDRASINHJI, MAHARAJASAHIB.
BORN FEBRUARY 16, 1888. INVESTED NOVEMBER 11, 1911.

1. MAHARAUL SHRI PRATAPSINHJI, MAHARAJASAHIB. Born November 23, 1864. Died September 20, 1911.

2. MAHARAUL SHRI GULABSINHJI, MAHARAJASAHIB. Born December 26, 1838. Died February 23, 1876.

3. MAHARAUL KUMAR SHRI PRAVATSINGHJI (BROTHER OF MAHARAJA INDRASINHJI).

4. MAHARAUL KUMAR SHRI NATVARSINHJI (BROTHER OF MAHARAJA INDRASINHJI). Born October 20, 1894. Died November 15, 1912.

5. MAHARAUL KUMAR SHRI KISHORSINHJI (BROTHER OF THE PRESENT RAJA SAHIB).

1. MAHARAUL KUMAR SHRI HARSHADKUMARSINHJI (SECOND SON OF MAHARAJA INDRASINHJI).
Born February 24, 1918. Died December 30, 1920.
2. MAHARAUL KUMAR SHRI DIGVIRSINHJI (HEIR APPARENT).
Born July 21, 1916.
3. KUNVARI SHRI SUSHILKUNVARBA (DAUGHTER OF MAHARAJA INDRASINHJI).
Born July 10, 1914.

THE STATE OF BANSDA.

1. Pratap Silver Jubilee Tower. 2. Remnant of Old Fort. 3. Dig Virnivas Palace.

THE STATE OF BANSDA.

1. Old Palace Gate. 2. Ancient Relics, Navanagar. 3. River Kaveri. 4. Shri Gulabsinhji Library and Town Hall.

year 1901 and the subjects of the State united in whole-hearted fashion in showing their appreciation of the benefits which they had received. With the object of commemorating the occasion in a suitable manner it was decided to erect a clock-tower in the centre of the town and also to construct another building in the upper and lower portions respectively, to be used as a town-hall and a public library. Several scholarships were also established for the encouragement of study in higher branches of learning. In 1903 His Highness the Raja had the honour of attending (with his son, the present Ruler), the second Imperial Durbar held at Delhi.

Great regret was manifested when it became known that a continuous strain of work had seriously affected the health of the Raja, who was advised to take a prolonged rest in a quiet and healthy place. He went to Deolali, but it was too late for any benefit to be derived from the change. He died on September 20, 1911, but before he passed away he expressed satisfaction that the reins of government would be taken up by his son, whom he had personally instructed in administrative matters.

His Highness Raja Pratapsinhji was succeeded by his eldest son, His Highness the Maharaul Sri Indrasinhji, the present Ruler, who was born on February 16, 1888. His Highness was sent to the Rajkumar College for his education when only 11 years of age, but before he could complete his studies he was compelled to return to his home owing to the indifferent health of his father. Private tutors were then engaged to give further instruction of a general character to the young Prince, while special officials were appointed to enable him to become conversant with administrative duties.

His Highness attended the notable Coronation Durbar held at Delhi in 1911, and on his return from the historic capital he devoted himself most assiduously to the task of introducing reforms calculated to improve the condition of his subjects.

Some of the most important matters which have engaged the attention of His Highness may be briefly summarized as follows: A revised survey and settlement of land for revenue purposes has been taken in hand; education in primary and secondary schools has been continued free throughout the State; a night school has been opened for men desiring to learn English and Gujarathi, and a class for training women in home industrial work has been started; local self-government by means of Municipal Boards and village *panchayats* has been made possible; every encouragement has been given to cultivators to take up areas of waste land, and a State Garden Department has been established for the growth and subsequent free distribution to *ryots* of grafts of fruit trees as well as vegetable seeds; excellent drinking water has been provided for the chief town; industrial enterprises have been fostered; an institution known as the Balsharam has been opened for boys belonging to the backward tribes to enable them to receive ordinary instruction combined with practical lessons in mechanics, carpentry, weaving and other subjects; the town of Bansda has been greatly improved by the construction of fine buildings and roads, and a new palace for His Highness has been erected.

His Highness the Rajasaheb was one of the first Rulers of Native States in India to offer his personal services as well as the resources of his territory for the help of the Allies in the Great War, and the small Principality of Bansda despatched several recruits to the front, contributed a large quantity of materials, and subscribed more than Rs. 2,00,000.

The year 1918 was a disastrous one for the State, as it was visited by widespread famine as well as an epidemic of influenza. His Highness quickly grasped the serious position in which his subjects were placed, and he gave direct personal attention to the adoption of measures for giving relief to the suffering inhabitants.

The rulers of Bansda enjoy independent sovereign powers with full civil and criminal jurisdiction, together with authority to make their own legislation.

The State formerly paid to the British Government an annual tribute of Rs. 7,351-8-0 and a *chouth* of Rs. 1,500, but a deduction from these amounts is now made of Rs. 8,608, this being the amount payable by the Paramount Power as compensation for the abolition of transit duty.

The State of Bansda is bounded on the north by the river Ambika, which divides it from the Mahuva and Vyara *talukas* of the State of Baroda; on the south by the State of Dharampur; on the east by the States of Dangs and Sulgana, the Kalvan *taluk* of the district of Nassik, and on the west by the Chikli *taluk* of the district of Surat, and a portion of Dharampur.

The State is hilly in character excepting in the north, where it merges in the plains of Gujarat, while in the south the land is covered with dense jungles interspersed with groves of mangoes and divided by ravines and rivulets. The Ambika, Wanki, and Kaveri rivers, together with their tributaries, are sufficient for the irrigation of the whole Principality.

The inhabitants, according to the census of 1911, were nearly 45,000 in number, consisting chiefly of Kunknas and Dhodias, known as the Kaliparaj people, to distinguish them from the upper classes of Hindus, who are termed Ujaliyats. The former are primitive in their habits and are persistent in preserving them, while the latter include Parsis, Mahomedans and Brahmans, who form the majority of the inhabitants of the chief town.

The soil is, generally speaking, black or loamy in character, while on the slopes of hills, being alluvial, it is exceedingly fertile. Rice—of which the best types are *kolum* and Bangaia—is grown to perfection. The staple food of cultivators is *nagali*, but *tur*, *juvari* and cotton are grown also.

Education is imparted in 15 institutions, including a High School in the town of Bansda, and a girls' school, which is greatly appreciated. Children of the forest tribes are being taught in schools with a free gift of all school materials.

Medical relief is given at hospitals situated in the capital, including one for males and another for females. There is also a "travelling" dispensary which makes periodical visits to various parts of the State.

The revenue of Bansda was Rs. 72,501 in the year 1862, but by the good government of His Highness the Raja and his immediate predecessors, by the encouragement given for the development of agriculture, the establishment of industries, and the building up of commercial enterprises, it has now reached the sum of Rs. 6,35,000.

THE STATE OF CHOTA-UDAIPUR

SITUATED within the territory under the control of the Political Agent of Rewa-Kantha, in the Bombay Presidency, is the second-class State of Chota-Udaipur, which has an area of 890 square miles.

The Rulers of the State belong to the Khichi clan of Chauhan Rajputs, and their progenitor, Anhal, is said, by tradition, to have been created by the sage Vasistha, out of the Agni Kund, on the summit of Mount Abu, in Rajputana. Ajayapal, a successor of Anhal, founded the city of Ajmer, and another successor, Manikrai, assumed and handed down to posterity the title of "Sambhari Rao," or "lord of Sambhar," or Ajmer. The Khichi Chauhan appears to have settled originally in Sind Sagar, and in the eleventh century Bir Bilander, a descendant of Manikrai, defended Ajmer against Mahmud of Ghazni. The next Ruler, Visaldev, occupied his position for a period of 60 years, until 1074, and it was he who founded the town of Visalnagar, in the northern portion of Gujarat. The most famous Ruler in the direct line of succession was the celebrated Prithiraj, whose name has been immortalized in the epic "Prithiraj Raso."

Prithiraj was killed in battle, and the family migrated to Malwa, and settled in a district which is to-day named after them, Khichi Vada. Khichi Hamir gallantly defended the stronghold of Ranthambhor about the year 1300, and after it had fallen a large body of Khichi removed to Gujarat, where in 1244 they, under the leadership of Palanshi, conquered the Kingdom of Champaner. The newly-acquired territory remained in the possession of the Palanshi family for several generations, but in 1484–5 the fortress of Champaner, through treachery and stratagem, fell into the hands of Sultan Mahmud Begda. This siege continued for about 12 years, and the loss of the fort caused the sons of Patai Rawal, known as Pratap Singh, the reigning Prince, to separate from one another, Prithiraj founding the State of Chota-Udaipur, and Doongerjee that of Devgad-Baria.

During the terrible days of the Sepoy Mutiny in 1857, Raja Jit Singhji, the Ruler at the time, manifested his loyalty to the English Throne by refusing to join hands with the rebel, Tantia Topi, who was defeated by General Parke while endeavouring by a display of troops to compel the assistance of the Chief.

The next Ruler (1881) was Moti Singhji, and he was succeeded by the present Chief, His Highness the Maharawal Shri Fatehsinghji Motisinghji Sahib, who was born on October 23, 1884, and was raised to the *gadi* in the year 1906.

Chota-Udaipur is bounded on the north by the State of Devgad-Baria and Kathiwara States, on the east by the State of Ali Rajpur, on the south by the river Nerbudda and the district of Khandesh, and on the west by the Sankheda Mewas Estates and a portion of the State of Baroda.

The inhabitants are about 104,000 in number.

The State is hilly in character, with a considerable area of forest and dense undergrowth, and it is practically divided into two portions by the Orsang river, which traverses it from the north-eastern boundary to the extreme west. The Heran river flows from east to west, and four other streams rise in the north, and after a course of several miles become a portion of the Orsang.

The State is divided, for purposes of land administration, into four *talukas*, namely, Chota-Udaipur, Jetpur, Kawant, and Karali, and each of these areas is controlled by a ***Thandar***, who is assisted by village Accountants and Headmen.

There are 417 "State," and 145 "alienated" villages. The former of these have been brought under the Survey Settlement, which is based upon the system adopted in British Indian territories, and at the present time arrangements are being made for the inclusion also of alienated lands.

The area of land under cultivation during the year 1918–19 was 142,685 acres in extent, the following being some of the principal crops: rice, 24,000 acres; maize, 15,000 acres: *jowar*, 16,000 acres; cotton, 31,756 acres: and ***kodra***, 10,830 acres.

Chota-Udaipur has a forest area of approximately 225 square miles, which is divided into blocks, classed as "reserved" and "protected." The timber in this extensive tract is of a very valuable character.

A potent factor in the development of commercial enterprises in the State was the opening in December 1917 of a branch line of the Bombay-Baroda and Central India Railway to the town of Chota-Udaipur.

The majority of the inhabitants consist of Bhils, Kolis, Dhankas, and

MAHARAWAL SHRI FATEHSINHJI RAJAJA SAHIB, OF CHOTA-UDAIPUR.

MAHARAJ KUMAR SAHIB NATWARSINHJI, OF CHOTA-UDAIPUR.

RAJ KUMAR SAHIB NAHARSNIHJI, OF CHOTA-UDAIPUR.

Naikras; Mahomedans are about 3,000 in number, high-caste Hindus may be put down at 10,000, and Parsis and other sects do not exceed one hundred in number.

The gross revenue of the State for the year 1918-19 was Rs. 8,88,516, and while tribute is not paid to the British Government, there is a liability to the State of Baroda for an annual subsidy of Rs. 7,805.

In the capital town there are the "State" hospital, named after a former Diwan, in which there is accommodation for nine patients; and a women's hospital, erected in memory of the late Raniji Saheba Shri Samaj Kunverba.

There is also a dispensary at the palace to which the general public are admitted for treatment. There are other dispensaries at Kawant, Jetpur, Chalamli, and Kadwal, and all of these institutions are well supplied with necessary equipment and drugs.

The total number of schools in the State is 31, which includes 27 in the various districts, to which girls, as well as boys, are admitted; while in the capital town there are an Anglo-Vernacular school, and Gujarati and Urdu institutions.

The prosecution of hostilities in the late Great War was the all-absorbing topic of conversation between the years 1914 and 1919. The Chief subscribed liberally to various war funds, and his example was worthily followed by State officials and others, but detailed particulars are only available for 1918. The State Administration Report for that year shows that His Highness's subjects regarded it as their privilege, as well as their bounden duty, to support the Allies to the fullest extent of their power. During the year just referred to His Highness contributed sums of Rs. 25,000 and Rs. 61,142 for general purposes, and he purchased War Bonds to the amount of Rs. 2,07,500. The Bhayats and other officials and subjects of the State also purchased Bonds and Cash Certificates for Rs. 1,50,675.

The heir-apparent of His Highness the Rajaji Sahib is Raj Kumar Natwarsinghji, and he and his brother, Raj Kumar Naharsinghji, are being carefully educated, while the other four children are daughters.

His Highness the Rajaji Sahib attends daily at the State offices when in Chota-Udaipur, and he is personally acquainted with, and supervises the work of, each Department, while all documents passing through the *Huzur* office are submitted to him for orders.

In December 1919 His Highness proceeded to Bombay, and was present at the various functions which took place on the arrival of His Excellency Sir Geo. A. Lloyd, G.C.I.E., D.S.O., the Governor-Elect of the Presidency, and the departure of the retiring Governor, His Excellency Lord Willingdon, G.C.S.I., G.C.I.E., G.B.E.

THE STATE OF DANTA

DANTA, situated as it is on the frontier of Rajputana and known as Nani Marwar, is a second-class State in the Mahikantha Agency in the Province of Bombay.

This State is bounded on the north by the State of Sirohi, on the south by territory of Baroda State, on the east by the State of Idar, and on the west by the State of Palanpur. Danta is 450 square miles in extent, and its chief town—Danta-Bhawanghad—and some 360 villages are occupied by a population of nearly 20,000 inhabitants.

The annual income is about Rs. 150,000.

The country is almost entirely hilly, abounding in forests covered with various kinds of trees, which afford picturesque scenery to the observer. Its western and southern portions are somewhat plain and open, while most of the country, having thick jungles and many hills on all sides, abounds in wild animals, such as tigers, panthers, bears, pig, roz, chital, deer, stags and buttal, and other species. The country is divided into four *talukas* for the purpose of administration, namely Hadad and Tarsang, each under a Mahalkari, and Mataji and Joita, each under a *Thandar* who is invested with powers of a Magistrate of the second class.

The State possesses mines of marble, a transparent brittle green stone (called *parevo*) and mica.

The principal products of the country are wheat, millet, maize, all kinds of seeds, *Gram*, sugar-cane and other varieties of cereals, in addition to different sorts of gum and spices. Owing to the abundance of large jungles in the State there are numerous valuable trees of great variety, all of which are useful for building purposes.

The Chief of Danta belongs to the illustrious Parmar race of Rajputs, originating from the Agni-cula, the ancestors of Bhoj, Vikramiditya and other rulers famous in the chronicles of early Indian history.

The Parmar family originally acquired an extensive tract of country in north-western India over which they held sway, and no fewer than 35 *shakhas* or branches have been established in many parts of India.

In 1878 there succeeded to the *gadi* of the State His Highness Shri Mahranaji Saheb Shree Jaswantsinghji Bahadur, who possessed all the qualifications of a great ruler. At the commencement of his reign His Highness was confronted with great difficulties owing to the rebellious character of the Bhil tribe, who had for many years previously been a source of terror to the State. These refractory people dwelt in mountain fastnesses, where dense vegetation afforded them almost complete security from attack. Their raids upon Danta increased in frequency as well as in severity, and the result was that neither the life nor the property of His Highness's subjects could be regarded as safe. Vigorous measures were undertaken against them, and thanks to the persevering efforts of His Highness, the marauders were eventually subdued and taught to recognize the principles of law and order.

The calamitous famine of 1900-01 was a severe strain upon the Government, the Rulers of Native States, and others holding positions of responsibility, but His Highness Maharanaji Jaswantsinghji laboured without ceasing in order to alleviate the terrible distress which existed in Danta. He opened the State treasury as well as his own private purse, and drew from them large sums of money for the purchase of food and clothing for his destitute subjects, and he characteristically made all possible provision for the preservation of the lives of cattle, which were practically the sole means of livelihood of the people.

Many valuable measures of reform were inaugurated, and in appreciation of his wise and liberal-minded administration, the Government conferred upon him the title of "Maharanaji Shri," and also granted him a personal salute of nine guns as a mark of special distinction.

His Highness died in the year 1908, leaving three sons, the eldest of whom, the present Ruler, succeeded to the *gadi*.

His Highness Shri Maharana Sahib Shri Hamirsinghji Bahadur was 39 years of age when he assumed control of administration, and in the few years since his accession he has shown himself to be a most painstaking, wise, and able Ruler. He was at first greatly assisted in his work by his uncle, Shri Raj Sahib Shri Mohobutsinghji, who had for a long time been officially connected with State affairs, but latterly he has been relieved of considerable responsibility by the heir-apparent, His Highness Shri Maharaj Kumar Sahib Bhawanisinghji, who has already inaugurated several useful reforms.

An important event of the Maharana's reign has been the settlement of an old dispute with the State of Palanpur, which ended by liberating Danta from the payment to Palanpur of an annual levy of Rs. 500. His Highness visited Bombay in 1911 in order to witness the arrival of Their Imperial Majesties the King-Emperor and Queen-Empress in anticipation of the Coro-

HIS HIGHNESS SHRI MAHARANAJI SHRI HAMIRSINGHJI SAHIB, RULER OF DANTA.

1. H.H. MAHARANAJI SHRI JASWANTSINGHJI, SAHIB BAHADUR, OF DANTA (THE LATE RULER).
2. RAJ SAHIBAN SHRI MOHOBATSINGHJI SAHIB.

1. H.H. MAHARAJ KUMAR SHRI BHAWANSINGHJI, SAHIB BAHADUR, OF DANTA STATE.
2. HIS HIGHNESS THE PRESENT MAHARANAJI SAHIB, WITH MAHARAK-KUMARS, SARDARS, NOBLES AND OFFICIALS.
3. H.H. MAHARAJ KUMAR SHRI BHAWANSINGHJI, WITH TIGER SHOT BY HIMSELF.

Photo by Haji Sant.

THE STATE OF DANTA.

1. The Bhawanghad Summer Palace. 2. The Famous Temple of Shri Mataji Amba-Bhawani, on Mount Arasur. 3. The Kumbharia Temples. 4. The Koteswar Temple, at the Source of the River Sarasvati.

nation *Durbar* held at Delhi in December of the same year.

The Great War of 1914-18 intensified the spirit of loyalty which has always characterized the people of Danta, and they manifested their earnest desire to help the Allies by contributing—inclusive of generous donations from His Highness the Maharana—the sum of Rs. 1,60,000.

His Highness the Maharana enjoys full powers of administration, together with supreme authority in civil and criminal matters. Danta is an important State from a social point of view, as it has marriage relationships with the States of Udaipur, Jodhpur, Banswara, Idar and Sirohi.

The heir-apparent, His Highness Shri Maharaj Kumar Sahib Bhawanisinghji, born in the year 1900, received the greater portion of his education at the Mayo College, at Ajmer, where his manly disposition and upright character won for him the approbation of the Principal as well as the confidence of his fellow-students.

For the past two years His Highness has taken a deep interest in State matters, and he has been primarily responsible for the revision and improvement of the tariff system, for discontinuing fees for education, and for the construction of, or repairs to, roads, tanks and other public works.

Shri Raj Sahib Shri Mohobutsinghji, uncle of His Highness the Maharana, was for several years associated with the late Maharanaji Sahib in conducting the affairs of the State, and his able services and ripe experience have been highly appreciated by the present Chief, especially the work performed by him in connection with the settlement of intricate boundary disputes. The Raj Sahib retired into private life about two years ago, but his advice is frequently sought upon important political and social questions affecting the welfare of the State. The result is that the sound methods of administration adopted under his direction have been continued and have been most effective.

GENERAL VIEW OF TEMPLES AT MOHANGADH, NEAR DHARAMPUR.

THE STATE OF DHARAMPUR

THIS is a second-class State in the Surat Political Agency, in the Presidency of Bombay, and it was formerly known as Mandvegan, and subsequently as Ramnagar. Its rulers belong to the Sisodia clan of Rajputs, and trace their descent from the same ancestors as the House of Udaipur. They are known as Ranas and are entitled to a salute of nine guns.

The Maharanas of Dharampur trace their descent from Ramchandraji of Ayodhia. Kanaksen, who was sixty-third in descent from Lava, one of the sons of Ramchandraji, in A.D. 144 defeated a Rajput ruler of the Parmar dynasty, and established himself in Kathiawar. The State of Dharampur was founded in 1262 by Ramraja, who is believed to be identical with Prince Ramshah of Mewar, a famous Rajput Chief. The history of the State was marked by the vicissitudes which are the common characteristic of Rajput dynasties. In 1787 the Ruler was one Rupdevji, and it was during his reign that the Treaty of Bassein, dated December 31, 1802, was concluded between the Peshwa and the British Government, which assigned in perpetuity all the claims of the Peshwa over the State to the Paramount Power. In this manner the direct connection of the State with the British Government was brought about.

Raja Vijaydevji came to the throne on the death of Rupdevji in 1807. He was of a generous nature and simple in his ways, but prodigal in his habits, spending an incredible amount of wealth in charities to Bhats, Charans, Brahmins, and other people. His style of living was splendid, but extravagant, and the inevitable result was that the State was burdened by a heavy debt.

His Excellency the Hon. Mountstuart Elphinstone, Governor of Bombay, in recognition of the independence of the State, presented the Raja with a medal and a *khilat*. Dharampur was the first of all the Native States of Gujarat to receive this honour at the hands of the Paramount Power.

In 1857, Raja Vijaydevji breathed his last, and his successor, Ramdevji III, ruled for about three years. The issue of his marriage with the daughter of Gumansinhji of Chhota-Udaipur was a son, born on September 3, 1840, named Narandevji, who ascended the throne on January 26, 1860, at the age of 19. After his accession he worked zealously for the good of the people.

A *sanad*, authorizing the Raja to adopt an heir to the throne on failure of a natural successor without paying *nazarana* to the Sovereign Power, was granted to him in 1862 by the Government.

Raja Narandevji took for his wives the daughters of Vansia Mohansingji, Chhasatia Sardar, Bhagubava of Dharampur, Vansadia Thakore of Nikora, the late Thakore Rayasinhji of Chhaliar in Rewa kantha, Akheraj of Bhavnagar, and the daughter of the Chavada Thakore of

HIS HIGHNESS THE MAHARANA SHRI MOHANDEVJI RANA, RAJA SAHIB OF DHARAMPUR STATE.

THE STATE OF DHARAMPUR.

1. Mohan Vilas Palace at Dharampur. 2. Radhakrishna Temple, Dharampur. 3. The Jubilee Charitable Dispensary.

Manekpur. Dharmdevji was born of the Vansadia Raniji, and Mohandevji, the present Chief, of the Chavada Raniji of Manekpur. Baldevji was born of the Chhasatia Raniji, Haridevji of Vansia Raniji, and Prabhatdevji of the Chhalior Raniji. Dharmdevji was the true heir to the *gadi*, but grim death claimed him as one of its youthful victims in 1879, whereupon the present Chief, Mohandeji, became the heir-apparent.

The Raja journeyed to Bombay in 1875 at the time of the arrival of His Royal Highness the Prince of Wales (afterwards His Majesty King Edward VII), in order to pay his respects to the Royal guest. As a memento of the memorable occasion His Royal Highness sent through the Agent to the Governor of Bombay at Surat a *khilat* and a medal for presentation to the Raja. His Highness was invited to be present at the grand *Durbar* held at Delhi in 1877 by His Excellency Lord Lytton, on the occasion of the assumption of the title of Empress of India by Her Most Gracious Majesty Queen Victoria, but he was prevented by ill-health from attending it.

Raja Narandevji died on August 7, 1891, and Maharana Shri Mohandevji Rana, who managed the affairs of the State during the last illness of his father, was duly installed on the *gadi*. He married one of the daughters of Shrimant Surshinji, Thakore Saheb of Virpur in Kathiawar, and the issue has been Kumars K. S. Vijaydevji Saheb (the heir-apparent) and K. S. Narsinhdevji Saheb, who died in January, 1920, at a comparatively early age.

In 1894 the Maharana Shri went to Surat and paid a visit to His Excellency Lord Harris, Governor of Bombay, who happened to be in that district at the time. On this occasion large sums of money were distributed by the Maharaja Saheb to several deserving funds.

The Moore Leper Asylum, named after Mr. R. A. L. Moore, the then Collector and Political Agent at Surat, was opened in the year 1898, and this institution has proved to be a veritable blessing by affording shelter and food to many unfortunate subjects of the State.

The Maharaja Saheb went to Bombay with a large retinue in November, 1905, on the occasion of the visit of His Royal Highness the Prince of Wales (now His Majesty the King-Emperor George V) and the Princess to India.

A High School, named the Maharana Shri Mohandevji High School, was opened in Dharampur in 1908, and not only is education, both primary and secondary, given free to pupils but school requisites, such as books, slates, and other requirements, as well as scholarships, are also provided gratis to the children of poor parents.

A telegraph office was opened here in 1905, and the long-felt want of the public and the State was thus removed.

On the occasion of the coronation of His Majesty King George V, the Maharana Shri Mohandevji proceeded to Delhi in 1911 and remained there for several days, taking part in the magnificent functions which had been arranged for that auspicious event. In commemoration of this ceremony a gold medal and a photo of their Imperial Majesties were presented to the Maharana.

In 1914 Maharana Shri Mohandevji went to Rumla, a large village in the northern territory of the State, for the purpose of turning the first sod of the road from Dharampur to Rumla. This road is now under construction, and has been named the Mohandevji Road.

In August, 1916, Maharana Shri Mohandevji completed 25 years of his brilliant and successful rule, and this event was celebrated by his *ryots* with great *éclat*. A considerable sum of money was voluntarily subscribed by His Highness's subjects and other well-wishers, and in memory of the event a magnificent building called "Maharana Shri Mohandevji Silver Jubilee Institute" has been erected. A marble statue of the Ruler will shortly be placed in front of the building.

The Chief is advanced in age, and not being conversant with the English language, he offered the services of his brother, Maharana Shri Prabhatdevji, in aid of the Allies, and he placed all the resources of the State at the disposal of the Government. As there is no military force in the State the dispatch of trained men for the front was out of the question, but more than 100 persons were sent, some of whom were selected to serve as soldiers, while others were employed as labourers. These recruits were given substantial sums of money by way of bonus or *inam*, and arrangements were made by the State for the maintenance of their families during their absence, while in case of their death, their children were promised free education, books, and other school requisites.

The sum of Rs. 35,000 was given annually towards war expenses, in addition to other amounts contributed to various war purposes, and grass to the weight of many thousands of pounds and bags of rice for the Army were also provided, free of charge, by the State.

The Raja Saheb took great interest in the two War Loans, and, as a result, the total amount subscribed in the State reached the sum of Rs. 5,25,000.

State contributions and donations for war charities and war relief objects amounted to over Rs. 1,00,000.

Maharana Shri Mohandevji has the interest of his *ryots* always at heart, and he rules the State wisely, with the able assistance of his present *Dewan*, Mr. Faramroze B. Garda.

The State is bounded on the north by the Chikhli *taluka* in the district of Surat and the State of Bansda; on the east by the State of Sulgana, and the Kalyan and Peint *talukas* of the district of Nasik; on the south by the district of Thana and the Portuguese territory of Nagar Haveli Pargana; and on the west by the Pardi, Bulsar, and Chikhli *talukas* of the district of Surat.

The area of the State is 704 square miles, and, according to the census of 1911, the inhabitants were 114,995 in number, the majority of whom are of the Kaliparaj race.

The State is divided into six *mahals* or divisions for the purpose of administration, each of which is in charge of a *Thanedar*, working under the supervision of the Revenue Officer.

Under an agreement dated April 6, 1870, a fixed amount of Rs. 9,000 is paid annually to the British Government in lieu of *chauth jakat*, which was formerly levied by them in the State.

The area of the State, which has already been surveyed, extends to 4,49,757 acres, and more than one-fourth of the total area is under cultivation. The rates of assessment prevailing in Dharampur are fair and reasonable, and the principal agricultural produce consists of rice, although *nagli jowar*, pulses, *kodra*, and other crops are also grown in large quantities.

There is no military force in the State. The regular police force is assisted by the *Huzur* palace guards, Arabs, and *Shirbandhis*, who hold service land free of assessment.

Justice is administered according to the principles of British Indian and local laws, the latter being to a large extent based upon the former. There are five Criminal and three Civil Courts.

There is a separate Municipal Board

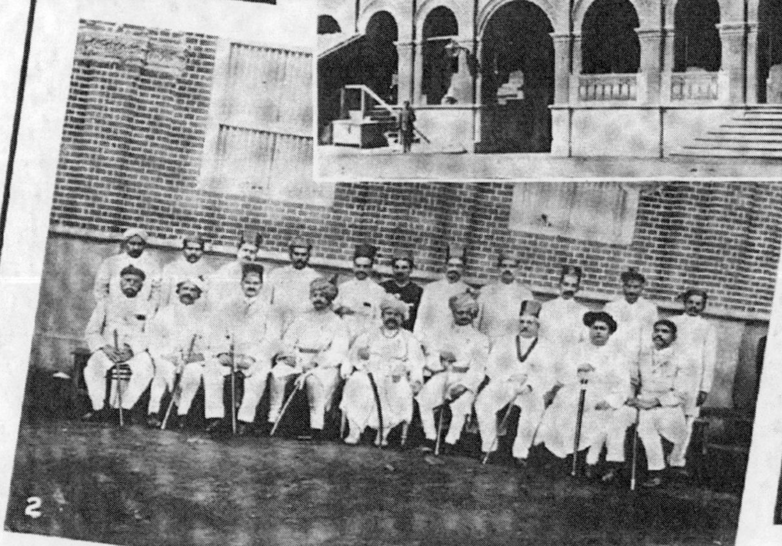

THE STATE OF DHARAMPUR.

1. Durbar Hall, Dharampur. 2. H.H. The Maharana Sahib of Dharampur, with Bhayata, Sardars and Officers of the State. 3. Dewan Sahib's Bungalow, Dharampur.

THE STATE OF DHARAMPUR.

1. H.H. the Maharana Shri Mohandevji Silver Jubilee Hall, Dharampur. 2. Shri Majiraba Girls' School, Dharampur. 3. Maharana Shri Mohandevji High School, Dharampur.

THE STATE OF DHARAMPUR.

1. "Narhemantalay" (under construction), at Dharampur. Bungalow of the Late Kumar Shri Narsinhdevji Sahib—Younger Kumar of H.H. Maharaja Sahib.
2. "Prabhat Nivas" (under construction). Bungalow of Maharana Shri Prabhatdevji, Sahib Brother of H.H. the Maharaja Sahib.
3. "Baldev Nivas." Bungalow of the Late Maharana Shri Baldevji Sahib, Brother of H.H. the Maharaja Sahib.

which looks after conservancy, sanitation, and other matters in the town of Dharampur, as well as at Nani Vahial, the seat of the Chief, and about six miles distant from the capital.

The chief exports are: Various kinds of grain, *timru* and *assindra* leaves, from which *bidis* (country cigarettes) are made, and *doli* (*mahua* fruit) and flowers of the same tree, from which valuable oil is extracted.

The country is hilly in character, and abounds in forests, in which panthers, leopards, and occasionally tigers are found.

A combined post and telegraph office has been opened in the town of Dharampur.

The following are the principal metalled roads: From Kharwel to Nanapondha, about 16 miles; Dharampur to Bilpudi, about 2 miles; and from Dharampur to Karanjveri, about 3 miles.

The majority of the inhabitants of the State are, as already mentioned, Kaliparaj people, who are very simple in their mode of living, and their wants are few. The greater portion of them depend upon the cultivation of the soil for their subsistence, and the remainder subsist upon wages as unskilled labourers on either field work or the cutting of forest trees. They are of migratory habits, and a trifling cause is sufficient to cause them to remove from one place to another.

The Ujaliats, consisting of Brahmins, Rajputs, Parbhus, Banias, and others, are in a great minority compared with the Kaliparaj, Dhodias, Kunknas, Warlis, Dublas, and others. The former carry on business as money-lenders, till the soil, and trade in corn and other local produce. Mahomedans are either State officials or cultivators of land, and Parsis, who are not numerous, either manage liquor or toddy stores or cultivate land.

The revenue of the State is nearly Rs. 10,00,000, of which more than one-half is derived from land.

The medical department of the State is efficiently controlled by fully qualified surgeons. The Jubilee charitable dispensary in the town of Dharampur is a well-equipped institution, affording relief there and in the surrounding villages. For the relief of the Kaliparaj *ryots* residing in distant villages, there are dispensaries at Godthal and at Balchondi. Besides these there is an itinerating dispensary moving about in the various districts for the purpose of giving treatment to sick persons, and there is also a leper asylum where patients are provided with board and lodging free of cost.

Education is imparted free in all the 26 schools of the State, including even the High School in the town of Dharampur.

THE STATE OF DHARAMPUR.

SUMMER VILLAS AT VAHIAL, NEAR DHARAMPUR.

THE STATE OF LIMBDI

THIS is a second-class State, situated in the eastern portion of the Kathiawar peninsula, in the Presidency of Bombay. It is bounded on the north by the State of Lakhtar and the British district of Viramgam; on the east by the British territory of Dholka; on the south by the State of Bhavnagar and the district of Dhandhuka; and on the west by the States of Wadhwan and Chula.

The Thakore Saheb of Limbdi belongs to the Jhala clan of Rajputs, and their succession to the *gadi* is governed by the law of primogeniture.

The present Ruler, His Highness the Maharana Shri Daulatsinhji, Thakore Saheb, is descended from Manguji, the second son of Harpaldeo, who lived in the days of Karan Vaghelo, the last Rajput King of Gujarat, from whom he received a grant of 1,800 villages as a reward for meritorious services.

The capital at Limbdi was founded in 1784 by Harbhamji I, who, dying in 1786, was succeeded on the *gadi* by Harisinhji, an able and intelligent administrator. This Ruler in 1807 concluded a treaty with Colonel Walker, who guaranteed permanantly to the Rulers of Limbdi, on behalf of the British Government, the enjoyment of the full powers hitherto enjoyed by them, and Thakore Saheb Harisinhji on his part promised to pay the tribute settled permanently by Colonel Walker, and to desist from internal warfare. The fourth succeeding Thakore was His Highness the late Sir Jaswantsinhji, who succeeded his father, Fatehsinhji, in the year 1862. During the minority of the young Prince the administration of the State was entrusted to his mother, but as she found the duties to be too arduous the Government in 1867 appointed an assistant to the Political Agent of Kathiawar, who relieved her of further responsibility.

The young Thakore Saheb became a student at the Rajkumar College, in Rajkot, where he gained the highest approbation of the Principal. His Highness manifested a remarkable degree of intelligence, and earned well-deserved popularity by reason of his frank and courteous nature and his exemplary moral character. His abilities were so pronounced that at the early age of 18 years he was invested with full powers.

The first visit to England of the Thakore Saheb was undertaken in 1876, and in 1887 he, as the representative of the Kathiawar Princes, proceeded to London, in order to be present at the Golden Jubilee celebrations of the reign of Her Majesty the late Queen Victoria. His Highness was on this occasion honoured by being created a Knight Commander of the Most Eminent Order of the Indian Empire.

Sir Jaswantsinhji died in 1907 without leaving issue. It appears, however, that the late Thakore Saheb had some years previously considered the question of a successor in the event of his dying without a direct heir, and he had been most favourably impressed with the personal appearance, as well as the great abilities, of Colonel Dadbha, then Commander-in-Chief of the Imperial Service forces in the State of Nawanagar. When the *gadi* became vacant the British Government acceded to the desire expressed by Sir Jaswantsinhji on his deathbed that Colonel Dadbha should be recognized as his successor, and the latter assumed the title under the name of Daulatsinhji. His Highness the Thakore Saheb had in earlier life received an excellent training in military matters, and he exemplified this by his great skill in organization and in the handling of troops. In 1901 he formed one of a party of military officers selected by the Indian Government to represent them at the opening of the Federal Parliament in Australia, and the tour was extended to New Zealand, where His Highness was the guest of the Rt. Hon. R. F. Seddon.

His Highness the Thakore Saheb was formally invested with full ruling powers on April 14, 1908, by Mr. P. S. V. Fitzgerald, C.S.I., Agent in Kathiawar to the Governor of Bombay.

In the year 1910 a most happy marriage alliance was formed between the ancient Houses of the Jhalas of Limbdi and the Rathors of Idar, by the betrothal of Kunvari Shri Nandkunvarba, the only daughter of His Highness the late Maharaja Sir Kesarisinhji of Idar, to the eldest son of the Thakore Saheb Yuvaraj Shri Digvijayasinhji, heir-apparent of Limbdi.

His Highness the Thakore Saheb has always been one of the most ardent supporters of education in India, and in order to commemorate the marriage of his eldest son, he established several scholarships for the assistance of students desirous of extending their collegiate work.

His Highness had the honour of being a guest at the Coronation Durbar of Their Majesties the King-Emperor and Queen-

HIS HIGHNESS SHRI DAULATSINHJI, THAKORE SAHIB OF LIMBDI.

1. YUVARAJ KUMAR SHRI DIGVIJAYASINHJI (HEIR-APPARENT OF LIMBDI).
2. KUMAR SAHIB SHRI PRATAPSINHJI, OF LIMBDI. 3. KUMAR SAHIB SHRI FATEHSINHJI, OF LIMBDI.
4. KUMAR SAHIB SHRI GHANSHYAMSINHJI, OF LIMBDI.

Empress at Delhi, in 1911, when he attended the various functions and festivities arranged for this auspicious occasion.

In 1912 His Highness proceeded to England to arrange for the admission of the heir-apparent as a student at Eton. While in London he had the honour of an audience with His Imperial Majesty King George V, and of being invited to attend a garden party, a State ball, and an Imperial levée at Buckingham Palace, and he subsequently visited France, Germany, Belgium, Switzerland, and Italy, in which countries he made a careful study of Western civilization in all its aspects, but more particularly as it was revealed in the manufacturing and industrial enterprises in large commercial centres.

Notwithstanding the immense responsibilities resting upon the shoulders of the chief representative of His Imperial Majesty in Bombay during the late Great War, His Excellency Lord Willingdon, Governor of Bombay, paid a visit to the State of Limbdi in February 1916.

His Excellency laid the foundation-stone of the " King George V Coronation Rajput Hostel." On the same day the formal opening took place of the Lady Willingdon Girls' School at the capital town.

His Highness the Thakore Saheb was born on July 11, 1868, and he has four sons and two daughters. He has won golden opinions in England, as well as in India, by his courteous and charming manners, and in India there is a wide appreciation of the intelligence and wisdom evinced by him in the administration of the State. He is regular in his attendance at the *Huzur* Office of the State, where he personally supervises the work of every Department, and the result of his untiring efforts for the amelioration of the condition of his subjects is seen in the deep affection entertained by them for their popular Ruler.

The State of Limbdi, about 350 square miles in extent, consists of 49 villages under its full jurisdiction, and it also owns 34 *Taluqdari* villages, situated within the British district of Ahmedabad.

The State consists of a dry flat plain. In the northern portion of the territory there is a marshy tract of low-lying land, called " Nalkantha," 20 sq. miles in extent, which is submerged during the greater portion of the year. Although the soil of Nalkantha is fertile and suitable for various crops, the prevalence of myriads of mosquitoes in the rank vegetation renders the area practically uninhabitable.

Speaking generally, the soil of Limbdi is of very unfavourable character, but that found in the *Bhal* villages is of a productive kind, yielding excellent crops, chiefly of wheat and cotton.

The following figures, extracted from a recent State Administration Report, show the area of land under cultivation : Cotton, 30,467 acres ; wheat, 22,825 acres ; gram, 3,200 acres ; winter *jowari*, 3,260 acres ; barley, 300 acres ; jowar, 15,985 acres ; *bajra*, 8,548 acres ; and other crops, including vegetables, making a total of 90,038 acres.

The cultivation of the land is an industry attended by very great risks, owing to variations in climate and rainfall, and in districts such as Limbdi, for example, there are recurring droughts, which very seriously affect the yields of harvests. In such seasons as these water is unobtainable from rivers for irrigation purposes, and many of the wells and tanks which have been constructed are practically useless to afford relief. In this matter, too, the Thakore Saheb has shown great foresight by his energetic action in commencing experimental irrigation works in the village of Gunjar, where he has sunk a huge well, from which water is raised to the surface by steam power. In the event of this trial being successful the new method will be tried in other places in the State.

Cotton grown in Limbdi has for many years been regarded with great favour by spinners, on account of its superior quality, but as there was not a single cotton press in the State the crop had to be conveyed in bulk to Wadhwan, where it was baled, prior to its export to Bombay. Not only was the cost of freight and pressing a hardship upon Limbdi cultivators, but it was also discovered that the consignments were frequently mixed with inferior cotton, and thus the reputation of Limbdi cotton began to suffer. His Highness was quick to realize the hardships imposed upon his subjects, and in 1909 he erected a fine cotton press in the town of Limbdi. Stores have also been built for the accommodation of bales until they are despatched to market, and a tramway for the transport of consignments has been constructed between the factory and the railway station. That these facilities have been duly appreciated is evident from the fact that cotton is now sent to the press from all parts of Limbdi, and from several neighbouring territories. During the year 1917–18 more than 23,080 bales were pressed in the factory. The idea of establishing a cotton market at Limbdi had its origin in the desire of His Highness the Thakore to attract purchasers to the State, and thus enable cultivators to sell their bales without the interposition of any other persons. The project was carried into effect in 1910-11, the building being situated near the ginning factory and the cotton press, and at the present time several well-known merchants of Bombay, Ahmedabad, Bhavnagar, and other famous cotton centres, have opened branches at Limbdi for the furtherance of their trading connections. Healthy competition, tending to increased prices, has thus been generated, and thus once again Limbdi cotton has established its superiority, and growers are receiving the full value of their crops.

There are now within the limits of the State three ginning factories, a cotton press, and a combined flour, rice, and saw-mill. The hand-loom weaving industry, also inaugurated by His Highness the Thakore Saheb, produces gold and silver thread embroidery work of exquisite patterns, and for the further encouragement of this industry the State has provided suitable quarters, free of rent, for the artisans.and has also arranged for the giving of financial aid in cases of necessity. *Dungari* cloth is woven in several villages, and the capital town is noted for the manufacture of ivory bangles, embroidery in silk, and various kinds of brass boxes, ornaments, and other articles. The principal imported goods are food-grains, cloth, sugar, and molasses, the value of these in the past year being Rs. 13,72,[illegible], while the chief exports are cotton, cotton-seeds, wheat, ivory, bangles, coarse cloth, and ghee.

The Limbdi State Bank has amply justified its foundation in 1910 by the valuable assistance it has given to merchants and cultivators in times of need.

In connection with the dispensation of justice the courts are guided mainly by the spirit of the laws prevailing in British India, although regulations and rules have been framed for dealing with certain special matters. The courts of criminal jurisdiction are the *Huzur* Court, which is the final authority in the State ; the Judicial *Karbhari's* Court, exercising power of a Sessions Court ; and the First Class Magistrate's Court. There are four Courts for the disposal of civil matters, namely, the *Munsiff's* Court, in which suits up to the value of Rs. 5[illegible]

THE STATE OF LIMBDI.

1. The Dig Bhuvan Palace. 2. The Bhavendra Vilas Palace. 3. The State Drawing-room. 4. Interior of the Durbar Hall.

THE STATE OF LIMBDI.

1. The Natwar Nivas Institute. 2. The Secretariat. 3. Shri Ghanshyamsinhji Club. 4. The Town Hall.

THE STATE OF LIMBDI

are heard; the Judicial *Karbhari's* Court, for the trial of cases beyond the powers of the Munsiff; the *Huzur* Court, with full powers of appeal; and the Small Causes Court, for deciding financial claims of not more than Rs. 100 in value.

His Highness the Thakore Saheb is an ardent and liberal supporter of education among his subjects, and it is his practice to pay periodical visits to every school in the State in order that he may give encouragement to teachers and scholars, and also with the object of satisfying him-

THE STATE OF LIMBDI.

1. The Hareshwar Temple. 2. The River-side, showing the Old Fortress.

self as to the suitability of the various buildings, and their general cleanliness, as well as the efficiency of the teaching staff. Both primary and secondary education is free to the subjects of Limbdi and Laktar States. Extremely moderate fees are payable by pupils belonging to places beyond the borders of the Limbdi and Laktar States.

At the close of the past year the teaching institutions comprised: the Jaswantsinhji High School, *Taluka* school, one girls' school, a *Pathshala*, and a *Madressa*, all at Limbdi; an English school, and one girls' school at Sihani; an English school at Barwala, and 20 primary schools.

Immediately upon receipt of news of the world's Great War in 1914, His Highness the Thakore Saheb telegraphed to His Excellency the Governor of Bombay, and to the Agent in Kathiawar, offering all possible assistance from himself personally and from the State. A public meeting was summoned, at which His Highness made a stirring appeal for help in aid of the righteous cause of the Allies, and a ladies' meeting was subsequently held, when definite steps were arranged for the collection of subscriptions to various Relief Funds, and for the making of articles of comfort for the troops.

There were no slackening of the energies of His Highness and his subjects in their support of war funds during succeeding years, and in the State Administration Report for 1917–18 it is stated that the total contributions to March 31, 1918, amounted to Rs. 47,000. This sum represented the cost of an ambulance car, together with the cost of its maintenance, two machine guns, contributions to the Imperial India Relief Fund, the Prince of Wales's Fund, the Belgian Relief Fund, "Our Day" Fund, and various other donations of money and clothing.

Special efforts were made to obtain subscriptions for the War Loan Funds, and the result was Rs. 3,00,000 from the officials and subjects of the State, Rs. 2,15,000 from the State and the Durbar family, and Rs. 43,950 from the inhabitants of the Barwala division, making a total of Rs. 5,58,950. His Highness was particularly anxious to secure recruits among his subjects, and he liberally offered a number of inducements, among which may be mentioned: a bonus of Rs. 100 to a combatant, and Rs. 50 to a non-combatant; a sum of Rs. 10 monthly to the family of a recruit on active service; and a grant of ten bighas of land, free of assessment, if the recruits were killed or permanently disabled.

It may be observed that the subjects of the State showed the greatest enthusiasm in their endeavours to curtail their ordinary expenses, and thus be in a position to contribute more largely to war funds, but it should be added that the success obtained was almost entirely due to the personal exertions of His Highness the Thakore Saheb, who spared no pains to exhort the people to render aid in every possible manner.

Limbdi, the capital of the State, with a population of more than 11,000 inhabitants, is situated on the bank of the river Bhogava. Among the most interesting features are the Durbar palace, the State offices in the centre of the town, surrounded by a wall called the ***Durbar Godh***, the "Wodehouse" Vegetable Market, the new State guest-house, and the clock tower over the Durbar hall. The old residential palace was destroyed by fire in 1906, and the present one is on the road to the railway station.

Thanks to the efforts of His Highness Limbdi now enjoys the benefits of a fine supply of pure drinking water, and of electricity for the lighting of the principal buildings.

The wedding of the Kunvari Shri Rupaliba Saheb, M.B.E., eldest daughter of His Highness the Thakore Saheb, with His Highness the Maharaja Rana Saheb of Porbunder, was celebrated in February 1920, at Limbdi, amid unprecedented rejoicings, with very great pomp and splendour.

From the foregoing notes it will be realized that His Highness the Thakore Saheb is a model Ruler and a sagacious administrator. His periodical visits to every village in the State, and his personal intercourse with the people, enable him to understand the conditions under which they live, and he is ever willing to redress grievances which may be put before him. In fostering commercial and industrial development, and in his persistent efforts to ensure the better education of the young people of the State he has few equals, and as a result of this paternal oversight His Highness rules over a contented and happy class of subjects.

THE STATE OF LOHARU

THE Mahomedan State of Loharu, 222 square miles in extent, in the south-eastern portion of the Province of the Punjab, is under the political control of the Commissioner of Delhi, and it is bounded on the north by the British district of Hissar; on the east and south-east by the States of Jind and Patiala; and on the west by Rajputana.

The founder of the State, Nawab Ahmad Baksh Khan (a Moghul), was in the employ of the British Government for about 30 years, towards the end of the eighteenth century, and served the Government with his men in a military capacity. Negotiations were at that time in progress between the British Government and a number of Rulers of Native States in India, and it was largely due to the influence and ability of Nawab Ahmad Baksh Khan, who acted as an Agent between the Alwar Durbar and Lord Lake, that Lord Lake was enabled to formulate an agreement which gave to that State—as well as to others—the protection of the Paramount Power. In recognition of the services thus rendered, the Maharaja of Alwar conferred upon Ahmad Baksh Khan, in perpetuity, through the British Government, the tract of land known as Loharu, and the British Government made a grant to him of the *pergana* of Ferozepur. The latter tract was, however, confiscated in 1835, when his son, Shams-ud-din Khan, was executed at Delhi for being concerned in the death of Mr. Fraser, the Political Agent. The possession of Loharu was transferred to Nawab Amin-ud-din, for the support of himself and his brother, Zia-ud-din, step-brothers of the assassin, who were found to have been entirely unconnected with the conspiracy which resulted in tragedy.

They were in Delhi during the Sepoy Mutiny of 1857, but there is absolutely no doubt as to their firm allegiance to the British, as the State possesses documentary evidences bearing direct testimony to this effect.

The hereditary titles of Nawab and Fakhr-ud-daulah were conferred upon Ala-ud-din (son of Amin-ud-din), who was succeeded in 1884 by His Highness the Nawab Sir Amir-ud-din Ahmad Khan Bahadur Fakhr-ud-daulah, K.C.I.E., who was born in the year 1860.

The aptitude of His Highness for administrative work was apparent soon after his accession to ruling powers, and he spared no pains to improve the State in every possible manner.

From 1893 to 1903 the Nawab was superintendent of the State of Maler Kotla during the minority of its Rulers, Loharu being in the meantime managed by the Nawab's younger brother.

In 1893 His Highness was created a Commander of the Most Eminent Order of the Indian Empire, and four years later he was raised to the dignity of a Knight Commander of the same order.

With the view of commemorating the famous Coronation Durbar, held at Delhi in 1903, His Highness established a charitable dispensary at Loharu, this being the first of its kind to be founded in the State, and in the same year a salute of nine guns was granted to him.

Not only through the dark days of the Mutiny, but since that time also, the Chiefs of Loharu have never for an instant wavered in their loyalty to the Throne, and the sincerity of their devotion to the British Government has been abundantly manifested on several occasions. The State provided 110 camels, with drivers, for transport service during the Afghan campaign of 1878, and it also rendered great assistance of the Government in the purchase of 400 other transport animals during the same war, and in the Tirah Expeditions of 1897–8 the State supplied 211 camels and 72 attendants.

His Highness the Nawab was at Srinagar, in Kashmir, in August, 1914, when news of the outbreak of the Great War was sent to him, and he at once telegraphed to the Government of India offering to provide 200 fully-equipped transport camels, with drivers and attendants, for service under the heir-apparent, in any theatre of war. These were despatched in December, 1914, and they were followed by 50 other animals in March, 1917, and a similar number in July, 1918. The State also sent to the front more than 400 recruits.

In addition to bearing the expense of furnishing the above-mentioned supplies, the State contributed the following amounts, among others: to the Imperial Indian Relief Fund, Rs. 1,500; H.R.H. the Prince of Wales's Fund, Rs. 250; the Punjab Aeroplane Fund, Rs. 1,000; the Kitchener Memorial Fund, Rs. 100; Lady O'Dwyer's Lucky Bag Fund, Rs. 100; "Our Day" Fund, Rs. 1,000; Indian soldiers' canteen, Rs. 100; and Sir Michael O'Dwyer's Memorial to soldiers, Rs. 250; the State also subscribed Rs. 20,000 for War Loan Bonds. The subjects of the Nawab contributed Rs. 400 to the Imperial Indian Relief

Fund, and the sum of Rs. 15,000 for purchase of War Bonds.

On the commencement of hostilities against Turkey His Highness the Nawab Sahib issued a manifesto, addressed to Mahomedans generally, to the effect that the conflict was the outcome of purely political questions, and had not the remotest connection with religious matters. Copies of this document were sent to newspapers throughout India and elsewhere. His Highness also composed an ode in the Persian language, in which he invoked the blessings of British rule, justice, and freedom, and also calling upon Mahomedans to stand firm in their loyalty to the King-Emperor. This poem was distributed in all parts of India, Mesopotamia, Persia, and Afghanistan.

In October 1915 His Highness went to Mesopotamia on a political mission, in connection with the prosecution of the war.

When disturbances, practically amounting to a rebellion, broke out in the Punjab in the year 1919, His Highness the Nawab Sahib offered the services of the heir-apparent, in command of 50 armed *sowars*, with fully-equipped camels, and two guns, and he was warmly thanked by the Government of that Province for this expression of his goodwill. The services of Nawabzada Aiz-ud-din Ahmad Khan, the heir-apparent, were accepted in connection with the latest Afghan trouble, and he was granted the honorary rank of Captain, being attached to the staff of the Inspector-General of Communications, Northern Division, and he was subsequently highly eulogized by General Sir A. A. Barrett, commanding forces on the northern frontier. The Nawab's third son, Nawabzada Aitezar-ud-din Ahmed Khan, after enrolment for service in the same war, became an attached officer on the staff of the General Officer Commanding in Baluchistan, from whom he received well-deserved praise for the exemplary manner in which he performed his arduous duties.

With the object of minimizing the destitution caused by the severe famine of 1900–01 His Highness sanctioned the construction, at a cost of Rs. 30,000, of a large masonry tank just outside of the northern gate of the capital town of Loharu.

His Highness was the recipient of several marks of distinction, among those being the Kaiser-i-Hind medal of January, 1877, gold medals issued in connection with the Coronation Durbar of 1903 and 1911, and other medals commemorating the late Great War.

Sir Amir-ud-din was for two years a member of the Council of His Excellency the Viceroy and Governor-General of India, and for a similar period of the Council of His Honour the Lieutenant-Governor of the Province of the Punjab.

His Highness the Nawab Sir Amir-ud-din Ahmad Khan abdicated in January, 1920, in favour of his eldest son, Nawabzada Aiz-ud-din Ahmad Khan, who was, on April 20th following, formally recognized by the Government as the Nawab of the State of Loharu.

The Political Agent paid a special visit to Loharu, when he presented a *kharita* from the Lieutenant-Governor of the Punjab, conveying congratulations upon his accession, and also handed to the Nawab Sahib a robe of honour. It was at the same time notified that Sir Amir-ud-din (previous Ruler) has been allowed to retain the title of Nawab, and that his salute of nine guns would be continued as a mark of personal distinction.

The present Nawab Sahib became actively connected with the administration of State affairs in 1903, when he was appointed Secretary to the Durbar; in 1908 he undertook the responsibilities of controlling the Financial Department; and in 1918 he assumed general administrative duties.

As an instance of the loyalty to the Throne of His Highness the Nawab Sahib, it may be mentioned that on the day of his installation he offered to raise an Imperial Service Reserve Transport contingent, composed of 200 fully-equipped camels, together with drivers and attendants, and this proposal is at the present time being considered by the Government of India.

The State of Loharu has a population of 20,614 inhabitants, this being a considerable increase over the figures given in the census report of the year 1901.

Loharu consists, for the most part, of a sandy plain, interspersed with a few hills, but with little in the form of vegetation to relieve the monotony of its physical aspect. The majority of the people find employment in agricultural pursuits.

Loharu, the capital of the State, is situated about 52 miles on the southern side of Hissar. The town derives its name from the *lohars*, or blacksmiths, employed therein. It contains the palace of the Nawab of Loharu, the State offices, a guest-house, hospital, jail, and postal and telegraph offices.

THE STATE OF LUNAWADA

LUNAWADA, a second-class Rajput State in the Rewakantha, Political Agency of the Bombay Presidency, is bounded on the north by the Rajputana State of Dungarpur, on the east by Kadana and Sunth-Rampur in Rewakantha, on the south by the Godhra Sub-Division of the Panch-Mahals, and on the west by Balasinor in Rewakantha and Idar in Mahikantha, and it has an area of 388 square miles.

His Highness the Raja of Lunawada is descended from the Virpura clan of Solanki Rajputs, which is the senior branch of the Waghelas of Rewah. His ancestors are said to have established themselves at Virpur as far back as the year 1223. Some two hundred years later the family removed to Lunawada, where Rana Bhimsinh founded the present State.

The direct line from Bhimsinh came to an end at the death of Akheraj, and Kumbho Rano, of a collateral branch of the family, was brought from the village of Gandhari and invested with the Chiefship. This Raja Kumbho Rano was succeeded by Jitsinh, who appears from his written grants to have ruled as late as 1618 A.D. Narsingh, who ruled from 1712 to 1733, laid the foundation of the Lunawada town wall in 1718. In 1812, through the medium of the Political Agent in Mahikantha, the State entered into an engagement to pay the Gaekwar a fixed yearly tribute of Baroda Rs. 6,000.

In 1819 an arrangement was entered into between Sindhia (who had wrested from the State a tribute of Baroda Rs. 12,000) and the Lunawada Chief, by which the British Government guaranteed the payment of the tribute on condition that Sindhia would not interfere directly or indirectly in the affairs of the State. In 1822 the engagements of 1812 and 1819 were renewed and made permanent, and the State became entitled to British protection, in accordance with the terms of a Convention of April 3, 1820. The Political control was, in 1825, transferred from the Mahikantha to the Rewakantha Agency, which was established in the same year.

Dalelsinhji was third in descent from Kumar Umedsinhji, third son of the above-named Narsinhji, fourteenth in descent from Bhimsinhji, and the present Maharana Shri Sir Wakhatsinhji, K.C.I.E., was adopted on October 7, 1867, by Motikunverba, widow of Dalelsinhji, and received instruction, first in the *Talukdari* School, Ahmedabad, and subsequently at the Rajkumar College, Rajkot. Between June, 1867, and May, 1879, the State was managed by an Assistant Political Agent. On August 28, 1880, the Maharana was invested with full ruling powers, and his accession was hailed with delight by the whole population, and was marked by general rejoicings.

Under His Highness's rule education has made considerable progress in the State. The latest progress consists in the opening of the Sajjan Kunver High School, on July 17, 1918, by Mr. W. W. Smart, Political Agent, Rewakantha.

The following buildings and institutions for public use were founded during this régime: A jail, the "Pollen" school, the "Barton" Library, a Municipal Hall, Lady Reay's Girls' school, the "Diamond Jubilee" rest-house, two clock towers, a public park, *dharamshal'as*, a vegetable market, the "Sajjan Kunver" Sanskrit *pathshala*, the "Sajjan Kunver" High school, and the "Daulat Kunver" charitable dispensary. The beautiful palace and the "Fatebag" bungalow are also worthy of note.

The Maharana has received various marks of approbation from the British Government. In 1889 he was created a Knight Commander of the Most Eminent Order of the Indian Empire, and he received a *sanad* of adoption in 1890.

The inhabitants, who were 75,998 in number at the census of 1911, comprise about 72,000 Hindus and some 4,000 Mahomedans, the former of these two races including Brahmins, Rajputs, Kunbis, and other tribes.

The principal crops are wheat, *bajri*, maize, cotton, sesamum, and paddy.

An excellent pasturage is obtainable in the greater portion of the State, pastoral farming is one of the chief sources of income for the inhabitants, and at the close of the year 1918 the agricultural live-stock comprised: 42,320 bullocks, 28,814 cows, 3,207 male buffaloes, 29,751 female buffaloes, 286 horses, 389 mares, 35 colts and fillies, 1,069 asses, and 14,026 sheep and goats; while farming implements comprised 31,365 ploughs and 2,653 carts.

The chief items of export, and the value of them in 1917–18, were as follows: Sesamum, Rs. 2,31,147; *ghee* (clarified butter), Rs. 1,97,848; foodstuffs of all sorts, Rs. 1,65,764; hides, Rs. 62,806; animals, Rs. 1,21,579; *mahua* flowers used in distillation, Rs. 11,642; and miscellaneous goods, Rs. 2,53,225; making a total of Rs. 10,44,011, as against Rs. 6,94,233 for the previous twelve months. An increase in value was notice-

HIS HIGHNESS MAHARANA SHRI SIR WAKHATSINHJI, K.C.I.E.

SHRIMAN SHRI MAHARAJ KUMAR SHRI RANJITSINHJI, HEIR-APPARENT.

able also in imports, as authorized statistics for the same period show: Cloth, Rs. 3,06,161; animals, Rs. 1,42,153; sugar and molasses, Rs. 69,784; metals, Rs. 24,421; foodstuffs, Rs. 1,12,062; *ghee*, Rs. 14,917; tobacco, Rs. 27,789; and miscellaneous, Rs. 1,29,154.

These amounts give an aggregate of Rs. 8,26,441, compared with Rs. 6,53,517 for the preceding year.

State forests have been placed in charge of a competent official, and the annual receipts from the sale of timber, *mahua* flowers, jungle produce, and miscellaneous items now amount to about Rs. 1,15,000. This sum, showing an increase over previous years, was due in part to the measures taken for securing a richer growth of timber, and partly to the reduction in the number of fires resulting from improved preventive methods.

Flowers and fruit obtained from *mahua* trees in the forests, in non-agriculturable areas, and on unoccupied land, provide a large amount of revenue. There are nearly 9,000 of these trees, and the income depends upon the total number of those which actually produce flowers and not upon the quantity or weight of the harvest.

The subjects of the State have during the past ten or fifteen years manifested a much greater interest in the question of providing educational facilities for their children, and this is one of the hopeful signs of increased prosperity throughout the principality. The *Durbar* now maintains a High School, Gujerati, and Girls' schools at Lunawada, and in various parts of the State there are 10 other teaching institutions. The scholars on the rolls in 1918 numbered 1,455, with a daily average attendance of 1,193.

Students of Arts Colleges and the High School are encouraged by State scholarships. The total amount expended by the State in the educational department in 1817-18 was Rs. 8,958, exclusive of a sum of Rs. 540 awarded in scholarships.

The *Durbar* affords medical relief at the Daulat Kunver dispensary, named after the junior wife of the Maharaj Kumar Saheb, who made a free gift of the building, which cost Rs. 20,000, and at the native "Ayurvedic" dispensary, called after the Uvraj Shri Ranjitsinhji. These two institutions give treatment annually to about 11,250 and 5,000 patients respectively at a cost of nearly Rs. 6,000.

The spirit of the Acts and regulations in force in British territories is followed in the Civil and Criminal Courts of the State. The two Courts of the original civil jurisdiction are presided over respectively by the *Dewan*, who has power to dispose of suits of the value of Rs. 5,000 and upwards, and the *Nyayadhish*, before whom cases involving a less sum than Rs. 5,000 are heard. Criminal justice is administered by First and Second-class Magistrates, while the *Dewan* is president of the sessions Court.

For the purpose of protection the State employs 43 cavalry, a few artillery, and infantry. The artillery are required to fire salutes on special occasions, and it is the principal function of cavalry to escort His Highness the Raja, the members of his family, and the chief officials of the State.

The police force has a strength of about 155 officers and men, comprising a superintendent, five chief constables, four head constables, an opium inspector, a drilling master, and graded constables, while the total annual cost amounts to about Rs. 16,000.

The average gross revenue of the State is Rs. 3,12,954, and the sums of Rs. 9,230 and Rs. 5,000 are respectively paid as tribute to the British Government and His Highness the Gaekwar of Baroda.

His Highness Maharana Shri Sir Wakhatsinhji, K.C.I.E., is a most capable Ruler, and the subjects of the State have profound faith in his ability and readiness to inaugurate measures for their welfare.

His Highness contracted marriage with a daughter of the Sesodia family of the Maharaval of Banswara, a first-class State in Rajputana. The heir-apparent, Shriman Shri Maharaj Kumar Saheb Shri Ranjitsinhji, received his education at the Mayo College, Ajmer, but the whole State was enveloped in sorrow in September, 1916, when Maharaj Rajkumar Shri Raghunathsinhji, the younger son of His Highness, succumbed to heart failure following an attack of diabetic coma. The heir-apparent is married to the sister of the Maharaja of Sitamau, a first-class State in Central India. In January, 1917, there were great rejoicings in the State owing to the marriage of Shri Bapulal Saheb, Ratnakuvern Saheb, daughter of the recently deceased younger Kumar Saheb, and the "Thread" ceremony of Bhamarlalji Saheb Lalsinhji, the eldest son of Shriman Shri Maharaj Kumar Saheb. About 4,000 guests attended the elaborate festivities.

These notes would be incomplete without reference being made to the assistance offered to the Imperial Government in support of the Allies in the late Great War.

The news of the declaration of hostilities was received in Lunawada with the deepest concern, and messages by telegrams and letter were immediately sent through the Political Agent expressing the intense loyalty and devotion of His Highness the Maharana and his subjects to the Throne, and at the same time conveying an intimation that the Maharana and his *Kumars* placed their personal services at the disposal of the Government in defence of the Empire. It was also announced that the resources of the State were at the command of the Government, and the letter concluded with an expression of the fervent hope that the forces of His Imperial Majesty and their comrades might emerge from the conflict with complete success and undiminished glory.

On August 26, 1914, a mass meeting of the residents in the chief town, Lunawada, was held with the object of considering the best means to be adopted for rendering practical assistance to the cause of the Allies, and the crowded assembly unanimously passed the following resolutions: (*a*) "that the residents of Lunawada, of all classes and creed, assembled at this public meeting, deem it their sacred duty to express on the occasion of this war, which our beloved King-Emperor has been obliged to declare, their unflinching loyalty and heartfelt devotion to His Majesty the King-Emperor, and beg to assure the British Government of their desire and readiness to render such assistance as might be required of them, and to pray for the success and glory of the British and their Allies"; (*b*) "that a committee be appointed to collect funds for the Indian Relief Fund"; and (*c*) "that the amount so collected be remitted to the Bombay Presidency Branch through the President."

The *Durbar*, on August 30, 1914, convened a public meeting for the purpose of counteracting evil and groundless reports concerning the Great War which irresponsible persons might spread. Shriman Shri Maharaj Kumar Shri Ranjitsinhji, on behalf of His Highness the Maharana, who presided at the meeting, expressed his satisfaction at the large number attending the meeting, giving practical expression of their deep and unswerving loyalty to the British Crown, and unflinching devotion to His Majesty, and of paying their quota towards the Indian War Relief Fund. He then

THE STATE OF LUNAWADA.

1. Shriman Shri Bhamarlal Shri Lalsinhji, Eldest Son of the Heir-Apparent. 2. The Palace, Lunawada.

THE STATE OF LUNAWADA.

1. Kisan Sagar Tank. 2. Fatehbag Bungalow. 3. Luneshwar Mahadev Temple. 4. Shri Sajjan Kunver High School.

described at length the circumstances in which the British Government were forced into this war, and pointed out the duties of all Indians at the present juncture. The meeting dispersed with three cheers for His Majesty, and the audience repaired to their respective temples to pray for the success of the British and their Allies. On September 21st, Ladiji Shri Sajjan Kunver Saheb convened a ladies' meeting in the *Durbar* Hall to raise funds for the Women's Branch of the War Relief Fund, Bombay Presidency, which proved a success. As a result Rs. 1,250 were collected and duly remitted.

In November of the same year the news of Turkey joining Germany and Austria as a result of German machinations was received with deep sorrow. The local Mahomedans realized the suicidal step the Turks had taken, and at a meeting they unanimously gave expression of their sorrow for Turkey's act, and emphasized the continuance of their loyalty to the person and the Government of His Majesty, who had kindly taken necessary steps for the protection of the pilgrims and their places of pilgrimage.

The Chiefs of the Solanki Rajput States in various parts of India desired to associate themselves, as a body, in giving a practical illustration of their loyalty to the British Throne, and they decided to raise a special fund for the construction of a number of aeroplanes to be presented to the Imperial Government for service in war, the gift to be called "The Solanki Flight of Aeroplanes." The offer was duly made to His Excellency the Viceroy and Governor-General, and was gratefully accepted by him, the contribution of the Lunawada State towards this fund being Rs. 10,000. The ladies residing in the State also contributed liberally to the Women's Branch of the India War Relief Fund, and they also forwarded a considerable quantity of clothing and other necessities for the troops.

Several other generous gifts of money as well as articles of comfort were made from time to time, and during the year 1917–18 War Loan Bonds of the year 1920 were purchased as follows: (*a*) Rs. 1,00,000 on behalf of the Lunawada State; of Rs. 2,000 by Kunveraniji Saheb Shri Sajjan Kunver; and Rs. 25,000 by the subjects of the State.

THE STATE OF MAYURBHANJ

THE Feudatory States in the division of Orissa, in the Province of Behar and Orissa, which area was placed under the administration of a Lieutenant - Governor at the time of the Imperial Coronation Durbar held at Delhi in the year 1911, form a succession of hill ranges rolling backwards towards Central India. From such sources of information as are available, it is believed that the State of Mayurbhanj was founded about the year 600 by Jai Singh, a relative of the Raja of Jaipur in the Province of Rajputana, who visited Puri with his two sons, Adi Singh and Jati Singh, the former of whom took for a wife a daughter of the Puri Raja.

During his return journey from Puri, Jai Singh conquered Raja Mayuradhwaja, a petty Chief occupying the *gadi* of Bamanghati (now a sub-division of the State of Mayurbhanj), which then became the headquarters of the Raj family, the State receiving its name from the deposed Ruler. The family title is Bhanja ("breaker"). The remains of ruined temples and tanks at Khiching, near Udaipur, indicate a condition of considerable prosperity in the past. The area of the State was, apparently, very much larger than it is to-day.

When the conquest of Orissa by the British took place in 1803–04, Mayurbhanj was, with the remainder of the Province, ceded by the Mahrattas, and treaties were entered into whereby the Ruler of the States undertook, among other things, to preserve loyalty and pay certain sums as tribute money. The State was at this time ruled by Rani Sumitra Dei Bhanj, and on her death in 1811 the succession devolved upon Tribikram Bhanj, who was adopted from the family of the Chief of the State of Keonjhar. In 1812 an agreement was entered into with the British Government whereby the annual tribute payable by the State was fixed at the sum of Rs. 1,001, the Chief at the same time agreeing that he would forego his claim to levy a tax on pilgrims who had to pass through the State on their journey to and from Jagannath, or Puri. This tribute subsequently rose to Rs. 1,067–11–9. A formal treaty engagement with the British was concluded by Raja Jadunath Bhanj in 1829. In 1866 the sub-division of Bamanghati was taken under the direct control of Government on account of the mismanagement of the Chief, but it was restored in 1878 to the grandfather of the present Ruler, Krishna Chandra Bhanj Deo, who was especially noted for his great ability and wisdom in administrative work and for his encouragement of the people to develop manufactures and industries.

He was created a Maharaja in 1877 for his good government and his liberal public benefactions, which included a sum of Rs. 27,000 towards raising the High School at Cuttack to the status of a college. The Maharaja's death in 1882 caused the greatest grief throughout the State, and in 1890 his son, Sriram Chandra Bhanj Deo, attained his majority and assumed management of the State, which for eight years previously had been controlled by the Government. He was another highly educated and enlightened Chief, who followed in the footsteps of his late father by the exercise of the greatest benevolence and by giving assiduous attention to all State matters, the administration being carried on according to British methods under his own personal supervision. The title of Maharaja was bestowed upon him as a mark of personal distinction at the Imperial Durbar held at Delhi in January, 1903, when he was also the recipient of a gold medal commemorative of the occasion. In 1910 the Viceroy of India, Lord Minto, conferred upon the ruling Chief the dignity of Maharaja as an hereditary family title. The Maharaja unfortunately received severe injuries while shooting in January, 1912, and in spite of the best medical and surgical skill given to him in Calcutta, to which city he was removed, his death took place on the 22nd of the following month. The management of the State was placed in the hands of a Superintendent appointed by the Government and the minor Chief, Purna Chandra Bhanj Deo, proceeded with his education at the Mayo College, Ajmer, where he distinguished himself as scholar, prefect, and captain of the College cricket eleven.

The betrothal ceremony of the minor Maharaja with the eldest daughter of Maharana Sir Amar Singhji, K.C.I.E., Raj Saheb of the State of Wankaner in Kathiawar, was fittingly celebrated on January 27, 1916, and the marriage took place at Wankaner on January 27, 1917.

The young Maharaja completed his College career in May, 1917, and very shortly afterwards he undertook a course of training as well as practical work in general administrative matters. He accompanied the Superintendent on his tours of inspection in practically every portion of the State.

The minor Maharaja, young as he was, realized the immensity of the burdens laid upon Great Britain and her Allies during the calamitous struggle of a few years ago, and the traditional martial spirit of his race prompted him to offer his services in any capacity, in the hope that he might render some assistance in the cause of Right against

LIEUT. H.H. PURNA CHANDRA BHANJ DEO, THE PRESENT CHIEF.

1. H.H. KRISHNA CHANDRA BHANJ DEO (GRANDFATHER OF THE PRESENT CHIEF).
2. H.H. THE LATE MAHARAJA RAM CHANDRA BHANJ DEO (FATHER OF THE PRESENT CHIEF).
3. THE MAHARAJA'S PALACE, BARIPADA. 5. THE BELGARIA RESIDENCY, BARIPADA.

THE STATE OF MAYURBHANJ.

1. The Victoria Diamond Jubilee Library, Baripada. 2. The King Edward Hospital, Baripada. 3. The High School, Baripada. 4. The Town Hall, Baripada. 5. The Maharani's Monument, Baripada. 6. The Protestant Church (Australian Mission), Baripada.

Might. The youthful age of the Chief naturally caused the military authorities to give serious consideration to his desire to participate in active hostilities, and in 1918 he was granted a commission as an Hon. Second-Lieutenant in the Royal Artillery then serving in France. He subsequently left Baripada, the chief town of Mayurbhanj, went to the front and thence to England, where he had an audience of His Majesty the King-Emperor and returned to the State on June 21, 1919, paying a short visit to the Maharana Saheb of Wankaner in Bombay.

An immense amount of money was needed for the war, but there never was a more generous response to an appeal for help in times of distress than was made in favour of the Allies of His Majesty the King-Emperor. Mayurbhanj, it is understood, contributed Rs. 89,217 towards various War Funds and invested Rs. 35,61,542 in Indian War Loans. Apart from this, great service was rendered by the State in obtaining recruits. The attempt to enlist coolies for the Labour Corps, far from being a success at first, led to the unfortunate Santal rising in the year 1917, to check which the State had to incur a heavy expenditure of Rs. 84,002. The work took, however, a definite shape in the early part of the year 1918, when one Shiba Jena, a subject of the State, returned from Mesopotamia to his home at Khuruntia in the Muruda *pergana*. It is said that this man spoke of the needs of the army in that country, and it seems tolerably clear that his advocacy, coupled with the great personal influence which the minor Maharaja exercised upon his people, did not fall upon deaf ears, as no fewer than 78 coolies were enrolled for the Mesopotamia Labour Corps between February 9 and 14, 1918. Mr. C. L. Philip, I.C.S., Political Agent, also personally supervised the work of enlistment, and he afterwards had the satisfaction of knowing that he had been instrumental in sending 2,452 men to the front.

The Durbar made grants of money by way of bonus to accepted coolies, and provision was made for the maintenance of those families who had been deprived of wage-earning fathers and brothers.

The greatest joy was manifested by the inhabitants of Mayurbhanj in February, 1918, when it was announced that His Majesty the King-Emperor had been graciously pleased to confer upon the Chief a permanent salute of nine guns in recognition of the valuable services rendered by him in various ways in connection with the late Great War.

On his attainment of majority the Chief was invested with full powers on August 6, 1920, by the Government, and an investiture ceremony was held at Baripada. Subsequently His Honour the Lieutenant-Governor of Behar and Orissa held a Durbar at Cuttack on November 20, 1920, and formally announced his succession to the *gadi*.

The State of Mayurbhanj, lying between 22° 34′ and 21° 17′ N. and between 85° 40′ and 87° 10′ E., is bounded on the north by the districts of Midnapore and Singbhum, on the east by the districts of Midnapore and Balasore, on the south by the Feudatory States of Nilgiri and Keonjhar, and the district of Balasore, and on the west by the State of Keonjhar and the district of Singbhum. It has an area of 4,243 square miles, and its physical aspects furnish almost every variety of scenery, a special feature being the large number of fertile valleys, while the vast extent of the territory is still covered with dense primeval jungle.

According to the census of 1911 the total population of the State was 730,000, of which there were about 95,000 Animists and 4,000 Mahomedans. According to the census of 1921 the total population of the State rose to 754,457. The population has greatly increased during the past half-century, owing chiefly to immigration from adjoining congested districts of persons who have been attracted to Mayurbhanj by the security to life and property which good government has assured.

Mayurbhanj is essentially an agricultural State, fully 95 per cent. of the inhabitants being wholly or partly dependent upon the products of the soil.

A geological survey of a considerable portion of India was made several years ago, and since that time it has been left to individual enterprise to ascertain the mineral wealth of a large number of districts as well as Indian States. During a survey recently undertaken in Mayurbhanj it was discovered that among the valuable deposits, iron-ore was undoubtedly the richest—in fact, it was stated that in all probability there were not more extensive or richer fields in India. Gold is found in several portions of the State, but at the headwaters of the Barhai river there is a tract of land some two square miles in extent where almost the whole of the alluvium is largely auriferous. About 50 families earn a livelihood by washing for gold in the river beds in this area.

A mining lease in favour of the Barhai river Gold-Mining Syndicate has been sanctioned by the Government of Behar and Orissa, but the document has not yet been actually completed. There are also extensive soap-stone quarries at Luloong which turn out large quantities of pots and dishes, which find a ready sale in neighbouring markets.

In the year 1909, shortly before the death of the late Maharaja, negotiations were commenced with the Tata Iron and Steel Company, Limited, for the lease of iron-ore deposits in the Gurumahisani Hills in the northern sub-division of the State, and the result was that the Company shortly afterwards obtained the rights over an area of about 5½ square miles in extent. Besides this the Company obtained a lease of more than six square miles for iron-ore deposits at Gurumahisani and Badampahar in the year 1919. The ore is transported to the Tata works at Sakchi by means of a branch railway connecting the mines with the main line to Bombay. The average quantity of iron-ore exported by the Company per year is nearly 390,863 tons, and the royalty paid thereon is Rs. 37,656.

The forests of Mayurbhanj are distributed over the central group of hill ranges and the plains sloping to the east and west of those hills. They are classified as (*a*) Reserved forests, having an area of 1,2[illegible]4 square miles, and (*b*) Protected forests, about 950 square miles in extent. A well-organized Forest Department was established, and full control of all forest matters is now vested in a Conservator, the position at the present time being held by Mr. A. H. Mee.

The average revenue derived from the forests, including the sale of minor products is about Rs. 4,00,000. Since the opening of the Mayurbhanj State light railway, very large quantities of wooden sleepers have been manufactured for export in the Simlipal forest area. A regular timber industry has now been established on a firm basis.

The State produces a large quantity of nux-vomica, used in the manufacture of strychnine, for which Messrs. Smith Stanistreet & Co., of Calcutta, held a lease; and the State forests supply myrabolams and other tanning products to which the late Great War has given a greatly enhanced value and a consequently accelerated development. One of the most promising side-products, from a remunerative point of view, is Sabai grass, from which an excellent quality of paper is made. The Titagarh Paper Mills Company, whose head-offices are in Calcutta, are now taking a very large supply for manufacturing purposes.

The first real aid to the opening up of the country on a more generous scale by the reclamation of jungles, thus giving

THE STATE OF MAYURBHANJ.

1. The Maharaja's Kutchery, Baripada. 2. The Jail at Baripada. 3. The Barni Ghat, Baripada. 4. The Leper Asylum, Baripada. 5. General View of Kutchery Buildings from the Roof of the Belgaria Palace.

THE STATE OF MAYURBHANJ.

1. The Burabalang River, Baripada. 2. The Baldiha Irrigation Bund. 3. A Bridge on the Old Bombay Road. 4. The Palpala River, on which the Bund has been Placed.

THE STATE OF MAYURBHANJ.

1. The Jaganath Temple, Baripada. 2. The Shandy Market at Baripada. 3. The Ranibag Garden at Baripada. 4. General View of the Main Bazaar Street, Baripada.

THE STATE OF MAYURBHANJ.

1. Cathedral at Arras. 2. Lens—after the War. 3. The Mole, at Zeebrugge, Belgium. 4. H.M.S. "Sydney" which sank the "Emden." 5. Lieut. Purna Chandra Deo in Military Uniform.

increased opportunities for obtaining greater productiveness from the land, was the construction of the Mayurbhanj State Railway; but the further possibilities which presented themselves for a much larger and more systematic trade in timber caused the formation of the Mayurbhanj Light Railway Syndicate, who extended the line from Baripada, the chief town in the State, to Talbandh, a distance of 32 miles.

The prosecution of the work was naturally delayed owing to the difficulties of transport during the late Great War. The line was, however, completed and opened to traffic on July 15, 1920. Another line, namely, the Badampahar extension of the Onlajuri-Sulapat Railway in the Bamanghati sub-division, is now being constructed, and it is hoped that it will be opened for traffic in the course of a few months.

Baripada, the headquarters of the State, is connected by a narrow-gauge branch with the Bengal-Nagpur Railway system. There are unusually good means of communication, not only within the State but also from its borders to important centres in other districts; and in addition to the railway facilities already mentioned there are about 150 miles of gravelled and 350 miles of unmetalled roads, while felled timber is floated down the Burabalang river.

For purposes of administration the State of Mayurbhanj is split up into four sub-divisions, namely, Mayurbhanj proper, or the Sadar sub-division, Kaptipada, Bamanghatty and Panchpir, and as far as is compatible with local environments and circumstances the work is carried on according to conditions obtaining in British India.

The Chief, with the Diwan or any other member of Council appointed by the Chief, form the Judicial Committee which hears appeals against the orders of all State Courts according to the provisions of the laws of the State. Subordinate to this authority are the State-Judge, Sub-Judges in the four sub-divisions above mentioned, and Magistrates.

There are 353 teaching institutions in the State, classed as follows: 1 English High School, 5 Middle-English, 338 Upper and Lower Primary, 7 for girls, one for the study of Sanskrit, and one Guru-Training School. The total number of pupils attending all schools is 9,658, of whom 773 are girls.

The State maintains one hospital at Baripada, in which separate wards for males and females of low-caste tribes have just been erected, together with eight dispensaries in suitable places. The average number of patients treated annually at the several dispensaries is 128,685, but nearly 5,415 other persons receive advice and medicine from two Sub-Assistant Surgeons who travel from village to village. The total average annual expenditure of the Department is Rs. 47,023.

The average yearly demand made for revenue upon land, including arrears, is Rs. 7,55,889 and as 96·89 per cent. of this sum is actually collected, indisputable proof is afforded of the capable management of the State authorities.

The general financial statement shows that the total average receipts amount to Rs. 44,06,756, while the average expenditure reaches a sum of Rs. 37,73,883.

THE STATE OF MUDHOL

THIS branch of the Bhosle Ghorpade family is one of the most ancient and distinguished among the Mahrattas. The original name of this family was Bhosle, but it has been superseded by the second name, which was acquired by one of the ancestors who, under the Bahamani dynasty, succeeded in scaling a fort in the Konkan, previously deemed impregnable, by fastening a rope round the body of a Ghorpad (iguana). There are many families now in the Deccan which bear this name. Different accounts are given as to how they are connected with this family. But the genealogical tree now in the possession of the family—the authenticity of which cannot be denied—does not contain any reference to any such branches.

The founder of this dynasty was of Rajput origin, and was descended from the Rana of Udaipur. The families of Ghorpade and Bhosle, of Satara, trace their descent to their common ancestor Baparawal of Chitoor, through his descendant Bhimsi, who founded the principality of Dongarpur and Baswara. This family played an important part in the history of the Deccan. Bhimsi's descendant, Sujansingh, came to the Deccan to seek his fortune, and was granted this State by Allauddin Hassan, the founder of the Bahamani kingdom, about the year 1347 to 1350. This grant was renewed by a fresh *Sanad* to the family about the year 1551.

It was then the practice to renew the *Sanads* from time to time to the successors of the original grantee, in which references are found about the original grant by Allauddin Hassan, though the exact date of the grant is not mentioned. At that time they held high positions at the Court of the Bahamani kings. It appears that Mudhol, along with its five *Mahals*, was held in *Saranjam* by this family until its grant by the Adilshahi dynasty, raising it to the status of a principality, and conferring upon this family the hereditary title of Raja, and the privilege of using the *Morchals* and *Chavaries*, and the dignity of exemption from *Mujara* (the obeisance of a subject). At this period Baji Ghorpade played an important part in the wars with Shivaji, who, in the seventeenth century, raised the standard of revolt in Maharastra, which caused the Bijapur kings to seek the capture of his father, Shahaji, who was a Sardar at the Bijapur Court. Shahaji was too sharp for them to be taken unawares. So the Emperor was obliged to seek in open Durbar the help of some willing person to capture Shahaji, and Baji Raje, who was never on good terms with Shahaji, willingly took the responsibility on himself, and was successful in capturing him.

The Bijapur kings raised an army to suppress Shivaji, and Baji Raje was appointed to conduct the operations. Baji left Bijapur for Mudhol a couple of days ahead of the army. Shivaji, who had an eye on him, finding him unattended, took advantage of the opportunity, left Panhala, and was before Mudhol when everybody thought he was engaged in making preparations for his defence. Mistaking Shivaji's company to be the advance guard of the Bijapur army, the gates of Mudhol were thrown open, thus leaving everything to his mercy. He found Baji Raje asleep with his family, and before Baji could leave his bed, he was killed by Shivaji. Shivaji also killed all the male members of the family, set fire to the house, and rushed back to Panhala. Thus the enmity between the houses of Mudhol and Kolhapur increased, until it was finally allayed by the marriage of the paternal aunt of the present Rajasaheb to a nephew of the Maharaja of Kolhapur in 1862.

After the downfall of the Bijapur kingdom, the Ghorpades of Mudhol for a time joined the armies of the Moghals, their *Saranjam* and *Inam* territories being continued to them by Aurangzeb. On the decline of the Moghal power in the Deccan, the Peshwas asked Malojirao to join the Marathas, but instead of doing so he gave up all the territories held under the *Saranjam* tenure to the Marathas.

Maloji, with his sons Shankroji and Ranoji, distinguished himself in the operations against the British in 1779. After the convention of Wadgaon, during the action that took place near that locality, Ranoji was killed and Maloji wounded. In consequence of this, the village of Padsalgi was granted to Ranoji's son Bahirjirao.

In the battle of Kharda, Maloji and his eldest son, Govindrao, were on opposite sides, and they met in a hand-to-hand encounter. Govindrao had, in consequence of a quarrel with his father, joined the Nizam, and received the *Pargana* of Patri before the action of Kharda, in which he was dangerously wounded by his father.

In 1805 Maloji died, and was succeeded by his grandson, Narayanrao, the son of Govindrao. In 1816 Narayanrao died,

THE RAJA SAHIB OF MUDHOL.

THE RAJA SAHIB OF MUDHOL.

leaving three sons, Govindrao, Luxmanrao, and Venkatrao. Venkatrao succeeded to the *gadi*. Though he was the youngest, he was the only son of the eldest wife of Narayanrao. Luxmanrao then went to Baroda, where he began to serve under the Gaikwar in the place of the substitute appointed by Malojirao.

It was in the reign of Venkatrao that a treaty was concluded with the British Government, and in 1854 Venkatrao Raje died, leaving a son, Balwantrao, then only 14 years of age. Government appointed a *Karbhari*, who looked after the work, until the State was handed over to Balwantrao Raje in 1859. Balwantrao's rule lasted only 14 months. He died, leaving an infant son, Venkatrao, heir to the State. Then there was a long minority of 20 years, during which period the State affairs were looked after by British Political Officers. Venkatrao Raje was handed over charge of the State in 1882 with full powers. His régime—which lasted until 1900, when he died of cholera at the early age of 39—was marked by works of great public utility. Thus, during the famine of 1895–6, which greatly affected the State, relief works were opened, corn brought in from a distance and distributed among the famine-stricken, and in this and other ways efforts were made to alleviate their sufferings.

The present Rajasaheb was born in 1884, and invested with full powers in 1904. Every department of State is receiving his personal attention ; and in this part of the country he was the first to make primary education free. The Rajasaheb also takes a keen interest in agriculture, as various experiments on modern lines, carried on under his personal guidance and supervision, testify. In recognition of his good work, Government has been pleased to confer on him a hereditary salute of nine guns.

The Rajasaheb enjoys all the rights, privileges and honours of a full power Ruler.

In the recent war the present Rajasaheb proceeded to the front, and remained in the Indian Expeditionary Force for about six months. He also placed all the resources of his State at the disposal of the Government, both as regards men and money, during the war. For the personal services rendered by the Rajasaheb, an Honorary Commission of a Second Lieutenant in the Army was bestowed on him, and in the recent New Year's Day Honours, His Majesty the King-Emperor was pleased to decorate him with the honour of a K.C.I.E.

GENERAL VIEW OF TEMPLES ON SHETRANJA HILL, PALITANA

THE STATE OF PALITANA

PALITANA is a second-class State in the Gohelwad division of the Kathiawar Political Agency in the Presidency of Bombay, and it is bounded on the north, east, and west by the State of Bhavnagar, and on the south by the Amreli *prant* of the State of Baroda.

The Rulers of Palitana are Gohel Rajputs who are descended from the famous Shalivahan, a king of Mewar, and therefore—according to Forbes' "Rasmala"—they have sprung from the solar race, to which also belonged the great Ramchandra and the Vallabhi dynasty, which migrated to Mewar after their defeat by Bhuvad Solanki. It appears that about the middle of the twelfth century the Gohels were established in Marwar with Khergadh on the river Luni as their capital town. Their Principality was, however, subordinate to the Dabhi dynasty whose headquarters were at Mehava. Sahar, *alias* Jhanjharsinh, the Gohel Ruler about the end of the same century, left Marwar for Gujarat where he accepted service under Sidharaja, the king of that Province, and his son, Sejakji, became Commander-in-Chief of the army. These two Rajputs with their followers, soon began to wield considerable power in Saurashtra (now Kathiawar and Gujarat), but in the year 1214 the relations between the Dabhis and Gohels were exceedingly strained, and the former having obtained the help of the grandsons of Jayachandra of Kanauj, overpowered the Gohels who left Khergadh never to return to it. The King of Saurashtra, Rao Mahipal, ruled over an extensive territory about this time, and Sejakji who had formed friendship with him, gave his daughter Amarkunvarba in marriage to Rao Khengar, the heir-apparent. Sejakji shortly afterwards received a grant of 24 villages (one of which he re-named Sejakpur) and he also obtained about 40 other villages by force of arms.

The step-brother of Amarkunvarba, who had founded the House of Bhavnagar, having appropriated these villages to himself that lady obtained 48 other villages, one-half of which she gave to her elder natural brother, Shahji, who founded the House of Palitana, and the remainder she handed over to her younger brother who established the Lathi family.

The modern history of Palitana may be said to commence with Noghanji III, who ascended the *gadi* in the year 1734. This Chief built the town wall of the chief town at enormous cost to the State Treasury and he is also distinguished as the originator of the formal capitation tax (*mudka vero*) which was levied upon all persons making pilgrimage to Shatrunjaya hill.

After a rule of 30 years Noghanji III was succeeded by Sartanji II, who was a brave soldier and a capable administrator, but he was unfortunately surrounded by a trio of conspirators, consisting of a Diwan, a Wazir, and a personal attendant. These three plotted with Alubhai, the youngest brother of the Chief, with the result that Sartanji was murdered in broad daylight

HIS HIGHNESS GOHEL SHRI BAHADURSINHJI, THAKORE SAHIB OF PALITANA.

in the Durbari stables which were situated immediately in front of the palace. An infant, the heir to the *gadi*, was killed by Alubhai's son, and Unadji, the next in succession, fearing that he was also to be a victim, fled to Damnagar to seek help from Ratanji Rangor, an old family priest of the Palitana house, who had been raised to a position of responsibility at the Baroda Court. Odha Khuman of Asodar also espoused the cause of Unadji, and these two repaired to Palitana and expelled Alubhai therefrom, but not before the latter had taken possession of all the money in the State Treasury in addition to priceless records and a large quantity of other valuable articles. Unadji was a man of warlike disposition, and although he made a determined effort to obtain Sihor from Vakhatsinhji of Bhavnagar, he was compelled to retire before the stronger force which had been sent against him. For some years the State was in a disturbed condition and its finances suffered grievously in consequence. A change for the better came in 1840 when Noghanji IV ascended the *gadi* and entrusted the financial business of the State to his son, Pratapsinhji. This prince reduced expenditure and generally managed affairs with such prudence and skill that he was able to liquidate the entire State debt.

Pratapsinhji was called to the *gadi* in 1860, and although he ruled for only about eight months his remarkable abilities enabled him to reorganize the various Departments of State and to evolve order out of chaos even in face of adverse circumstances.

Surshinhji, the next ruler, continued the good work commenced by his late father, and he introduced some of the most beneficial reforms ever instituted in Patiala. One of his first acts was to introduce cash assessments upon land in place of revenue consisting of a share "in kind" being handed over to the State, thus avoiding the expensive machinery of survey and classification of holdings. That plan—which has stood the test of experience for a period of nearly 50 years—defines the maximum amount that can be levied, although provision is made that reductions can be made in unfavourable years according to the circumstances of each village. Sursinhji gave encouragement to the irrigation of land from wells by abolishing the special assessment upon crops watered by artificial methods, and owing to his generous support of the industry of agriculture larger tracts of waste land were brought under cultivation.

Sursinhji was the first Ruler of Palitana to obtain (in October, 1881) from the Government a recognition of its right to levy a capitation fee of Rs. 2 upon each pilgrim worshipping on the Shatrunjaya hill.

Sursinhji, son and successor of Pratapsinhji, was a man whose progressive ideas led him to do all in his power to bring the administration of his State into closer conformity with the practice prevailing in British Indian districts, and it may be mentioned that he reorganized the police force and the judicial department, he established schools in villages, constructed metalled roads and fine buildings in the chief town, and considerably enlarged and improved the palace.

Sursinhji died of heart failure in 1885, while returning from a visit to Mahabaleshwar, to which place he had gone to meet His Excellency the Governor of Bombay.

Mansinhji, the next occupant of the *gadi*, was born in the year 1862. In 1896 Her Imperial Majesty the late Queen Victoria was graciously pleased to confer upon the Thakor Sahib the distinction of Knight Commandership of the Most Exalted Order of the Star of India, and on December 15 in the same year the Garter King of Arms, acting on behalf of Her Majesty the Queen-Empress, issued a duly signed and sealed Warrant granting and assigning hereditary Armorial Ensigns and Crest to Sir Mansinhji. Following in the footsteps of his father, Sir Mansinhji established new villages, these being Manpur, Mangadh, Manvilas, Bahadurpur, and Bahadurgadh the first three named after himself and the other two after his son and heir, Bahadursinhji. Considerable additions and improvements were effected in the State palaces at Palitana and Gariadhar, a new palace was erected in the village of Nani Vavdi. Further means of communication were opened up by diverting watercourses or by throwing bridges across them, the beautiful temple of Bhairavnathji was constructed, the "Harris" English school a teaching institution for girls, and the "Jubilee" public park was laid out in a thoroughly picturesque manner. Sir Mansinhji had taken full advantage of the educational privileges secured for him by his father, and his knowledge of the English language was of a high order. He composed poems in Gujarathi and Hindi, chiefly of a devotional character and such was the versatility of his attainments that he was credited with the authorship of some entertaining plays. He died from the after-effects of small-pox on August 29, 1905, leaving behind him a son, the heir to the *gadi*, one daughter and three widows.

The heir-apparent, the present Ruler, Thakor Sahib Bahadursinhji, succeeded to the *gadi* at the early age of five years, he having been born on April 3, 1900. Mr. W. C. Tudor-Owen, Political Agent of the Gohelwad *prant*, took charge of the State as Administrator, and he was also appointed guardian of the young Ruler during minority.

When 11 years of age the Thakor Sahib was admitted as a student at the Rajkumar College, Rajkot, under the care of Lieut. L. S. Harbord, I.A., and during his residence there for about two years he not only proved himself to be a painstaking pupil but he also acquired a proficiency in outdoor games, particularly in cricket and tennis in which he played in the College teams.

In 1911 he had the great privilege of being an invited guest at the Imperial Coronation ceremony at Delhi, but the greatest honour was paid to him when he was selected as the senior Page to Her Majesty the Queen-Empress.

In March 1913 the Thakor Sahib, together with his two cousins Mulrajsinhji of Virpur and Madhavsinhji of Chok (who had been his companions since infancy, and who were with him at College at Rajkot), sailed for England under the guardianship of Mr. and Mrs Tudor-Owen, who also had charge of the minor Nawab Sahib of Junagadh. After spending a year at a preparatory school at Rugby the Thakor Sahib, modestly styling himself "B. Palitana," became a pupil in King Edward VI Public School at Shrewsbury, and he remained there until the end of the summer term in 1918. Mention has already been made of the Thakor Sahib's prowess as a cricketer, and therefore it may not be out of place to refer here to some of the games in which his skill was abundantly manifested. He quickly earned a place in the first "Eleven," and having played for the team in four seasons he was the senior member of it when he left the institution. His most successful season was in 1918 when he scored three "centuries," namely, 125 runs when playing against the Masters of the school, 150 against Repton School, and 104 against Clifton College, while he won the challenge bat for the year. During the holidays in the same year he was engaged in two matches at Lords' ground in London, and in one of these he played for public schools against a team captained by P. F. ("Plum") Warner.

The young Ruler was fired with enthusiastic loyalty to the Person and Throne of His Imperial Majesty the King-Emperor in the fateful month of August 1914 when the clouds of war burst upon the greater portion of the civilized world, and although he was

THE STATE OF PALITANA.

1. Hawa-Mahel, Palitana. 2. Darbargadh Frontage, with Marriage Mandap. 3. Durbar Hall, Palitana State.

THE STATE OF PALITANA.

1. Shri Bhairavnathji Temple, Palitana. 2. Entrance to Palitana. 3. Ruined Wall at Mandvi Village. 4. View of Mandvi Village, showing Musjid. 5. Mokhadka Paddock.

THE STATE OF PALITANA.

1. School at Gariadhar Town. 2. Dispensary at Gariadhar Town. 3. Nandkunverba Anath-Ashram. 4. Sir Mansinhji Hospital.

not permitted, as he was still at school, to participate in active service in battle, he and other students "did their best" during the summer vacation of 1917 and 1918 by working on agricultural farms in place of those who had responded to the clear call of duty.

During the residence of the Thakor Sahib in England he was twice honoured by being presented to Their Imperial Majesties the King-Emperor and Queen-Empress. When returning to India after an absence of nearly five and a half years he travelled by way of Paris, Rome, Taranto, Port Said and Cairo, and on November 1, 1918 he again set foot on the shores of his native land. Almost immediately after his arrival at Palitana the Thakor Sahib attended the Public Offices of the State in order that he might receive training in general administrative work under the direct personal supervision of Mr. Tudor-Owen, but as that gentleman was also responsible for duties as Political Agent in Gohelwad, and as Manager of the States of Lathi, Jasdan, and Bhavnagar during the minority of their respective Rulers, he soon began to place greater responsibilities upon the shoulders of the Thakor Sahib. Full powers of a Ruler of a Native State of the second class were conferred upon the Thakor Sahib on November 27, 1919, the customary ***kharita*** being presented by Mr. E. Maconochie, C.S.I., I.C.S., the Agent in Kathiwar to the Governor of Bombay, in a grand Durbar attended by a large audience consisting of European officers, ruling Princes and other distinguished guests. The Thakor Sahib was married at Palitana on December 2, 1919 to Shrimati Sitaba Saheba, eldest daughter of Prince Bhojrajji, heir-apparent of His Highness the Thakor Sahib of Gondal.

Notwithstanding the fact that the finances of the State had been seriously reduced on account of famine and cost of measures of relief, the State loyally supported the cause of the Allies by contributing in money and materials to the best of its ability. The sum of Rs. 30,000 was given in aid of various war relief funds, the subjects of the State contributed Rs. 25,980, war bonds of the value of Rs. 1,57,200 were purchased (all interest being paid over to war funds), the sum of Rs 8,000 was presented towards the Kathiawar motor ambulance, tents to the value of Rs. 3,000 were supplied, the materials together with trucks for a light railway two miles in length were provided, ten remounts bred on the State stud farm and valued at Rs. 6,325 were given to the Government, and miscellaneous items amounted to Rs. 10,405.

Many wounded and convalescent officers were accommodated in the Hawa Mahal palace, where they enjoyed the greatest kindness and attention from Mr. Tudor-Owen.

The State also supplied 20 recruits, and the cousins of the Thakor Sahib, namely, Mulrajsinhji—attached to the 5th infantry—and Madhavsinhji—the 3/39th Garhwal regiment—who were educated in England at the expense of the State, served in the trenches in Europe and were subsequently transferred to positions on the north-west frontier of India. The State does not pay any tribute to the British Government, but it is liable to the States of Baroda and Junagadh for *peshkash* and *jortalbi* respectively amounting to Rs. 7,874 and Rs. 2,400.

The Thakor Sahib is a member of the Chamber of Princes in virtue of his own right, he has been appointed an Hon. A.D.C. to His Excellency the Governor of Bombay, and he is entitled to a dynastic salute of nine guns.

The State of Palitana with an area of about 300 square miles, has a population of more than 59,000 inhabitants, and its revenue reaches a sum of more than Rs. 6,50,000. The culturable land in the State occupied by some 3,020 tenants, comprises

THE STATE OF PALITANA.
SHRI ADESHWAR TEMPLE ON SHETRANGA HILL, PALITANA.

94,000 acres, and it produces a revenue of about Rs. 5,50,000, while the portion which is unsuitable for tillage (nearly 66,000 acres) consists chiefly of hills and river beds. The Bhayats are owners of 24 villages with 19,840 acres under plough, and the total alienated revenue is approximately Rs. 1,30,000.

Long-stapled cotton of the Dhumar, Vagadia, Kanvi or Lalui types were formerly cultivated in the State, but when the "Mathia" short-stapled variety was brought to the notice of *ryots* they speedily gave it the preference on the ground that it did not need such a large quantity of rain, that it was able to withstand frosts, and that it reached maturity at least three months before any other variety, thus enabling them to sow another crop on the same land. Other cottons realized higher prices, but the hardiness of the "Mathia" and its greater yield per acre gave to cultivators a sense of security against positive failure which was frequently the experience of their neighbours. Fashion, however, is the most autocratic power in the world, and at the time of writing (1921) an unwritten edict has gone forth that articles manufactured only from cotton of long staple will meet with customers in foreign markets. Holders of land in Palitana, however, are fully alive to the new departure, and with the encouragement of their practical Thakor Sahib they are determined to enter into strong competition with other agriculturists.

In the year 1911 the State established a demonstration and experimental farm for the benefit of occupiers, and about the same time the Durbar undertook the maintenance of a stud farm which in the year 1919–20 accommodated three stallions, three entire colts, 10 brood mares, 43 foals, 33 horses for carriage work, 35 for mounted police, and 12 trained to go under saddle. Stud bulls, cows, buffaloes, calves, and camels are more than 130 in number.

In connection with the administration of justice the State has the Court of the *Nyayadish* who exercises the powers of a Magistrate of the first class in criminal matters, and has jurisdiction to hear civil cases up to Rs. 5,000 in value. The *Shri Nyayadish* is virtually a District and Sessions Judge, as well as Judge of a Court for the hearing of suits of small value. The Thakor Sahib has full judicial powers and presides over the High Court.

The State does not maintain any military force, but it has about 270 police of all ranks, the proportion of men to population being one in 2,491, and to area one man to 1·23 square miles.

Education is practically free in the State, but a very small fee is charged to students in the High School who are receiving instruction in the English language.

Palitana is 488 miles distant from Bombay by the Bombay-Baroda and Central India Railway, and the Bhavnagar-Gondal-Junagadh-Porbandar branch of the same system.

THE RAJKUMAR COLLEGE.

THE STATE OF RAJKOT

THIS is a second-class State in the Halar division of the Kathiawar Political Agency in the Presidency of Bombay, and the chief town of the same name has attached to it a military cantonment and the headquarters of the Agent to the Governor in Kathiawar.

The State is bounded on the east by the State of Nawanagar and some Kathi estates; on the south by the State of Gondal and the *taluka* of Kotada; on the west by the State of Dhrol and *talukas* of the Halar Prant; and on the north by the State of Wankaner and other *talukas* of Halar.

The ruling Chiefs of Rajkot, who are Jadeja Rajputs, have sprung from the main stock of the Jam of Nawanagar. It appears that in the year A.D. 1608 the death occurred of Jam Sataji, who had reigned in Nawanagar for several years, and it was his grandson, Vibhoji, who founded the Rajkot State. The history of the State is a record of the usual vicissitudes which marked the existence of the Rajput principalities in the period of Mogal decadence. Approaching the nineteenth century we find the *gadi* occupied by Ranmalji, the eldest son of Prince Mehramanji, who succeeded Thakore Saheb Lakhoji, on the death of the latter in Nawanagar, in 1796. He was a very pious king, and his memory is still held sacred by the people of Rajkot. Thakore Saheb Ranmalji took the lead in helping the Government to stamp out the nefarious practice of drowning newborn girls in milk, which was then prevalent among Rajputs. On the death of Ranmalji in 1825, Suraji, his son, ascended the *gadi*, and after a peaceful reign of 19 years, he was followed by Mehramanji IV, who was presented by the Government in 1857 with a gold necklace in appreciation of the excellent results achieved by him in suppressing the cruel practice above referred to. Mehramanji was succeeded in 1862 by His Highness Thakore Saheb Bavajiraj, the late Chief. The latter was only six years of age at the time of his accession, and the administration of the State was carried on by his grandmother, Naniba, and Captain Lloyd, Political Agent, until 1867, when limited powers of rulership were granted to the young Chief. He had received an excellent education at the Rajkumar College at Rajkot, and he had also been well trained for the responsible position which had devolved upon him.

The Thakore Saheb specially interested himself in the ceremonies connected with the celebration of the fiftieth anniversary of the illustrious reign of Her Imperial Majesty the late Queen Victoria, and the day set apart as a holiday in Rajkot was marked by great rejoicing, and an abundant distribution of food, sweets, and clothing to school children as well as to a large number of needy persons. On behalf of the Thakore Saheb, his mother,

1. H.H. SIR LAKHAJI RAJ, K.C.I.E., THAKORE SAHIB OF RAJKOT.
2. RANJIT VILLAS PALACE. 3. RANJIT VILLAS PALACE GARDENS.

THE STATE OF RAJKOT.

1. Darbargadh. 2. The Amarsinhji Secretariat. 3. View from Grain Market to Raiya Gate.

THE STATE OF RAJKOT.

1. Bird's-eye View of Rajkot City. 2. View of Rajkot City from the Aji Bridge.

Naniba Saheb, gave some 385 acres of land, in addition to the area rented in 1822, in order to meet the increasing needs of the *kothi* which had grown into the Agency Headquarters, and the annual rental was increased to Rs. 4,303.

Thakore Saheb Bavajiraj was very bold, yet affable and learned. He was gifted with great legal acumen, and he laboured hard for the prosperity of his State. It may be said that it was during his reign that the State of Rajkot entered upon its modern phase. Great grief was manifested in Rajkot, as well as in neighbouring States, in 1889, when the announcement was made of His Highness' death at the early age of 33 years. His successor, the present Prince, His Highness Thakore Saheb Shri Sir Lakhaji Raj Bahadur, K.C.I.E., being then a child of six years of age, the administration of the State was entrusted to the *Karbhari* of the previous Ruler, subject, however, to the control of the Political Agent. The Thakore Sahib's course of studies at the Rajkumar College was marked by diligent application and a thoroughness which evoked the highest praise from the tutors, and since he took up the reins of government he has been unwearying in his efforts to promote the prosperity of the State.

The Thakore Saheb was installed on the ancestral *gadi* on October 21, 1907, and was invested with full powers of a second-class Chief. During the year 1908-9 His Highness visited England, where he remained for about five months, and on his return to Rajkot he was accorded a flattering reception by his beloved subjects. March 5, 1910, witnessed the birth of the present heir-apparent, Yuvraj Kumar Saheb Dharmendrasinhji, when His Highness the Thakore Saheb granted several concessions to the people, which included remissions of arrears of rent, of overdue interest on advances, and of municipal taxes; the granting of scholarships for the encouragement of education in agricultural or technical knowledge, and for good conduct of boys or girls, while primary education was made entirely free, excepting in the town of Rajkot.

In May, 1910, the sad tidings of the death of His Majesty the King-Emperor Edward VII reached Rajkot, and at a mass meeting of European and Indian inhabitants, His Highness the Thakore Saheb delivered a touching address, dwelling on the late monarch's virtues and statesmanlike qualities.

During the same year His Highness the Thakore Saheb established a State Council, comprising the heads of all important departments, who were required to confer monthly with the object of securing more efficient control of State affairs. A State Bank was opened in July, 1910, and it has, during its nine years' existence, given a great impetus to trade and industries.

His Highness gladly availed himself of the privilege of attending the Coronation Durbar at Delhi, in December, 1911, when he took part in the various functions which had been arranged for the numerous visitors. The twelfth of that month was a day of festivities throughout the whole State, and at a Durbar held at the capital, under the Presidency of Mr. A. T. Mehta, the Sar Nyayadhish, the Royal proclamation was read in the English and vernacular tongues, this being followed by the firing of a salute of 101 guns. Food and

THE STATE OF RAJKOT.

1. THE ALFRED HIGH SCHOOL. 2. THE KARANSINHJI MIDDLE SCHOOL.

sweets were distributed to poor people as well as to scholars, and hay was served to needy cattle in the villages.

When intimation reached Rajkot of the outbreak of the Great War, His Highness the Thakore Saheb addressed a letter to the Political Agent in Kathiawar, in which the following words (*inter alia*) occur: "It is the bounden duty of the Indian Empire, in which we have the privilege of being colleagues and partners, to rally enthusiastically to the support of England, and I, as a humble partner, earnestly give full assurance of all loyal support from me and my State." His Highness the Thakore Saheb not only gave valuable financial help to a number of War Relief Funds, but he also addressed public meetings, and in various other ways encouraged the inhabitants of the State to contribute to the best of their ability. From the commencement of hostilities the State has contributed, up to the present time, approximately Rs. 1,64,590 to the several War Funds and beneficent activities in aid of war, to which officials and the public added their mite of Rs. 11,000. The munificent sum spent by the State included Rs. 52,500 paid to the Imperial Indian Relief Fund; Rs. 33,500 paid to the Women's Branch (Bombay) of the War Relief Fund; Rs. 29,920 disbursed in the enlistment of 241 recruits provided by the State; Rs. 17,170—the value of a Lanchester motor-car, presented for war work (together with its upkeep charges); Rs. 10,000 paid to the "Our Day" Fund of the Red Cross Society; Rs. 7,500 to the Prince of Wales's War Fund; Rs. 6,000, the value of 12 horses given for remount purposes; Rs. 2,000 donated to the Lady Hardinge War Hospital; and Rs. 1,500 to Queen Mary's Silver Wedding Fund. Moreover, the State by itself and through its Bhayats, Official Subjects, and *ryots* purchased War Loans, War Bonds, and Postal Cash Certificates of the value of Rs. 3,53,850. As a fitting conclusion to this war of "Right" versus "Might," in which Right at last prevailed, the Thakore Saheb drew up a very comprehensive programme of Peace celebrations, which continued for four days from December 13, 1919.

The untiring efforts made by the Thakore Saheb to help to bring the titanic struggle to a victorious termination elicited from the Bombay Government a letter, dated July 8, 1919, which says: "On behalf of His Majesty the King-Emperor, His Excellency the Viceroy, and His Excellency the Governor, I am directed to thank you warmly for the aid rendered by the Rajkot State during the last four and a half years. Besides giving horses and a motor-ambulance, you made a gift of Rs. 2,000 towards the expenses of the Lady Hardinge War Hospital. You have thus manifested your steadfast loyalty and devotion to His Imperial Majesty the King and the British Empire, and have shared in the great struggle for justice and freedom in which India has so nobly borne her part."

THE STATE OF RAJKOT.

1. THE RAJKOT COTTON MILLS CO., LTD. 2. THE LAKHAJI RAJ ROLLER FLOUR MILLS CO., LTD.

The Rulers of the State exercise full administrative powers, and are entitled to a dynastic salute of nine guns. The Birthday Honours for the year 1918 elevated the Thakore Saheb to the dignity of a Knight Commander of the Most Eminent Order of the Indian Empire, and the investiture was made in Bombay at the hands of His Excellency Lord Willingdon on December 7th of the same year.

THE STATE OF RAJKOT.

1. Lalpuri Lake. 2. The Darbargadh at Sardhar. 3. Tank, showing Village and the Darbargadh, Sardhar.

THE STATE OF RAJKOT

Political Agents and other officials who have visited Rajkot during the course of the past 10 or 15 years have given personal testimony as to the remarkable progress made in all State departments during the occupancy of the *gadi* by the present Chief. In spite of the various social and other engagements for which a ruling Prince has to provide, the Thakore Saheb presides at the *Hazur* Office from about 1 p.m. to 5 p.m. in the newly-built Amarsinhji Secretariat, where he controls the work of all departments. Mr. Harjiva Bhawanbhai Kotak, B.A., LL.B., has been his able and far-sighted Diwan for more than 12 years, and he deserves well of the State for having contributed to its financial and commercial prosperity, and of the people for having brought about their general contentment. Besides the Heir-Apparent, the Thakore Saheb has two other sons, K. S. Kishorsinhji and K. S. Pradumansinhji, respectively aged eight and seven years.

The State is of a gently undulating character with stony soil, and well watered by several streams of which the Aji is perennial.

The State is divided into four *mahals*, namely, Rajkot proper, Rajkot-Chibhada, Sahrdhar, and Kuvadava; and there are three different systems of collection of land revenue. These are known as (1) *bhag batai*, or a share in cash and kind; (2) *vighoti*, or cash assessment according to the classification of soil; and (3) *udhad*, or cash taken in a lump sum upon each holding. Cultivators are tenants-at-will of the Durbar, so that they have no right to alienate any portion of their holdings by sale or mortgage.

The area of the State is 282 square miles in extent, and during the year 1917–18 there were 1,07,745 acres of cultivable land, of which 32,874 were under cotton, 9,253 acres under wheat, and 458 acres devoted to sugar-cane.

Several years ago the State established a paddock for stud horses, to which is attached a cattle-breeding department and a model farm. As many as 40 or 50 brood mares were at times to be found in the paddock.

With the object of affording greater facilities to cultivators in securing loans of money for the purchase of livestock, seeds, and implements, the State, on November 1, 1914, established village co-operative agricultural banks, which are connected with the State bank in the town of Rajkot. There are 25 village banks, three urban banks, and the initial capital of Rs. 44,630 has been provided by the purchase of 2,261 shares of Rs. 10 each by the cultivators, and of 2,202 shares by the State.

The State of Rajkot, commanding a very central position in Kathiawar, carries on an increasing trade in nearly all kinds of merchandise. It has several industrial enterprises, the principal articles of manufacture being cotton and woollen fabrics and copper and brass ware.

His Highness the Thakore Saheb is profoundly interested in the spread of education, and probably there is no other branch of work where his enthusiastic encouragement has been more conspicuously manifested.

The inhabitants of the State, according to the census of 1911, were 50,638 in number, and they were classified as follows: 41,254 Hindus, 5,894 Mahomedans, 3,276 Jains, 48 Christians, 6 Parsis, and 169 undefined.

The gross revenues of the State (inclusive of sums realized by sale of land for building purposes, amounted in 1918–19 to Rs. 7,56,850, as compared with Rs. 8,53,732 for the previous 12 months, and gross expenditure for the same periods were respectively Rs. 6,03,806 and Rs. 6,43,898.

THE STATE OF RAJKOT.

THE CITY WALL AT SARDHAR.

THE STATE OF SANGLI

THE State of Sangli, having an area of 1,112 square miles, is included in the territory under the control of the Political Agent of Kolhapur and the Southern Mahratta *jagirs* in the Presidency of Bombay, and, according to the census of 1911, the inhabitants were nearly 228,000 in number.

The Chief of Sangli is a Chitpawan Brahmin belonging to the historic family of the Patwardhans, who originally came from the Konkan in the early portion of the eighteenth century and rose to distinction under the Peshwas of Poona. The founder of the family of the present Chief was Harbhat, who was born in 1655, at Kotawada, a village in the district of Ratnagiri. Harbhat acquired fame on account of his great piety and profound study of Vedic literature, and he eventually became the family priest of Naro Mohadeo, the Ruler of the State of Ichalkaranji.

During his incumbency of this office his saintly virtues attracted the attention of Balaji Vishwanath, the first Peshwa of Poona, who raised him to a position of great responsibility in the Mahratta kingdom. Harbhat died at Poona in the year 1750, and his name was commemorated by his son, Govind Hari, who founded the village of Haripur near Sangli, on the bank of the River Krishna. Three of the seven sons of Harbhat won distinction as fearless warriors in the Mahratta army, and Govind Hari—who had entered the service of the Peshwa in 1719—had by sheer ability and high character risen in 1741 to the command of the cavalry of Balaji Bajirao I. Govind Hari rendered excellent service to the Peshwa in his campaigns against Hyder Ali, the Nizam of Hyderabad, and other formidable opponents of the Mahrattas. As a reward for his valour he was made a *jagirdar* under Balaji. In the majority of the sharp conflicts in which Govind Hari was engaged he was ably supported by his son, Gopalrao, and the brilliant deeds performed by these two brave soldiers were highly praised by the Peshwa, who made grants to them of Mangalwedha, Miraj, Dodwad and other places now in the territory of the State of Sangli. Govind Hari established the capital of his *jagir* at Miraj, where he resided until his death in 1771. His eldest son, Wamanrao, succeeded to the *jagir* of his late father, and he was invested by the Peshwa with a dress of honour. He had already won his spurs by his courage and skill by inflicting a crushing blow upon Hyder Ali; but his brilliant prospects were unfortunately terminated by his death, which occurred in 1775 at Warangaon, where he had encamped with the Peshwa's army. This was a sad calamity for the Patwardhans, and their bright hopes for his successor, Pandurangrao, were in a somewhat similar manner doomed to disappointment. The *jagirdar* had barely entered into possession of his estates when he was called upon to oppose Hyder Ali, who was advancing at the head of his troops with the avowed intention of seizing the whole of the Mahratta country lying in the southern side of the Krishna. Mahomed Ali, who was leader of a large section of Hyder's army, disposed his forces in such a manner as to give Pandurangrao the impression that he was retreating. This stratagem was completely successful, and when the Peshwa's cavalry led a hot pursuit of the enemy the latter's reserves poured upon them a deadly fire on the flank and completely routed them. This is known in the Mahratta history as the famous Battle of Sawashi. Pandurangrao, one of the prisoners of battle, was taken to Seringapatam, where he was placed in confinement. The Court ministers at Poona thereupon selected Hariharrao, the eldest son of Pandurangrao, as the rightful heir to the *jagir*, and a robe of honour was accordingly presented to him on October 1, 1778. Owing to the minority of Hariharrao, the leadership of the family devolved upon Parasharam Bhau as its senior member. The latter performed his duties as foster-father in a most praiseworthy manner, but his charge had scarcely reached the age of manhood when he succumbed to illness in 1782. The claims of Chintamanrao, second son of Pandurangrao, were then placed before the Poona Durbar, and on February 6, 1783, the Saranjam *jagir* was conferred upon him; but as he was only nine years of age at the time, the management of the estates was entrusted to Parasharam Bhau. The young Chief subsequently became the famous Chintamanrao Appa Saheb, the actual founder of Sangli, and the real history of the State commences with him.

When Chintamanrao was only about 17 years of age a compact was made between the Mahrattas, the Nizam, and the British, under which the allied forces were to march against Tipu Sultan, son of Hyder Ali, who had become a constant source of danger to their power. The details of the numerous battles which took place in this campaign have frequently been chronicled, but it may be observed here that all historians agree that the Patwardhans rendered the greatest help to the British, especially at the time when " the provisions

LIEUT. SHRIMANT CHINTAMANRAO APPASAHIB PATWARDHAN, CHIEF OF SANGLI.

of Lord Cornwallis and General Meadows were exhausted at Seringapatam." The war was concluded in 1792 by a treaty of peace with Tipu, who "agreed to cede to the allies, from the country adjacent to theirs, one-half of the dominions possessed by him before the war, and to pay a sum of Rs. 3,30,00,000." The ceded territory extended to Harihar on the Tungabhadra, over which the Patwardhans virtually ruled till the end of the eighteenth century.

The most important event of the year 1800 was the rising of marauders led by Dhondia Waugh, and his subsequent overthrow by General Wellesley.

As soon as hostilities were concluded the question arose of the appropriation of the conquered territory; but the subject bristled with difficulties, as the country ravaged by Dhondia was originally under the rule of the Peshwas, although virtually it was in the possession of the Patwardhans, to whom it had been assigned "as a payment for expenses in the former Mysore War." Sindhia was opposed to the claim of the Patwardhans, but Wellesley not only defended their rights, but actually handed over the territories to them. During the absence of Chintamanrao owing to the Dhondia insurrection, his uncle Gangadharrao—who had acted as administrator during the minority of his nephew—appropriated to himself a considerable portion of the ancestral domains, and this act of his resulted in serious differences among the various members of the family. A settlement of the trouble was arranged in 1801, under which a portion of the *jagir* was given to Gangadharrao, while Chintamanrao was granted possession of the remainder, he establishing himself at Sangli, then a small village on the River Krishna, but now a flourishing town and capital of the Sangli State.

In the year 1802 serious disputes arose between Sindhia and Holkar, ambitious leaders of the Mahrattas, and the trouble became so acute that the Peshwa was deposed and compelled to seek protection from the Bombay Government. General Wellesley, whose troops were strengthened by the Patwardhan's army, marched to Poona, and succeeded in restoring the Peshwa to his original position of power; but during the next few years there were many complaints as to the attitude of the Peshwa towards the southern *jagirdars*. The Resident at Poona in 1811 strongly urged the necessity of settling all differences between the Peshwa and the southern *jagirdars*, and in the following year an agreement was made which confirmed the Patwardhans in the peaceful possession of their territory. The Peshwa, who had for some time been chafing against the British Government owing to their protection of small principalities, broke off all friendly relations with the Paramount Power in the year 1817, and this was the commencement of events which led to his downfall in the year 1818. His next act was to make a sudden attack upon the Residency at Poona, and war was at once declared against him by the British Government. The Patwardhans were friendly with the British, although they were feudatories of the Peshwa, and therefore General Munro, who was entrusted with the duty of suppressing the Peshwa in the Carnatic, was authorized to deal with the southern *jagirdars* in an amicable manner. The British general performed the latter part of his task in a most generous spirit, and in inducing the Patwardhans to remain neutral he assured them that "their position would be better and not worse" by leaving the standard of the Peshwa. The revolution which ensued at Poona resulted in the establishment of British supremacy in the Deccan. This was effected solely through the masterly statesmanship of General Munro and Mr. Mountstuart Elphinstone, who subsequently became Governor of Bombay. The Patwardhan Chiefs, with their oriental natures, took some exception to the new arrangements involved by the terms of peace, which "reduced their independent position of an ally to that of a feudal Chief." Chintamanrao, who was dignified in demeanour, was jealous of his rights, but after some correspondence with the representatives of the British Government he submitted to the proposed terms and entered into an agreement with the British in May, 1819. On the downfall of the Peshwa British rule was firmly established in the Deccan, and Chintamanrao—as well as other Chiefs—quickly learned to appreciate the wise policy of Mr. Elphinstone, who was gifted with talents of the highest order.

Chintamanrao manifested his loyalty to the British in 1838 by offering his personal service in expeditionary measures rendered necessary by troubles in Persia, and in 1839 he expressed a desire to aid the Government by proceeding with his troops to take part in the Afghan War. It is probable that the most valuable help given by Chintamanrao to the British was rendered in 1844 when a serious revolt occurred in the State of Kolhapur. The trusty Chief despatched a strong military force to co-operate with British troops, and referring to these services the Resident wrote: "This help can only be faintly represented by the record of Government." The Supreme Government warmly thanked Chintamanrao and presented him with a valuable sword of honour "in testimony of their respect for his high character and in acknowledgment of his unswerving fidelity and attachment to the British nation."

Chintamanrao ruled over the Sangli State, under the British regime, from 1818 to 1851. Mr. Townsend, for many years Political Agent in the Carnatic, and who knew Chintamanrao intimately, wrote concerning him: "His character was marked by an integrity of a high order, by a desire to do absolutely equal-handed justice between man and man, and by whole-hearted affection both for the rich and the poor."

This famous Chief died on July 15, 1851, and his memory is still cherished with honour and respect by the people of Sangli.

The late Chief was overwhelmed with grief at the death of his son, Ganpatrao, in 1826, and his daughter-in-law adopted Vinayakrao Bhausaheb as the heir-designate of Chintamanrao, but in 1838 a son was born to the latter, who succeeded to the Chiefship of Sangli in 1851 under the title of Dhundirao Tatyasaheb. This Ruler attained his majority early in the year 1857, shortly before the outbreak of the Sepoy Mutiny, and it was at once apparent that he had inherited the martial spirit of his forefathers, and that he was, like his immediate predecessor, a staunch and true ally of the British Government. He rendered very substantial aid in crushing the rebellion, and at a grand Durbar held at Sangli he received the cordial thanks of the Supreme Government, which were formally presented to him by Colonel (afterwards Sir L. G.) Jacob, the local Political Agent. Dhundirao Tatyasaheb availed himself of the advice and help of the British representative during the 40 years of his Rulership, and he died in December 1901 without leaving male issue, and the State of Sangli consequently came under British management. The duty of selecting a successor devolved upon the Paramount Power, which supported the claims of Vinayakrao, the great-grandson of the previously-mentioned Vinayakrao, the adopted son of the widowed daughter-in-law of Chintamanrao, the first Chief of Sangli. The young Ruler was renamed Chintamanrao Appasaheb, and he was formally invested with powers of administration on June 2, 1910. He was educated at the Rajkumar College, Rajkot, and is an enlightened and intelligent Chief, devoting direct personal attention to the details of work in the several departments

SHRIMANT SOUBHAGYAVATI SARASWATIBAISAHIB, RANI OF SANGLI.

1. SHRIMANT MADHAVRAO RAO SAHIB, YUVRAJ OF SANGLI. 2. THE CHIEF OF SANGLI AND FAMILY. 3. THE CHIEF OF SANGLI AND PRINCIPAL OFFICERS OF THE STATE.

THE STATE OF SANGLI.

1. Chief's Residence, Sangli. 2. Guest house, Sangli. 3. Entrance to the Fort, Sangli. 4. The Palace (Fort) Sangli.

of State. He is a thorough believer in efficiency, and his energies are constantly employed in promoting measures for the improvement of the State and the true welfare of his subjects.

His full title is Shrimant Chintamanrao Dhundi Rao Appasaheb, Chief of Sangli.

The State of Sangli is divided for administration purposes into six widely scattered *talukas* spread over four Collectorates of the Bombay Presidency, the territory extending from the River Bhima in the north to the Tungabhadra on the south. "Monotony" is the only word by which the general aspect of the four northern *talukas* can be described, as they are typical of the flat and tireless plateau of the Deccan.

The whole of the State, with the exception of a few *Inam* villages, has been brought under the operations of the Revision Survey, which was carried out under the personal control of Colonel Anderson of the Revenue Survey Department.

There are 41 *Inam* and *Saranjam* villages in the State, and 39 of these enjoy the privileges of the revised rates. The land revenue demand for the year 1918–19 amounted to Rs. 7,54,852, and the arrears of collection during the same period, amounting to Rs. 2,29,707, were due to suspensions granted according to rules on account of a deficiency in the rainfall which rendered it impossible to cultivate a very large proportion of the land. The area actually cultivated during the past year was 6,05,839 acres, and at the present time the acreage of cultivable land which is still untilled is exceedingly small. The practice of agriculture is the mainstay of the people, and with the object of improving the methods a State model farm has been established. This farm, some 50 acres in extent, is exceedingly valuable from an educational point of view, as demonstrations are constantly given upon the most approved systems of cultivation, and instructive experiments in the growing of various kinds of crops are conducted by experts.

The State gardens, which are in a thriving condition, are stocked with coco-nut, betel-nut, mango and other valuable trees. The animals in the State cattle farm are of superior quality, and they were highly praised by His Excellency Lord Willingdon, the Governor of Bombay, and the Director of Agriculture of that Province, who inspected them at the Sangli Livestock Exhibition held in 1916–17.

About a quarter of a century ago the forests of Sangli were in a pitiable plight owing to the ruthless destruction year by year of the portion containing the best trees. With the advent of British administration, however, a definite system of forestry was adopted, as it provided for demarcated blocks, roughly equal in size, which were to be cut down in rotation once in 30 years, thus allowing time for the raising and maturing of transplants.

In 1902 an official trained at the Dehra Dun College was appointed as Chief Forest Officer, and he is now supported in the work of conservancy by a Head Assistant, a Surveyor, and about 30 guards.

A very noticeable improvement has taken place in the commercial activities of the State during the past 20 or 30 years, and at the present time a flourishing trade is carried on in *jaggery*, turmeric, *ghee*, tobacco, cotton, chillies, and ground-nuts, but unfavourable weather conditions are apt to interfere with the aggregate turnover. The town of Sangli is now regarded as an important trading centre in the Southern Mahratta Country States, and this fact is very largely due to the opening of the Sangli State Railway and to the establishment of the State Bank, which is of the greatest assistance to merchants and others. The other business towns in Sangli are Shahapur and Rabkavi, which export a considerable quantity of cotton piece-goods, coloured cotton and silk yarn, and it may be observed that the towns just mentioned have for a very long period been noted for the permanency of the colour of their cotton and silk goods. The town of Sangli is famous for its copper and brass pots, and its ornaments and various other articles made of gold, silver and steel; copper and brass pots of large sizes are manufactured at Terdal and Gundi; country blankets are woven at Shirhatti and adjoining villages; glass bangles are made in several districts; and utensils of domestic use are made at Belhatti from soft stones which are found in quarries in the neighbourhood. The State has also a number of cotton ginning and pressing factories, weaving, grinding, and oil mills, as well as ground-nut and turmeric factories.

Prior to the year 1851–2, when a regular system of civil and criminal procedure was introduced into the State, there was neither a recognized code of laws nor a prescribed form of trial, nor any Courts for the administration of justice. A great change has, however, been effected since that date, and there is now a permanent set of codes and regulations based to a very considerable extent upon laws in force in British India, but especially upon those prevailing in the Courts of Bombay.

There are at present 25 ordinary Criminal Courts, and the Sessions and Appellate Courts, comprising the Courts of the *Huzur*, the *Nyayadish*, and the District Magistrate. The Civil Courts are six in number. The Chief is invested with powers to hear cases of all kinds, including those of capital offences.

In connection with the question of education it may be observed that, prior to the year 1857, there was not a single teaching institution maintained by the State in Sangli. After the lapse of 20 years there were 45 schools, in which there were 2,200 pupils, and at the close of the year 1918–19 these numbers had been increased to 176 and 10,131 respectively.

The gross income of the State, exclusive of *Inam* adjustments, amounted during the past year to Rs. 11,26,623, this sum being about Rs. 30,000 less than in the previous 12 months owing to the unfavourable harvest and consequent scarcity of all kinds of agricultural produce.

The State does not pay any tribute to the Supreme Government, which in 18[illegible] accepted in commutation the cession of territory then yielding an annual revenue of Rs. 1,35,000. The State Bank was established in 1893, with the view of finding profitable employment as well as security for a large sum of money which had accrued to the State in previous years of prosperity, and secondly with the object of benefitting agriculturists and traders by making advances to them during periods of commercial depression. Branch banks have been opened in six *talukas*, and this system of investment of surplus savings and at the same time assisting deserving occupiers and traders has proved to be highly advantageous to the State. Financial help is also afforded by about 25 Co-operative Credit Societies, in which there are nearly 2,300 members, and which have a reserve fund of nearly 8,000.

The steadfast loyalty to the Throne of the Chief of Sangli, which is his cherished inheritance from his staunch predecessors, was never more practically manifested than it was by his whole-hearted labours and sacrifices during the dark days of the Great War.

In this connection reference may be made to paragraphs in the State Administration Report for the year 1916–17, where it is stated that the Chief had just then subscribed a sum of Rs. 3,00,000 to the Indian War Loan Fund. The people rallied to the call of their Chief, and contributions were sent to a considerable number of funds established for the successful prosecution of the conflict. Among other items in the

THE STATE OF SANGLI.

1. Amrai Gardens, Sangli. 2. Ghaut Scene on the River Krishna, Sangli. 3. Waterworks, Sangli. 4. Water Reservoir, Sangli. 5. Shri Ganpati Temple, Sangli.

accounts there are sums of Rs. 58,000 and Rs. 30,000 raised partly by subscriptions and partly for the supply of motor-ambulance cars, and an amount of Rs. 20,000 subscribed for grants to hospitals, relief funds, and for the purchase of comforts for soldiers. The State has for many years past been regularly supplying recruits for the Indian Army, and during the years 1914–18 no fewer than 938 men were recruited. With the view of encouraging enlistment the Chief offered many inducements, including cash bonuses, promise of employment by the State on retirement from the army, allowances to sick or wounded, and pensions to the relatives of soldiers killed at the front. The news of the cessation of hostilities was received in Sangli with the greatest enthusiasm by all classes of the people. The Chief gave instructions that a day should be set apart in order that the momentous occasion might be celebrated in a fitting manner. Thanksgiving services were held on the morning of November 17, 1918, by all communities in their respective temples and places of worship, and the remainder of the day was spent in distributing gifts and sweetmeats to aged people as well as children and in various entertainments.

THE STATE OF SAVANTVADI

THIS Principality is one of the ancient Mahratta States in Western India which is now under the control of the Government of the Bombay Presidency. It is bounded on the north and west by the British district of Ratnagiri, on the east by the Sahyadri range of mountains, the territory of Kolhapur, and the district of Belgaum, and on the south by the Portuguese territory of Goa.

The Rulers of Savantvadi belong to the old Bhonsle family and trace their descent from Mang Savant, a feudatory of the Mahomedan dynasty of Bijapur, their title of *Sar Desai* having been conferred, it is alleged, by the kings of Bijapur. The successors of Mang Savant endeavoured to throw off their allegiance to Bijapur, but it was not until the decline of that kingdom that actual independence was gained by Khem Savant I. Early in the eighteenth century his grandson Khem Savant II received from Shahu, successor of the great Shivaji, a deed confirming him in his possessions in full sovereignty. Phond Savant ascended the *gadi* in 1709, and he was the first Chief with whom friendly relationship with the British Government was established, the treaty concluded in 1730 being offensive and defensive against Kanoji Angria, the piratical Chief of Kolaba.

Phond Savant was succeeded in 1738 by his grandson, Ramchandra Savant, and on his death in 1755 the *gadi* fell to the lot of his son, Khem Savant III, who is usually referred to in history as "Khem Savant the Great." He married (in 1763) Laxm Bai, daughter of Jayaji Sindhia, and he subsequently obtained from the Moghul Emperor of Delhi the title of Raje Bahadur, this honour being recognized by the British Government. The long period of Khem Savant's administration was marked by a practically continuous struggle with chiefs of various Mahratta States, particularly the Maharaja of Kolhapur, and with the Portuguese, in the course of which he lost several important districts of his territory. Raja Khem Savant died in 1803 without leaving male issue, and dissensions which arose regarding the succession to the *gadi* resulted in civil war in the State. Hostilities continued until 1805, when Laxmi Bai, widow of the previous Raja, adopted from the junior branch of the ruling family, Ramchandra Savant, or Bhau Savant, who was murdered about four years later, and Phond Savant, one of the same Bhonsle family, was called to the *gadi*.

The chief event of this reign, which terminated in 1812, was the enforced cession of the fort of Vengurla owing to a sequence of piratical acts on the part of subjects of the State. The Raja left behind him a minor son, who in 1822 was entrusted with the administration of the State under the title of Khem Savant IV. In the year 1838 the Raja transferred to the British Government the right to levy customs on land and sea, he receiving in return a fixed annual sum of money. The affairs of the State began to get into such disorder that in 1838 the British Government, with the consent of the Raja, assumed administration of the State. Rebellions broke out in the State in that year and again in 1844, but they were soon suppressed by the British iauthorities. The successful control of the State by British officials was signalized in 1861 by the restoration of the Raja to his rightful position as Ruler, subject to the following conditions, namely, (1) that the Raja would pay the sum of Rs. 5,50,000, the cost of the second rebellion; (2) that he would pay a succession fee equivalent to one year's revenue; (3) that he would secure proper protection for his subjects; and (4) that he would bear the expenses of a British Resident and his necessary establishment.

It should be mentioned here that Anna Sahib, son of the Raja, who had joined the rebels in 1844, was pardoned and duly recognized as heir-apparent to the *gadi*. After the arrangement made with Khem Savant, referred to in the previous paragraph, the Political Superintendent endeavoured to persuade the Raja to take a greater personal interest in the welfare of the State, but as his efforts proved to be unavailing the administration was continued by the British Government through the Superintendent. Khem Savant IV died in October 1867, and was succeeded by his son, Anna Sahib, who ascended the *gadi* as Phond Savant IV. This Ruler lacked the ability to control the affairs of the State owing to his habit of indulgence in drugs, and the British Government accordingly proposed that he should remain as nominal Ruler but that his powers should be restricted.

Before full effect could be given to this project, however, the Raja died, and he was succeeded on August 29, 1870, by his son, Raghunath Savant, as Sar Desai of Savantvadi. The young Chief was only six years of age at the time of his father's death, and therefore the Political Superintendent retained control of State affairs while he (the minor) received his early training at Kolhapur under the supervision of the Resident.

The Chief subsequently became a student at the Rajkumar College at Rajkot, and in 1878 a magnificent Durbar was held at the chief town of the State, when he was presented with the Delhi banner, sent by His Excellency the Viceroy and Governor-General of India, in commemoration of the assumption by Her Majesty the late Queen Victoria of the title of Empress of India. In the following year the Chief married the daughter of the late Maharaja Khanderao Gaekwar of Baroda. The British Government doubted the ability of the young Sir Desai to undertake the duties of a Ruler, and therefore he was not invested with administrative powers, the Political Superintendent remaining at the head of affairs. The Sar Desai died in 1899, and was succeeded by his cousin Shri Ram Savant Bhonsle, the father of the present Chief, who was installed on the *gadi* on July 23, 1900. Once again the British Government resolved that the Political Agent should carry on the administration under the name and seal of the Raja, but the Sar Desai was entrusted with the direct management of the *Paga*, *Durbar* and *Devasthan* departments of the State.

The Sar Desai died on April 24, 1913, leaving an only son, the present Chief, who was born on August 20, 1897.

The full title of the young Ruler is Captain Raje Bahadur Khem Savant Bhonsle Sar Desai Prant Kudal and Mahalanihaya, Sar Desai of Savantvadi.

When the young Prince was six years of age he was placed under the care of Miss L. C. Moxon, at Poona, in order to undergo a course of preliminary training. He subsequently studied with Lieut. Tate at Kolhapur for nearly two years, and during the first week in January 1912 he travelled with Miss Moxon to England, where his education was proceeded with at a preparatory school and afterwards at the College at Malvern. On the death of his father in 1913 the Prince was recognized by the Government of India as Sar Desai of the State. When the Prince's collegiate term had been completed at Malvern he was permitted to offer his personal services to His Majesty the King-Emperor in connection with the prosecution of the late Great War. He joined the 2nd Officers' Cadet Battalion, and on passing out was subsequently gazetted 2nd Lieutenant, and attached to the 116th Mahrattas.

Prior to leaving England the Chief had the honour of being received by His Majesty the King-Emperor in London, and on returning to India he paid a flying visit to Savantvadi, but left on October 6, 1917, for Mesopotamia in order to join the Expeditionary Force in that country. He remained with his regiment at the front until the cessation of hostilities, and returned to India on March 4, 1919. The Chief was accorded a magnificent reception by the subjects of the State on his arrival at Savantvadi, and a congratulatory address, enclosed in a silver casket, was presented to him. On July 23, 1919, His Majesty the King-Emperor conferred upon the Sar Desai the permanent honorary rank of Captain, and he has since that date been permanently attached to the 1st Battalion 116th Mahrattas.

The Sar Desai, a Mahratta according to caste, is related by marriage with the ruling families of Gwalior, Baroda, Dhar, and Akalkot, and he is entitled to a salute of nine guns.

The gross revenue of Savantvadi, based upon the average of the past five years, is Rs. 5,46,985; and the State does not pay tribute to the Supreme Government nor to any other State.

The territory of Savantvadi covers an area of 925 square miles, and the inhabitants are nearly 218,000 in number, these being chiefly Hindus and Mahomedans, together with a small proportion of Christians.

The surface of the land rises rapidly from the sea coast (from which the State is separated by a narrow strip of Ratnagiri) as far as the Sahyadri range, and the scenery, which is of a most charming character, is marked by wooded hills, verdant valleys, luxuriant gardens, and groves of coco-nuts and palms, interspersed with a considerable number of peaks varying in height from 300 feet to 3,000 feet. Many of these summits are crowned with forts of historic interest, and one, at least, of them dates from the time of the *Mahabharata*.

Savantvadi is a land of hills and streams, and the combination of a salubrious climate with fertile soil rarely lacking in moisture has enhanced the natural beauty of the districts of the State. The principal rivers are the Karli or Sarambal, which flows from the village of Shivapur on the Sahyadris for a distance of 35 miles to the Arabian Sea at Malvan; and the Terekhol or Banda which, rising in the same range, marks off the State from the Portuguese territory of Goa and is navigable for a distance of 15 miles from the sea.

Prior to assumption of control of the State by the British Government there was no organized system of land revenue administration, the amount collected by the State being usually based upon a bird's-eye view and valuation of a growing crop. A certain proportion of the amount of the appraisement—usually about one-sixth of the entire yield—was paid, "in kind," to the State. Innumerable taxes were also levied upon traders, and upon tobacco and other merchandise, but the whole procedure was most unsatisfactory, especially in connection with the recovery of assessments, as the expenditure was frequently as great as the income itself. No more conclusive proof of the mismanagement in those days could be given than that which is contained in the following cryptic sentence: "When the British Government took over the administration of the State on September 17, 1838, there was a balance of only Rs. 53 in the State treasury."

From this date the system of recovering land revenue was properly regulated. The practice of paying the salaries of servants directly from the villages was abolished, and it was ordered that all the dues should at first be credited in the treasury and should then be issued in cash to the payees. For administrative purposes the area of the State was divided into three sub-divisions of Vadi, Banda, and Kudal, and the charge of each of those fiscal areas is placed in the hands of an officer styled a *kamavisdar*.

Under British administration the lands were surveyed, classified and assessed, and all advantages of survey secured by the completion of the Survey Settlement in 1895-6 in the land revenue was increased from 1·8 to 2·7 lakhs.

In early days the procedure in civil disputes was based to a large extent on native usages and local customs.

After the advent of the British the Courts were guided by India, and especially Bombay Government, Acts, as far as they might be applicable to Savantvadi.

Before 1842 there were two civil tribunals, the Chief's Court and the Magistrates' (*Mansabdar's*) Court; the latter consisting of a bench of three judges who decided all cases after consulting a council of three persons of rank and intelligence. In 1842 the Chief's Court was abolished and a new court established under a native judge, *Nyayadhish*, with jurisdiction over the Banda and Vadi sub-divisions and the town of Vadi. In 1858 a Court with jurisdiction over the whole of Kudal and thirteen villages of Vadi was established under a native subordinate judge. [illegible] In 1878 three civil courts existed: original, and one (that of the Political [illegible]

1. HIS HIGHNESS CAPTAIN RAJE BAHADUR KHEM SAVANT BHONSLE, SAR DESAI OF SAVANTVADI.
2. MUSEUM AND CHIEF JUDGE'S COURT, SAVANTVADI.

tendent) exercised appellate jurisdiction. Before 1885 only a few enactments were formally introduced, although as many as thirty-five were followed. Since 1888 a number of British India enactments have been introduced in the State, or acts on British India models have been passed. The Legislative Committee, consisting of the Political Agent, the State *Karbhari*, and the Judicial Assistant (now Chief Judge), was constituted under the orders of Government in 1888, and legislation was introduced in the State upon the advice of this Committee. In 1897 the Court of the Political Superintendent was invested with the powers of a High Court. The Court of the Judicial Assistant exercising the delegated appellate powers of the Political Superintendent was constituted a Court of First Appeal, and the designation of the officer presiding over that Court changed from Judicial Assistant to Chief Judge. Many important British India enactments have all been introduced into the State, and civil justice is now administered on the same lines as in British Courts.

From October 14, 1916, the post of the resident Political Agent, who exercised the powers of a High Court in civil matters, was abolished, and the Court of the Administrator was created in its place to exercise those powers.

In connection with the administration of criminal justice, and in accordance with instructions issued by Government in 1838, an officer, called a *Mansabdar*, was appointed as magistrate with limited powers of punishment, with also certain clerical duties in civil causes. Serious cases were transferred to the Political Superintendent. In 1842 the State was divided into three parts, each of which was placed under a manager or *Kamavisdar*, who, besides hearing land and rent suits, was invested with magisterial powers of simple imprisonment up to twenty days and of fining up to Rs. 15. All cases of importance were referred with the documents of the case to the Political Superintendent, who was invested with powers of a Sessions Judge, and in dealing with such matters he was empowered to select from amongst the officers of the State and *Sardars* three assessors, who, after the hearing of the evidence, were required to record their opinions. The sentence then passed by the Political Superintendent had to be submitted for the confirmation of Government. In 1877 the Political Superintendent was invested with powers of a High Court to enable him to revise the sentences of the subordinate magistrates under Section 439 of the Criminal Procedure Code. In 1876 a new appointment of State *Karbhari* was created, and this official was invested with the powers of a District Magistrate, which had hitherto been exercised by the Political Superintendent.

From October 14, 1916, the post of the resident Political Agent was abolished, and the Administrator was appointed to carry on the duties under the superintendence of the Collector and Political Agent, Belgaum.

In 1874 a regular police force was organized. The total strength of this force is at present 187 armed and 137 unarmed men. Taking 925 square miles as the area of the State and 2,17,240 as its population, the strength of the Savantvadi unarmed police is one policeman to every 6·7 square miles and to every 1,585 persons. The total cost of the whole police force is Rs. 55,363-3-5, or Rs. 60 a square mile, or nearly four annas a head of the population.

The total culturable area of the State is about 3,80,000 acres, rice being by far the most important crop.

The forests of the State are 34 855 acres in extent; those classified as reserved cover 34,340 acres, and protected forests 515 acres. The total income of the Forest Department, from all sources, amounts to about Rs. 54,000. The forests literally abound with wild animals of numerous species, which include tiger, panther, bear, bison, sambhur, pig and wild cat.

There are no manufactures or industrial enterprises of importance, but a knitting factory has been opened recently; weaving is carried on in the jail at Vadi; bricks and tiles are made in various places; beautiful embroidery work is done at Vadi; and inlaid coco-nut shells and lacquered ware articles, the latter being famous all over India, are skilfully made in the capital town.

Before the advent of the British into the State, Savantvadi was almost cut off from the outer world excepting by certain exits through the *Ghats* and various difficult passes through the Sahyadri mountains. All these mountain passes were crossed by foot passengers, and merchandise was carried on pack bullocks. No vehicular traffic then existed in the State. Heavy tolls were collected and consequently trade was much hampered. Roads had not then been constructed in the State with the exception of the Ramghat road connecting Belgaum with Vengurla, which was made by the British Government about the year 1820 for military purposes. Its length in the State is 43 miles from Tulas *Ghati* to Ramghat. In subsequent years road construction was prosecuted in various directions. In the period of Colonel Westropp's supervision of the State an extensive programme was carried out, with the result that the total length of roads, including cart tracks and footpaths, which was 155 miles when Colonel Westropp assumed charge in 1876, had increased to 412 miles at the time of his retirement in 1888. The State now possesses 440 miles of road, including 30 miles of footpaths in the several *ghats*, and 75 miles which are bridged and metalled.

Eighty years ago there were practically no means for giving even primary instruction in the State. In 1839 Mr. Richard Spooner, the first Political Superintendent, brought to the notice of the Government the deplorable state of ignorance in which the people of the State were steeped, and with the permission of the Government he opened a school in the town of Vadi for the teaching of Marathi. The pioneer work of Mr Spooner had a most beneficial effect upon the all-important question of education and in almost each succeeding year there was a substantial increase in the number of scholars receiving instruction. Notwithstanding discouragements, the State authorities persevered with their good work, and statistics show that in 1870—that is [illegible] years after the beginning of British administration—40 schools had been established and the roll-calls contained the names of 1,869 pupils.

In 1912-13 the State Educational Department was placed under the control of Rao Sahib R. G. Sabnis, with the title of State Educational Inspector, and this official has made it a special feature of his work to establish as many schools in villages as the funds allotted for building purposes will allow. English schools for boys are now to be found at Vadi, Kudal, Banda, Aronda, Ajgaum and Tulsuli, while one for girls, in which teaching is imparted up to Standard V, has been opened at the capital town.

Three well-equipped libraries have been opened in Vadi, Kudal and Banda for the use of the general public. They have 82, 41 and 47 subscribers, and contain 4,004, 1,120 and 3,540 volumes respectively.

The total annual expenditure on Education is Rs. 56,000, of which Rs. 33,0[illegible] are paid from the State funds and the balance is made up from local funds and fees.

The State has made adequate provision for rendering medical aid and relief: the Westropp Civil Hospital, the lunatic and leper asylums and the dispensaries at Kudal, [illegible]

THE STATE OF SAVANTVADI.

1. General View of the Moti Tank, with Leseer Gate. 2. Savantvadi High School.

THE STATE OF SAVANTVADI.

1. British Military Pensioned Subhedars from the Savantvadi State. 2. Savantvadi Armed Police.

Mangaon, and the Itinerant Dispensary. The amount expended by the Medical Department in 1918–19 was Rs. 24,840.

Before concluding these notes a brief reference should be made to the very substantial aid rendered by Savantvadi in support of the Allies in the Great War.

In the State Administration Report for 1917–18, it is shown that 986 recruits were obtained during the year under notice; the total investment from the State in the First Indian War Loan was Rs. 3,13,385–12–0. Rs. 6,741–3–1 were also contributed from the State to the "Our Day" Fund; Rs. 2,500 to the Imperial Indian War Relief Fund, and Rs. 1,000 to the Women's Branch of the Bombay Presidency War and Relief Fund, and a monthly contribution of Rs. 25 was made to the East Indies Station Naval Fund.

The Administration Report for the following year contains these remarks: "The signing of the armistice and the cessation of hostilities with Germany were celebrated with great rejoicings and in a manner befitting the occasion all over the State on November 27, 1918, and thanksgiving prayers were offered on that day by all communities. Sweets were also distributed to the school children, and alms were given to the poor. The number of recruits obtained during the year was 397 up to November 11, 1918, when recruiting of men for the Army was stopped under the orders of the British military authorities. Altogether 2,232 men out of a total population of all ages and sexes of 2,17,240 took part in the Empire's military service, an achievement of which any State could be proud.

It will be evident from the foregoing pages that immense improvements have been effected in the State since British control was inaugurated in 1838, and one has only to travel through the various districts to observe that the people appreciate the progressive policy which has been the most prominent feature of government during the past three quarters of a century. Occupants of land have been placed under more favourable conditions; courts of justice have been established on modern lines; cultivators are benefitting by the practical aid in agricultural matters rendered by the Durbar; education has spread in a remarkable manner; the State has a network of roads which afford good access to centres of trade; post offices have been opened in several large villages, and Vadi and Arouda have been provided with telegraphic facilities; and finally, the State Exchequer is in a flourishing condition, a sum of Rs. 7,00,000 having been recently invested as a reserve fund. There are few States which can boast of a better all-round record.

THE STATE OF SUNTH

SUNTH is a second-class State in the Rewa Kantha Political Agency under the Bombay Government, and the ruling family is a very ancient one, as it traces its lineal descent from Vikramaditya of Ujjain and Raja Bhoj of Dhar, both of whom were famous in the early history of India. The Chiefs belong to the Mahipawat branch of the *Puwar* or Parmar clan of Rajputs, and it is related that in the tenth or eleventh century a Prince of that race, named Jalamsinghji, left the neighbourhood of Mount Abu, the headquarters of the Rajputana Political Agency, and made a home for himself and his followers in Gujarat, where he founded the city of Jhalod and made it the seat of his government. Four succeeding Rulers did not experience serious trouble from external sources, but the fifth, Jalamsinghji II, was, in 1247, sorely oppressed by the Mahomedans, who eventually overran the country and put to death all the members of the Ruling House excepting a son named Sant and his uncle. These two became outcasts, hiding among the jungles in the district occupied by the Bhil tribes, but in 1255 the former founded a kingdom for himself, the capital of which was at a village which he named Sunth.

Direct descendants of Sant occupied the *gadi* for a number of years, during which period there were not many events of great importance to record, but after the death of Ratansinghji II, in 1753, the Chief of the State of Banswara, who had married a daughter of the Sunth family, put to death three of the late Ruler's sons and tried to seize the *gadi*. The fourth son—an infant—was concealed by the Kolis, or Khants, in Malwah, who were greatly enraged at the violent treatment meted out to the State in which they had previously enjoyed a peaceful home. Several years later the Kolis made a sudden attack upon Sunth, and succeeded in expelling the Banswara troops from the State, whereupon they produced the young Prince, Badansinghji, and placed him on the *gadi* of his father. This Ruler died in 1774, and was followed by his son, Shivsinghji, during whose time a treaty was, in 1803, entered into with the British Government. This alliance was practically set aside owing to the non-intervention policy of Lord Cornwallis with regard to Rajput States. When Kalyansinghji was Ruler in 1819 troops of horse belonging to the State of Gwalior began to make raids upon Sunth, but they were speedily driven away by British forces under Sir John Malcolm. Six years later the State was included in the jurisdiction of the Political Agent at Rewa Kantha.

Raja Kalyansinghji died in 1835, and as his heir was a boy of three years of age, his widow became Regent. The methods of government adopted by this lady were of an irritating character, and in 1854, before her son, Bhawanisinghji, attained his majority, the Khants rose in rebellion and went so far as to plunder peaceable occupiers of land. The Raja, who had, in the meantime, been installed on the *gadi*, realized his inability to check the operations of the marauders, and having appealed to the British for assistance, the Political Agent visited Sunth and forced the rebels to abstain from further attacks. He also exacted from them an undertaking to reimburse Sunth for the damage occasioned by them. The year 1860 was an eventful one for the State, as, after an exchange of territory between the British Government and Sindhia had taken place, Sunth was placed under the direct protection of the former, who from that date have received the tribute of Rs. 7,000, *shiyashai* (*i.e.* Rs. 5,385), originally paid to the State of Gwalior. The useful reign of Raja Bhawansinghji was cut short by death when he was only 40 years of age, without leaving an heir to succeed him.

The choice of a new Ruler fell upon Pratapsinghji, who was remotely connected with the family of the late Raja, and who was then only 12 years of age. The British Government retained control of State affairs during minority, and in 1880 the successor was invested with full ruling powers. His Highness received a first-class education in the English and vernacular languages at the Rajkumar College at Rajkot, and his accession to the *gadi* was marked by intelligent government sympathetically administered, and by a firm determination to promote the happiness and welfare of his subjects. In 1890 a *sanad* conferring a right of adoption was granted to the Ruler of Sunth. To the great sorrow of his people the Raja passed away in 1896 without leaving issue.

An appointment of a successor was made in the person of the present Ruler, whose title is Maharanaji Shri Jorawarsinghji Rajaji Sahib of Sunth.

His Highness was born in the year 1880, and on May 10, 1902, a grand Durbar was held by the Political Agent at

MAHARANAJI SHRI JORAWARSINGHJI, RAJAJI SAHIB OF SUNTH.

MAHARAJ KUVAR SHRI PRAVANSINGHJI,
HEIR-APPARENT OF SUNTH.

MAHARAJ KUVAR SHRI PRAVANSINGHJI.

Heir-Apparent of Sunth.

THE STATE OF SUNTH.

1. Sunth Palace from the West. 2. Sunth Palace from the North. 3. Entrance Gate to the Palace Fort. 4. Jorawar Nivas, in the Garden at Rampur. 5. Jorawar Clock-tower at Rampur.

THE STATE OF SUNTH

Rampur, the capital town, where he delivered an impressive address as he formally invested the Raja Sahib with full ruling powers. In replying to the remarks of the Political Agent His Highness thanked him for his encouraging words, and also tendered his acknowledgments to the Government for the admirable manner in which the State had been managed prior to his installation.

On January 1, 1903, a special Durbar was held for the purpose of celebrating the Coronation of Their Imperial Majesties the late King-Emperor Edward VII, and the Dowager Queen-Empress Alexandra. In the year 1905 His Highness the Raja Sahib went to Bombay for the purpose of taking part in the various functions which had been arranged in connection with the visit to India of Their Royal Highnesses the Prince and Princess of Wales, and in November of the same year he was presented to the illustrious visitors at an interview which had been graciously granted to Chiefs of second-class States. It was with the greatest regret that His Highness was compelled —owing to circumstances beyond his control–to crave permission to be excused from attendance on the occasion of the Coronation ceremony of Their Imperial Majesties at Delhi in 1911, but this unique event was suitably celebrated throughout the State by the Rajaji's subjects.

In the year 1913 a rebellion broke out among the Bhil tribe on the Sunth-Banswara border, but it was speedily suppressed.

His Highness the Raja Sahib takes the keenest interest in the administration of State affairs, and his intelligent rule (aided by his present Diwan, Mr. Nicchabhai K. Desai, B.A., LL.B., has been productive of great progress in every department of State.

Education is imparted free of cost in all parts of the State, and a good English school was opened in the capital town about five years ago.

His Highness is a first-rate horseman, but if there is one particular form of sport in which he excels it is that of shooting, and his skill in handling a rifle may be gauged from the fact that since the year 1905 he has bagged 52 panthers, in addition to a considerable number of other species of large game.

The Chief is entrusted with unlimited powers in civil actions, and also in criminal matters, with this exception, that foreign subjects cannot be tried for capital offences without the consent of the Political Agent of Rewa Kantha. His Highness is entitled to a salute of nine guns.

The heir-apparent, Maharaj Kuvar Shri Pravansinghji, now 12 years of age, is receiving instruction at home under a graduate tutor, but he will shortly proceed to one of the Colleges in India specially designed for the education of sons of Rulers of Indian States.

The State of Sunth, 394 square miles in extent, is bounded on the north by the Kadana, Dungarpur, and Banswara States; on the east by the British district of Panch Mahals; on the south by the State of Sanjeli and the Godhra taluka; and on the west by the State of Lunawada.

The territory of Sunth is divided by a range of hills into two parts, named respectively the Eastern and Western *Mahal*. The former of these consists largely of rich soil capable of producing two crops annually, but the methods of agriculture practised by the Bhil occupiers leave much to be desired. The western half, inhabited by Kumbis and Kolis, is even more productive owing to the fact that they are better farmers.

The State forests would be a much more valuable asset if the projected railway scheme had been carried out, thus affording facilities for the removal of timber to markets where satisfactory prices could be secured.

The annual tribute paid to the British Government amounts to Rs. 5,385, while on the other hand Sunth receives *chouth* from certain districts of the total value of nearly Rs. 500.

As soon as the news of the unfortunate outbreak of hostilities in Europe reached Sunth, His Highness the Raja Sahib sent a telegram and a letter to the Political Agent at Rewa Kantha, in which he gave expression to the loyalty and devotion to the Throne of himself and his subjects, and at the same time he placed his personal service as well as the resources of Sunth at the disposal of the Government. During the whole of the four years' struggle the inhabitants of the State were kept well-informed as to the progress of the war, and they were constantly attending their temples and mosques in which fervent prayers were offered for a speedy and complete victory for the Allies. Her Highness the Raniji Saheba subscribed liberally from her own purse to various War Funds, and she also contributed clothing and other articles for the comfort of the troops. Nearly 230 recruits were enlisted by the State, forty-six of these being actual combatants, and the remainder consisting of followers and labourers.

The total amount expended by the State in connection with recruiting amounted to Rs. 10,560.

The State contributed the sum of Rs. 1,00,000 and Rs. 52,787 to the First and Second Indian War Loan Fund. His Highness's subjects subscribed Rs. 29,787 to the latter of these two funds.

THE STATE OF WANKANER

WANKANER, a State in the Halar division of the Kathiawar Political Agency of the Bombay Presidency, is bounded on the north by the States of Morvi and Dhrangadhra, on the south by Rajkot, Bamanbor, and Chotila, on the west by Morvi and Kotda, and on the east by Than Lakhtar. It has an area of 417 square miles, and consists of 104 villages, exclusive of its *talukdari* village of Khasta, having an area of eight square miles. The soil is chiefly light and the territory is hilly. The population of the State, according to census returns of 1911, was 32,653 in number, of whom one-half are Hindus and the remainder consist of some 8,000 Mahomedans, 2,000 Jains, and others of various races. The gross revenue of the State for the year *Samvat* 1974 (1917–18 A.D.) was Rs. 7·16,000, while the average for the past quinquennial period was Rs. 502,200. A sum of Rs. 18,879 is paid in tribute to the British Government, including Junagadh *Jortalbi*. The Ruler of the State is Captain His Highness Sir Amarsinhji Bahadur, K.C.I.E., Maharana Rajsaheb of Wankaner, and he is entitled to a personal salute of 11 guns.

The State was founded by Rajshree Sartanji, grandson of Chandrasinhji, Ruler of the State of Halvad (now Halvad-Dhrangadhra) in Kathiawar, in the year 1605.

Among the brilliant successors of Sartanji (the founder) may be mentioned Raj Bharaji (1749 to 1783), who consolidated the dominions already acquired by his ancestors. Another famous Ruler was Chandrasinhji, *alias* Dosaji, who commenced to reign in 1787. He was a man of great physical strength and courage, and defended his State successfully against formidable rivals.

In 1807 Raj Chandrasinhji (Dosaji) entered into an engagement or settlement with Colonel Walker, representing the East India Company, and Babaji, on behalf of the Gaekwar, the terms of which govern the relations of the State with the paramount power. Raj Chandrasinhji's death took place in 1839, when he was succeeded by his eldest son, Raj Vakhatsinhji.

His Highness Vakhatsinhji was a benevolent and religiously inclined Prince, and while on the throne he performed pilgrimages to many of the famous Hindu shrines in India. On his death he was succeeded by his grandson Banesinhji (Vinayasinhji), in 1861, as his eldest son, Jasvantsinhji, had already predeceased him. His Highness Banesinhji occupied the *gadi* from 1861 to his death, in 1881, when the State passed to the present Ruler.

Captain His Highness Maharana Rajsaheb Sir Amarsinhji, K.C.I.E., born on January 4, 1879, was installed on the throne of Wankaner on June 25, 1881, in the presence of Colonel Nutt, the then Assistant Political Agent, Jhalawad, but the Prince being only two years of age, the State was placed under an Administrator specially appointed by Government. In 1887 the young Prince joined the Rajkumar College, Rajkot, for his education, and he was placed under the special care of Mr. Macnaughten, and, later on, under Mr. Waddington, Principals of the College. Having successfully passed through his course of studies at the College, the Prince visited the principal cities of India (including Ceylon) in 1898, and in May of the same year he started on his European tour in the company of Major F. De B. Hancock. Having spent about four months in seeing the various interesting places in England, the minor Prince returned to India, spending a few days in Paris on the way, reaching Wankaner on October 22, 1898. The Government of Bombay having been completely satisfied with the progress and achievements of the young Prince, soon decided to hand over complete powers of administration into his hands, and, accordingly, Colonel J. M. Hunter, the then Political Agent in Kathiawar, in a famous Durbar, specially held for the purpose in Wankaner, announced the decision of Government to place the reins of administration in the hands of His Highness the Rajsaheb on March 18, 1899.

In the very first year of His Highness's reign the State was confronted with one of the direst famines that ever visited Western India. The monsoon of 1899 failed entirely, and consequently the State was unprepared for the terrible catastrophe which followed. The Durbar energetically took up the work of famine relief, imported a large amount of grain and fodder, together with good bullocks, from Malwa. It made large advances to cultivators by way of *taccari*, and started several famine relief works in order to provide employment for the labouring classes. The Jasvantsar and Vinaysagar tanks were constructed in this year. Owing to these heavy charges the State was compelled to incur a debt of about

HIS HIGHNESS SIR AMARSINHJI, K.C.I.E., MAHARANA RAJSAHIB OF WANKANER.

HIS HIGHNESS SIR AMARSINHJI, K.C.I.E., MAHARANA RAJSAHIB OF WANKANER.

YUVARAJ SHRI PRATAPSINHJI AND HIS YOUNGER BROTHERS.

five lakhs of rupees, on Government loan, and during the succeeding years the State had to practise the greatest economy in order to pay off the liability incurred.

The lesson of the severe famine of 1899 was not lost upon His Highness. Since then the State has been regularly storing a large quantity of cheap grains in specially constructed pits, and it has also been keeping a considerable amount of fodder in store by building large stacks of hay in good seasons to meet future contingencies. Since the famine of 1899 there have been not less than three famines and lean years, but during all these, owing to the foresight of the present Ruler, it has been possible for the State to meet them all successfully.

His Highness the Rajsaheb was invited to the Imperial Coronation Durbar at Delhi in 1911, and in view of the success which His Highness had been able to achieve in the administration of his State, His Imperial Majesty was pleased to confer upon him the insignia of a Knight Commander of the Most Eminent Order of the Indian Empire. On the outbreak of the war with Germany in 1914 His Highness the Rajsaheb, as an outcome of his attachment and loyalty to the Throne, placed the entire resources of his State at the disposal of His Majesty, and also offered his personal services on the battle fronts. As soon as the Bombay branch of the Imperial Relief Fund was started to afford help to distressed and disabled soldiers, His Highness the Rajsaheb subscribed a sum of Rs. 4,000, and convened a public meeting of Wakaner citizens at which Rs. 2,800 more were subscribed. His Highness further subscribed a sum of Rs. 1,000 for providing artificial limbs to Indian soldiers wounded during fighting. A further sum of £200 was presented to His Royal Highness the Prince of Wales's War Relief Fund; Rs. 1,000 more were subscribed to the Bombay branch of the Imperial War Relief Fund; and a further sum of Rs. 500 was offered to the Hindu Division of the St. John's Ambulance Corps, Bombay. To the Women's Branch of the War Relief Fund, opened by Her Excellency Lady Willingdon, Her Highness the Rani Saheb and Raj Matushri (Queen Mother), Ba Shri Jamba Saheb, subscribed Rs. 1,000.

His Majesty's Government was pleased to accept the offer of personal services of His Highness, and a temporary rank of Captain was conferred upon him, together with the rank of Second Lieutenant on the one officer and two cadets who accompanied him. His Highness the Rajsaheb sailed on November 14, 1915, for France in one of His Majesty's troopships, and while His Highness was on a short leave in London he was received in audience by their Imperial Majesties, the King-Emperor and Queen-Empress, on March 14, 1916. His Highness the Rajsaheb subscribed Rs. 3,000 to different War Funds in England at that time.

In 1916 His Highness gave a 60 h.p. Berliet motor-car to the Red Cross Society at Delhi for the use of wounded soldiers. On the occasion of his daughter's marriage in January, 1917, His Highness the Rajsaheb announced a donation of Rs. 5,000 to Lady Willingdon's Women's Branch of the War Relief Fund. In the course of the year a fancy fête and war sale was held at Ahmedabad, to which His Highness the Rajsaheb sent two cubs, one of a lion and the other of a leopard, the proceeds of which were to be devoted to the War Relief Fund. In March, 1917, His Highness subscribed Rs. 50,000 to the Indian War Loan, with a further offer that the interest on half the amount was, during the continuance of the war, to be placed at the disposal of His Excellency Lord Willingdon for such use in connection with the war as His Excellency deemed proper. During the same year a committee was appointed to encourage recruiting and to induce the subjects of Wankaner to invest in the War Loan. A total of Rs. 1,26,000 was subscribed to the War Loan owing to the efforts of this committee. Liberal concessions were announced to those who were willing to enrol themselves as recruits for the army. A sum of Rs. 5,300 was offered to Queen Mary's Technical School for disabled Indian soldiers at Bombay, and a further sum of £200 (Rs. 3,000) was placed at the disposal of His Imperial Majesty the King-Emperor on His Highness' birthday in 1917 for such purposes in connection with the war as His Majesty thought proper. Three Indian cavalry horses and two mounted infantry ponies were presented to the Government from the State paddock. A sum of Rs. 4,000 was collected on December 12, 1917, towards the "Our Day" Fund. In May, 1918, in response to the stirring call for men and money made from all parts of the Empire by the Prime Minister, Mr. Lloyd George, His Highness the Rajsaheb remitted to His Excellency the Viceroy a sum of Rs. 20,000 as a contribution towards the general expenses of the war. In March, 1919, His Highness contributed Rs. 5,000 to the Imperial Indian Relief Fund.

His Highness the Rajsaheb was obliged to return to India in July, 1916, in order to take part in the wedding ceremony of his eldest daughter, Ba Shri Takhtakunverba Saheb, with His Highness the Maharaja Shri Purnachandra Bhanj Deo of Mayurbhanj, the premier State of Orissa. In August, 1916, the *Samurtan* (betrothal) ceremony was performed at Wankaner by a deputation headed by the Maharaja's uncle, Shri Dam Chandra Bhanj Deo, and January 27, 1917, was fixed as the auspicious day of the marriage. The marriage party, consisting of several distinguished Princes and European officers, arrived at Wankaner by a special train on January 26th, and the ceremony was performed with great pomp and splendour on the day following.

Shortly after the marriage ceremony, Rao Bahadur Nathabhai A. Desai, Chief *Karbhari* of the State, who had served the State honestly and faithfully for a period of nearly 18 years, requested His Highness to be relieved of his duties owing to failing health, and His Highness the Rajsaheb, while accepting the resignation, appointed him advisor to the State with the view of continuing his connection with the State, and as a mark of appreciation of his long and meritorious services. Mr. Devshanker J. Dave, who had been employed as Deputy *Karbhari* under Mr. Nathabhai for the previous four years, was appointed to succeed him, as he had by dint of his fine character and ability already won the esteem and regard of His Highness the Rajsaheb.

In January, 1918, His Highness the Rajsaheb was granted a personal salute of 11 guns, and the permanent rank of honorary Captain in His Majesty's army. His Excellency the Viceroy, in a congratulatory telegram, informed His Highness that His Most Gracious Majesty was pleased to confer on him the above distinctions in recognition of his valuable services rendered in connection with the war. His Highness, in view of these personal honours, is now entitled to all the complimentary honours due to Chiefs of first-class States in Kathiawar, and his *Karbhari* is entitled to be styled as "Diwan."

His Highness the Rajsaheb has three Kumars (sons) and three Kunvaries (daughters). The eldest and heir-apparent, K. S. Pratapsinhji, aged 12 years, is now studying at the Rajkumar College and is progressing very favour-

THE STATE OF WANKANER.

Bird's-eye View of Wankaner City.

THE STATE OF WANKANER.

1. The Amar Villas and Lasbendra Villas Palaces. 2. The Ranjit Villas Palace.

THE STATE OF WANKANER.

1. The Jadeshwar Temple. 2. The Wankaner High School.

ably in his studies. The eldest daughter, Ba Shri Takhtakunverba Saheb, is now Maharani of Mayurbhanj. The names of the other two Kumars are K. S. Chandrabhanusinhji and K. S. Rasik Kumar.

The State is divided into four *mahals*, called Tithwa, Mesaria, Lunsar, and Talpad. The revenue system in force is what is popularly called *bhagbatai*, in which the State share is levied partly in kind and partly in cash, the proportion varying according to the nature of the soil, but a cash assessment system has been introduced of late in a few villages.

The principal crops are *juvari*, *bajri*, cotton, pulses, sesamum, *gram*, wheat, barley, and sugar-cane, of which cotton plays an important part in the export trade. The "Kanmeri," or Wagadio variety of cotton, which, like the "Wadhwan" type, has a long staple, is grown with considerable success in the State.

In order to encourage habits of thrift amongst the cultivators, and also to provide means for giving them loans at a moderate rate of interest, His Highness decided to establish an agriculturists' co-operative bank. The year 1910 seemed to present a favourable opportunity for commencing the scheme, and at a meeting held at Wankaner it was resolved that each occupier should contribute Rs. 10 per *santi* (about 30 acres) of land held by him for a period of four years, the State agreeing to pay a similar amount at the same time. The amount thus collected was to be utilized in granting loans to cultivators under certain limitations. Nine years have since elapsed and the bank is now working very satisfactorily.

The Durbar has also established a model experimental farm of about 90 acres situated on the banks of the river Machhu, near Kerala, and, in addition, a separate farm, established some years ago at Rampara Vidi for the breeding of good strains of cattle.

On the whole the State is making steady progress in agriculture, as the following figures will show: At the commencement of the Agency administration (1881) there were 21,333 acres under cultivation and 743 wells were in use; at the commencement of the present rule (1899) the respective figures were 70,073 acres and 1,483 wells, and in 1918 they were 87,252 acres and 1,985 wells.

The average annual revenue and expenditure for the period covering the years 1877 to 1881 was respectively Rs. 1,67,854; from 1894 to 1898 they were Rs. 2,88,908 and Rs. 3,33,615; and from 1914 to 1918 they were Rs. 5,43,468 and Rs. 4,05,405.

While giving the above figures of expenditure, it is necessary to point out that they include the amounts spent every year upon works of public utility. The construction of roads and bridges, school and hospital buildings, court-houses, jail and office accommodation, travellers' bungalows, and guest-houses, points to the care with which State money is utilized.

The State maintains one hospital at Wankaner and a dispensary at Tithwa, the headquarters of the division of the same name.

The State maintains one High School, 14 vernacular schools for boys, one girls' school, and one Urdu school. Besides these there is one aided *Pathshala* for teaching Sanskrit only, and one indigenous school for children of the Bohra community. Primary education is absolutely free of charge throughout the State, and 30 per cent. of the fees for students is permitted in the High School.

Both civil and criminal courts follow the procedure and adopt the enactments usually enforced in British Indian districts, and the judges frequently obtain assistance by referring to decisions of the High Court of Judicature in India, as well as to the Reports of the Privy Council in England. The *Huzur* Court, the highest authority, is presided over by His Highness the Rajsaheb and the Chief *Karbhari*, or either of them.

The import trade principally consists of cloth, piece-goods, yarn, rice, food-grains, sugar, molasses, salt, spices, groceries, timber, metals, iron, kerosene oil, tobacco, glassware, tanned leather, and various other goods, while the chief exports include cotton, wool, hides, *ghee*, stone, and clay, the principal being cotton and *ghee*.

The handloom weaving industry, which produces coarse country cloth, has been revived here and show signs of returning prosperity. The various kinds of clay found in the State are of proved value, and a company has recently been started, with a capital of more than Rs. 1,00,000, for the manufacture of pottery ware of various kinds. There are also a cotton press and two ginning factories in the State.

BALCHANDRA VILLAS PALACE.

THE STATE OF WADHWAN

WADHWAN, a second-class State in the Jhalawad *prant* of the Kathiawar Political Agency, is bounded on the north by the State of Dhrangadhra, on the south by the States of Chuda and Limbdi, on the east by Limbdi, and on the west by the Muli and Sayla territory. It has an area of 242 square miles, and a population of 35,831 inhabitants, but this does not include the population of 3,300 souls in the *Zilla* villages. About 6 per cent. of the people are Mahomedans, the rest being Hindus and Jains. Banias and Brahmins form the bulk of the population in Wadhwan proper, and their general occupation is trade and service.

The Wadhwan family, who are Jhala Rajputs, trace their ancestry from Rajoji, grandson of Chandrasinhji, Chief of the Dhrangadhra State. Prithiraj, the father of Rajoji, as heir-apparent of Dhrangadhra, was, according to custom, granted Wadhwan in *appanage*, but as he was taken by the Viceroy of Gujarat, as a prisoner, to Ahmedabad, it was not until his death in 1630 that Rajoji assumed possession of Wadhwan and established it as a separate Principality. A successor, named Arjunsinhji, displayed great tact in his administration of the State, which prospered greatly under his rule, but he also extended the area of his possessions by the acquisition of extensive tracts of land adjoining Wadhwan.

Upon his death in 1739, his wife, Dev Kunvarba, sacrificed her life on the funeral pyre of her late husband, and in commemoration of the event a beautiful temple was erected, to which newly-married couples, connected with Wadhwan, resort for the purpose of offering worship.

Thakore Arjunsinhji was followed successively by Sabalsinhji, Chandrasinhji, and Prithiraj, all of whom were constantly engaged in feuds with Dhrangadhra, Limbdi, and other neighbouring States. Wadhwan was placed under British protection at the time of the Kathiawar Settlement in 1807.

Jalamsinhji became entitled to the *gadi* on the death of his father, Prithiraj, in 1807, but as he was then an infant the management of State affairs was entrusted to his mother, Bai Rajba. This lady was a most capable administrator, and she made a distinguished name for herself by her efforts to repair the great damage done to the State and its capital city during many years of warfare. Her son, Jalamsinhji, was unfortunately removed by death in 1827, just at the time that he was about to take over the reins of government. He left a son, Rajsinhji, who was born in 1826, and Bai Rajba retained the control of the State until 1823, when a dispute arose between her and Baji Rajba, the mother of the infant heir, as to the guardianship of the latter. Baji Rajba was eventually entrusted with the task, and although she endeavoured

THAKORE SAHIB JORAWARSINHJI JASVATSINHJI, OF WADHWAN.

THE STATE OF WADHWAN.

1. Madha Vav. 2. Hava Mahel (Incomplete Palace). 3. Daji Raj High School. 4. Cricket Bungalow.

to promote the interests of the State to the best of her ability she was continually disturbed by Bai Rajba, who made several attempts to be reappointed. Rajsinhji died in 1875, and was succeeded by his grandson, Dajiraj, who was entrusted with ruling powers on attaining his majority in 1881. The young Thakore Sahib quickly won the hearts of his subjects by his painstaking efforts to assist them in every conceivable way, and it is recorded that he inaugurated measures of useful reform and progress, including the construction of works of public utility.

The Thakore Sahib expended a sum of Rs. 30,000 in the construction of schools and dispensaries, and Rs. 75,000 in the erection of a bridge across the river Bhogawa.

He visited Europe in the company of the Assistant Political Agent of Kathiawar, but the experience gained during the tour was destined to be of little real value to him, as he was unfortunately called away by death in 1885, and in the twenty-fifth year of his age.

He died on May 25, 1910, without male issue, and Maharana Shri Jasvatsinhji Becharsinhji was declared by Government as the successor to the *gadi*. He was duly installed on March 20, 1912, the installation ceremony being performed by Major F. De B. Hancock, Acting Agent to the Governor, Kathiawad.

The year 1918 was an exceedingly sad one for the Wadhwan family, as on the 5th February Rana Shri Jivansinhji, step-brother of His Highness the Thakore Sahib, died after a protracted illness, and on the 22nd of the same month the Maharana himself passed away at Bombay at the comparatively early age of 42 years. His Highness was greatly respected by a large circle of friends, and his subjects realized their irreparable loss of a capable Ruler and sincere friend.

The Minor Thakore Sahib Jorawarsinhji, who was born on July 23, 1899, was then a student at the Rajkumar College at Rajkot, and the control of the State was placed in the hands of Khan Bahadur Syed Shamsuddin Kadri, I.S.O., as Administrator. The other members of the family of the late Maharana are: Kumars Sahibs Karansinhji, Banesinhji, Surasinhji, and Harishchandrasinhji, and Kunvari Shri Nand Kunvarba.

Two most important events took place in the State in the early portion of the year 1919. The first was the betrothal of His Highness the minor Thakore Sahib to the Kunvari of the Rajadiraj of Shahpura, and the other was the marriage of his sister.

The betrothal ceremony was performed in the city of Wadhwan on February 3, and the alliance is noteworthy on account of the fact that it is the first time in the annals of the Wadhwan State that a daughter of the distinguished Sesodia family of Mewar has been connected with the Jhalas of Wadhwan. The marriage of the Kunvari Shri Mati Nandkunvarba Saheba with the Maharaj Kumar Birsinhji of Orchha was celebrated on March 4, and all the customary ceremonials were carried out according to established usage.

The minor Thakore Sahib having completed his course of education, subsequently received instruction in the details of administrative work in the Revenue, Judicial, and Executive Department of the State, and two months prior to his investiture with ruling powers he toured through India with his companion, Capt. R. P. Henstock.

The present Thakore Sahib Jorawarsinhji Jasvatsinhji attained his majority on July 23, 1919, and in due course he received an intimation from the Government that ruling powers would be conferred upon him at an early date.

The ceremony of installation took place at Wadhwan on January 16, 1920, in the presence of a large and distinguished company, including a number of brother Chiefs and Princes, British officials, and others.

The marriage of the Thakore Sahib took place at Shahpura on February 22, 1920, with Kunvari Shri Laxmikunverba, daughter of His Highness Sir Naharsinhji, K.C.I.E., Raja-dhi-raj Saheb of Shahpura, in Mewar.

His Highness left Wadhwan for Shahpura by special train on February 20th, and returned to his palace with his bride on the 26th of the same month.

The State of Wadhwan consists of a flat plain, unbroken by hills, and although there is a comparatively large quantity of land capable of cultivation the area under crops is frequently less than it should be, owing to recurring seasons of drought, and the hardships caused by famines. The total area brought under cultivation in 1918 was 1,08,079 acres, and it comprised the following: cotton, 70,548 acres; *jowar*, 14,156 acres; *bajri*, 19,528 acres; wheat, 507 acres; *gram*, 159 acres; and miscellaneous, 3,181 acres.

Wadhwan has earned a reputation for its indigenous soap, which is made in 12 factories, and then exported to various places in Kathiawar and Gujarat, to the value of Rs. 60,000 annually. The *khatris* of Wadhwan, Vastadi, Khodu, and Nagnesh are professional dyers, who produce several kinds of coloured dresses, which are still popular with the women of Kathiawar.

Primary education is entirely free in the State.

The financial year of the State commences on November 1st, and the income for the 12 months ending on October 31, 1919, was Rs. 5,86,023, while the disbursements were Rs. 5,14,551. This last amount was considerably greater than in 1918–19, but the increase was caused by additional expenditure at the marriage of His Highness, and also the high prices paid for practically all commodities.

The State enacts its own laws for the administration of justice in civil and criminal actions, and the Courts in existence are: (1) the Nagnesh Thandar Court; (2) the Nyayadhish Court; (3) the Sar Nyayadhish Court; (4) the Huzur Court.

In common with other Native States in India, Wadhwan manifested its devotion to the cause of the Allies in the world's Great War by doing its utmost to subscribe money, collect gifts, and enlist recruits, but a succession of unfavourable seasons naturally had a prejudicial effect upon this noble work. Subscriptions were sent to various funds from the commencement of hostilities, and the following statement contained in the Administration Report for the year 1919–20 may be of interest.

The total contributions by the State for war purposes may be summarized as under: Rs. 10,202-15-0 to the Imperial Indian Relief Fund, Bombay branch; Rs. 2,302 to the Imperial Indian Relief Fund, Women's branch; Rs. 5,269 to the motor ambulance fleet; Rs. 6,000 to the Jhalawad Red Cross Fund; Rs. 600, for clothes and medical treatment for the Indian Sepoys on the front; Rs. 522-15-9, the value of articles sent to the Great War Sale and Fête, Bombay Women's branch; Rs. 240, the value of articles sent to the Ahmedabad Fancy Fête; Rs. 15,000, contribution to the "Our Day" Fund. Rs. 283-7-9, contribution to the "Our Day" Fund at Rajkot; Rs. 182 to the Dhar State War Fête; Rs. 550 to the "Our Day" Kathiawar Lucky Bag, Rajkot; Rs. 323 to the Recruiting Fund.

THE STATE OF WADHWAN.

1. Hadi Ma Temple. 2. Ranakdevi Temple. 3. Wadhwan City.

Rs. 500 to the Poona Pageant and Fête; Rs. 1,000, the value of arms and ammunition supplied to Her Excellency Lady Willingdon; Rs. 1,000, contribution to the Silver Wedding Fund of Their Imperial Majesties, for the education of the children of Indian soldiers who have fallen in war; Rs. 2,200 to Queen Mary's Technical School for disabled soldiers; Rs. 1,575 to the Jhalawad branch of the Women's Relief Fund (by monthly instalments); Rs. 1,000 to the Imperial Relief Fund; Rs. 631, contribution to the Peace "Celebration Fund," and making a total of Rs. 49,381-5-9.

The sums of Rs. 3,00,000 and R. 1,56,790 were respectively subscribed to the first and second Indian War Loan Funds.

Substantial concessions were offered to encourage the enlistment of recruits for the Kathiawar contingent, and a special officer was deputed to visit each district in the State for the purpose of obtaining men for the colours. The news of the signing of the armistice in November 1918 was received with the greatest enthusiasm in Wadhwan. Thanksgiving services were attended by all classes of the people in every village, and at the invitation of the administrator 1,600 girls and boys walked in procession through the streets of the city, singing songs of joy to the accompaniment of bands of music, and finally assembling in a large marquee, where they were presented with gifts, including books and sweets.

The State pays to the British Government as under: *peshkashi*, the sum of Rs. 25,922-8-0; *zortalbi*, Rs. 2,682; Ahmedabad *sukhdi*, Rs. 87-0-8, *jama* and local fund cess for the villages in the Dhandhuka Taluka, Rs. 9,523-1-0; summary Settlement cess for wantas in the Viramgam and Sanand Talukas, Rs. 873-15-10.

The State receives: Rs. 1,033-12-0, *jama* from the *Talukdars* of Gundiala, Jhampodar, Jhamar, Kherali, and Bhalala; Rs. 2,431-8-0, *jama bandhi* from Bhayats; Rs. 2,083-4-9, *sudharo* cess from Bhayats; Rs. 2,250, rent from the British Government for the site of Wadhwan Civil Station leased under an agreement; and Rs. 5,000, customs of Wadhwan Civil Station as per agreement with the British Government.

THE STATE OF WADHWAN.

1. Rang Mahel (Palace). 2. Chandra Bhuvan Palace.

THE STATE OF AKALKOT

AKALKOT, a Mahratta State situated on the confines of the Bombay Presidency, is bounded on one side by the Dominions of His Exalted Highness the Nizam. At the beginning of the seventeenth century it formed part of Nizamshai territory at Ahmednagar, but was at a later date taken by the Moghul Emperors and given by them as a grant to Shahu, the Mahratta king, who transferred it to the founder of the Akalkot dynasty.

The Rulers of Akalkot thus became feudatories of the Satara *Raj* or kingdom, and claim a proud descent from the great Raja Shivaji, Ruler of the Mahrattas, through his grandson, Shahu, Raja of Satara. This story forms an interesting episode, and it is referred to in all histories of the Mahratta Empire.

Raja Shivaji, the founder of that Empire, died in 1680, leaving two sons, Sambhaji and Rajaram, the former of whom succeeded his father, but was not long afterwards captured and slain by the Emperor Aurungzeb, while his infant son, Shahu, was also made a prisoner and taken to Aurungzeb's Court where he remained for several years. After the death of the *Padshaha*, Shahu was liberated and returned to claim his kingdom, but in this he was opposed by Tarabai, widow of Rajaram, who ruled the Mahratta Empire in the absence of Maharaja Shahu.

During Shahu's march southwards, his army was attacked by a force commanded by Sayaji, *Patil* of Parad, an adherent of Tarabai, but fortune smiled on Shahu, and Sayaji was defeated and slain. After the battle the widow of the Patil surrendered to the victor, and throwing herself and her three children at his feet, implored his forgiveness. Shahu, touched with pity for the fatherless little ones, agreed as a mark of gratitude to God for his victory, to take the eldest orphan, Ranoji, and adopt him as his own son, and to this proposal the mother gladly acceded. The lad was brought up as a soldier, becoming much attached to his father by adoption, and in course of time he was successful in several warlike actions. Shahu changed the boy's name to Fatehsinh, and, besides conferring on him the hereditary title of "Raja," and his (Shahu's) own surname of "Bhosle," gave him the State of Akalkot, made him *Senapati*, or General-in-Chief of his army, Fatehsinh thus being always kept in close association with the Raja Saheb.

This Fatehsinh, first of the line, passed away in 1760, and after his death the Rulers of the Akalkot *gadi* were as follows :—Shahaji I, Fatehsinh II, Maloji I, Shahaji II, Maloji II, Shahaji III, and the present Ruler, Fatehsinh III.

The last-named prince, Captain Meherban Shrimant Fatehsinhrao Shahaji, alias Bapu Saheb Raje Bhosle, is therefore the third Fatehsinh to succeed, and the eighth Raja of the line. He is the son of Ganpatji Raje Bhosle of Kurla, a direct descendant of Shahaji I and was born on August 24, 1894. In 1898 Shahaji III having died without a son, this boy was chosen by the British Government to succeed, and his adoption into the elder line by the widow of the late Raja was also permitted. Being then 4½ years of age he was placed by Government in the charge of an English lady, named Miss Moxon, who controlled his upbringing and education until his thirteenth year, and it may be added that the Raja has always shown the most loving gratitude and filial affection towards his early instructress.

In 1907, when nearly 13 years of age, the young Raja Saheb was sent for further studies to the Rajkumar College, Rajkot where he remained for about three years. During this period the College authorities spoke highly of his conduct and abilities, and, on his leaving Rajkot at the age of 15½, he took with him many well-earned prizes, having also, young as he was, carried off the highest honour of all, by passing with honours the final diploma examination.

Shortly after this time the Raja Saheb remained for a few months with a young relative under the charge of Captain Tate of the Political Department, at Kolhapur, and of this officer both pupils have many pleasant memories.

In June 1911 the Raja Saheb joined the Imperial Cadet Corps at Dehra Dun which was then commanded by Major R. L. Ricketts, 10th Lancers, a gentleman for whom the Raja always felt the greatest affection and esteem. By the end of March 1914 Raja Fatehsinhrao's military training was completed by successfully passing the final examination for a Commission, which in due course was granted to him. While at Dehra Dun, the young Raja continued his training in polo, cricket, tennis, and shooting, sports in which he is much interested. He and his brother cadets had the opportunity of meeting many first-class players in various polo matches, thus enabling them to acquire considerable proficiency in the game, and during his last year the Raja Saheb was a member of the Imperial Cadet Corps' polo team. Of all sports, however, shooting has always been his favourite, and although at Dehra Dun there was not much opportunity for him to hunt large game, he has recently been able to obtain a fair amount of this sport.

During his stay at Dehra Dun, the Raja Saheb had the honour of being officially

CAPTAIN MEHERBAN SHRIMANT FATEHSINH SHAHAJI, alias BAPU SAHIB RAJE BHOSLE, RAJE SAHIB OF AKALKOT.

1. SHRIMANT RAJE SAHIB, SHRIMATI SOUBHAGYAVATI RANI SAHIB, YUVRAJ VIJAYSINH, AND SHRIMATI LEELAVATI RAJA AKKA SAHIB.
2. YUVRAJ MEHERBAN SHRIMANT VIJAYSINH.
3. "FATTESINH MAHAL," RAJE SAHIB'S NEW PALACE AT AKALKOT.

THE STATE OF AKALKOT.

1. Raje Sahib with State Officials. 2, 3. Armoury Hall in the Old Palace, Akalkot.

THE STATE OF AKALKOT.

1. Raje Sahib's Old Palace at Akalkot. 2. Bronze Fountain near the Palace at Akalkot. 3. Tomb of the Late Raje Sahib at Akalkot.

present at Their Majesties' Coronation Durbar at Delhi in 1911, the Imperial Cadet Corps having the proud privilege of forming the Royal escort at all great functions during the ceremonies. He was also on escort duty to His Excellency the Viceroy, Lord Hardinge, on December 23, 1912, when the latter was injured by a bomb, the Raja Saheb's position being quite near to His Excellency.

The Raja Saheb's marriage took place in April, 1912, the bride being Shrimati Tarabai, daughter of the Chief of Kagal (Senior), and niece of His Highness the Maharaja of Kolhapur. He has had a family of four children, two of whom, a boy and girl, survive, the others having died in infancy.

On the conclusion of his military course in May, 1914, the Government sent the Raja Saheb, accompanied by the Rani Saheb and Miss Moxon, for a trip to England. While in that country the Raja Saheb had the honour of a personal interview with Their Majesties the King-Emperor and Queen-Empress, this being the second time such a privilege had been accorded to him, the first occasion being when Their Majesties visited India in 1905 as Prince and Princess of Wales. The Raja of Akalkot was then only eleven years of age, and together with his nephew and companion, Shrimant Bapu Saheb Bhosle of Savantwadi, aged eight, and accompanied by their guardian, Miss Moxon, they were granted a special interview by Their Royal Highnesses. The two little fellows in their gorgeous Durbar dress greatly interested the Prince and Princess and, owing to the boy's command of good English, Their Royal Highnesses were enabled to have a pleasant conversation with them. At the close of the visit the Raja Saheb was presented with a silver-mounted hunting crop and Shrimant Bapu Saheb received a nice book, both of which were gifts from Her Royal Highness the Princess as a memento of the occasion.

In addition to the private reception accorded to the Raja Saheb by Their Majesties, he and his family received a Royal invitation to be present at the ceremony of the trooping of the colours in the presence of Their Majesties, and the Raja Saheb was also personally commanded to a Court at Buckingham Palace. He attended the India Office reception at Whitehall, and was present at a banquet given by the "Overseas" Club. He also had the opportunity of seeing the huge naval review at Spithead just before the opening of hostilities, where he was the guest of the Captain of one of His Majesty's battleships.

Upon the declaration of war between Great Britain and Germany in August, 1914, the Raja Saheb at once offered his personal services to the King-Emperor, and a Commission was subsequently given him in His Majesty's Army, he being posted to the 9th Reserve Cavalry, a Corps affiliated to the 3rd Hussars, which was then at Shorncliffe, near Folkestone. Thanks to his previous training, the Raja Saheb was able at once to be useful in training recruits urgently needed to replenish the ranks of the armies in France. He was placed in command of the 2nd troop of 'D' squadron, then 250 in number, and his work was exactly the same as that of other British Officers of his rank. The Raja Saheb is the only Indian ruling Prince who has personally served and worked with a British regiment during the War; being on the same footing and having the same duties as the regular Officers, a fact of which he is very proud. His superior Officers reported well of him, and he much enjoyed his term of service in the Corps.

After spending some months at Shorncliffe the Raja Saheb earnestly requested to be sent on active service to France, whereupon he was posted to the staff of an Indian cavalry division fighting near Albert and Thiepval in the north-east of France and in close touch with the German line. There, at his own request, he took his turn of duty in the front-line trenches with the other Officers, lived in a dug-out and narrowly escaped death on more than one occasion, but particularly when a German shell fell so near, when he was crossing an exposed situation, that several men were blown to pieces at his very side.

At the end of October, 1915, the Raja Saheb's health being much weakened, he returned with his family to India, where, though no longer personally serving in the army, he was still able to assist Government, after being formally put in possession of his State in August, 1916, in doing his best to secure recruits for the Indian Army. In this work he met with some success, and Akalkot, though a very small State, was only beaten by four or five Principalities out of the total of about three hundred in the Bombay Presidency in the number of recruits that were sent to the colours. Besides this the State of Akalkot had contributed largely to the various War charities by gifts of money and materials.

The Raja Saheb was promoted to the rank of Captain in 1918.

The State of Akalkot is 498 square miles in extent. The area under actual cultivation during the past year was nearly 260,000 acres; and there were only 113 acres of waste land, while forests covered 4,272 acres. *Jowar* (the larger millet) is grown more extensively in the State than any other crop, forming, as it does, the staple food of the people, and very large quantities of this kind of grain are disposed of in States and districts in various parts of India.

The average amount of revenue paid during the past five years was Rs. 5,11,246, and the inhabitants of the State at the census of 1911 were 89,082 in number.

The family of the Raja Saheb consists at present of the Yuvaraj, Meherban Shrimant Vijaysinh Raje Saheb, just five years of age, and his younger sister, Shrimati Leelavati Raja Akka Saheb, aged three.

The State enjoys full powers in civil jurisdiction, but in criminal matters cases brought under a certain section of the Indian Penal Code were, until quite recently, transmitted for trial to the Court of the Political Agent. This practice has, however, ceased, and the State now exercises full criminal jurisdiction. The State of Akalkot has power to make its own laws, and to levy taxes.

The only important Treaty formed by the British Government with the Akalkot State was that of 1820, which guaranteed to the State its province, its dignity, and its uncontrolled sovereign powers which it has exercised since its foundation. Agreements regulating the consumption and sale of opium and other goods, and others dealing with the leasing of the State *abkari* revenue to the British Government for certain fixed periods, have been entered into on various occasions.

Akalkot town, the capital of the State, is seven miles distant from Kadabgaon, a station on the Great Indian Peninsula Railway, with which it is connected by a first-class metalled road. Near the station the State has provided a bungalow and a *dharmashala*, which are reserved for the use of travellers.

At Akalkot itself there are two guest-houses, both fully furnished, one situated near the Raje Saheb's own residence and the other not far from the old Palace. The last-named is situated in a picturesque stone fort with great bastions at each angle, one of which supports the Raje Saheb's Observatory, containing a 10 ft. refractor telescope, the largest of its kind in use in India. The fort walls also serve to guard the State armoury, one of the finest collections of ancient weapons treasured in India and the East. The majority of these date from old Mahratta times, and many of them are now exceedingly scarce and of priceless value.

THE STATE OF AUNDH

THE State of Aundh, under the Political Superintendence of the Collector of Satara in the Bombay Presidency, lies within the Deccan trap area and is 501 square miles in extent. The inhabitants at the census of 1921 were 64,504 in number, and they reside in about 72 scattered villages.

The Chiefs of Aundh bear the title of "Pratinidhi," meaning "the representative of the King," and such officials were entitled to sign and seal papers and to issue orders in the absence of the Ruler.

The post of Pant Pratinidhi was created during the reign of Rajaram, Maharaja of Satara, a younger son of Shivaji, the founder of the Mahratta Empire, and a person holding this office exercised powers over all ministers of the Mahratta Court including the Peshwas. The first occupant of the position under Rajaram was Pralhad Niraji.

Parshuram was the ancestor of the present Pratinidhi family, and he was born in the year 1660, his father being a devotional and pious village officer of Kinhi, named Trimbak Krishna. He began his business life by serving as an ordinary clerk, but his abilities and valour enabled him, during the reign of Rajaram, to repel the attacks of the Moghul Emperor in Maharashtra, and he succeeded in recovering the Satara, Panhala and other fortresses, and in re-establishing the Mahratta power. He had already been created a nobleman, but in view of his meritorious services Rajaram now conferred upon him the title of Pratinidhi, after the death of Pralhad Hirajee, the first holder of the office. Rajaram was succeeded by his wife, Tara Bai, who retained Parshuram Trimbak his Pratinidhi.

Parshuram died in 1718, and was succeeded by his third son, Shrinivas Rao, alias Shripat Rao, who won the favour of Shahu by his brilliant efforts as a soldier fighting many battles in defence of the kingdom. He was succeeded in the year 1746 by Jagatjeevanrao his brother, who carried on independent administration, but he was not so able a man as his late father. The Peshwa about this time decided that all nobles as well as the eight ministers of his kingdom should reside at Poona, and he further declared that in the event of their refusing to comply with his order their posts should be forfeited. Bhawanrao, who, by the way, was an able and courageous man, was one of those who declined to remove, and therefore his position as Pratinidhi was given by the Peshwas temporarily to his cousin, Bhagawantrao. Bhawanrao was subsequently reinstated as Pratinidhi, but he died in 1777, and on the day following his demise, his wife Kashibai gave birth to a son, who was named Parshurampant. Nana Farnavis, a friend of the late Chief, heard of the news, and at once obtained the armorial bearings of the Pratinidhi from the Chhatrapati Maharaj and sent them to be given to Parshurampant. On attaining the age of early manhood the latter proved to be remarkably capable and brave, and he personally manifested great valour when fighting in the battle at Kharda. Baji Rao II subsequently interfered in the private conflicts of the Pratinidhi, even sending Bapu Gokhale to attach his *jagir*, and after many battles had taken place between Parshurampant and Bapu the final struggle took place in the year 1806 at Konegaon, between the Stations of Karad and Masur. This resulted in the capture of the former, who was sent to Poona for imprisonment. His wife Laxmibai, with the help of Appasaheb, Chief of Sangli, endeavoured to induce the British Government to compel Baji Rao to return Pratinidhi's *jagir* which had been illegally attached. In the year 1811 Parshurampant was released, and he was granted a *jagir* of the annual value of Rs. 2,00,000, which now forms the principality of Aundh. About seven years later, when the kingdom of Baji Rao was annexed by the British Government, the Pratinidhi's *jagir* was secured to him, but the supervision of it was placed in the hands of Chhatrapati Maharaja Pratapsinha of Satara. Parshurampant was greatly respected by the British Political Residents, and one of them, in 1820, entered into a treaty with the Pratinidhi in which it was promised that his rank and position would be maintained as they had been since the days of the Peshwas. Having no issue he was permitted by Shahaji Raja of Satara, with the consent of the British Government, to adopt Annaji Hari, the brother of Abaji Hari Kulkarni, of Hivare, to whom he gave the name of Shrinivasrao. Parshurampant died on May 10, 1848, and his tomb may be seen at Mahuli in the sandy tract opposite the temple of Shri Vishweshwar.

He was succeeded by his adopted son Shrinivasrao. After the death of the Raja of Satara Aundh became a feudatory State, as Satara then lapsed to the British Government. During this regime a very great advance was made in the management of the State, as the Chief thoroughly reorganized the State departments and brought the administration more into conformity with British standards.

The next Chief was Parshuram Shrinivas (1902–5), during whose rulership considerable encouragement was given to the improvement of methods of agriculture, the construction of schools and other public buildings, and the opening of means of com-

SHRIMANT BHAWANRAO SHRINIVASRAO, alias BALASAHIB PANDIT PRATINIDHI, B.A. (BOM.), FIRST-CLASS SARDAR OF THE DECCAN, CHIEF OF AUNDH.

THE STATE OF AUNDH.

1. Shrimant Trimbakrao, *alias* Rajesahib Pant Pratinidhi, B.A., LL.B. (Bom.), Heir-Apparent to the Chief of Aundh.
2. Temple of the Goddess Shri Yamai, the Family Deity of the Chief of Aundh, together with the Dipmal (Light Pillar) and Palace.
3. Temple of the Goddess Shri Yamai, on the Mool Peeth Hill.

munication by the making of good roads. Gopalkrishna, his successor, was deposed in 1907 just two years after his accession.

The present Chief, Bhawanrao Shrinivasrao, alias Balasaheb Pandit Pratinidhi, a Deshastha Yajurvedi Brahman by caste, was born on October 24, 1868, and was installed on the *gadi* in the year 1909 in the presence of a very large and distinguished gathering. The Chief was educated at the High School at Satara and at the Deccan College. He graduated as a Bachelor of Arts, and it is noteworthy that he was the first Prince of a Native State in the Southern Mahratta Country to obtain this distinction. The Chief at an early age showed that he not only had an aptitude for learning but that he also possessed natural qualifications which enabled him to make the best possible use of the education which he had acquired. He is an eminently progressive Chief, and there is not a single department in the State which has not been reorganized and improved under the capable supervision of the Pratinidhi.

The Chief is a great and renowned artist. He had a natural liking for Art. He imbibed a great taste for drawing and painting from his very boyhood, and during the course of his education he developed this art to a remarkable extent. His drawings are very much appreciated by the people. As the author of the unique work of "Picture Ramayan," he is greatly admired for his high artistic skill as displayed in the illustrations. The Chief has promised a donation of Rs. 1,00,000 towards the publication of a new and a critical edition of the Mahabharat which has been undertaken by the Bhandarkar Oriental Research Institute, Poona, under his patronage. He has been contributing Rs. 5,000 every year towards this great work since its commencement, and has also undertaken to prepare himself the illustrations required for it.

The whole of the State, with the exception of three villages, has been surveyed, and the revenue settlement, which is fixed for a period of 30 years, is so light a burden that complaints are rarely heard. The demand for the year 1919-20 amounted to Rs. 2,77,481, and of this sum Rs. 2,57,882 were recovered. The total land under cultivation in the State is about 2,85,000 acres, and the principal crops are the Indian millet, *jowar*, wheat, cotton, sugar-cane, *gram*, linseed, and ground nuts. The Chief is deeply interested in fostering the cause of agriculture, and an Agricultural Inspector has been appointed to deliver lectures and to teach holders of land new methods of cultivation, the use of modern agricultural implements, the selection of pure seeds and the application of artificial manures. Under the auspices of the Chief several new industries have been established in recent years. The largest of these concerns is the factory and works of Messrs. Kirloskar Brothers, Limited, situated at Kirloskarwadi, near Kundal road station. These were established more than thirty years ago at Belgaum, but when the site on which they were built was required by the municipality, they were at the instigation and with the assistance of the Chief of Aundh, removed to a suitable locality in the State now under notice.

His Excellency the Governor of Bombay visited the factory in July, 1920, and he was conducted through the offices, smithy, machine, and pattern shops, foundry, implement shop and finishing sections, and the electric power house. An inspection was then made of the model village of Kirloskarvadi, founded for the employees, which is situated on the slope of a small hill and presents a most picturesque appearance. His Excellency was also shewn the stores for the sale on co-operative principles of grain and cloth, the sports ground, library and school and the dwelling-houses which are lighted by electricity. Special interest was taken in the large stock of modern agricultural implements, including seed drills, iron ploughs, pumps, hoes, harrows, and machines for cutting fodder, and grinding corn as well as sugar-cane. There is also a glass factory in the Kundal *taluka* in which the manufacture of lamp-ware such as chimneys, globes, and other similar articles is carried on. The Aundh State Laboratory manufactures chemicals for photographic and other purposes; the preparation of sugar from jaggery is now being taken in hand, and steps are being taken for the crystallization of sugar and the extraction of oil and the making of transparent soap. A large number of persons are engaged in their homes in weaving blankets, *khadies*, *saris*, and other articles of apparel, and in order to make this industry more profitable the weavers are to be supplied with improved types of looms.

With the object of encouraging industrial enterprises and with the view of inducing the inhabitants of the State to cultivate habits of thrift the Co-operative Societies Act No. II of 1912 was introduced into Aundh in the year 1917.

The Chief exercises full civil and criminal powers. Criminal matters are dealt with in the *Huzur* court presided over by the Chief, who exercises the powers of a High Court. In addition to these there are the courts of the District Magistrate, a Sub-judge and Magistrates of the 1st, 2nd and 3rd classes.

There are four Courts for the trial of civil actions, and objections to the decisions of these tribunals are heard by the Appellate Courts of the Chief of Aundh and the District Judge. With the object of providing speedy and inexpensive settlement of petty civil and criminal cases the Chief has introduced the system of village *Panchayats*, the members of which are selected from the most intelligent persons in each village.

Public instruction is given in the Sri Yemai Shrinivas High School, three middle schools, thirty-four primary schools for boys, four of a similar character for girls, a Mahomedan school, one low-caste school, and three aided schools. In addition to these, however, there are thirty-four compulsory schools in various parts of the State, the pupils being taught up to the vernacular Standard IV, and subsequent instruction is given in ordinary primary schools.

The gross revenue of the State, based on the average of the past five years, is Rs. 3,31,871 including alienations, local funds and all other items. The principality does not pay tribute to the Paramount Power nor to any other State.

The Chief has three sons and one daughter. The heir-apparent, Trimbakrao, alias Rajesaheb, is a B.A., LL.B. of the Bombay University. He received training in administrative work according to British method, his instructor being the Political Agent at Satara. During the year 1920 Rajesaheb, who is in his twenty-eighth year, expressed a desire to proceed to England in order that he might obtain a knowledge of economic and industrial problems in the old country, and the Chief, realizing the immense advantages which might ultimately accrue to the State as a result of the visit gladly gave his consent to the proposal.

THE STATE OF ALI-RAJPUR

THE State of Ali-Rajpur, one of the guaranteed Chief-ships under the Political Agent in the Southern States of the Central India Agency, is bounded on the north by the district of the Panch Mahals and the State of Baria in the Bombay Presidency; on the south by the Narbada river which divides it from the State of Barwani and the district of Khandesh; on the west by the State of Chhota-Udaipur; and on the east by the States of Gwalior, Indore, Jhabua and Jobat. The ruling family of the State belongs to the famous Rathor clan of Rajputs, and are descended from the same stock as Jodhaji, the founder of the State of Jodhpur. The Ali-Rajpur State itself is traditionally believed to have been founded in the years from 1414 to 1443 by a chief named Anand Dev or Ude Dev. A descendant of this prince was the founder in 1644 of the family of the Sondwa Thakur from whom the present ruler of Ali-Rajpur is descended. British supremacy was established early in the nineteenth century, during the rulership of Rana Pratap Singh I (1765–1818), and about the year 1817 the State was practically controlled by the minister named Musafir Makrani, who was in reality an adventurer. On the death of the Chief in 1818 the Makrani became Manager of the State for Jaswant Singh, a posthumous son of Pratap Singh. This arrangement was opposed by Kesri Singh, a nephew of the late Chief, who desired to succeed to the *gadi* but the British authorities upheld the claims of Jaswant Singh and placed the Makrani in the position of Superintendent of the State during the period of minority. A written engagement was at the same time entered into between the Superintendent and the Paramount Power, which contained the following among other clauses: "That Bhabra shall be given up to Kesri Singh; and that in exchange for the fixed sum of Rs. 20,000 tribute to the State of Dhar, the exact amount of the taxes of the Raj of Ali as collected by me shall be given up to the Government of Dhar; that the charge of keeping the road through the Raj of Ali free from the danger of plunderers belongs to me; and that without the orders of the British Government I will on no account maintain any intercourse with other Rajas." Instead of an amicable settlement of disputes with Dhar being arrived at, the proposals contained in the above-mentioned document led to endless troubles between the officials of the two States in question, but in 1821 a settlement was effected, the terms being that the Dhar Durbar should hand over the *pargana* of Berasia to British management, that the Government should pay to Dhar the sum of Rs. 10,000 (Hali) yearly in lieu of tribute and that it should collect Rs. 11,000 from Ali-Rajpur, all feudal rights of Dhar over Ali-Rajpur ceasing with this new arrangement.

Rana Jaswant Singh died in 1862, dividing by his will the State of Ali-Rajpur to his two sons in equal shares, but the Government set aside the document and declared that the elder son Ganga Dev should succeed as ruler, suitable provision being at the same time made for his younger brother. Ganga Dev was deposed on the ground of incompetency in the year 1869, and the State was again placed in the hands of a Superintendent, Rup Dev, the brother of the Chief, being also appointed to a place in the administration. Ganga Dev passed away about two years later and was followed by his brother Rup Dev, whose rule of about ten years was devoid of any events of striking importance. On his death in 1881 without issue, the British Government agreed that, in the absence of a *sanad* of adoption, a youth named Bijai Singh, of the Sondwa Thakur's family, should be raised to the *gadi*. Objections to the proposed appointment were raised by a number of the Makranis as well as by the Thakur of Phulmal (Jitsingh), who was desirous of following the late rulers on the *gadi*. The Makranis, who by this time had lost much of their former power, were joined by the Bhils, who were in a most discontented state owing to the unwarrantable exactions of assessments made upon them by district officials. Both tribes, therefore, were ripe for rebellion, and after throwing in their lot with Chhitu Bhil, *Patel* of Sorwa, and Bhawan Tarvi of Tokria-Jhiran, villages in Ali-Rajpur, they placed themselves under the command of Jit Singh and began to plunder the *parganas* of Nanpur, Chhaktala, and Bhabra. Dad-Mahomed, the actual leader of the Makranis, was powerful enough to add to his followers with a considerable number of men from Gujarat, the district of Khandesh and the State of Chhota-Udaipur. The British Government was at last compelled to interfere, and a detachment, composed of the Malwa Bhil corps and the Central India Horse, attacked the rebels at the Sorwa Pass, where Dad-Mahomed was killed and the marauders were utterly routed. Jit Singh managed to escape to Gujarat where he died, and his State became forfeited to the Ali-Rajpur Durbar. Chhitu Bhil and Bhawan Tarvi were imprisoned at Indore. Rana Bijai

Singh died in 1890 without issue, and his cousin Pratap Singh (the present Ruler), son of Thakur Bhagwan Singh of Sondwa, was selected by the Government of India to succeed to the *gadi*. He was born in September, 1881, and his accession was recognized on June 10, 1891. He was educated at the Daly College, Indore, and after a most successful scholastic career he in 1901 was entrusted with the administration of the two *parganas* of Nanpur and Khatali. He was honoured in 1902 by being appointed a Magistrate of the first class, and full ruling powers were granted to him in 1904. His Highness the Raja Saheb was married in the year 1900 to the daughter of the late Thakur Bahadur Singh of the Kathiwara Estate, and again, in the year 1902, to the daughter of the late Maharawal Chandra Singh, uncle of the present Chief of the Chhota-Udaipur State in the Rewa Kantha Agency. The second Rani Saheba has since died. The Raja's son and heir, Rajkumar Fateh Singhji, was born on August 22, 1904, by the senior Rani Saheba. The Raja Saheb has also two daughters, with the elder of whom a marriage has been arranged with the Raja Saheb of Nilgiri, a feudatory State in Orissa.

The grand Imperial Durbar held in December, 1911, in connection with the Coronation ceremonies of Their Imperial Majesties, with its gorgeous functions and processions, its reception of Indian Chiefs, its garden parties and other pleasurable social entertainments, will long live in the memory of H.H. the Raja Saheb of Ali-Rajpur. H.H. the Raja Saheb journeyed from Rutlam by special train, engaged for him and H.H. the Rana Sabeb of Barwani, and they were received on arrival at their destination by a number of British Officers and other distinguished persons. On December 11th H.H. the Raja Saheb was highly delighted when he heard that the hereditary title of Raja was to be conferred upon him, and on the morning of the 12th the Chief had the honour of receiving the Durbar gold medal at the hands of His Imperial Majesty. A special Durbar was held at the palace in Alirajpur on December 29th, when *Sardars* and officials of the State as well as a large number of private individuals assembled to offer their congratulations to H.H. the Raja Saheb upon the honoured distinction which has recently been bestowed. Early in February, 1912, the Hon. Mr. O'Dwyer (subsequently Lieutenant-Governor of the Province of the Punjab) formally opened the "Edward VII" School buildings which were erected to commemorate the memory of the late lamented King-Emperor.

On June 4th the Raja Saheb received the *sanad* conferring upon him the hereditary title of Raja, which had been announced during the Coronation ceremonies at Delhi in the previous year.

Included in the list of birthday honours bestowed by His Imperial Majesty the King-Emperor in June, 1915, was the name of Raja Saheb Pratap Singhji, who was created a Companion of the Most Eminent Order of the Indian Empire, and it was further stated that the Government of India had decided to extend his judicial powers.

Early in the year 1915, arrangements were made for the marriage of Rajkumar Fateh Singhji, the heir-apparent, with Kunwari Sahiba Rajendrakunwar Ba, the daughter of the Raja Saheb of Devgad-Baria. The betrothal ceremony was performed in open *Durbar* on July 19th in the presence of a large number of distinguished guests.

In October, 1915, H.H. the Raja Saheb travelled to Mhow, where the Agent to the Governor-General in Central India handed to him the insignia of the recently bestowed distinction of C.I.E. and at the same time presented him with the official *sanad* extending his judicial powers.

In 1917 the valuable services rendered by H.H. the Raja Saheb to the St. John's Ambulance Association in India were recognized by His Imperial Majesty the King-Emperor by conferring upon the Chief the Order of the Hospital of St. John of Jerusalem.

On January 1, 1920, His Majesty's Government conferred upon the Raja Saheb a personal distinction of an addition of two guns to his salute, whch was subsequently made permanent on January 1, 1921. The Chief now enjoys a hereditary salute of 11 guns.

H.H. the Raja Saheb was in August, 1918, invited to Indore to meet His Excellency the Viceroy and Lady Chelmsford, and after paying ceremonial visits to His Excellency he joined with other Central India Chiefs in giving an entertainment to the illustrious visitors in the Daly College Hall.

The Rajkumar received his early training in the home of his parents, but in July, 1916, he was admitted as a student of the Daly College, Indore. The severance of the affectionate ties which bound him to his revered father and mother was naturally a source of great grief, but H.H. the Raja Saheb did not allow his parental feelings to interfere with his sense of duty to his son, and it was therefore on this account that he insisted upon a course of collegiate study. In August, 1918, when the Daly College was placed at the disposal of the Government for military purposes the Raj Kumar Saheb was transferred to the College at Rajkot. After spending a year at Rajkot, where he found the climate uncongenial to his health, he returned to Alirajpur in September, 1919. He is, at present, prosecuting his studies under the guidance of a European tutor.

The State of Ali-Rajpur, about 837 square miles in extent, is almost entirely hilly in character, although there are several ranges of low hills densely covered with jungle, which are interspersed with valleys, some of which are moderately fertile. The main ridges stretch diagonally from east to west but the highest peak does not rise to a higher elevation than 2,200 feet above the level of the sea. With the exception of a few small rivulets, which are dry during the hot weather, the rivers in the State are: the Narbada which forms the southern boundary of the State, the Hatni which flows from north to south, eventually joining the Narbada, and the Sukkad and the Ankhar which discharge themselves into the Hatni.

The inhabitants of the State are over 89,000 in number, and about 90 per cent. of them are Bhils and Bhilalas, who are engaged almost entirely in agricultural pursuits. The State is divided for administrative purposes into five *tahsils* or *parganas*, and each is placed in charge of an Executive Officer called a *Kamasdar*, who has general control over his area, supervising the work of land administration and collecting revenue.

The administration of forests is in the charge of a Departmental Officer who is assisted by Range and Subrange Officers and several guards. The reserved portion is 289 square miles in extent, and it is composed chiefly of mixed species of trees, a large quantity of teak being grown in some areas. A considerable quantity of timber and bamboo is exported to Dohad and Chhota-Udaipur, while the minor products of the forests consisting of *doli*, lac, honey, wax, *safed-musli*, *chironji* and *temru* leaves are disposed of chiefly at Bombay and Dohad in the district of Panch Mahals, and mangoes and *mohwa* flowers are exported in large quantities to the neighbouring States of Dhar, Indore, Gwalior, Jhabua and Barwani. The total receipts during 1919-20 amounted to Rs. 1,15,3[illegible] showing a substantial increase in revenue over the previous year which is attributable

HIS HIGHNESS RAJA PRATAP SINGH, C.I.E., OF ALI-RAJPUR.

THE STATE OF ALI-RAJPUR.

1. Rajkumar Fateh Singh, of Ali-Rajpur. 2. His Highness Raja Pratap Singh on his Favourite Polo Pony "Darbar."
3. His Highness Raja Pratap Singh and the Team with the Cup won at Mhow in the Polo Tournament, March 1920.

Photo by Herzog & Higgins.

THE STATE OF ALI-RAJPUR.

1. The Palace, Ali-Rajpur. 2. The Fateh Club, Ali-Rajpur. 3. Pratap Bhawan (a Guest-house), Ali-Rajpur. 4. The Bridge on the Sukkhar River, near Ali-Rajpur.

to a larger sale of timber, bamboos and miscellaneous produce.

The principal centres of trade in the State are Alirajpur, Bhabra, Nanpur, Khatali, Ambua and Umrali, but goods received at, or despatched from, these places have to be conveyed generally by carts to Dohad and Chhota-Udaipur railway stations—the former on the Rutlam-Godhra branch of the Bombay-Baroda and Central India Railway, and the latter a terminus station of the Miyagam-Chhota-Udaipur section of the Gaekwar's Dabhoi Railway. Dohad is 44 miles from Alirajpur, and a good metalled road is being constructed which is nearing completion, while Chhota-Udaipur is situated about 30 miles distant, and a fair-weather road runs to it from Alirajpur.

Administration of justice in the State is conducted in accordance with the spirit of the Civil and Criminal laws of British India. There are eight Courts of Justice in the State. The police force comprises 258 men, including 75 semi-military Sepoys, five of whom are trained to fire heavy guns on special occasions.

The State maintains one hospital at Alirajpur and a dispensary at Bhabra, both of which are fully equipped with surgical instruments and appliances in addition to an ample stock of medicines.

The gross yearly revenue of the State based on the average of the past five years is Rs. 4,21,568, the chief items of receipts being under the following headings. Land Revenue, Forests, Excise, *Sayar* and Customs.

Some reference must now be made to the assistance rendered by H.H. the Raja Saheb and the people of his State in support of the Allies during the late Great War. As soon as the declaration of war with Germany was publicly made in August, 1914, the Raja Saheb manifested his loyalty to the British Throne by offering his personal services and the resources of the State for the benefit of the Allied cause. With the object of pressing upon the minds of the people the fact that Great Britain had been forced to take up arms, copies in Hindi and Urdu of official correspondence which passed between England and other European Powers prior to hostilities were freely distributed by the Durbar. In response to the appeal issued by His Excellency the Viceroy to the Ruling Chiefs, Nobles and others in India to contribute to the best of their abilities for the alleviation of distress and suffering caused by the war, H.H. the Raja Saheb and H.H. the Rani Saheba subscribed Rs. 5,000 and Rs. 1,000 respectively towards the Imperial Indian Relief Fund. A public meeting of State officials and the people of Alirajpur was held under the presidency of H.H. the Raja Saheb on September 9th when the objects of the Relief Fund were clearly explained, and subscriptions amounting to Rs. 1,500 were collected on the spot. Other meetings of a similar character were held at Bhabra, Nanpur, Ambua, and Khatali, at which the sum of Rs. 907 was received and subsequently remitted to the Political Agent in the Southern States of Central India. Later, in 1919, H.H. the Raja Saheb contributed a further donation of Rs. 5,000 to the (Central) Fund in response to the special appeal made by His Excellency the Viceroy. His Highness the Maharaja Saheb Scindia of Gwalior shortly afterwards launched a scheme for offering to the Allies the hospital ship *Loyalty*, and H.H. the Raja Saheb was glad to have the privilege of contributing Rs. 10,000 to its maintenance. H.H. the Raja Saheb of Ali-Rajpur, together with the neighbouring Chiefs of Dhar, Jhabua and Barwani, approached the military authorities and expressed their willingness to supply despatch riders, bearer corps or motor cars for duty at the front, but the Government of India after due consideration suggested the supply of motor ambulances. As a result of these negotiations six motor ambulances were purchased at a cost of Rs. 36,000, and it was arranged that they should be used in Europe and be employed as near to the fighting line as possible and be in charge of His Highness the Rana Saheb of Barwani. During the year 1915–16, another motor ambulance was added to the six already purchased by the joint contributions of the Chiefs of Barwani, Dhar, Jhabua, and Ali-Rajpur, and the whole convoy was presented personally to His Imperial Majesty the King-Emperor by Captain His Highness Rana Saheb Ranjit Singhji of Barwani. The Ali-Rajpur Durbar consequently paid, as their share Rs 8,650 towards the cost of the ambulances.

KHAN SAHIB SORABJI COWASJI DOTIWALA, DEWAN, ALI-RAJPUR STATE.

His Highness the Raja Saheb was, as has already been observed, extremely anxious that the truth concerning the actual cause of the war should be clearly made known to his subjects, but especially to young people, and in furtherance of this desire he ordered that facsimile copies should be distributed in all schools of the famous "scrap of paper"—the treaty made in 1839 between the principal Powers of Europe which guaranteed the neutrality of Belgium.

In the year 1916–17 His Highness the Raja Saheb contributed Rs. 3,000, being half of the initial cost of converting the Chief's guest-house at Indore into a hospital for convalescent soldiers, and he also took upon himself the burden of meeting one-half of the expenses of maintenance, roughly estimated at Rs. 750 per month; while from January, 1918, he raised his contribution to Rs. 500 per month. The total expenses incurred on this account amounted to Rs. 12,500.

In June, 1918, His Highness the Raja Saheb contributed a sum of Rs. 15,000 for war purposes, and in addition promised to subscribe Rs. 10,000 annually until the close of the conflict.

Among other contributions the following may be mentioned: the sum of Rs. 15,000 subscribed by His Highness the Raja Saheb to the Imperial War Loan Fund; Rs. 35,320, the value of war bonds and post-office cash certificates purchased by the subjects of the State; a sum of Rs. 300 presented by His Highness the Rani Saheba in each of the years 1914, 1915 and 1916, together with Rs. 500 in 1917, to the St. John's Ambulance Fund; Rs. 3,000 by His Highness the Raja Saheb to the "Our Day Fund"; Rs. 3,664, the share of expenses of the Ali-Rajpur State in holding a war fête at Dhar; Rs. 4,480 contributed by the people of the State to a war lottery held at Dhar; Rs. 1,000 subscribed by the Durbar to the Officers' War Hospital at Indore; Rs. 500 to the Kitchener Memorial Fund; Rs. 200 to the Indian St. Dunstan's Hospital Fund; Rs. 3,670 to the Despatch Riders' Fund; Rs. 626 to various bearers' corps; Rs. 1,000 to the Silver Wedding Fund; and Rs. 1,500 to the Disabled Officers' Fund.

THE BALRAMPUR RAJ

THE Estate of Balrampur, with an area of about 1,300 square miles, comprising more than a thousand villages, inhabited by half a million people, is situated in the districts of Gonda, Bahraich and Lucknow, in the United Provinces of Agra and Oudh.

Among the famous clan of Rajputs, the aristocracy of India, there is none which is more celebrated in its traditional and historical records than the Janwars, who are descended from Arjun, one of the five Pandavas mentioned in the ancient epic known as the ***Mahabharata***. The Balrampur family belongs to this clan, and they trace their ancestry to Bariar Shah, the youngest son of a Sombansi Chief, named Raja Mansukh Deo, of Pawagarh, in descent from Arjun. Bariar Shah entered the service of the Mahomedan Emperor of Delhi about the end of the fourteenth century, and as a reward for his meritorious conduct, he received the Cawnpore ***madade*** as a grant. He was also promoted to the rank of ***Risaldar***. In the year 1414 Bariar Shah settled at Ikauna and in the district of Bahraich, and subsequently became the founder of the family of Balrampur. One of his successors, Ganesh Singh, who held the title of Raja (which is said to have been hereditary in the family from the thirteenth century), had a brother named Madho Singh, who, about the middle of the sixteenth century, seized a large extent of territory between the Rapti and Kuana rivers, situated in the district of Gonda, and it was in this area that he established a separate ***raj***. During the reign of the Moghul Emperor Jehangir, Balram Shah, son of Madho Singh, founded the present town of Balrampur.

Passing over the next few years, in which there are not many events of outstanding importance to record, in a general way it may be said, that during the seventeenth century the principality attained great power, and successfully resisted the inroads and exactions of the Wazirs of Oudh, who were bent upon imposing unjust taxation upon the Balrampur Raj. It is ascertained that in 1777 Raja Newal Singh became owner of the ***Raj***, and history establishes the fact that he was one of the most distinguished soldiers of his race. His grandson, Raja Jai Narain Singh, died in 1836 without issue, and was succeeded by Raja Digbijai Singh, who was then 18 years of age. The events of the next few years were not marked by any serious troubles, but, as will be seen later, they were the prelude of stirring episodes which accompanied the horrible massacres of the Sepoy Mutiny of 1857. It may be mentioned here that in February, 1856, the Kingdom of Oudh was annexed by the British Government, and the Raja of Balrampur loyally recognized the new form of government. Mr. (afterwards Sir Charles) Wingfield was at that time Commissioner of the Bahraich Division, which comprised the three civil stations at Bahraich, Gonda and Mullapur. This gentleman had for some time previously noticed that there was considerable unrest among Indian troops, especially at the military station at Sikraura, or Colonelganj, where he resided. His suspicions that a serious rebellion was imminent led him to communicate with the Raja of Balrampur, in whose staunch adherence to the Paramount Power he had supreme confidence. He further made arrangements that, in the event of an actual rising, all British officers in his Division should immediately seek refuge with the Raja of Balrampur. On the 9th of June Mr. Wingfield was perfectly satisfied that the Sepoys had become rebels, and that the lives of Europeans were in great peril. He accordingly set out for Gonda, where he also found a similar danger confronting him. On the following morning the military officers and other officials at Sikraura escaped from the station and proceeded to Balrampur. On the 10th of June Mr. Wingfield, accompanied by several officers from Gonda and Sikraura, reached Balrampur, where he and his party (numbering about 30, including children) were heartily welcomed by the Raja.

The troops stationed at Sikraura and Gonda broke into open mutiny on the 10th and 11th of June, and forthwith began to commit acts of atrocity, at the same time enriching themselves by breaking open and despoiling the public treasury. The whole Province of Oudh was at this juncture in a state of open rebellion ; the Raja was surrounded on all sides by insurgent Chiefs, mutinous soldiers and deadly enemies, and the British authority was superseded by a rebel Government at Lucknow, which was prepared to impose the severest treatment upon all who sympathized with the British. The Raja, notwithstanding the extremely dangerous position in which he was placed, stedfastly refused to have anything to do with the rebels, but, on the contrary, he loyally supported the British in every possible

THE MAHARAJA BAHADUR OF BALRAMPUR.

THE BALRAMPUR RAJ.

THE PALACE, BALRAMPUR.

way in their attempts to crush the rebellion. In view of the possibility of Balrampur being overrun by the mutineers, Mr. Wingfield deemed it advisable to remove his friends to a place of safety, and he accordingly transferred them, under an escort of 500 faithful retainers, under the command of the Raja himself, to Bansi, and subsequently to Gorakhpur, where he arrived on the 26th of June.

The mutiny in Oudh was concluded in December, 1858, by the trans-Ghagra campaign, in which the Raja of Balrampur joined the British forces, under the command of General Sir Hope Grant, he being especially zealous in procuring supplies and obtaining accurate information as to the movements of the rebels, and he remained in this arduous service until the last band of insurgents had, in May, 1859, been driven across the Serwa Pass into Nepal.

The unswerving allegiance of the Raja to the end of the rebellion was suitably recognized in several documents by the Paramount Power, and by many of its officials in high positions, but it may be interesting to quote here the terms of a certificate given by Mr. Wingfield, which contains the following passages: " When, in consequence of the mutiny arising among the troops at Gonda, Kra-ara and Bahraich, the European Civil and Military Officers were compelled to seek safety in flight, they were sheltered and hospitably entertained by the Raja of Balrampur, Raja Digbijai Singh, who, despite the threats of the mutineers, continued to afford them all the aid and protection in his power; and on their deeming Balrampur no longer a safe place of refuge, from its proximity to the insurgents, sent them on, under a strong escort of his own followers, to his relative, the Raja of Bansie, accompanying them half the distance himself.

" For the aid thus generously extended to the British Officers, he is sure, during the temporary abeyance of our rule in Oudh, to be marked out for the vengeance of the mutineers and the malcontent Rajas, who detest him for the attachment he has uniformly shown to our Government. If I succeed in reaching a place of safety, I shall deem it my first duty to bring to the notice of the Government of India the magnanimous conduct of the Raja, and impress on it a sense of the obligations it lies under to him, and point out the proper mode of acknowledging them. If, on the other hand, I am not enabled to plead his cause in person, I earnestly call on the Government to bestow some most signal mark of its favour on the Raja, by conferring the title of Maharaja or some higher degree on him, and by making him a large grant of confiscated lands, or by giving him an *istemraree* grant of the zemindari of Balrampur at a *jumma* of Rs. 50,000."

In recognition of his unswerving allegiance and untiring energy in rendering assistance to the British, the Government subsequently granted him a *khilat* of Rs. 7,000, together with the whole of the confiscated *pargana* of Tulsipur, besides large portions of the Ikauna, Charda and Bhinga Estates in Bahraich. He was further honoured by having a remission of 10 per cent. of the Government revenue on his ancestral property, and the revenue assessed thereon at the first regular settlement of 1871–72 was fixed in perpetuity. He was also exempted from attendance in Civil Courts; and the retainers of the Chiefs of Balrampur have been permanently exempted from the operation of all prohibitions contained in sections 13 to 16 of the Arms Act. He was also honoured by the bestowal of the title of " Maharaja Bahadur," while at a Durbar held in Agra on November 20, 1866, he was created a Knight Commander of the Most Exalted Order of the Star of India. Probably the principal distinction conferred upon the Chief, however, was the granting of a salute of nine guns—an honour which is seldom conferred on any one below the rank of a Ruling Chief—this dignity being awarded at an Imperial Assembly, held at Delhi on January 1, 1877, in celebration of the assumption by Her Majesty the late Queen Victoria of the title of Empress of India. The Maharaja was elected President of the Taluqdars' Association of Oudh, and was for some time an Additional Member of the Council of the Governor-General of India. During the last few years of his life the Maharaja was engaged in carrying out works of utility, and in other ways he manifested the greatest solicitude for the welfare of the inhabitants, to whom he was constantly dispensing charitable gifts. Sir Digbijai Singh, K.C.S.I., died in May, 1882, as the result of a fall from an elephant while tiger-shooting at Allahabad.

He was succeeded by his senior Maharani, Indra Kunwar, who, in the following year, adopted as her son, in accordance with her husband's Will, the present Maharaja Saheb, who is a relation of the late Chief.

A statue was erected at Balrampur to perpetuate the memory of His Highness the late Maharaja, and it was unveiled on December 21, 1888, by the Hon. Sir Auckland Colvin, Lieutenant-Governor of the North-Western Provinces and Commissioner of Oudh. In the course of his address His Honour observed: " I have heard all who knew him speak in the highest praise of his character as a landlord, and, in common with all the rest of us in India, I know how eminent his services were in 1857. When the events of that year overtook us, and when for a moment the power of the British Government suffered eclipse, the Maharaja, with a sagacity which all tell me pre-eminently distinguished him, never for a moment hesitated as to the course he should pursue. From first to last he threw in his lot with the English Government, and that at a time when he was almost the only man of position in Oudh who dared to do so, and when he was surrounded by a population in open arms against Her Majesty."

In November, 1892, Col. G. W. Anson, Agent of the Balrampur Estate, addressed a letter to the Government of India stating that, in view of the eminent services of the late Maharaja, his position as the first Baron of Oudh, and his vast possessions then held by his widow, the Maharani Indra Kunwar, he trusted that the lapsed salute of nine guns, granted as a personal distinction to her late husband, might be continued to her in appreciation of the very great assistance rendered to him in the administration of the Raj, and of her loyal obedience to the wishes of the Government.

In reply to the above recommendation, a communication dated March 29, 1893, was received from the Under-Secretary to the Government of India, Foreign Department, which contained the following words: " I am to say that although the grant of salutes to *zemindars* and others below the status of a ruling Chief is considered by Her Majesty's Government to be undesirable, yet, in the special circumstances of the case, Her Majesty the Queen-Empress has been graciously pleased to sanction, as a mark of Her Royal favour, the continuance to the Maharani of Balrampur, for *her life*, of the salute of nine guns." The Maharani Sahiba did not, unfortunately, live long to enjoy the distinction conferred upon her, as she passed away on the 28th of June following.

This lady was succeeded by her adopted

THE STATE OF BALRAMPUR RAJ.

1. Statue Hall. 2. Macdonell Orphanage.

son, the Hon. Maharaja Sir Bhagwati Prasad Singh, K.C.I.E., and the management of his extensive *Raj* was entrusted to him on attaining his majority in July, 1900. The assumption of his duties by the Maharaja was celebrated in a fitting manner in November of the same year, and in a speech delivered by Sir Anthony (afterwards Lord) MacDonnell, the following remarks were made: "The Balrampur Raj dates from high antiquity. It was an important chieftainship in the reign of the Emperor Jehangir, and, though never independent, it maintained with varying success its place among the chieftainships of Oudh throughout those troublous times when Might was Right, and the only reliable title-deed was the sword. The advent of British influence in Oudh in the early part of the nineteenth century found the Chiefs of Balrampur maintaining the traditions of their House for unyielding firmness in the defence of their patrimony, but we who see the Oudh of to-day, with its peaceful fields and its industries, can with difficulty conceive what its state was eighty years ago. Your father, the late Maharaja Sir Digbijai Singh, was engaged for years after his succession to the *Raj* in constant fighting and, as you know, he had to fly from Balrampur to escape the hostility of the Court of Oudh. . . . In the early days of the mutiny, some of the great Talukdars held aloof, doubtful as to what side they should join; a few joined the wrong side; but from the outset there was no standing aloof and no doubt in the mind of Sir Digbijai Singh of Balrampur. It is a matter of history how he rescued the District Officers at Sikraura, and how, having sent them in safety to Gorakhpur, he faced the mutineers. This loyal behaviour so incensed the rebel Government at Lucknow, that it issued a *Firman*, dividing the Balrampur Raj between its old enemies, the Rajas of Tulsipur and Ikauna, and at the same time directed the rebel Commander to burn down this town.

"Without going into details, I will sum up the result of those stormy days by saying that the Tulsipur Raj and the Ikauna Raj are things of the past; while the Balrampur Raj has waxed greater from their ruin. . . . He was made a 'Maharaja' and a 'Knight Commander of the Most Exalted Order of the Star of India'; while the final honour of a salute of nine guns, an honour given to very few subjects, was conferred upon him. It is in this open-handed way that the British Crown rewards the loyalty of those who stand by it in times of trial.

"Raja, you are now entering on a great heritage; the fortunes of half-a-million of people depend upon you. . . . Your education has led you across the threshold of Western knowledge, and it has sharpened your tastes for manly sports without in any way denationalizing your feelings or beliefs. I am glad to know that you have begun your independent life in friendship with all the influential *Talukdars*, who are here to-day to show their regard for yourself and their respect for your family.

"His Excellency the Viceroy, remembering the services which your family have rendered to the British Government, recognizing your high position, and wishing to encourage you in all ways to follow your father's footsteps, has ordered me to deliver to you this *Sanad*, which confers on you the title of 'Maharaja' as a personal distinction."

In the month of June, 1906, the Maharaja was created a Knight Commander of the Most Eminent Order of the Indian Empire.

The Maharaja's deep personal interest in the welfare of his people was never more clearly manifested than in the severe famine of 1907–8, which spread throughout the northern districts of the Province of Oudh. He organized relief works on a liberal scale on his vast estates in his own, and other, districts, and he supported gratuitously many thousands of persons until the end of June, and undertook 70 unaided works, as well as maintaining two poor houses.

The title of "Maharaja," conferred upon the Chief in 1900, was made hereditary in the family in January, 1909, and His Honour Sir John Hewett, the Lieutenant-Governor of the United Provinces, in presenting the customary *Sanad*, remarked (*inter alia*): "In the speech delivered at your installation, on November 30, 1900, Lord MacDonnell announced to you that His Excellency the Viceroy had directed him to deliver to you the *Sanad*, conferring on you the title of 'Maharaja' as a personal distinction. He told you that the conferment of this honour on you, as you entered public life, should stimulate you to high endeavours, and should confirm you in your resolve to lead in private a blameless life, and in public a beneficent one. This resolve you have firmly kept before you, and you have proved yourself a worthy successor to the late Maharaja Sir Digbijai Singh, whose statue will be unveiled at the Kaisarbagh to-morrow. The Government has done you honour by making you first of all K.C.I.E., and now by giving a *Sanad*, making your title of 'Maharaja' hereditary. I believe that you are the first *Taluqdar* of Oudh to receive this distinction. I know that it is highly appreciated by your fellow-*Taluqdars*, and, I believe, by all residents of Oudh, whether Hindus or Mahomedans; and on behalf of the European community, I beg to assure you that they unite in the universal approval with which the announcement of the honour has been received. No act that I am likely to perform during my tenure of office will give me greater pleasure than to hand you this *Sanad*."

In 1909 the members of the British Indian Association—which was founded by His Highness the late Maharaja Sir Digbijai Singh, K.C.S.I.—erected a statue at Lucknow to his memory. An address of welcome to the Hon. Sir John Hewett (who had undertaken to perform the unveiling ceremony) was read on the 19th of January of the year just mentioned, by His Highness the Raja-i-Rajgan of Kapurthala, and in reply His Honour made the following remarks: "Your Highness, I am very pleased that you should have been induced to accept the invitation of the Maharaja of Balrampur and other *Taluqdars* to act as their spokesman on this occasion. . . . Sir Digbijai Singh held a unique position among his brother *Taluqdars*. He was the first President of the British Indian Association, and he directed their counsels for the long period of 22 years. He busied himself on the Legislative Council of the Governor-General in securing legislative recognition to the special rights of inheritance upon which the *Taluqdars* of Oudh rightly set so much store. It is only proper and just that the British Indian Association should raise a statue to his memory, and give it a home in their hall, where it will recall him to future generations of the *Taluqdars*, for whom he laboured so well. . . . His successor, the Maharaja Sir Bhagwati Prasad Singh, was adopted by Sir Digbijai Singh's widow, and came into his property (which is the largest estate in Oudh) after it had been managed by the Court of Wards for seven years. Maharaja Sir Digbijai Singh lived partly under the old and partly under the new régime; and if, in his early years he had to fight for his own land, he showed, by his generosity towards charitable objects in his later years, that no

THE BALRAMPUR RAJ.

Lyall Collegiate School.

one could realize better than he did the responsibilities and the duties of his great possessions. He rendered most important service to the British Government in the stormy days of the Mutiny, and in the peaceful times that followed it, he devoted himself to the careful management of his estates and to works of public utility and benevolence. At Balrampur and Lucknow his name is kept green by the hospitals which he built and endowed; and he established the Lyall Collegiate School at the head-quarters of his estate, and a number of schools in the villages belonging to it. When his death occurred, as a result of an accident, while he followed the sport to which he was so devoted, every one felt that one had been removed from among us who had played his part equally well in troublous and in peaceful times, and whose like we could not expect to look upon again.

"It is a privilege to have been invited by the British Indian Association to unveil the Statue, and with Your Highness's permission, I will now proceed to do so."

The Maharaja was educated privately under English and Indian tutors; he speaks the English language fluently, and is also acquainted with Hindi, Urdu and Persian. His Highness has a son and heir, now seven years of age, who bears the title of Maharaja Kumar Sahib.

One who knows the Chief of Balrampur, has written concerning him as follows: "The present Maharaja, I believe, has the reputation of being a quiet, unassuming, well-meaning man, keenly solicitous about the welfare and happiness of his tenantry . . . fond of manly sports, public-spirited and munificent in his benefactions . . . and, above all, loyal to his finger-tips." The Maharaja is a highly respected nobleman of the United Provinces of Agra and Oudh. He is well educated, and is naturally desirous of making it easy for his people to enjoy every facility for obtaining instruction in order to fit them for becoming better citizens. He is President of the Taluqdars Association of Oudh; a member of the Legislative Council of the United Provinces and Honorary Fellow for Life of the Allahabad University; Chairman of the Balrampur Municipality, and an Honorary Magistrate.

The beneficence of His Highness the Maharaja has always been of a most princely character, and his charitable gifts have always been dispensed with an utter disregard for all questions of caste or creed. He has set a laudable example to others in furthering the cause of education, in giving encouragement to agricultural and other industries, in providing facilities in obtaining medical advice and treatment, and in supporting any scheme which has for its object the improvement of the moral and social status of his fellow men.

The contributions made by the Balrampur Raj, during the time of His Highness the present Maharaja, up to December, 1918, include the following: for educational purposes, Rs. 7,22,200; including maintenance of schools at Balrampur, a Girls' School, and the Canning College at Lucknow, and contributions to a Hindu University at Benares; (2) dispensaries, Rs. 6,98,000, including maintenance of dispensaries on the Estate, hospitals in the capital town and in various parts of the Raj, and donation to King George's Medical College at Lucknow; (3) the MacDonnell Orphanage, Rs. 47,000; (4) other charities, Rs. 8,07,800; (5) sanitary improvements, Rs. 2,58,000; (6) famine relief, Rs. 5,00,000; (7) other relief granted, Rs. 15,500; (8) contributions amounting to Rs. 175,000 towards Provincial and all-India Victoria Memorial Funds, the Allahabad Exhibition, and other objects; (9) Rs. 3,94,969, representing war donations from the estates and *thikadars*, a monthly war contribution of Rs. 5,000, the cost and maintenance of a Daimler motor-car for sick and wounded soldiers, and subscriptions to sundry war funds; (10) war loan subscription from the estate amounting to Rs. 28,21,487. These sums make a grand total of Rs. 64,39,956.

It may not be out of place to mention here that an address was presented by the Committee of the Medical College, Lucknow (one of the charitable objects mentioned in the foregoing list), on the auspicious occasions of the laying of the foundation-stone of that institution by His Royal Highness the Prince of Wales (now King-Emperor George V), and that the reply of the Royal visitor was as follows: "On behalf of the Princess of Wales and myself, I thank you sincerely for the very kind sentiments to which your address gives expression. We also thank you for affording us this opportunity of identifying ourselves with an institution which must have a marked influence on the health and happiness of the vast population of these provinces. I gather from the papers which I have read, that for many years the need of a Medical College has been recognized. I rejoice to think that, thanks to the noble liberality of the Maharaja of Balrampur, and of others, whose names will be gratefully remembered by future generations, this great need will now be supplied. . . . I shall be delighted to lay the foundation-stone of the College, and we are proud that our names will be respectively associated with the institution and its branch college for women."

THE STATE OF JAMKHANDI

THE Principality of Jamkhandi, situated in the Bombay Presidency, and under the Political Resident in Kolhapur, is bounded on the north by the Athni Taluk of the district of Belgaum, on the south by the State of Mudhol, on the east by part of the district of Bijapur, and on the west by the State of Sangli.

The founder of the Patwardhan family, to which the Chief of Jamkhandi belongs, was one Haribhat of Kotawada, a village in the district of Ratnagiri. He was in somewhat straitened circumstances, but he became the family priest of the Chief of Ichalkaranji. He had seven sons, but only three of them distinguished themselves in Mahratta history, they being the founders of three Patwardhan Jahageers. They were introduced at the court at Poona by the Chief of Ichalkaranji, who was a relative of the Peshwa. In 1740 Haribhat received a grant of land from Shri Chhatrapati Shahu Maharaj of Satara, but he died in 1749.

Ramchandra Rao I was the sixth son of Haribhat. He, with his brother Govindrao, came to prominence at the siege of Bassein in 1737. The two were first given a *Saradari* in the Khasgee *Pathak* of the Peshwa. Ramchandra died in 1749 while serving in the Northern Expeditions led by the Peshwa. He left behind him his only son Parashuram, nine years of age, who under the better known name of Bhow was destined to be one of the most famous Mahratta Generals and Sardars at the Peshwa's Court. The life story of this great chief is a part of the history of the Mahratta nation. It suffices here to note that after the British subjugation of the Mahratta power brought the military career of the Mahratta Sardars to an end, the Tasgaon Jagir, part of the hereditary Patwardhan estate, was divided into two tracts known as Chinchani and Jamkhandi, the latter remaining in the possession of Gopalrao as the senior representative of Bhow's line of descent. In 1822 the Bidri Mahal, valued at 30,000 rupees, was given to the Chief as a Saranjam by the British Government. In 1826 Gopalrao was granted permission to adopt a son in case he had no male heir. He was a man of considerable ability, and managed his *jagir* with tact and skill. In 1840 he adopted as his heir Ramchandrarao Appa, who was seven years of age at the time, and he died on the following day.

A *nazarana* of 170,000 rupees having been paid to the British Government, the administration of the State was entrusted to his mother, but serious mismanagement soon took place for which the Karbhari and the others were tried and punished. The Regent Radhabai died in 1853, and the young Chief, who had been well educated, was invested with ruling powers in the same year. He remodelled his administration on the lines laid down in British India, and introduced reforms in almost all the departments of the State. In 1858 he was removed to Belgaum on suspicion, but the Imperial Government, being satisfied as to his innocence, reinstated him on his *gadi* in 1859, while in 1861 an adoption *sanad* was granted by Lord Canning to him as Chief of Jamkhandi. Ramchandrarao Appa Saheb was a man of considerable intelligence and a capable administrator. He removed his capital to Ramtirth, a hill near Jamkhandi, where beautiful temples, halls, and bungalows add greatly to the natural beauty of the place. Having no male heir, Ramchandrarao Appa Saheb adopted Parashuramrao, *alias* Bhausaheb, the present Chief, a lineal descendant of the lapsed Chinchani family. Ramchandra died in 1897, whereupon his adopted son ascended the *gadi*. A *nazarana* of about 5,00,000 rupees being paid to the Imperial Government during the minority, the State was managed by the representatives of the British Government. The Chief received careful training during his educational career at Kolhapur, and while his guardians were British officials, his tutors were of Indian birth. He travelled throughout India in order to become acquainted with the people of that vast country, their institutions, industrial enterprises, systems of government and their general social surroundings. He was installed on his *gadi* in 1903, and since that date he has administered the State with great tact and zeal, sound progress having been made in practically every department. With the object of gaining insight into Western civilization he visited Europe with his Rani, and has brought to bear his wide experience on all branches of administration. As a token of appreciation of his ability as a ruler, His Imperial Majesty in 1913 bestowed on him the honour of a Knight Commandership of the Most Eminent Order of the Indian Empire. During the late Great War he offered his personal services to the Imperial Government and served for about four months with the British Indian Expeditionary Force, on the Western Front in France. In 1918 he was granted the honorary military rank of Captain, together with a personal salute of nine guns, in recognition of his valuable services in the war. He was subsequently deputed as an Indian Representative to proceed

CAPT. MERHERBAN SIR PARASHURAMRAO, alias BHAUSAHIB PATAWARDHAN, K.C.I.E., CHIEF OF JAMKHANDI.

FAMILY GROUP.

with Major S. F. Madden to Mesopotamia to inquire and report on the work of the Red Cross Society in that country. He also acted as an honorary A.D.C. to His Excellency Lord Willingdon, the late Governor of Bombay, and is also an honorary A.D.C. to His Excellency Sir George Lloyd, the present Governor. He has a son named Shankarrao Appa Saheb and a daughter named Keral Tara, *alias* Akkasaheb. He is a man of high literary ability; is a staunch patron of learning, and at the same time he is an excellent all-round sportsman, being fond of all healthy, manly exercises. He manifests the greatest kindness towards his subjects, and has always been extremely solicitous for their material, social and moral welfare.

The Chief of Jamkhandi is a First Class *Sardar* of the Deccan and a Ruling Chief of the second class of States in India, having full powers over his State. The total area of Jamkhandi is about 525 square miles. It is divided into three *talugs* and two *thanas* in which there are 80 villages and 20 hamlets, seven of the former being Inams. The total population of the State according to the census of 1911 was 1,00,304, the majority of whom speak the Kanarese tongue. Forests and hills cover about 30 square miles of the total area of the State, while the remainder of the land is under cultivation. The total acreage is 3,04,355, and the Government assessment and *judi* thereon amount to Rs. 3,90,273. The revenue from all sources reaches the sum of Rs. 6,36,725 and the average expenditure is about Rs. 6,00,000. There is no legislative body in the State, nearly all laws in force being in accordance with those adopted by the Government of India and Bombay. There are 691 men in the Police Force, and of this 363 are termed "district men," while the remainder are employed in villages.

The policy of the State with regard to education is that all instruction shall be imparted entirely free of cost. There are in all some 76 schools, including the P. B. High School at Jamkhandi and the F.G.A.V. School at Kundgol, all the others being of the vernacular kind.

The Public Works Department has been profitably employed during the past 40 years in carrying out undertakings of utility, and among these may be mentioned about 250 State buildings, costing more than Rs. 14,00,000, and the construction of 140 miles of good roads in areas where such means of communication were urgently required. The total initial cost of all works carried out by this department to the present time is not less than Rs. 30 00,000.

THE STATE OF JATH

THIS State is one of those in the Deccan under the Political Superintendence of the Collector at Bijapur, and it is surrounded by the British Districts of Sholapur, Bijapur, and Belgaum, and by the State of Sangli.

The ruling family was founded by Satwajirao, son of Lakhamojirao Yeldojirao Chavan, *Patil* of Daflapur, a village in this State. His bravery attracted the notice of Ali Adilshah, Emperor of Bijapur, who took him into his service in 1672 and conferred upon him in perpetuity the *Deshmukhi Watan* of the four *Mahals*, namely, Jath, Karajgi, Bardol and Vhanwad on payment of a *Nazar* of 3,000 *mohors*. Satwajirao continued to be one of the leading noblemen at the Bijapur Court until its final overthrow by the Emperor Aurangzeb in 1686.

After the downfall of the Bijapur Kingdom Satwajirao assumed entire independence and began to exercise his own authority over a large portion of the Bijapur Empire and further to molest the Moghul Emperor Aurangzeb, who ordered his Generals to capture Satwajirao and to convey him to the Royal Court. The Moghul Generals could not secure Satwajirao, but they obtained his brother Dhondjirao and took him to the Emperor. Satwajirao loved his faithful brother dearly, and fearing lest any calamity should befall him, he had no other alternative but to surrender himself to Aurangzeb. He accordingly saw the Emperor and expressed his willingness to serve him faithfully, and he pledged his word of honour to this effect. The Emperor Aurangzeb took his son Bawajirao into his Army and raised him to a very high position. In 1700 the Emperor Aurangzeb besieged the fortress of Ajimtara, in the district of Satara.

The Mahrattas defended the citadel with great bravery, resolving to fight to the last. The Moghul Army, however, was making all possible attempts to capture the stronghold, and in one such effort when the bastion near the Manglai Goddess was mined and blown up, causing a breach in the wall, Bawajirao was the first to enter, gallantly leading his troops and then planting the Moghul Emperor's flag on the bastion, which is still known as the "Dafle's Bastion." He received many serious wounds in the battle, and he soon died of them.

The Emperor Aurangzeb being pleased with Bowajirao's gallant and meritorious services, called Satwajirao to him and bestowed on him the *jagir* of the Jath and Karajgi *mahals*, with a command of 5,000 horse in about the year 1704.

Satwajirao then made the town of Jath his capital. He thus rose from an ordinary rank of a *Patil* to that of a king, but unfortunately he did not live long to enjoy his honours, as the death of Bowajirao, his beloved son, and the premature death of his second son Khanajirao had such an effect on his mind that he passed away in 1706.

A succession of Rulers occupied the *gadi* with varying success until the nineteenth century, when we find the State in the hands of Khanajirao. This Chief died about 1810, and after his death his senior widow Renukabai began to rule. On April 22, 1820, she entered into a treaty with Captain James Grant on behalf of the East India Company, and in the same year she also made a similar treaty with the Raja of Satara. Although a woman, she was very strict in her administration, but being very generous, she granted many *Inams* during her reign. She died in 1822 and after her death, Salubai, the younger widow of Khanajirao, ascended the *gadi*, but she unfortunately died in the following year.

Ramrao, alias Abasaheb, was then invested with ruling powers by the Raja of Satara, but he died in 1835 whereupon his widow Bhagirathibai succeeded him. Having no son she adopted Bhimrao, the son of Bhagwantrao bin Bavajirao, from the Dafle Bhauband family at Umrani. He was named Amritrao alias Raosaheb. Bhagirathibai died on July 29, 1846, and Amritrao began to rule after attaining his majority in 1855.

Amritrao died on January 11, 1892, leaving behind him two widows—the senior Laxmibai Saheb and the junior Anandibai Saheb alias Maisaheb, as well as a daughter named Yeshodabai alias Akkasaheb.

The *gadi* thus being vacant was conferred on Bowanjirao, the fourth son of Parshramrao Dafle of Umrani, whose selection to succeed the late Chief was sanctioned by the Government of India in December, 1892. The Bombay Government also acceded to the request of Laxmibai Saheb, the senior widow of the late Chief, that she might be allowed to adopt Bowajirao, and a proclamation to this effect was duly published.

In officially recognizing this adoption a Durbar was held at the palace on January 13, 1893, at which *Inamdars*, *Jamedars*, *Mankaris*, *Darakdars*, village officers and a large number of town people were assembled. Colonel Woodhouse, Political Agent, Kolhapur, gave an address suitable to the occasion, and then installed Bowajirao on the *gadi* with due ceremony. The Jagirdar has been

SHRIMANT MEHERBAN RAMRAO AMRITRAO, alias ABASAHIB DAFLE, CHIEF OF JATH.

SHRIMATI SOUBHAGYAWATI BHAGIRTHIBAI DAFLE, RANI SAHIB OF JATH.

1. YUVRAJ MEHERBAN SHRIMANT VIJAYSINHA DAFLE (Seated),
AND SHRIMANT KUMAR AJITSINHA DAFLE.
2. SHRIMATI KUMARI PREMILA RAJE (Seated), AND SHRIMATI KUMARI KAMALA RAJE.
3. SHRIMANT KUMAR UDAYSINHA DAFLE.

THE STATE OF JATH

named Shrimant Ramrao Amritrao alias Abasaheb Dafle. The customary religious rites were performed on February 21, 1893.

Shrimant Ramrao Amritrao was born on January 11, 1886, and was brought up for some years at Kolhapur under European guardians, and he subsequently received his education in the Rajkumar College of Rajkot, where he had a very distinguished career. Having completed his training course at Rajkot, he returned to Jath in 1906, and commenced a course of administrative training. He was formally installed on the Raj *gadi* on July 11, 1907, and since then he has exercised full powers of administration of the State. He is a hard worker, and takes a keen interest in the welfare of his subjects. He is a high-caste Mahratta, and is married to Shrimant Putala Raje, second daughter of the late Rajasaheb of Akalkot State, who is a kind-hearted lady and has great sympathy for the welfare of women, and has started a Ladies' Home Class for giving instruction to those who are untrained.

The Chief has three sons and two daughters, the heir-apparent being Kumar Shri Vijayasing alias Baba Saheb, a smart and promising youth.

Daflapur and other villages which had been granted to Bahinabai and which were resumed after her death by the State were restored in 1841 to her grandson Ramchandrarao, who died without a male issue in 1850. The villages were continued to his widows during their lives, and the last of them having died in 1917, the villages known as Daflapur Estate reverted to the Jath *jagir* in accordance with the decision of the Court of Directors in 1861, and have accordingly been incorporated in the *jagir*.

The surname of the Dafle family was originally Chavan, but after the *jagir* was bestowed, and Jath was made the capital, the ruling family and its *bhaubands* came to be known as the "Dafles" from the Daflapur village of which the original ancestors were *Patils* or headmen. The Daflapur *Patilki* still continues to be enjoyed by the ruling family.

The present Chief's adoptive sister, Yeshodabai Akkasaheb, was given in marriage to Shrimant Sardar Pratapsingh alias Bhau Saheb Bhosle of Satara, descendant in direct line of the great Sivaji Maharaja, founder of the Mahratta Empire.

Since the installation of the present Chief many reforms have been made in the various departments of the State. Education has been made compulsory and free both to the rich and poor alike throughout the whole of the principality.

Since December, 1920, the British Government has very generously restored to the Ruler of the State full powers in criminal matters which were curtailed in 1850.

The State pays Rs. 6,400 in lieu of service of a Horse Contingent, and Rs. 4,847 for *Sardeshmukhi* rights to the British Government.

The State is 980 square miles in extent, and at the census of 1921 it had a population of 82,649 inhabitants, who reside in the capital town of Jath and some 118 villages. The annual income from all sources is about Rs. 3,36,932.

The Chief is entitled to visit, and be visited by, His Excellency the Governor of Bombay.

THE STATE OF KANKER

THE Feudatory State of Kanker, in the Central Provinces, is under the Political Agent attached to the district of Raipur. Its origin is traced back to a certain Bir Kanker Deo, ruler of a small principality in Orissa, who, migrating to the Central Provinces, found favour with the people of what is now the Kanker State, and was made their king.

An ancient inscription discovered at Sihawa states that the descendants of Bir Kanker Deo ruled many years at that place, and it is generally understood that the third Chief in succession annexed the Kanker *pergana* and transferred his capital from Sihawa to the small town of Kanker, while the fourth Ruler seized the *taluq* of Dhamtari. During the period when the Haihaivansi dynasty was at the height of its power the Ruler of the State is said to have been its feudatory, exercising sway, however over the Dhamtari tract. It was about this time that the Mahrattas held supremacy in Central India, and the Kanker State was required to do feudal service by furnishing a military contingent of 500 men whenever called upon.

Rudra Deo, a succeeding Ruler, constructed a temple on the bank of the River Mahanadi, near Dhamtari, and named it Rudreshwar, after himself. He also founded the village of Rudri at the same place, and built a fort at Dhamtari, the outer ditch being still in existence.

A succeeding Ruler named Harpal Deo gave his daughter in marriage to the Chief of the Bastar State, at the same time transferring the *pergana* of Sihawa as dowry.

Bhup Deo, when on the *gadi* in 1808, went to the assistance of Bastar, which had been attacked by the Mahrattas, but he was eventually compelled to leave his home and take refuge in Jheria, a village in the *tahsil* of Dhamtari. He remained for nearly 10 years at Jheria, where his wife bore a son, named Padam Singh, and in 1818 the British Resident administering the Nagpur territories restored him to Kanker on payment of an annual tribute of Rs. 500, a liability which was remitted in 1823.

Maharaja Dhiraja Narhar Deo ascended the *gadi* in 1853, and was succeeded by the present Chief, who was installed in 1904 with the title of Maharaja Dhiraj Shri Komal Deo.

His Highness made himself exceedingly popular in all parts of the State soon after his accession to power, and his ability as a Ruler has been marked by the introduction of many measures of reform which have won the approval of the British Government. In 1911 he attended the Coronation ceremonies at Delhi, when His Imperial Majesty conferred upon him a personal salute of nine guns. In November, 1917, His Highness presented to the town of Raipur a statue of His Majesty the King-Emperor, which was unveiled amid the enthusiasm of the spectators by the Hon. the Chief Commissioner of the Central Provinces.

The State of Kanker has an area of 1,429 square miles, and is bounded on the north by the districts of Drug and Raipur, on the east by Raipur, on the south by the State of Bastar, and on the west by the district of Chanda.

The Mahanadi river enters the State at a short distance from its source, and flows through the eastern portion of the area, receiving the water of several small streams rising on the hills.

The greater portion of the State consists of hilly land and forests, and even in the extensive tract of fertile soil in the valley of the Mahanadi outcrops of rocks and scattered boulders are found. Iron and gold have been discovered in certain areas but the yield of these valuable metals is scarcely sufficient to make mining a profitable concern.

About one-third of the total area of Kanker is composed of hills and forests, and although only a small quantity of timber is extracted there are valuable trees comprising teak, *sal*, *sisa*, and other varieties.

The inhabitants of the State about 127,000 in number, comprise nearly 80,000 Gonds, Halbas (who have migrated from Bastar), Rawats Kalars, Telis and Malis and the major portion of these are connected in one way or another with agricultural pursuits.

About 500 square miles of the State are under cultivation.

A branch line of railway from Raipur to Dhamtari, connected with the Bengal-Nagpur system, which has recently been opened has been of immense value to the State in transporting forest and general agricultural produce.

The State has provided dispensaries at Kanker and Sambalpur, the latter being called the "King Edward" dispensary.

His Highness the Maharaja, who belongs to the Somavanshi Kshatriya branch of an ancient Rajput family, administers the State personally, and he is assisted by his Diwan, Rai Sahib Pundit Durga Prasad Tiwari.

The headquarters of the State are at Kanker, a village with 3,906 inhabitants and it is situated about thirty-nine miles distant by road from Dhamtari railway station.

The gross revenue of the State is about Rs. 2,63,360, the annual net income is nearly Rs. 2,60,000

1. MAHARAJA DHIRAJ SHRI KOMAL DEO, PRESENT FEUDATORY CHIEF, KANKER STATE.
2. GUEST-HOUSE (RADHANIWAS), KANKER. 3. VIEW OF THE OLD FORT, SHOWING SONADAI TANK.

THE STATE OF KANKER.

1. Crawford High School, Kanker. 2. The Katcherry, Kanker. 3. General View of Kanker Town.

KHAIRAGARH STATE

KHAIRAGARH, a Feudatory State under the supervision of the Political Agent of the Chhatisgarh in Central India, is most irregular in formation, its boundaries intermingling with those of the States of the Chhuikadhan, Kawardha, and Nandgaon, and also the district of Drug which lies on its eastern side.

The ruling family are Nagvansi Rajputs connected with the House of Chhota-Nagpur, and the present Chief is able to trace a direct line of descent through the long period of nearly 1,200 years.

Kamal Narain Singh succeeded his father in November 1890, at the age of twenty-three, and in 1898 the title of Raja was conferred upon him. Keen administrative abilties were manifested by the Chief upon his assumption of the management of the State, but to the great regret of his people he succumbed to an attack of paralysis on October 7, 1908. His eldest son, Raja Lal Bahadur Singh, born in June 1889, ascended the *gadi*, but owing partly to his minority and partly to the unsatisfactory financial condition of the State the date of his formal installation did not take place until December 13, 1912, when all liabilities had been discharged.

Raja Lal Bahadur Singh gained the approval of the Government, as well as the affection of the inhabitants, by the wisdom displayed by him in managing the affairs of the State, by his lofty character, and by the strict sense of justice which marked his actions. Although he was assiduous in his attention to official duties, he was a fine athlete and encouraged by practice, as well as precept, all manly games, especially cricket, of which he was no mean exponent. The promise of his future career was bright indeed, but he unfortunately died from an attack of influenza in October, 1918.

He was followed by his elder son, Lal Birendra Bahadur Singh—born in November 1914—whose succession was duly recognized by the Government and upon whom the hereditary title of Raja was bestowed. The younger son, Lal Bikram Bahadur Singh, was born in December, 1915. Bhuneswari Babi, elder sister of the late Chief, is married to Raja Bahadur Ram Gopal Singh of Manda, in the United Provinces of Agra and Oudh, who belongs to a distinguished family of the Rathor Gaharwar Kshatriya Rajputs, and the younger sister is wife of Rana Kharag Jung Bahadur, of Allahabad, who is younger brother of the present Rani Sahiba of Khairagarh.

The State, which is 931 square miles in extent, has a population of 124,770 inhabitants.

Nearly the whole of the western portion of the State consists of hills which are intersected by tracts of light sandy soil, but the eastern part is an extensive plain of rich black soil of great fertility upon which excellent crops of *kodon*, rice and wheat are grown.

The forests, which are 165 square miles in extent, are a valuable asset as they contain a large number of timber trees, including teak and *bijaral*, while a considerable revenue is derived from bamboos and minor products such as flowers, fruit, wax and resin.

Owing to the minority of the present Ruler the State is administered by a Superintendent named Rai Bahadur S. R. Pandit, whose services have been lent to Khairagarh by the British Government. This official is invested with powers of criminal matters similar to those exercised by District Magistrates and Sessions Judges, while in the disposal of civil suits he has the authority of the District Judge. The Assistant Superintendent is on the same status as a District Judge in civil matters, and he enjoys the powers of a Magistrate of the first class, having summary jurisdiction under section 260 of the Code of Criminal Procedure.

The gross revenue of the State based upon the average of the past five years is Rs. 4,53,937. The actual income of the State for 1920 was Rs. 5,02,950 and Rs. 4,66,590 respectively.

Nearly thirty teaching institutions are maintained by the Durbar, including a high school, a normal school, and one academy for girls at Khairagarh; together with middle schools at Khairagarh and Dongargarh.

The Bengal Nagpur Railway passes through the southern portion of the Principality, and stations have been opened at Bortalao, Dongargarh and Musra.

Khairagarh, the headquarters town of the State, is situated at a distance of 23 miles by road from the railway stations of Dongargarh and Rajnandgaon on the Bengal-Nagpur system. The area and population of the town (according to the census of 1921) are 165 acres and 4,046 persons respectively. The most important public buildings in the town are the Raja's palace, the Victoria High School, a dispensary, court-house, jail, town hall, and a *dak* bungalow.

The State is well administered and has a promising future.

1. THE LATE RAJA KAMAL NARAIN SINGH, FEUDATORY CHIEF, KHAIRAGARH STATE.
2. THE LATE RAJA LAL BAHADUR, FEUDATORY CHIEF, KHAIRAGARH STATE.
3. RAJA BIRENDRA BAHADUR SINGH, PRESENT MINOR CHIEF, KHAIRAGARH STATE.

THE STATE OF KHAIRAGARH

1. Palace, Khairagarh. 2. Court House, Khairagarh. 3. Town Hall, Khairagarh.

SIDE VIEW OF THE PALACE.

THE STATE OF KHILCHIPUR

KHILCHIPUR is a mediatized Chiefship in Central India under the Political Agent in Bhopal.

Its area of 273 square miles, in which there are more than 40,000 inhabitants, is bounded on the north by the State of Kotah in the Rajputana Agency, on the east by the State of Rajgarh, on the west by the State of Indore, and on the south by the State of Narsingarh.

The Rulers of the State are Khichi Rajputs, a section of the famous Chauhan clan, and they trace their descent from Ugrasen, who left the Khichi capital of Gagraun owing to family dissensions and established himself in 1544 at Khilchipur. He subsequently obtained from the Moghul Emperors certain *perganas*, which now belong to the States of Gwalior and Indore. This loss of territory occurred in 1770, when Abhey Singh, the Chief at that time, was compelled to yield to the terms of Sindhia at the conclusion of hostilities. In 1819, when the settlement of Malwa took place, disputes arose regarding the succession, but at the request of the Gwalior Durbar the British authorities intervened, and approved the claims of Dewan Sher Singh, a boy of five years of age. He was followed in 1869 by his nephew Amar Singh, upon whom the hereditary title of "Rao Bahadur" was conferred in 1873 for his services during the Mutiny. This Chief abolished all transit duties in the State, and he in many ways proved his ability as a progressive ruler.

Rao Bahadur Bhawani Singh ascended the *gadi* in 1899, and after a rule of about 10 years died in 1908.

Rao Bahadur Durjansal Singh, the present ruler, was born on August 26, 1897. He succeeded his father, Rao Bahadur Bhawani Singh, in 1908, when he was in his eleventh year. In 1916 he was married to the third daughter of His Highness Raja Sir Jaswant Singh Bahadur, K.C.I.E., of Sailana. He was invested with full ruling powers on February 22, 1918. The Rao Bahadur is an enlightened ruler, having received a liberal education at the Daly College, Indore, and subsequently training in administration work in the Central Provinces. He is a good shot and an excellent rider. Since his investiture he is taking keen interest in the administration of his State.

The greater portion of the State is situated in what is known as the Deccan trap area, but sandstone of the Kaimur and other types are prominent in its northern villages.

There are 307 villages in the State, which are mostly inhabited by the Sondhias, Dangis and Lorhas.

The total area of the State is 273 square miles. Of this 64,909 acres are cropped and new fallow, 100,406 acres are culturable waste, part of which is included in holdings, and the rest is unculturable. The soil in the south-west is rich black type which produces excellent crops of all kinds of grain, but that found in the northern portion is too rough and stony to give good crops, and is chiefly utilized in raising *til* and *jowar*.

1. RAO BAHADUR DURJANSAL SINGHJI SAHIB.
Present Chief.

2. MAHARAJ KUMAR YASHODHAR SINGHJI SAHIB.
Heir-Apparent.

THE STATE OF KHILCHIPUR

1. Chhatris of Late Chiefs. 2. The Late Rao Bahadur Amar Singhji Sahib (Grandfather of the Present Chief). 3. The Late Rao Bahadur Bhawani Singhji Sahib (Father of the Present Chief). 4. General View of Khilchipur Town. 5. Temple of Kalayan Raiji.

THE STATE OF KHILCHIPUR.

1. Mr. S. Shaukat Ali, B.A., Dewan. 2. Rani Jodhpuriji's School. 3. Bejeygarh Kothi. 4. Davis Club. 5. Guest-house.

The principal crops are *jowar, til*, cotton, wheat and sugar-cane.

The State is divided for administrative purposes into two *tehsils*, each of which is under the control of an official styled a *Tehsildar*. The Chief has recently been invested with full criminal powers, including sentence of death.

The strength of the Military Force and Police is 94 and 86 respectively.

The gross revenue of the State is Rs. 2,11,078.

The State pays a tribute of Rs. 11,134-3-6 to the British Government, and a "Karar Dad" of Rs. 866-12-0 to the Kotah State annually.

The Chiefs of Khilchipur are entitled to a salute of nine guns.

THE STATE OF KHILCHIPUR.

1. Front View of the Palace. 2. Temple of Narda.

THE STATE OF KURUNDVAD (SENIOR BRANCH)

KURUNDVAD is a Native State under the Political Agent for Kolhapur and the Southern Mahratta country in the Presidency of Bombay. The territory was originally granted in *inam* by the Peshwa to Trimbak Rao, a member of the illustrious Patwardhan family on the condition that he, in return, would render military service to the granter. The State was in 1811 divided into two portions named respectively Kurundvad and Shebdal, but the latter subsequently lapsed to the British Government in default of male heirs. About the year 1855 the Supreme Government effected a partition of the State between Raghunath Rao and Ganpat Rao on the one hand and Vinayak Rao and Trimbak Rao on the other, and the two branches were respectively known by the names of Kurundvad Senior and Kurundvad Junior. Trimbak Rao died in 1869 without leaving a lawful heir, and his share of the *jagir* was transferred to Ganpat Rao and Vinayak Rao. The interest of Trimbak Rao in the *inam* formerly given to him was passed on to the senior Chief, Raghunath Rao, whose grandson, Shrimant Balchandra Rao Chintaman, is the present Ruler. The Chief, who takes rank as a *Sardar* of the first class in the Southern Mahratta country, exercises full powers of administration, and is invested with authority to try his own subjects for capital offences. Succession is governed by the law of primogeniture, although the family have been granted a *sanad* of adoption.

The State is 185 square miles in extent and its inhabitants, some 50,000 in number are composed almost entirely of Hindus. The majority of the people find occupation in agricultural pursuits, but some industrial enterprises include the manufacture of coarse cotton cloth and articles of apparel for women. The principal crops raised are rice, millet, wheat, gram, and cotton.

A desire for educational facilities for the young has been unmistakably manifested by the people in recent years, and the Chief, gladly recognizing the movement, has established more than twenty schools in various parts of the State.

The State also maintains two dispensaries for granting medical advice and treatment to sufferers.

The sum of Rs. 9,619 is paid annually by way of tribute to the British Government.

THE STATE OF NANDGAON

NANDGAON is one of the important Feudatory States under the Government of the Central Provinces, and it consists of the four *perganas* of Pandadah, Nandgaon, Mohgaon, and Dongargaon, all of which were originally separate *zemindaries* subordinate to the Bhonsla Raja of Nagpur.

The circumstances under which these areas came into the possession of the Nandgaon ruling family vary considerably, but in each instance the early history must be traced from one Prahlad Das, a *Bairagi* shawl merchant, who towards the end of the eighteenth century established himself in business at Ratanpur. This enterprising trader became a very wealthy man, and upon his death the whole of his possessions devolved upon his *Chela*, or "disciple," named *Mahant* Hari Das. It may be mentioned here that *Mahants* in those days strictly observed the rule of celibacy. The Mahratta Chief, Bimbaji, who was then living at Ratanpur and was locally regarded as a Raja, had seven Ranis who not only made Hari Das their spiritual adviser but also empowered him to collect Rs. 2 from each village throughout the whole of the Ratanpur territory.

This gave the *Chela* an opportunity of extending his business connections, and his next important step was to commence lending money to landholders and others in the district. One of the borrowers was the Zemindar of Pandadah, who was granted a loan on the security of his property, but as the debt was not repaid at the proper date Hari Das took possession of the above-named *zemindari*, which was placed in charge of Ram Das, his own *Chela*. After the death of Hari Das, *Mahant* Ram Das took over the Nandgaon *pergana* in discharge of a liability owing by a Mahomedan *zemindar*.

Mahant Ram Das was succeeded, on his death, in the ownership of the *perganas* of Pandadah and Nandgaon, by *Mahant* Raghubar Das, and afterwards by *Mahant* Himanchal Das. This worthy was of very liberal disposition; in fact, his benefactions were so great that he was unable to pay his annual tribute to the Nagpur Raja.

In consequence of this default in payment the *Mahant* was ordered to appear before the Raja, who was prepared to listen to any explanation which might be tendered. In the result the Bhonsla King was so impressed by Himanchal's eloquence that he freely remitted the debt, and in addition made the *Mahant* a grant of the Mohgaon *pergana*.

Himanchal Das did not live long after the acquisition of this property, and the whole of his estates passed to *Mahant* Mojiram Das. Shortly after the latter's accession he was called upon to suppress a revolt instigated against the Nagpur Raja by the *zemindar* of Dongargaon and his brother, and as an acknowledgment of his valuable services he was rewarded by the gift to him of the Dongargaon *pergana*.

Thus the four separate *perganas* became united and formed the State of Nandgaon.

Mahant Mojiram adopted Ghasi Das, his *Chela*, as his successor, but he subsequently married and had a son, Ghanaram Das, who succeeded to the *gadi* in due course, but he died after ruling for only three years.

It should be observed that this was the first instance of a son, instead of a *Mahant*, succeeding a deceased Chief.

Mahant Ghasi Das was then (1865) recognized by the British Government as Feudatory Chief of Nandgaon, and he was further given a *sanad* which conferred upon him the right of adoption.

Ghasi Das was a very capable administrator, and took active measures to consolidate his territories and place them on a sound financial basis. He selected Raj Nandgaon as his capital town, and made it an important trading centre by the establishment of a mart; he developed the indigenous resources of the State; and he constructed a noble palace and laid out two beautiful gardens at the chief town.

During the second Afghan War the Chief, true to the acknowledgment of fealty which he had previously made, very greatly assisted the British forces by presenting them with supplies to the value of Rs. 1,10,000.

Mahant Ghasi Das died in 1883, and was succeeded by his minor son, Balram Das, the administration of the State being entrusted to the young Chief's mother, who was assisted by a Diwan. In 1887 Balram Das was honoured by the bestowal of the title of Raja as a mark of personal distinction, and four years later he was formally installed on the *gadi*.

The Raja had progressive ideas, and what was of still greater importance, he laboured incessantly to give effect to them The Government recognized his public-spirited policy by conferring upon him the honoured title of Raja Bahadur in the year 1893. Great grief was manifested at his death in 1897, and he was succeeded by his adopted son, *Mahant* Rajendra Das, who died a minor in 1912.

The present Chief, *Mahant* Lal Sarveshaar Das, now in the thirteenth year of his age is being educated at the Rajkumar College at Rajpur, and the administration of the

1. THE LATE RAJA BAHADUR MAHANT BALRAM DAS, FEUDATORY CHIEF, NANDGAON STATE.
2. THE LATE MAHANT RAJENDRA DAS, MINOR FEUDATORY CHIEF, NANDGAON STATE.
3. MAHANT SARVESHWAR DAS, MINOR FEUDATORY CHIEF, NANDGAON STATE.

THE STATE OF NANDGAON.

1. The Palace, Raj-Nandgaon. 2. Rani-[illegible] and Rani-[illegible], Raj-Nandgaon. 3. Court-house, Raj-Nandgaon. 4. Guest-house, Raj-Nandgaon.

State is now in the hands of a Superintendent, who is an Extra-Assistant Commissioner in the service of the British Government, and who is under the direct control of the Political Agent for the Feudatory States.

The name "Nandgaon" is believed to be derived from the words *Nand* (the father of the god Krishna), and *gaon*, a village.

The State of Nandgaon, 871 square miles in extent, lies between 20–50 and 21–22 N. and 80–26 and 81–13 E., and it has a population of 167,258 inhabitants, more than two-thirds of whom are dependent upon agricultural pursuits for a livelihood. The principal castes among the people are *Telis*, *Gonds*, *Chamars*, and *Rawats*.

The gross revenue of the State is about Rs. 4,25,000, and the tribute payable annually to the British Government amounts to Rs. 80,000.

THE STATE OF PHALTAN

THIS Indian State, under the political superintendence of the Collector of Satara, in the Bombay Presidency, lies within the Deccan trap area.

The present Chief, Malojirao Mudhojirao Naik Nimbalkar, a *Kshatriya* by caste, belongs to a very old Mahratta family, and is descended from one Podaka Jagdeo, who fell in battle in the year 1327, while fighting under the Emperor of Delhi. His son, Nimbraji, followed in the footsteps of his father by accepting military service under the same Ruler, and he found such favour at the Royal Court, that the Emperor conferred upon him the *jagir* of Phaltan, and further bestowed upon him the title of Naik. The State remained in the possession of the lineal successors of Podaka Jagdeo until the year 1825, when it was attacked by the Raja of Satara, but it was shortly afterwards restored to Banaji Naik on payment of a succession fee of Rs. 30,000. Somewhat later the State was again held by Satara, and it was released in 1841, almost immediately prior to the death of the Chief, whose widow adopted the late Ruler, Mudhoji Rao Jan Rao Naik Nimbalkar, who was then three years of age. This Chief was invested with full administrative powers in 1860, and for several years was a member of the Legislative Council of Bombay, while his wise and intelligent rulership and his deep concern for the welfare of his subjects was rewarded at the Delhi Durbar of 1911, by the bestowal of the insignia of a Companionship of the Most Exalted Order of the Star of India.

The most important event of the year 1913 was the marriage of Shrimant Maloji Rao, otherwise known as Nanasaheb, the bride being Shrimati Lakshmibai Saheba, daughter of Raja Shambhu Singh Jadhavrao of Malegaon, in the district of Poona. The ceremony was performed on the 18th of December, in the presence of a very large number of European and Indian guests.

Mudhojirao Naik died on October 17, 1916, at the advanced age of 79 years, and his funeral was attended by a vast concourse of people of various castes and creeds, as the late Chief was greatly beloved by all who knew him. He was virtuous, kind-hearted and generous, and the majority of the improvements which have been effected in the State are the result of his wisdom and forethought.

The present Chief succeeded to the *gadi* under the title of Malojirao Mudhojirao Naik Nimbalkar, and the State was placed under the management of a British Official. A special Durbar was held at Phaltan on November 15, 1917, when Mr. B. A. Brendon, I.C.S., handed to the Chief the customary *Kharita*, conferring full administrative powers upon him. In replying to the excellent speech of Mr. Brendon, in which good advice was given to the young Ruler, the latter emphasized the fact of his sincere loyalty to the King-Emperor, and his determination to introduce measures of progress and reform for the benefit of his subjects. Intense gratification was manifested by the inhabitants of the State on August 28, 1918, when the wife of the Chief gave birth to a son and heir to the *gadi*. In December of the same year the Chief journeyed to Bombay in order to take part in the functions connected with the departure of His Excellency Lord Willingdon, the Governor of Bombay, and the arrival of his successor, Sir George Lloyd, G.C.I.E., D.S.O.

The State of Phaltan is 397 square miles in extent, and the inhabitants, according to the census of 1911, were nearly 56,000 in number.

A revision survey settlement of the State was carried out in the year 18[illegible], and the rates of assessment then fixed will remain in force until 1924, when a new valuation will be made. The total land revenue demand for the year 1919-20 amounted to Rs. 2,01,804, inclusive of a sum of Rs. 75,025, representing arrears. Remissions and suspensions of payment were put down at Rs. 42,834, and Rs. 1,58,970 were entered for collection from occupiers. The exceedingly just manner in which the assessments were made is evidenced by the fact that Rs. 1,57,416 were actually received by the Treasury without resort to coercive measures.

There is no military force in the State, but included in the police roll of 104 officers and men, about 33 armed with rifles are employed in guarding the palace, treasury and jail; and eight *sowars*, carrying swords and spears, act as an escort to the Chief. The *Huzur*, or chief criminal Court, is presided over by the Chief, but cases involving sentences of death or transportation are disposed of by the Political Agent at Satara, although the preliminary proceedings are heard by the Chief. The State *Karbhari* is invested

SHRIMANT NANASAHIB NAIK NIMBALKAR, CHIEF OF PHALTAN.

with the powers of a District Magistrate, but he occasionally presides in the capacity of a Sessions Judge. There are also several stipendiary and three honorary Magistrates. The administration of civil justice is carried out in the *Huzur* High Court, the first Appellate Court (presided over by the State *Karbhari*), and one first-class Sub-Judge's Court exercising original jurisdiction.

The majority of the inhabitants are agriculturists, and the season of 1919–20 was far more favourable, both for cultivation and harvesting, than had been experienced in previous years, which had brought the State almost to the borders of famine. The River Mira supplies water for the irrigation of a portion of the territory, but the major portion of the crops are dependent upon rainfall, which for the past five years has reached an annual total of 20·35. The quantity registered during the period under report was 17·92 inches, and although the early rains were not sufficient for *Kharif* sowings, the subsequent downfall relieved cultivators in an anxious situation.

The chief products of the soil are *jowar*, *bajri*, wheat, rice, *gram* and *tur*, and as the market value of these kinds of grain remained at a high figure, the material prosperity of the *ryots* was increased.

The forests in the State, 13.757 acres in extent, are scattered over various parts of the territory, but there is not, at present, any regular system of conservancy for their protection beyond that furnished by police and village watchmen. The Durbar is, however, raising plantations from seedlings raised in well-prepared nurseries, and it is hoped that, by these means, damage caused by illegal felling or by fires may, in course of time, be repaired. The total receipts from all forest produce during the year under report amounted to Rs. 3,815, as against Rs. 3,478 for the previous 12 months, and the expenditure of Rs. 705 showed an increase of Rs. 113.

Manufactures in Phaltan are few in number and of little importance, although coarse country blankets, *dhotis* and *saris* are made in a few places. The handlooms actually at work increased from 125 to 156 during the past year, and it may be added that the weaving industry, generally, is improving in nearly every part of India owing to the extremely high prices charged for imported goods.

There is a combined post and telegraph office at Phaltan, in addition to branch offices at Taradgaon and Walhar, which are under British management.

Statistics relating to revenue and finance show that the opening balance for the past year was Rs. 76,802, and that the total gross revenue was Rs. 2,71,612, these figures exhibiting a marked improvement in the position of the previous 12 months. A comparative table of increases and decreases in receipts under several heads reveals the fact that land revenue produced Rs. 1,58.421, against Rs. 47,670 of the previous year, this being due to the recovery of suspended arrears; repayments of advances, Rs. 16.923 against Rs. 3,646; irrigation fees. Rs. 1,964 against Rs. 448; and miscellaneous items, Rs. 13,308 against Rs. 3.816. Decreases of revenue occurred with regard to hemp drugs and opium. On the expenditure side of the account there were increases in establishment charges, Public Works, Law and Justice, Police and Education Departments.

The total gross receipts for the past year were Rs. 4,24.732.

The State maintains one charitable dispensary at the chief town, at which medical advice and treatment was given to 5,955 persons, but in the previous year the staff gave their services to as many as 9,000 persons, this large number being accounted for by the prevalence of a severe form of influenza. A travelling assistant, connected with the dispensary, gave advice and medicines in nearly 200 cases of ordinary ailments.

Every possible encouragement is given by the State to the establishment of schools in Phaltan, but the success of its efforts must not be estimated by statistics of scholars on the rolls, or of average daily attendances, as continued agricultural depression and epidemics have been responsible for the absence of pupils, and even the closing of schools.

The teaching institutions, 37 in number, comprise the Mudhoji High School, 34 primary schools for boys, one of a similar kind for girls, and one Vedic school, in all of which there are 1,825 pupils. The Political Agent, Satara, after visiting the High School recently, reported as follows: "The building is a very good one, and education being free, attendance is good. It seems that there are not enough qualified masters, but graduates are expensive, and I think that the State might consider the question of charging some fees in order to improve the quality of the teaching. The Head Master evidently has the interest of the school at heart, and the appearance and manners of the boys are good. The Middle School building is also good." Education in this establishment is imparted free up to the Matriculation and school final standards. Mr. Moysey, I.C.S., referring to the school for girls, observed: "There are 120 girls in this school, of whom 102 are present. The attendance is very good, and the girls are neat and intelligent. The Head Master is doing very well, though, of course, it is desirable to have mistresses, but these are hard to get. The State might send intelligent girls for training. The Chief intends to build a separate school-house for girls, and this will doubtless lead to girls prolonging their studies, especially if mistresses are obtained." It is an undoubted sign of progress in the State that the attendance of pupils at the school specially set apart for low-caste children is steadily increasing, and that the night school continues to attract students.

The establishment of Co-operative Societies, commenced in the year 1917-18, is an admirable fulfilment of the address of the Chief on the occasion of his being invested with full ruling powers, in which he emphasized his determination to make his administration marked by progressive reforms for the good of his people. The objects of these Societies was fully explained to the inhabitants of Phaltan by an official deputed for the purpose by the Government of Bombay, and the utility of such institutions in granting relief in times of necessity now appears to be fully realized.

The first results of the movement were the inauguration of Co-operative Stores and a Weavers' Society. Efforts were made during the past year to consolidate and improve existing societies rather than to expand the movement, and there are now 13 societies with 431 members, the total assets are Rs. 2,81.486; the working capital is Rs. 68.364; deposits received during 1919–20 amounted to Rs. 7,222, and the Reserve Fund stands at Rs. 503.

The Phaltan Bank, Limited, is purely a private enterprise, which was promoted in July, 1918, with the main object of financing co-operative societies, and for conducting all branches of banking business by raising local capital. The institution is registered under the Indian Companies Act, VII of 1913. In the State Administration Report for 1919-20, it is remarked that the Bank was gaining in popularity; that the total receipts for

THE STATE OF PHALTAN.

1. Shri Rama Temple, Phaltan. 2. Shri Nageshwar Temple, Phaltan.

that year amounted to Rs. 2,13,049; that the disbursements were Rs. 2,09,661; that eight societies had been granted loans totalling Rs. 20,016; and that a dividend of seven per cent. to the shareholders had been declared.

The Victoria Diamond Jubilee Public Library, at Phaltan, is a fine, spacious building in the heart of the town, and is well supplied with a large number of books, newspapers, the Bombay Government Gazette, and the Gazette of the Government of India. The library is maintained partly by private subscriptions, and partly by State and Municipal funds.

Immediately after the outbreak of war between His Imperial Majesty's Government and Germany, the Chief convened a public meeting at Phaltan, at which the real cause of hostilities was explained to the people, and a sum of Rs. 800—exclusive of the donation of the Chief—was collected and sent in aid of the Bombay branch of the War Relief Fund.

When the Imperial Government, in 1917, announced its intention of raising a War Loan, the Chief took great pains to explain the necessity for such a proceeding, and he succeeded in obtaining the consent of cultivators to contribute amounts equivalent to their respective annual land revenue assessments, and the sum thus received, together with the contributions of merchants and others, reached a total of Rs. 1,75,333. The State, from its treasury, invested Rs. 59,850 in the same fund, and the present Chief—then Kumar Shri Malojirao—sold some of his own jewellery and raised Rs. 51,065, which he paid into the Loan account; and in the following year he contributed a further sum of Rs. 50,000.

Soon after the Chief's assumption of government he visited nearly every part of the Principality, promising liberal concessions to encourage the work of recruiting, and he authorized the appointment of a special recruiting staff, which was maintained at the expense of the State. An enlisting depôt was opened at Phaltan, where recruits were clothed and fed, and the sum of Rs. 10 was given to each man on enrolment. Assessments upon lands of recruits were remitted during service, and other great inducements enabled the State to send 250 men in aid of the Allies.

Accounts published by the State show that up to the close of the year 1918 the State had contributed Rs. 250 to the Lady Willingdon Memorial Fund; Rs. 300 to Lord Kitchener's Biography Fund; Rs. 2,721 to the "Our Day" Fund; Rs. 584 to the Women's Relief Fund; Rs. 480 to the Recruiting Fund;

THE STATE OF PHALTAN.
MUDHOJI MANMOHAN PALACE, PHALTAN.

Rs. 200 to the Poona pageant and fête; Rs. 300 to Their Imperial Majesties' Silver Wedding Fund; and Rs. 2,000 to the Imperial War Relief Fund. A list of donations subsequently published contains the following items: Rs. 200 to the Children's Guild of Service; Rs. 904 being the value of two pearls for the Children's Welfare Necklace; Rs. 290 to the Wrestling Tournament, Poona; Rs. 200 to the Maharashtra Girls' Education Society; Rs. 600 to the Indian Olympic Association, and Rs. 360 to the King Edward Memorial Hospital at Poona.

In recognition of the very valuable services rendered in obtaining recruits and in making suitable provision for their families, the Government presented the Chief with the prescribed recruiting badge, which was handed to him at a Durbar held in Phaltan on December 11, 1919, by Mr. E. L. Moysey, I.C.S., Political Agent, Satara. It may not be out of place to quote a few sentences from Mr. Moysey's excellent address on this occasion. He remarked: "My principal object in coming here has been to present you with the Recruiting Badge, which the Government of India have awarded for the great assistance you have given in recruiting. I learn that 250 recruits were secured in the State, and that by far the greater number were secured in the year which elapsed between your installation on the *gadi* and the conclusion of the war. I consider this result of a year's work very praiseworthy, since I am told that before the war very few men enlisted in the Army from this State. I know myself, by personal experience in a district in Sindh, which had not previously given any recruits, how hard it is to obtain recruits from an area without previous military traditions, and I can see that you and your officers must have worked very hard to obtain this number. The recruits were very well treated in the Recruiting Depôt, and considerable concessions were made to those who enlisted and to those who obtained recruits. In other directions, also, you and your people joined wholeheartedly in the efforts of the people of India to relieve distress and to bring the war to a victorious conclusion. You rightly say, in your administration report, that the value of the help given by your State lies not in its magnitude, but in the spirit of devotion and loyalty in which it was offered. But in comparison with the resources of your State, and considering the degree in which it has been affected by failure of rains, the assistance given by you compares favourably with many other parts of India. I learn that, in order to invest in the War Loans, you even sold a large portion of your private jewellery.

"I now have great pleasure, Meherban Chief Saheb, in presenting you with the Recruiting Badge, which, I hope, is the precursor of many honours. I am glad to see that the anticipations of Mr. Brendon, when he installed you on the *gadi*, are being fulfilled, and the administration of the State is being conducted on enlightened and liberal lines."

The State pays an annual tribute of Rs. 9,600 to the British Government.

The chief town of the State, Phaltan, was founded in the fourteenth century by Nimbraji, and it is situated about 37 miles on the north-eastern side of Satara. The Political Agent, when visiting the town on a recent occasion, made this observation: "The sanitation of the town seems to me to be excellent, and the street drains are kept in a very good condition. The management of the Municipality seems very efficient."

Trees have been planted on the sides of roads, and endeavours are being made to improve the architectural features of the town. The general effect of the measures is to enhance the importance of the place as the State capital.

THE STATE OF POLO

THIS second - class State in the Mahi Kantha Political Agency in the Bombay Presidency is bounded on the north and east by the State of Udaipur, and on the south and west by the State of Idar.

The Agency of Mahi Kantha, meaning " Bank of the Mahi," is thus named from the fact that the territory is traversed by the Mahi river, and it contains nearly 60 Chiefships, the only important one being that of Idar.

On the borders between Mahi Kantha and Rajputana, General Sir John Outram did excellent service for the British Government many years ago in connection with the civilizing of the turbulent Bhils and Kolis. The whole area is about 4,000 square miles in extent, and the inhabitants are nearly 500,000 in number.

The Raos of Polo as the Rulers are termed—trace their descent from Jaichand, the last Rathor Rajput sovereign of the Kingdom of Kanauj. Jaichand's grandson, Seoji, founded the Rathor dynasty in Marwar. This Seoji had three sons, namely, Asodham, Soningji, and Ajmalji. Asodham established himself in Marwar; Soningji, dethroning the Bhil Chief, Samalia Sordh of Idar, established himself at that place under the title of Rao of Idar about the year 1257; and Ajmalji conquered Okhamandal in Kathiawar.

A successor of Soningji, Rao Chando, occupied the *gadi* of Idar early in the eighteenth century, but his weak rulership tempted the Vaghela and the Rahewar Rajputs to encroach upon his villages, with the result that a considerable area of territory was occupied by them. At this juncture the death occurred of the Thakore of Palya, and, according to custom, it became necessary for the Idar Chief to present a sword and dress of honour to the successor.

Rao Chando prepared to leave Idar ostensibly with the object of making the presentation, while in reality he journeyed to Polo, a village then occupied by his wife's relation, to whom he expressed his intention of proceeding to Kashi, where he had elected to spend the remainder of his days. After remaining at Polo for about two months Rao Chando determined to visit the holy city of Benares, but when he reached Sarsao, about 10 miles distant from Polo, he addressed an invitation to his friends at the latter place to join him in a farewell feast. The banquet took place in due course, and when the Polo Rajputs had partaken " not wisely but too well " of strong drink, the host caused every member of the party to be put to death. Rao Chando then returned to Polo, where he established himself as Ruler, assuming the title of the Rao of Polo.

Rao Hamirsinhji XVI, in descent from Rao Chando, had three sons, Prathisinhji, Mohobatsinhji, and Bhupatsinhji, of whom the eldest son, Prathisinhji, came to the *gadi* of Polo, and his second son, Mohobatsinhji, went to Verabar ***Taluka***, as his uncle, Thakore Parabatsinhji, died without leaving any son behind him. As Rao Prathisinhji died without any issue, he was succeeded by his youngest brother, Bhupatsinhji, who, also dying without an heir, was succeeded by his elder brother, Mohobatsinhji, who ascended the *gadi* of Polo without relinquishing the Verabar *Taluka* already held by him.

Rao Mohobatsinhji died on November 27, 1914, and the heirs and claimants for the Polo *gadi* were Dalpatsinhji, Thakore of the Tuntiabar estate in Banswara, in the Southern Rajputana States Agency, and his two cousins, named Gopalsinhji and Hindusinhji. These three persons appeared before the Political Agent of Mahi Kantha, and in consequence of old age or infirmities they renounced their claims of succession in favour of Hamirsinhji, who had already been adopted as the heir of Dalpatsinhji.

It should be mentioned here that the Thakore of Valasna, Pahala, and Pal, as well as His Highness the Maharaja of Idar, claimed the vacant Chiefship, but the Government turned a deaf ear to these aspirants for the honour, and declared that Hamirsinhji, the nearest available next-of-kin of Rao Mohobatsinhji, should become Rao of Polo. Further than this, the *Durbar* of Idar laid claim to the estate of Verabar, but the Government declined to admit the validity of the proposal. and conferred the vacant position of Thakore upon Kumar Jorawarsinhji, the younger brother of Rao Hamirsinhji. The latter and the Kumar are now studying at the Scott College at Sadra, where excellent progress is being made with their education, and during the period of minority the Political Agent, Mahi Kantha, is undertaking the management of Polo and of the Verabar Estate.

It is not certain whether the State of Polo and Verabar were acquired by the ancestors of the present Rao by conquest, or whether by grant from the early Rajas of Idar, but according to Mr. Kinloch

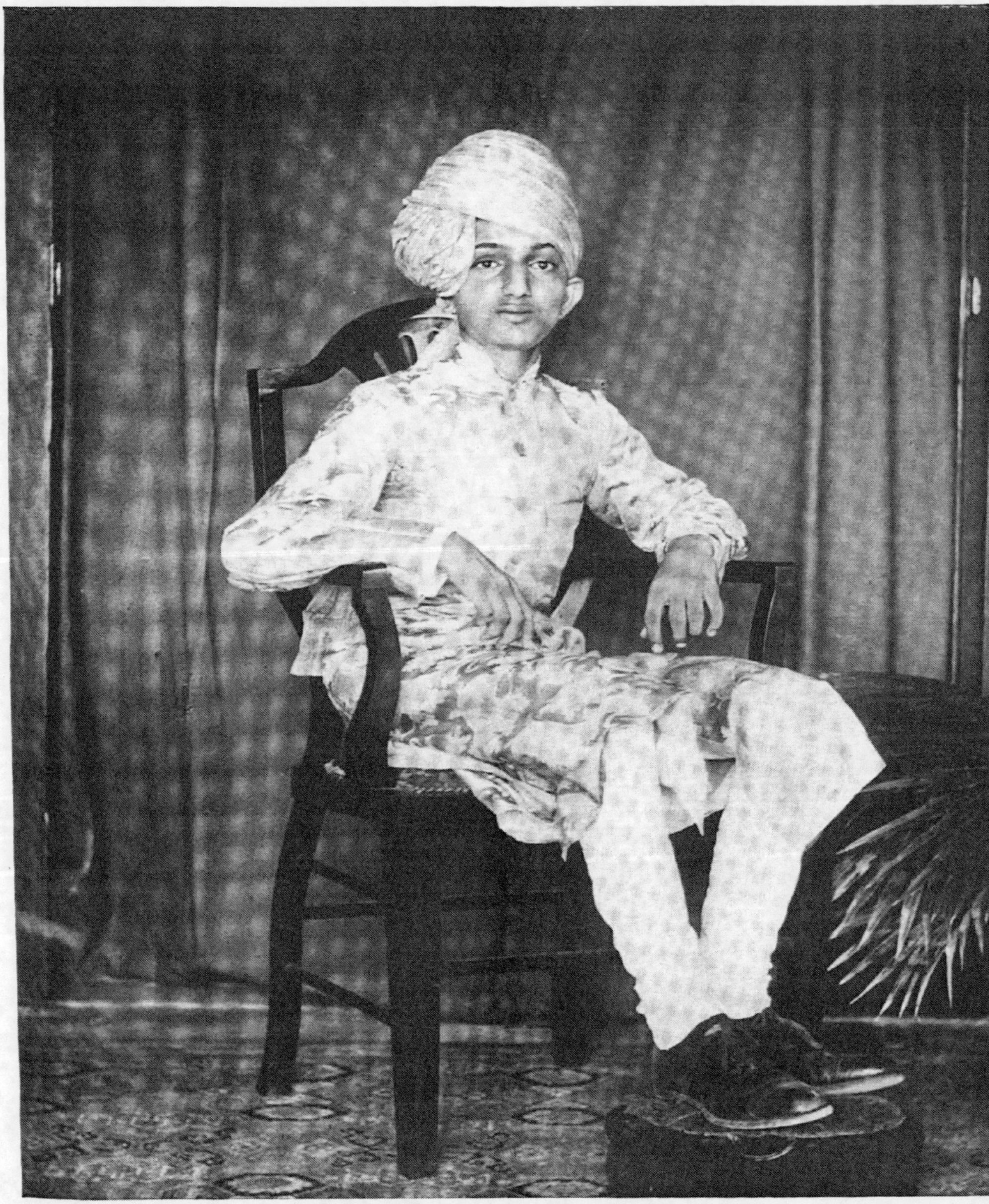

MINOR RAO SHRI HAMIRSINHJI, OF POLO STATE.

THE STATE OF POLO.

1. [illegible] 2. [illegible] at Old Polo. 3. Sarneshwar Temple.

THE STATE OF POLO.

1. Bird's-eye View of Ghodadar, the Present Capital of Polo State. 2. Darbargadh Ghodadar. 3. Types of Bhils.

Forbes, in the *Rasmala*, they were originally separate Principalities, acquired at different times by various members of the family, and not therefore dependencies, one of the other, and that Verabar was never transferred by the present dynasty of Idar.

According to a custom still prevailing, however, the Thakore of Verabar is usually promoted to the Chiefship of Polo in the event of there being no direct successor to the *gadi*; and the State of Polo provides a successor when the office of Thakore of Verabar is vacant. Regarding the *Pattawats* of the Rao of Polo, Colonel Miles says: "The *Pattas* are derived from the former Race of Idar, and it does not appear that service can be claimed from them by Idar, nor that any interference of control in their respective *Pattas* would be attempted or allowed."

In addition to what has already been stated, it may be remarked that Idar has the right of *Khichadi* over Verabar which appears to have been levied about the year 1808, when the ruling Maharaja attached it. Idar, however, cannot seize the Verabar *Pattas* in default of direct heirs, nor can it determine the succession thereto. If the succession be disputed, the British Government as Paramount Power decides the matter, after careful examination of the pretensions of the candidates. Even the Rao himself is excluded from the succession, as, by the custom of Gujarat and of his own family, he cannot hold Verabar as well as Polo, at any rate so long as there is a true heir available.

The State of Polo is 135 square miles in extent, and it comprises 85 villages - including 26 which are at the present time deserted. The State is sparsely populated.

The general appearance of the State is of a most pleasing character. The northern and eastern portions are intersected by wooded hills, which increase in breadth and altitude near the boundary line, and the intermediate valleys are noted for the great beauty of their natural scenery. The most highly cultivated tracts in the State are found in the northern and eastern districts, while there is a considerable quantity of fertile land in the south and west which is still lying fallow owing to the turbulent and unsettled habits of the tribes who have settled there.

Trees of various descriptions, including species of mango, *mahua*, tamarind, *pipal*, wad, timber, kher, bamboos, and others, are scattered in the wildest profusion in various parts of the State, but the jungles have during the past few years been greatly diminished in density, and valuable cleared land is being taken up by occupiers, who appreciate the great security of life and property now afforded by the State authorities. This protection has resulted in the foundation of many new villages, all of which are being rapidly populated.

The principal crops are *maize*, rice, *kodra*, *barta*, *banti*, and wheat and other cereals, while vegetables, which are largely cultivated, comprise brinjal, rataloo, suran, valar, gaja, naldi, and onions.

In consequence of the hilly nature of the country camels are generally used for transport purposes.

The village of Polo was originally the headquarters of the State, but as it was found to be unhealthy, the seat of Government was transferred to *Ghodadar*, in which there are about 950 inhabitants.

Polo State does not pay any tribute or any other *Hak* either to British Government or to Baroda State, but on the contrary it realizes *chouth*, Tika (Installation Hax), *Hathgarana* (marriage cess), and several other *Haks* from some of the villages of the Idar State. There are three Vernacular schools in the State, and a well-furnished dispensary at Ghodadar. It appears from old views in the possession of the State that the Jain temple Lakhena and the Shive temple of Sharneshwar in ruins convey the idea that the village of Polo was in ancient times a prosperous and a well-populated city.

Polo, being a second-class State in the Mahi Kantha Agency, exercises full criminal jurisdiction as well as civil jurisdiction for suits up to the value of Rs. 20,000.

THE STATE OF SAKTI

THERE is a curious legend regarding the origin of the ruling family of Sakti, one of the Feudatory States in the Chhattisgarh division of the Central Provinces. The tradition is that their ancestors were twin brothers named Hari and Gujar, who were soldiers in the army of Raja Kalyan Shah of Sambalpur. Their only weapons were two wooden swords, and the Raja, displeased at their arming themselves in so useless a manner, determined to punish them by directing that at the next succeeding *Dasehra* festival the brothers should slaughter the sacrificial bullock. The men were filled with alarm as they reflected upon the serious consequences which would inevitably follow non-fulfilment of the order, but the goddess Devi appeared in a dream and assured them that all would be well. On the eventful day the head of the animal was severed with one stroke, and the Raja, delighted with the marvellous performance, undertook to make a grant to them of the area of land over which they could walk in one day. The actual distance covered was 20 miles in each direction, and the territory thus obtained has remained in the possession of the descendants of the brothers to the present day. The swords have been preserved, and are worshipped at the annual *Dasehra* ceremonies. The older branch of the direct line ended with Shew Singh, who died without issue, but his widow adopted Kalandar, a cousin of her late husband, and he became Feudatory Chief The next Ruler, Ranjit Singh, was deposed in 1875 on account of certain irregularities, and the administration of the State was assumed by the British Government. In 1892 Raja Rup Narayan Singh, son of the ex-Raja, was installed as chief. Upon the death of Rup Narayan in 1914, his son, Liladhar Singh, the present Ruler, succeeded to the *gadi* as Raja of Sakti.

His Highness was duly installed by a British Government official in January, 1915, and he was invested with full ruling powers in January, 1917. He personally supervises the work in each department, although he is assisted by a Diwan and an Assistant Diwan. His Highness is an intelligent Ruler, and his chief ambition is to see Sakti become an ideal State both as regards administration and general material prosperity. Notwithstanding the demands made upon the time of the Chief in the revenue, judicial, educational, and other State Departments His Highness never

THE CHIEF OF SAKTI.

neglects his regular religious exercises, in which he is guided by well-known *Pandits* of Benares. His Highness has inaugurated many useful reforms, and at the present time he is considering the adoption of other progressive measures, but special reference should be made to his advocacy of scientific agriculture, which is the principal industry in the State.

While the majority of the subjects of the State are keen agriculturists, it is unfortunate that the methods of cultivation are still of a very primitive character.

At a public meeting held in February, 1919, His Highness the Raja spoke strongly in favour of arable farming according to the principles of modern science. As a result of the discussion which took place, an Agricultural Association was formed, and the "Clouston" agricultural demonstration farm was established.

Another outcome of the meeting referred to was the decision to establish stores on a co-operative basis in each village, in order that cultivators may at any time obtain a sufficient supply of seed in ordinary seasons as well as in the event of failure of harvests.

The necessity for irrigation is fully realized, and in addition to a considerable number of tanks already in existence the State is now constructing a large one capable of supplying water to more than 2,000 acres.

The headquarters town of Sakti, which has a population of about 2,500 persons, is situated about three-quarters of a mile distant from the station of the same name on the Bengal-Nagpur railway system.

The State is being administered on good progressive lines and should be prosperous.

THE INDIAN RULING STATES.

The following is the list of Indian States as given in the *India Office List* :—

Salute Guns.

21
- Baroda.
- Gwalior.
- Hyderabad.
- Jammu and Kashmi.
- Mysore.

19
- Bhopal.
- Indore.
- Kalat.
- Kolhapur.
- Travancore.
- Udaipur.

17
- Bahawalpur.
- Bharatpur.
- Bikaner.
- Bundi.
- Cochin.
- Cutch.
- Jaipur.
- Jodhpur (Marwar).
- Karauli.
- Kotah.
- Patiala.
- Rewa.
- Tonk.

15
- Alwar.
- Banswara.
- Bhutan.
- Datia.
- Dewas (Senior Branch).
- Dewas (Junior Branch).

15
- Dhar.
- Dholpur.
- Dungarpur.
- Idar.
- Jaisalmer.
- Khairpur.
- Kishangarh.
- Orchha.
- Partabgarh.
- Rampur.
- Sikkim.
- Sirohi.

13
- Benares.
- Bhavnagar.
- Cooch Behar.
- Dhrangadhra.
- Jaora.
- Jhalawar.
- Jind.
- Junagadh.
- Kapurthala.
- Nabha.
- Nawanagar.
- Palanpur.
- Porbandar.
- Rajpipla.
- Ratlam.
- Tripura.

11
- Ajaigarh.
- Alirajpur.
- Baoni.

11
- Barwani.
- Bijawar.
- Bilaspur.
- Cambay.
- Chamba.
- Charkhari.
- Chhatarpur.
- Faridkot.
- Gondal.
- Janjira.
- Jhabua.
- Jhalawar.
- Maler-Kotla.
- Mandi.
- Manipur.
- Morvi.
- Narsingarh.
- Panna.
- Pudukkottai.
- Radhanpur.
- Rajgarh.
- Sailana.
- Samthar.
- Sirmoor.
- Sitamau.
- Suket.
- Tehri-Garhwal.

9
- Balasinor.
- Banganapalla.
- Bansda.
- Baraundha.
- Bariya.

9
- Chota-Udaipur.
- Danta.
- Dharampur.
- Dhrol.
- Fadthli.
- Haipur.
- Hsipaw (or Thibaw).
- Jawhar.
- Karond.
- Kengtung.
- Khilchipur.
- Kishn.
- Lahej.
- Limbdi.
- Loharu.
- Lunawada.
- Maihar.
- Mayurbhanj.
- Mudhol.
- Nagod.
- Palitana.
- Patna.
- Rajkot.
- Sachin.
- Sangli.
- Savantvadi.
- Shehr.
- Sonpur.
- Sunth.
- Wankaner.
- Wadhwan.
- Yawnghwe.

INDEX

INDEX

INDEX

3 H

INDEX

INDEX

S

T

U

V

W

Y

Published by

Facsimile Publisher
Ashok Vihar, Delhi-110052 (India)
Website: www.facsimilepublisher.com

Distributed by

Gyan Books Pvt. Ltd.
5, Ansari Road, Daryaganj, New Delhi-110002 (India)
E-mail: books@gyanbooks.com, Website: www.gyanbooks.com

4 444006 999559